A GIANT FROM GEORGIA

MERCER UNIVERSITY

MERCER UNIVERSITY PRESS

Endowed by

TOM WATSON BROWN
and
THE WATSON-BROWN FOUNDATION, INC.

A GIANT FROM GEORGIA

The Life of U.S. Senator Walter F. George, 1878–1957

JAMIE H. COCKFIELD

MERCER UNIVERSITY PRESS
Macon, Georgia
1979–2019
40 Years of Publishing Excellence

MUP/ H955

Published by Mercer University Press
1501 Mercer University Drive
Macon, Georgia 31207

9 8 7 6 5 4 3 2 1

Books published by Mercer University Press are printed on acid-free paper that meets the requirements of the American National Standard for Information Sciences—Permanence of Paper for Printed Library Materials.

Printed and bound in Canada.

This book is set in Adobe Caslon Pro.

ISBN 978-0-88146-676-8
Cataloging-in-Publication Data is available from the Library of Congress

To

Emily Bailey Walker

One of the South's great ladies

CONTENTS

PREFACE

On a hot August day in 1957, twelve-year-old Frank Horn was playing golf at a country club outside Cordele, Georgia, when he saw a fleet of large planes fly into the small Cordele airport. The passengers in these planes disembarked into a chain of waiting limousines that made a convoy headed north, as it turned out, to Vienna, Georgia, a town ten miles away. "I didn't know there were that many limousines," Horn, who would one day himself serve in the Georgia legislature, told this author. He did not know that the passengers consisted of much of the cream of the Washington power structure headed to the funeral of Senator Walter George, one of the most powerful men in Washington and a true giant in the Senate.

After moving to Georgia almost a half century ago, I was surprised that no one had ever written a biography of Senator Walter George, since I had even heard of him as I grew up in South Carolina. I discovered that he had ordered all of his personal papers be burned upon his death, so I assume that in the absence of a huge personal collection that survives most famous men, no one had ever attempted a biography. I learned later that the University of Georgia and the Georgia State Archives had pleaded with the family not to dispose of his papers, but they did anyway. When I asked his law partner, T. Hoyt Davis, why George had instructed his heirs to do such a thing, he replied, "He just didn't want people to know what other people had asked him to do for them." If that was indeed George's reason, it has a hollow ring to it. Donors can make papers inaccessible for long periods if they do not want their secrets revealed soon after the owner's demise, so the mystery remains.

Senator George served in the US Senate from 1922 to 1957, so he was there during some of momentous events in American history. Consequently, with his papers' destruction, an enormous amount of American history literally went up in smoke. A neighbor, Frances Coley, told me that she thought she remembered a cedar chest with some papers in it in a barn on the George farm, but they were destroyed by a leaky roof. If these papers ever existed, they have been permanently lost—unless they are part of the "George Collection" in the Walter George Museum in Vienna, Georgia. The archive in the museum is not extensive and consists of bits and pieces of correspondence and newspaper and magazine clippings. At the time I read these holdings, they were not organized, and the Vienna Historic Preservation Society (VHPS) was searching for someone to arrange the collection. At one point, there were discussions with the Walter F. George School of Law to transfer these materials to the law school, but as of this writing, the VHPS and the law school have not reached an agreement.

There also exists a collection of George materials in the Special Collections Room of Mercer University's Jackson Tarver Library, but it consists mostly of printed materials and focuses largely on George's time as a Mercer student. There is a collection in the Georgia State Archive in Morrow, Georgia, and in the Eisenhower Library in Abilene, Kansas, but in both cases, most of the materials are newspaper clippings. A sprinkling of his correspondence does appear in the collections of people with whom George interacted (e.g., Franklin Roosevelt, Harry Truman, and various senatorial colleagues), but these are few. Since I had to rely heavily on newspapers and magazine articles, I was handicapped by the fact that what any politician states publicly does not always reflect his or her personal thoughts. I found some non-public sources in other diaries, papers, and memoirs, but these sources, while valuable, were limited. These limited sources on any politician would be a major roadblock to any biographer, and it certainly was a daunting one for any would-be George historian. The writer, still, must be satisfied with these scraps.

Although I defended post-Reconstruction American history for my master's degree, I trained primarily as a European historian, with emphasis on Russian history. Still, I have always had as an avocation twentieth-century American politics. Years ago, as I was writing Russian history, I put it in the back of my head to one day "do something on Walter George." Several years ago, while talking with a Mercer student, Rusty English, I asked him where he had been reared. He said, "A town you've never heard of." I said, "Try me." When he said "Vienna, Georgia." I said, "Well, you're not so obscure. Your town boasts a United States senator." Then I told him that I had tentatively planned one day to write a biography of Walter George. He eagerly advised that I had to talk to his mother, Beth English, who was then president of the Vienna Historical Preservation Society. This conversation did start my thinking: I could always research the printed materials on Walter George, but my time to interview anyone who knew him personally was limited. Although I was up to my eyebrows in a work on General Aleksei Brusilov, Russia's greatest World War I general, I decided I should probably interview those people who had known the Georges before they were gone. If I ever did write the biography, I would at least have that information.

Fortunately, I was able to speak with several dozen people who had been acquainted with Walter George. The above-mentioned Mrs. Frances Coley was over a hundred when we talked, and Mrs. Sally Mae Childs, one of Walter George's last nurses, was ninety-nine when I met her. Both had minds as sharp as proverbial tacks; Mrs. Coley had even mowed her own grass into her nineties. There followed many others (listed in the bibliography) to whom I owe a great debt of gratitude. These interviews got me started, and then I began to work in libraries and archives before I really had planned to do so. I soon found myself working on two distinctly different books at the same time, a task I would *strongly* discourage others to undertake.

I quickly encountered a couple of problems. First, I realized there are probably two dozen or more articles, master's theses, doctoral dissertations, and even books that might be written titled "Senator Walter F. George and ____________________." Having served more than three decades in the US Senate as one its most influential members, Walter George left his mark on many historical events. It is impossible to write a one-volume definitive biography on his career because giving definitive treatment under one biographical title to every project in which he played a role is impossible. Such a study, if completed, would be encyclopedic, even with the absence of personal papers. There will doubtless be readers who will feel I have not plumbed the depth of George's activities in certain phases of his life, but I have chosen in many cases to leave these "deficiencies" to the revisionists due to lack of time, space, and resources. To those who would like to pursue facets of his life more deeply than I have, I can only say, "Have at it!"

A second difficulty facing a George biographer is the near-universal popular perception of George himself. It seems almost everyone who knew him held him in the highest regard. He is praised by most people in the superlative degree of comparison only: *greatest*, *smartest*, *most perceptive*, *most diplomatic*, etc. With all the encomiums, the work might quite naturally take on the strong flavor of hagiography, and no one is that good or perfect. I therefore actively *tried* to find flaws in the man. Those few that I eventually unearthed had no exhaustive proof (e.g., in his later years he seems to have begun drinking a bit too much; he might have been somewhat anti-Semitic; he may have had an affair with his secretary), but I have presented them with the limited materials that I had. The reader can be the judge.

A book never consists of only the writer's efforts. I must say a special thank-you to Janet Joiner, executive director of the Vienna Historical Preservation Society, whose help was invaluable. She has been from the beginning my "go-to" person on all matters. She arranged interviews with local citizens who knew George personally and always found time to go with me to visit with these people. She served as a reference librarian on matters like individuals' first names, and she performed a myriad of other duties. I could not have done this work without her. I also must thank two presidents of the VHPS, Rusty's mother, Beth English, and Diane Couch. These ladies helped and encouraged me from the beginning of the project, and I hold all three as valuable personal friends. Finally, I must thank the many underpaid and overworked librarians and archivists who cheerfully—and anonymously—assisted me. These people range from those in the Dooly County Public Library and the Georgia State Archive to the *Archives du ministère des affaires étrangères* in Paris, France. I owe all of them an enormous debt.

I also owe a tremendous obligation to the fellows who answer the phone in the Mercer University's Information Technology Department. Over the years, a number helped me when my computer played tricks on me, but it seemed to be the misfortune of Joey Tant and Ben Kienker to be on duty most often when I was in crisis. The university gave me a new computer in mid-project, and everything I had done had to be transferred to the new device, which in no way performed as my old one did. Documents disappeared, margins appeared where they were not supposed to be, and a myriad of problems occurred that only an expert could untangle. So my thanks to Joey, Ben, and all the others. I could never have finished without their assistance, which they always gave cheerfully. Another computer assistant who helped me in another way was Ricky Varga. He had the tedious task of "computerizing" the manuscript so that it would fit the format needed by the Mercer University Press.

Another individual I must especially thank is the Honorable Ray Hill, a political scholar who contacted me on learning of my work on Walter George. A past member of the Tennessee legislature, of the Knox County Commission, and currently an official in juvenile court in Knox County, Ray Hill is easily the most knowledgeable person I have ever met about American political history. He can tell you off the top of his head by how many votes Estes Kefauver beat Senator Tom Stewart in the 1948 senatorial primary or the first name of some obscure congressman from Arkansas and the years he served. He has supplied me with pictures for this work and read the entire manuscript as a fact-checker. His help, like that of Janet, Joey, and Ben can have no price. I must say, however, that any errors in the text are totally mine. Thanks also to the University of Georgia student Ryan Reeves who researched forced retirement for me.

I also found invaluable the help of friends and colleagues who read chapters of the manuscript for style as well as facts. Given their busy schedules (some were currently writing books themselves), I generally asked no one to read and edit more than one chapter. They are, in order of the chapters they read, Robert Good, Laura Moody, Wayne Mixon, Buck Melton, Wallace Daniel, John Dunaway, Douglas Steeples, Catharine Savage Brosman, Olivia Pass (she read two chapters), and Mary Faith Pankin. After the work was more or less complete, George Conyne of the University of Kent at Canterbury, England, read almost all of it again and gave me invaluable editorial help. Again, any stylistic or factual shortcomings are entirely my own.

Finally, a word about the person to whose memory I have dedicated this work: Emily Bailey Walker. If she were alive now, she'd be well over a hundred years old. I met her, as I have met so many friends, through the card game of bridge, and I spent many delightful weekends playing the game with her and her husband at their hunting preserve, "Pretty Pond," in Lee County, Georgia. To get there, one has to pass through Walter George's hometown, Vienna, Georgia, and it was Miss Emily who first pointed out to me Walter George's two houses in the town long before I seriously thought about writing this book. We formed a real friendship despite our age difference, and after her husband died, the two of us made long trips together a number of times to play bridge other places. It was during these excursions that I really came to know "Miss Emily." A loquacious Southern lady and voracious reader, she virtually consumed books and had a perfect command of the English language, correctly using words and idioms that many literate people could not or did not use correctly. Our long travel conversations revealed a depth of character and human understanding that few people have, and in a case or two with me, these personal traits were shown in all their perceptive incisiveness. For that reason, I dedicate this work to her memory. It is my great regret that she did not live see it finished.

So, here is a seminal effort to write the life of a man I have chosen to call "A Giant from Georgia." I do not think there could be a more appropriate title.

I

A Son of the South

Georgia! 'Tis a glorious name
As ever bard inspired
Or swelled the breast of orator
Or heart of warrior fired.
Old Georgia, with her thousand streams,
That ripple toward the sea,
And sing her clearness in numbers sweet
And raise these thoughts in me!
—John Roach Straton[1]

Walter George is a man whose roots, like those of a mighty oak, are planted deep in the soil of his native Georgia.
—President Lyndon Baines Johnson[2]

Fishing is a disease, and I am glad that science has not been able to find a cure for it.
—Macon Attorney T. Baldwin Martin[3]

WALTER F. GEORGE: EARLY YEARS

One January 29, 1878, in an unpainted, sun-blistered, pine-framed tenant house on a ninety-five-acre farm in Webster County, Georgia, near the Elliot Wilson farm, Walter Franklin George was born.[4] He was the first child of Robert Theodoric and Sarah Stapleton George.[5] They chose the

[1] *Kinetoscope*, 1898, 143.

[2] *Congressional Record* (hereafter cited as *CR*), 84th Congress/2nd session (hereafter cited as 84/2), p. 6967.

[3] "Scattered Recollections," by T. Baldwin Martin, p. 20, Martin memoir, Special Collections, Jackson Tarver Library, Mercer University, Macon, GA. A copy also is on file in the Special Collections of the Washington Memorial Library, Macon, GA.

[4] Biographical sketches of WFG exist, but there is no full-length biography.

[5] Jarman, "Taxpayer's Senator," 41. For the birth and death dates of the children, see *The History of Webster County*, 427, with this page copied in the Walter F. George file, Spe-

name "Walter" perhaps because it was popular at the time and "Franklin" after the famous founding father Benjamin Franklin. George's father, a man of "limited education," George would later say, was a tenant famer who grew cotton, cowpeas, and sweet potatoes in the poor, sandy soil of Webster County, named for one of the great orators of the early American republic. Despite his own limited education, Robert knew its value, and he would move the family to see that his son got the best education available in that part of Georgia.[6]

Young Walter's parents were of English and Welsh stock. His mother, born Sara Louwicie Stapleton (called "Wice") in 1847, was married to Robert on December 28, 1875, three years before their first child was born. She was a native of Webster County and the daughter of Nancy Beatty Stapleton and James Franklin Stapleton. James' paternal great-grandparent was Capt. George Stapleton, a Revolutionary War soldier from Virginia, who was in Savannah when the war ended. He took off into the hinterland of Georgia and settled in what became Jefferson County. One of his sons, Major Thomas Stapleton, was killed in the Seminole War; another, his name lost to history, settled in another part of the state where he married Senator George's maternal grandmother. From this side, at any rate, the *Atlanta Journal* once told its readers George's family was "good solid colonial stock, a blend of English and Welsh, seasoned by a good American upbringing."[7]

Robert was born in Decatur County and grew up in farming, which became his lifelong profession. In the late 1920s, when he was in his seventies and after his son Walter became a senator, he moved to Florida to raise oranges near Lakeland.[8] He also was four years Wice's junior.[9] Apparently, they moved to Florida shortly after their marriage but returned to Preston the year Walter was born. Robert was one of eleven children, and several of his brothers had been killed in "The Lost Cause," but he was only ten or so

---

cial Collections, Jackson Tarver Library, Mercer University, Macon, GA. Hereafter cited as WFG-MU.

[6]Jarman, 41.

[7]"George Is Lauded," *Atlanta Journal*, June 30, 1931, RCB-5804, box 15, biographical questionnaire, Walter F. George file, Georgia State Archives, Morrow, GA. This collection is hereafter cited as WFG-GSA.

[8]"Meteoric Rise of George…," Unidentified clipping, ibid.

[9]Western Woman's [*sic*] Club, *The History of Webster County*, 168. At one point after George had become famous, *Mercer Cluster,* the student newspaper of Mercer College, later Mercer University, stated that George's father had been a Mercer graduate, but that information is not correct. See *Mercer Cluster,* October 20, 1922, 1, Jackson Tarver Library, Special Collections, Mercer University, Macon, GA.

at the time and was too young to serve.[10] In his nineties, he would visit the Georges, probably even live with them, and would walk into town from their house on the outskirts of Vienna. He developed dementia before he died.[11]

George had only one sibling, a sister, Wilna Nancy George, born on October 9, 1878, just shy of nine months after Walter was born, although her death certificate lists her birth year as 1879.[12] In 1894, she married John Nelson King of Cordele, where she lived until her death in 1960.[13] Little is known about her, and there is no evidence that she was close to her brother, but there is likewise no evidence of an estrangement.

Like most farm boys, George grew up strong and tough. Years later his father remembered that as a boy, Walter would never give up in a wrestling match with another boy. He recalled, "No one ever discovered how to make Walter say 'uncle,' no matter how long gone was his breath nor how blue he became in the face."[14] Even at seventy-seven, George was described by *Collier's* as "compact and broad shouldered" and his gait as "firm." The only sign of feebleness were his thick glasses worn because of a 1939 cataract operation, which ended his bird hunting.[15]

What very early education the young Walter obtained is unknown, but he must have studied somewhere, probably a one-room schoolhouse. Indeed, his grandfather (some say his father) subscribed to the *Congressional Record*, and these pages of sometimes ponderous speeches supplied young Walter's first serious reading.[16]

Like most politicians, George always stressed his humble origins, but certain points raise doubts about this claim. Not many tenant farmers subscribed to the *Congressional Record,* and in his maiden speech in the Senate in 1923, George noted that he had first met Senator Tom Watson, whom he replaced, when the senator was a guest in his home in 1893. Despite his reputation for being a champion of the poor, Watson was not likely a guest in a tenant farmer's home. Webster County local historian Rena Cobb affirmed that George's grandfather Stapleton was a large landowner and was comfortably well-off, which explains both the *Congressional Record* and

---

[10]"Meteoric Rise…," WFG-GSA.

[11]John Bonner interview.

[12]Western Woman's [*sic*] Club, *The History of Webster County*, 427, WFG-MU.

[13]Western Woman's [*sic*] Club, *The History of Webster County*, 427.

[14]*This Is Senator George of Georgia.*

[15]Donovan, "Senator George," 33.

[16]Chandler, *Natural Superiority of Southern Politicians*, 323; Mellichamp, *Senators from Georgia*, 230.

George's education in schools that would have been beyond the reach of the son of a tenant farmer.[17] Though George's father was indeed a tenant farmer, his mother's family appears to have been quite comfortable, so he probably saw Senator Tom Watson at his grandfather's house.[18]

Given the small community, *The Congressional Record* was among the limited reading materials available to him. "The style was ponderous, but I learned to like it," he remembered.[19] It was said that he sometimes memorized the speeches; one day he demonstrated the flowery nature of the oratory of that period when he rode the family mule into Preston. In what became in an oft-quoted (and likely embellished) story, one of the local beauties saw him on the animal and laughed at him. Perched on the mule as his stage, George addressed what must have been a small crowd, saying, "This mule of mine is a worthy burden-bearer on our farm. He does his work most uncomplainingly. To laugh at me, miss, is a reflection cast upon this good animal." The girl blushed in embarrassment, and the small crowd fell silent.[20] His quick response and the eloquence of his language indicate both some good education and a quick mind. Another version describes a second encounter with the girl in which he adds that the mule, having worked five or six days, was entitled to some sort of recreation, presumably the trip into town.[21]

When George was ten, the family moved to Cordele, then in Dooly County (some accounts state Arabi, a town not far from Cordele), where George was able to attend public schools that were probably better than the ones in Webster.[22] The *Mercer Cluster* reported that he had already learned "to read, write and cipher" when he entered the Cordele schools, but in 1893, when George was fifteen and had become a "promising and performing pupil," he was admitted to "a splendid new school at Arabi," later known as the Houston Public School, an institution created for the children of

---

[17]Several telephone conversations with Ms. Rena Cobb, a citizen of Webster County. She told me that much of her information came from her uncle Mancie Cato, also of Webster County.

[18]*CR*, 67/4, 2132.

[19]Chandler, *Natural Superiority of Southern Politicians*, 323.

[20]Mellichamp, *Senators from Georgia*, 232; "Voice of the 84th," 23.

[21]*Atlanta Journal*, June 30, 1931, WFG-GSA. Another version has the young girl as "Miss Lucy," his future wife, which is untrue since she lived nowhere near Preston. See *This Is Walter George*, 3, in Walter F. George file, Dooly County Public Library. File is cited hereafter as WFG-DCPL.

[22]In one of his campaign speeches in the 1938 Senate race, he speaks of Cordele as being "one time my home" (George, *Addresses*, Vienna Historic Preservation Society (hereafter cited as VHPS), September 6, 1938, 7).

farmers. Here George distinguished himself such that when his family returned to Webster County, the principal prevailed upon Robert George to allow his son to remain in Arabi to finish his education.[23] As a further inducement, he was given his room and board free.[24] He ultimately graduated with distinction, despite taking a year off when he was sixteen to teach grade school at Patesville, Georgia.[25] He also taught for two years after graduating before he entered college.[26] While in high school, he decided to become a dentist,[27] but all of that reading of the *Congressional Record* had honed his natural skills of debate and declamation, and young George turned instead to a legal career, and then, as many do, to politics.[28] A skillful debater and speaker in high school, he nailed down his love for the speaking stump and a political career thanks to a chance event when he was sixteen.

On Confederate Memorial Day in Preston in 1894, a crowd had assembled at a Methodist campground near Cordele to hear Judge U. V. Whipple, a man whose career would be intertwined with George's. Either Whipple failed to appear or canceled at the last minute, and young George, whose reputation as an orator was already locally known from his high school performances, was tapped to give an impromptu speech. He had only thirty minutes to prepare, but he then gave a forty-minute address on Robert E. Lee. As it happened, there had appeared in a recent *Congressional Record* a speech on Lee, which had plainly stuck with George.[29] "The beardless boy magnetized the crowd," his alma mater's newspaper reported some years later, demonstrating the "electrifying manner so natural to him."[30] The crowd wildly cheered him, and their adulation completed the change his life's course from dentistry to law and politics.[31] This speech was the first public demonstration of not only the power of his speaking voice, but his ability to move people by his speech. "[His speaking] was a natural gift," his Vienna neighbor John Bonner remembered.[32] Later as a senator, he was of-

[23]*Mercer Cluster*, October 20, 1922, 1.

[24]"George Is Lauded," *Atlanta Journal* clipping, June 30, 1931, WFG-GSA.

[25]"Voice of the 84th," 23; *Mercer Cluster*, October 20, 1922, 1.

[26]Kay Tipton to Herman Talmadge, February 23, 1956, VI, A-1, box 1, f. 2, Talmadge papers.

[27]Chandler, *Natural Superiority of Southern Politicians*, 323.

[28]Jarman, "Taxpayer's Senator," 41.

[29]Mellichamp, *Senators from Georgia*, 232; Jarman, "Taxpayer's Senator," 41; "George Is Lauded," *Atlanta Journal* clipping, June 30, 1931, WFG-GSA; "Voice of the 84th," 23.

[30]*Mercer Cluster*, October 20, 1922, 3.

[31]Mellichamp, *Senators from Georgia*, 232; Chandler, *Natural Superiority of Southern Politicians*, 323.

[32]John Bonner interview.

ten the only member of that body who could change votes "simply by his incomparable rhetoric," the *New York Times* told its readers. While most votes were changed in discussions in the cloakroom, George could, and often did, change votes on the floor.[33] A Senate booklet that answered 291 questions on that deliberative body included the question, "Is legislation much influenced by oratory?" to which the answer was given, "Not much." His long-time friend Senator Carl Hayden (D-Arizona) told people that he had seen George do it "with his appearance, manner and dignity." He noted that "disagreeing with George could seem almost sacrilegious, like questioning Moses on the authenticity of the Ten Commandments."[34] It was an innate power, and it would carry him far from the courtroom to the halls of Congress.

Any detail about George's life in these adolescent years is lost. We know that he finished high school and that while still in high school, he taught grammar school. Why he chose Mercer College, today Mercer University, we do not know. Probably George's Baptist roots swayed him; Mercer was also the nearest three-year degree-granting institution to his native area. He had by this time proved to be an excellent student, and we can be certain that his teachers must have encouraged him to obtain a college education. During campaign speeches later in his life, George credited his father for his attending college.[35] He also would later say that it was his teaching experience that showed him the need for vocational education, which he would champion for the remainder of his life. While teaching for the pittance of a salary, he realized that if he never earned a college degree, he would be condemned to teach for the remainder of his life. Had he received a good vocational training in high school, he would have had other options, so he would fight throughout his political career to see that other high school graduates had vocational education.

George's interest in politics must have encouraged his interest in law, yet prior to both he needed an education. He later would dramatically recall for campaign audiences nights of lying in bed and "long[ing]...for the opportunity to acquire an education." He told his audiences, "the walls of Mercer...seemed as far away from me as the castles in Spain."[36] Exactly where the funds for his education came, we do not know, but they seem to have been adequate. He may have taught while attending Mercer, especially the

---

[33]White, "Senator George, Monument Determined," 44.

[34]Arthur Edson, *Atlanta Constitution,* August 6, 1957, 17, WFG-GSA.

[35]George, *Addresses*, Macon, August 19, 1938, 2–3.

[36]Ibid., Rome, August 24, 1938, 5.

summer before he entered law school in 1900. He does not seem to have been impoverished while there, given his memberships in a number of societies, including a social fraternity. Photographs of him at the time show a well-dressed young man—although he may be wearing the same suit in all of them. In one of his campaign speeches in 1938, he said, "When I finally got to Mercer, I probably made as little of my opportunities as any boy who ever entered that institution,"[37] a curious statement to make, especially since he seems to have exploited every opportunity available to him. Perhaps it was made in false modesty.

Mercer College at that time was an institution that granted a degree in three years; a student started as a freshman, then became a junior, and finally a senior. In the third year of the presidency of Pinckney Daniel Pollock, who also doubled as an English teacher, Walter F. George arrived at Mercer. George later remembered of Pollock, "Among my fellow students while there, he was held in universal high esteem."[38]

In 1897, Mercer's liberal arts faculty consisted of twelve professors, only one of whom had a doctorate. That was Dr. G. W. Macon, who was a professor of the unlikely combination of modern languages and biology. The institution was organized into twelve "schools," which roughly correspond to "departments" today: Latin, Greek, English, modern languages, math, astronomy, natural history, physics, chemistry, history, philosophy, and Bible.[39] To be admitted, students had to be "at least fifteen years of age" and have "a thorough knowledge of technical English grammar" and the ability "to write fair [?] English."[40] Each "school" had its own entrance requirements, such as proficiency in Latin, which was rigorously pushed, and Greek, although Greek was not required of those desiring a B.S degree. "Proficiency" in Latin was defined as the ability to read Caesar's *Gallic Wars* as well as Cicero's orations, but Virgil's *Aeneid* could be substituted for Cicero.[41] All students had to take courses in English, Latin, Greek, mathematics, history, physics, and psychology. Curiously, Bible was optional in this Baptist institution.[42]

Tuition and fees for freshmen were $46.00, with another $48.00 for board, laundry, coal, and kerosene. Room furnishings, books, and stationery

---

[37]Ibid., Macon, August 19, 1938, 2–3.

[38]Bryant, "Walter F. George," 4.

[39]*Catalogue and Annual Announcements of Mercer University*, 1897–1898, 4.

[40]Ibid., 8 9.

[41]Ibid., 10.

[42]Ibid., 21–22.

cost an additional $13.65, with another $3.50 tacked on for unspecified "incidentals," for a total annual expense for a year at Mercer College of $111.40. These figures, the catalogue warned, were only for "*necessary* [italics original] expenses" and noted that "Many of our students get through the college year on $150.00."[43]

George was actively involved in campus activities from the very beginning. He joined the yearbook staff, where he served on the board of editors and on the subscription committee. Given his later victories in oratorical contests, one might have expected him to have won an oratory event his first year, but if he entered, he did not win. He pledged Sigma Nu and remained in it until his graduation three years later.[44] His glory days would be in speech in his work in Mercer's Ciceronian Society, a literary and debating society founded on August 15, 1838 (when Mercer was still at Penfield). It had then become the Franklin Society, but a split had formed the Phi Delta Society and then the Ciceronian Society.[45] The Ciceronian Society's alumni include former governors, senators, and congressmen.[46] George, who would later become one of the most powerful men in the United States, was elected to the Ciceronian Society in September 1897.[47] He was first called on to "declame" early in October, and at the same meeting he was elected to the important post of "critic," the member who analyzes other members' speeches.[48] The minutes of the October 2 meeting noted, "Mr. George made an able report as critic."[49] For some reason, there was a completely new election on October 30 in which someone else was elected critic, but George was reappointed critic pro-tem on November 22. He also joined a deputation to approach the rival Phi Delta Society to match the Ciceronian Society's pledge of $10.00 for magazines for the college's reading rooms.[50]

George moved right to the top of the Ciceronian Society. In January 1898, George, still a freshman, was elected to the society's executive committee, and the minutes show that he was frequently called on to speak in the place of absent declaimers.[51] They also show that he was active in debate, was frequently summoned to make impromptu speeches, and elected

---

[43]Ibid., 60.

[44]*Kinetoscope*, 1898, 31.

[45]Ibid., 1897, 39.

[46]Ibid., 39.

[47]Phi Delta Society minutes, September 25, 1897, 88.

[48]Ibid., 199.

[49]Ibid., 200.

[50]Ibid., 212.

[51]Ibid., 215.

to represent the society in debates with other schools.[52] He was on the finance committee when it voted "not to spend more than $7.50 on the annual college present this year."[53]

In 1899, at the end of his juior year, George was elected editor-in-chief of the *Mercerian*, the campus literary magazine, with the understanding that "he is to serve the whole year,"[54] but for uncited reasons, the Society accepted his resignation on February 10, 1900.[55]

The typical debates of the society seem amusingly lofty in hindsight. Others, however, are rather weighty. For example, "Resolved: That the orator has been a greater factor in the civilization of the world than the poet,"[56] or in December 1897, the members debated, "Resolved: That the reading of fiction improves the mind."[57] On a pacifist note, the society discussed on October 2, 1897, "Resolved: That the statesman has done more for the advancement of civilization than the warrior."[58] On December 11, 1897, their debate centered around this. Resolved: that wealth wealth has a favorable influence upon morals of a people."[59] On another lofty note, the Society debated on February 12, 1898, "Resolved: That men of thought have done more for civilization than men of action."[60] In one meeting they debated the question of women's suffrage.

Reflecting the times, there were a surprising number of resolutions debated on the place of the Negro in American society: "Resolved: That lynching in the popular sense of the term is justifiable," "Resolved: That the Negro should be colonized,"[61] "Resolved: That the Negro has retarded the progress of our country,"[62] and "Resolved: That the Negro not be allowed to derive more from the education fund than he puts in [*sic*]."[63]

The minutes of the society do not reveal what individual members said on these topics, so we have no idea of George's views on such matters. Our only clues are his comments in the Ciceronian Society's *Critics' Book*. Even

[52]Ibid., 241.
[53]Ibid., 270.
[54]Ciceronian Society minutes, June 3, 1898, 291.
[55]Ibid., 319.
[56]Ciceronian Society minutes, 1891–1902, 204.
[57]Ibid., 212.
[58]Ibid., 200.
[59]Ibid., 213.
[60]Ibid., 217.
[61]Ibid., 295.
[62]Ibid., 230.
[63]Ibid. 210.

here, we learn little except that young George had a good knowledge of English grammar, for his remarks are largely corrections of the flaws in a speaker's English. In one meeting on October 16, 1897, he notes that "double negatives are used frequently," and in others he corrects subject-verb agreement errors. ("Mr. Sims' verbs are often plural when they should be singular and singular when plural verbs are required."[64]) He notes that "zenit" should be "zenith," and another time he corrects "an important part" with "an important past."[65] He must have made major contributions overall, for in April 1898, while still a freshman, George was placed on the Ciceronian Society's executive committee. [66]

George's association with the Ciceronians was not always pleasant and triumphal, however. For example, his first time in the "Ready Speakers' Contest," he had to yield victory to his opponent J. R. Jester on the debate, "Will the United States become the Greatest of Nations?" In such competitions, each speaker was given the topic ten minutes before he had to speak, and George lost this one. The minutes do not record what his position was. The literary journal *The Mercerian* had expressed the hope that each society would encourage speaking *extempore* because "the man who can think upon his feet and express his thoughts clearly and forcefully will always have power with [over?] men in the world."[67] Even in his senior year, in a debate on the resolution, "Resolved: That a federal income tax should be beneficial to the people of the United States," he was criticized for referring to "Massachusetts" as "who" in a number of places and "which" in one place.[68] At another point, George was fined a quarter for failing to declaim at a meeting.

As a sophomore, George demonstrated his literary skills in the campus annual, *Kinetoscope*, of which he became editor. Where we learn most of George's college years and of his literary ability is from his editorship of *The Mercerian,* Mercer's literary journal. His writing, while typical of the time's style, is highly readable and perfectly written grammatically. His pieces show an erudite command of the English language and a broad knowledge of great writers, and his writing style reveals a deep knowledge and profound use of language beyond the years of the average sophomore either then or since. There are frequent quotes from Shakespeare, Tolstoy, Emerson, and Plato. He wrote on such editorial themes as would have been of interest to

[64]*Ciceronian Society: Critics' Book*, March 20, 1897, 13.
[65]Ibid., 11.
[66]*Mercerian* 1/7 (April 1989): 17.
[67]*Mercerian* 8/6 (March 1898): 17.
[68]*Ciceronian Society: Critics' Book*, March 20, 1897–November 4, 1899, 107.

most college students, such as "A Summer Trip," or "Clean Athletics," but he also wrote on subjects that reflected a deeper intellect and wider reading background than the average student of his day, such as an analysis of Edwin Markham's "The Man with the Hoe," a poem that had recently appeared and caused some ripples in the literary world, and the unveiling of Zolnay's bust of Edgar Allen Poe.[69] In his essay on "Christmas—Good Will toward Men," he wrote, "Yet the rational basis of Christmas and its charities are beautiful after the similitude of the foundation stones of a great temple, and in the slow construction and probable defects of the super-structure will be revealed to men the imperfections of their methods."[70] On the "law of giving," he wrote, "Every ripened head of wheat, locked in the tender embrace of its fellows, murmurs the message in every golden billow of the broad wheat field."[71] He was equally eloquent when he held forth on democracy: "In the realm of free thought," he told his readers, "Democracy holds an honored place.... It is the only medium through which Free Thought makes known its laws and applies its teaching to the children of men.... Free Thought respects neither class nor rank. It bows before no king, it supplicates no throne. It sees in the monarch's jeweled crown the badge of servitude, and seeing this, it bids defiance to the decrees of prince and pope."[72]

In another essay, he praised Edgar Allen Poe as the "greatest Southern poet," overlooking the local "Poet Laureate of the South," Sidney Lanier, and strongly criticized the lack of homage paid to him. "For many years our book writers have said repeatedly that the South has produced no literature previous to the Civil War," he intoned. "Often have we searched the pages of our *textbooks* [emphasis original] in vain for the most meagre account of Southern poets. It is so unfortunate that the South has [been] given so little recognition to her men and women in the field of letters. It is unfortunate that that the Southern student should look upon his land as a literary desert." Then he added, "The former misfortune was perhaps unavoidable; the latter is the natural result of the former." He condemned Southerners for not having recognized their greats, adding that Southerners are now only "beginning to know...our poets and story writers." Mentioning Sidney Lanier, Timrod, and Poe, he asks, "Can the opulent and imperial North exhibit such a trinity of Genius."[73] In non-Southern themes, he shows a strong

[69] *Mercer Cluster*, October 20, 1922, 1.
[70] WFG, "Christmas—Good Will toward Men," 35–36.
[71] Ibid., 36.
[72] WFG, "The Expression of Free Thought," WFG-MU.
[73] WFG, "On the Unveiling of Zolnay's Bust of Poe," 21–23.

grasp of literary criticism made all the more remarkable when one considers that he was only a few years from his humble tenant-farmer origins.

In discussing Markham's "The Man with the Hoe," he wrote,

> The poem itself has a strong theme, a theme running itself out in Mr. Markham's later poem 'Dreyfus.' The Poem has strong expressions and is the most remarkable production of several poetic decades. In many parts its strength is as powerful as the best poems of [Rudyard] Kipling—the men who express what English statesmen and philosophers fail to imitate and what Anglo-Saxon history itself is slowly writing out.[74]

His analyses of oratorical speeches were equally eloquent. In an editorial in *The Mercerian* in February 1900, he praised the speeches at the Founders' Day exercises. Of the speech of W. Cole Jones of the Ciceronian Society, he wrote that he had "delighted his audience with a carefully prepared and well-delivered oration on 'Unhistoric facts,'" adding, "Mr. Jones adds to his fine sense of literary appreciation the charm of his graceful personality." Of the performance of O. A. Thaxton of the rival Phi Delta Society, he wrote, that he had "charmed his audience with a well-thought out oration on 'William the Silent, Prince of Orange.'" Thaxton's delivery was "marked by its calm rationality and his composition was singularly free from that high-flown bombast so common to the schoolboy orator." He summed up the whole speaking at the event with the observation "The '99 program was conceded on all sides to have been the best presented in several years."[75]

Although George was supposed to serve out the year 1900 as the *Mercerian* editor, the position passed mysteriously in March to a Walter M. Lee. The reason for George's replacement can only be guessed. In the February issue, he had written two editorials, "The Story or the Essay—Which?" and "Clean Athletics." The first seems to have been in response to criticism of his editorial choices. Noting that college literary magazines should "contain both stories and essays, with a leaning toward the essay," he then added that such good stories "it must be admitted…are like the visits of angels—few and far between." Students were better at writing essays than stories, he felt, and so when the latter are chosen for publication, they should be "chosen with great care and a well-trimmed blue pencil."[76] "Clean Athletics" decried the rule-breaking that some athletes had used to win, making the point that it would be better to lose than to win by cheating. College athletics do not

[74]WFG, "Edwin Markham—The Man with the Hoe," 8–10.
[75]Editorial, biographical folder, WFG-MU.
[76]WFG, "The Story or the Essay—Which?" 33–35.

seem to have changed that much from George's day to ours. After these two editorials, he was no longer the editor. The first is clearly a response to criticism of his editorial policy. His support of college athletics probably stepped on the toes of some administrators, but beyond what can be surmised form these themes, we do not know what led to his departure.

On the question of athletics, George highly favored a college athletic program. His first attack on Mercer's limited athletics came in the 1899 issue of *Kinetoscope* where he wrote, "Candor demands that it be said of Mercer's athletics that they are not what they should be." His specific criticism was that the university had no football team. He suggested that Mercer students needed a greater interest in athletics generally, and he criticized the college for not having given enough attention "to this very important phase of college life." Mercer was constructing a new gymnasium, and George felt that this construction "bespeaks a more healthful stimulus in all departments of our athletics."[77] One of his primary criticisms of college athletics was the "unfair methods in making up their [college] teams," apparently referring to illegal recruitment and the use of athletics to recruit students for colleges, but he does not explain further. George also criticized the "professional element" of the hunger to win. Both the desire to win at any cost and illegal recruitment "defeat the real aim of college athletics" and are equally "injurious." He wrote in "Clean Athletics," "There can never be in any college a successful team until the idea that every game must be won, by fair means or foul, is dismissed." He insisted that the Mercer athletic program "remain honest," implying that it was currently not, and concluded with the prediction that "the time will come when we will no more feel the need of importing athletes than we now feel of importing debaters."[78] This editorial was the last George wrote for the *Mercerian*; the March issue, as noted above, had a different editor. It is difficult to know if the end of his tenure as editor was a result of the editorials or due to another cause. Interestingly, in his one year in law school, 1900–1901, he served on the college Athletic Council, so his criticisms must have been taken somewhat to heart.

George's greatest accomplishments in his four-year stay at Mercer (un dergraduate and law) were in his speaking and debating successes. Memorizing the speeches in the *Congressional Record* as a young man honed his natural speaking skills, which were so improved in his Mercer competitions that as a politician he easily fit into the mode of the Southern politician with the thunderous voice. When he was later on the Mercer Board of Trustees,

[77] *Kinetoscope*, 1899, 98.
[78] Ibid., 35–37.

the *Mercer Cluster*, by then the student newspaper, described his college speaking and debating career in the most florid of terms by quoting a source from George's student days: "Honors have rolled down upon our heads in boundless confusion [as a result of Walter F. George's victories]," the papers told its readers. "Our admirable Crichton, Walter George, together with his famous colleague, Mark Bolding...many times vanquishes our inveterate foes, are resting quietly on their oars, having defeated everything in sight."[79] George had early joined the debating society and as a junior gained wide recognition for his oratorical skills when Mercer's team bested a team from the University of Georgia in a tournament promoted by *Atlanta Journal* editor John Temple Graves in 1898.[80]

That same year, George won a smashing victory in Atlanta in the Southern Oratorical Contest, where both he and his partner Mark Bolding represented the college. They competed against students from North and South Carolina and Alabama. Governor Candler, a Mercer graduate, presided over the event, and George spoke on the US Constitution. An entire trainload of Mercer students attended the event to support the two orators.[81] Word of the pair's success reached the campus before they did, and the students who had remained behind decided to celebrate with a huge bonfire, a typical rallying point for a celebration. In searching for wood, a gang of students noticed a chicken coop behind President Pollack's house, and without too much thought, proceeded to dismantle it, when reason took over. After a discussion, the group decided not to raze the coup for firewood and was about to depart when a woman's voice pierced the darkness from an unlit window of the president's house. It was that of the president's wife. "Young gentlemen," she said, "this is my coop. Use it as you like." They dismantled it, adding it to the fire, and in the process emancipated the chickens, which were found wandering aimlessly about the campus "with a look in their eyes as though they remembered well the night when everyone went wild but they and when dawn appeared on the campus at an unusually early hour."[82]

In spring 1899, George's sophomore year, he won a first-place medal in the Ready Speakers' Contest, where each contestant was given only ten minutes of preparation.[83] The topic may have been "The Bases of Peace."[84]

---

[79]*Mercer Cluster*, October 20, 1922, 1.

[80]Bryant, "Walter F. George," 4.

[81]Ibid., 1.

[82]Ibid.

[83]*Kinetoscope*, 5, 1901, 81.

[84]*Catalogue and Annual Announcements of Mercer University*, 1898–1899, 51; *Kinetoscope*, 1901, vol. 5, 341-343.

His delivery was described as an unusually "slow and...formal manner of speech,"[85] which the *Mercer Cluster* later translated into his being "the logical orator."[86] In these contests, George defeated students from all over the South, but he modestly spread the glory, writing, "Since '97 Mercer has engaged in three outside debates and four contests and has not a single defeat to her account," victories he credited to "our institution's true life and work." He gave credit to everyone, never mentioning himself. "Let us not forget that one man, one set of men cannot win our battles. Let us not forget."[87]

George's greatest oratorical victory came when he was in law school in 1901 in the Georgia Oratorical Contest, which was held in the Grand Opera House in Macon to a packed standing-room only crowd. George was Mercer's orator, and the Mercer delegation was confident that he would win. His supporters stopped yelling when he rose to speak on one of his old topics, the "Bases of Peace." One account stated that he "stepped at once into the very heart of his subject, and stayed there dealing with fundamentals until his speech was finished." It was accounted by all who heard it or read it tobe the greatest speech ever delivered in Georgia by a college man. George, of course, won the competition. [88]

MERCER LEGACY

George never lost his gift for speaking. Even in his late seventies, his voice still thundered when he spoke.[89] One journalist at the same time noted that his "resonant, compelling voice" could create "a thundering effect in both the courtroom and the Senate."[90] Mrs. Prescott Bush, the mother and grandmother of a president, wrote of the content and organization of one of George's speeches that "The Senator, never looking at a note, gave a thirty-minute speech in perfect, logical order, which could be heard without the slightest strain by everyone. It was a beautiful job...."[91] George had cut a wide swath at Mercer in both his undergraduate and law years, where one contemporary wrote that he had held the student body "in the palm of his hand." Judge R. C. Bell of the Georgia Supreme Court told George's longtime friend, Macon attorney T. Baldwin Martin, "I never think of Mercer

[85]WFG, *The Dictionary of Georgia Biography*, vol. 1, 1983, copy in WFG-MU.
[86]*Mercer Cluster*, October 20, 1922, 3.
[87]WFG, "The Oratorical Contest," 28–29.
[88]Kinetoscope, 5 (1901), 78, Special Collections, Tarver Library, Mercer University.
[89]Donovan, "Senator George," 32.
[90]"One of the Greatest," *Newsweek*, 50, (August 12, 1957), 34.
[91]"Washington Life," clipping, WFG-VHPS.

but that I think of Walter F. George. He was a BMOC ...."[92] For the remainder of his life, he would maintain a close association with the school that had given him his higher education. Having always been an active alumnus, he was elected to the board of trustees in 1922, the year he was elected to the Senate, and he served proudly for a number of years. On his election to the board of trustees, the student newspaper the *Mercer Cluster* wrote, "Walter George is already [a thorough gentleman]—a Christian gentleman—as thoroughly made in the manner as his brilliant genius is conspicuous and proud as we are of him.... Mercer will be prouder yet to claim him as one of her noble sons."[93] Mercer's high regard of George culminated in 1947 at a testimonial dinner held in the dining hall of Mary Erin Porter Dormitory, when the law school was named for him. US Supreme Court Chief Justice Fred M. Vinson attended. Every year thereafter, George attended Law Day at the institution.

In the years that followed, he was often active in Mercer affairs, and he was frequently called on to speak at graduation, baccalaureate, chapel, and Founders' Day events. He was instrumental in naming of Dr. Rufus W. Weaver, a distinguished educator, president of the institution in 1924.[94] He hired the institution's graduates in his offices.[95] In 1932, George gave the major address when a new law school building was dedicated.[96] Many years later, he was made honorary president of the Washington, DC, Mercer Alumni Chapter at a dinner attended by a number of members of Congress who were also Mercer graduates.[97] At the graduation exercises in June 1957, after Walter F. George had announced that he was leaving the Senate, President George Connell announced that George would receive a Doctorate in Humane Letters.[98] Later that year, he was declared Mercer's most distinguished alumnus and described in the most laudatory terms: "Alert mind, lofty ambition, sound judgement, judicial temperament, high ideals, faultless

---

[92]T. Baldwin Martin, "Walter F. George," *Mercerian* 33/3 (February 1947): copy in WFG-MU; "Walter George was Senate's Workhorse," *The Advantage*, March 9, 1992, WFG file, Vienna Historic Preservation Society, Vienna, GA. Cited herafter as WFG-VHPS.

[93]*Mercer Cluster,* October 20, 1922, 3.

[94]*Mercer Alumnus* 2/4 (December 1924): 2; *Mercer Alumnus* 2/4 (October 1924): 11.

[95]*Mercer Alumnus* 2/4 (December 1924): 2.

[96]Program on the dedication, 2 June 1932, WFG-MU.

[97]"The Washington D. C. Alumni Dinner," *Mercerian,* n. d., WFG-MU.

[98]That same day, Mercer awarded to George's colleague, Richard Russell, a doctorate of laws ("Four Leaders to receive Honorary Decrees," *Mercerian*, April 1957, 4, clipping in WFG-MU.

character, complete dedication and innate courtliness" and "a peerless Christian Statesman."[99] The encomia sounded like an epitaph and might well have been as they were written just nine months before his death.

Upon graduation in 1900 with a BS degree, George taught school,[100] but in the fall, he matriculated into Mercer's law school, which was temporarily housed in one downstairs room that would later become a dining room in Sherwood Hall (now a residence hall).[101] It was later "permanently" located in a room in the present-day Willingham Chapel. The school was not accredited when George entered, nor would it be for a quarter of a century, until under the leadership of Dean Rufus C. Harris, the school finally received its accreditation.[102] Although not accredited when he was a student there, an act of the Georgia Legislature in 1875 gave graduates the right to practice law in Georgia.[103] The school consisted of eight professors and opponents, and the law course was only one year long, as was typical at that time. The year's tuition and diploma cost $65.00, with board estimated to be $10–15.00 per month. The total cost of the textbooks came to a pricy $28.00.[104] George's class enrolled a total of twenty-one students.

George continued to distinguish himself academically and oratorically. In his one year of law school, he won the Georgia and Southern States oratorical championship. He graduated with a Bachelor of Laws degree. The University of Georgia awarded George a Phi Beta Kappa key in 1944.[105]

By the time that George left law school, he had had acquired a very dignified demeanor. Not surprisingly, all extant pictures of him from this time onward show him in a suit and tie, a form of dress he never abandoned, even when in Vienna after he had entered the Senate. Even when he had no plans to leave the house, he still put on a tie every morning.[106] For someone who came to climb so high, he never developed an arrogance or personal

---

[99]"Highlights of Sen. George Citation," *Mercerian* (December 1957): 11, clipping in WFG-MU.

[100]Mellichamp writes that George taught for two years in Dooly County to pay for his legal training, but that cannot be correct as he entered law school in fall 1900 immediately after graduating in May (Mellichamp, *Senators from Georgia*, 232).

[101]*Mercer Cluster*, April 18, 1956, 3.

[102]Rufus Harris would go on to become the dean of the Tulane Law School and then Tulane's president. On retiring from Tulane, he returned to Mercer to serve first as its president and later as its chancellor.

[103]*Catalogue and Annual Announcements of Mercer University*, 1897–1898, 35.

[104]Ibid., 1900–1901, 55.

[105]A phone call to the Phi Beta Kappa National Headquarters in Washington, DC.

[106]Interview with John Bonner. In time, he developed the manner of a Southern aristocrat ("One of the Greatest," 34.).

vanity. He never developed a phony political persona, like suspender-snapping or baby-kissing, and he never traveled with a washboard band.[107] No man was too lowly for his attention, and when he was in Vienna after a grueling congressional session, he gave time to anyone who came to the door of the small bungalow that he and Miss Lucy eventually came to call their home.[108] Even in the last years of his career, when he needed to burnish his image in the expected race with Herman Talmadge, he avoided self-promotion when he was the most instrumental figure in bringing about of the first conference in 1955 of an American president and the Russian leadership in ten years, nor was he eager to attend such a conference himself. "If he does decide to go," Newsweek reported, "it will be from a sense of duty, not vanity."[109]

Pictures of him in his last days of college show man of rather average build if a bit thin. Over time, he gained a middle-age paunch, but he never became fat. The *Atlanta Journal* described him in 1931 as having "a peaceful countenance from which peer kindly gray eyes." Unlike some senators who exuded self-importance, George was always cordial and gentle, "yet dignified with those rugged qualities so appealing in men."[110] His Mercer graduation picture shows a certain school-marmish air about him. Few people would call him good-looking. He was one of those people whose looks improved with age.

Even after he joined "the most exclusive club in the world" in 1922, few friends called him by his first name, with even members of his own family addressing him as "Senator."[111] He did not seem to have ever acquired much of a sense of humor. Once, when a reporter told him that he had been named honorary president of the "Society for the Prevention of Calling Pullman Porters George," he replied in all seriousness, "That seems a queer society. Why not just call them by their right names?"[112] Observing his style when he ran against Governor Gene Talmadge, arguably one of the most colorful politicians Georgia ever produced, his son Herman, who was managing his father's campaign, thought the race between George and his father would be a "duck shoot".[113] The one trait he had that usually accompanied

[107]"Political Test," 33.

[108]Conversation with Janet Joyner, director of VHPS, who remembered hearing her parents tell this story.

[109]Freedman, 279–80.

[110]"George Is Lauded," *Atlanta Journal* clipping, June 30, 1931, WFG-GSA.

[111]Mellichamp, *Senators from Georgia*, 238.

[112]Jarman, "Taxpayer's Senator," 23.

[113]Talmadge, *Talmadge: A Political Legacy*, 39.

the successful Southern politician was his remarkable speaking ability, which George of course had, and sometimes even that seemed like he was "handing down an important religious or legal tenet."[114]

George was a religious man, but not conspicuously so for that day and time. He rarely mentioned God in his speeches. He had grown up in the Old Macedonia Baptist Church in Webster County, and in Vienna he was a deacon in the First Baptist Church, where he taught a men's Bible class. One of the few revealing statements of his Christianity came in a speech he gave at the Old Macedonia Baptist Church. He informed, or rather reminded, the congregation that "It was here in this little church where I met Christ as my Savior. It was here in this little church where I was taught those great principals [*sic*] by which I have sought to live and which have guided my life."[115] After he had been in the Senate a number of years, he sent a birthday greeting to Bishop W. A. Chandler of Atlanta, saying, "May I not [*sic*] now add my voice to the multitude who rejoice with you today among the living preachers of the Gospel.... Your unfaltering faith in Jesus Christ is a consolation and hope to Christians the world over."[116] His devout origins remained influential.

In his personal life, he enjoyed mystery novels, which, especially in his elder years, he consumed with great enthusiasm. His great love, though, was hunting and fishing, especially the latter. One of his favorite foods was catfish, and he was known for his ability to fry them.[117] Until his cataract surgery, he was a crack shot with both a shotgun and a rifle, and he was known as the best wild turkey shot in Dooly County—no casual accomplishment because wild turkeys are especially hard to hit.[118]

George smoked cigars and cigarettes in public, but in his early days in the Senate, he smoked a corncob pipe in the privacy of his office using tobacco he had grown on his Dooly County farm.[119] He also drank alcoholic beverages, usually on hunting and fishing trips, and well out of the sight of his wife Miss Lucy, who thoroughly disapproved.[120] There are some indications that after World War II, he may have begun to drink to excess. Vice President Henry Wallace noted in his diary that at a dinner meeting to dis-

[114]Jarman, "Taxpayer's Senator," 23.

[115]John H. Robson, "Sen. Walter F. George: A Distinguished Georgia Baptist," WFG-MU. Robson was the pastor of Vienna First Baptist Church.

[116]WFG to Bishop W. A. Candler, 23 August 1927, box 64, f. 4, Candler papers.

[117]T. Hoyt Davis interview.

[118]"One of the Greatest," 31.

[119]Ibid.

[120]Henry Woodward interview.

cuss post-war aid to Britain George appeared "tight."[121] George was away from Miss Lucy and possibly used the occasion to overindulge.

On finishing law school in the early summer 1901, George moved to Vienna, Georgia, which he would call home for the remainder of his life. To this point, his life had been rather remarkable, given his background and origins. From this point, it would become what one journalist said resembled "a Horatio Alger novel." "It is no wonder," the journalist notes, "that this legend appears on his campaign pamphlets: 'I stand where I have [always] stood...on my record."[122] He would make a stellar rise from this small town to become one of the most powerful men in the United States.

Why George picked Vienna, a town of only about 1,500 citizens, is unclear. With a formal law degree in a time when people could practice law by simply "reading the law" for a period of time in a law firm, he could have had a most lucrative practice in Atlanta. Perhaps he chose Vienna because it was close to his birthplace and because he had lived and gone to school in nearby Cordele. Perhaps he chose Vienna because it offered opportunity; George had somehow learned of a law practice that was for sale there. (A local lawyer had decided to go west to seek his fortune, for oil had just been discovered in Beaumont, Texas.) George and Z. H. Copeland, a fellow Mercer law school graduate, visited the town a week before they were to graduate, and it must have been then that he made arrangements to purchase the practice, its six cases, and its law library of fifty volumes. *The Vienna Progress* (later to be renamed *The Vienna News*) noted their visit and wrote that the two men "would be heartily welcomed here, not only at the bar but in social circles."[123] George departed Macon the night after graduation for Vienna, where the court would open in two weeks.

George came to Vienna with his old debating and oration partner Marc Bolding, not Copeland, who had come down with him only to scout out the territory. Bolding and George formed a "co-partnership for the practice of law." The *Vienna Progress* enthused over "these two young men of more than ordinary ability" and indeed informed its readership that "they will have a bright future before them" and that they were "heartily welcomed to Vienna."[124] The two men went into partnership with an M. A. Flournoy, forming the firm, albeit a short lived one, of Flournoy, George and Bolding. Not

[121] "Personalities in your government," 26 June 1955, 8, WFG-MU.

[122] *Vienna Progress,* May 30, 1901, 1.

[123] Ibid., June 13, 1901. Pages were not numbered in most issues, but the paper was usually only a few pages.

[124] Ibid.

much is known about M. A. Flournoy, but an ad for legal services in the local paper had billed him as having "special attention to bill collections,"[125] so we might surmise that this form of practice was the focus of this newly created firm. Individual lawyers were advertising in the local paper, but Flournoy, George, and Bolding seem have been the only "law firm," although each seemed to practice independently. Their office was in a small brick building on courthouse square, called rather grandly the Stoval Corner Brick Building, and George thus joined a surprisingly large community of nine lawyers in Vienna.

For some reason, Bolding and Fleming, who had replaced Flournoy, do not seem to have stayed long, for by November, there are no further mentions of them in the newspaper, and George's law partner is A. W. Copeland. It's unclear if this might have been the same Copeland who accompanied George on his exploratory visit, and the paper may have simply gotten the initials wrong.

George was admitted to the bar on June 7, although there is some question about exactly where he was admitted. It was not, interestingly enough, in the Southwestern Circuit, in which he would be practicing law, because there is no record that he took the oath in either Americus or Vienna. George Connell (president of Mercer University in the late 1950s) felt that he probably was admitted to the bar in the Southeast Georgia Circuit.[126] Wherever he was admitted, he quickly acquired the typical Southern courthouse title of "colonel" and was so addressed.

Assuming that the young lawyer would ask for a delay because he would not have had time to prepare the six cases he had purchased in the two weeks before the court session began, the attorneys for the other side showed up at the appointed hour unprepared. They were surprised to learn that George was quite ready to try the cases. George won every one of them, for he had been furiously preparing in the two weeks he had been in Vienna. He very rapidly became the town's leading attorney, and within five years he had taken so much of the local legal work that many of the Dooly County lawyers had to resort to other forms of work, like selling insurance, to make a living.[127]

We do not know the reason for the changing partnerships, nor what happened to Bolding or Flournoy, who likewise disappears. George was so immediately successful that he may have decided that he would be better

[125]Ibid., February 27, 1902.

[126]Vienna Historical Preservation Society, *The Kingdom of Dooly*, 18–20.

[127]*Vienna Progress*, July 11, 1901.

served by going it alone. An inexhaustible worker, with a courtroom demeanor that his obituary years later called "majestically calm and patient," he was also known to be "fair and legally learned." His success was great enough that the *Vienna Progress* commented that George "enjoys the confidence of the entire community"[128] and reported within months of his arrival of his many trips to court in the surrounding counties. Within a few short weeks of his arrival, he had legal work in both Preston, his hometown, and Americus.[129] In September, the *Vienna Progress* reported that he had just returned from Stewart County on a visit to friends and relatives, but while in Limpkin, he argued two cases involving a thousand acres of land. Two weeks later, he was back in Stewart County Superior Court with more legal business, and the *Vienna Progress*, which had become the great champion of the young lawyer, enthused to its readers, "This is indeed a compliment to the young attorney who is in his first season of practice."[130] Within two years, his practice took him to courts in Macon and even Atlanta, to say nothing of work in Florida, where he was handling legal business for the Spring Hill Naval Stores and Lumber Company.[131] By 1903, he was so busy that he hired Miss Beatrice Nelves of Macon as a stenographer, and he moved to a larger office in the Stoval Corner Brick Building. In 1906, he partnered with L. L. Woodward, and the two men bought a building from Colonel G. W. Wooten, who had purchased it for his own law office years before. In 1924, two years after George went to the Senate, he sold his interest in the building to Woodward, who in time sold it to H. C. Lee for a bicycle shop. The Vienna Historical Preservation Society bought it and moved it to its present site on Fourth Street. They began restoring it and converting it into a museum honoring George in 1984. It was dedicated upon its completion in 1991.[132]

MARRIAGE AND FAMILY

In Vienna Walter George met and married his lifelong companion, the redoubtable "Miss Lucy" Heard. "Miss Lucy" was born May 5, 1882, one of eleven children.[133] She attended Vienna schools and then later took her

---

[128]Ibid., July 25, 1901.

[129]Ibid., September 1901 and October 17, 1901.

[130]*Vienna News*, May 29, 1903. *Vienna Progress*'s name changed 1903 to *Vienna News*.

[131]"Historical Society Works...," unidentified copy of clipping in WFG-DCPL.

[132]Jake Gregory interview.

[133]"Thirty-one Year Span in Capital," unidentified clipping, Lucy Heard George File, Vienna Historic Preservation Society, Vienna, GA. Cited herafter as LHG-VHPS.

higher education at LaGrange Female College.[134] *Time* called her "bouncing" and "irrepressible," and she was reputed to be a great beauty in her youth.[135] Apparently the editor of the local paper had a crush on her, because she could not take a step outside her home without its being reported in the paper, always in the most gushing, fawning manner. Once calling her "one of the noblest little women in Georgia," the editor even noted to the public when she was sick,[136] and when she got a job as a bookkeeper at the Vienna Drug company, he reported that, too.[137] When electricity came to Vienna in 1903, six young ladies were chosen to throw the switch sending current throughout the city. Naturally Lucy was among them.[138]

Unlike George's family, the Heards were wealthy and prominent, and Lucy Heard was one of the town's most sought-after young women. Jake Gregory, a local citizen, commented on the Heards, "If you did not know that they were wealthy and prominent, they would tell you."[139] Joseph P. Heard, Sr., Lucy's father, was a cotton farmer, undertaker, warehouseman, wholesale grocer, building contractor, mule trader, and a dry goods merchant, with a store that sold everything from underwear and corsets to buggy whips. Moreover, his interests were not confined to the small town of Vienna; he was part-owner of Heard Brothers of Macon, which sold buggies and carriages. According to the *Vienna Progress*, when George came to Vienna, Heard's Macon concern alone was worth about $125,000, an enormous sum at the time.[140] His home and major interests were in Vienna, and every issue of the *Progress* contained ads for his dry goods enterprise. He enticed his customers with lines such as, "Silks at cotton Prices" and "The place where quality and LOW prices reign supreme."[141] One ad informed potential customers, "Exquisite don't [*sic*] express it." In an ad for wood stoves, Heard guaranteed "to make it warm for the cook if you will buy one of our Jewel, Tallulah, or Gott City stoves."[142] Every one of Heard's ads stressed the high

---

[134]"Senator Walter F. George, A Distinguished Georgia Baptist," unidentified clipping, *The Christian Index*, July 6, 1972, 4, in WFG-DCPL.

[135]*Vienna Progress*, especially issues July 18, 1901 and October 23, 1902.

[136]Ibid., September 12, 1901.

[137]Ibid., April 9, 1903.

[138]For example, she held a dinner party in honor of her house guest, Miss Pauline Martin of Cuthbert, in January 1902 (*Vienna Progress*, January 10 [?], 1902).

[139]*Vienna News*, July 17, 1903.

[140]Ibid.

[141]*Vienna Progress,* August 1, 1901.

[142]For example, see *Vienna Progress,* August 22, 1901.

quality of the product at low or reasonable prices.[143] Whatever the Heard family did was major news. Indeed, sometimes what they did not do made the papers as well. In June 1901, the *Progress* reported the J. P. Heard, Jr., and his wife had just returned from a trip to Virginia and New York, but "they did not attend the Pan American Exposition at Buffalo, however."[144] Excursions to less exotic places like Charleston, South Carolina, were always noted, and even their opinions made news.[145] In June 1901, the *Progress* reported, "J. P. Heard was driving over the country last week and says he never saw the crops in worse condition, especially the cotton crop."[146]

All of this adulation and money produced an arrogant bunch of unruly children. Lucy's numerous brothers, Jake Gregory remembered, were "rounders." One Sunday a number of them dynamited the pond dam on their father's property, taking what fish they wanted, leaving the rest to die.[147] The family threw its weight around in other ways as well. When the railroads were trying to decide on a place for a four-way junction, they wanted to place it in Vienna. The Heards, however, would not give them the right of way, so the connection went to Cordele, ten miles south. As a result, Cordele grew and Vienna withered.[148]

Miss Lucy was not immune to this snootiness. She frequently bossed her husband, and when they needed a car in 1934, she insisted on an expensive one. George suggested that they get a Ford, but Miss Lucy told him in no uncertain terms that she would not be seen around Washington in a Ford, and she made him buy a Lincoln-Zephyr from a dealer in Cordele. In the depths of the Depression, when most political families tried to hide their wealth, Miss Lucy ran around Vienna in this expensive car.[149] She seems to have sometimes treated George's Washington staffers as though they were her personal servants. Jessie Nichols, a black Mississippian who worked for the Finance Committee on which George served, told the story that "at her whim, whenever she wanted to go somewhere, she would call Nichols and order him to drive her. She would just say to him, 'Come on!' He would try to beg off, telling her, 'My time's on that committee.' Then she'd say, 'Well, we'll work it out.' And he would go drive her."[150]

143 Ibid., June 20, 1901.
144 Ibid., May 8, 1902.
145 Ibid., June 27, 1901.
146 Jake Gregory interview.
147 Ibid.
148 Henry Woodward interview.
149 Jesse Nicholas, oral history, 31.
150 WFG, estate tax record, Davis & Forehand Law Firm, Vienna, GA.

Miss Lucy frequently visited friends in surrounding towns and often had visitors to her home for several days, as was the custom of the day.[151] Like her brothers, she seemed to feel that she could do no wrong and could always have what she wanted. Jacob Gregory recalled his mother's live-in domestic employee, Lucinda; one day, Mrs. George, in need of some extra domestic help herself, simply showed up at the Gregory household and asked (more likely demanded) that Lucinda come to work for her that day. On this occasion, Miss Lucy did not get her way, and the refusal came not from Mrs. Gregory: Lucinda herself simply refused to go.[152]

Others sometimes put her in her place. Once when Senator Theodore Green of Rhode Island, a good friend of the Georges, mentioned that he only drank a quarter of a cup of coffee in the morning, Miss Lucy, in her abrupt way, said, "If that's all you drink, why do you mess up a cup?" To this rebuke, Senator Green shook his head and said, "I knew it was right. It was the best thing I ever did." "What's that?" Miss Lucy snapped. "The best thing I ever did," the senator replied, "was never to get married."[153]

Perhaps she met her match in Walter F. George, but it does not seem that he handled her by confrontation. She would not get her way with him because he would just passively ignore her. From the time they met until the end of her life, he was to her "Mr. George," and to him, she was "Miss Lucy."[154] This form of address among married couples was common in the South in those days, to some Washington reporters' amusement. When one asked her about her form of address for her husband, she replied in her frank manner, "I always call him Mr. George, no matter how sweet I feel, nor how mean."[155]

In a town the size of Vienna, Lucy Heard and Walter George certainly would have been introduced, but their meeting was somewhat delayed by the fact that Miss Lucy was visiting her friend Pauline Martin in Cuthbert when George arrived. Her departure for the neighboring Cuthbert was heralded with the usual rapture by the editor of the paper: "Miss Lucy Heard, one of the reigning belles of Vienna, and a young lady whose friends and admirers are not limited to her acquaintances," had departed for Cuthbert. Probably speaking more for himself than for other Viennese, he concluded

---

151Jake Gregory interview.

152Thayer, "She Voted," *Washington Post,* n. d., Miss Lucy's scrapbook, LHG-VHPS.

153T. Hoyt Davis interview.

154"Voice of the 84th," 24.

155*Vienna Progress,* May 30, 1901.

the announcement, "Her return will be anxiously looked for here."[156]

Miss Lucy stayed in Cuthbert long enough to receive a letter from a friend, informing her that there was "an attractive new man in town" and suggested that she come home. "I did," she told a reporter more than fifty years later, "and we were married in 1903."[157] Her return was loyally noted by the newspaper editor between an ad of H. B. Thompson and Co, which "always had on hand," the newspaper informed its readers, "fresh eggs," and an ad of the Vienna Drug Co. which advertised "the best cooking soda at 4 cents a pound."[158]

They likely first met at a lawn party given a few days after her return, where "the young men were spruced up in 'store clothes'" and the ladies were in "handsome costumes." Ice cream, cake, sherbet, and cold drinks were served, and the paper reported, "The evening was spent in social conversation." Among the "gay throng present" were "Messrs. Walter George... [and] Lucy Heard...."[159] most assuredly the first of many times their two names would appear together in print.

Apparently love blossomed eventually, but we do not know how quickly. It was more than two years before the "reigning belle" of Vienna, born to privilege, and the young lawyer, who had by intelligence and hard work clawed his way up from a tenant farm, finally married. There was most probably opposition from the Heard family, although the only evidence we have of that was in a *Newsweek* article after his death, when Miss Lucy's father Joseph Heard was quoted saying to Lucy, "Don't see what you want to waste time on Walter George for. He will never amount to anything, hunting and fishing out on the [Flint] river all the time."[160] Any objections, however, were overcome because "Miss Lucy" and "Mr. George" were married at 5:00 p.m. on July 8, 1903.[161]

The wedding was quite the event in Vienna, as one would imagine. In previous issues of the *Vienna News* in the two years that George had lived there, weddings had not been mentioned, but Lucy and Walter's wedding covered the front page. Lucy's father's prominence was certainly a factor, but the editor's obvious admiration for "Miss Lucy" in previous issues likely also

---

[156]"Thirty-one Year Span in Capital," unidentified clipping, LHG-VHPS.

[157]*Vienna Progress*, June 13, 1901, 1.

[158]Ibid., June 26, 1901.

[159]"One," 34.

[160]One journalistic change in the local press as the Heard-George romance heated up and the marriage date approached was a noticeable decline in the number of times the local paper reported on Miss Lucy, and absent were the glowing encomiums to her beauty.

[161]*Vienna News*, July 10, 1903.

had something to do with it. The wedding was held in the Heard home, and the out-of-town guests formed an impressive list, sort of a who's-who from the surrounding towns as far as Macon. On the list were, of course, Mr. and Mrs. Robert P. George of Preston, Georgia.[162] The Heard parlor, where they were married, was decorated with Southern bamboo and cut-glass vases of roses and maidenhair fern. Miss Roberta Render of LaGrange, likely a college friend of Miss Lucy, sang "Sweethearts and Violets," and the couple entered the living room to the strains of Mendelsohn's "Wedding March," played on the piano by Mrs. O. M. Heard, probably one of Miss Lucy's sisters-in-law. There was a wedding party complete with flower girls. George himself entered with his best man, Tom Royal of Arabi. Miss Lucy entered with a white *crepe de chine* gown trimmed with pearls.[163] The paper reported on the front page that an "elegant supper" was served at 7:00 p.m., and that the bride's table was decorated with the same ferns and roses that had been in the parlor. The couple received many presents, the newspaper noted, which "tested [*sic*] the popularity of the couple." At 8:00 p.m., the newlyweds departed on the A and B Railroad for Tate Springs in Tennessee for their honeymoon.[164] The couple returned home from their wedding trip on July 21, apparently taking up residence in boarding house conditions "at the residence of Mrs. L. Davies."[165]

Thus began the partnership of over half a century of two sharply different people: The staid Walter George and the vivacious, willful Miss Lucy. One gets the impression from the evidence that she tended to nag him, with few results. He hated Washington social life, while Miss Lucy loved it. As chair of the Senate Foreign Relations Committee for a number of years, he had many social demands, including numerous dinners and receptions at the White House. He would always, if possible, beg off, and under the Eisenhower administration, when Ike asked him personally to accept the chair of the Foreign Relations Committee, George received formal permission to avoid most required evenings at the White House. Miss Lucy, on the other hand, "went to everything she could get to,"[166] often in the company of the bachelor Senator Theodore Green of Rhode Island, a man fourteen years her senior. George would stay at home in the Mayflower reading committee

[162]Ibid.

[163]Ibid.

[164]*Vienna News*, July 24, 1903.

[165]G. Dixon, "There's no one…," *Macon Telegraph*, May 21, 1956, scrapbook, LHG-VHPS.

[166]*Vienna News*, May 11, 1906.

reports or murder mysteries. Lucy and Walter did, however, do many things together, and she would even go fishing with him on the Flint River, where they eventually made a river cottage by joining several railroad cars (some accounts say street cars).[167] Here they would entertain as well. Though they often went their separate ways, they were devoted to each other, despite the formal way they always addressed each other. One day he sat next to a colleague in the Senate and said, "Now I'm here and I'm here to vote, but about 5:30 I'm going to see Miss Lucy."[168] Once someone asked them, "When are the two of you going to get to know each other well enough to call each other by just your first names?"[169] Apparently, they never did.

They often quipped and joked with each other. "That's grounds for divorce!" she snapped at him once. "All right," replied Mr. George calmly, "you just go and get one, and don't let's have any more unpleasantness about it."[170] She had always wanted to travel, especially to go to Europe. George did not but once leave the country, despite that fact that he often chaired the Foreign Relations Committee, and that was only a trip to Cuba. Once after she had nagged him about going to Europe and he had refused, she told him, "When I'm lying in my coffin, I hope friends will take Mr. George aside and say, 'See, there's poor Miss Lucy. She's never been to London or Paris'— and that should make him feel bad."[171]

Although the *Washington Post* reported that she generally "stayed out of her husband's politics,"[172] one gets the impression that she influenced his political thinking behind the scenes from time to time. When a special committee was constituted to determine whether or not Senator Joseph McCarthy should be censured, "several persons" tried to persuade George to serve on the committee because his stature would add weight to any decision rendered. Finally after much conversation, he said, "I'll have to ask Miss Lucy." After talking it over with her, he did not serve.[173] In 1955, when he was addressing the National Conference of Editors in Washington, he began by saying, that "Since Mrs. George is here, I am under strict admonition not to

---

[167]"They Like to Sit Next to Miss Lucy," *Washington Post*, August 22, 1954, LHG-VHPS.

[168]Ibid.

[169]Mary Thayer, "Paris Calls Miss Lucy," *Washington Post*, May 10, 1956, scrapbook, LHG-VHPS.

[170]Ibid.

[171]"They Like to Sit Next to Miss Lucy," LHG-VHPS.

[172]Ibid.

[173]*CR*, 84/2, April 25, 1955, 4226.

talk very long about anything."[174] While the remark was meant as a quip, it had the ring of truth.

At least once she intervened to gain a raise for Jesse R. Nichols, the black government documents clerk for the Foreign Relations Committee. He was having trouble with Christie Bell, Senator George's secretary, and was about to resign, when Mrs. George found out about it. "Don't you ever worry," she told him. Nichols figured that "she must have given the senator holy hell" that night. The next day, Ms. Bell was much nicer to Nichols, and a day or two later called him into the senator's office and told him that Senator George had gotten him a raise. Nichols expected that there were strings attached and asked what they were. The condition was that he refrain from talking to Mrs. George.[175]

In 1956, Washington journalist Mary von Renssallaer Thayer called Lucy Heard "Washington's most engaging personality."[176] That same year, the Washington reporter for the *Macon Telegraph* echoed these sentiments back home, stating, "Miss Lucy…is the gayest lady for her age, size, weight, and social position that this or any other world capital has ever had the privilege of harboring."[177] Mrs. Prescott Bush felt that "If a vote were to be taken for the most popular of the Senate wives, I am sure 'Miss Lucy' George…would be unanimously elected," and she added that she was "more fun than a barrel of monkeys."[178] She organized congressional wives into needlepoint groups and groups that sewed for the Red Cross. When the groups assembled, she made cheese cookies (probably cheese biscuits, a Southern favorite) for the group and told funny stories.[179]

The Georges' first child, Heard, arrived on April 2, 1909, almost exactly nine months after their wedding. When Heard was born, the *Vienna News* announced his birth with the laconic words, "Col. Walter George is all smiles this week. He has a fine boy at his home."[180] Heard grew up to be an amiable, well-liked fellow who got along well with people, often going around town giving out vegetables from his garden. He seems, however, not

---

174Jessie R. Nicholas, oral history, 30–31.

175"Paris Calls Miss Lucy," *Washington Post*, May 10, 1956, scrapbook, LHG-VHPS.

176G. Dixon, "There's no one…," *Macon Telegraph*, May 21, 1956, scrapbook, LHG-VHPS.

177News Release of Mrs. Prescott Bush, June 13 and 14, 1956, scrapbook, LHG-VHPS.

178"They Liked to Sit Next to Miss Lucy," *Washington Post*, August 22, 1954, LHG-VHPS.

179*Vienna News*, April 6, 1904.

180Conversations with several local citizens in Vienna.

to have inherited either his father's political savvy or his mother's refinement, and locals today remember his frequent use of profanity.[181] One friend, Henry Woodward, recalled that sometimes Heard's bluntness "shocked him," but then added that he had "not a mean bone in his body" and had a good sense of humor.[182] Woodward remembered being on a dove shoot with Heard, when two birds flew directly at them. Heard, a crack shot, shot one and then turned to get the second, which had flown over them. At that point, the one that he had shot hit him in the back of the head. "You could have heard him cussing in Atlanta," Woodward recalled.[183] Heard served as his father's administrative assistant, and once when a staffer in the office mentioned on a memo that he was going to the beach the next week, Heard scribbled on the note, "Have a good time—legally!"[184]

The amiable elder son may have been considerably less than a ball of fire and perhaps would not have had a good job had his father not given him one. After his father left Washington, Heard, who hated Washington and could not wait each year to return to Vienna when the end of a session permitted, later "dabbled in farming" and worked for the Georgia Power Company.[185] He also tried to develop a subdivision, but he would sell the lots for as little as $25.00 when he needed a little cash.[186] He married Irma Grace, a native of Vienna, whom neighbors remembered was "rather snooty"[187] but "very attractive."[188] She must have been somewhat sentimental, for once when she and Heard were moving, a mover dropped and broke a barrel of their china. She was crying so that Senator George told her that he and Miss Lucy would buy her another set, to which she replied that this set was special because it was one that she and Heard had bought when they were "struggling."[189] They had no children.

Heard entered Mercer, his father's alma mater, in 1921, and later went to law school in Washington. Although he had some sort of law practice in Vienna, he does not seem to have done much with it. He shared none of his father's political ambitions.

---

[181] Henry Woodward interview.

[182] Ibid.

[183] Frances O. Wilcox to Heard [George], August 19, 1955, WFG-VHPS.

[184] T. Hoyt Davis interview.

[185] Conversations with Hattie Conner, whose husband chaired the Dooly County Commission and was at one point in business with Heard George.

[186] Grace Slade Crevett interview.

[187] Henry Woodward interview.

[188] Jake Gregory interview (although his wife, Ethel, who was present, told this story).

[189] Henry Woodward interview.

Marcus, the second George child, was another matter. Born Joseph Marcus George on November 16, 1911, he was the one who seemed destined for politics had it not been for his untimely death in World War II. He was taller than Heard, and one of his Riverside Military Academy classmates recalled that he was "a fine-looking man—very handsome...darker complexioned man—almost Spanish."[190] He resembled his mother's family. Neighbor Frances Coley spoke of his good looks, adding "All the girls lined up to date him."[191] He was just a "good ole boy," one neighbor recalled.[192] "I don't know of any boy who did not think of Marcus as a friend." [193] He was very affable and "never got into fights." He was not an exceptionally good student, but he was an excellent outdoorsman. One time he even took a boat trip down the Flint River to the Gulf, camping out along the way.[194] He went to the University of Georgia, where he "majored in liquor," his friend Henry Woodward remembered.[195] One time Woodward went by his fraternity house to see him and found him passed out on the floor.[196]

Marcus George loved Dooly County, and after leaving for school he returned there as often as he could. A pilot in the war, he would sometimes fly home to a small air strip near Vienna. On arriving over the town, he would pass over the small grocery store of a friend, cut the engine off to kill the sound, and yell down to the owner to come to the air strip to get him. Then he would start up the engine again before the plane had fallen.[197] So attached to the part of Georgia he loved, he carried a small packet of Dooly County soil with him when he went off to war, so if he was killed, he would die on "Dooly County soil."[198] Marcus, such a popular figure and so different from his staid father, likely would have been his father's political successor.

He married in the early 1940s a prominent Washington socialite with the ironic family name of "Senate." They had one daughter, Mary Senate, a few months before Marcus was killed. "This town did grieve at his death, [in 1993]" John Bonner, a close neighbor remembered[199]

[190]Frances Coley interview.
[191]John Bonner interview.
[192]Ibid.
[193]Ibid.
[194]Ibid.
[195]Ibid.
[196]Gene Methvin interview.
[197]Jake Gregory interview; T. Hoyt Davis interview.
[198]WFG-VHPS.
[199]Woodward interview.

Marcus's widow remarried, and although Mary Senate George kept the George name all of her life, she does not seem to have been especially close to her paternal relatives. There is a picture of a very pretty teenager autographed to "Uncle Heard and Aunt Irma" in the George papers, and she reportedly called Walter George "Father George."[200] As a young woman, she co-hosted a radio show in Washington in the early 1960s called "Breakfast with Bill and Senate," and at this writing, she lives in California.[201]

There is not much evidence to indicate what sort of family life Walter, Lucy, Heard, and Marcus had together, but the devil-may-care attitude of both boys might indicate a neglectful upbringing typical among busy Washington parents, and Marcus's attendance at Riverside Military Academy might indicate he needed discipline that his parents waited too long to instill. Nevertheless, both were popular and neither ever got into trouble with the law.

George's political career began when in April 1906 he was elected city solicitor of Vienna in what the local paper described as "a campaign [that was] exceedingly quiet and free to a great extent from mud-slinging." George received 714 votes to 575 for two other candidates combined.[202] It is not clear whether he ever served in that position because shortly after, when the new five-county judicial circuit was created, he resigned his new post and ran for solicitor general of the Cordele circuit. It was said later that he entered the race at the encouragement of the local lawyers, who had seen their practices suffer because his successful record had caused a flood of clients to George, meaning the other lawyers in town had to take side jobs to support their families.[203] Not surprisingly, therefore, that the Dooly County Bar Association gave him a strong endorsement: "We heartily endorse Col. George, knowing him to be of high moral character, well versed in the law and untiring and devoted to his profession."[204] George himself ran in the same edition of the paper a more modest call for his election: "I will feel grateful for a strong vote in my home county."[205] At the time Walter George had no idea where his entry into politics would eventually lead.

Georgia politics in this day, and for many years thereafter, was a blood

---

[200]Efforts to interview her proved fruitless.

[201]*Vienna News*, April 20, 1906. In the same election, his father-in-law, J. P. Heard, was elected to another position.

[202]*Vienna News*, August 8, 1957, 2, in WFG-MU.

[203]*Vienna News*, August 17, 1906.

[204]Ibid. Jarman states that he was elected prosecuting attorney (Jarman, "Taxpayer's Senator," 41).

[205]*Vienna News*, February 27, 1904.

sport, and Dooly County did not even have the (Australian) secret ballot.[206] Moreover, the people of the state liked their politicians flamboyant, loud, and theatrical. George, on the other hand, was quiet, self-effacing, austere, no self-promoter, and as one historian has put it, "with the mien of a corporation lawyer."[207] He was not a back-slapper, and even years later in the middle of his political career, Jarman of the *Saturday Evening Post* wrote, "He probably never kissed a baby for political purposes in his life,"[208] adding that "[h]e is one of the rare Southern Democrats who have been elected to important political office without benefit of concerts of hillbilly musicians, free fish fries, watermelon cuttings, barbeques and suppers, [or] an established political organization."[209]

George was assisted by the fact that Georgia had no two-party system. The Republicans had imposed Reconstruction and freed the Slaves, so *ipso facto*, all white Georgians were Democrats.[210] As one observer of the time wrote,

> The Democratic Party [in Georgia]...stands for nothing, practically, except the exclusion of negroes [*sic*] from public affairs. It makes only conventional pretense of adhering to the various principles in the party's national creed.... Few of them ever think of the issues when they vote the party ticket, because they would vote it anyhow.[211]

Noting that it was a white man's party, the anonymous person quoted observed, "Within the party, a man may advocate anything he pleases, barring certain phases of the race question, and still run no risk of losing his credentials. He may denounce the party itself...and yet remain a Democrat."[212]

One calls to mind Will Rogers's famous statement that he was not a member of an organized political party, he was a Democrat. The "Georgia Democracy" was a conglomeration of political fiefdoms ruled by political warlords, who constantly entered into shifting alliances and allegiances, de-

---

[206]Hopper, "The Purge," 56.

[207] Ibid., 157.

[208]Jarman, "Taxpayer's Senator," 23.

[209]Ibid.

[210]As late as 1964, an uncle of this author cited the fact that the Republicans had freed the slaves as the reason he would never vote for a Republican. When I burst out laughing at the statement, he exploded, "You don't understand. My granddaddy had 'em like mules, and they [the Republicans] come [*sic*] along and turn [*sic*] 'em loose."

[211]"Why Was Frank Lynched?" 681.

[212]Ibid.

pending on the ebb and flow of political fortunes and the distribution of patronage. This political terrain prevented any strong organized party opposition against the candidate of one party and created a political ice floe through which individuals with relatively small backing could rise to the top. This curious situation enabled Walter George to rise to the United States Senate, but sadly it enabled the election of demagogues and Ku Klux Klan members to the governor's mansion.

From the position of Cordele solicitor general, George was appointed in 1911 and then later elected to the position of superior court judge in 1912, a position he held until 1917. His circuit was Dooly, Crisp, Wilcox, Ben Hill, and Irwin counties. Strangely, this boost to George's career came at the resignation of Judge U. V. Whipple, the man whose failure to show at the Confederate Memorial Day event in Preston in 1894 had given George his first broad recognition—at the age of sixteen—as a public speaker. Whipple had resigned effective January 1, 1912, and Governor Slaton appointed George to complete the term on December 20, 1911.

A sitting judge, Max Land however, opposed George's election to superior court judge. Slaton was in Waycross at a political meeting, but an intense lobbying skirmish occurred between the partisans of both men. Both George and Land "worked like Trojans" campaigning for the job, and Governor Slaton received scores of endorsements on behalf of both men. Slaton "played Solomon," the *Vienna News* informed its readers: He made George the judge, and Land the solicitor for the same circuit, thus ending "a red-hot fight for the judgeship."[213] George was elected to the full four-year term on November 3, 1914.[214] In this capacity, he once faced down a lynch mob on the steps of the Cordele Opera House and, using his incredible oratory, talked the members of the mob out of killing a white man who had shot a county official.[215] He had in his study and practice of law developed a reverence for the court and judicial system. Courts and judges must be obeyed, regardless of whether one agreed with the decisions handed down, and courts must be independent. George maintained this mentality whether it was on a criminal case, the court-packing of President Roosevelt in 1937, or a US Supreme Court order to integrate schools. George was often called

---

[213] *Vienna News*, December 22, 1911.

[214] Ben Fortson to Hatten Lovejoy, October 20, 1958, T. Hoyt Davis papers, Davis & Forehand Law Firm, Vienna, GA.

[215] *Vienna News*, August 8, 1957, 2; Mellichamp, *Senators from Georgia*, 233. In 1915, 25 percent of all lynchings in the US took place in Georgia ("Law and Lynching in Georgia," 484).

"Judge George" long after he had ceased to serve on any bench, and it was a title he carried proudly.

One judicial issue that hit the Georgia courts when George was on the superior court bench (but did not pass through George's courts) was the infamous episode of the lynching of Leo Frank, a Jewish accountant in an Atlanta pencil factory, for the murder of Mary Phagan. Like the Alfred Dreyfus case in France a few years before, Frank was suspected solely because he was Jewish and was convicted on absolutely no evidence. Frank was condemned to death, but when a brave governor commuted his sentence to life, a mob stormed the jail and lynched Frank.[216] What George thought of the terrible murder we do not know, but given his respect for the court system, he must have deplored it. Rev. Randolph R. Claiborne expressed his horror: "A century will hardly wipe out the stain...on Georgia's honor [which] rests upon the men whose consciences led them to defy the courts."[217] George might well have written those words.

When the legislature created three new judgeships for the State Court of Appeals in 1916, friends and members of the bar in his circuit urged George to run although in the very early speculation, no one advanced his name. On August 24, two days before qualifying would end, the *Macon Daily Telegraph* announced that George would announce "in a few days." By the closing of qualifying on Saturday, August 26, thirteen men had put their names forward, and George was the next to last to qualify[218]—and the only one of the thirteen to be presently serving on the Superior Court bench.[219] The *Atlanta Journal*, reporting on his announcement, gave his candidacy a boost by saying, "His career as a lawyer and jurist has been one of success and has gained for him an enviable reputation...."[220] The *Vienna News*, always in George's corner, opined that "It is safe to predict that he will have the unanimous support of the voters of this circuit" and went on to give him a formal editorial endorsement as well, calling him "a man of high character and purpose, clean, honest, and unsullied by political mire."[221] The campaign was statewide, and George quickly garnered a number of endorsements, including every member of the Americus Bar Association and Congressman Charles Crisp as well. By September 5, George had received the

216"Outlaw State: Lynching of Leo Frank," 946.
217Ibid.
218*Macon Telegraph*, August 27, 1916, 1.
219*Atlanta Journal*, September 6, 1917, 14.
220Ibid., August 27, 1916, 4.
221*Vienna News*, August 31, 1916.

endorsements of the bars in the Southwestern Judicial Circuit, as had the bars of Coffee, Harrien, Dodd, Telfair, and Pulaski counties.[222] Within four days, George had been endorsed unanimously by the bars in thirty-three counties, as well as by a number of prominent individuals,[223] and W. H. Dorris, one of his campaign agents, predicted that George would lead the ticket on the September 17 vote.[224]

In the September primary, George received 60,762 votes, coming in fifth of the thirteen candidates in the popular vote, but third in the then-used county unit system. He trailed only O. H. Bloodworth of Forsyth, who got 174 county unit votes, and Frank Jenkins of Eatonton, who received 170 votes. George had garnered 149.[225] None of the candidates had therefore received a majority of the county unit votes. Since the Democratic convention would formally decide the nominee from those who had been in the primary, George's third-place finish at first seemed to assure him of a place on the November election ballot.[226] Within a few days, there was speculation around Atlanta that the convention nominees would be Bloodworth, Stephens, and John B. Hutchinson of Ashburn—who had run ahead of George in the popular vote but secured fewer county unit votes—because the "powers" wanted to punish George and Jenkins "for their past political affiliations."[227] One cannot even guess to what they are referring.

From across the state, Democrats poured into Macon for the state convention set to open on Monday, September 25, where the major point of interest was the judicial contest. There began a "threshing out of candidates," and prior to the opening, it seemed that George might be eliminated even though he had placed among the top three candidates. When the first vote was taken, Bloodworth led on with 184 votes, George finished second with 170 votes, and Alexander Stephens was third with 77 votes. But on the second ballot, "the George tide rolled high," according to the *Macon Telegraph*, and he was nominated by 219 votes as one of the three new justices.[228] The *Telegraph* wrote, "Walter F. George showed strength from the beginning.... The first mention of his name brought forth what had then been

[222]*Atlanta Journal,* September 5, 1916, 4.

[223]Ibid., September 9, 1916, 3.

[224]Ibid., September 10, 1916, 2.

[225]Ibid., September 18, 1916, 9.

[226]*Vienna News,* September 14, 1916.

[227]*Atlanta Journal,* September 19, 1916, 16.

[228]*Vienna News*, September 28, 1916; "George Is Lauded," *Atlanta Journal* clipping, June 30, 1931, WFG-GSA.

the greatest demonstration of the entire session."[229] The "election" in November was in those days merely a formality in the one-party state, and it would be George's first statewide political victory. There would over the next thirty-five years be many more. It would also be ironic that he won only because of the feudal county unit system, whereby the 121 smallest counties (37 percent of the population) cast 242 county unit votes (60 percent of the total county unit votes), with only 168 votes (40 percent of the total county unit votes) cast by the 38 larger counties, which contained 67 percent of the population.[230] This system had been used off and on, depending on the circumstances, since 1898 but became law under the Neill Primary Act of 1917.[231] Under this scheme, it was possible, if unlikely, for a governor to be elected with only 5 percent of the popular vote. This very undemocratic system that elected him would one day end his political career.

George began another term on January 1, 1917, but he held the position for only nine months, for in October 1917, he was appointed associate justice of the Georgia Supreme Court, on which he served until January 1922. Little is known about his stay on the court, but with five years remaining on his term, George suddenly announced on October 26, 1921, that he would leave the bench at the end of that year to return to Vienna to practice law. His reason for leaving was that he was not making enough money to give his family a comfortable living "at his present business."[232] In other sources he stated that he was leaving to manage his father-in-law's estate. His father-in-law had died in 1912, and although he had extensive businesses and several sons who helped manage them, it seems the estate would have been settled by 1921. In later sketches of his life, it was written that he had left "in disgust over crooked Georgia politics."[233] If that reason is correct, we do not know what specifically annoyed him though there would have been many possibilities. He and his family returned to Dooly County

[229]*Macon Daily Telegraph*, September 27, 1916, 1. Ironically, neither Bloodworth nor Stephens was chosen. Instead, the nods went to Roscoe Luke of Thomasville and W. Frank Jenkins of Eatonton.

[230]Coleman, et al., *A History of Georgia*, 392.

[231]Lynwood M. Holland, "The County Unit System in Georgia," *The Emory University Quarterly* 2/4 (December 1946): 198, cited in Fossett, "The Impact of the New Deal on Georgia Politics, 1933–1941," 23. See also Bonner, "Legislative Appointment and the County Unit System." Under this undemocratic scheme, it was possible, if not likely, for only 5 percent of the popular vote to elect a governor in Georgia. See also Rigdon, *Georgia's County Unit System*.

[232]"Judge George to Retire," *Thomasville Times-Enterprise* clipping, October 26, 1921, WFG-GSA.

[233]"Old Independent," 21; *Vienna News*, August 8, 1957, 2.

early in 1922, and he settled into the tranquil life of a prosperous country lawyer.[234]

FIRST SENATE CAMPAIGN

This idyllic life came to an abrupt halt September 26 of that year when popular US senator Tom Watson, Populist presidential candidate in 1904 and 1908 and the tsar of Georgia politics, died suddenly in Washington of an asthma attack. Senator Watson's health had impaired his official duties in recent months. His health had been improving when he was stricken after dinner on Monday, September 15. He was able to attend the closing session of the Senate on Friday, September 22, and he died about 3:00 the next morning.[235]

Always championing the farmer, Watson had in his earlier career supported political equality for the newly freed blacks.[236] By the end of his life, however, Watson had make a total reversal, becoming a rabid racist and virulent anti-Semite. He had whipped the state into a fury over the shameful Leo Frank affair in 1913, and his agitation had been a major contribution to the lynching of the innocent man in 1915. A strong isolationist, he opposed American entry into the Great War in 1917, contending that in doing so, the United States would be fighting for "international bankers."[237] Elected to the US Senate in 1920, defeating one of his protégés, he used that forum to attack Jews and Catholics.[238] When he died, a Georgian wrote former president William Howard Taft, "I have literally worn myself out, financially and otherwise, fighting Tom Watson in this state—until the Lord took a hand and helped out...."[239] Ten to twelve thousand people came to pay their respects at Hickory Hill, his plantation in McDuffie County, not far from

[234]It is interesting to note that no major state paper announced his departure from the court.

[235]*Augusta Herald*, 26 September 1922, 1. The best biography of Watson is C. Vann Woodward's *Tom Watson: Agrarian Rebel* (New York: Macmillan, 1938).

[236]Woodward, *Tom Watson*, 220–21, cited in Fossett, "The Impact of the New Deal on Georgia Politics, 1933–1941," 15; Woodward, *The Strange Career of Jim Crow*, 62–63.

[237]Tom Watson to M. G. Reynolds, June 29, 1920, series I, box 1, folder 6, "Democratic Convention, 1920," Hardwick papers.

[238]See C. C. Moseley, "Invisible Empire: A History of the Ku Klux Klan in Twentieth Century Georgia, 1915–1965," 64–66.

[239] H. Smith to Chief Justice W. H. Taft, October 20, 1922, series II, box 14, folder 9, Hoke Smith papers.

Augusta, and the Ku Klux Klan sent an eight-foot-high cross of roses.[240] While revered by many of his contemporaries, his fulminations of hate in his later years left his memory on a dark page of history.[241]

George was fishing on the Flint River when he learned of Tom Watson's death.[242] When he returned home, there were numerous telegrams from all over the state encouraging him to run for the seat although he was not really considered a politician.[243] Moreover, state senator Edgar Brown Dykes visited George and suggested that he run. This meeting was apparently a major encouragement because Dykes became his campaign manager when he finally entered the race.[244] George's name also began to appear in the press as a possible candidate, but always among "others mentioned."[245]

Before he entered the race, George first wanted to determine that former senator Hoke Smith, who was practicing law and managing real estate in Washington, would not enter the race as many speculated that he would. Smith had run in 1920, and he would be a formidable opponent. George wrote Smith's son Marion to ask and eventually learned that the former senator would not enter the race although George ultimately declared before he received Marion's reply.[246] Smith had assumed a number of legal cases involving large amounts of money, and he did not feel he could abandon these clients.[247] With requests for his candidacy coming from all over the state, George decided to enter the race.

---

[240]Woodward, *Tom Watson*, 421; The *Savannah Morning News* estimated the crowd at only 7,000 (*Savannah Morning News*, September 29, 1922, 1).

[241]So bad is Watson's reputation among scholars from his last years that when the Watson-Brown Foundation offered Mercer University a million-dollar grant to create a chair in his honor in the Walter F. George School of Law, the law faculty rejected it. Then, Mercer President R. Kirby Godsey suggested that it be given instead to fund a chair in the Mercer history department. The history department suggested such a chair be named the Tom Watson Chair of Racial Reconciliation. The Watson-Brown Foundation, which generously helped fund research for this book, refused the changes, and the university returned the money (Conversation with President R. Kirby Godsey and history department members).

[242]T. Hoyt Davis interview.

[243]Jack Stinnett, "Washington Daybook," clipping *Atlanta Journal*, December 12, 1940, WFG-GSA.

[244]"Remembering Edgar Brown Dykes," *News Observer*, May 2, 1991, clipping, WFG-DCPL.

[245]See *Atlanta Journal*, September 27, 1922, 1; October 2, 1922, 1.

[246]Hoke Smith Bell to Sen. Hoke Smith, November 9, 1922, series 22, box 14, f. 10, Hoke Smith papers.

[247]Marion Smith to WFG, October 2, 1922; to Smith, October 2, 3, 14, 1922, in Marion Smith Papers, in Grantham's *Hoke Smith*, series II, box 14, f. 1 & 2, Russell Library. See also Grantham, *Hoke Smith*, 366.

The political jungle into which Walter George entered was a rough-and-tumble, undemocratic wasteland in which elections resembled barroom brawls more than democratic contests. There was, of course, at this time, nothing that could be called a Republican Party organization.[248] Frequently, the candidate receiving less than a majority and even fewer than another candidate won the election. [249] The reader will remember that George, who won the race for his judgeship in 1916, actually came in fifth in the popular vote.[250] The average voter outside of Fulton County had 11.5 times the voting power of a citizen in Atlanta.[251]

This inequality was reflected in the legislature whereby Fulton County (Atlanta) had only three representatives in the state legislature, with Echols County, which had only 1 percent of the population of Fulton, had a single representative. One journalist called the body "the creature of peasants,"[252] and calls for a more equitable distribution of seats were shouted down with "the hoots of the yokels."[253] This blatantly undemocratic system was upheld in the courts in 1950 but was finally struck down in the early 1960s after Mayor William Hartsfield of Atlanta took the issue to the US Supreme Court.

Furthermore, the 154 rural counties paid little in the way of taxes to the state while the seven most urban (Fulton, Chatham, Bibb, Muscogee, Richmond, DeKalb, and Daugherty) provided most of the state budget. John Hammond, the Atlanta correspondent for the *Macon Telegraph*, wrote that without these burden bearers, "the State of Georgia...would have to stop functioning and the other 154 counties would...starve to death."[254] Also, one extremely powerful force in the state was the newly revitalized Ku Klux Klan—with national headquarters in Atlanta.[255] In 1922, the Klan had elected Clifford Walker, an admitted Klansman, as governor. Several of George's opponents in the race (Judge Gus H. Howard of Fulton and Muscogee counties and Carl E. Hutcheson of Atlanta) were open Klan mem-

---

[248]There were only nine counties in which any noticeable Republican vote was ever cast in those days: Fannin, Union, Towns, Pickens, Haralson, Gilmer, Cherokee, Poke, and Whitfield (Tucker, "Nine Orphan Counties," 2).

[249]A phone conversation with Hon. Buck Melton mayor of Macon.

[250]Jones, "The Georgia Plan," 313.

[251]Cited in Moseley, "Invisible Empire," 31.

[252]Bergman, "How the Supreme Court Helped the Dixiecrats," 13.

[253]*Augusta Chronicle*, October 6, 7, 1922, cited in Moseley, "Invisible Empire," 49.

[254]Jones, "The Georgia Plan," 311.

[255]Ibid., 312.

bers.[256] The Klan would play a crucial role in electing Walter George.

It is no surprise that Watson's death threw the state into a feeding frenzy for his Senate seat. The deceased senator was not yet in the ground before jockeying had begun, and the *Atlanta Constitution* warned that the state "will soon be engulfed in a raging flood of politics,"[257] which the *Savannah Morning News* called a "Political Stampede."[258] On the trains returning from Watson's funeral, Georgia political figures huddled in groups, holding whispered conversations. The names most frequently mentioned were Governor Hardwick, Hoke Smith, Clark Howell of the *Atlanta Constitution* and Walter F. George.[259] Moreover, there was the question of how the replacement could be made. The state Democratic convention was scheduled to meet on October 4 and could nominate a Democrat. Others were calling for a primary, which would have to be held with time for a run-off in the likely event that no one received a majority on the first vote. The primary would also have to be before the November general election, as set by the US Constitution.

Governor-elect Clifford Walker favored a primary. His campaign manager, Judge Gus Howard of Columbus, was considered the most likely successor to Tom Watson. He had managed Governor Hardwick's successful Senate and gubernatorial races in the past as well, and the smart money was certainly on him.[260] Howard was initially from Columbus (Muscogee County), where he still maintained a home, but he now formally lived in Atlanta. He could easily pass himself off as a candidate for South Georgia. Howard was the first to announce informally, through his friends, on Thursday, September 28. There quickly appeared a boomlet for state senator Herbert Clay, the president of the state senate, who the next day was the first to announce formally.[261] Many still thought Hoke Smith would run, and someone reserved rooms for him in the Kimberly House in Atlanta, a hotel that would house the headquarters of a number of candidates. Maconite John T. Boifeuillet, the retiring railroad commissioner, entered the race on September 29. He might well have been the most qualified and was certainly well known throughout the state. A most distinguished man, and probably too

[256]Ibid.

[257]*Atlanta Constitution*, 29, 1922, 1.

[258]*Savannah Morning News,* September 27, 1922, 1.

[259]*Atlanta Georgian*, September 27, 28, 29, 30, and October 1, 1922, cited in Talmadge, *Rebecca Latimer Felton*, 140.

[260]*Atlanta Constitution*, September 29, 1922, 1, 3; *Savannah Morning News*, September 27, 1922, 1; *Augusta Herald*, September 27, 1922, 1, 28.

[261]*Augusta Herald,* September 29, 1922, 1.

polished for the job, Boifeuillet had been the clerk of the Georgia House of Representatives in 1916 and that year had spoken all over the state for the candidacy of Governor Harris. He then had served as a special attaché to the American Embassy at the Court of St. James in London.[262] Recently defeated Governor Hardwick, vacationing in Canada, rushed back to Georgia and was soon mentioned in the running.[263] Except in the discussions on the train, none of the early press speculation mentioned Walter George, and he was not seen as a possibility until he was suggested in the *Augusta Herald* on Thursday, September 28,[264] but by Saturday, September 30, the *Savannah Morning News* reported that Judge Walter F. George of Vienna was "being genuinely talked of."[265]

George in effect announced that day, with a more positive statement on Sunday, October 1, when he told the press that he had been "in conference" with his friends across the state and would be formally announcing. When he did so on October 2, he was the sixth candidate to enter the race, a group that included Howard, Clay, Boifeuillet, Judge Horace Holden of Athens, and Carl Hutcheson of Atlanta. A lawyer, John R. Cooper, a political unknown from Macon, had also entered. Several persons entered and dropped out, including the very powerful Senate president Clay.[266] The chemistry changed with the formal non-entry of Hoke Smith, and the newly returned lame duck Governor Hardwick jumped in on Tuesday, October 2.

Hardwick had been defeated for governor by Clifford Walker a few weeks before, and on returning from Canada, he stopped in Washington to visit with President Warren Harding in the White House. Since he was still governor, he had the power to appoint an interim successor to Watson's seat. The conventional wisdom held that it would be W. C. Vereen, a prominent farmer and businessman from Moultrie and the father of W. J. Vereen, the chair of the state Democratic executive committee.[267] Whatever his thoughts about Vereen, the politician instincts kicked in, and he first offered the interim appointment to Watson's widow. She declined it because of her health, and then in what was probably a political move to gain the women's vote, Governor Hardwick appointed eighty-seven-year-old political activist Rebecca Latimer Felton, "now in the sunset of a splendid, useful life," to the

[262] *Atlanta Constitution*, August 23, 1916, 7.
[263] *Savannah Morning News*, September 28, 1922, 1, 3.
[264] *Augusta Herald*, September 28, 1922, 1.
[265] *Savannah Morning News*, September 30, 1922, 1.
[266] *Atlanta Constitution*, October 5, 1922, 5.
[267] *Atlanta Journal*, September 26, 1922, 1.

seat.[268] It was an empty political gesture because she could not be sworn in until Congress, having adjourned on September 22, opened again on November 15, by which time Watson's successor would be elected. As a result of the equally political motivated actions of Walter F. George, she would be sworn in as the first woman in the United States Senate.[269] She would also hold the record of being the oldest person sworn in for the first time, and serving only one day, she holds the title of having served the shortest tenure in that body.[270] Hardwick's entry was to become part of the political alchemy that would eventually elect Walter F. George to the Senate. Hardwick had been a rather liberal governor, which had rankled the reactionary machine of Tom Watson, who had regarded Hardwick, off and on, as his protégé, and his machine had elected Hardwick two years before. As governor, Hardwick had introduced the secret ballot and voting booths for elections. He had urged at least one consolidated high school in each county. He tried to reorganized state government, combining some departments and abolishing others, thus cutting patronage jobs, but was stymied by the legislature. He also tried but failed to pass a state income tax and to inaugurate prison reform. It did not help that Republican president Warren Harding, a friend of Hardwick's in the Senate, had him in line for a high appointment when Watson died.[271]

Hardwick put the final nail in his political coffin, however, when he became the first governor to condemn Klan violence and then tried to unmask them.[272] This "liberalism" was more than Tom Watson could stand, and he had thrown his enormous weight against Hardwick's gubernatorial reelection in 1922. In 1920, with Watson's support, Hardwick had beaten Walker 84,000 to 68,000 votes. With Watson wanting to punish his former protégé, Walker beat Hardwick 123,000 votes to 86,000.[273] Watson had been taking political potshots at Hardwick since fall 1921, and the heretic Hardwick's entry galvanized the Watson-Walker forces into an "anybody-but-Hardwick" stance.[274] They sought a man to rally around to beat him.[275] Moreover, what Woodrow Wilson Democrats there were in Georgia opposed him for his opposition to Wilson's policies on foreign affairs, and dur

[268]Talmadge, *Rebecca Latimer Felton*, 140.
[269]Coleman, et al., *A History of Georgia*, 306.
[270]Dole, *Historical Almanac of the United States*, 208–209.
[271]*Atlanta Constitution*, September 26, 1922, 3.
[272]Coleman, et al., *A History of Georgia*, 309.
[273]Heard and Strong, *Southern Primaries and Elections*, 52.
[274]*Atlanta Journal*, October 1921, *passim.*
[275]*Savannah Morning News*, October 4, 1922, 1.

ing his tenure as Senator in 1917, they had led an unsuccessful call to remove him from the Senate for his anti-Wilson remarks. He was everyone's candidate to beat, but at this point, Walter George was still not on anyone's short list for the job.

The rancor between Hardwick and the Watson-Walker faction deepened when Hardwick, still governor of Georgia and still legally the leader of the Georgia Democratic party, convened a meeting of the "Hardwick" Democratic Central Committee at the Hotel Lanier in Macon on Saturday, September 30, four days before the originally scheduled state Democratic convention, since they would have no power after the convention met to ratify Walker's election.[276] Making the most of the vanishing shreds of power, Hardwick's committee established the senatorial primary date for October 17, with a $250.00 qualifying fee, with a runoff, if necessary, to be held on October 24, in time for the Democratic nominee to appear on the ballot for the general election on November 7.[277] Moreover, the committee postponed the Democratic state convention to October 28, at which time it could certify both Walker's gubernatorial nomination and the senatorial nomination that would have been by then decided. Walker had been invited to the Macon meeting by Vereen (though he did not come) and apparently agreed to the changes at first with Vereen by telephone.[278] On the same page of the *Atlanta Constitution*, however, it was stated that he had opposed the changes, and he strongly urged his supporters to come to the scheduled convention on October 4 in Macon as originally scheduled.[279] Declaring after the fact that he "had never been more shocked in my life than at the high-handed juggling with so important a matter," Walker called on his supporters to appear in Macon anyway. Several days earlier the *Atlanta Constitution* had predicted that the Walker forces would not like these changes and would raise "a howl…at the state convention which will be heard from…Rabun's Gap to the justly famous Tybee Light."[280]

On October 2nd, George proceeded to Macon to attend the state convention. He was expected to open a state campaign headquarters in Atlanta before the end of the week.[281] The Hardwick people announced that they would bolt the October convention, which they did, and if the *Augusta Her-*

[276]Ibid., October 1, 1922, 1; *Atlanta Constitution,* September 29, 1922, 2.
[277]*Atlanta Journal*, October 1, 1922, 1.
[278]Ibid.
[279]*Atlanta Constitution,* October 1, 1922, 1.
[280]Ibid., September 29, 1922, 2.
[281]*Atlanta Journal*, October 3, 1922, 12.

ald is correct, 2500 people, largely Walker supporters, assembled in Macon at 10:30 a.m. on Wednesday, October 4, for the "Walker Convention."[282] It duly assembled, nominated Walker, and adopted a resolution condemning the Hardwick state committee's actions and then promptly ratified the very primary election dates that the committee had set. Everything had gone smoothly until it broke for lunch at 2 p.m. The only friction came in the afternoon, when some delegates wanted to nominate the Democratic senatorial candidate at the convention, bypassing a primary. This move was defeated. They "recessed" the convention until October 28, the date that the Hardwick committee had chosen for the postponement.[283] The only suspense was created by those of the Walker faction (who were for some unfathomable reason were called "Bolsheviks" by the *Augusta Herald*), who wanted to have the convention nominate also the senatorial candidate, a move Walker himself opposed.[284] This bit of rancor could only have added fuel to the anti-Hardwick feeling of the Watson-Walker crowd, which initially was thought to be supporting Seaborn Wright, a strict prohibitionist.[285] After this rump convention, the election had shaped clearly into a Walker-Watson faction vs. Hardwick, with the newspapers never mentioning George as a major player, if they mentioned him at all.

There had been much juggling to force others out of the field so as not to split the vote against Hardwick, and it must have worked. Judge Horace Holden, a brief entrant, dropped out of the race, claiming someone had paid his filing fee without his knowledge, and his withdrawal was followed by that of Clay, Flint, and Hutchinson, leaving seven candidates including George for the nomination. A disgusted Clay, who had apparently been forced out of the race, told a reporter, "If the people of Georgia knew all the political juggling that went on in Macon, they would wake up."[286] Then Hoke Smith left the race, leaving six candidates. After the "Walker Convention," the leaders of the Walker-Watson camp repaired to Atlanta to plan reducing the field further and getting behind one man to beat Hardwick, and they did not seem too concerned who it was. It was logical that a south Georgian would have the best chance, given the county unit system, and

---

[282]*Augusta Herald*, October 4, 1922, 1; *Atlanta Constitution*, October 4, 1922, 4. The *Atlanta Journal* stated that there were 1200 delegates, a more likely figure (*Atlanta Journal*, October 4, 1922, 1).

[283]Ibid.

[284]*Augusta Herald*, September 28, 1922, 5; *Savannah Morning News*, October 5, 1922, 1.

[285]*Augusta Herald*, October 6, 1922, 1.

[286]*Atlanta Journal*, October 5, 1922, 2.

south of Macon, George was the only one in the race.

On October 5, however, the *Atlanta Constitution* listed George last as a possible candidate of the Walker-Watson faction, but he does not appear to have been considered too seriously only twelve days away from the election.[287] There seems to have been an inability of the Watson people to center on a candidate to support against Hardwick, whose defeat more than supporting a special candidate was their goal. W. T. Anderson, editor and owner of the *Macon Daily Telegraph* and who had himself been mentioned earlier as a possible candidate, reflected on this lack of decision, calling the Walker convention in Macon an "unled horde." He felt that "this mess seeks the spirit of the leader [Tom Watson] who perhaps held Georgia more firmly in his grasp than has been the case in her entire history." Although noting that Tom Watson had "gone to his reward," Anderson felt that "his ghost walks the earth," adding that the composition of the Walker convention "would give their right arms…to know what their dead chieftain would like to have done in filling the position made vacant by his death." Noting that all candidates claimed to have inherited Watson's mantle, Anderson called for "a man to stand in the breach…. A man…who has his eyes toward heaven instead of his ear to the ground."[288] George launched his campaign headquarters in rooms 201 and 202 in Atlanta's Kimball House, along with Judge Howard and John T. Boifeuillet, who had done so as well, on October 5 or 6. The next day, a "George for Senator Club" popped up in Savannah and organized a group of speakers to work throughout the community for George.[289] Judge U. V. Whipple of Cordele, whom we have seen was ubiquitous in George's life, endorsed him in a letter to the *Macon Daily Telegraph*, writing, "By reason of his temperament, training and qualifications, he would render ideal and distinguished service as a senator."[290]

On Sunday, October 8, George issued his platform, which reflected the popular isolationist attitudes of the 1920s and played on the various fears and prejudices of the time. George called for "no entangling alliances with foreign countries" and "economic rehabilitation." He called for a "restrictive policy" against "wholesale immigration." He expressed strong support for the Monroe Doctrine yet demonstrated a measure of moderation when he called for cooperation with all nations "to restore the economic balance." He called for the popular notion of collecting all foreign debts but tempered his

[287] Ibid., 1.
[288] *Macon Daily Telegraph*, October 4, 1922, 1.
[289] *Atlanta Constitution*, October 8, 1922, 4.
[290] *Macon Daily Telegraph*, October 6, 1922, 1.

position with the caveat that the United States should "assume the attitude of a wise and helpful rather than a harsh creditor." He proposed, way before his time, federal funds for highway construction.[291] He announced that he was a strict prohibitionist and wanted to restrict immigration.[292] There were really few true issues in the Senate campaign, since all of the candidates held basically the same positions, especially in their opposition to the League of Nations, immigration, or weakening the Volstead Act.[293] The only real issue was whether the state would be for or against Hardwick. The Walker faction hoped to winnow the field further, and pressure shortly after the convention was put on George to leave the race in favor of Howard, although they did not seem to care which one left the race—just so one of them did. Sensing he had a good chance for victory by sweeping all of Georgia south of Macon, George flatly refused, telling the press that he would be eliminated only "by the Democrats in the state in their primary" on October 17. "I have surveyed the situation and I know exactly what my chances are.... Therefore you may announce that I am in this race...to win." The elimination of other candidates by various means, however, had indeed put George, who was not really the darling of the Watson-Walker faction, in an enviable position. The faction wanted Hardwick beaten, and George's geographic position and good name over the state made him probably the man to do it.

That same day, events started breaking George's way. Since the only sources of the campaign are newspapers, there is no way to know what subterranean deals in whispered talks were produced, but at this point, the Watson-Walker faction began clearly to move to George as their candidate. On the day he issued his platform, another major figure left the race, Judge Howard. It had been rumored on Friday, October 6, that he would withdraw, but the Judge had held a press conference denying that he would.[294] What deals were made or what arm-twisting had taken place in the following two days, we will never know, but on Sunday, October 8, Judge G. H. Howard withdrew, curiously, "because of the principals involved," whatever that meant, and endorsed George. Moreover, he became one of George's campaign managers.[295] There were rumors of deals of support in future campaigns, for either governor or senator, which probably had taken place, but what appears certain is that the Watson faction was beginning to settle,

[291]*Atlanta Constitution*, October 8, 1922, 1.
[292]*Atlanta Journal*, October 8, 1922, 1.
[293]Ibid., October 17, 1922, 9.
[294]*Atlanta Constitution*, October 7, 1922, 1.
[295]*Augusta Herald*, October 9, 1922, 1.

for whatever reason, on George as their candidate. He had spent the weekend in Vienna certain of his strengthening position and receiving assurances of supporters south of Vienna that he would sweep south Georgia.[296] The Watson-Walker forces were gathering behind him, and this alliance meant that the Walker organization, fresh from its electoral triumph a few months before, would be behind him as well. This support was underscored when the next day, *The Searchlight,* a paper connected with the Ku Klux Klan, came out for George as "the strongest and best possibility" to defeat their nemesis Hardwick, who had, the reader will remember, called for their unmasking.[297] Ironically, George was the only major Georgia politician (other than Hardwick), who was not associated with the organization,[298] and indeed *Searchlight*'s endorsement devoted more space to denouncing Hardwick than to praising George.[299] Two decades later, the *Atlanta Journal* refreshed the memory of the campaign to its readers, noting that George's style was "a sharp contrast...[to] that of Tom Watson, Mississippi [Senator James K.] Vardaman, or [South Carolina Senator 'Pitchfork'] Ben Tillman,"[300] all crude, racist rabble-rousers. Ironically, it would be George's moderation on the question of race that would make him a victim of another politician of the Vardaman ilk more than three decades later.

A clear indication that the powers had lined up behind George came with his prediction on October 10, a week before the voting and only a short time after his name appeared for the first time in the "might-runs," that he would win without a runoff, coupled his statement that he would make no speeches in the remainder of the race, "confining his activities to correspondence."[301] This stance is certainly not the behavior of a candidate who is in a close race or who is behind. The press did not report of any speeches he had even made to date, only that twenty-five prominent men in Augusta had wired him an invitation to speak in Richmond County.[302] George apparently never went.

What George had promised the powers, either sincerely or to gain their support, we will never know, but the endorsements of the Watson-Walker forces began to fall in line. Walker himself returned from a fishing trip on

---

[296]*Atlanta Journal*, October 9, 1922, 1.
[297]*Atlanta Constitution*, October 10, 1922, 1.
[298]Moseley, "Invisible Empire," 60 ff.
[299]See editorial quoted in *Atlanta Constitution*, October 10, 1922, 1.
[300]*Atlanta Journal*, December 20, 1942.
[301]*Augusta Herald*, October 10, 1922, 3.
[302]*Atlanta Constitution*, October 7, 1922, 3.

October 12 and announced that he was "for George."[303] The *Greensboro Herald-Journal*, a consistently anti-Hardwick, pro-Walker paper, curiously called for an end of factionalism, which had been the "curse of Georgia," and the putting aside of animosities to "pull for George and Georgia."[304] Walker's formal endorsement was important because Walker had, from his recent gubernatorial campaign, an organization on the ground which George did not have, and which Hardwick, having just run a campaign for governor two months before, did.[305]

An endorsement for George from Congressman William Upshaw followed the next day. Upshaw had been a student at Mercer when George was, but he was a dry leader and an official in the Anti-Saloon League. Calling George "one of the keenest, cleanest and most inspiring characters I have ever known," he issued a statement of "100 per cent support." He praised him as a dry advocate, calling him "dry as a bone,"[306] a position George would not maintain all of his life. On the Saturday before the election, the Georgia Federation of Labor endorsed him as the Klan had done, which was more an attack on Hardwick than support for George.[307]

At this point, whatever was left of Hardwick's campaign began to unravel. In an effort to prove to the voters that he was frugal, he announced on October 12 that if elected to the Senate, he would resign the governorship to save the taxpayers money, presumably his salary. His resignation would make Clay governor for eight months, so it is difficult to comprehend how this move would save the taxpayers anything, and it brought cries of "deal" from the Walker forces.[308]

On Saturday, October 14, Georgia's other senator, Senator Harris, appeared in Atlanta on his way home to vote in Cedartown. Having missed the Atlanta-Cedartown train, he took advantage of the large press coverage to attack Hardwick, whom he had beaten in 1918 running against his antiwar record. From Washington Harris had called for a strong coalition to defeat Hardwick, and announced in Atlanta that Tom Watson, who could neither confirm nor deny the statement, had shortly before his death denounced Hardwick, saying that he was only running to build a machine to use against Harris in 1924.[309] He added that Tom Watson had said that he

303 *Augusta Herald*, October 12, 1922, 9.
304 *Atlanta Constitution*, October 12, 1922, 6.
305 *Augusta Herald*, October 10, 1922, 1.
306 *Atlanta Constitution*, October 12, 1922, 2.
307 Ibid., October 14, 1922, 1.
308 *Atlanta Constitution*, October 15, 1922, 1, 8.
309 *Savannah Morning News*, October 13, 1922, 1.

would resign from the Senate before voting for Hardwick.[310] Harris followed up this attack with a statement on election day accusing Hardwick of "ingratitude," coupled with an endorsement of George in Watson's paper, *The Columbia Sentinel*, claiming to have one of Watson's last letters, dictated a few hours before his death, claiming that Hardwick had called him "the Hound from McDuffie [County]" and promised even to come to Thomson and denounce Watson before his wife.[311] George weighed in with a Watson statement of his own on the same day to the effect that Watson had endorsed him shortly before his death as "a man for public office."[312] Even from the grave, Tom Watson was influencing Georgia politics. Hardwick tried to counter these "from the grave" endorsements by saying that "among gentlemen" it was not appropriate "to quote alleged conversation with dead men" and even questioned that the conversations had even taken place.[313]. Nevertheless, these endorsements seem to have had little effect.

George received two boosts when on Sunday, Boifeuillet also left the race, leaving George the only candidate that could claim to represent south Georgia. Boifeuillet had been the brunt of a dirty campaign claiming that he was a Catholic, the kiss of death in the Georgia of that day (a campaign likely part of the Watson-Walker winnowing process). In his vitriolic withdrawal statement, he blasted unknown persons who were employing this tactic, asserting that he was "a Presbyterian by baptism, a Baptist by training, and a Methodist by marriage."[314] Quite probably, his family had been Huguenots, given his Calvinist baptism, but with his French name, the "Catholic" label easily stuck. He probably knew the origin of the rumors, and he did not go gracefully, blasting Harris's character as "bootlicking President Wilson" when he was powerful but one who, when Wilson was "broken in health and mind," tried to "grab onto the coattails of Senator Watson."[315] His departure consolidated George's vote from middle Georgia southward.[316]

The other boost that came to George that day was the endorsement of organized labor, although in the Georgia of the 1920s, the labor endorsement carried few votes. John G. Valentino, head of the State Federation of Labor, came out for George, although nine railroad conductors held a public

[310]*Atlanta Constitution*, October 13, 1922, 1.
[311]Ibid., October 17, 1922, 1–2.
[312]*Augusta Herald,* October 17, 1922, 1.
[313]*Savannah Morning News*, October 17, 1922, 1.
[314]Ibid., October 16, 1922, 1.
[315]*Augusta Herald,* October 16, 1922, 1.
[316]Ibid., October 17, 1922, 1.

press conference and said that labor would go for Wright.[317]

In the eleventh hour of the campaign, George received some quixotic attacks from his two leading opponents. W. W. Phillips with the Hardwick campaign wrote to George's headquarters demanding to know how George had voted in the 1920 presidential and Senate primaries, which had been a contest among Tom Watson, Hoke Smith, and A. Mitchell Palmer of Pennsylvania for president and Tom Watson, Hoke Smith and Hugh Dorsey for the Senate.[318] The letter went unanswered. Wright accused George of duplicity, attacking him for claiming that he had voted for Walker for governor when in reality he had met with the Hardwick people several weeks before the primary to discuss their campaign in his area of Georgia.[319] On the weekend before the election, George, Hardwick, and Wright all claimed victory, but only George's claims sounded real. Spending Friday night in Macon at the Dempsey Hotel to confer with his local supporters, he reported that developments of the previous days showed that the powers of the state were coalescing around him to defeat Hardwick. In a statement to the press, he said, "I have sought to conduct the campaign on the plane above factionalism,"[320] which was a curious bit of hypocrisy, since he had become the candidate of the Watson-Walker faction. Early the next morning, he left for Atlanta to wait out the remaining days of the election, obviously feeling secure that Dooly County would be his without his own personal vote. The next day, most agreed that with Hardwick on the defensive from Harris's attacks and Boifeuillet's departure from the race, George was guaranteed a sweep of all counties south of Macon. His campaign manager Dykes announced on Monday that reports coming into his office for the past twenty-four hours guaranteed George a sweep of south Georgia "almost to a county." This sweep had been boosted by Senator Harris's "strong and forceful" statement that he hoped that a south Georgia man would be sent to the Senate and that the Watson people were behind George ninety percent.[321] By election day, there were only two real candidates, Hardwick and George, and the anti-Hardwick forces (Watson-Walker machine and the Klan) were behind George, who had by some sort of curious political Darwinism survived to the end.[322]

---

[317] *Atlanta Journal,* October 16, 1922, 1.
[318] *Atlanta Constitution,* October 16, 1922, 2.
[319] *Augusta Herald,* October 12, 1922, 9.
[320] *Macon Daily Telegraph,* October 14, 1922, 1.
[321] *Atlanta Constitution,* October 16, 1922, 1–2.
[322] *Savannah Morning News,* October 17, 1922, 3.

George never rebuffed Klan support. Wright issued a statement to the effect that he would not win, and Howard and Boifeuillet had not withdrawn in time, so their names had to be hand scratched off the ballots before they were issued to voters. George's last appeal was a clarion call for his supporters to "man the polls" to see that they were open.[323] Hardwick's last attacks were on Harris, not George, on Monday, October 16. Calling Harris the leader of "a dirty gang of politicians," he claimed that it had been Harris and his group that had caused trouble between him and Watson. Then, as if not feeling that Harris's attacks would hurt, he predicted that he would win the primary without a runoff the next day.[324]

In the last day, the Senate race was pushed off the headlines by other things. The last appeals in the campaign were not for votes but a call for volunteers to staff the precincts. Hardwick had called as early as October 11 for all of the candidates to "chip in" to keep precincts open, since a primary would cost $12–15,000.[325] W. J. Vereen, chairman of the state Democratic executive committee, announced four days later that there were not sufficient funds to staff all the precincts in the state[326] and warned that some polling places might not open if volunteers did not come forward. Apparently, there were a number of precincts throughout the state that never did open, but the closed precincts attracted little attention. The voters seem to have been more titillated by an unrelated scandal that emerged just before the election: The founder of Coca-Cola, Asa Candler, Sr., dumped his fiancée, a Mrs. DeBouchel of New Orleans. The story included such French farcical scenes with frivolous lawsuits and stolen love letters retrieved from force-opened file cabinets and the like. This sordid soap opera drew much more attention in the last days before the vote than the election did.[327]

The election the next day seems, by today's standards, a most haphazard affair. In a number of rural counties, some polling places never opened. Rural precincts that did provide workers closed at 3:00 p.m., with more urban polling places remaining open until 7:00 p.m. The final vote was very light, primarily because it rained all day over most of the state, and the turnout was one of the smallest in years. In Dalton, a relatively large town, only

[323]Ibid.

[324]*Atlanta Journal*, October 16, 1922, 1.

[325]*Augusta Herald*, October 12, 1922, 1.

[326]*Savannah Morning News*, October 16, 1922, 3.

[327]*Atlanta Journal*, October 10 ff, 1922.

eighty votes were cast by 10:00 a.m.[328] By one hour after the polls closed, George was ahead in the vote count, and his lead only widened as the night wore on.[329] When the votes that were cast were counted (and probably some were counted that had never been cast), Walter F. George had routed his opponents, having received 60,436 votes to 36,328 for Hardwick. Wright received only 12,820 votes, with Cooper bringing up the rear with 1,018. George had carried 132 of the 160 counties, with no returns reported from Peach County. George had, as expected, run well in rural counties but he had also carried several large ones: Fulton and DeKalb (Atlanta), Bibb (Macon), and Muscogee (Columbus), losing only Richmond (Augusta) and Chatham (Savannah).[330] George had carried every ward in the city of Atlanta and every congressional district except the 10th. Hardwick had run less well than he had for governor two months before.

There were some surprises: George carried Bartow County, the home of Mrs. Felton, and Hardwick carried McDuffie County, home of Tom Watson, whom he had supposedly called "the Hound of McDuffie."[331] Although Wright had carried the six-vote county Floyd, his own, George had carried Wright's own precinct by 49 to 28, with 3 having been cast for Hardwick.[332] George had won 318 county unit votes, more than a hundred more than needed to win.[333] It had, however, been a vote against Hardwick, not one "for" George, but many elections have been won or lost that way. The *Savannah Morning News* put it correctly: "The ghost of the late Senator Thomas E. Watson bobbed up from his grave long enough…to send Governor and former Senator Thomas W. Hardwick down to defeat."[334] In his victory statement, George appeared quite humble. "I am profoundly grateful for the confidence that the Democrats of Georgia have place in me," he said in a public statement. "I shall serve the state in the Senate to the limit of my ability."[335]

Even with the completion of the vote tallies, Hardwick was not done. The day after the election, he praised George as a "gentleman" who had

---

[328]*Atlanta Journal*, October 18, 1922, 1. In fact, George received in his landslide county unit victory almost the exact same number of votes that he had received in his 1916 judicial race, when he had come in fifth in the popular vote.

[329]*Atlanta Journal*, October 18, 1922, 1.

[330]Heard and Strong, *Southern Primaries and Elections*, 61–62.

[331]*Savannah Morning News*, October 18, 1922, 9

[332]*Atlanta Constitution*, October 18, 1922, 12.

[333]*Macon Daily Telegraph*, October 19, 1922, 1.

[334]*Savannah Morning News*, October 18, 1922, 1.

[335]*Atlanta Journal*, October 18, 1922, 1.

"conducted a clean campaign," but leveled on Senator Harris, whom he termed "a disgrace to the state," a "coward," and a "liar."[336] George returned to Vienna on Wednesday, the day after the election, to a hero's welcome. Dooly County had given him 770 votes to 18 for all other candidates. The local citizens held a reception for him, which included about 2,000 people from surrounding counties, and Vienna businesses were closed for the occasion. George was carried on the shoulders of the crowd to the town square, where the festivities were to be held. Watts Powell, George's campaign manager in the county, made a speech before George spoke himself.[337]

George filed a financial report for the election with the secretary of state stating that he had received no contributions and had had no expenditures made either "by himself or any agents." This report is very suspicious, since he obviously traveled about and had a headquarters in Atlanta. It is so unusual that it even drew the attention of the *New York Times*.[338] By the first of November, George had filed an amended report to the effect that he had received $1,697 in contributions and had expended $7,357, which had mostly been spent on "advertising" in the ten-day period before the primary.[339] There were no George ads in the major newspapers, so that meant a lot was spent on road posters or probably payoffs. Some senators were taking Attorney General Daugherty's interpretation of a Supreme Court ruling to mean that senators did not have to file a financial report. Also, other senators had reported strange figures. Senator Henry Cabot Lodge, the Republican leader in the Senate, reported only $3,870 spent in his race in Massachusetts, while Senator Henry Ashurst of Arizona reported receiving only $100 in contributions and having spent only $17.00.[340] Campaign finance was of course far more casual in that day, and a carefree approach continued even after the laws became stricter. One politician who failed to change with it was George's last political nemesis, Herman Talmadge, with his famous overcoat that ended his career.

George rested there for a short time before returning to Macon to accept the Democratic senatorial nomination at the postponed state Democratic convention held in the Macon City Hall Auditorium on October 28. Here Walter George was to sound a conservative theme that would not

---

[336]*Savannah Morning News*, October 19, 1922, 1. Hardwick and George remained friends and continued a correspondence until Hardwick's death in 1944.

[337]*Atlanta Journal*, October 18, 1922, 16.

[338]*New York Times*, October 28, 1922, 14, column 6.

[339]Ibid., November 2, 1922, 21:8; *Savannah Morning News*, November 2, 1922, 13.

[340]*Savannah Morning News*, November 2, 1922, 13.

change for the remainder of his political career: He was a strong believer in states' rights, and time and again, he would defend the states' power whenever possible. His name was placed in nomination by Judge U. V. Whipple of Cordele, a man so often in and out of George's life. In his speech, the *Atlanta Journal* told its readers that the new senator-elect "drew an oratorical sword and sliced it right and left."[341] "The framers of our constitution," he thundered to the state's Democrats, "did not claim absolute power for themselves and could not admit that it resided anywhere. They recognized the supremacy of man's law, and laws much rest on something higher than the mere will of a majority." He felt that the founders had intended "expressly limited powers" for the national government, leaving the states with the right to "all acts and things, which independent states may do." He called for a "limit to lawmaking" and stressed that the growth of federal power "usurped the powers of the states."[342] To make his point, he attacked the Dyer anti-lynching bill, which was the civil rights issue of its day. The bill, he said, "proceeds directly upon the assumption that the states or the people have lost the capacity to govern themselves," and that the extension of such federal power "destroys the capacity of the people for self-government."[343] The writers for the *New York Times* must have shaken their heads, thinking that Georgia had elected merely another racist Southern Senator Cleghorne, little imaging that they would one day trumpet George's many virtues.

George's election in the general election on November 7 was merely a formality since he had no Republican opposition, but he was not to face his first political test as a senator over the curious appointment by lame duck Hardwick of "Grandma" Rebecca Felton. Since the Senate had not been in session, she could not be sworn in, and the law provided that an appointee could only serve until which time that a replacement was elected in a general election. Since George had been elected in a general election on November 7, legally Ms. Felton could not take her seat. Helen Longstreet of Gainesville, a feminist widow of Confederate General Longstreet, had suggested that President Harding convene Congress solely to swear in the first woman senator. Harding refused.[344] A similar situation had occurred earlier when South Carolina's colorful senator "Pitchfork" Ben Tillman died. Christie Beret was appointed to replace Tillman, but the Senate did not convene be-

[341]*Atlanta Journal*, October 28, 1922, 1, 7.

[342]*Augusta Herald*, October 29, 1922, 1.

[343]*New York Times*, October 29, 1922, II, 1:7.

[344]Longstreet telegram to Felton, Felton Collection, University of Georgia, cited in Talmadge, *Rebecca Latimer Felton*, 142.

fore his replacement was elected. Vice President Marshall ruled that Ms. Beret could not be sworn in after the election of Tillman's successor, because on the election, she ceased to be a senator.[345] This situation would be the exact case of Mrs. Felton.

A curious collection of events, some real, others probably contrived, happened to make Ms. Felton the first woman sworn in as a United States Senator. Georgia Secretary of State S. G. McLendon, a relative of Ms. Felton's by marriage, told her that George, because of "technicalities," would not be certified in time to reach Washington by the time Congress resumed on November 20 since some returns were not in and since Governor Hardwick, this time vacationing in New York, would not be here to convene the canvassing board.[346] McLendon seems to have been dragging his feet, but then Walter George made it plain that he was in no hurry to be sworn in himself. In a phone conversation with Ms. Felton from Atlanta to her home in Cartersville, George said that he did not want to force Governor Hardwick to cut short his vacation and was willing to have her sworn in ahead of him if it was at all legally possible. He suggested that she leave for Washington ahead of him on Friday, November 17, and he would follow when he could. He promised to delay his swearing in by any means "all in his power" so that "this honor may be conferred on this lady."[347] She left for Washington alone on Friday, November 17, at 11:45 from Atlanta with her appointment with her wrapped in brown paper.[348] Her arrival on Sunday, November 19, at Washington's Union Station went unnoticed because there had been some misunderstanding on when she would arrive, so there were no reporters to greet her. She went to the Lafayette Hotel, where reporters finally found her. Hoke Smith gave a dinner in her honor, and Senator and Mrs. Harris gave a luncheon the day she was sworn in.[349]

George, meanwhile, received his commission shortly after noon on Saturday, November 18, after the returning Hardwick, who thought he had done everything necessary for George's certification before his departure, signed the necessary papers. Hardwick congratulated George on handing

[345]*Atlanta Journal*, November 18, 1922, 1.

[346]*Macon Daily Telegraph*, November 16, 1922, 1.

[347]*Atlanta Constitution*, October 1922, 1.

[348]*Savannah Morning News* stated that she, George, and Senator Harris all left for Washington on Saturday, November 18, on the same train (November 17, 1922, 1), but that apparently is not so.

[349]Frank Gilreath to Hoke Smith, December 12, 1922, series 2, box 14, folder 12, Hoke Smith papers.

him his commission, wishing him a "long and successful career."[350] Then the two drove across town together in Hardwick's car. George was also collared by the redoubtable Ms. Longstreet, who had blown into town to further encourage George to delay his swearing in.[351] George had received in the final count 76,374 votes with 158 counties reporting, nothing having been heard from Columbia and Telfair counties, whose final returns would make no difference.[352] According to the *Savannah Morning News*, which had gotten things wrong before, he left for Washington on Sunday evening.[353] He actually reached Washington on Sunday evening by train with Miss Lucy and Marcus, seeming to have taken their time getting there. Louis C. Russell, brother of Richard Russell and George's newly appointed secretary, drove up, stopping off in Macon to pick up Heard.[354]

Rebecca Latimer Felton appeared as the Senate reconvened on Monday morning, November 20, but it stayed in session only long enough to pass a resolution of "deep regret" at Watson's passing and then adjourned until the next day. She reappeared with Senator Harris early on Tuesday morning and asked to be sworn in at 1:30 p.m. on Tuesday, November 21, 1922. George seems to have avoided coming to the Senate Chamber and spent the time of Mrs. Felton's Tuesday appearance moving into his Senate office, suite 129, on the first floor of the Senate Office Building, into the same office Watson had occupied. There are indications that at one point he was in the Senate cloakroom while Mrs. Felton was on the Senate floor receiving the oath as the first woman ever seated in the US Senate, and in her one and only speech, she thanked Senator George for "letting her have her day in the Senate."[355] All of the senators were not a gracious as was George. Because women could now vote, they were hesitant to prevent her taking the oath—but the entire body agreed that she could not receive mileage or any pay for her half hour of service. Eventually Senator Harris was able to obtain for her $287.87, $280.00 of which was for mileage.[356] Walter F. George was sworn in on Wednesday, November 22, 1922, immediately after Mrs. Felton made her one and only speech. That body would be his professional home for over three decades. That evening the Georgia Society in Washington gave a party in George's honor at the home of Mr. Theodore Tiller, the president of the

[350] *Atlanta Journal*, November 18, 1922, 1.

[351] Ibid., 2.

[352] *Savannah Morning News*, November 19, 1922, 1.

[353] Ibid., November 19, 1922, 1.

[354] *Atlanta Journal*, November 20, 1922, 2.

[355] *CR*, 67/3, 23.

[356] *New York Times*, November 20, 1922, 19:2.

society. The house was decorated with yellow chrysanthemums, and the hostess served cake, ice cream, and punch. Dancing followed. Most of the Georgia delegation was there, as well as journalist Colonel and Mrs. John Temple Graves.[357]

Rather unknown and probably dismissed by the Northern press as a less flamboyant version of Tom Watson, George would in time become one of the most famous of its members and arguably the second most powerful man in Washington. Journalist W. S. White noted in his book *Citadel* that a lot of history was made in the George's Mayflower apartment when in the 1950s, Secretary of State John Foster Dulles stopped by weekly to have breakfast, which Miss Lucy cooked, and direct the nation's foreign policy.[358] Perhaps foretelling George's greatness, even before he was actually sworn into the Senate, on Saturday, November 11, a group of his friends organized a "George for President" club in Savannah to support his candidacy for the Democratic presidential nomination in 1924.[359] Walter F. George, a tenant farmer's son, was well on his road to greatness.

[357]Ibid., November 23, 1922, 6, column 6.
[358]*Atlanta Journal*, November 23, 1922, 16.
[359]*Savannah Morning News*, November 12, 1922, 32.

2

THE GENTLEMAN FROM GEORGIA, 1922–1932

He [Walter F. George] is a worthy successor [to Tom Watson]. I want to plead for your gracious attention to him. He has been most chivalric.
—Senator Rebecca Latimer Felton[1]

The Senate and Walter George seem to be made for each other.
—Senator Mike Monroney (D-Oklahoma)[2]

One of the great assets of Democracy is its ability to thrust up from its chaste, diverse and free soil unforeseen resources to meet the need of a certain hour. Senator Walter F. George…son of a tenant farmer, illustrated well this political fertility.
—The McClatchy Newspapers Sacramento, California[3]

Therefore, on November 22, 1922, Walter Franklin George began his thirty-four years, one month, and four-days in the United States Senate. He was elected as an avid "dry," a strong opponent of the League of Nations, and vigorous antagonist of foreign loans.[4] By the time he ended his career, he would reverse himself on all three of these positions, by no means being the first politician to grow in office. In the years of his career, he served on twelve committees, both standing and special, and chaired five. His first assignments were boring: the Committee on Post Offices and Post Roads, the Committee on Immigration, and the Committee on Civil Service, but two of these gave its members rich patronage plums to dispense.[5] In the 68th Congress in 1926, he was moved to Finance, Military Affairs, and Elections, and in 1931 he joined the Foreign Relations Committee. It would be on Finance and Foreign Affairs on which he would make his greatest marks in history.

On the Finance Committee, he would demonstrate an inordinate talent

---

[1]*CR*, 67/3, 23.

[2]Albert Riley, "Reporters' Request…," WFG-GSA.

[3]"Senator George Plays a Key Role in Nation," McClatchy Newspapers, scrapbook, LHG VHPS.

[4]Mellichamp, *Senators from Georgia*, 233.

[5]*CR*, 67/3, 272.

for mastering the arcane intricacies of tax law, and on Foreign Relations, he would be a major force to lead an isolationist-minded nation onto the world stage. His role there in the 1950s began the process that ended in time the Cold War. One national magazine observed that though the House of Representatives is "constitutionally supposed to initiate tax legislation, of late years, it is the Senate's bill that is most likely to become law. One substantial reason for this procedure is Senator George himself."[6] As for his being placed on Foreign Relations, the *Augusta Chronicle* told its readers,

> That group of statesmen [the men on the Foreign Relations committee] is usually recognized the world over as being the most brilliant, diplomatic, and well-informed members of the Senate. America's great position in the world demands that the best men be there. The fact that Senator George of Georgia, young in years and in service, has been named on this committee raises him even above the prominence of a national figure.[7]

George used to tell the story that on his arrival in the Senate, he was taken aside by the famous Mississippi senator John Sharp Williams, who quoted a philosopher (George could never remember whom) who told his son, "I want you to go to all parts of the world. Especially I want you to visit all the capitals of the world and see what little wisdom the world is actually run with."[8] This statement is reminiscent of the famous remark of Harry Truman about the Senate: "When you get to the Senate, you spend the first six months wondering how you got there. Then you spend the rest of the time wondering how everybody else got there."

Many successful politicians are somewhat dim-witted, but Walter George was not one of them. Early in his Senate career, he did not speak often, observing the Senate protocol that new senators do not address that body. Once when a freshman senator made a lengthy speech, he afterward sat with Walter George. Wanting to appear personable, he asked the veteran senator how the Senate differed from when he first arrived. George curtly replied, "Freshmen didn't used to talk so much."[9] George certainly maintained that rule. For years after arriving in the Senate, George rarely made a speech. He did frequently ask questions of a speaker, but he rarely spoke himself. Not until the late 1920s did his participation increase. Involvement

---

[6] *Vienna News*, August 8, 1957, 5.

[7] This statement is probably the first bit of gushing praise of the "Man from Georgia" that would not stop until his death. Clipping from the *Augusta Chronicle*, May 1, 1928, WFG-GSA.

[8] *CR*, 84/2, April 25, 1955, 4266.

[9] Cited in Caro, *The Years of Lyndon Johnson*, 81.

in later years, however, frequently manifested itself in unprepared speeches that went on for over an hour.

His personal demeanor was not that of the typical politician. He was not garrulous nor did he draw attention to himself. He had a noble manner, which his Vienna neighbor John Bonner described as "stately dignity."[10] *Newsweek* called it "aristocratic aloofness," adding, "No one would ever call him 'Walter,' or slap him on the back."[11] Secretary of State Dean Acheson remembered, "I should say that he had no humor, but rather a regal geniality. He spoke slowly and ponderously [in conversation]...dispensing the benediction of a sentence here and there.[12] Although praising George's abilities, Acheson found him "less admirable in basic human qualities, less kindly, less generous, less outgoing, and much—much—more pompous."[13] With this seeming *froideur,* there went a common touch that was not an act. The *Atlanta Journal* observed that at his office in Washington, "the humblest citizens are just as welcome as the mightiest and richest man in the nation." He rarely took a vacation, except when he went home to Vienna, where he would fish and stroll around town visiting with the folks there—"including Negroes."[14] This sense of formality extended to other associations as well. Lyndon Johnson's protégé, Bobby Baker's "baptized" name was "Bobby," not Robert, and George told him one day that he should have a "man's name," now that he was a man. Baker changed it. George was delighted and thereafter treated Baker in the warmest possible fashion. George's stiffness extended to his mode of dress. He was always fastidious and wore double-breasted suits and starched white shirts, even when at home in Vienna in the summer heat though he hated formal dress. Once when he was invited to the White House to a formal dinner to discuss taxes, he expressed his horror at "trying to talk taxes in a stiff shirt." When the White House learned of his annoyance, the mode of dress was changed to business suits.[15]

Formality extended into his Senate speeches. William S. White in his book *Citadel* described George's speaking style as that of the stereotypical Southern senator. "He [George] will begin softly with wry self-deprecation, almost with an embarrassment of humility," White wrote. "He will say that he has, of course, only a few words...aware that it is not for him to intrude

[10]John Bonner interview.

[11]"George of Georgia: Ike's Friend in Need," 29.

[12]Acheson, *Sketches from Life of Men I Have Known*, 142.

[13]Ibid. This coming from one of the most pompous secretaries of state in recent times.

[14]*Atlanta Journal,* December 20, 1942, 6-B.

[15]Baker, *Wheeling and Dealing*, 37.

upon the deliberations." As he continued, almost imperceptibly, his voice, having begun so low and quietly, "will begin to rise in volume and fall in tone. And at the end, it has become a commanding pipe organ, rolling and thundering before the wicked, the foolish, and the insensitive."[16] Moreover, George did not speak unless he had something to say. "It has not been my habit to fill the *Congressional Record* with speeches or even speak unless I had a real conviction," he told a reporter, adding "If I have any influence in the Senate today, it is because the Senate generally credits me with being sincere."[17] Senator Ralph Flanders of Vermont underscored this idea in his memoirs by saying "The senior senator from Georgia seldom took the floor, but when he did, the effect was all the greater for the rarity of his appearance."[18] Harry McPherson on Lyndon Johnson's staff remembered that on the rare occasion that George made a set speech, "it was something to hear. Powerful tuba-tones, absolutely uninterruptible."[19] Floyd Riddick, a Senate parliamentarian, remembered that when speaking on an issue, George usually did not need the assistance of a staff person sitting next to him, feeding him information the way other senators did.[20] He knew his material well, and that reinforced the influence of his words. Senator Flanders said that only three times in his Senate career did he change his mind on an issue because of the debate on the Senate floor, and one of those times, it was Walter George's speech that did it by delivering a speech that "was impressive, both in content and delivery."[21] Colleagues recognized George's speaking abilities early on; in 1927 he was chosen to read to the Senate Washington's farewell address.[22]

Moreover, George came to possess a number of qualities not typical in a politician. For example, he did not seek publicity. *Saturday Evening Post* observed in the latter third of his career that "as a personality…he is almost unknown to the general public. The name is familiar…but the man is not. The reason for this…is that he has little knowledge of how to achieve personal publicity and [has] no apparent desire for it. This makes him a phenomenon in American politics."[23] He also rarely attended private social

---

[16]Ibid.

[17]White, *Citadel*, 73; William M. Bates, "Newsmen Held George…," *Atlanta Constitution*, August 7, 1957, 36, box 15, f, WFG-GSA.

[18]*Atlanta Constitution*, August 5, 1956, 5, clipping in box 1998–1980 A, f. WFG-GSA.

[19]Flanders, *Senator from Vermont*, 212.

[20]McPherson, *A Political Education*, 35.

[21]Francis O. Wilcox, oral history, Eisenhower Library, 149.

[22]Flanders, *Senator from Vermont*, 212.

[23]*CR*, 69/2, 4396–400.

functions, almost never in his later years, preferring to remain in his suite at the Mayflower Hotel reading mysteries while some brilliant diplomatic or social event to which he had been invited was raging in the ballroom below.[24] He would sometimes spend an evening with North Carolina governor-turned-lobbyist Max Gardner, his close friend, but only because Gardner lived in the Mayflower himself, and he could make the trip without leaving the building.

Moreover, George would compromise, but he would not cut a deal. The *Atlanta Journal* told its readers, "No one would dare suggest a deal to him. The brashest of lobbyists wouldn't think of button-holing him."[25] He always maintained an open mind in any argument. Walter Robertson in an oral interview at the Eisenhower Library remembered, "Well, I don't think anyone could come in contact with Senator George who didn't think he had an open mind. He was a man of strong convictions...but you were always conscious that he was trying to ascertain all the facts before making up his mind."[26] This quality contributed to George's reputation of bipartisanship throughout his career. Rabbi Manfred M. Rechtshoffen, a guest Senate chaplain who knew George well, remembered, "Party lines fell away before this great American."[27] A quality that was always in evidence was George's incredible mental power. Senate employees nicknamed him "the Brain."[28] Noted above was his ability to speak on an issue without an assistant feeding him information. Time and again he entered the debate unplanned on certain subjects and relayed statistics and information that contributed to the debate that simply came spontaneously out of his head.[29] When this intellect was combined with what the reader will remember were his debating, speaking, and legal skills, he was indeed a formidable opponent. Journalist W. S. White observed, "Those who seek to engage him...[in details] are wasting their time; he will peer at them in moral lofty indifference."[30]

When George interrupted a speaker on the Senate floor, as he often did, he must have cast fear in all but the most secure of speakers. When he

---

[24]Jarman, "Taxpayer's Senator," 22.

[25]Ibid., 22.

[26]"When Georgia's Sen. George Speaks Out," *Atlanta Journal*, 1955, clipping in scrapbook, LHG-VHPS. This observation was also made voluntarily by Senator George Smathers (D-Florida) in an interview with the author.

[27]Walter Robertson, oral history, Eisenhower Library, 121.

[28]*Vienna News*, August 8, 1957, WFG-GSA.

[29]White, *Citadel*, 205.

[30]One such example was his entering a debate on tariffs on ammonium nitrate and nitrate of sodium. See *CR*, 68/1, 3526.

did interrupt, he would interrogate the speaker like a prosecutor, always posing the question in such a way that he appears to want to enlighten himself when he really always knows the answer and is trying, by the Socratic method, to enlighten the speaker. His questions often dealt with congressional protocol, or language, or the use of a word, or some tedious point of order. For example, on May 16, 1929, when Senator Wheeler of Montana was calling for an investigation of a tariff question involving issues in three states, George interrupted and first questioned Wheeler's right to call for investigation since tariffs questions had to originate in the House. Then he asked if a study should not first be made to see if tariffs on farm products were effective. Finally, he questioned using only three states for the point in questions. Then, George would invariably add something like, "Personally I have no objection to the investigation, but…it seems to… me exceedingly strange that the senator would have singled out only three states, because the tariff applies universally in the country."[31]

His legal, judicial background, reinforced by his exceptional knowledge of English grammar, often led George to introduce an amendment that merely refined the language to fine-tune the piece of legislation.[32] One example: George took the floor in a debate to offer an amendment: "I desire to offer an amendment on page 18, line 23, of the committee amendments, to strike out the semi-colon and to insert a period and to strike out all after the semi-colon including the word 'violation' in line 25."[33]

George's changes would often tighten the language and improve the bill. Once he interrupted the redoubtable Huey Long. "Mr. President," he said, "if the senator will yield, may I suggest to the senator from Louisiana that if he will include the word "exclusively,' so as to read, 'payable exclusively out of taxes," then he will [better] accomplish what he is undertaking to do."

Long, on thinking it over, said, "I think that would be a great improvement." George, however, was not finished. "Or the word 'solely" might be used, so as to read 'solely out of taxes." Long changed his amendment to include George's language.[34]

George's daily work routine had him up at the crack of dawn, and he would eat a large breakfast of grits, eggs, and country ham with red-eye gravy cooked by Mrs. George, who had no personal help. He would be in his

[31]White, "Senator George, Monument Determined," 42.
[32]*CR*, 71/1, 1382, 1384.
[33]For some examples, see *CR*, 67/4, 2673–674; *CR*, 68/1, 4726; *CR*, 72/2, 3767.
[34]*CR*, 72/2, 3767.

office on the third floor of the Senate Office Building before 7:00 a.m., although by the time he was in his late sixties, his arrival time became the decadent hour of 8:30. Before the staffers appeared, he would read the morning mail, make appointments, and answer the phone incognito.[35] He took Lewis Carolyn Russell, the sister of Judge Richard Russell, who would be his adversary in the 1926 Senate race, with him to Washington as his executive secretary and had a long string of secretaries and office managers throughout his career, including his own son Heard George, who seems to have had trouble making a living much of his life.[36]

Like many freshman senators, George's early years were rather obscure until he was nominated for United States president in 1928. In these times, he staked out his territory and developed his persona. He was very thrifty with his personal finances, so it is not surprising that he was thrifty with government money, and the debates from the beginning of his career show him often questioning the necessity of spending money.[37] His early interest in fiscal matters and his contribution to these debates show a deep and perceptive understanding of money matters, and hence taxing. He would become a senator without equal in financial matters, easily mastering the arcane points of tax law.[38] There were, however, certain pet items on which he did not pinch pennies: vocational education, soldiers' and veterans' benefits, agricultural matters, and any pork for Georgia. Money was sought to build a bridge across the St. Mary's River, erect a statue to a local war veteran, and build a dairying and livestock experiment station in Tifton, Georgia.[39] Moreover, when his pet projects were up for a Senate vote, he made it strict policy to be there.[40] A second area that established his conservative credentials was his strong belief in the constitutional question of states' rights. It would guide many of his actions for the remainder of his life.

George's feet, however, were not always in concrete. The reader will recall that he ran for the Senate as a "dry" and an isolationist, opposing the League of Nations and foreign loans. He would in time reverse himself on all of these issues, and, in fact, lead the opposition to his former positions in the Senate.

On some issues he never wavered. He would until his dying day remain

[35]Ibid., 72/2, 2406.

[36]Jarman, "Taxpayer's Senator," 41.

[37]Russell, *A Heart for Any Fate*, 206–207.

[38]Some examples: *CR*, 67/4, 2396; *CR*, 68/1, 6694.

[39]Some examples: *CR*, 68/1, 7133, 7544, 7545, 8015, 8107.

[40]Certain examples: *CR*, 68/1, 494, 10448, 8963.

a fervent defender of the Jeffersonian concept of states' rights and a vigorous opponent of too much federal government power. Even when he might favor a position, he always applied to it the litmus test of states' rights before giving it his full backing. For example, in January 1923, Congress was considering the Sterling-Towner bill, which would have established a Department of Education, an idea that did not come into being for decades in the future. George, a conservative Southerner, favored this modern proposal. In his mind, such a department did not impinge "upon the rights, powers and duties of the several states" or permit the federal government "to dictate the course of study, the methods and practice, the terms and requirements, direction and the full control by the state authorities as to the management of schools."[41] With all of that eliminated, one wonders what he felt a Department of Education should do.

In 1924, he fought a bill that would abolish any statute of limitations the federal government would have to prosecute a citizen for failure to file a tax return. Moreover, the bill, as George saw it, enabled the government to call a simple tax return error "fraud."[42] That same year he opposed a bill that would regulate child labor in the United States because he felt that any law that gave the federal government the right to protect children in the workplace "will necessarily carry with it the power to regulate any industry in which they labor."[43]

George articulated his position on Jeffersonian democracy in a speech in Boston in 1928. To his skeptical audience he intoned, "If states are to be submerged, their initiative, self-reliance and power lost to an overshadowing federal government...[then] the states for which Lee drew the sword are endangered. History proclaims one truth: Free government rests at last on local self-government."[44] The author of the article posed the question, drawing on a comment in the *Macon Telegraph*, which had raised the same question: If George favored states' rights, how could he at the same time advocate federal Prohibition? Like most men, George was not free of hypocrisy, and we shall see that there were times in his life that he took positions that were unabashedly hypocritical.

George introduced his first bill shortly after coming to the Senate on December 21, 1922. It was S. 4219 to amend Section 13 of the Federal Re-

---

[41]See *CR*, 68/1, 8789.

[42]*Atlanta Constitution*, January 6, 1923, 13:3.

[43]*CR*, 68/1, 7133. He did, however, favor no limitation on genuine fraud.

[44]Ibid., 10005.

serve Act to the committee of Banking and Currency.[45] His first resolution, S. Res. 405, was entered in January 15, 1923. A surprisingly clumsily written document for a man with his skills, it called on the president to purchase the 28,000 tons of nitrate held for sale by the War Department "for distribution," presumably to make fertilizer.[46] Most of the other bills of his first Congress were minor in nature, such as relief for individuals, the removal of a tariff on ammonium nitrate, or relief to small businesses such as the Georgia-Florida-Alabama Railroad Company.[47]

George's first speech, like many he would deliver in his long career, was rather lengthy and was on his predecessor Tom Watson. It was a beautifully written paean reminiscent of the prose he wrote for student publications while a student at Mercer. "Of Tom Watson as a Senator, I shall not speak," he told his colleagues. "I prefer," he said, "rather to acquaint you with his life, which is part of the history of my state." He then traced Watson's family history and praised Watson's reading of the law "by the light of the pine-knot." Extolling his virtues, he told his colleagues that Watson "loved the common man. He was his champion, his tireless thinker, worker, and dreamer. His passion was always for the weak...."[48] Conspicuously absent was any mention of Watson's infamous role in the terrible Leo Frank lynching.

From the beginning, George became recognized for his constituent services, for both the great and wealthy and the poor and lowly, and he arranged, or tried to arrange, meetings of his constituents with prominent government figures. He intervened to get a Mr. Cox of the Kentucky distillers' Association of Louisville a meeting with the British president of the board of trade and the chancellor of the exchequer.[49] He reconstructed tax laws to spare Coca-Cola, of course a major industry in his home state, additional taxes.[50] He arranged for his close friend and fishing buddy, Macon lawyer T. Baldwin Martin, to have a meeting with the attorney general by telling the attorney general, himself an avid fisherman, that so was Mr. Martin.[51] He readily rushed to the assistance of one Thomas F. C. Napier of Ringgold, Georgia, to help him gain the entrance to sell certain products to

---

[45]*New York Times,* March 3, 1929, III, 2:6.
[46]*CR*, 67/4, 798.
[47]Ibid., 1731.
[48]Ibid., vol. LXV, part 12, 157.
[49]Ibid., 67/4, 2132.
[50]William Brown to Carl March, April 24, 1956, GFR-VHPS.
[51]"Old Independent," 20.

both the state and federal governments.[52]

Early in his career, George began to make himself known. Raymond Carroll later wrote of his early Senate speeches as "mild but convincing and minus the sensational element which some of the other gentlemen of the South like to inject into debate." George's first major accomplishment in the US Senate was the first piece of comprehensive legislation for protecting veterans of the Great War. By 1923, he was prominent enough to be asked to deliver a major radio address on the *Atlanta Constitution*'s radio station on American politics and the upcoming 1924 elections. Of this address, the *Atlanta Constitution* wrote, "Senator George was a forceful speaker and by his address...added his name to the already long list of well-known men who have spoken on the Constitution's station."[53] By 1928, he was already what is called "presidential timber," and indeed was the "Southern candidate" at the Houston convention. Carroll also wrote that year "about the steadiest and strongest voice from the Democratic side of the chamber" and noted him as carrying on "in spirit of the New South." Raymond G. Carroll, the Washington correspondent of the *Philadelphia Public Ledger*, wrote that year, "Perhaps no other men of his time, certainly no southern public official, has come to the front more rapidly than Senator Walter George." In a feature article in the *Ledger*, Carroll called him "a man who is always prepared for an emergency and is an outstanding personality of character, ability, and force."[54] By 1932, he was being prominently mentioned to replace Senator Joseph Robinson, the Senate Democratic leader, should he retire.[55]

George's first important assignment was to the Post Office Committee. The work of this group could be quite boring, but at the same time it was a committee in which there was much control of patronage. One of his first actions in this area was a bill to reduce postal rates on second class mail. His bill called for the restoration of the 1919–1920 rates, for George felt that restoring the rates would increase revenues because the recent increases had reduced the number of pieces in the mail system by six million. Reducing the rates would bring them back.[56] He generally supported increases in sala-

---

[52]Martin memoir, n.p.

[53]See December 19, 1928, September 29, 1942, October 20, 1943, in Rainey papers. This is simply not the senator's signature, but to more important constituents he did personally sign his letters (WFG to Bishop Warren A. Candler, March 18, 1933, box 75, f. 1, collection # 2, Candler papers).

[54]*Atlanta Constitution*, July 3, 1923, 7:6.

[55]The quotes in this paragraph can be found in "Meteoric Rise of George," unidentified clipping, n. d., RCB-5804, box 15, f. WFG-GSA.

[56]*Vienna News*, November 17, 1932, 1.

ries for mail carriers,[57] and in a surprise move, he opposed a provision in the 1930 tariff law that would give the post office the right to seize any literature held to be "obscene, immoral, and treasonable."[58]

Work in postal matters invariably dealt with sale of post offices and kickbacks. In spring 1925, George and Senator Harris together asked President Coolidge to have the Justice Department examine the question of the sale of federal jobs, especially post masterships, in Georgia. William J. Donovan, assistant attorney general in charge of investigations, had done so in the past, and as a result, several officials had landed in the federal penitentiary.[59] The dealing in post offices in the South had been the major activity of the Republican Party since Reconstruction since it rarely had any elected officials. They were generally referred to cynically as "Post Office Republicans." George had no problem with the dispensing of patronage, just so long as the jobs were held by "clean men," and he even offered the opinion that he would not mind the current chairman of the state Republican committee dispensing patronage because he was an honorable man, unlike other Republican operatives, who had sold offices.[60] Both George and Harris singled out in 1927 the GOP patronage referee, Benjamin Jefferson Davis, a black newspaper editor, as someone with whom they did not like to deal because often his recommendations "do not always have smooth sledding when they arrived in the Senate."[61]

In 1928 George had a particular dustup with US Postmaster General Harry New, who in testifying before the Post Office Committee, had noted that when the Democrats were in power, they had forced federal appointees to give a kickback to the Democratic Party. In a hearing in Atlanta in July 1928, George produced canceled checks to prove that Republican office holders were giving kickbacks to the Georgia Republican executive committee. He pointed out that some individuals in dealing out patronage enriched themselves.[62]

LEGISLATIVE PRIORITIES AND EXPERTISE

Vocational Education. George's first legislative love, and one that would remain a major interest of his for the remainder of his years in the Senate,

---

[57]*Atlanta Constitution*, January 28, 1925, 8:6; *New York Times*, January 25, 1925, 15:1.

[58]*Vienna News*, February 21, 1929, 1.

[59]*Atlanta Constitution*, March 19, 1930, 1:4.

[60]Ibid., March 2, 1925, 1:6, 2:3; *New York Times*, March 2, 1925, 6:5.

[61]*New York Times*, March 4, 1925, 18:2.

[62]Moore, "Public Office on Easy Payments," 206.

was vocational education. His son Heard George said it was always his father's favorite legislation.[63] George later explained his interest stemmed from the fact that 75 percent of boys never go to college and that these boys "should be taught some field of service."[64] After the Smith-Hughes Act of 1917, every piece of legislation on vocational education was to bear George's name. The George-Reed Act, the George-Ellzey Act, the George-Deen Act, and the George-Barden Act.[65] Moreover, George adopted Dudley Hughes's position that vocational education should be extended to agriculture. Hughes had noted that "to rebuild our agriculture, we must return intelligence to the operation of farms." Boys growing up in the cotton fields learned to farm only as their fathers had, acquiring no innovations."[66]

George introduced his first vocational Education bill (S. 1731) on December 15, 1927, which was sent to the Committee of Agriculture.[67] It was reported out favorably in March 1928 and became law shortly after. It was no hindrance that it received the support of the Republican leader, Senator Charles McNary of Oregon. It stressed rural education, and starting in 1929, a half-million dollars would be budgeted for that year and would increase to the much larger sum of $6 million per year, which would supplement the Smith-Hughes Act, which already granted $3 million. The money would largely go to salaries of teachers and supervisors of rural education.[68] It did not hurt that since Georgia had the third highest percentage of farm population that it received an additional $175,000. The act made it possible to double the enrollment in vocational education classes.[69] Moreover, it extended agricultural education into fields like cattle breeding and food canning and encouraged farmers to convert from corn to farming chickens. The vocational education journal wryly noted in 1954, "Old King Cotton is still a $100 million crop, but no longer does the state rise and fall with the lint harvest."[70] In 1936, George introduced a bill to provide vocational education funding on a permanent basis. Since the Smith-Hughes bill of 1917, which

---

[63] *Vienna News*, July 12, 1928, 1; July 19, 1928, 1; *New York Times*, July 17, 1928, 23:4.

[64] "Senator Walter F. George: A Distinguished Baptist," copy of unidentified newspaper, July 6, 1972, WFG-MU; "Address of Cong. Stephen Pace at Unveiling of Senator George's monument in Vienna, Georgia," RCB-5804, box 15, f. WFG-GSA.

[65] "George Given Citation," *Atlanta Constitution*, March 18, 1954, 20(?), scrapbook, LHG-VHPS.

[66] *CR*, Congressional Digest, 23:53; "The Journal Salutes Georgia," 5.

[67] Ibid.

[68] *CR*, 70/1, 677.

[69] *Vienna News*, March 8, 1928, 1.

[70] Ibid., February 7, 1929, 1.

did provide for a continuing appropriation, additional appropriations had been made for limited periods. George's 1936 bill provided a continuing appropriation to cover and increase the appropriation heretofore made for a limited time.[71]

By 1950, there were 141,000 vocation educational students in Georgia and two million in the country.[72] By 1954 Georgia had 299 white and 113 black vocational schools.[73] Dudly Hughes's wife had told her husband, "Remember the girls. Don't leave out the homemakers," and the act likewise promoted home economics. By 1954, 98 percent of all Georgia high schools had home economics.[74] In 1956, the Eisenhower administration tried to abolish the vocational education appropriation, but George got it reinstated in full.[75] The vocational education people would not forget Walter George and his useful work. In June 1950, there was the unveiling of a statue of Walter George at "Walter George Day," in the town square in Vienna, with 3,000 people in attendance to recognize his work with vocational education. A lot of distinguished people were on hand: Janet Barber, president of Vocational Association, Dr. M. D. Mobley, Georgia state vocational education director, and M. D. Collins, state superintendent of education. Congressman Stephen Pace made the address, and Jacqueline Sumter, president of Future Homemakers of America, unveiled the statue.[76] In 1954, the American Vocational Association gave Walter George the first-of-its-kind citation at a luncheon attended by most of the Georgia delegation. Rep. Paul Brown of Elberton made the presentation. "If I should call the role of great men of the nation in my lifetime," he told the audience, "the senator would be among the first I would mention. He is the leading spirit and co-author of every vocational education act passed since 1917."[77] Its imprint is with us today.

States' Rights. Still, the conservatism that would be the trademark of his career, although it would modify in time, was manifestly evident from the beginning. His ardent belief in states' rights would lead him to challenge on constitutional grounds many pieces of legislation. One of the first was his

---

[71]"The Journal Salutes Georgia," 6–7.

[72]*CR*, 74/2, 6268–70.

[73]"Address of Congressman Stephen Pace at the unveiling of George's statue," 2, box 15, f. WFG GSA.

[74]"The Journal Salutes Georgia," 7.

[75]Ibid.

[76]*This is Senator George of Georgia*, George Museum, Vienna, Georgia.

[77]*Vienna News*, June 22, 1950, 1.

opposition to child labor restrictions introduced in 1924, made all the more curious because the issue was a constitutional amendment and therefore if passed would not be "unconstitutional." George wanted such matters as child labor left to the states and therefore opposed the amendment. In the debate, when even the working child's education was in question, George even defended the states on this matter, noting that "I dare say that such a provision is in the child labor law of every state of the Union." George feared that the amendment would lead to government interference in other areas. When a senator from Wisconsin told George that the labor laws of Wisconsin did not permit child labor unless the child was in school, George rejoined, "For so many months…Or, for so many years….? If Congress can regulate conditions under which the child shall labor [,] it can effectively impose any condition on educational requirements."[78] George feared that if the amendment passed, "the power to regulate…the labor of persons under eighteen years of age would necessarily carry with it the power to regulate any industry in which they labor….and the labor of adults in the industry in which they are permitted to labor."[79]

George's argument here demonstrates how he always looked several steps beyond the present legislation into what other points could result beyond the apparent goals of the legislation. He will repeat this argument, always very carefully articulated, for the remainder of his Senate career. Big government would always be an anathema to the gentleman from Georgia, and he would fight its growth for the rest of his life.[80]

Taxation. It would be, nevertheless in the area of taxation that George would make one of his greatest, if unnoticed, marks on American history. The gentleman from Georgia had an incredible ability to understand and ferret out the minutiae of tax law. One Harvard Economics expert said of George after a tax bill hearing, "George is a man of great intelligence and experience…. [He] was the only one [of the committee] who understood the testifying tax and insurance experts, and he seemed to grasp what was going on."[81] In time, it came to be accepted that although the House was supposed to initiate all tax measures, it would be George's bill in the Senate that would become law. Since tax law does not generally interest most peo-

---

[78]"George Given Citation," *Atlanta Constitution,* March 18, 1954, 20(?), scrapbook, LHG-VHPS.

[79]*CR*, 68/1, 9998.

[80]Ibid., 10005.

[81]The child labor constitutional amendment passed on June 2, 1924.

ple, and certainly not in detail, this aspect of George's work was never as well known, but through his work in wartime taxation during World War II, he was able to arrange a taxing policy that would not only pay for more than 40 percent of the war but also allow for such economic growth during the war that the standard of living of the average American rose.

Constitutional Law. A more visible area in which George would become well known was in constitutional law, and within a few years of his entry to the Senate, he was mentioned for the first of a number of times for a position on the US Supreme Court. When Justice Edward Terry Sanford of Knoxville, Tennessee, passed away, the Georgia delegation recommended to President Hoover that George should be his replacement. Hoover was cordial at their meeting but remained non-committal. Thinking of politics, he felt that naming George would not help elect a Republican to Congress in Georgia but naming a North Carolinian or a Tennessean might elect one there since the mountainous part of both states had often elected Republicans. If Hoover ever seriously considered George, a revolt in the GOP lawmakers precluded his nomination, and he nominated Judge John J. Parker of North Carolina, a Republican. The Senate eventually rejected his nomination, so the slot was again open. It ultimately was given to Charles Evans Hughes, the former Supreme Court justice, secretary of state, and Republican presidential candidate. Hughes served again for more than a decade.[82]

George was again prominently mentioned among the twenty or so who were discussed when Oliver Wendell Holmes resigned in January 1932.[83] Again in 1937 and 1938, George's name continued to appear. In 1938, George announced that he "preferred" that his friends abandon the effort, adding "I would appreciate it if I am left entirely out of the matter."[84] At this point, George knew that Roosevelt would never name him, and within seven months, the president would even try to defeat him for his reelection to the Senate.

Isolationism. Over the years 1922–1932, George's adherence to rigid isolationism mellowed. He originally ran for the Senate as a strict isolationist, opposed to the League of Nations and US loans to foreign countries,

---

[82] Gene Methvin, "Statesmanship," *Vienna News*, August 8, 1957, box 15, f. WFG-GSA.

[83] *Vienna News*, March 13, 1930, 1; May 8, 1930, 1; and January 21, 1932, 3. "Very Serious Consideration" *Atlanta Journal*, March 23, 1930, WFG-GSA.

[84] *Vienna News*, January 21, 1932, 3.

especially "Negro Liberia."[85] Nevertheless, when Woodrow Wilson died just two years after George's election, George praised him because "he saw very clearly that the machinery for peace must be provided," which was mild praise for the League of Nations.[86] In 1927 he even supported, with conditions, a treaty with Turkey that would "take care of our moral obligations as well as our purely commercial interests."[87] In 1923, he had even suggested abandoning the World Court[88] when he shortly championed our entry into a World Court created by the League of Nations, within certain conditions.[89] We have seen how Russell tried to make it a campaign issue in 1926.

Nevertheless, much of his old isolationism remained. He voted in 1923 to withdraw troops unilaterally from the German occupation of the Rhineland.[90] He strongly opposed American intervention in Nicaragua, when the Coolidge administration sent troops in to support anti-revolutionary factions. To a joint session of the Georgia legislature, he condemned our taking sides with internal factions within a country. "The use of American troops in Nicaragua is endangering American goodwill in South America," was his theme.[91] His speech was so well recognized that it was reported in the *New York Times*.[92] He opposed in 1926 the cancellation of foreign debts of $12 billion owed the US, noting that we were paying a half million in interest a year on that part of our national debt.[93]

These early years likewise saw the appearance for the first time of two related foreign policy themes that would be the core of George's foreign policy thinking for the next three decades: A strong search for peace, not through isolation but through preparedness for war. Coupled with this idea was a fervent desire to see that any war that would involve the United States would be fought "over there," not on American soil. He strongly supported the naive 1928 Kellogg-Briand Pact "outlawing war" as an instrument of foreign policy. When Professor Glenn Rainey, a Georgia Tech English teacher, wrote George calling on him to support the treaty, George *wired* Raney back two days later, saying, "I voted to report Kellogg treaty out to

---

[85]Ibid.

[86]"Voice of the 84th," 23.

[87]*Atlanta Constitution*, February 4, 1924; *New York Times*, February 1924, 3:1.

[88]WFG to Bishop W. A. Candler, January 11, 1927, box 62, f. 7, Special Collections, Woodruff Library, Emory University, Atlanta, Georgia.

[89]*New York Times*, July 1, 1923, section 7, 9:1.

[90]Russell, *A Heart for Any Fate*, 217.

[91]*New York Times*, January 7, 1923, 2:2.

[92]*Vienna News*, July 21, 1927, 1.

[93]*New York Times*, July 20, 1927, 2:6; *Atlanta Constitution*, July 20, 1927, 1:1.

Senate and will continue my deep interest."[94]

In a speech three years later to the Georgia Legionnaires, he underscored for the first time the second component to his peace theme: preparedness "to defend the cause of peace." A nation that is prepared for war is not as likely to have to fight one. He told the legionnaires, and as he would frequently do in speeches throughout his career, that he would cover all bases: "There is no need to burden ourselves with the support of an [unnecessarily] great military program, but we cannot afford...to be less armed than others."[95] George, like George Washington, feared "entangling alliances" that might drag the American nation needlessly into a war. In March 1930, the United States sent a delegation to the London Naval Conference, headed by secretary of war Henry Stimson. While at the conference, Stimson issued a statement to the effect that the delegation would consider proposals for a pact committing the US to consult with other powers "if danger of war was [*sic*] threatened." Misuse of "was" aside, the isolationists in Congress feared that this agreement might drag the US into war, and Senator Borah, an unreconstructed isolationist, called it "a pious fraud." Others attacked it as well. George returned to the Senate floor from a White House visit with Atlanta Boy Scouts and entered the debate. He, like Senator Borah, condemned the provision and afterward told reporters that even if a consultative pact would not require force, "it would be interpreted by some [as such], and might place the administration in a war. He warned that any such pact would meet "determined opposition in the Senate." He feared that in time of war, other nations might think differently "and thus involve the US in war."[96] Here is some of George's natural isolationism, yet when Senator Kenneth McKellar of Tennessee had several weeks before suggested that the American delegation be recalled from the conference, George staunchly opposed him. Calling American non-involvement "a most disappointing blow to the hopes of mankind," he stressed that "[t]he prevention of another war like the recent world struggle is an ideal toward which our strength should be turned."[97] In the end he supported the London Treaty.

George opposed the recognition of the Soviet Union, but like all good politicians would bend his views if the interests of his state were involved. Refusal to recognize the Communist government in Moscow did not include an unwillingness to trade with it. When the Cotton Stabilization

[94]*Atlanta Constitution*, September 2, 1928, 2:1.

[95]WFG to Glenn Rainey, December 19, 1928, box 1, f. 1, Rainey papers.

[96]*Vienna News*, July 9, 1931, 1.

[97]*New York Times*, March 28, 1930, 1:6 and 2:4.

Board refused to sell cotton to the Russians, George came out strongly *for* trade with the Communist giant. Calling the situation among cotton growers "desperate," George said the Stabilization Board's refusal to sell cotton to Amtord Trading Corp., a Russian dummy corporation to facilitate trade with the West, because we do not "officially recognize Russia" is not "sufficient reason to justify its course in the present emergency. If Russia is willing to pay a fair price, there is no reason why the board should not sell."[98]

As late as 1927, however, he could still be classified as an isolationist. In a speech to the Americus Kiwanis Club, he spoke of disarmament, the prevention of wars, and the promotion of peace with the nations of the world. "We cannot continue to police the world with our marines...with justice to ourselves without making a declaration of our position. While policing South America will not get us into war at this time, eventually it might do so."[99] Walter George's foreign policy ideas evolved in the early years of his Senate tenure, but the blind isolationism of his 1922 campaign, sincere or not, had begun to show signs of breaking down. Even he would not do a *volte face* on the question, and almost a decade later, his actions would still be laced with notions of detachment of the US from world affairs. He likely could have never predicted the internationalist he would be a quarter of a century later.

One area in which he had made a complete turnaround was on the question of Prohibition, or at least a complete change from his stated position in 1922. In 1928 he stated, "The wets have every right to oppose the Eighteenth Amendment and the Volstead Act, and do all within their power to take the federal Government out of a domain where it has no business to be—the regulation of a private citizen's habits and wishes."[100] He does not seem to have voiced this view too loudly in Georgia, but it was a complete reversal from the position on which he ran—if he believed it then.

ELECTION OF 1926

In 1926 George was up for reelection for a full term. His future colleague Richard Russell famously said that a Southern senator could be a statesman for two years, but then had to be a politician for the second two, and a demagogue for the last two. His Mississippi colleague at the time, the stately Pat Harrison of Mississippi, put it a bit more crudely: "[A Southern

---

[98] *Atlanta Constitution*, March 4, 1930, 3:1; *New York Times*, March 4, 1930, 6:1.
[99] *New York Times*, July 11, 1931, 24:4.
[100] *Vienna News*, October 6, 1927.

senator] could be a statesman for five years, but on the sixth election year he went back home 'to sling the shit.'"[101] What both meant was that as reelection neared, senators had to engage in race baiting, which could cloud all other issues, leading one political observer of Georgia politics to remark, "In Georgia primaries, everything will be ventilated but the real issues."[102]

One of the reasons for this behavior was the power in the 1920s of the Ku Klux Klan in the country, especially in the South. George's great patron in the 1922 race, Governor Clifford Walker, was a major figure in the national Klan organization, so much so that he gave a major speech in Kansas City at the national "Klanvocation." Walker had so detested Hardwick, to Walter George's benefit in 1922, because of Hardwick's opposition to the Klan. In his unsuccessful attempt to regain a seat in the Senate in 1922, he had summed up his opposition to the Klan by questioning in his candidacy announcement, "If good men insist upon wearing masks, what is to prevent bad men from wearing them also?"[103]

There is no indication that George ever even remotely considered Klan membership (as Richard Russell did, but decided better of it), but he never openly opposed it as Thomas Hardwick had, and given his political survival in the 1920s and 1930s, we can probably safely assume that he played footsie with the organization, since the organization was so powerful it could even influence the vote for mayor of Atlanta.[104] In 1926, the Klan endorsed George, and he was the only Klan-endorsed candidate that won.[105] Klan potentate Walker was still governor, and had George displeased him, Walker would most assuredly go after him in 1926. Walker's signature on George's letter of reelection certification meant a great deal.[106]

George's only serious opponent in 1926 was Georgia Supreme Court Justice Richard B. Russell Sr., a somewhat shopworn perennial candidate who had run for other offices but had been successful only in being elected to the state supreme court, which he had won in 1922, with his son's help. Richard B. Russell Jr., a rising star in Georgia politics, planned to run for speaker of the Georgia House as well for as other offices. He also had built a network throughout the state for his future use, and his father benefited

---

[101]"George would prefer...," January 7, 1938, *Atlanta Journal* clipping, WFG-GSA.

[102]Egerton, *Speak Now against the Day*, 119.

[103]McMillan, "So Goes the South," 43.

[104]*Atlanta Constitution* clipping, October 16, 1924 in series I, box 1, f. 20, Hardwick papers.

[105]*Announcement of Thomas W. Hardwick for U. S. Senator*, July 5, 1924, series 1, box 1, f, Hardwick papers.

[106]Moseley, "Invisible Empire," 40.

from that network. Russell Jr. was close to the Klan, if he actually was not a member, and he had supposedly withdrawn from the 1924 Senate race at the request of Klan officials, who wanted to see incumbent Senator William J. Harris reelected.[107] Russell attended at least one Klan-hosted dinner, the guest list of which included many state government officials.[108]

The elder Russell entered the 1926 race himself only after trying unsuccessfully to recruit a candidate to take on George.[109] He ludicrously claimed that he was running "purely as a matter of conviction and duty, totally divorcing any personal interest and ambition whatsoever."[110] He ran what some politicos in the state called "a foolish campaign," and the press generally ridiculed him, calling him "an old stager and stump artist" and a "tragedy who had been feeding at the public trough all his life."[111] The *Macon Telegraph* called Russell a "misfit" and a "boozer," and told its readers that his election would be "a tragedy." He was in general made a laughing stock.[112] He erroneously thought he had a winning issue in denouncing George's support for the League's World Court, which he claimed incorrectly that George had run against in 1922. He also felt that George had done little for the farmer and was "too cozy with railroads, power companies, and banks,"[113] a charge that would follow George much of the rest of his political life but never hurt him.

Russell Sr.'s reluctant campaign manager was his son, Richard B. Russell Jr., with his father's hope, one guesses, that Russell Jr. could work the same magic for him that he had done in his Supreme Court race. An aunt remembered that son Richard opposed his father's entry into the race against George because he admired Walter George, and he realized the futility of the whole venture.[114] Dick Russell's sister remembered that George and Russell Sr. had earlier been friends and "grown up together in Georgia, both [being] in judicial [matters]." George had even given Richard Sr.'s brother Lewis a job in Washington. She also remembered that "Dick thought that was a tragic thing to do, and all of us did....We didn't think my father had a chance to beat him.... I can remember how he would dread to have to go out and make those speeches around in Georgia...begging the

[107]*CR*, 69/2, 2414.
[108]Moseley, "Invisible Empire," 103.
[109]Ibid., 46.
[110]Russell, *A Heart for Any Fate*, 217.
[111]*Atlanta Constitution*, September 1, 1926, 7:1.
[112]Caro, *The Years of Lyndon Johnson*, 170.
[113]Fite, *Richard B. Russell, Jr., Senator from Georgia*, 49.
[114]Russell, *A Heart for Any Fate*, 217.

people to vote for his father...when in his heart he was so sorry that his father was running."[115]

The race was run on a shoestring out of Judge Russell's judicial office in Atlanta, where he had one stenographer. All of the family pitched in without pay in various capacities, even his son-in-law Gordon Green, who was living in Washington and who had the job of monitoring George's speeches from the Senate gallery to try to catch him saying anything that might be of use in the campaign.[116] As his campaign manager, Russell Jr. seems to have worked harder than his father, who seems to have run a front porch campaign while his son was out on the hustings, working like "a Trojan," Robert Caro wrote.[117] Russell had invited George to debate him, but George always declined, one family member suggested seriously that "because he was not an orator in Russell's class and would not, he felt, come out on top in a toe to toe standoff;" to debate Russell would only have given him needless publicity.[118]

The campaign was nasty from the beginning with some incidents of near violence. Russell Jr. was even threatened by thugs in George's interest at a campaign rally in Kirkwood.[119] Russell Sr., who made his first public statement of the campaign only on September 1, with little over a week left in the campaign, made a number of reckless charges that could readily be proved wrong, especially his spurious charge George had voted for the joining of the League of Nations' World Court, which Russell claimed that George had promised in the 1922 campaign he would oppose. What George had done in 1922 was oppose entry into the League of Nations, a position he still held in 1926, and the court he suggested that the US join did not even exist in 1922. Moreover, he accused George of failing to help farmers. George, by making two campaign appearances a day all over Georgia in the sweltering heat, showed in speeches in the *Congressional Record* that he had repeatedly supported farm programs. In turning the court question back on Russell, George pointed out that he only favored joining the court if American sovereignty would be maintained, and he had seen to that. In a stump speech, he told the crowd that he had visited military hospitals with a 100,000 permanently maimed "boys," and he would never close the

[115]Russell, *Roots and Ever Green*, 228n.

[116]Mary Willi Russell Green, oral history, 17, 18, 21. Dick Russell was also working for himself, laying a network for any future races of his own.

[117]Russell, *A Heart for Any Fate*, 218.

[118]Caro, *The Years of Lyndon Johnson*, 170.

[119]Russell, *A Heart for Any Fate*, 220.

door on a proposal to make war "impossible." He added, "By entering the World Court, we can settle disputes other than by the sword and cannon."[120] His argument resonated well with voters. What is more, George had the support of his colleague, Senator Harris, who had also voted for the World Court.[121]

A few days before the election, George's campaign manager, E. H. Dykes, predicted victory, adding that George would carry more counties than he had in 1922, when he had won 133 counties out of the 159, adding that he would concede only two counties. He added that the "court issue" that Russell had hoped to ride had been a "most disappointing [?] failure."[122] The election for his campaign was held on Wednesday, September 9, and George made his final campaign speech on Monday, September 6, in Gainesville, saying, "The generous and loyal support of my friends in all parts of the state has made it possible for me to conduct this campaign and also furnished absolute assurance in an overwhelming victory in the Democratic Primary.... I am deeply grateful. I am certain of victory and feel that the result is apparent.... As to preclude the making of extravagant claims of any kind at this time."[123]

On September 9, although the weather was good, the turnout was light, but George rode to a landslide to victory. At midnight, the total popular vote was George, 39,428, to Russell's 20,737, or 229 unit votes to Russell's 40. In Fulton County (Atlanta), George had crushed Russell 5,864 to 3,946, and he had carried his birth county Webster 196 to 7. He also handily carried Richmond and Chatham counties, both of which he had lost in 1922. In the final tally, George received 128,179 votes to Russell's 61,911, which translated into 242 county unit votes for George to Russell's 32.[124] In the November general election, George received 100 percent of the vote.[125] George was confirmed as "reelected "in a letter by the governor, the comptroller general, and the secretary of state.[126] It would be twelve years before

[120]Caro, *The Years of Lyndon Johnson*, 170. He cites an interview with Rev. Henry E. Russell.

[121]*Atlanta Constitution*, September 5, 1926, 12:6.

[122]Ibid., September 9, 1926, 8:1.

[123]Ibid., September 5, 1926, 3:7.

[124]Ibid., September 7, 1926, 1:1.

[125]Dubin, *United States Congressional Elections*, 468.

[126]Russell, *A Heart for Any Fate*, 221; *New York Times*, September 10, 1926, 1:6; Heard and Strong, *Southern Primaries and Elections*, 63–64; Russell's loss of eight county unit votes on election night, which switched to him the next day, was probably due to some typical flip-

George would face serious opposition again.

The evidence is skimpy, but it seems Richard Russell Jr. never fully forgave George for the nastiness of this campaign although George does not seem to have been directly involved in the more negative aspects. Jake Carlton, who worked for a number of Georgia politicians over his long career, said in his oral history at the University of Georgia that he once asked Dick Russell about his relationship with George, and Russell replied, "It really was a bitter campaign [in 1926] and so there was a hostility between the Russells and the Georges for a long time."[127] Erle Cocke, one of George's close associates, stated in his oral interview that the two families "were against each other until the '36 race,"[128] when George endorsed Russell in his reelection to the Senate. Russell even asked George to make his nominating speech at the Democratic convention for his unsuccessful race for the presidency in 1952. However, Russell never paid him back when George needed him most: Russell remained silent in George's desperate campaign in 1938, and when George was seventy-eight and running for reelection in 1956, Russell ignored George's plight when a simple endorsement would have saved George's career, but he owed George his intervention in these two crucial ones. Bitter feelings sometime die hard.

LIFE IN WASHINGTON

George's life in Washington was relatively simple. It was rumored that the Georges had no housekeeper and that Miss Lucy did all of the cooking and cleaning, but it seems unlikely she would not have had domestic help.[129] At least hotel housekeeping must have given the apartment a weekly cleaning. Miss Lucy may have cooked breakfast, which was usually orange juice, eggs, fried Georgia country ham (his favorite dish), and grits.[130] George ate breakfast early, dined out infrequently, and almost never dressed for dinner.[131]

His work, especially on the Foreign Relations Committee, required that he attend some formal functions, and he did buy a formal cutaway coat

---

flopping of small counties whose local politicians did not want to be on the losing side. This type of manipulation often happened.

[127] *CR*, 69/2, 2414.

[128] "Jake" Carlton oral history.

[129] On coming to Washington, Richard Russell rejected staying there, feeling that it was too expensive.

[130] "Old Independent," 21.

[131] Ibid.

and striped pants, but they hung in his closet unused for a decade. By then he had outgrown it, so he bought another one, which shared the same lonely fate for many years. When Queen Wilhelmina of the Netherlands came to Washington, George was required to go to some function with her and tried to find the formal wear. It was not in the closet because a month or so before, Miss Lucy had had it made into a suit for her, since he didn't use it, so he escorted the Queen of the Netherlands around Washington in a gray business suit, but he generally never went out in the evening.[132] Once when Miss Lucy asked him what he wanted to do after dinner, he replied, "Rest, Lucy. I recommend it for you. Rest."[133] He also might allow himself to enjoy the strains of the orchestra in the ballroom below, if there was such a function, or at lease use it as background music while he worked on one of his tax bills, or lacking ballroom music, he would turn the radio up as background noise. Sometimes he would stop to listen to Fibber McGee and Molly or Charlie McCarthy, while Miss Lucy sat on the other side of the room doing needle point or jigsaw puzzles.[134] The one social function George would attend was Senator Harry Byrd's famous annual Apple Blossom luncheon at his farm in western Virginia, but generally he spent his evening in his apartment.[135] He avoided dinner parties, receptions, balls, and parties, and as one journalist put it, "George usually begins his working week with meditation on how to escape social events." When an invitation arrived at his office, he usually threw it away before going home. "He has become as skillful at avoiding a reception as he is at piloting a tax bill through the Senate," another journalist wrote.[136] Whereas George hated to go out, Miss Lucy loved it. Dinner parties and receptions were a delight for her, and George's refusal to attend usually did not stop her if she found out about an invitation. These social preferences and their going of separate ways seem to have suited them both.

Home for George was, and always would be, Vienna (pronounced "Vay-enna"), where certainly throughout most of his career, he and his family spent at least half the year, where even before his career in the US Senate, George was known as "the Sage of Vienna." They could leave Washington by train at 6:00 in the evening and be in Vienna by lunch the

---

[132]Ibid.

[133]Jarman, "Taxpayer's Senator," 39.

[134]Mellichamp, *Senators from Georgia*, 238.

[135]Jarman, "Taxpayer's Senator," 23.

[136]P. Borsh, "Washington Life," *Advocate* (?), April 27, 19??, UNC, Sen. G(NC), VHPS.

next day. "It was here [in Vienna] that I met Miss Lucy. It was here that our two sons were born. It was here that you gave me my first chance to be of public service," he would reminisce in 1950, and despite the fact that he walked with the mighty of the nation in Washington, it was here that he was totally himself.[137] Even Miss Lucy said that she preferred Vienna to Washington although she "enjoys Washington."[138] His neighbor John Bonner's most outstanding recollection about the Georges was "the simplicity of their lifestyle,"[139] and social events there were not shunned. George was teaching a Sunday school class of young ladies at the First Baptist Church in Vienna at the time he was elected to the Senate,[140] and the Georges were regularly feted there.[141]

His daily routine did not vary much from that in Washington. He often went to bed by 8:00, never later than 9:00, after watching television or reading. While sitting, Mrs. George's parakeet, "Bobby," occasionally would perch on his shoulder.[142] During the day, he would come into town and sit in his little office there. Twice a day he would cross Cotton Street to get his mail, and there he would be bombarded with citizenry and their good wishes. Traffic would stop and business would come to a halt.[143] When he was in his office, no one bothered him with visits, and no one called on the phone. He was known to be a private person, and the locals respected that.[144] One day some people from Vienna came all the way to Winder, Georgia, home of Richard Russell, for help with a problem. Surprised, when Russell asked why they did not talk to George in their own hometown, the reply was, "Oh, we wouldn't want to bother Senator George about a matter like this."[145]

When he was not in his office, he was often fishing or hunting, but unlike many other politicians, George never played a round of golf.[146] He liked

---

[137] Isabelle Shelton, "The Congress goes to the White House," UNC, f. Sen George (NC), VHPS.

[138] *Vienna News*, June 22, 1950, 1.

[139] Ibid., June 14, 1928, 1. This statement, given her personality, is open to question.

[140] John Bonner interview.

[141] Jarman, "Taxpayer's Senator," 41.

[142] *Vienna News*, June 14, 1928, 1, such as the banquet honoring him given by the United Daughters of the Confederacy.

[143] Donovan, "Senator George," 33.

[144] Baldwin Martin, "Walter Franklin George," *Mercerian* 3 (February 1947), WFG-MU.

[145] Frances Coley interview, March 16, 2004.

[146] John Carlton interview, oral history, 21.

to fly fish and had a great touch.[147] She told this author that he had a farm on the Flint River with neighbor Pat Butler. Miss Lucy never went to the farm, saying all she wanted from it was a ham or two a year.[148] George, who had been an ardent prohibitionist early in his life, began imbibing at some point later. He and son Marcus went with Henry Woodward to a deer drive on the 140,000-acre plantation of a George Varn in South Carolina, and apparently it was on these hunting and fishing trips that George learned to "take a drink," well out of the sight of Miss Lucy. After a day's hunting, the men would sit around and have drinks and "tell lies," Mr. Woodward remembered. George usually did not say much in these sessions, but one day when he had killed a pair of turkeys on the day's hunt, "that night you couldn't keep him from talking."[149]

LIFE IN VIENNA

Over the years, the Georges stayed in a number of places in Vienna. They initially lived in what was then known as "Miss Lucy's house," a large white-columned home on Union Street, built by a Dr. Stoval, who in turn sold it to Senator George, who then sold it to the Woodwards.[150] The front porch of the house came to be called "the first Walter F. George School of Law" because on that porch he would tutor young lawyers who were "reading the law," as people often did in those days.[151] The Georges sold that house early in his Senate career because it was too expensive to maintain only to sit empty much of the year.[152] Sometimes the family lived with George's sister Wilna, but most frequently they lived in the ramshackle Virginia Hotel, which seems to have been more of a boarding house. In it they had a suite. It was owned and managed by Nell Heard, Miss Lucy's sister-in-law, wife of her brother Julius Heard.[153] As Mrs. Coley remembered,

---

147 *Atlanta Journal*, December 20, 1942, 6-B

148 Frances Coley interview.

149 Ibid.

150 Henry Woodward interview.

151 Frances Coley interview.

152 T. Hoyt Davis interview.

153 Gene Methvin told me that he clearly remembered that Judge Walter McMillan of Sandersville, Georgia, whose father was somehow involved in the loan, told him that the Georges were about to have it foreclosed on them during the Depression, but the bank decided that to have a U. S. senator's house taken would be such a bad morale blow to the nation that they did not do it. I called Judge McMillan, who had no recollection of the near-foreclosure. He did remember, however, that Gene Talmadge, Senator Herman Talmadge's

Miss Lucy "got enough of that" and had an old tenant house moved to a 132-acre farm they had on the outskirts of Vienna on the Unadilla Road next door to Mrs. Coley's house, and Miss Lucy "fixed it up, put her touch on it."[154] In addition to whatever changes Miss Lucy made inside the six-room cottage, she also added a large screened porch, which was open to breezes from three directions and shaded by a large oak tree covered with ivy.[155] His son Heard managed the farm on which they raised pecans, peanuts, tobacco, cotton, and cattle, which George enjoyed watching from the porch.[156] Next door was Irma and Heard's house, linked to the George's home by a stone walk. The Georges later made a lake house on Lake Blackshear by putting together several street cars in which their faithful housekeeper Ada Durham even had a room, but the main purpose of this get-a-away was for fishing.[157]

Though Miss Lucy had become a fixture in Washington, and according to Mary Lou Davis, social editor of the *Dekalb New Era*, she was "the Dolly Madison of the Twentieth Century, everywhere and into everything," she remained the uncrowned queen of Vienna.[158] She came into town often to shop and frequently would go to Emmett Stephens's grocery store to buy something for dinner, saying to him, "What have you got for me today?" He would go back to the meat counter and cut her something.[159] The Merita bread delivery man would leave a complimentary angel food cake for the Stephens family each week, and sometimes they would be eating it in the back of the store when Miss Lucy came in. She would tear herself off a piece and quip, "It's such a good vegetable."[160] Mrs. George was always active in her community and close with her neighbors. She always had a country ham at her house, neighbor Frances Coley remembered, and whenever she baked a ham or a turkey, she would always send some of it to her neighbors. Sometimes the Georges would have parties in their front yard. The Coca-Cola Company would supply the cokes and Miss Lucy would call neighbors and

---

father, owed his father $200.00, but every year would pay only the interest, using as an excuse that "The legal business is tight right now" (McMillan interview).

[154]Henry Woodward interview.

[155]Frances Coley interview.

[156]George, *Addresses*, Dublin, August 30, 1938, 7, VHPS.

[157]Donovan, "Senator George," 34; the tobacco allotment was in Heard's name, not the senator's, and it was the only tobacco allotment in Dooly County.

[158]Grace Slade Crovett interview.

[159]"Potomac Press Meat," *Dekalb New Era*, February 3, 1955, VHPS.

[160]Jack Stephens interview.

ask them to fix sandwiches.[161] She often shopped in a "Ten-cents store" (the ancestor of the Dollar Stores of today) wherever she was, and once she lobbied a chain mogul to locate one in Vienna. He did not put one there, supposedly because he could not find Vienna on a map.[162] She was an active member of the Ladies' Sewing Club in Vienna, one similar to one she had founded in Washington among senators' wives. Members would come once a week and bring their sewing baskets, and they would spend the afternoon knitting and crocheting.[163] Their husbands called it "The Gossip Club."[164]

When he was not in Washington running his father's office, Heard George lived in Vienna, too. He married Irma Elizabeth Grace in December 1933. She was a striking blond with a charming personality. Although a native of Vienna, she went, the local paper informed its readers, to Mullins, West Virginia, for "special training," whatever that was. Locals in Vienna remembered her as being somewhat stuck on herself.[165] Most locals did not remember Heard doing much but hunting and fishing, but he always shared what he caught, often bringing dressed fish to the bank to give away.[166] Several people remember him fondly but noted that he had a foul mouth. He had graduated from Tech High in Atlanta and attended Mercer for two years before getting a law degree from National Law University in Washington, DC. After law school, he worked in DC running his father's office, but he generally could not wait for the Congressional session to end so he could return to Vienna.[167]

Marcus, the younger son, graduated from Riverside Academy in Atlanta in May 1929.[168] Many people expected Marcus to follow his father into politics. Handsome and debonair, he was a flier and man about town. He would fly to Vienna in his own plane and buzz a local grocery story of a friend. Flying low over the store, he would cut the engine and yell down for someone to come to the Cordele airport to get him, then start up the engines again.[169] He married a Washington socialite who was a divorcée with

---

[161]Ibid.

[162]Frances Coley interview.

[163]"Potomac Press Meat," *Dekalb New Era*, clipping in f. WFG-VHPS.

[164]Frances Coley interview.

[165]*Vienna News*, November 18, 1933, 1.

[166]This information was mentioned in several interviews.

[167]Conversation with Mary Branch, at the time the executive director of the VHPS. Mrs. Coley did not remember his bringing them dressed.

[168]*Vienna News*, November 16, 1933, 1.

[169]Ibid., May 30, 1929, 4. Strangely, a year later the *Vienna News* reported that Mrs. George planned to attend Marcus's graduation on May 5, 1930.

the ironic name Mary Senate (Mrs. Whiting Wicker), and in 1942, their daughter was born on Marcus's birthday, November 16, in a Washington hospital.[170] She went on to become in the late 1950s a Washington radio hostess.

One fixture in the George household who was not strictly a family member was the George's longtime housekeeper, Ada Durham. She also served the community as a midwife although she did not deliver the George children.[171] She not only ran the Georges' household when they were in Vienna but also oversaw the property there even when the Georges were in Washington. She was assisted by a black man named Bass, who also tended the yard and cleaned Heard's fish and game.[172] She also accompanied the Georges to their lake house, where she had her own room. She was "quiet and kept in the background," one family friend remembered.[173] She was an outstanding cook, and when several people drove to Florida to pick up Mrs. George when she would visit her sister in Bradenton, Ada would always pack a lunch of fried chicken, ham, and the trimmings.[174]

When Miss Lucy entertained, Ada would wait the table, and at least once she embarrassed Miss Lucy in front of some Washington guests who happened to be in Vienna. Miss Lucy had told her to cook "a basic Southern meal," and while the assembled guests were in the living room, not at the dining room table, in walked Ada with a stack of hoe cakes, saying, "Any of you people want some fried cornbread?"[175] Miss Lucy seemed to take Ada in stride. At breakfast, Ada would say to the Georges, "Do you want your coffee het [heated] up?" One time after she had refilled their coffee cups and left the room, Heard, a little annoyed, said to his mother, "Mother, why don't you do something to improve Ada's English?" Mrs. George quickly replied, "No, I might want my coffee het up sometime."[176]

One aspect of George's life in Vienna that changed over the years was his drinking. He had run as pro-prohibition in 1922 but voted to repeal Prohibition a decade later. At some point, he began drinking alcoholic beverages, usually bourbon and water, and by the late 1940s, he would drink when his wife was not around, such as on the above-mentioned hunting

[170]Gene Methvin interview.

[171]Mary Senate Wicker to Friedin, August 20, 1957, in "George, Walter F. (Estate folder), Davis and Forehand Law Firm archives, Vienna, Georgia.

[172]John Jacob Gregory interview.

[173]Ibid.

[174]Grace Slade Crovett interview.

[175]Ibid.

[176]Frances Coley interview.

trip. In time, he came to drink openly, even in Vienna. He would sit on his screen porch, looking at the cows in the adjacent pasture, and at 5:00 p.m., he would simply call out, "Ada?" That was Ada's cue to bring him a toddy.[177] There are some indications that later in life, George was drinking too much. At a dinner party at secretary of state Jimmy Byrnes's house, Henry A. Wallace, former vice president, remembered that "George was pretty 'tight' and at the start of the meeting was brutal in his treatment of both [secretary of the treasury] Fred Vinson and [assistant secretary of commerce] Will Clayton."[178] He seems to have been often in Senate leader Lyndon Johnson's private office in the Capitol, where a lot of drinking went on,[179] and Dean Acheson remembered that George would even have a drink before lunch each day in the office of Leslie Biffle, the secretary of the Senate.[180] If indeed he was over-indulging, there is no evidence it affected his work or his performance in the Senate.

GROWING NATIONAL RECOGNITION

One accompaniment to his visits home was a barrage of speaking engagements, especially as he became a more nationally known figure. He would be asked to speak at historical commemorations such as the unveiling of the Stone Mountain memorial, college commencement addresses, or to a local Kiwanis Club.[181]

George was often invited to speak out of state. In 1928, he gave the graduation address at North Carolina Women's College, where he called for training women for public service.[182] The next year at the Duke commencement on the themes of public service as well.[183] In 1929 he spoke at the "Dixie Dinner" of the Southern Club at Boston, where he spoke on George Washington and Robert E. Lee, "two of the greatest figures of Southern History."[184] Harlee Branch in the *Atlanta Journal* called it the greatest speech since Henry Grady's talk forty years earlier.[185] In 1937 he was invited to address the Florida legislature, giving a memorial to Florida senator Duncan

[177]John Bonner interview.

[178]Frances Coley interview.

[179]Blum, *The Price of Vision*, 526.

[180]For an example, see Caro, *The Years of Lyndon Johnson*, 338.

[181]Acheson, *Sketches from Life of Men I Have Known*, 142.

[182]WFG to Hon. W. M Camp, March 14, 1928, series I, sub-series I, box 6, f. 4, Stone Mountain Collection.

[183]*Vienna News*. June 7, 1928, 1.

[184]Ibid., May 16, 1929, 6.

[185]Ibid. January 24, 1929, 6; speech reprinted in the *CR*, 70/2, 4709.

Fletcher.[186]

No request seemed too lowly for his appearance, as his speech at the Vienna Kiwanis Club, of which he was a member, shows.[187] The next year he spoke at a joint meeting of the Vienna and Cordele clubs.[188] Even as late as his last year in office, when he could have avoided many invitations, he spoke to the North Georgia Conference of Women's Society of Christian Service at the First Methodist church of Griffin, Georgia, speaking on the role of women in the Methodist movement.[189]

PRESIDENTIAL ELECTION OF 1928

One clue to George's prominence was his being touted as a presidential candidate as early as 1927, less than five years after having been elected to the Senate. As early as April 1927 there was already a growing movement, "Georgia for George," to send a favorite son delegation to the 1928 convention pledged to vote for George as the presidential nominee. The newspaper correspondents in Washington had already identified George as having "an outstanding Democratic figure." It was obvious to them that George was becoming a national figure, and they observed that had he been from the North or the West, "he would be a serious contender."[190] By early fall 1927, there was much talk that the next nominee would be from the South, which the *Vienna News* termed "America's great barn and smokehouse," and much national attention was focused on Walter George, with many predicting he would be much more than just "Georgia's favorite son." Opinion had it that he would be a strong candidate in the North and West, in addition to sweeping the Solid South. Again, the *Vienna News* reported, "On the floor of the Senate, there is not a more popular member nor one that commands a more respectful hearing nor welds a more powerful influence."[191] Granted, much of his support came from his hometown newspaper, but frequently it was merely reporting what others were saying outside of Georgia. Thirty years later, Senator Olin Johnson of South Carolina remembered how "almost thirty years ago" in the late 1920s that George was "mentioned in the legislative halls of South Carolina" as presidential timber.[192] Clearly by the

---

[186]Ibid.

[187]*CR*, 75/1, 5512.

[188]*Vienna News*, January 9, 1930, 1.

[189]Ibid. July 2, 1931, 1.

[190]Jarman, "Taxpayer's Senator," 41.

[191]*Vienna News*, April 7, 1927, 5.

[192]Ibid., September 22, 1927, 1.

late 1920s there was a "George groundswell," if only a minor one.

The animus against a Southerner was not as strong as it would become later, but even then, George would have been recognized as a strong right-of-center conservative. His support of business was well known, and he openly defended the inequality endemic in Southern race relations, which was not yet the issue it would later become. As late as January 1928, he defended the all-white primary in Georgia in the Senate; when it was attacked by Senator David Reed of Pennsylvania, he invited anyone in the body to test Southern electoral laws before the US Supreme Court. "We have not integrated our primary laws," he told the Senate. "The primaries are purely party affairs. We may run them as we please." He did say that blacks were free to vote in the general elections: "More than 3,000 of them in a single city in my state did qualify and vote for the president of the United States. True, that was not a primary[,] but it shows the negroes [*sic*] are not disqualified [from voting]." Then he defended the social system of the time, which today is chilling in its inequality when saying, "Whatever the South may have done[,] she has acted in an honest and abiding belief that it was necessary for her to act to preserve her own civilization."[193] When Senator George made this statement, a majority of Americans would either have agreed with him or been indifferent to the plight of African Americans.

By January 1928, the movement of "George for President" was gaining noticeable momentum, and he was often asked about his interest. When asked if he might consider the position of vice president, he stated plainly that he was not a candidate for vice president, but then added coyly that he was not "an active candidate for president" either. His hometown paper editorialized that it would be a loss to give him the vice presidency, which it termed an "empty honor."[194]

In January, the Georgia congressional delegation in Washington met at a dinner at the Mayflower and unanimously endorsed George for president. John S. Cohen, Georgia's Democratic National Committeeman, wired the *Vienna News* their resolution: "Resolved, that it is the sense of the Georgia delegation in Congress [and] the Georgia Democratic committee men that Walter F. George be, by the state of Georgia, offered to the nation as the candidate of the Democratic Party for President of the United States." It had been written by Congressman Eugene Cox and seconded by Congressman Carl Vinson.[195] The *Augusta Chronicle* opined that George should be

---

[193] *CR*, 84/1, 12574.

[194] *Vienna News*, January 19, 1928, 1.

[195] Ibid., January 26, 1928, 4; Timmons, *Jesse H. Jones*, 147.

given a totally free hand to choose all the delegates to the Houston convention.[196]

Support began to appear for George in other Southern states. Members of Congress from South Carolina, Florida, and Alabama returned to Washington after the 1927 Christmas break reporting that George had support in their states and that they would send delegations supporting George to the Houston convention.[197] In February, the *Tampa Times* came out "flatfootedly for George" as did many weekly papers, and John Temple Graves was writing editorials favorable to George for the *Jacksonville Journal*. Moreover, Dr. E. C. J. Dickens, a well-known evangelist from Georgia and a Mercer classmate of George's now living in Florida, declared the "Florida Democrats are rapidly turning to Sen. W. F. George as the logical standard bearer of the Democratic Party." He had been traveling about the state of Florida and observed, "I find the sentiment for Senator George growing at an amazing rate." He predicted that Florida would send a "George delegation" to Houston.[198]

Meanwhile, George's presidential campaign began to catalyze invitations to speak in other parts of the South. On February 4, 1928, he was asked to address the South Carolina Legislature, and later that month he spoke at the Ninth Congressional District Convention in Virginia.[199] At that gathering, he told the 1500 delegates that the Coolidge administration had instituted a "bureaucratic rule" in administrating laws for "the privileged few." "Boards and bureaus are all right so long as they serve the people," he told his audience, adding, "I did not come to Virginia to teach Democracy but to drink from the fountain from which Democracy springs, the home of Jefferson...." George was introduced to the convention by W. H. House, who had been nominated for Congress from the 9th district. After his speech, White told the delegates, "The party could not select a better candi-

[196]*Vienna News,* January 12, 1928, 1. It's unclear why the Democrats would choose Houston for their convention late in June. Not only was the weather hot, so was the city's water. The pipes were so close to the surface that the water stayed around 85 degrees. To remedy this problem, the convention organizers would have to install oversized Frigidaire water coolers to produce cold drinking water. Someone estimated that the coolers would provide the equivalent of nine tons of melted ice daily, or the equivalent of fifteen pounds of ice daily for drinking water.

[197]"Give Senator George Full Freedom," *Augusta Chronicle,* February 12, 1928, WFG-GSA.

[198]Ibid., January 5, 1928, 1.

[199]*Vienna News,* February 23, 1928, 8. Much of the boomlette for George was reported largely in *Vienna News,* his hometown newspaper. The Atlanta papers do not seem to have been as interested at this point.

date nor the people of the United States a better president than the man who has just addressed you, Senator George."

The next month he spoke in New York at the fifteenth annual banquet of the National Association of Waste Material Dealers at the Hotel Astoria on the subject of "Government and Business." From there he returned south to speak to the North Carolina Pine Association convention, which strangely was meeting in Norfolk, Virginia. After just six years in the Senate, newspapers all over the nation were citing his speeches, and "scores of invitations" to address groups flooded in.[200]

By late March 1928, he had gone from Georgia's "favorite son" to the South's candidate. People were optimistically predicting that he would arrive at the convention in Houston with 100 pledged delegates: He was receiving twenty-eight delegates from Georgia, twenty-four from Alabama, twenty-four from North Carolina, and ten from South Carolina, giving him a total of ninety-four. His supporters expected additional delegates from Virginia, West Virginia, Oklahoma, and Tennessee.[201] At the state democratic convention in Macon, he had named his delegation to be headed by Senator William J. Harris of Cedartown, and it included Governor Clifford Walker and two women, one of whom was Mrs. Emily Woodward, editor of the *Vienna News*, and individuals from each congressional district. Those chosen included even some of his political enemies.[202]

In May, the Georgia delegation wrote a letter, signed by Senator Harris and all members of the Georgia delegation, to all unpledged delegates, praising George's ability as an orator, his character, and so forth. George requested that the letter be brief and non-controversial. Starting with the belief that the entire country would profit from the election of a Democratic president, who would "act wisely," the letter informed the reader that Georgia was presenting to the convention such a man, who after only five years in the Senate "has taken a prominent place in that august body." It concluded with, "We recommend him to you and the country."[203]

It was probably an exercise in futility. Al Smith, the governor of New York, had the nomination more or less sewed up by June, and it seems that much of the George candidacy attracted more light than heat.[204] Even the Atlanta papers paid so little attention to it. When the *Atlanta Constitution*

---

[200]Ibid., February 9, 1928, 1, 8.
[201]Ibid., March 22, 1928, 1.
[202]Ibid.
[203]Ibid.
[204]Ibid., May 31, 1928, 6.

did report on his presidential campaign, the articles on it are placed deep in the paper, rarely on the front pages. George, though, continued his candidacy to the bitter end.

George returned to Georgia for only five days early in June 1928 before returning to Washington on June 12 via White Sulphur Springs, West Virginia, to speak to a state bankers' convention. In Washington, he attended committee meetings to investigate the violation of civil service laws.[205] Before leaving for Washington, George announced that he would go to Houston. Typically candidates for presidential nomination remained aloof in another city during the nominating process, but George wished to be at the convention itself. He did not say whether he would be on the floor of the convention, but the newsmen assumed that he would be near enough to "remain in personal touch with his floor managers." At any rate, he planned to return to Atlanta on June 21 or 22 to confer with his staff, and then he would go to Houston on June 23 with the Georgia delegation on the "Walter George Special." The Georgia delegation planned to have the South Carolina delegation accompany them on the same train.[206] The delegates were to gather at the Henry Grady Hotel and leave for Houston at 8:00 p.m. A round trip ticket was a rather pricy $64.16.[207]

Miss Emily Woodward, managing editor of the *Vienna News*, and Miss Lucy went to Atlanta to join the Georgia delegation on Friday, June 22. The next day, four of George's supporters, J. N. Hargrove, president of the local Kiwanis Club; T. Hoyt Davis, the solicitor general (who would later become the federal judge who struck down the all-white primary in Georgia); Reverend August Walters, a local Baptist minister; and J. B. Walters, a local farmer and merchant, left for Houston by automobile. Ed Dykes, the state senator in the area, left on Monday by himself, having delayed his departure because of business matters.[208]

George's main campaign emphasis was the plight of the farmer, he told the press on the eve of his return to Washington. "I am quite aware," he added, "that the farm problem is not to be solved by any single legislative proposal." He added, "'This great and scary problem will not be solved until we [The Democrats] elect a president and Congress in full sympathy with the farmer and his business." For a bit of comic relief, a reporter asked George, an avid fisherman, if he had had any time while in Georgia to fish.

[205]Nevins, *Herbert A. Lehman and His Era*, 97.
[206]*Atlanta Constitution*, June 13, 1928, 10:8; *Vienna News*, June 14, 1928, 1.
[207]*Atlanta Constitution*, June 13, 1928, 10:8.
[208]Ibid., June 10, 1928, 8:5.

He did not reply in words, only with "a pained wistfulness" on his face. The interviewer suggested that George probably had a policy "of less government and more fishing for the republic."[209]

On George's arrival in Houston, Rep. Thomas M. Bell of Texas predicted that George would go into the convention with a hundred delegates, thus denying Smith a first ballot victory. Then the real bartering would begin. George also learned that he was still being mentioned for the vice-presidential position on the ticket, and because of this discussion, for the first time, an article on George's candidacy appeared on the front page of the *Atlanta Constitution*.[210] He opened his headquarters on the mezzanine floor of the Rice Hotel, with the Georgia delegation staying either in the Rice or the nearby Sam Houston Hotel. His campaign center "hummed with activity all day yesterday," the *Atlanta Constitution* relayed to its readers, adding, "and between convention sessions today."[211] All of the George delegates wore a badge with a picture of Senator George with the inscription "For President, George of Georgia." Still, the *Constitution*'s front-page headlines read, "Democratic Convention Opens Today as Smith in Complete Control," and "Quick Nomination of New Yorker Freely Forecast."[212]

On June 26, George spoke to the first Georgia caucus. The Prohibition issue had become the elephant in the room because Al Smith was a "wet," and the Georgia delegation had planned to issue a "dry" platform plank supporting the Eighteenth Amendment. By this time, George had begun to rethink his dry stand, but more importantly, he saw the platform fight as disrupting the party's success in November. In a stirring speech, George stressed the need for convention harmony and declared that "great issues were at stake, which demand this last ounce of energy." A fight over Prohibition would only distract the party from important issues and weaken it for the fight in the fall election.[213] This performance of George is all the more amazing because the Prohibition forces had caucused at the convention and elected George as their champion. George himself had told the AP that if any effort is made to write a pro-liquor plank in the platform, he (George) would join the drys in a floor fight.[214]

Congressman Charles Crisp had begun work on George's nominating

[209]*Vienna News*, June 28, 1928, 1.
[210]Ibid., May 24, 1928, 2.
[211]*Atlanta Constitution*, June 10, 1928, 6 7; June 24, 1928, 1:2.
[212]Ibid., June 27, 1928, 6:7.
[213]Ibid., June 10, 1928, 8:5.
[214]Ibid., June 27, 1928, 6:7.

speech on June 15, and he was the first nominator to take the floor at the convention.[215] At the mention of George's name, the Georgia delegation held up a thirty-foot banner proclaiming "The Constitution Must Be Preserved," famous words of Andrew Jackson. A demonstration led by Ralph Rosser of Lafayette, Georgia (an alternate who should not have even been on the floor), erupted and lasted for fifteen minutes. The band played a quickstep medley of Southern tunes, including "Dixie" and "Dear Old Georgia," and anti-Smith delegates, most of them "drys," did all they could to help the George demonstration. After fifteen minutes, Senator Joseph Robinson of Arkansas, chairing the convention, banged the gavel, and the band stopped short. Deprived of music, the George demonstrators took their seats. At the rollcall, Alabama voted unanimously to yield to Georgia to nominate George, making his name the first to be put before the convention. There had been some fear that the state's delegates would vote to yield to Tennessee so they could place Cordell Hull's name, but their apprehension proved groundless.[216]

Crisp spoke for half an hour on the convention floor to deliver an extraordinary nomination speech, which hardly mentioned Walter George. He first lashed out at Republican corruption and mismanagement as "a shameful betrayal of public trust." He read a litany of great Georgians who had served the country well, twice mentioning Alexander H. Stephens, who had served as the vice president of the Confederacy and was regarded by much of the country as a traitor. He stated that this man, whom he still had not mentioned, was sympathetic with the "toiling masses." Crisp called on other Southern states to rally to George (still without actually naming him), especially reminding Alabama that Georgia had supported Alabamian Oscar W. Underwood four years earlier.[217]

Other names placed in nomination were Cordell Hull of Tennessee, James A. Reed of Missouri, and Pat Harrison of Mississippi; however, New York Governor Al Smith had the nomination before the convention even began.[218] He arrived at the convention with an overwhelming number of delegates, 733 to be exact, the second most ever after Woodrow Wilson in 1912, and he lacked only 48 votes to win the nomination.[219] As was usually the case, "favorite sons" usually hoped to create a bloc of delegates over one

[215]*Vienna News*, June 28, 1928, 1.
[216]*Atlanta Constitution*, June 16, 1928, 4:6.
[217]Ibid., June 28, 1929, 4:1.
[218]Ibid., 1:6 and 2:6.
[219]Warren, *Herbert Hoover and the Great Depression*, 41.

third to deny a first-ballot victory for the leading candidate.[220] To be nominated, the Democratic Party required a two-thirds majority for a candidate, not a simple majority. Smith had received a boost a week earlier when Governor Albert Ritchie of Maryland withdrew and threw his support to Smith.[221] Franklin Roosevelt, the Democratic candidate for governor of New York, placed Smith's name in nomination.

Smith won the nomination in a rout, a clear sign that the Democratic Party was not overly dedicated to Prohibition. He received 849 votes on the first ballot, giving him the nomination. Talk of George's receiving a hundred votes never materialized, but he came in second with 52½ votes. He had received eight of the twenty-four from Alabama, all of Florida's twelve, all of Georgia's twenty-eight, and four and a half of West Virginia's sixteen.[222] Although he was the only deep-South candidate, George received no other votes from any other Southern states. Given all the hype and optimistic predictions, his performance was terribly disappointing. His second-place finish wasn't even much consolation; he exceeded the third-place candidate, Senator Reed of Missouri, by only one-half vote. Pre-convention talk of George for vice president didn't materialize, either. George had, of course, said that he did not want the vice-president slot before the convention "under any circumstances regardless of the identity of the presidential nominee."[223] However seriously he might have been considered, he was not offered the job, and it went to Senator Robinson of Arkansas only after Jesse Jones, the Reconstruction Finance Corporation (RFC) chief, had turned it down.[224]

As soon as he returned to Vienna, George and his son Heard went fishing so that he could avoid the press.[225] He did later address several Georgia organizations, such the Georgia Editors Annual Convention, but for a while, he somewhat vanished.[226]

[220]*Atlanta Constitution*, June 26, 1928, 1:7, 8.

[221]Ibid., June 17, 1928, 1:8. This article on the convention does not even mention George on its first page.

[222]Ibid., June 21, 1928, 15:5.

[223]Ibid., June 29, 1928, 1:8 and 4:1.

[224]*Vienna News*, October 25, 1928, 4.

[225]Timmons, *Jesse H. Jones*, 147.

[226]*Vienna News*, July 5, 1928, 1.

GEORGE CAMPAIGNS FOR AL SMITH

One of the few issues on which Northern and Southern Democrats could agree was that the Republican Party was the "party of the rich," even though Southern Democrats often sided with them in Congress.[227] Even wealthy Southern Democrats felt this way. George was frequently one of them; likely his reason for doing so was to "preserve the Constitution" or because of his belief in states' rights—while in so doing he supported the desires of the wealthy. At a convention of postmasters in Macon in 1927, George said, "There was never a greater need for liberalism…than at the present time."[228] But he himself repeatedly sided with big business, not just in 1928, but throughout his political career. He suffered in these early years from the paradoxical malaise of many Southern Democrats in that they voted for northern liberals for president and in so doing were voting against everything in which they believed. It is hard to imagine someone of George's intelligence not noticing the contradiction in his beliefs and his actions. It would later not be so contradictory in either case. Although his views were much closer to those of Herbert Hoover, the Republican nominee in 1928, than they were to those of Al Smith, he endorsed Al Smith out of party loyalty.

Many Democrats abandoned the party that year, and as a result, the "Solid South" was broken for the first time since the end of Reconstruction. Reverend John Roach Straton, a prominent New York clergyman and, ironically, a friend and former roommate of George's at Mercer, publicly called on him to leave the party and "turn to the moral and religious forces that will at least sweep the South." Appealing to George as "my old-time friend and roommate during the happy college days in Georgia," he called on him to "make a temporary break…with the Democratic machine as now dominated by the forces of Tammany Hall corruption" and to "ponder long and well before you throw yourself into any active advocacy of the candidacy of Al Smith." Warning that "dark and sinister forces are working for his election," Straton had attacked Smith from the pulpit, accusing him of being backed by "the forces of gambling and prostitution."[229] George, held by his ties to the Democratic Party, had by this time already endorsed Smith in his first speech since Houston at a rally in Webster County before a crowd of 2,000, where he called for loyalty to the Democratic Party and branded

[227]Ibid., August 9, 1928, 1.
[228]White, *Citadel*, 103.
[229]*Vienna News*, July 28, 1927, 1.

those who vote Republican in 1928 as having "joined forces with the ancient enemy. My mother, who lies sleeping in yonder churchyard, taught me…that my first and highest duty was fidelity to my obligations…. Can it be that my mother was entirely wrong…?" He returned to loyalty to the Democracy: "I am going to faithfully observe…my obligations to the Democratic Party of the south [*sic*]. It is the party that protected us during Reconstruction days… It is the party that has preserved white rule."[230]

Although "dry" Georgia Democrats met in Macon to organize against Al Smith, gradually by the end of August, Georgia's leading Democrats had rallied, if unenthusiastically, for the Democratic national ticket.[231] Smith was endorsed on August 8 by Democratic National Committee chairman John S. Cohen, former senator Hoke Smith, W. T. Anderson, the Macon newspaper owner and former governor T. W. Hardwick.[232] J. M. Busbee, a political ally of George's in Dooly County, however, endorsed Smith, hitting on an issue even bigger than Prohibition—his Catholicism: "With the present Senate make up of 92 senators, only six of whom are Catholic, it would be extremely difficult for a Catholic president…to deliver the United States to the Pope."[233] One delegate at a meeting in Columbus, observing that support was solidifying behind Smith, told a reporter, "You cannot get one outstanding Democrat in Muscogee County to state openly that he will vote for Hoover."[234] On a more colorful note, the first bale of Georgia cotton sold in 1928 was a donation to Smith's campaign. It had been flown in a plane to New York, where it had brought $5,000, the largest amount ever paid for a bale of cotton, before or since.[235] Although George did not seem to have been embraced by the local Democrats, candidate Al Smith invited him, Senator Carter Glass, and Josephus Daniels to come to New York for a "conference" with him on the campaign and was scheduled to meet with Smith in Albany on Thursday, August 16.[236] Indeed, he even invited George to stay in the governor's mansion. While there, Smith showed them his acceptance speech, and George gave his advisors his views on Smith and his chances in the South. With great assurance, George stated that Smith would

[230]*New York Times*, August 16, 1928, 4:2; *Atlanta Constitution*, August 16, 1928, 2:2.

[231]"Senator George Urges Loyalty," *Columbus Enquirer-Sun*, July 17, 1928, WFG-GSA.

[232]*Atlanta Constitution*, August 9, 1928, 7:1.

[233]Ibid., 1:4.

[234]*Vienna News*, August 2, 1928, 1.

[235]*Atlanta Constitution*, August 21, 1928, 1:2.

[236]Ibid., August 16, 1928, 1:1.

carry Georgia.[237] The *New York Times* reported that as one of the "dry chieftains," and "Since he comes from a state where dry sentiment is predominant [*sic*] and the K-K-K has been at times exceptionally strong, his...air of confidence was encouraging to the governor's supporters."[238] After the meeting, George went to New York City, and Governor Smith arose earlier than usual to see George off.

In New York City, George made a speech at Democratic headquarters. He prefaced his remarks with, "Of course you know my position—I am supporting the ticket." Then he took on first the religious question. "The religious question exists in all parts of the country," he said to his listeners, adding, "It is a factor that exists here in New York." He felt that the religious question will "clear itself." More serious, George thought, was the question of Prohibition. Known as a prohibitionist, George said, "But Governor Smith recognizes that I have a right to my views and he has a right to his. As a Democrat, we would never find a leader with whom we would agree on every possible question. But on the essentials on true democracy, Governor Smith impresses everyone as one of the outstanding Democrats of all times." George had been impressed that on the liquor issue, the governor had approached the question "honorably and openly," and George felt that "this will appeal to the people of the South."[239] Later, before leaving New York, he issued this statement, "The South is bound to recognize that a man may be in thorough agreement with Democratic doctrines and yet have the views of Governor Smith on Prohibition. They are bound to respect him as a great Democrat..."[240]

Until Franklin Roosevelt started the tradition of accepting the nomination personally before the convention in 1932, successful nominees rarely attended the conventions, and their acceptance speeches were simply made public sometime in the weeks after the convention. When Smith did make public his acceptance, the speech that he had shown George in Albany, George was quick to praise it. "In his acceptance speech, Governor Smith shows a remarkable grasp of national and international problems," he announced to the press. "It is a speech by an honest man with an honest mind and a human heart." George then stressed what he felt was the key component part of the message: Smith's pledge to enforce the Eighteenth Amendment "and the laws enacted pursuant there to the last degree."

[237]Ibid., August 14, 1928, 1:3.

[238]Ibid., August 17, 1928, 1:7.

[239]*New York Times*, August 17, 1928, 1:7.

[240]*Atlanta Constitution*, August 19, 1928, 1:8.

George felt that his assurances that he "will ruthlessly stamp out corruption in the enforcement agencies carries conviction." Moreover, he felt that the speech "breathes the fine spirit of progress and reform."[241] He also presciently noted that Smith's speech "effectively destroyed the myth of Republican prosperity."[242] George's statement on the speech was his first salvo in the campaign for Smith's election.

Curiously, in the beginning at any rate, it was George's colleague Senator Harris who did most of the campaigning for Smith in the state of Georgia, while George at first worked actively outside of the state.[243] When vice-presidential candidate Senator Robinson campaigned in Savannah, it was Harris who greeted him. George was not even there; he was already on his speech swing—elsewhere.[244] George was still called on for speeches out of state, and indeed he was better known outside of Georgia than was Harris. Senator Millard Tydings was arranging the speech schedule for campaign surrogates, and Tydings had George, described by the *New York Times* as "a bone dry," speaking in other Southern states and in the Midwest.[245]

George first stumped for the ticket in Tampa, Florida, and in so doing "opened the national campaign in the South." Repeatedly, George warned that if Smith were defeated by the defection of "a single Southern state," the Democratic Party, as a national organization, "faces its supreme crisis." As usual, George played both sides of the issue: "I do not question the sincerity of any man...who asserts he...will vote a protest vote against the party nomince in 1928...and return to the party hereafter," but George warned that the party "cannot be held together as a national party if Democratic votes...insure the election of the Republican candidates." He feared, he said, that these people who planned to return to the Democratic Party after the election might not have "any national Democratic party to which you can return."[246] His first campaign tour in Florida included speeches in Lakeland, Bradenton, and Tallahassee as well. In Lakeland, Florida's junior senator, Park Trammell, introduced him, and C. A. Boswell from Bartow, member of the state Democratic committee, presided over the meeting and said that George's tour of Florida "had done much to clear the air and unify the Democrats."[247] The Palm Beach County Democrats asked George to come

---

[241] *Vienna News*, August 23, 1928, 1.

[242] *New York Times*, August 23, 1928, 5:4; *Atlanta Constitution*, August 23, 1928, 1:1.

[243] *Atlanta Constitution*, August 23, 1928, 1:1.

[244] Ibid., September and October 1928, *passim.*

[245] Ibid., September 16, 1928, 5:1.

[246] *New York Times*, September 13, 1928, 4:4.

[247] *Atlanta Constitution*, August 26, 1928, 1:7.

there, along with Senator Robinson, for a rally since the county had gone for the GOP in 1924, but George was already headed back north.[248]

Passing back through Georgia, he spoke in Thomasville, then Bainbridge, then Unadilla near Vienna, joining Robinson for a rally in Atlanta on September 18 as he headed north.[249] His Thomasville speech was his first in the city since his 1926 campaign, and in it he called for "coordinated support for the Democratic national ticket." His talk was repeatedly interrupted with bursts of applause. He raised several issues he would hammer to the end of the campaign: Prohibition, corruption, Smith's religion. He prefaced his remarks by noting that he had opposed Smith's nomination, but he had "cheerfully bowed to the will of the party." He noted that Smith's platform called for "enforcement" of Prohibition, which the Republican Platform only pledged to "observe" it, whatever that meant._Then he asked rhetorically, "How can we expect Andrew Mellon, the distiller, to observe the Prohibition law when he has whisky to sell?" To those who might doubt Smith's sincerity when he said he would support the law, he said, "To doubt a man who by the honesty of his whole life…is so foreign to an unbiased conception that it is useless to argue the point." He then spoke to a collateral fear of his own: the destruction of the Democratic Party. "Necessarily in life people differ," he told his audience, "and to drive from the party all with whom we do not fully agree will destroy the party system."[250]

George next addressed the fear that a Smith administration would be controlled by the corrupt New York democratic political machine Tammany Hall. He likened such charges to "ghost stories constructed to frighten children," but then added that instead of being controlled by Tammany, Governor Smith "dominated Tammany," a curious slip in logic that would hardly allay the concerns of those who feared the machine.[251]

Finally, George turned to the issue he felt was the most damaging of all: Smith's Catholicism. This issue was probably the one most lethal, nationally, to his campaign. Calling for religious tolerance, he noted that "everyone within the hearing of my voice cherished the religion of his…[dear parents]," saying that Smith "was in a similar situation. Religious liberty was one of the cornerstones of American freedom. When an unknown soldier was brought from the foreign land where he gave his life for his native soil…no one asked if he might be Protestant or Catholic, Gentile or Jew."

[248]Ibid., August 30, 1928, 3:5.
[249]Ibid., September 6, 1928, 3:2.
[250]*Vienna News*, September 13, 1928, 1.
[251]*Atlanta Constitution*, September 15, 1928, 8:1.

George was just warming up. In Unadilla he delivered another thunderous oration in the school auditorium, and the *Vienna News* reported that George "has never delivered a more impressive address." Here he hit boldly on the religious issue by stating that Smith was "an honest-to-God Catholic and Robinson a Methodist," but then he informed his audience that Hoover had been married by a Catholic priest and Curtis was baptized one when he was a baby, but "neither seems to be sure what he is as to creed." One old man who was there remarked, "It has been my privilege to listen to Tooms, [Alexander] Stephens, [William Jennings] Bryan and other famous orators, but never had I heard anything more eloquent than his ringing plea for Democracy made by Senator George.[252]

George was then headed to a super rally in Atlanta with Senator Robinson, whom he was to introduce. Senators Harris and Harrison of Mississippi were to be there, as well a collection of political figures from across Georgia. Special seats were to be reserved on the dais for Confederate veterans since Robinson was the son of a Confederate veteran.[259] This rally was canceled, however, due to flooding between Jacksonville and Atlanta caused by a hurricane,[253] so Robinson, when he arrived on the 19th gave only a short speech at the Terminal Station.[254] On September 26, however, there was another major rally in Atlanta where Franklin Roosevelt spoke. Former Governor Hardwick spoke as well and was very well received.[255] George was not there because he had already begun his national swing for the ticket. He spoke in Lynchburg, Virginia, on October 1, and speaking in Charlottesville, Virginia, on October 2, George defended Smith's views on Prohibition, saying, "The Lord only knows where Hoover stands."[256] From Charlottesville, he went like a whirlwind, to Stanton then Newport News, Virginia, to Murphreesboro, Tennessee, then into Arkansas, Kentucky, Missouri, and as far west as Oklahoma. At this point it was not certain where he would go, perhaps into Nebraska and Illinois, but most likely eastward to Delaware and other eastern states.[257] His tour made him optimistic that the Smith candidacy was gaining ground. He told the *Vienna News*, "I am convinced that the tide is running strongly towards the Democratic ticket." He predicted with certainty that Virginia, Tennessee, and

---

[252]Ibid.

[253]Ibid.

[254]Ibid., September 16, 1928, 1:1.

[255]Ibid., September 19, 1928, 10:1.

[256]Ibid. September 20, 1928, 1:4.

[257]Ibid., September 27, 1928, 1:1, 10.

Missouri would go for Smith, adding, "Democratic strength is growing daily in Kentucky and Oklahoma."[258]

It is difficult to tell whether George believed the Democrats were gaining ground or was just blowing smoke. Smith did not carry one of the states other than Georgia in which George campaigned, so if George believed his rosy prognostications, he had badly misread the political mood. One suspects that his optimism was real. His zeal in the campaign gives strong indication of that premise.

Suddenly, however, the Georgia Democratic Party called George back to the state to work for the ticket there. There were some real fears apparently that the state might go for Hoover, and the party wanted to use its heavy artillery. It was announced on Saturday, October 20, at the state Democratic headquarters that he was returning and would be speaking in Swainsboro on Wednesday, October 24, Waycross on Thursday, Moultrie on Friday morning, and Bainbridge, Ashburn, Cordele, Cornelia, Gainesville, making one speech a day in each of these cities. On November 1, 2, and 3, he would make a tour of the 7th Congressional district, ending in Augusta, where he would be introduced by Congressman Carl Vinson.[259] Speaking "with the ability of a master," he attacked the Republican "old lease thievery," the absence of a farm program, and deplored the introduction of race into the campaign when an African American was named civil service commissioner in New York by the mayor, not by Smith, as they implied. He struck at corruption, claiming in Waycross, "If Herbert Hoover had no knowledge of the corruption, then he is not wise enough to be president."[260] He drew large crowds everywhere, usually standing room only, his voice becoming more and more hoarse.

Toward the end, his speeches began to get a trace of demagogic hysteria, and in Marietta, George did something that he had almost never done, either before or after, to the end of his career: He played the race card. On November 1, he asked the crowd rhetorically, "Are you going to lie down with Ben Davis [and] Marie Williams, [black leaders of the Georgia Republican Party]?"[261] He might have used less suggestive words than "lie down," but he did not, and he was too great a wordsmith not to realize the implication of his language.

Of course, Smith lost in a landslide, carrying only the Deep South. For

[258]Ibid., October 3, 1928, 2:6.
[259]*Vienna News*, October 4, 1928, 1.
[260]Ibid. October 25, 1928, 1.
[261]*Atlanta Constitution*, October 21, 1928, 1:5.

the first time since the end of Reconstruction, the South was not "Solid." Hoover had carried Virginia, North Carolina, Tennessee, Florida, and Texas, and Smith had carried Georgia by only 33,000 votes, not the 40,000–50,000 votes that George had predicted. Even Fulton County had gone for Hoover. George probably derived little consolation from the fact that Dooly County cast 745 votes for Smith, with only 156 for Hoover.[262] There is no statement in the press indicating what George thought of the disaster. Shortly after the election, he went deer hunting in Ivanhoe, Georgia, a small town near Statesboro. Two deer were killed, neither one by George. After the hunt, he spent the day in Statesboro and took the midnight train to Atlanta.[263]

THE GREAT DEPRESSION

On October 23, 1929, the American stock market, fueled by speculation on money borrowed by people who could not afford to borrow it, had a sudden sharp fall in the last hour of trading. Margin calls after closing and the next day led to a crash, and Thursday, October 24 became known as "Black Thursday." Monday and Tuesday of the following week prices fell even lower. With some up-ticks, the market finally bottomed out in summer 1932.[264] It would be almost a quarter of a century before stock prices would reach the levels of summer 1932.

Americans generally cite this debacle as the cause of the Great Depression, but it was far more complicated than a single financial disaster. One problem was a weak farm economy, which the reader will remember, George had often pointed out and called on the Republicans to remedy, to no effect. The Depression made the farm situation even worse. For products affecting Georgia farmers, the average price of corn fell from 80 cents a bushel in 1929 to 31.5 cents in 1932; the price of a pound of raw cotton fell from a low 19 cents in 1929 to 6.5 cents in 1932; tobacco fell from 18.5 cents a pound in 1929 to 10.5 cents in 1932.[265] From 1929 to 1932, farm income in Georgia fell from $206.00 per person in 1929 to $83.00 per person in 1932.[266]

With the advent of the Great Depression, George became decidedly more active in Congress; his name appears much more in the *Congressional*

---

[262]Ibid., October 26, 1928, 1:5 and 6:7.
[263]Ibid., November 2, 1928, 1:3.
[264]*Vienna News*, November 8, 1928, 1.
[265]Ibid., November 15, 1928, 4.
[266]Morrison, *The Oxford History of the American People*, 940.

Record, and he was frequently chosen to serve on conference committees to iron out differences between House and Senate bills. It was during these years that George began to be a major player in the Senate, not just a popular, hardworking member.

The first area of relief in which George became very active, and the only area he later promoted enthusiastically under Roosevelt, was aid to the farmer. Having been reared on a farm, owning a farm himself, and representing a farming state made his interest a natural one. One of his biggest criticisms of the Republican administrations of the 1920s was the absence of a farm program. When the Hoover administration did finally propose a "farm bill," George worked hard to get Georgia farm products included in the bill. Cotton and tobacco were easy, but George was able to get turpentine, resin, and gum termed "farm products."[267] Later that year George took one of Huey Long's programs, the guaranteed payment of 6 cents a pound for cotton of the 1931 crop and 6 cents again next year, for all who would not plant cotton in 1933, and he proposed this move to the farm board. Probably to gain broader support, he included wheat in the suggestion, since little of it was grown in Georgia. He wired the suggestion to both Long and Hoover.[268] He at one time angrily opposed a senator's reference to the farm loans in drought conditions as "a dole," since they were loans to be repaid. "The Senator [Watson of Indiana] used the word [dole]," he said testily, "and I did not think he wanted to go to the country in that light, because that is a loan...that has been repaid in practically every incidence...There is not an element of dole in it."[269] Linked with this concept, he demanded in October 1932 that the tobacco and cotton farmers receive the same credit breaks that the wheat farmers received. Wheat farmers throughout the country (few of which were in Georgia), but not the tobacco and cotton farmers, had been given a moratorium on repayment of these loans. He wired his criticism to President Hoover, who never replied, but the president was on the eve of his defeat and had more important issues to concern him.[270]

In the last month of the Hoover administration, George and his colleague Senator Russell joined forces to get delays on farm foreclosures. Pri-

[267]Ibid., 123, 296, 302.

[268]Friedel, *Franklin Delano Roosevelt*, 38. For other statistics on the Georgia economy in the 1920s and 1930s, see Fossett, "The Impact of the New Deal on Georgia Politics, 1933–1941," 42–46.

[269]*Vienna News*, March 5, 1931, 1.

[270]Ibid., August 20, 1931, 1.

vate lending companies were granting moratoriums, but the Federal Land Bank was taking farms from delinquent lenders. George fired off a letter to Paul Beston, the federal farm loan commissioner in protest.[271]

As critical as George had been of Hoover and the Republicans, Hoover turned to him late in 1931 for help, probably because of his work on the Finance Committee. He was invited to the White House and told to come "after supper." In addition to George, Senator Jim Watson of Indiana, Senator Carter Glass, Senator Pat Harrison, and Tom Connally were also there. On arrival, they were taken to the East Room, where Hoover, with bloodshot eyes, was seated with Bernard Baruch, George Harrison, and Owen D. Young. Hoover seemed to be sleepwalking, and Senator Connally said that his eyes were "begging for help." In a shaky voice, Hoover told these men that they were called to discuss "economic conditions." He added, "There is a great danger that we are going to slip off the gold standard." He then read a statement of the economic situation in different parts of the nation and asked for their opinions of "general business conditions." Connally could not later remember what he or anyone else said to this "inane" question."[272] The Hoover administration was paralyzed, and it would take a different sort of leader to put America back on the proper road.

George's conservatism, however, came through in a number of his actions. When in February 1932 he was promoting federal relief, he wanted it only for states that could not afford relief themselves. When asked by Senator William H. King of Utah if he favored emergency appropriations if "any state is able to care for the situation"? George's reply was a curt, "No, I do not." In one of those alleged duels in which both senators agreed and were trying to make the same point, Senator King replied, "The federal government has no business to interfere in their [states'] affairs or to assume this responsibility," to which George replied, "I am disposed to agree with the senator from Utah."[273]

One area where George was often a thorn in the side of the Hoover administration was on the question of tariffs, and since he held a seat on the Finance Committee through which all tariff legislation had to pass, he was in an excellent position to ambush it. The Republican Party had always been the party of high tariffs, which were generally protective of northern industry and not protective of agricultural or raw products that industry would need. This policy made the industrial manufactured products that the farmer

---

[271] *Vienna News*, February 9, 1933, 1.
[272] *CR*, 71/3, 699.
[273] *Vienna News*, October 6, 1932, 1.

had to buy artificially high in price. George, who often masked as a free trader when it came to protection of industrial manufactured products, was quick to promote tariffs protecting agricultural production.[274] Such a position is not unusual for a politician, but in George's case, his actions were blatantly hypocritical, easily the most flagrant of his entire political career.

As early as 1926, George had declared that the South needed "reasonable protection to industry," that is, lower tariffs on manufactured products, but tariffs nonetheless.[275] The fact that he had recognized the need for them for industry gave him license to demand them for agriculture—and not just agricultural products but other produce such as *kaolin* (China clay), of which Georgia is blessed with rare deposits just as West Virginia, Kentucky, Ohio, and Pennsylvania are blessed with deposits of coal. When the question came before the Senate, George so skillfully argued for increase tariffs on English and other foreign *kaolin* that Senator Walter Edge of New Jersey said, "to me it is so impressive to have the senator from Georgia making this eloquent plea for protection that I am not inclined to combat any of his arguments."[276]

When the tariff question came to be debated during the first year of the Hoover administration, George continued to make this pitch. On the 1929 tariff bill, later known as the Hawley-Smoot tariff, George said, "While I do not look for drastic increase on duties on industrial products, it is equally certain that the disparity between prices of manufactured articles and farm products remain virtually the same after the tariff act is passed."[277] When the question of a tariff on tobacco, a major crop of the Georgia farmer, was being debated, George continued to straddle the fence. "While not committing myself to the high protective theory as a wise policy," he argued, "I am convinced that if the system is to be continued...the benefits...ought to be equally distributed and protection extended to farm products." For good measure, he also threw in peanuts and cotton substitutes such as jute. He felt that as a member of the Finance Committee, he could insist on adequate protection for these products.[278] His true feelings came out when he tried to make the tariff bill "an all agricultural bill," which lost by a single vote.[279]

A special session was called to discuss tariffs on agricultural products.

---

[274]Ibid., February 9, 1933, 1.

[275]Connally, *My Name is Tom Connally*, 136–37.

[276]*CR*, 72/1, 3924–25.

[277]For one of the many examples, see *CR*, 73/1, 1349.

[278]William J. Robertson, *The Changing South* (New York: Boni and Liveright, 1927), cited in Tindall, *The Emergence of the New South*, 135.

[279]*CR*, 71/1, 5144.

In a Senate floor tangle with Senator Reed Smoot of Utah, one of the authors of the bill, George declared that this bill would be of little benefit to farmers. Smoot replied that George's remarks were "not only unfair but misleading." George replied, "Under the 1929 tariff act, agriculture has a rate of protection of 25.85 percent…. Under Fordney-McCumber tariff of 1922, Industry has an average rate of protection of 42.03 percent and [under this bill it will rise] to 47.07 percent. The disparity of the two rates is thus widened against farm products."[280] Several days later, George attacked the Republicans for wanting to reorganize the Tariff Commission on a partisan basis since the commission had some leeway to adjust tariffs by themselves. Noting that the efforts raise the Fordney-McCumber tariff was already losing steam, the supporters of upward revision were trying to circumvent Congress by packing the commission with partisans of higher rates. "[If the commission is given the power to adjust tariff rates], the beneficiaries of existing rates will not need to come to Congress for higher duties."[281] "However, the fight," he warned, is not won. It's just beginning."[282]

On leaving for Vienna in mid-July, after the end of the special session, he excoriated President Hoover for his indirect contribution to the tariff debate. "I believe Mr. Hoover desires…to see a tariff bill carrying rates as high as will not endanger its passage. He had not indicated anything to the contrary." He felt that the special session on agriculture was worthless, and he blamed the president, saying, "The president has stepped out of the picture and not even his shadow has since been discernable." He contrasted the Republican position with that of the Democrats, arguing that the Democrats want a "fair bill," one that "should be so adjusted as to equalize the economic conditions of agriculture and industry."[283]

As the debate continued into the fall, Hoover, who had said nothing at this point on the question, letting the Republican leaders carry the ball, finally weighed in on the bill. He asked for the inclusion presidential authority to raise and lower tariffs on certain products, and George took the floor and spoke for two hours, a performance described by the *Atlanta Constitution* as "one of the most vigorous speeches heard on the floor this session."[284] George accused President Hoover of siding with industry over agriculture. Opining that the session was supposed to help farmers, George argued it

---

[280]*Vienna News*, August 15, 1929, 1.
[281]Ibid., January 10, 1929, 6.
[282]Ibid., July 4, 1929, 6.
[283]*New York Times*, July 4, 1928, 2:2.
[284]*New York Times*, July 6, 1929, 2:1.

had made their plight worse. Noting that Hoover had been "silent as a tomb until now," had entered the fray only when industry, "the highest protected sector in the country," was threatened.[285] He did, however, make the observation that Hoover's attempt to obtain control of the commission was politics that any partisan would do, admitting, "I do not say a Democrat would not try to do likewise."[286] George lost another battle with the Republicans, who wanted to give the president the authority to make discretionary changes in tariff rates when Congress was not in session. Despite his failure to delete it from the bill, his hometown newspaper, *Vienna News,* praised George's leadership in the matter: "His logic was unassailable and his conclusions that the provision is contrary...to the intents and prescriptions of the Constitution was inescapable."[287] As we shall shortly see, George would later call on the president to use this power he so strongly opposed.

George continued into 1930 to fight a rearguard insistence on the tariff question. He succeeded on preventing an increase in tariffs on wool hats, which gained him some national attention, but an alliance of northeastern manufacturing states and wool state interests blocked Democratic efforts led by George to reduce tariffs on raw wool.[288] His amendment to reduce rates on wool was defeated 41–31. "It was apparent that this amendment was calmly and deliberately framed in greed," he said, as though that might be a surprise to anyone. "This initiates a new principle in the making of tariffs based on greed...and not upon the needs of trade or consideration of the consumer," he added. Then he threatened Hoover with political defeat in 1932. "If Mr. Hoover wishes to succeed himself, he will hesitate a long time before he will approve the same kind of tariff bill which sealed Mr. Taft's doom," adding that Taft's bill was almost a "free trade policy compared to Hoover's bill."[289]

In March, George the free-trader favored protectionism when manufacturing tariffs were proposed supported raising tariffs on tobacco.[290] When Senator James Watson of Indiana criticized the Democrats' votes for tariff increases while attacking the overall bill and its impediments on free trade, George fired back, rather disingenuously and ineffectively, that Watson's remarks were merely a smoke screen "to buffer against popular disapproval

[285]Ibid.

[286]Ibid., 1:3.

[287]*Atlanta Constitution*, September 26, 1929, 1:6.

[288]Ibid.

[289]*New York Times,* September 26, 1929, 4:2.

[290]*Vienna News*, October 10, 1929, 4.

of the Grundy-Smoot-Hawley tariff bill," and he defended the Democrats by saying that they had voted for some raises and not others because the GOP Old Guard had voted consistently "solid" for higher duties on sugar, lumber, cement, and brick."[291] In July, George attacked the tariff again, stating that it had not benefited the farmer and had resulted in the fall of agricultural prices. He again defended the Democratic votes for higher tariffs on some items by saying that they had felt that the farmer should get something out of the tariff bill.[292]

After Smoot-Hawley passed, trade did begin falling. George pounced on the decline with glee. Calling Hoover's signing of the bill the killing of "the goose that laid the proverbial golden egg, with one stroke of his pen." He noted that in 1929 Canada had bought $948,000,000 worth of American goods, while we had bought $503,000,000 from them, giving us almost a half billion trade surplus in our favor, but the new tariff had "strangled Canadian trade" by 1931. He predicted "economic calamity" from it.[293] In February 1931, because "we recklessly undertook to exclude Canadian imports by duties virtually prohibitive, George gleefully noted that Canada had retaliated by raising duties on American cars that would in effect exclude high-priced American cars from Canada. "The Canadian government is simply following a program of retaliation," he observed, and then he proceeded to show how trade between the US and Canada continued to fall.[294] Total statistics on world trade for 1930 bore out his argument. In July 1931, he also pointed out that overall, in the first six months of 1931, US exports to European countries had fallen by 21 percent. Claiming that his charges did not indicate "the slightest disposition to criticize or embarrass the president," something he had been trying to do all through the debate, he again called for downward revisions of the rates before it was too late.[295] That same month he called on Hoover to use the provision on Hawley-Smoot that gave the president discretionary powers to adjust tariff rates (a provision he previously strongly opposed), to lower rates, and then mildly accused Hoover of hypocrisy by noting that since Hoover had insisted on this provision of the bill and was not using it, he was being held hostage to his supporters "among the high tariff barons."[296] Before leaving for Vienna, he pro-

[291]Ibid., January 23, 1930, 1.
[292]*New York Times*, February 25, 1930, 3:5.
[293]Ibid., March 18, 1930, 26:3.
[294]Ibid., April 4, 1930, 5:2.
[295]Ibid., July 21, 1930, 5:1.
[296]Ibid., July 10, 1930, 9:3.

posed that those "unwarranted and especially burdensome duties on the trade and commerce of so many of our best customer nations" be lowered by use of the president's discretionary powers in Smooth-Hawley that George himself had opposed.[297] While in Georgia, he addressed the Georgia General Assembly, and not surprisingly the subject was tariffs. In it he accused the Republican Party of thinking that "a country may isolate itself by excessive tariff barriers and [still] enjoy the maximum of prosperity."[298]

On returning to Washington, George was thrust into the center of the tariff debate by an open letter to him and Senator Pat Harrison of Mississippi from senator Smoot and Dickenson of Iowa in which they asked Harrison if he was interested in reducing rates on cotton, naval stores, etc., "products in which Mississippi is interested," and they asked George if he wished to lower tariffs on *kaolin*, sole leather, hides, jute, tobacco, and cotton. Smoot then specifically asked George, "I now ask you as an outstanding spokesman for Democracy to clarify the position of your party. Are you against the tariff act simply in the hope of making political capital...or have you some specific items in mind which in your opinion, make the measure objectionable?"[299] Smoot was clearly exposing George's hypocritical position on the bill.

George lamely replied on August 2, specifying that the tariff on sugar (a major ingredient in Coca-Cola, an Atlanta-based company) was too high, and he questioned the tax on jute. He then tried to muddy the water by accusing the Republicans of muddying the water to distract the public from "idle money, a surplus of commodities, widespread unemployment, and the general distress of the people."[300] Smoot theatrically replied to George from a sugar beet field in Utah, his home state, pointing out that George had supported a seven-cent tariff on long-staple cotton while opposing a two-cent tariff on sugar. Then pointing out the obvious, he hammered George with, "the senator's statement is inconsistent and irreconcilable."[301]

George became engaged in a similar tangle in 1932 with a fellow Southerner Huey Long over the question of a tariff on oil, which Louisiana had and Georgia did not. The anti-tariff groups were filibustering the entire appropriations bill, and George criticized Hoover for not using his influence with his party's leadership to eliminate the tariff from the appropriations

---

[297]Ibid., July 10, 1930, 9:3.

[298]Ibid., February 23, 1931, 2:3.

[299]Ibid., July 14, 1931, 5:2–3.

[300]Ibid., *Vienna News*, July 23, 1931, 4.

[301]*Atlanta Constitution*, July 14, 1931, 5:5.

bill. In the debate, George seems to have lost his cool, at one point shouting, "The fight has just begun!"[302] Still by a narrow vote, the tariff stayed in the appropriations bill. Then Senator Long of Louisiana took the floor and read a list of items that George had put into the Hawley-Smoot bill, which included one on vegetable oil. Long then wryly noted, "It's all right for the Georgia senator to vote for oil from his state...." George lashed back at Long, whom he does not seem to have liked anyway: "Perhaps I ought not to rise to answer the plainly irresponsible talk of the senator from Louisiana, but no senator has ever come into this body who has the authority to criticize and censure, and the senator from Louisiana will not be accorded that privilege." Then pointing to Long with a finger shaking with rage, he said, "I am different from the senator from Louisiana because I am not [tied] to the special interests in my state.... Perhaps when he has been here longer, he will respect the honest convictions of his colleagues."[303]

In fall 1931, George called for a world parley to cut tariffs, calling it "an international trade armistice." Again, his motive was assistance for the farmer. "The farm problem is far from solved and the real hope of agriculture is a downward revision of our tariff [*sic*]." He did put his finger on the possible evil of tariffs, saying excessive tariffs "constitute one of the chief causes of our present world depression. They [have] brought stagnation in trade...."[304] When in Vienna for the Christmas holidays, he attacked President Hoover for not calling an international conference and accused the president of failing to do so because he did not want "political repercussions" from big business.[305] By this time, however, the political paralysis of the Hoover administration had set in, and the presidential election of the next year would send Hoover's party into political oblivion for fourteen years.

WALTER GEORGE, RICHARD RUSSELL JR., AND THE ELECTION OF 1932

The last two years of George's first decade in the Senate saw the political emergence of Richard Russell, Jr., the son of the man George had beaten in 1926. Russell had grown up in a large political family and had himself been elected to the Georgia House of Representatives in 1920 at the age of twenty-four. His rise in that body was nothing short of meteoric. In 1923 and again in 1925 he was unanimously elected speaker pro-tem. In June

[302] *New York Times*, August 3, 1931, 2:3.
[303] Ibid., July 30, 1931, 6:4.
[304] Ibid., August 3, 1931, 2:3.
[305] Ibid., August 4, 1931, 6:2.

1927, he was elected speaker and reelected again in 1929. The following year he was elected governor at the age of thirty-three. There was the usual crowd of candidates in the Democratic primary, but only three other than Russell were serious contenders for governor: George Henry Carswell, the secretary of state; John Holder, past chairman of the State Highway Commission; and Eurith Dickenson "Ed" Rivers, a state legislator but the only candidate from south Georgia.[306] Since Walter George was up for reelection in 1932, he must have had some anxious moments wondering if the popular *Wonderkind* would take him on. As luck would have it, and George had a lot of political good luck in his career, his colleague Senator William J. Harris died in April 1932, creating an open seat. Whether Russell had planned to run against George had Harris lived, we do not know. We can probably safely assume that he at least thought about it.

Russell and everybody else naturally chose not to oppose the popular incumbent Walter George and instead chose to run for the open seat. Several days later Russell declared for the open seat, and Congressman Charles Crisp, sixty-one years old, thirty-six of it spent in the US House of Representatives, jumped into the race as well. The reader is no doubt aware that he was Walter George's congressman and had delivered his nomination speech at the Houston convention in 1928.[307] Again there is no evidence, but it seems likely that Crisp talked to George before entering the race. We can also assume that George had voted for him.

In his race, George had no opposition in the Democratic primary and only token Republican opposition. Clarence E. Dunbar, the former speaker pro-tem of the House, had announced against George but quickly withdrew. Gene Talmadge apparently considered running against George but decided against it because of what he believed to be George's "massive state organization."[308] He decided to run for governor instead. No doubt grateful for not having any opposition, George issued a statement, "I am deeply grateful for the confidence placed in me by the people of this state, and I am now under renewed obligation to spend my time in the public service."[309]

George then became officially nominated at the Democratic State Convention on October 5 in Macon. A Democratic rally was held the night before with Senator Alben Barkley, who had given the keynote address at the Democratic Convention that had nominated Roosevelt, as the main

[306]*Atlanta Constitution*, May 20, 1932, 1:8, 5:4.

[307]Ibid., May 21, 1932, 1:8, 6:6.

[308]*Vienna News*, November 26, 1931, 1.

[309]Ibid., December 31, 1931, 1.

speaker at both the rally and the convention. George had introduced him.[310] The 4,700 delegates and guests roared as Barkley ripped into Hoover. According to the *Atlanta Constitution*, the crowd "cheered until the rafters of the auditorium rang."[311]

George did have Republican opposition in 1932, the Republican National Committee chairman from Georgia, Athens native James W. Arnold, but in the Georgia of that day, the general election was, to quote one historian, "like a mother-in-law's kiss: A perfunctory performance."[312] Arnold was the major speaker at Republican rallies around the state, making, fifty-six speeches in his campaign, and he seems to have been treated courteously everywhere he went. He claimed that many Democrats had told him they would vote the Republican ticket this time, but if some did, it was not enough. He garnered only 18,152 votes (7.18 percent) to Walter George's 234,490 (92.82 percent).[313] Arnold carried only Fannin County in north Georgia, in the part of the state that came closest to being a Republican stronghold.[314]

As governor, Russell could appoint someone to fill the remainder of Harris's term. He wanted the seat for himself, and since he was too shrewd to incur the political liability of appointing himself, he named a close political ally, John Sanford Cohen, editor of the *Atlanta Journal* and the Democratic National Committee chairman from Georgia, to hold the seat until he could run for it himself in 1932. Though raised Christian, Cohen was a son of a Jew who had married a gentile. Still, the Klan supported him for Democratic National Committeeman when he ran in 1924, despite that some had used his Jewish heritage against him at the time.[315] Probably with great relief, George wired Russell his support of Cohen's nomination: "Permit me to congratulate you sincerely on the appointment of Major John S. Cohen to the Senate [stop] Major Cohen is splendidly equipped to assume immediately the responsible duties of the present session."[316] Russell replied warmly to George's telegram: "I thoroughly appreciate your endorsement of Major Cohen. It has been my privilege to claim him as a loyal friend during my entire public career, and I am sure that he is eminently qualified to serve the

[310]Kelly, "Richard B. Russell," 70–123, cited in Hassett, 6.

[311]Russell lost Dooly County in the runoff by 318 votes to 174 for Russell. "Scores 333 Unit Votes," clipping, series 1, box 1, f. 1, Russell papers.

[312]*Vienna News*, April 26, 1932, 1.

[313]*Vienna News*, June 9, 1932, 1.

[314]Ibid., October 6, 1932, 1; *Atlanta Constitution*, October 4, 1932, 1:2.

[315]*Atlanta Constitution*, October 5, 1932, 1:1.

[316]Jones, "The Georgia Plan," 314.

people of Georgia." Then he added, "I am indeed happy to know that the appointment is pleasing to you and that you share my high opinion of Major Cohen and his ability."[317]

In the November election, Russell won the seat easily, having spent the princely sum of $12,589.00 on his campaign.[318] George wrote him immediately to offer his congratulations and best wishes. "Accept my congratulations on your decisive victory," he wrote, "and my assurance of full cooperation in the best service of our beloved state. Walter F. George."[319] "My dear Senator," Russell replied, "your kind message of congratulations is deeply appreciated. I keenly feel the great responsibility that will be mine in assuming my duties in Washington, and I am grateful for your assurance of cooperation. In turn, I can assure you of my desire to work with you for all things that will advance the welfare of the people of Georgia." Though the message seems notable for its lack of personal warmth, he added, "I shall feel free to call on you for advice from time to time, for I realize that there is a great deal for me to learn."[320].

Several months later, when the town of Vienna gave George a dinner honoring his service in the Senate, George invited Russell. He had apparently accepted, but the sudden death of an aunt caused him to decline at the last minute by telegram. "Deeply regret that it is impossible for me to attend the dinner given you by the citizens of Vienna this evening[,] but death of an aunt makes it impossible for me to be with you [stop]." Then he continued with more geniality than he had shown in the reply in September: "It would be a real pleasure to join with your neighbors in bearing testimony to the high esteem of all the people of Georgia and the confidence and pride they feel in your splendid service in the Senate."[321] George replied three days later with a warmth of his own; "My dear Governor Russell," he wrote, "We were indeed sorry that you could not come to Vienna last Friday night. The little dinner was most enjoyable, and we very much appreciated your telegram."[322]

---

[317]*Atlanta Constitution*, November 6, 1932, 7:1.

[318]Dubin, *United States Congressional Elections*, 499.

[319]Heard and Strong, *Southern Primaries and Elections*, 63–64.

[320]Moseley, "Invisible Empire," 84.

[321]Telegram from WFG to Russell, 25 April 1932, VI-F, f. 7, Russell papers.

[322]Richard B. Russell to WFG, April 29, 1932, Russell papers. George seems to have worked well with Cohen during his short tenure, and when he died on April 13, 1935, George praised him highly in the *CR*, 74/1, 7446.

As was customary, George escorted Russell down the aisle to his swearing in on January 10, 1933, and a partnership began that was over the next quarter of a century most beneficial to the state of Georgia. There was still a lingering bitterness between the Georges and the Russells because of the bitter 1926 campaign, but Russell later told Colonel Jake Carlton, a friend and neighbor, that when he "came up here I went to Sen. George and he and I reached an agreement that I would be the North Georgia Senator and he would be the South Georgia Senator.... Our friendship ripened on this agreement." Later he told Carlton, "I've really gotten to be very...fond of him and our personal relations are almost perfect."[323]

The two men were radically different in both their public image and their private personalities. Russell was much more the "political animal" one observer remembered. George was "a jurist, had never been a handshaker...."[324] George was very warm in a one-on-one meeting, but we have seen he had an austere public persona. "He would have graced the office of the Chief Justice of the Supreme Court," John Carlton remembered, "but you could sit down and chew the fat with Senator George. Russell dispatched you quickly."[325] Georgia state senator Spence M. Grayson remembered Russell and George as "two entirely different types of people." "Dick was a cautious man, much more cautious in politics than Walter George was. Dick would weigh things carefully...but Walter George would make up his mind as to what was right...and he followed it in an unswerving manner."[326] Perennial speaker of the Georgia House Roy V. Harris put it differently: "Dick wasn't too much of a fighter.... He didn't take much of a definite position. He was always staying on neutral ground.... He went up to the Senate, [and] he was pretty much the same way."[327] Grayson felt if you were Walter George's friend, "he stuck with you." On that same line, Grayson seems to have started to say that Russell was not generally loyal, but then seems to have thought better of it, saying only, "I would say that he [Russell] was both cautious and expedient.... Politics is a ruthless game."[328] Jimmy Bentley, a political force in Georgia in the 1960s, described Russell as being

[323]Jake Carlton Oral History, Russell Library, 21.

[324]WFG to Richard B. Russell, 15 September 1932, series VI-F, box 140, f. 2, Russell papers.

[325]Jake Carlton, Oral History, 22.

[326] Richard B. Russell to WFG, December 2, 1932, (Winder Collection).

[327]Ibid.

[328]John Carlton interview, oral history, 21, Russell Library; Spence M. Grayson, Oral History, Russell Library, 27-28.

"much more personable," but he tended to blame George's aloofness on George's age ("he was quite ancient"), but still he added, "There just wasn't a great deal of warmth [in George]."[329]

There were other personal differences. George spoke in grammatically correct, long, and convoluted sentences in which he seemed to try to touch every shade of a question and every possible point of an argument. He was the ultimate trial lawyer. Russell, on the other hand, spoke little, but when he did, people listened because he would likely resolve an issue in a few words. *Life* noted that reporters interviewing Russell did most of the talking. When Russell did speak, reporters would "get from Russell in a sentence or two an answer which is complete, well thought out, and authoritative."[330] George was more interested in international affairs, Russell domestic and military matters. Russell was a rabid racist, who even once considered joining the Klan.[331] George was certainly no integrationist, but he never spewed hatred against the blacks and rarely played the "race card."[332] In time, both men would become giants in the Senate, or "Senate Bulls," as Senate powers were called, and it would be the general consensus in Washington that no state had senators as powerful as George and Russell. In some instances, as in the cases of Pat Harrison and Theodore Bilbo of Mississippi, senators did not speak to their home-state colleague. Olin Johnston and Strom Thurmond of South Carolina went so far as to instruct their respective staffs not to speak to one another.[333] Francis O. Wilcox, the chief of staff of the Foreign Relations Committee, felt that Russell and George were "probably the best team in the Senate at that time," and he called the two "the best examples of statesmanship and ability in the Senate."[334] He was not alone in thinking so.

1932 PRESIDENTIAL ELECTION

The last year of George's first decade in the Senate was consumed with the watershed 1932 presidential contest. The enormous Democratic gains in

---

[329]Ibid.

[330]Robert Troutman, Jr., oral history, 16, Russell Library.

[331]John Carlton interview, oral history, 22, Russell Library.

[332]Roy V. Harris, oral history, 26–27, Russell Library.

[333]Spence M. Grayson, oral history, 27–28, Russell Library. Curiously, almost the exact same comparison of the two was given me by Senator George Smathers (D-Florida) in my phone interview with him in 2009. He described George as a "straight up kind of person," but Russell was "a deal maker." He clearly started to make a rather pejorative description of Russell, but the politician kicked in, and he caught himself. Then his voice trailed off.

[334]James L. Bentley, Jr., oral history, 10, Russell Library.

1930 elections foreshadowed a Democratic victory in the presidential race in 1932. Despite the Democratic victories, when George returned to Washington in December 1930 for a special session, he called for moderation and bipartisanship and felt that the Democrats "should pursue a constructive and not an obstructionist course."[335] In retrospect this attitude might foreshadow George's opposition to the not yet born New Deal. Indeed, even President Hoover, who still had a one-vote Republican majority in the Senate (48–47) in 1931 suggested that control already be given to the Democrats, who would be better at reform than the Republicans, but the GOP majority would not hear of it.[336] After the 1932 elections, they would not have a Republican majority in the Senate for fourteen years.

George readily felt that the Democrats would win everything in 1932, and in a speech to the Georgia general assembly, he blamed the Depression on Harding, Coolidge, and Hoover, and he told the assembled legislators that "the Democratic party [*sic*] must equip itself to assume control of the government in 1932." He especially, and not surprisingly, attacked the Republican tariff policies, which he felt had caused a 21 percent decline in American exports. He attacked "selfishness and greed" as the "base for nearly all of our difficulties," adding that "these blind us to the true interests of the people." He also blamed some "timid Democrats for not acting."[337]

As in 1928, George's name surfaced again in the presidential sweepstakes, especially when Southerners were mentioned. George rebuffed these suggestions, probably because he was up for reelection himself, and given that the other seat was open, his absence or possible election to another office might draw him opposition. Moreover, Roosevelt was an early-on favorite, the "outstanding tentative candidate," one journalist put it.[338] Even the *New York Herald Tribune* wrote as early as June 1931 that he could be a serious contender, calling him "a man who has received prominence by moderate and quiet persistence."[339] In these months, George visited Roosevelt at Warm Springs often, and on one occasion when he did not see Roosevelt on one of his trips to Georgia, he wrote a note of apology.[340] Roosevelt already had a great deal of Southern support by 1932 from Tennessee senator Cor-

---

[335]McConaughy, "Patriarch," *Life*, 36 (April 19, 1954), 112..

[336]Russell, *A Heart for Any Fate*, 220.

[337]Vienna News, 30, 1831, 1.

[338]"Southerners Mentioned," June 15, 1931, *Atlanta Journal* clipping, f. WFG, FDR; PPF box 107-117, 109, Roosevelt papers.

[339]Russell Library, 711, "George Lauded" Atlanta Journal, June 30, 1931, quotes the *New York Herald Tribune*.

[340]*Vienna News*, December 4, 1930, 1.

dell Hull, Mississippi senator Pat Harrison, and future New Deal enemy Senator Harry Byrd.[341] He would not have their full allegiance again until December 7, 1941.[342]

Roosevelt had secured enough delegates for the nomination by the end of May 1932, with George nowhere counted among his supporters.[343] Despite the visits to Warm Springs, George did not endorse Roosevelt for the nomination, despite the fact that in the March 1932 primary, Roosevelt got 377 votes in Dooly County against a stand-in Judge G. H. Howard's 35.[344] George does not seem to have been supporting anyone else either, but Roosevelt was too shrewd a politician not to have noticed. Late in July after the Democratic convention, George did issue a statement that "the Democrats have nominated a ticket which promises more to the average citizen, more to agriculture, and therefore more to the country as a whole than any since the first administration of Woodrow Wilson."[345] He then went fishing and was, except for a few exceptions in the fall, largely silent during the fall campaign. Seventeen years later, *US News* told its readers that "Roosevelt didn't forget it," but soon Roosevelt would have stronger reasons for disliking Walter George.[346]

Other members of the Georgia delegation were active, however. Senate stand-in Cohen campaigned, and Congressman Eugene Cox, the National Chairman of the Speakers' Bureau, campaigned for the Democratic ticket as far away as Ohio and Michigan. Senator-elect Richard Russell spoke in Florida, Tennessee, and North Carolina, and he rode at one point on Roosevelt's train.[347] George did give the keynote address at a Young Men's Democratic League at Atlanta's Piedmont Hotel early in October, and he spoke in Clayton county the next day, but that seems to have been the extent of his campaigning in Georgia.[348] George did make a campaign swing for Roosevelt in Florida, addressing crowds in Ocala, St. Petersburg, Bradenton, and Orlando late in September, but it seems to have been somewhat of a vacation trip. Miss Lucy went to Florida with him but visited

---

[341]Dole, *Historical Almanac of the United States*, 218.

[342]*Vienna News*, July 30, 1931, 1.

[343]"Southerners Mentioned," June 15, 1931, *Atlanta Journal* clipping, f. WFG, box 107–117, f. 109, president's personal file (hereafter cited as PPF), Roosevelt papers.

[344]"George Is Lauded," *Atlanta Journal* clipping, June 30, 1931, WFG-GSA.

[345]WFG to FDR, October 10, 1931, f. WFG, PPF, box 107–117, f. 109, Roosevelt papers.

[346]Freidel, *FDR and the South*, 30.

[347]Ibid., 34.

[348]*Atlanta Constitution*, May 30, 1932, 1:8.

with her sister Mrs. Argyle Crocket in Bradenton. George's performance seems to have been unenthusiastic, but he did agree with Jim Farley that Roosevelt would win by ten million votes.[349] Toward the end of the race, Roosevelt held a giant rally in Atlanta. Richard Russell introduced him, and Gene Talmadge was there, along with an estimated 25,000 people, but there is no mention of Walter George, and he is not listed among the dignitaries present.[350] George was still in Florida at the time, but his stay in the state was long after his campaign swing there, and he was at his sister-in-law's house in Bradenton. The Georges announced that their son Marcus was hospitalized in Bradenton, but no reason was given for his illness. This family matter could have indeed genuinely prevented his return in time for the rally, and George did return to Atlanta, leaving Miss Lucy with their son, but he did not arrive in time for the Roosevelt rally.[351] He also surfaced in New York with Senator Cohen at Democratic National Headquarters, where he predicted that a Roosevelt victory would bring some sort of modification of Prohibition legislation, and he expressed his belief that, given the "desperate" nature of the Republican campaign in recent days, Farley was not too far afield when he had predicted a ten million vote majority for Roosevelt.[352]

Had George intentionally avoided appearing in Atlanta with Roosevelt? Few politicians would have failed to appear before such crowds with such a popular leader. There is no evidence that he purposely avoided Atlanta, but a lack of evidence either way leaves George's motives obscure. Perhaps he seemed indifferent because he felt he should have been given the vice-presidential nomination. Perhaps he was not invited to speak any more than he did, but that seems unlikely. His law partner T. Hoyt Davis remembered that "He [George] and Roosevelt were apart," but George supported the New Deal legislation.[353] Since Roosevelt sounded much like a conservative before he became president, it is unlikely that George was beginning the distancing from the left wing of his party that would come later. Weeks after Roosevelt's victory, George wired his congratulations to the president-elect in a short telegram: "Without thought of partisan exultation, [I] heartily congratulate the country on your election and renew pledge of

[349] *Vienna News*, March 24, 1932, 1.
[350] Ibid., July 28, 1932, 1.
[351] "Senator George, Who Is Saying 'No' to President on Tax Rise," 48.
[352] *Atlanta Constitution*, October 29, 1932, 6:89; November 5, 1932, 6:7.
[353] Ibid., October 7, 1932, 7:4.

cooperation."[354]

Roosevelt was too shrewd and perceptive a politician not to have noticed George's lack of enthusiasm for his campaign, and Roosevelt did not forget such things. With 3,000 Georgians attending Roosevelt's inaugural for Georgia's "adopted son," one of the largest representations from any state,[355] there is little wonder that he would think that he had the popularity to delve into Georgia politics as he would do six years later.

[354] *Vienna News*, September 29, 1932, 1; *Atlanta Constitution*, October 27, 1932, in Coode, "Georgia Congressmen and the New Deal, 1933–1938," 17.

[355] *Atlanta Constitution*, October 24, 1932, *passim.*

3

A MARGARINE NEW DEALER, 1932–1938

I am a liberal but a liberal within the Constitution.
—Walter F. George[1]

I don't consider Mr. George a New Dealer. Yet, when I try to diagram the proof out of the record, I can't do it. You have to give Mr. George a Scotch verdict—guilty but not proven.
—Journalist Raymond Clapper[2]

While I am a Republican, I have always thought that Senator George was one of the great statesmen that our times have produced and during the years of the New Deal did more probably than any other Senator to preserve some semblance of the system that made this country great.
—Victor Emanuel to President Dwight David Eisenhower[3]

When Roosevelt was elected in 1932, there were an estimated 13,000,000 people out of work, and in some states 40 percent of the population was on relief.[4] The country had never been in such desperate economic condition. On Saturday, December 3, 1932, George left for Washington for a special session of Congress to try to deal with the problem. He also was probably glad to get out of Georgia because since the election he had been besieged with patronage seekers. In returning, George, always a champion of rural interest, hoped first that something should be done for the farmers, and at the same time, he somewhat naively aimed to cut government expenses. In a statement given to the press on departing, the latter seemed more important that the former. "President Hoover has the power to effect [*sic*] far-reaching economies, and I believe he will do it," he told the *Vienna News*. He had already predicted a treasury deficit of nearly $750,000 million,

[1]"Senator George, Who Is Saying 'No' to President on Tax Rise," 39–40.

[2]"Voice of the 84th," 22–23.

[3]Victor Emmanuel to Dwight David Eisenhower, January 5, 1957, f. 72-A-2, Walter F. George, box 287, Central files, official file, Eisenhower papers.

[4]Coode, "Georgia Congressmen and the New Deal, 1933–1938," 53.

with a budget shortfall by the end of the year of $1,250,000,000.[5] His solution was one we know would only make things worse: He wanted to raise taxes and cut spending by abolishing some governing boards and merging others.

At first, George supported New Deal programs in the "Hundred Days" tidal wave of legislation that characterized the early period of the Roosevelt presidency, but then most people did. Where George was most surprising was in his support of the National Industrial Recovery Act (the NIRA), which promoted industry. He defended his action by saying, "I went along with the NRA [National Recovery Administration, created by the NIRA] at the behest of the president because we need something drastic to break the logjam of business…." He told a Macon luncheon club in August 1933 that the NRA would be a "pronounced success," adding as almost an afterthought that "there would probably be an improvement in farm prices" as a result of it. He had been working hard to get NRA money released in Georgia, but the state government had not met requirements demanded in the law.[6] This position is all the more amazing since of the thirteen Southern congressional figures who voted against it, five were from Georgia. Congressman Cox, one of George's allies, was one of the most vociferous in his opposition.[7] George even opposed giving federal relief monies to the states' governors to dispense, citing "the possibility of abuse amounting to scandal" in the administration of the fund. This staunch advocate wanted to see relief distributed by the local taxing authorities.[8] Eventually funds were spent lavishly. Between 1933 and American entry in World War II, the federal government had spent a quarter of a billion dollars in Georgia, a princely sum at the time.[9]

Given his work on the Finance Committee, George was especially involved in all aspects of New Deal financing, and a major concern across the country was the failure of the banks. Georgia banks, for whatever reason, were not in as bad a shape as banks were in other parts of the country. By March 13, 1933, all Atlanta banks were in full operation, and by mid-May, all but four of the state's 217 banks that had been functioning at the time of the bank holiday were working.[10] George still became heavily involved in the

[5] *Vienna News*, December 1, 1932, 1.
[6] Ibid., August 31, 1933, 1.
[7] Coode, "Georgia Congressmen and the New Deal, 1933–1938," 66.
[8] *CR*, 72/2, 4338.
[9] Coleman, et al., *A History of Georgia*, 312.
[10] Coode, "Georgia Congressmen and the New Deal, 1933–1938," 38–39.

national banking problems. He was a manager of the famous Glass-Steagal Banking Act, and as the reader is aware, he applied his skillful use of words to anything he did. While he was a great supporter of the bill, George did his usual micro-managing. On January 24, 1933, when the bill was being discussed even before Roosevelt took office, George introduced an amendment employing his usual attention to detail: "The paragraph on line 5 of page 8 subjects member banks to the same limitations and conditions with respect to our purchasing, selling, underwriting, and holding of investment securities and stock as are applicable in the case of national banks under paragraph seventh [*sic*] of section 5136 of the Revised Statutes, as amended...."[11] His conservatism on money matters led him to oppose the issue of "silver certificates" because it would deflate the currency and cut the obligation of foreign debtors (mainly World War I allies). "It is a gift to our debtors...of about if not exactly 30 percent of the amount of principal now due," he told the Senate, indicating that perhaps it was even more. "If we are to cancel the debts," he advised, although this action was not the intention of the bill, "let us do it openly, candidly and frankly.... This [bill] is a mere cancellation *pro tanto* of the debt due."[12] Since the former allies never paid the debt anyway, this concern made little difference, but it is evidence of how sharply he was in tune with finance. Like a number of conservative Democrats, he became terribly concerned about the deficits that Roosevelt was incurring despite his pledge to balance the budget. This worry led him to support cuts to veterans, his greatest interest next to agriculture. He supported the 1933 Presidential Economy Bill in the Senate Finance Committee, which called for, among other things, cuts to veterans' funds, and his reason was his fear for the financial stability of the government as a whole. "If the financial stability of the government is not preserved," he opined in a press release, "our disabled veterans will suffer far greater hardships...than the partial sacrifice they are now called upon to share." He blamed the cuts on "the unhappy condition of the country" and the need "to sustain national credit."[13] Tied in with his desire to balance the federal budget was his concern with taxes. Again, being on the Finance Committee placed him in the middle of the tax question from the beginning of the New Deal until he began chairing the Foreign Relations Committee in 1955, at Eisenhower's request. George believed that growth was the key, and the key to growth was a moderate tax policy. A saying he had on taxes, and he would repeat it

[11] *CR*, 76/2, 2408.
[12] *CR*, 73/1, 2542.
[13] Telegram to the Georgia press, *Vienna News*, March 16, 1933, 1.

throughout his career, was, "A government can confiscate only once, [but] it can tax forever, provided it preserves free enterprise and the American way of life."[14] For the remainder of his career, he championed low taxes as a source for growth, tempered with the knowledge that revenue has to be first raised to pay the government's bills, and that there was a golden mean in planning a budget between taxing and spending. In his view that there were definite states' rights, he saw the need for a balance of federal taxation with that of the states, so that the states could raise the money to allow the federal system to work. In 1933 he complained that "the primary cause of our suffering is the heavy burden of taxation which is literally exhausting the American city, the American state, and the Nation as well." He felt that the "primary responsibility" of the federal government was to realize that "we can extend...federal functions, drying up the resources of the states...."[15] When in 1934, Senator Bob La Follette of Wisconsin proposed an amendment to increase the tax rate on small businesses beyond that recommended by George's committee, George fought back with an argument still heard today:

> We may close our eyes if we want to, but...the men who have money to invest are looking for tax exempt securities...so there is a point beyond which we cannot carry rates without endangering our economic and financial...progress.... We can tax income until the tax will tend to discourage business enterprises.... The mere arbitrary redistribution of the wealth of the country means chaos. The redistribution must come through the application of sound principles of public justice...and by the adoption of wise policies.[16]

He further examined La Follette's measure. Pointing to a rather unrealistic figure of $100,000 (few small businesses made that much in 1934), he showed that under the finance bill under discussion, the company and person would pay $30,810 in taxes. Under La Follette's amendment, the tax bill would be $42,915, a huge difference.[17] The $12,000 difference would have provided jobs for almost a dozen people in unemployment-plagued 1934. The next year he went so far as to introduce a bill to allow charitable deductions by corporations, which has meant so much over the years in so many ways.[18]

---

[14]*Atlanta Journal,* December 20, 1942, 6-B.
[15]*CR,* 73/1, 1039–41.
[16]*CR,* 73/2, 6086–88.
[17]Ibid., 6087.
[18]*CR,* 74/1, 11275.

George did not oppose all tax increases, however, and the almost hopeless quest for a balanced budget led him to support some tax increases as long as they did not punish work. In his 1938 campaign he noted that while he had always opposed "a federal sales tax in any form," he had found it necessary to vote for one occasionally "in order to raise the necessary revenue for the support of the government."[19] This increase did not punish the people who were working and making money, only those who had it to spend. In this tax, he might achieve the golden mean he sought.

The Roosevelt Administration, however, had to raise taxes in 1936 because the Supreme Court had struck down the Agricultural Adjustment Act, which hurt income from the progressive tax. Roosevelt tried to cover the shortfall by taxing "undistributed earnings of corporations" and by repealing the exemption of taxation on dividends. When the bill to implement these taxes reached the Senate floor, George praised Roosevelt's "revision of our tax laws" because he saw that they "removed undoubted inequalities in our taxing system."[20] For reasons that are unclear, however, George reversed himself and opposed the law, and he rushed a number of amendments into the bill before it went to conference.[21] When the conference bill came before the Senate, minus George's amendments, George did not show up for the vote and is listed as being "unavoidably detained."[22] His amendments were apparently expunged from the bill, but the next year he was able to moderate it successfully.[23] In time, Roosevelt's antipathy for George became intense, and it came to be believed that George's conservative view on taxes was the reason.[24]

George seemed to support publicly any New Deal programs that had anything to do with agriculture. Georgia's rural population peaked in 1920 and has declined ever since, but federal help for agriculture has almost continually risen.[25] In 1930, there were 225,598 farms in operation in the state (the average one being 86.4 acres), but the average income per farm was $677 in 1931, and in 1932 when the Depression hit bottom, the per capita

[19]George, *Addresses*, Vienna, July 4, 1938 and September 13, 1938, 10.

[20]*CR*, 74/2, 3476.

[21]Altman, "Second Session of the Seventy-fourth Congress," 1094, cites *CR*, 74/2, 9230.

[22]Ibid., 1094.

[23]"Senator George, Who Is Saying 'No' to President on Tax Rise," 40.

[24]"Conservative George," *St. Louis Post Dispatch*, July 18, 1956, scrapbook, LHG-VHPS.

[25]Bonner, "Legislative Appointment and the County Unit System," 371.

cash annual farm income in Georgia was a meager $46.00.[26] George voted for every major farm bill between 1933 and 1938, and throughout his career he was always quick to fight not only for cotton, tobacco, and peanuts, but less lucrative farm productions as well, such as produce. Federal payments to American farmers in 1933 totaled $208,410,866, of which Georgia received $8,015,855.[27]

As we will see, Georgia congressmen such as George readily supported agricultural programs but balked on the creation of government agencies like the Security and Exchange Commission, using words like "Russianize," Sovietize," and "Bolshevize" to describe it.[28] In the debate on the Agricultural Adjustment Act (AAA), George spoke forty-six times.[29] Even on agricultural questions, George's conservatism came through time and again. On the debate on the AAA in April 1933, a bill on which all Georgia House members voted "aye," George hammered away in his prolix fashion about the question of constitutionality of the act itself. "I know that we have with a high degree of indifference passed many legislative acts that might have been subjected to very serious constitutional questioning," he lectured the Senate. "I also know that there is a disposition…to raise constitutional questions simply because we do not favor a proposition. I am wholly unable, however, to see any ground upon which the validity of this particular part of the bill [an effort to create minimum prices for agricultural products] can possibly be [constitutionally] sustained." He added that he would vote against it because "the price is controlled ultimately by the laws of economics."[30] Although having taken that position, George hypocritically promoted the government's buying of cotton directly from producers, which would artificially raise the price of the commodity and essentially achieve the same thing.[31] He tried to encourage the same policy with peanuts, peaches, and watermelons.[32]

George and Georgia Congressman Cox teamed up to pass a bill reducing mortgage payments on farming families by refinancing farm mortgag-

[26]*A Century of Georgia Agriculture, 1815–1950* (Athens: University of Georgia Press, 1954) 269, in Coode, "Georgia Congressmen and the New Deal, 1933–1938," 26–28.

[27]US Department of Agriculture, *Agricultural Statistics, 1937* (Washington: Government Printing Office, 1937) 98, 384, 414–15, cited in Hassett, 40.

[28]Coode, "Georgia Congressmen and the New Deal, 1933–1938," 75 ff.

[29]*CR*, 74/1, 11295, 11401 et al.

[30]*CR*, 73/1, 1633–34.

[31]*CR*, 72/2, 4389–93.

[32]George, *Addresses*, Monroe, August 22, 1938, 7.

es.[33] The average income farm owners (not laborers) in Georgia in 1934 was a little more than $500.00 per year. The average sharecropper earned only about $150.00 per year.[34] The bill doubtless saved many Georgia farms from foreclosure, and by 1934, prices were slowly rising. The Department of Agriculture reported at the end of 1934 that for every dollar a Georgia farmer made in 1932, he had more than doubled that income to $2.40 in 1934.[35]

By the late 1930s, when conditions were much better, George still continued to hammer away for the Georgia farmer. In August 1935, George introduced a resolution to form two committees to study cotton and to report their findings back in the next session of Congress. One committee was to be composed of seven men "who have experienced utilization and distribution of cotton," while the other was to be "three distinguished technical experts and scientists" to research various ways cotton and cotton products could be further used.[36] In 1938, when the second AAA was in force, George joined Senator Michael Andrews from Florida in an amendment to increase tobacco and cotton allotments.[37]

Another unlikely feature George championed was the Rural Electrification Administration. George voted for the act when it originated in 1935, and at the time he voted against every amendment to weaken it.[38] In early 1938 he was still championing the REA.[39] When in June of that year, there were efforts to cut REA funding from $100 million to $25 million, George joined Representative John Rankin (D-Miss) in leading the defeat of the amendment. In calling for the restoration of the full appropriation, George, using hyperbole and apparently having forgotten the AAA, told the Senate, "The Rural Electrification Administration has done more for farm relief, done more for the comfort, done more for the pleasure of farmers, done more for the value of the American farms than almost any other thing...during the past five years."[40] The Senate restored the appropriation, and Rankin wrote George to thank him for "the splendid speech on rural electrification.... You helped greatly in getting my amendment...adopted by the House...restored by the Senate. You have rendered a great service to the

[33]*CR*, 72/2, 1283–84.

[34]Stolberg, "Buzz Windrip, Governor of Georgia," 317.

[35]*Vienna News*, January 3, 1935, 2.

[36]This piece came to him in a letter from Lincoln McConnell, the Georgia state employment director, which George put into the *CR*, 73/2, 27 (February 1934), 3312.

[37]*New York Times*, August 19, 1935, 29:5.

[38]*CR*, 75/3, 4141.

[39]George, *Addresses*, Thomson, August 26, 1938, 11.

[40]*CR*, 75/3, 2441.

farmers of this country." The first electrification project to be filed in Georgia and second in the nation was in Crisp County, adjacent to Dooly. One can well imagine George's fine hand in the choosing of the location. There had been certain legal complications, and George had intervened and smoothed them out. The county delegation wrote him a grateful letter of thanks. "It seemed hopeless for us to overcome these difficulties," the delegation said, "until you came to our assistance. Without your aid it is doubtful if we could have been able to secure the benefits our rural residents have enjoyed from the REA projects.... To you...we will ever be grateful."[41] Harry Hopkins, Roosevelt confidante and administrator of the Federal Emergency Relief Act, included some of George's provisions on education in the Federal Emergency Relief Act (FERA) making money available to pay teachers' salaries,[42] and in 1934 George introduced a bill providing $50,000,000 to keep the public schools of poor states open in order to "meet the crisis in public education."[43] Senator David Walsh, chair of the committee, got the monies extended to colleges and universities, but the bill died in committee.[44]

Throughout the 1930s George continued to fight for everything that affected Georgia, be it soil conservation, which he championed in a speech in Metter,[45] or the elimination of a tax on tung seed oil, since tung trees were being grown by then in south Georgia.[46] He always fought for lower freight rates so that Georgia commodities could be cheaply shipped to other parts of the country, and in 1934, George called on the Interstate Commerce Commission to investigate the inequities in freight rates. Due to his and others' complaints, the ICC finally ruled in November 1939 to lower the rates on ten of the fourteen requested items.[47] Then there were the grants for Georgia of a more local nature. In February 1933, he introduced a bill allowing Georgia to build and operate a toll bridge over the Savannah River.[48] In the next few years he introduced a bill that established the famous Ocmulgee National Park at the Indian mounds in Macon and the

---

[41]Rankin to George, June 2, 1938, letters and speeches folder, WFG-VHPS.

[42]County Commissioners to WFG, August 10, 1938, letters and speeches folder, WFG-VHPS.

[43]*CR*, 73/2, 2118–119, 2830, 73/2, 911.

[44]*Vienna News*, February 22, 1934, 1.

[45]*CR*, 73/2, 2118–119.

[46]George, *Addresses*, Metter, July 28, 1938, 4.

[47]*CR*, 74/1, 11295. This crop never became a major money maker.

[48]Henderson, *The Politics of Change in Georgia*, 119–122; *CR*, 73/2, 10345; 1110–11.

well-known Fort Frederica National Monument on St. Simon's Island.[49] In 1933, he proposed a centennial commemorative stamp for the 100th anniversary of the founding of Wesleyan College, the oldest chartered women's college in America.[50]

In the early New Deal days, however, George's politics, or rather what he said his politics were, were somewhat contradictory, and it is on these contradictions that this historian most wishes that he could consult a diary or some correspondence, not just public utterances. For example, at a speech delivered to the Valdosta Rotary Club in July 1934, George called for "a more equitable distribution of wealth," a statement at odds with his general position in almost any other times in his life. "Civilization cannot go on," he told the Rotarians, "if the great majority producing the wealth of the country are not allowed to participate in its benefits." He continued to praise Roosevelt for redistributing the wealth.[51] A month and a half later, he defended the New Deal in Statesboro by telling the audience that he wished to allay the fear of all "that we are not headed for 'isms' of other countries [i.e., fascism, socialism, or communism]," but then he went on to add, "Real democracy cannot exist where the masses are denied access to the means of producing wealth" and spoke of all elements in society receiving "a fair share of the national wealth."[52] He returned to Statesboro several weeks later to tell a crowd of 700 at the Georgia Teachers' College that despite the Democratic majorities, the party had not exercised any power that was not given it by the people, and then he went on to state the time-worn leftist concept of "returning the government to the people."[53]

George was too intelligent and knowledgeable about politics and economics not to know what he was saying, so we can only assume that he meant it or was indulging in some mild demagoguery. These views were not normally those expressed to a Rotary Club. Perhaps he was in a window of time when his views were truly liberal. If that was the case, it was a relatively small window because statements like these were totally antithetical to most of what he had said otherwise, both before and after his political career. Unless some other evidence emerges, his public utterances in the first years of the New Deal will forever remain a mystery.

---

[49] *CR*, 72/2, 4300; *CR*, 73/2, 2151.

[50] *CR*, 74/1, 13197.

[51] *CR*, 74/2, 8414.

[52] *Vienna News*, July 26, 1934, 2.

[53] "On A Safer Course," *Savannah Morning News*, 9:4, 1934, PPF, box 107–117, folder 109, Roosevelt papers.

By 1934, though, Southern Democrats were beginning to question the general direction of the New Deal although they continued to support Roosevelt on agricultural programs.[54] Frequently, Georgians were among the few Democrats to oppose Roosevelt's programs by 1935. When the House voted $4.8 billion to "attack unemployment," the bill passed 329–78. Ten Democrats were among the seventy-eight who were opposed, five of them from Georgia.[55]

The actions of a number of academics around Roosevelt likewise took their toll. Rex Tugwell's intellectual condescension was not taken well, nor was Frances Perkins's insulting remark that if people of the South would wear shoes, "a social and economic revolution would occur."[56] Georgians were so indignant at this remark that the legislature overwhelmingly rescinded an invitation to Secretary Perkins to speak in Georgia on child labor laws.[57]

Southern Democrats in general (and people such Carter Glass and Harry Byrd of Virginia, Thomas P. Gore of Oklahoma, Millard Tydings of Maryland, Josiah W. Bailey of North Carolina, and Ellison D. "Cotton Ed" Smith of South Carolina, in particular) began to bail on the New Deal in 1935.[58] Walter F. George joined their ranks, and not hesitantly, making a strong *volte face* from his days of praising Roosevelt and the New Deal just the year before. What seems to have soured George most of all was the growth of the power of the executive branch at the expense of the legislative branch.[59] George styled himself as an 80 percent New Dealer, and in numbers that statement is probably correct. As several of Roosevelt's henchmen noted, however, George would often amend "to death" New Deal legislation before voting for it.[60]

Like many Southerners, George was, or became, a "Jeffersonian Democrat," who felt that one cannot base his liberty "upon a central govern-

[54]*Vienna News*, October 4, 1934, 1.

[55]Coode, "Georgia Congressmen and the New Deal, 1933–1938," 75.

[56]Ibid., 121.

[57]Swint, "Northern Interest in the Shoeless Southerner," 457.

[58]*Atlanta Constitution*, May 23, 1934, February 15, 1935, cited in Coode, "Georgia Congressmen and the New Deal, 1933–1938," 101.

[59]George T. Mazuzan, *The Hoover Presidency,* Fausold and Mazuzan, eds., 190 n.

[60]William Harris, congressional secretary, to Rep. Hugh Peterson, September 15, 1965, cited in Coode, "Georgia Congressmen and the New Deal, 1933–1938," 99.

ment."[61] The power grabs of the Roosevelt administration had pushed, or at any rate, *confirmed* his beliefs in that direction. Beginning in these years, George first expressed the philosophy, "I am a liberal within the Constitution.... Let that Constitution be liberally construed...but I do not travel beyond the Constitution.... And I will follow no man beyond the known and fixed...limitation of our Constitution."[62] He either felt, or came to feel, that the expenditure of government money "is not any *final* [emphasis added] answer to the problem of America."[63] By 1936 he certainly had come to see the New Deal as a temporary measure, not a permanent fix. This rush to the right, at least from some of his positions expressed above from the early days of the first Roosevelt administration, was indeed genuine, if he really was traveling that far.

Whereas George became increasingly hostile to the New Deal, he does not seem to have become hostile to Roosevelt the man. From the beginning of Roosevelt's presidency, George praised him warmly and openly. At the time of Roosevelt's inauguration in 1933, George was so overwhelmed with Finance Committee work on disabled veterans' affairs that he was unable to reply to constituent correspondence on Roosevelt, so he sent a telegram on March 13 to most Georgia newspapers praising the new president—and also forwarded a copy to Roosevelt. Roosevelt warmly thanked him in a letter on March 15 for the "fine telegram which you sent the papers of Georgia."[64] Roosevelt called on George for advice in January 1934 when he was planning to abandon the gold standard. The two men met for two hours, and on leaving the White House, George declined to give reporters anything specific but he announced that he supported the president's new monetary policy.[65] That same month, Roosevelt demonstrated his appreciation by inviting George to a 200-guest dinner at the White House honoring Albert Einstein.[66]

When a revolt against Roosevelt and the New Deal erupted in 1934 in the Georgia Democratic Party, led by Georgia governor Eugene Talmadge, George took Roosevelt's side. At the state convention to renominate

[61]Sec. 5, Income tax, untitled report on George's voting record, attached to Clark Howell to Tom [Corcoran], August 1, 1938, FDR's presidential secretary file (hereafter cited as PSF), box 136, f. Georgia Campaign, 1938, Roosevelt papers.

[62]George, *Addresses*, Eastman, August 17, 1938, 6.

[63]Ibid.

[64]George, *Addresses*, Macon, August 19, 1938, 5.

[65]WFG to FDR, with copy of the telegram; FDR to WFG, March 15, 1933, PPF, box 107–117, f. 109, Roosevelt papers.

[66]*Vienna News*, January 18, 1934, 1.

Talmadge for a second term as governor met in Macon, the assembly became a rally to attack the president. At first no one rose to speak for Roosevelt until one man placed his political career on the line and walked into the lion's den and took Roosevelt's defense. That was Walter George, who rose to defend the president before the hostile crowd.[67] A number of other members of the Georgia delegation followed George's example in speeches around the state in the months that followed, and George himself expressed complete support for the president and his New Deal philosophy in a speech he gave in June 1935 at the graduation at Emory University. He told the graduates that there was a "new social philosophy" in America that was now a "permanent fixture" and legislation would follow that reflected the new mood.[68] Just a week before, George had introduced into the *Congressional Record* an editorial from the *Augusta Chronicle* titled, "We are with you, Mr. President," which praised his programs, especially the NRA, which had just been declared unconstitutional by the Supreme Court.[69]

Later in the fall, George promoted "Roosevelt Day," a "homecoming" celebration to honor Roosevelt in November when he was to visit Warm Springs for Thanksgiving.[70] On the day of the event, Roosevelt supporters formed a motorcade at 5:00 a.m., which assembled in Vienna, Unadilla, and Pinehurst with signs stating "Vienna, Georgia, Dooly County for Roosevelt." As the motorcade passed Macon, it gathered other cars and a police escort as it approached Atlanta, where a parking lot was reserved for the participants.[71] The press estimated the number of cars at 250 and the passengers at a 1,000. School classes had been canceled for the event.[72] Politics, specifically, and history, in general, are replete with irony. This warm reception for Roosevelt, which George organized, had to have been a contributing factor to Roosevelt's imagining that he was so popular in the state that he could defeat George in his bid for reelection three years later.

In fall 1936, George campaigned for Roosevelt in New York and New England, and he was genuinely delighted when Roosevelt won overwhelmingly.[73] The president had carried Dooly County by 1339 to 41 for Gover-

---

[67] *Vienna News*, February 1, 1934, 1.

[68] George, *Addresses*, Macon speech made by General Walter Harris, August 19, 1938, 2.

[69] *Atlanta Constitution*, June 11, 1935, cited in Fossett, "The Impact of the New Deal on Georgia Politics, 1933–1941," 155.

[70] *CR*, 71/2 November 14, 1938, 8749.

[71] Tel. to McIntyre, October 10, 1935, PPF, box 107–117, f. 109, Roosevelt papers.

[72] *Vienna News*, October 30, 1935, 1, 8.

[73] Ibid.

nor Alfred Landon, the Republican presidential candidate, and George expressed himself as being "very pleased" at the results, adding that the vote had "surpassed even my fondest hopes," and he predicted that the Democratic Party "will stay in power for many years to come." The *Vienna News* reminded its readers, incorrectly as it turned out, as an afterthought that "Senator George has been an ardent supporter of the president and the New Deal."[74] The last sentence, however, was not by 1936 completely true.

Another partnership of George of a different type emerged in the early 1930s that would endure for a quarter of a century and would be highly beneficial to the state of Georgia. It was the cooperation of Walter George with Richard Russell on issues beneficial to the state. When both men hit their stride, perhaps during World War II and certainly afterwards in the late 1940s and 1950s, it can easily be said that no state was better represented in the Senate than Georgia, nor had two more powerful senators. Both men, dead for half a century, are largely forgotten today outside of Georgia, but in their heyday, both typified men, to use Carl Sandburg's famous phrase, "who left footprints on the sands of time." Even in just day to day politics, Spence Grayson, once city attorney of Savannah, remembered that "I used to get a lot through Senator Russell and Senator George. They were very influential up there. They both had power."[75]

There is a strong feeling, if not concrete evidence, that Russell never forgave George for his father's defeat and the rough 1926 campaign. Whereas George often helped Russell, Russell was never eager to assist George although they would work together for Georgia. Two times when his support might have made a difference, in 1938 and 1956, Russell maintained a sphinxlike silence when he could have helped George a great deal. The two men also do not seem to have had much to do with each other outside of Senate work although they both at one point lived in the Mayflower.[76] Both men agreed that Russell would have control of the patronage of North Georgia, while George would control the patronage of the southern part of the state, while they would agree on what was in between.[77] They had not had their arrangement more than a year when they disagreed on a

---

[74]*Atlanta Constitution*, September 13, October 16, October 18, October 22, 27, 28, and November 1936, cited in Coode, "Georgia Congressmen and the New Deal, 1933–1938," 177.

[75]*Vienna News*, November 5, 1936, 1.

[76]Spence M. Grayson, oral history, 36, Russell Library.

[77]Russell lived there in the 1930s but found the place too expensive and was always threatening to move. Richard B. Russell to Mother [Ida], February 4, 1938, V-I, box 41, f. Family papers, 1938, Russell papers.

candidate for the collector of revenues for the Port of Savannah and also over the district attorneyship for the southern district of the state.[78] In 1937 they differed on a candidate for Collector of Revenue for the state of Georgia.[79] Such disagreements were rare. They both voted in 1934 to override Roosevelt's bill to veto higher pay for veterans and federal office holders. The *New York Times* felt that Russell had his eye on the 1936 elections, when he had to run for the full term, but George's vote remained a mystery to the paper, which told its readers, "Admirers of Senator George are still wondering about his vote."[80] The writer for the *New York Times* obviously did not know that George was always on the side of veterans, regardless of the political risk. Both cooperated to obtain money for a new Savannah River bridge at Augusta[81] and jointly introduced a homesteading bill in 1939.[82] There would be many such instances of cooperation.

From the beginning the partnership would be somewhat one-sided, as is manifested by the 1936 Senate race. Gene Talmadge, the "wild man from Sugar Creek," had come out of nowhere to be elected commissioner of agriculture in 1926, then elected governor in 1932. Reelected in a landslide in 1934, carrying 156 of the 159 counties, Talmadge saw himself as unbeatable. The famous Huey Long of Louisiana dismissed Talmadge as "not being smart enough for his ambitions," but he was an extremely shrewd politician of the rabble-rousing Southern type, usually running a race-baiting campaign and planting hecklers in the audience to call on him to mention something he had done for them. His usual histrionics led him once to tether a cow on the lawn of the governor's mansion in Atlanta. One historian noted, "Gene stirred men's souls and left them howling like dogs."[83] He never mentioned to his redneck followers that he was a second-generation college graduate and that his father had been instrumental in the founding of Fort Valley State College, the major black institution of higher learning in the state. Given what he saw as his great popularity, Talmadge decided to take on Richard Russell in 1936.

Walter George had not endorsed anyone in the race except Roosevelt and the general New Deal Program, which he ironically was already turning

---

[78]Mark Dunahoo, oral history, 64, Russell Library.

[79]*Vienna News*, September 21, 1933, 1; see letter from M. H. McIntire to George et al., box 22, file 4, president's personal file, Roosevelt papers.

[80]*New York Times*, April 8, 1934, IV, 7:4.

[81]*CR*, 74/2, 6144.

[82]Fite, *Richard B. Russell, Jr., Senator from Georgia*, 154.

[83]Anderson, *Wild Man from Sugar Creek*, 158.

against.[84] Talmadge was so hostile to the New Deal that some felt George's endorsement of it was an endorsement of Russell. Whereas Russell could be a demagogic orator himself and engage in campaign theatrics (he would campaign door to door at night, waking people up under the notion that if he did that, they would definitely remember his name), he could not out-demagogue Talmadge. In a hot, crowded tobacco warehouse on August 1 during a torrential rainstorm in Adel, Georgia, a crowd had gathered to hear several speakers, and both Richard Russell and Walter George happened to be there. George used the opportunity to endorse Roosevelt "as the greatest friend of Southern agriculture since the War Between the States. No one with decency and honesty would [want to] wipe that out [by electing Talmadge]." George did not mention Russell by name, but it implied his support of Russell, given Talmadge's hostility to the New Deal.[85] Russell and his operatives seized on George's remarks as an endorsement. Russell stepped forward to remind those present that he supported the New Deal: "I have no apologies to make for supporting President Roosevelt in his efforts to relieve economic distress. On the contrary, I am proud that I have been able to be of some assistance."[86]

Talmadge's biographer makes the point that George had wanted to avoid the Russell-Talmadge race, but he realized a Talmadge victory would be an endorsement of Talmadge's anti-New Deal program in a way George would not like, and given Talmadge's wild antics, he would dominate Georgia politics and steal the limelight from the more aloof and distant Walter George.[87] Russell and George had not been able to handle Talmadge, his biographer wrote, and now this gave them something to use. They later saw George's endorsement as the turning point of the campaign and the boost that Russell's candidacy needed.[88] George had the most sophisticated political organization in the state, and with his endorsement, it would swing into action. What role George's "endorsement," and it could only be taken as such, had on Russell's campaign cannot be measured, but Russell buried Talmadge 256,154 votes to 134,695.[89]

---

[84]Fossett, "The Impact of the New Deal on Georgia Politics, 1933–1941," 202.

[85]Anderson, *Wild Man from Sugar Creek*, 159; *Atlanta Journal*, August 1, 1936, cited in Fite, *Richard B. Russell, Jr., Senator from Georgia*, 142.

[86]Anderson, *Wild Man from Sugar Creek*, 159, quotes the *Atlanta Journal*, July 22, 1936, days before the event.

[87]Ibid.

[88]Ibid.

[89]Ibid. Kytle also gives a good overview of the county unit system ("A Long, Dark Night for Georgia?" 55–64).

We have seen how George had generally worked behind the scenes to undermine much New Deal legislation, voting, for example, for weakening amendments, but then voting for the final passage of the bill. The year 1935, however, saw George openly oppose a major piece of New Deal legislation: the Social Security Act, and in his opposition, he stood like Horatius at the bridge holding back the forces of Lars Porsina. As early as May 15, 1935, George had introduced a substitute bill to the Wagner bill, adding in his usual gentle way, that his substitute was not being offered "in a spirit of hostility to, or criticism of, the general objectives…[of the Wagner bill] ." He claimed that Social Security was "the most important program submitted in this session of Congress," and claimed that it was "critically important to adopt [some such program] in the near future."[90] George's bill seems to have contradicted itself, reflecting that it might have been hastily written. In some ways, it was more generous than Wagner's bill. It placed the payment totally on industrial enterprises employing more than fifty persons, and in effect created two systems: (1) old age and child and maternal aid in one system and (2) permanent old age and unemployment in another. It would, however, be financed through the states with federal "grants in aid."[91]

As was often the case of George and other conservative opponents, the major argument used against Social Security was that it was unconstitutional, and since George was a well-recognized constitutional scholar, his objections carried some weight. "I do not believe that any lawyer of experience would assert," he told his Senate colleagues, "that the bill is free from constitutional question." He felt that its "unconstitutionality" lay on the fact that it was a tax on specific employers, not everyone, i.e., those not under the bill. He also added a caveat that passage of the bill would result in the abolition of private pension plans maintained by employers, and he supported that same day an amendment exempting from coverage all private pensioners from inclusion in coverage.[92] He felt great certainty that the Supreme Court would rule it unconstitutional, and when it did, individuals who had had private pension programs that were given up would then have no protection.

George first dueled with Senator Robert Wagner of New York, who was the chief author of the bill. Wagner felt "very confident that the bill would [successfully] run the gauntlet of the courts." George strongly disagreed with his fellow Democratic senator. "Why strike down with a proba-

---

[90] *CR,* 74/1, 7750.

[91] Untitled review of George's record, attributed to Clark Howell to Tom [Corcoran], August 1, 1938, PSF, box 136, f. Georgia campaign, 1938, Roosevelt papers.

[92] *CR,* 74/1, 9514–15.

bly unconstitutional act," he told his colleague, "the private pension system...by passing a bill which will probably not stand the test of the courts?" He then rather wildly accused the opponents of the amendment as being "motivated by an overwhelming desire to concentrate in Washington all power and reduce the states to vassalage."[93] The next day, June 19, George introduced his weaker substitute Social Security bill that would permit the federal government to set a standard schedule of benefits but take the management of Social Security out of its hands and permit industry and the states a large degree of freedom in controlling the system. Henry E. Jackson, an expert in the field of social insurance, had sounded an even more strident alarm than George by stating the "Wagner bill meets the problem by the use of state socialism; the George bill uses the principle of democracy."[94] The substitute bill was very pro-business, as much of George's thinking went and would continue to go for the remainder of his life.

His substitute was defeated resoundingly by 15 votes for and 63 against, with even Richard Russell's voting against it. A number of Republicans and conservative Democrats voted against it, such as Senator Kenneth McKellar of Tennessee while a number of prominent conservative Democrats such as Harry Byrd, Carter Glass, and Champ Clark did not vote.[95] Having lost in his effort to substitute a "states' rights" version, George then supported the motion of Senator Michael Hastings to strike the Wagner bill out altogether, which failed.[96]

When the Senate bill passed 77–6, George's vote was among the "ayes." Strangely, given George's virulent opposition to the measure, or perhaps because of it, George was one of three Democrats on the conference committee with the House bill "getting it through," a fact that he used in his reelection campaign in 1938 when he was trying to bolster his New Deal credentials.[97] He never mentioned that he had voted to scrap it altogether. George had used, as many members of Congress do, these behind-the-scenes tactics to scuttle some piece of legislation that they do not wish to oppose publicly, but this struggle was the first time that George so openly opposed New Deal legislation. He got his second chance to "come out"

---

[93] *Vienna News*, June 20, 1935, 1.

[94] *CR*, 74/1, 9644–45.

[95] Ibid., 9648.

[96] Untitled review of George's record, attributed to Clark Howell, to Tom [Corcoran], August 1, 1938, PAF, box 136, f. Georgia campaign 1938, Roosevelt papers.

[97] George, *Addresses*, Clarkesville, August 8, 1938, 13. All ten Georgia House members voted for Social Security (Coode, "Georgia Congressmen and the New Deal, 1933–1938," 136).

within two months of the passage of Social Security.

August 1935 saw the appearance of the Bituminous Coal Conservation Act of 1935, better known as the Guffey Coal Act, which created the Bituminous Coal Commission to set the price of coal, another red flag before Walter George. It was predicated on the claim that it would protect the industry from low competitive rates by creating the Bituminous Coal Labor Board to regulate maximum working hours and minimum wages. In the debate on August 21, 1935, George roundly condemned the bill and told the Senate that it would not find five lawyers who would defend its constitutionality. He strongly criticized the way it was written—by the United Mine Workers and a group of bituminous operators and their lawyers—stating, "If groups are to legislate for themselves, the end [of the country] isn't very far distant."[98] The bill passed 45–37, with Richard Russell and the entire Georgia House delegation joining George in opposition. The bill was less easily defended than Social Security, and senators on both sides of the argument commented that George had made "the most masterful arguments against the measure" than any arguments made in the current session. Exasperated at the way the Democratic liberal majority was ramming through legislation that George considered unconstitutional, he asked rhetorically of his opponents, "What does a majority need with a constitution (*sic*) if it is not going to uphold it?"[99]

Then George's old nemesis from the Social Security bill appeared with another piece of legislation that enraged George, the Wagner-Ellenbogen bill, which would put government in the low-cost housing business by creating large multi-unit housing projects, a novel concept. Congress had already passed the National Housing Act of 1934, but it had only helped keep people from losing their houses in the bad economic climate. Senator Wagner introduced a public housing bill in three successive congresses from 1934–1936. The bills never left the House Banking Committee because the chairman, Rep. Henry Steagall (D-Alabama), thought the concept favored big cities and was "socialistic."

With public housing appearing on the horizon, the Roosevelt Administration introduced a bill in March 1936 allowing the federal government to pay certain municipal services fees in lieu of taxes on low income housing since the comptroller general had ruled that rental money could not be used to pay local taxes and city governments had balked at providing municipal services. George had introduced a bill on March 27, 1936, requiring federal

[98]*New York Times*, August 22, 1935, 31:1.

[99]*Atlanta Constitution*, August 22, 1935, 10:1.

low-cost housing to pay municipal taxes, and even liberal Secretary Harold Ickes had recommended it.[100] Atlanta alone would collect under the bill $18,000 a year, George told the mayor of Atlanta.[101] Other bills to sweeten the notion of public housing, promoted by Senator Wagner, arrived in the Senate. When one of Wagner's bills reached the Senate floor on June 3, 1936, conservatives of both parties delayed it a day to move Walter George front and center in the debate as the best chance to stop it. George spoke, imploring his colleagues "to turn back before we have gone into a state of socialism," but his objections were swamped in a tsunami of aye votes, and the bill passed 42–24.[102] The omnibus Wagner-Steagall bill (Steagall having somehow overcome his fears of socialism) did finally reach the Senate floor in summer 1937. In the debate on August 7, 1937, George tangled with Senator Wagner again. In a rather patronizing manner, Wagner told George, "It is difficult to explain complicated legislation to a statesman not in sympathy with it." George replied, "The senator is arrogating to himself the right to sit in judgement upon his fellows in this body." He then back-handed Wagner with, "I am not in sympathy with any fraud in this bill." To this Wagner thundered, "Does the senator suggest that I am indulging in fraud?" At this point Senator Matthew Neely of West Virginia intervened with a plea for the restoration of senatorial courtesy.[103] The bill subsequently passed and was signed into law by President Roosevelt on September 1, 1937. George had lost another open battle with the New Deal. His opposition, of course, did not go unnoticed by the president himself.

The president likely also noticed George's move to override Roosevelt's veto of the Veterans' Bonus bill, which would allow 23,000 veterans to renew their temporary life insurance for five more years. It had been voted out of committee by a 15–2 vote. Secretary of the Treasury Henry Morgenthau opposed it, stating that it would add $2 billion to the national debt, bringing it to $36.5 billion.[104] Roosevelt had vetoed it, but George asked the Senate to override the veto, arguing by some convoluted arithmetic that it would be no additional cost to the treasury.[105] The Senate overrode Roosevelt's veto by a vote of 69–12, a public insult to the president that was openly engineered

[100]*New York Times,* March 28, 1936, 2:8.

[101]*Atlanta Constitution,* March 28, 1936, 7:3.

[102]*CR,* 80 (?), 9557 ff, 9564–66, cited in Huthmacher, *Senator Robert F. Wagner,* 214–15.

[103]*New York Times,* August 8, 1937, IV, 7:1.

[104]Ibid. January 15, 1936, 1:8.

[105]Ibid., June 8, 1937, 15:1.

by Walter George.[106]

Then, in 1938 came the Fair Labor Standards Act (FLSA), known also as the Wages and Hours bill, which set a national minimum wage for industry and regulated the number of hours employees could work. Something like the bill had first been drafted in the last year of the Hoover administration by Alabama Democrat Hugo Black. Black's bill, more radical than the one that passed six years later, met with very stiff opposition. George immediately joined the opponents when the bill gained steam by 1936, and he attacked it with a blind fury, and as was often the case when George opposed something strongly, his arguments sometimes became irrational. He called the Forty Hour Week bill a "spendthrift policy [?]," adding that it ran counter "to every dictate of prudence."[107] The next year when the bill was taken seriously, George argued that it would "crucify" Southern industry by not taking into account differentials in the cost of living and different pay scales in different parts of the country. "In arguing against it," the *New York Times* wrote, "he stated that '[In passing the bill] we undertake to do what nature, what economic laws, what the development that has gone on in this country...says we cannot do unless we want to disrupt... the industries in some parts of the country....This is the wildest dream that was ever presented to the American Congress.'"[108] An adequate minimum wage in New York would break Southern business owners, whose workers could live on less. He led the effort to return the bill to committee, and when unsuccessful, he voted against it. Strangely, Senator Russell did not vote.[109] Still attacking the bill in 1938 after its passage, George presciently argued, "What does it profit a man if he has a guarantee of wages but hasn't any job? What does it profit a man if he has a guarantee of a minimum wage, if your industries...cannot operate under it?"[110]

George had succeeded in exempting agriculture and industries closely allied with agriculture such as processing of cotton goods and the canning industry, so in that way he won a partial victory. Senator Allen Ellender of Louisiana wrote him to say that the House and Senate conferees would produce the final bill in the next few days and that he was "delighted that many of the suggestions made by you...were incorporated in the bill," especially

[106] *Atlanta Constitution*, June 2, 1936, 3:1; Altman, "Second Session," 1102. The House followed suit by a vote of 368–13.

[107] Ibid., June 28, 1936, 8:5.

[108] *New York Times*, July 30, 1937, 5:2.

[109] *Atlanta Journal*, August 1, 1937, in Fossett, "The Impact of the New Deal on Georgia Politics, 1933–1941," 281.

[110] George, *Addresses*, Decatur, August 25, 1938, 2–21.

those exempting agriculture, "which if placed under the Wages and Hours bill, might have imposed greater burdens on the shoulders of farmers of our nation."[111] In 1939, after the bill had become law, George had the dark pleasure of reporting to the Senate that "Throughout the South many small industries have closed since the law went into effect…because the management could not pay the wage required by the act."[112] Likely World War II might have saved further businesses from failure. Again, George had altered, if not crippled, a major piece of New Deal legislation.

One area in which Southern legislators in general and George in particular were especially successful against a New Deal program was their opposition to the civil rights question of the day: anti-lynching legislation. Lynching of blacks (and Catholics and Jews) had happened since the end of Reconstruction, with periods of greater intensity here and there. The large spate came after World War I, when black soldiers returning from France—where they had been treated like human beings—naturally wished to be treated similarly in the country for which they had fought. This desire had led to "uppity behavior" on returning home, and their new attitude had led to an explosion of lynchings in the early 1920s. The issue, if not the intensity, was still present at the time of the New Deal. Roosevelt, encouraged by his wife, who was more liberal than he on the question, favored greater civil rights for black Americans but not to the point of pressing the cause to the detriment of other New Deal legislation. Any anti-lynching legislation would be filibustered and that would delay or even block the passage of important New Deal programs. Moreover, Roosevelt feared that his support for anti-lynching legislation might unify Southerners in a way nothing else would. Southerners traditionally chaired committees because of their seniority, and their power could be used to block other New Deal legislation if Roosevelt promoted this civil rights issue of the day. In May 1934, Roosevelt told Walter White, the secretary of the National Association for the Advancement of Colored People, "If I came out for the anti-lynching bill now, they will block every bill I ask Congress to pass to keep American from collapsing. I just can't take the risk."[113] Though sympathetic, Roosevelt stayed on the sidelines and let liberal senators from the North promote the hopeless issue. As a result, during the 1930s there was almost always an anti-lynching bill in some Congressional committee.

One such bill, the Costigan-Wagner Anti-Lynching bill, reached the

---

[111]Allen Ellender to WFG, June 13, 1938, Sen. G (L and S) folder, VHPS.
[112]*CR*, 76/1, 6266.
[113]Freidel, *FDR and the South*, 81, 86.

Senate floor in spring 1935. It called for punishment for sheriffs who did not try to block lynch mobs. George's actions on civil rights will be discussed in a later chapter, but suffice it to say at this point that George's campaigns were generally free of the wild race-baiting of so many Southern politicians On this issue, nevertheless, George joined forces with South Carolina senator "Cotton Ed" Smith, whose campaigns were not free of such demagoguery, to try to defeat the bill by filibuster.

In the debate, George argued that such questions were better left to the states. He reminded, or perhaps informed, his colleagues that he himself had risked his life to protect men from mob violence. He stressed that the South had made great progress on the issue, which he compared to the violence in 1920, and added, "We went through one bloody war through a misapprehension of the social structure of the country," which seems to be a condemnation of slavery, in itself at the time a rather liberal statement for a Southerner.[114] He then attacked the measure on its constitutionality, a recurring theme of his: "I have not a shadow of doubt in my mind that the whole scheme is unconstitutional. The states can handle this better without federal intervention." He also added, incorrectly in the case of southern states, that "better steps are being taken [by the states] for the safety and security of life against mob violence than this bill will ever do."[115]

George argued that the South deplored lynching more than any other part of the country, a questionable statement, to be sure. Then calling lynching "primitive humanity in motion," he added truthfully, "I have never been an apologist for lynching and never will be.... We have made major progress in every part of the country of ridding civilization of the blot of this abuse."[116] George was correct that lynchings had declined, having reached a national average of twenty per year, considerably down from 1920, but the evil was still there and would continue to be for several decades.[117] Noted journalist Arthur Krock wrote in an editorial in the *London Times* on April 17, 1935, that opposition to the lynching bill would be led by "the ablest men in the Senate." Walter White, a noted civil rights activist until his death in 1955, cited a number of senators who were among the ablest in Senate who promoted the legislation, and were more outstanding so than

---

[114]It is not clear that Walter George made this statement. The next day, the *New York Times* reported that "Cotton Ed" Smith had made it, which is surprisingly liberal for him (*New York Times*, April 18, 1935, 10:30). The remainder of the statement is vintage George.

[115]*New York Times*, April 17, 1935, 5:1.

[116]*Atlanta Constitution*, April 17, 1935, 15:6.

[117]The Costigan-Wagner bill died by the mid-1930s because lynchings declined to very few.

Krock's anonymous "ablest men." Krock fired back to the editor of the *Times*, "I'll match Senator George...individually against a dozen named in Mr. White's list," adding that he (Krock) was not "unique among Washington correspondents in that estimate."[118]

The bill, of course, went nowhere in 1935, and when in 1936 supporters acquired enough signatures on a discharge petition to force a similar bill out of the committee, it was too late before the August adjournment for a vote to be taken.[119] In 1937 Senator Royal Copeland of New York tried to attach the anti-lynching bill to the minimum wage bill, but Senator Hugo Black moved that it be stricken, which it was by a vote of 46–29.[120] Victor Hugo famously said that no army has the power to stop and idea whose time has come, but it would be three decades before the idea would really come on civil rights.

Cotton remained king in the 1930s in the South, although tobacco was gaining. As a money crop, tobacco did not replace it until America's flirtation with synthetic fabrics in the late 1960s and early 1970s eclipsed it, only to have it return in importance in the 1980s and 1990s. Ever mindful of dangers to farming interests, and like most politicians playing to the galleries, George sounded an alarm in March 1935 about the dangers present to the cotton textile industry. He said that "possibly" a hundred mills had closed in the past two months. "The cotton textile industry is facing a situation so grave that only prompt and drastic action will prevent a large-scale shutting down of mills," which George said would result in "dumping of perhaps 400,000 employees on the relief roles." Sounding an alarm that was still off, he blamed Japanese competition "foremost among the factors militating against normal operation in the industry." He called for a limited embargo to save the industry, and he called on President Roosevelt to deliver one. He then threw into the pot a number of unrelated factors that he said were causes, but probably were not: taxes, price of raw cotton, and NRA restrictions. Warning that Japanese imports were increasing, he noted that 24 million square yards of Japanese cloth had been imported in the first two months of 1935, three times the amount for all of 1934. He felt that a tariff would be ineffective, for reasons he did not state, and announced that he and Senator Walsh were going to meet with Roosevelt on the question.[121]

How much of this cry was political grandstanding is hard to say. The

[118]*New York Times*, April 19, 1935, 20:7.

[119]Altman, "Second Session," 1088.

[120]*Atlanta Constitution*, August 1, 1937, 1:8.

[121]*New York Times*, March 19, 1935, 39:1.

Japanese had probably bought the cotton to make the cloth largely from the United States, which helped the Southern farmer, and George could not have been unaware of that fact. Further, an increase of raw cotton prices could hardly have helped keep cotton mills open. George certainly knew these facts, but the rhetoric played well back home.

In the midst of George's private war against the New Deal, he found an ally: the United States Supreme Court. In 1935 the Supreme Court, populated by twelve years of Republican appointees, began striking down like bowling pins elements of the New Deal. One of the first major institutions to fall was the NRA, which George had opposed but for which he had voted. George was not alarmed at the court's ruling. In an interview with his hometown newspaper, he said that the ruling "won't greatly disturb business nor shake the US" Noting that he did "not think that this is an hour of great excitement," he added that in a couple of days, "the country will breathe easier."[122] He was not openly jubilant, but it is obvious that he was pleased with the decision. He was more openly delighted with a statement he made on the Senate floor at the end of May. "I see nothing in the decision which has not been well recognized in the law from the beginning," he told his colleagues. He continued,

> [t]he difficulty has been...that we have tried to circumvent in too many instances the very clear application of well-decided constitutional principles, and it has led us into some difficulty.... The difficulty has been upon the part of those who wish to stretch the plain provisions of the Constitution...so that the hand of the federal authority might reach into the remotest hamlet and so disturb the citizens so that he [*sic*] could not know what to expect tomorrow morning.

He did add that the NRA did "some good," but he did not call for its renewal "because the backbone of the Depression, Mr. President, is broken...and the American people are ready to govern themselves...."[123] George had met with Roosevelt on March 6 and told him that Congress wanted any duties of the NRA divided between the Federal Trade Commission and the Labor Department, with outright abolition of the NRA bureaucracy, but he told Roosevelt that it could not continue as a separate entity. He suggested that what was needed was a voluntary system and much greater revision than Roosevelt had indicated in a speech two weeks earlier. He also had advised the president that no legislation of this sort would pass

---

[122] *Vienna News*, May 30, 1935, 1.
[123] *CR*, 74/1, 8300.

Congress unless the powers of a similar institution were "drastically curbed without the first NRA's complicated code structure." He wanted mandatory codes replaced by voluntary ones, calling it a "return to self-government."[124] In short, he wanted the NRA, if resurrected, to be totally gutted.

In January 1936, the Supreme Court declared unconstitutional the Agricultural Adjustment Act.[125] George had voted for it though he did not want to, and as usual he thought it "unconstitutional." Richard Russell immediately issued a statement calling the decision "amazing" and noted that unless the government assured farmers that they could obtain a decent price for their cotton, the country will face a depression that will make the period from 1931 to 1933 "look like a prosperous era."[126]

Unlike with Russell's reaction, in the days following the decision, there was only silence from George. Not until February when Senator Joseph Robinson of Arkansas, the Democratic Senate leader, blasted the court for its decision, did George have anything to say. In response to Robinson's outburst, George expressed "keen regret" that the senator had attacked the Supreme Court, adding that "the expressions coming from this side of the Senate [the Democratic side]" are "entirely without real foundation or justification." Again stressing the unconstitutionality of the program, George added, "I will not support a program looking to the destruction of the dual [i.e., federal] system of government in this country because as I see it, my...duty to my country is superior to my obligations to my party." The AAA, for which George was not to be caught voting against, "invades the reserved rights of the states," since it was a "plan to regulate and control agricultural production, a matter beyond the powers delegated to the federal government."[127] Again, a program that George opposed but dared not vote against was defeated by the judiciary.

Roosevelt won reelection in 1936 with a landslide that would not be duplicated in American politics until 1964 and 1972. Alfred Landon of Kansas, who campaigned as a governor who had cooperated with the New Deal, was buried, having carried only two states. The country had clearly endorsed the New Deal, which had been a slow-motion revolution in reforms, the likes of which the country would not see until the presidency of Lyndon Johnson in the 1960s. It would have been a rare man indeed who could have this adulation shown to him and not have it affect notions he had

[124]*Atlanta Constitution*, March 7, 1935, 1:2; *New York Times*, March 7, 1935, 1:1.
[125]*Atlanta Constitution*, January 7, 1936, 1:6.
[126]Ibid., 4:6.
[127]*Atlanta Constitution*, February 16, 1936, 2A:4.

of himself. Roosevelt had a taste of the dictator in him; he demanded fast action on anything that he wanted, and the niceties of democratic give and take were alien to his nature. With this national show of adulation on election day, and given his personality, it is not surprising that Roosevelt, with lopsided majorities in both houses of Congress, simply assumed that he could do anything. He took his victory as an important mandate to push the social legislation he wished to promote. He had said in his inaugural address that he would be "taking the [American] people along the path they have chosen to advance."[128] It soon became obvious that the consequence of his first two attempted changes was to enhance the power of the presidency.[129]

One of his first actions was a plan of government reorganization to be an economy measure. It was in no way a power grab, and it certainly was not as sinister as it was later portrayed by the conservatives. In fact, Herbert Hoover had suggested it when he was in the White House, and he endorsed it when Roosevelt attempted it, as did Richard Russell in 1937. Walter George had endorsed it as well in January 1932, when he said, "If we are to do more than pay mere lip service to economy…it seems to me to be necessary to confer upon the president of the United States blanket authority to consolidate offices…within the executive department…."[130]

The Reorganization Bill called for the addition of two new cabinet members and six additional secretaries (called "assistant secretaries"). It also called for the abolition of the bipartisan civil service commission with a single civil service commission appointed by and responsible to the president, with members removable at the will of the president. The bill was finally amended to create only one new cabinet position, but what must have rankled Roosevelt the most was George's amendment removing from control of the president all civil service employees.[131] George had for some time lamented what he saw as the loss of power of the legislative branch, and over a PWA appropriation matter as early as a year before, George had decried what he called "surrender of congressional appropriation authority" and the "further sinking of the legislative branch and putting the power in the executive."[132] For reasons that are not clear, George saw this as another step in

[128]"Mr. Roosevelt's Court Plan Dies," 5.

[129]Altman, "First Session," 1071.

[130]Section 2, 1, of untitled report on George's record, Clark Howell to Tom [Corcoran], August 1, 1938, PSF, box 136, f. Ga. Campaign 1938, Roosevelt papers; see also Clark Forman to Rudolf Fester, August 5, 1938, PSF, box 136, F. Georgia campaign, 1938, Roosevelt papers.

[131]George, *Addresses*, Macon, August 19, 1938, 23.

[132]*New York Times*, March 3, 1936, 8:3.

that direction. The whole bill was derailed, and Walter George had been partially instrumental in its demise.

The most egregious Rooseveltian move, however, was indeed a power grab: His attempt in 1937 to pack the Supreme Court, which had dug the graves of so much New Deal legislation. Roosevelt in a campaign speech as early as 1932 called the court "a mere annex of the Republican administration."[133] In winter 1936–1937, there was general talk in Washington about doing something about limiting the court's powers. There was another action of the court that also rankled Roosevelt. He had dismissed William Humphries from the Federal Trade Commission, and Humphries had taken his dismissal to court. He died before the issue was decided, but Humphries had pressed on until it reached the Supreme Court, which ruled that Roosevelt did not have the right to dismiss Humphries and ordered that his salary be paid. Journalists Joseph Alsop and Turner Catledge in writing on the court-packing imbroglio, wrote that Roosevelt was "infuriated" and that the court had "outraged his love of power."[134]

Technically the court had overstepped its power early in the nineteenth century by declaring something unconstitutional, and no one had pointed out that it did not have a right to declare things unconstitutional, so this power became a court prerogative. Whether Roosevelt knew this arcane point of judicial law is not known, but in February 1937, Roosevelt friend and former secretary of the navy Josephus Daniels wrote Roosevelt and pointed this fact out, adding, "It is a pity [that] Jefferson and Jackson and Lincoln did not…[determine]…once and for all…that the Supreme Court has no authority to declare an act of Congress…unconstitutional."[135] Roosevelt was a good enough lawyer to know that he could not undo the court's "right" to declare something unconstitutional, nor could he pass a constitutional amendment changing this power, but he decided that he could weaken this conservative bastion. The Constitution did not specify that the court had to have exactly nine justices either, so Roosevelt felt he could alter the conservative majority by adding additional justices.

Exactly who was behind the plan is not fully known. Senator Claude Pepper of Florida felt the idea came from Attorney General Homer Cummings, who had been a longtime ally of Roosevelt.[136] Alsop and Catledge

[133]Alsop and Catledge, *The 168 Days*, 15.

[134]Ibid., 13–14.

[135]Josephus Daniels to FDR, February 27, 1937, box 269, f. Supreme Court file, Correspondence D-G, Corcoran papers, Roosevelt Library.

[136]Pepper, *Eyewitness to a Century*, 57.

felt that it was Tom Corcoran and Ben Cohen.[137] These two were indeed the Goldust Twins of the whole affair, and if they had not come up with the idea, they certainly led the promotion of it. At any rate, the plan as Roosevelt announced it in February 1937 called for the creation of fifty new federal judgeships in the country and one Supreme Court justice for each jurist on the court over seventy years of age. Since six of the nine justices were over seventy, Roosevelt would have six new appointees. Moreover, in the future, if any justice who turned seventy and did not retire within six months, the president had the right to appoint another justice. The plan was all the more odious even for many Democrats because it had been hatched among a small group around Roosevelt and then presented to the Democratic majority as a *fait accompli*, which they were expected to rubber stamp.

When Roosevelt did announce the plan to congressional leaders shortly before the public announcement, the congressional delegation was stunned. Congressman William Bankhead and Vice President John Nance Garner said little in the meeting or immediately after, but on the return ride to Capitol Hill, Representative Hatton Sumners, chair of the House Judiciary Committee, told his fellow representatives, "Boys, here's where I cash in." It fell to Sumner's liberal colleague from Texas, Maury Maverick, to sign it and drop it in the hopper.[138] Initially, before people thought about it, the plan had considerable support, even in the conservative South. An American Institute of Public Opinion poll reported that more Southerners favored the plan than opposed it,[139] and there was considerable grassroots support for it in Georgia, where three counties had a referendum, Mitchell County (home of Congressman Cox), Randolph County, and Seminole county, all passing it with lopsided majorities.[140] Even Richard Russell's father, Chief Justice Richard Russell, supported the court-packing plan.[141] In the days following the announcement, a tide of opposition rose all across the country from both Republicans and Democrats.

Walter George did not immediately join the opposition.[142] Probably George had prickly feeling about court-tampering because he himself had

---

[137]Alsop and Catledge, *The 168 Days*, 75.

[138]Burns, *Roosevelt: The Lion and the Fox*, 293–94.

[139]*Atlanta Constitution*, February 23, March 17, March 23, 1937, cited in Coode, "Georgia Congressmen and the New Deal, 1933–1938," 186.

[140]Ibid., March 12, 17, 18, 20, and April 17, 1937, cited in Coode, "Georgia Congressmen and the New Deal, 1933–1938," 192.

[141]*Walton Tribune,* March 27, 1937; *Atlanta Constitution*, May 8, 1937, cited in Coode, "Georgia Congressmen and the New Deal, 1933–1938," 190.

[142]Alsop and Catledge, *The 168 Days*, 88.

been a judge, but he had been privately challenging critics of the Supreme Court even before Roosevelt dropped his bomb.[143] On February 16, however, for the first time he broke his public silence and announced that he opposed the bill. With his picture on the front page of the *Atlanta Constitution* and a headline "George Strikes at Judiciary Plans as 'Unwise,'" (one can be certain that George's feeling went far stronger than simply "unwise"), the senator, in a briefly worded statement, offered that he had not planned to comment on the proposal until the "legislation had taken final form." However, since some of his letters on the subject had leaked out, he "had no hesitancy in announcing his position." He was rather gentle, however, in his criticism of the proposal. "In my opinion[,] this particular recommendation of the president is unwise," he said. "[I]f approved will impair the independence of the federal judiciary.... A subservient judiciary is worse than no judiciary at all."[144] With his affirmation, declared opponents of the Supreme Court reform moved into a majority in the Senate, 30–29.[145]

George's role in the opposition fight of the court plan was not a major one. The opposition forces met for an organizational dinner at Senator Millard Tydings's house, and George was there, but the conservatives felt that they would be more effective if their leader was a liberal, so they chose liberal Democrat Senator Burton K. Wheeler of Montana,[146] a Republican, and Senator Edward Burke of Nebraska, a Democrat.[147] Senator Tom Connally was often mentioned as a major leader as well.[148] Present, however, were Harry Byrd of Virginia, McKellar of Tennessee, and Burke of Nebraska, all leading Senate conservatives. Though there were several Republicans in the fight (e.g., Wheeler and Arthur Vandenberg), the group was largely composed of Democrats.[149] *Newsweek* reported that the GOP Senate leader Charles L. McNary "crossed his long, thin legs and enjoyed the show."[150] A "Steering Committee," which would lobby other members of Congress was formed, and George was not on it.[151] In fact, in the publicity of the fight,

[143]Coode, "Georgia Congressmen and the New Deal, 1933–1938," 188.

[144]*Atlanta Constitution*, February 17, 1937, 1:7.

[145]*New York Times*, February 17, 1927, 1:8 and 2:8.

[146]Cole, *Roosevelt and the Isolationists, 1932–45*, 214.

[147]"Mr. Roosevelt's Court Plan Dies," 5.

[148]"New Team," 15.

[149]Mulder, *Insurgent Progressives in the United States Senate*, 178.

[150]"Champions of the Senate," 8.

[151]Cole (*Roosevelt and the Isolationists, 1932–45*, 214) cites Wheeler, *Yankee from the West*, 322–23.

George was not prominently mentioned at all.[152] George's secondary role, therefore, makes Roosevelt's behavior to George the next year all the more puzzling.

The most prominent efforts George made were two radio addresses, one in February, the other in July. In his February speech, he began by saying how much he admired Roosevelt, but noted "without warning, the executive has demanded of the national legislature a subservient judiciary." He stressed that he did not challenge the president's right to appoint to the court, but he denied the right to appoint "wholesale merely because of dissatisfaction with the decisions of the tribunal." If this change would be enacted, George warned, "It will become a prey of faction. When democracy is everywhere challenged," he said without noting wherever else it was being challenged, "it would seem the part of wisdom to sustain that branch of our government…which has remained the stabilizing force…in the American system. A subservient judiciary…will provide shackles for the liberties of the people."[153] George's speech resonated well back home. The *Atlanta Constitution*'s headlines reporting George's broadcast read, "Roosevelt is repudiating Loyal Democrats, George Charges in National Address." George reminded the home folks that he had been on the Democratic Party's platform committee in 1936 and had, with Roosevelt's consent, put in the platform that the Party would take no shortcuts to put in place its program, adding "In the campaign that followed, no responsible voice was raised…for the legislation which is now demanded of the Congress."[154] George seems to have honestly wanted Georgians to hear both sides. After Robert Jackson, who would later serve on the Supreme Court himself, testified for the bill on March 12, 1937, George encouraged Archibald Lovett, later a federal judge in a district court in Georgia, and Alexander W. Smith, Jr., president of the Georgia Bar Association, to invite Jackson to speak to the Georgia Bar Association. Not wanting to play Daniel in the lion's den, Jackson declined, saying that since his and George's positions were clear, any speech he made in Georgia would be mistaken as an attack on Senator George. Probably knowing Jackson's wariness, George replied, "The people of my state are entitled to hear both sides of this question. A good many of them, perhaps most of them, will agree with you." Then George added, with a more accurate position than he at the time imagined, "I shall not be surprised if the position I have taken means the end of my political life, but I do not feel that I could do any dif-

---

[152] Altman, "First Session," 1085; Alsop and Catledge, *The 168 Days*, 104–105.

[153] *New York Times*, March 1, 1937, 1:1; *CR*, 75/1, appendix 362–63.

[154] *Atlanta Constitution*, March 1, 1937, 1:8.

ferently, no matter what it meant for me." He again issued the invitation to come to Georgia and "say to them [the people of Georgia] just what you think without regards to its effect on me." Jackson did indeed go to Georgia late in May 1937, but avoided mentioning the court plan directly.[155]

George's July 19 radio speech was much longer than the first. Meanwhile the Senate Judiciary Committee had reported out the bill adversely by a vote of 10–7. George reviewed the history of the bill to his listening audience and pointed out that the Supreme Court had sustained Social Security and the Labor Relations Act, proving that this bill was not needed. Putting another knife into the bill, which by now was already on life support, he admonished that the bill "intends to create a Supreme Court that will approve and validate the will and legislative program of the party temporarily in power.... [In such a case] stability in government is threatened...and the Constitution cannot long survive without the aid of the independent, uncontrolled Court."[156]

Again the speech played well back home. The next day the *Atlanta Constitution* proclaimed, "George brands Plan as 'Glorified Carpetbaggery,'" referring to the part of the bill that allowed federal judges to be moved around the country. Recognizing that Congress should have the power to add new justices when and only when the business of the country demanded it, George intoned, "Congress can never...interfere with the normal orderly discharge of the functions of the court." Then patting the opponents on the back, he opined, "Those who oppose the bill know how to save our government."[157]

Finally, after eighty-five witnesses, 1.5 million words of testimony, and one senator dead over the matter,[158] the full Senate voted overwhelmingly on July 22, 1937, to return the bill to the committee.[159] Vice President Garner, on returning from Robinson's funeral, went by the White House and told Roosevelt that the Supreme Court plan was dead, having helped scuttle it himself.[160] His reasoning, as he later put it, was "I want to do everything I

---

[155]Jackson, *That Man*, 54 and 233n.

[156]*CR*, 75/1, appendix, 1828–829.

[157]*Atlanta Constitution*, July 20, 1937, 6:3. George was even critical of a substitute bill, thought by Roosevelt as more palatable, stating that it would "wipe out state lines" (*New York Times*, July 20, 1936, 2:5).

[158]Senator Joseph T. Robinson, the Democratic leader in the Senate, who had tried to appease the opponents with weakening amendments, died of a heart attack in his apartment in the midst of the fight.

[159]Altman, "First Session," 1086.

[160]"Mr. Roosevelt's Court Plan Dies," 5.

can to help my country, but I also want to preserve the Democratic Party. The president is licked and he knows it.... Let's get together and be brothers again."[161] Georgia's congressional representatives were almost universally against the court packing bill. Representative Stephen Pace, who would later become George's campaign manager in his ill-fated 1956 campaign, called the court plan "damnable, detestable, abominable and outrageous," adding "but not necessarily in that order."[162] Moreover, polls showed little alienation for opponents of the court bill. A national poll showed that only 26 percent of Democrats responding favored punishment of the renegade Democrats. In the South it was only 20 percent.[163] One Southern voice that had remained silent was that of George's colleague Richard Russell. Apparently not wanting to alienate Roosevelt, or else standing in awe of him, he wrote his mother, "When and if the Supreme Court issue ever reaches the floor of the Senate...I think I should leave for a trip of several days and do nothing but laze around."[164]

As Senator Tom Connally remembered the whole affair, "The court fight was Roosevelt's first major defeat as president. He never forgot it."[165] Seething with rage, Roosevelt told Farley, his campaign manager, "They'll [the conservative Democrats who opposed the court plan] be sorry yet."[166] While personally affable to their faces, he withheld patronage and retaliated by inviting Senator James E. Murry aboard his train in an October tour out west, but did not invite Burton Wheeler.[167] When Senator Pat McCarran (D-Nevada) asked Vice President Garner about political reprisals, Garner replied soothingly, "There will be none of that. I can promise you that I will do everything I can to prevent it."[168] In the privacy of his office, Roosevelt was quite "peevish." He told Farley, "And I won't go along with Walter George [on patronage appointments] in Georgia. That's final!" Farley reminded Roosevelt that if he played that game, the president would not get by the Senate any appointments that George felt were "personally obnox-

161Allen, "Roosevelt's Defeat," 124.

162Congressman Pace to Coode, July 27, 1965, cited in Coode, "Georgia Congressmen and the New Deal, 1933–1938," 187.

163Fagin "Franklin D. Roosevelt", 33.

164Richard B. Russell to Mother, May 19, 1937, (Winder), V-I, box 41, f. Parents—1937, Russell papers.

165Connally, *My Name is Tom Connally*, 192.

166Farley, *Jim Farley's Story*, 96.

167Cole, *Roosevelt*, 220.

168Allen, "Roosevelt's Defeat," 124.

ious." Roosevelt snapped back, "We'll see about that."[169]

In a speech in his roughhouse campaign in 1938, Walter George explained to his constituents why he had taken his position the year before on the court plan. "I know that human liberty cannot be secured or retained if you had in one man, however great or noble…all of the powers," he told an audience in Decatur late in August 1938—and knowing Roosevelt, he knew that he was not always so noble.[170] The year before, he had expressed the opinion that if the administration did try to persecute Court bill foes, the party "will be disorganized and faction-torn in 1940." He felt, however, that "if the president lets the party in each state act [on its own] in the 1938 election, we will come back here united." On the other hand, he felt that if there were an attempt to control the primaries in individual state, "We will come back here with an uncertain situation as far as party harmony is concerned."[171] The court itself was changing, however, and even before Roosevelt had offered his plan. In January 1937, Justice Owen Roberts switched his vote with a majority to uphold Washington State's minimum wage law when he had voted to nullify New York's although the decision was not announced until March 29.[172] Apparently Chief Justice Charles Evans Hughes convinced the court to rule favorably on several pieces of legislation, having the effect of rendering Roosevelt's court plan unnecessary. In May, in the midst of the court fight, Judge Willis van Devanter retired, giving Roosevelt a chance to nominate a liberal. It could not be known at this point, but between 1937 and 1941, Roosevelt would have the chance to appoint seven of the nine justices on the court. Unquestionably, though, the court fight removed much of Roosevelt's luster. At the start of the struggle, he enjoyed more power than probably any other president had ever possessed. By the close of it, he had been humiliated and was powerless to get his way.[173] It was, in any case, a defeat Roosevelt would neither forget nor forgive. A journalist writing for *Nation* summed up Roosevelt's feelings: "Although the president took his licking calmly and pleasantly, the victorious rebel Democrats have no illusions about the depth of his smile." Adding that they know that there can be no lasting peace between them, he suggested that "if the opportunity arises[,] he will retaliate…. He is putting on a good show of affability, but he hasn't forgotten or forgiven a thing." As for Roosevelt him-

[169]Farley, *Jim Farley's Story*, 172.

[170]George, *Addresses*, Decatur, 25 August 1938, 15–16.

[171]*New York Times*, August 28, 1937, 1:2.

[172]Alsop and Catledge, *The 168 Days*, 140.

[173]Ibid., 13.

self, he continued to deny the existence of any bipartisan conservative union, long after it was obvious that there was one. At a news conference in November 1938, Peter Brandt of the *St. Louis Post Dispatch* asked Roosevelt if he thought he was facing a "Conservative coalition," the president replied, "I don't think so." To that remark Brandt shot back, "I do," to which everyone, including Roosevelt, laughed.[174]

Roosevelt had also sundered the Democratic party, making the bulk of the Southern Democrats almost a separate party within the party, a situation that would last until the Southern Democrats became true liberals and aligned with the national party, many of them replaced by Republicans, not just in voting record but in name as well. This large part of the Democrats in Congress joined with the Republican minority to form a conservative majority, which would largely dominate the US Congress for the next three or more decades. It was generally called the "Conservative coalition" though it was never given a formal name by anyone other than journalists. Immediately after the court fight, it joined against other New Deal measures and other liberal issues as well, so much so that except for the Fair Labor Standards Act and the Second AAA, which George himself supported, Roosevelt was unable to get any domestic programs passed between 1937 and his death in 1945. Harry Truman inherited the same problem, so much so that not only did this "unholy alliance," as Senator Hubert Humphrey of Minnesota called it, block many of his congressional initiatives, it helped the Republicans pass the Taft-Hartley Act and override Truman's veto. The price the Republicans had to pay for conservative Democrats' cooperation was simply to turn a blind eye to civil rights, which they did until the late fifties and early sixties, by which time it became embarrassing for them to do so. By that time, conservative Southern Democrats began to be replaced with Southern Republicans. Therefore, it can be said that many years after his death, Roosevelt finally achieved the realignment of political parties that he sought.

Some historians have suggested that the court-packing scheme created the Conservative coalition, but that argument is too simple.[175] A better answer would be that it was achieved by the New Deal itself. We have seen how George and other Democrats began slowly distancing themselves from it well before 1937. George, the reader will remember, first openly opposed the New Deal in 1935–1936, with his open opposition to the Wage and Hours Act, the Guffey Coal Act, and the housing legislation of 1935–

[174]Ibid., 123–24.

[175]Clapper, *Watching the World*, 51–52.

1936.[176] The court-packing move was simply the final straw.

Another consequence of the Conservative Coalition was the work on a "Conservative Manifesto." It was technically bipartisan, but in reality, it was a Republican proposal offered by conservative Democrats. It was not a particularly successful movement, but it was another warning sign for Roosevelt that he could no longer send a new program to Congress to be rubber-stamped. The chief architect of the manifesto was Walter George's close friend, Democratic Senator Josiah Bailey of North Carolina. There seems to have been talk behind the scenes, but a formal meeting to draft the document occurred on December 2, 1937, and in several days afterward. Republican senators John Townshend and Arthur Vandenberg were in the group, but it was composed largely of conservative Democrats such as Harry Byrd, Carter Glass, "Cotton Ed" Smith, Frederick Van Nuys, Copeland, and a number of others. The group drafted a manifesto that made five demands the group felt would energize business and get the economy moving again: Tax reduction, a balanced budget, curb on labor violence, promotion of free enterprise and states' rights.[177] At a meeting, a document was drafted calling for these principles, and the members tried quietly to gather support. Less than two weeks later, as members quietly tried to gather support for their demands, newspapers broke the story leaked to them by Senator McNary of Oregon, the Republican leader. Most involved members ran for cover and few people ever signed it. Senator Bailey did read it on the floor of the Senate, but in general the whole thing fell flat.[178] It was, nevertheless, a symptom of the mood of the conservative Democrats, who made up a large chunk of the party's representation in Congress. The Civil War and Reconstruction was still too fresh in Southerners' minds to bolt the party as many did in the 1960s and the decades after. As one journalist put it, "The [Democratic] Old Guard is after the scalp of the New Deal and *not* of the Democratic Party."[179] That was still decades away.

Roosevelt's handling of the court-packing imbroglio seriously damaged his popularity, but it did not cripple him or his presidency. Still, it was obvious he was wounded to some degree. The fight over the issue was the "Stalingrad" of his presidency; he still had a lot of support, but the court fight

---

[176]Cited in Fagin, "Franklin D. Roosevelt", 50; Chandler, *Natural Superiority of Southern Politicians*, 205.

[177]Jarman, "Taxpayer's Senator," 41; Schlessinger, *The Coming of the New Deal*, 503; Hooper, "The Purge," 158; Leuchtenburg, *Franklin Roosevelt and the New Deal*, 239.

[178]*New York Times*, December 16, 1937, 15:7.

[179]Dunn, 90–91.

showed that he could be beaten and that he did not have a solid Democratic Party behind him ready to do his bidding. He would be further hurt by the recession of 1937–1938, known as the "Roosevelt Recession," which largely erased gains made since 1935. Industrial production had fallen 33 percent. National income declined 13 percent, and manufacturing employment decreased by 23 percent.[180] Much of the old despair returned, and it could not be blamed on Hoover this time. Roosevelt's arrogance and the recession, combined with political bungling in the form of an attempted purge of conservative Democrats the next year, would reap a bitter harvest in the 1938 congressional elections.

[180]Allen, "The New Deal Fights for Its Life," 35–36.

4

THE BARNESVILLE MANIFESTO, AUGUST 1938

I ruined their country, their home, and then,
I placed the blame on "Nine Old Men."
—Roosevelt on his admission to Hell (political jingle)[1]

It was President Franklin Roosevelt, who made me a Republican overnight, back in 1938.
—Macon Attorney T. Baldwin Martin[2]

purge…fr. L. *purgare,* to cleanse, purify… **1b** to make free of physical impurities: make clean by removing whatever is foreign, soiling or superfluous…**c.** to make morally or spiritually clean. **d.** get rid of (as disloyal or suspect elements from a group)[3]

In the election of 1936, Franklin Roosevelt's landslide clearly demonstrated the love of an adoring nation, for he had produced a whirlwind of legislation that had lifted the United States from black despair onto a road of hope. He had inspired a nation with confidence, and there was abundant evidence that the economy was improving. Ford Motor Company was producing as many cars as it had been making in 1928, and unemployment was far below the levels it had been when he had taken office four years before. Although the US Supreme Court had declared much of the New Deal unconstitutional, Roosevelt had fought on with a Second New Deal, and to millions of Americans, he was a messiah. There are indeed few men whose egos could handle such electoral adulation. It would later destroy several presidents who would come to think that their victories enabled them to run roughshod over the laws and Constitution of the American nation. Without World War II, perhaps it would have destroyed Roosevelt as well.

---

[1]"Rejection," series 1, box 2, f. 16, Hardwick papers.

[2]Bryant, "Walter F. George," 5.

[3]*Webster's Third New International Dictionary*, ed. Philip B. Gove (Springfield, MA: Merriam Webster, 1986) 1845.

There were, nevertheless, rumblings of desertion within his own party. Increasingly by 1936, Democrats were abandoning him on such questions as the minimum wage, labor reform, and government reorganization. This segment of his own party was beginning to call his programs "socialism" and voting against them. In many cases, if indeed these Democrats had voted for the final piece of legislation, they had also voted for every Republican amendment to gut it.

Two of the first to jump ship were Walter George and Josiah Bailey of North Carolina. When George began to have doubts is impossible to say, but Senator Bailey was, by spring 1935, accusing the Roosevelt Administration of following policies "which will change the United States from a republic into a federal soviet,"[4] and writing condemnatory articles like Bailey's "Bricks without Straw: Fabian Socialism in the United States."[5] These vitriolic denunciations enabled Bailey to be reelected in 1936 by a majority of 330,000 votes in the Democratic primary, 60,000 votes more than North Carolina's Democratic nominee for governor that year. In a letter to George in November after his victory, the North Carolina senator observed that "my somewhat conservative course" had not been a "detriment as a candidate." Curiously noting that the "conservative leadership" was passing to the Democrats (he must have meant Southern Democrats), he added, "I think you are better prepared to guide us than anyone else."[6]

George and Bailey both served on the Democratic Party platform committee that year, and Roosevelt had given the committee a proposed draft that called for a constitutional amendment on wages and hours. These two members immediately struck a sentence from the plank abolishing the no-man's land between state power and federal power, proclaiming that it is "everyone's land, that is the land of rights reserved to the people" by the federal system. Later, in a three-way phone conversation among George, Roosevelt, and Jimmy Byrnes, Roosevelt was rather jocular in his discussion of George's and Bailey's removal of this effort to limit states' rights, stating that they had "dealt with it like Philadelphia lawyers."[7]

This action was George's first openly defiant move against Roosevelt. George knew that other moves would follow. He also guessed that his con-

---

[4]See unidentified clipping attached to J. W. Bailey to Stella L. Thorpe, May 20, 1936, box 474 (54-F), f. 1934 August–1935 July, Bailey papers.

[5]Ibid.

[6]Sen. J. Bailey to WFG, November 18, 1936, box 475 (54-F), f. Polit. Nat. 1936 October–December, Bailey papers.

[7]J. Bailey to Burton K. Wheeler, April 15, 1936, f. 1936, January–July, Bailey papers.

servative stance could not help his reelection in 1938, not because at this point he thought that he would catalyze overt Rooseveltian opposition, but because he knew that Roosevelt was still extremely popular in Georgia; opposing Roosevelt's wishes would probably hurt him with the electorate. Roosevelt's overwhelming victory in November did not mute George's stance, however. "In Georgia, I am sure of the course I should follow to be reelected," he wrote his friend Bailey in late fall 1936. He added, "I am not quite willing to do it." George's main concern at this point was Roosevelt's support of the minimum wage bill, which George had opposed and which had been defeated.[8] At this point, George had no idea that something much greater would drive a bigger wedge between him and the popular president.

With all of his popularity, Roosevelt could not see how "nine old men," his derogatory metaphor for the Supreme Court, could thwart his administration, and with the Republican minority reduced to eighty-nine Republicans in the house and only sixteen in the Senate in the 75th Congress, Roosevelt decided to go after the court with his famous court-packing plan, which would give him the right to appoint one justice for each Supreme Court member over the age of seventy with a maximum of six, thus placing more liberal members on the court.

What Roosevelt could never have guessed is that the serious opposition to the proposal would come largely from within his own party. Initially fifteen Southern Democratic senators did endorse the bill, with four (Andrews of Florida, Bankhead of Alabama, Overton of North Carolina, and Russell of Georgia) taking no position. Several were entirely supportive but most who declared for it were unenthusiastic, and many were like Senator Pat Harrison of Mississippi, who tepidly endorsed it and then faded permanently into the background. Senator Joe Robinson of Arkansas, the Democratic VP candidate with Al Smith in 1928, supported it because he wanted a Supreme Court appointment. When Senator Bankhead did finally come out for it, he continued to say in private that what was needed was a constitutional amendment. Vice President Garner avoided the issue by simply leaving Washington for Texas.[9]

Senator Millard Tydings (D-Maryland) hosted a barnstorming dinner session at his home in Washington, and this group became the steering committee for the anti-court packing fight. At the meeting were Walter George, Tydings, Wheeler, and a few other conservative Democrats. The men picked Wheeler to lead it because they thought it would look better if a

---

[8]Ibid., WFG to J. W. Bailey, November 20, 1936.

[9]Tindall, *The Emergence*, 621–22.

liberal was in the vanguard of the opposition.[10] Senator Peter G. Gerry of Rhode Island was the whip.[11] The group met often to plan strategy, and it was around this committee that all opposition congealed.

Walter George had formally come out against the bill less than two weeks after its introduction. Having been a judge himself, he was a great believer that courts had a certain sacred aura about them, a view that led him not to attack with any vigor the 1954 *Brown v. Board of Education* decision sixteen years later, a lack of action that helped seal the fate of his political career two years later. In criticizing the bill to the *New York Times* in mid-February, he opined that "a subservient judiciary is worse than no judiciary at all."[12] It was true that the Constitution did not specify a set number of judges for the Supreme Court, but George questioned whether a stable government could "long survive without…an independent, uncontrolled court,"[13] and he feared the dangers in a judicial system that could be controlled to approve the "programs and policies, however wise and right" of any political party in power.[14]

Although little of his Senate work had been in judiciary matters, George was regarded throughout the country as a leading constitutional attorney,[15] and even Yale law professors had been for some time quoting his opinions to their students.[16] Although his actions, or lack of them, show otherwise, George came to be regarded as the leader of the opposition to the court-packing movement.[17] He had not, curiously, even been one of the first to attack Roosevelt's movements, primarily because he was up for reelection in 1938.[18] He spoke in the Senate on the issue only six or seven times, and his comments, the *Congressional Record* shows, were usually in the form of questions, usually challenging the bill on arcane points of constitutional law.[19] In one of his few debates on the matter, George possibly even comes

---

[10]Wheeler was strongly encouraged by his wife, who worked in a supportive role of the movement. Roosevelt caller her "the Lady Macbeth of the Court Fight" (Cole, *Senator Gerald P. Nye*, 214).

[11]John Moore, 130, Electives A to Z.

[12]*New York Times*, February 17, 1938, in Thomas, "Roosevelt vs. George," 6.

[13]*Atlanta Constitution*, July 20, 1938, cited in Fossett, "The Impact of the New Deal on Georgia Politics, 1933–1941," 278.

[14]Ibid., 279.

[15]Thomas, "Roosevelt vs. George," 6.

[16]James MacClamoch to WFG, 16 August 1938, box 476, f. 1938, June–August, Bailey papers.

[17]Thomas, "Roosevelt vs. George," 7.

[18]Patterson, *Congressional Conservatism and the New Deal*, 99.

[19]See *CR*, 75/1, 1285, 1649, 1720, 2828–29, 7044, 7381.

out second best in an exchange with Senator McKellar of Tennessee, a supporter of the measure. McKellar argued that the actions of the executive and the legislative branches were essentially superior to whatever the judicial might do and somewhat boxed George into a corner, making the point that the Constitution does not give the Supreme Court the power to abolish in effect legislation produced by these two branches.[20]

McKellar was indeed correct in asserting that the Constitution does not expressly give the Supreme Court the right to rule laws "unconstitutional," but it had begun to do so in the early years of America's history, and by use it had in effect become "constitutional." George continued to argue that it was Congress's duty to pass laws "in pursuance of the supreme law found in the Constitution," and therefore it was the court's purpose to determine if Congress had superseded its constitutional authority with any given piece of legislation.[21] George's major contribution to the court fight came near the end of February 1937 when he made an American Bar Association-sponsored national radio address, which drew wide attention. In it, George presented the most detailed, legalistic attack on the court bill yet. Although expressing the highest regard for Roosevelt, he condemned his efforts to create a subservient judiciary, and added, not completely truthfully, that "no responsible voice in any quarter was raised for the legislation now demanded of Congress," a slap, intended or otherwise, at the members of Congress who supported it. He criticized the president for attacking Democrats who opposed his shortcuts to reach "the [party's] worthy objectives," and he continued by lecturing the American public saying, "Conditions never demand abandonment of tested principle," and that an independent court was "a safeguard of liberty."[22] It was rumored that in the original draft of the speech, George called Roosevelt "a traitor to the Democratic party," a supposition that is highly unlikely given George's personality and personal regard for Roosevelt at the time. The comment was supposedly deleted before the broadcast, the rumor went, but many reporters published it with the statement included.[23]

Judge Mark Dunahoo, who worked in Washington for years in various capacities and for various members of Congress, felt that the speech in itself stopped the bill. "But with that forty-minute speech, Walter George killed

[20]Ibid., 1284–86.

[21]Ibid.; see also Thomas, "Roosevelt vs. George," 7.

[22]Speech in the appendix of the *CR*, 75/1, 362.

[23]See *Atlanta Constitution,* August 13, 1938, in Fossett, "The Impact of the New Deal on Georgia Politics, 1933–1941," 278.

that bill so dead," he remembered years later. "When it was finally voted on, they defeated that bill something terrible."[24] Dunahoo has most likely overstated the impact, but in certain quarters, rightly or wrongly, George's influence was perceived to have stopped the bill. In blurring of recollections, it could have been this speech that gave George the reputation of having led the whole court fight. Often in politics, the truth is not important. What is important is what is *believed* to be the truth, and George emerged from the speech in the minds of many as the major figure that caused its defeat.

The bill was soon returned to the Judiciary Committee, where on July 22, it was rejected again as "a needless, futile and utterly dangerous abandonment of constitutional principles." Twenty Senate Democrats accepted the committee's majority vote, ten of them from outside the Southern bloc. Even Vice President Garner had worked against it behind the scenes. Twenty years later, his son, Heard George, remembered that the court fight was when his father really broke with the Roosevelt administration, but as we have seen, George had already begun to join with the conservative Southerners in Congress to form an anti-New Deal bloc that looked with horror on the latest parts of the Roosevelt program.[25]

There followed curiously for years continued support for the Democratic Party in local elections, while the South began to shift its popular votes to the Republican party in presidential contests, beginning with Eisenhower's carrying four Southern states in 1952 (Virginia, Tennessee, Texas, and Florida) and six in 1956 (those four plus Kentucky and West Virginia). That Nixon carried four of these (Virginia, Florida, Tennessee, and Kentucky) and lost two more in very close tallies (South Carolina and Texas, the latter of which may well have been stolen) is evidence that Eisenhower's breaking of the Solid South was not just due to his personal popularity. By the presidential elections of 1968, every one of the Southern states except Texas denied its electoral votes to the Democratic Party.[26]

By 1938, Byrd, Carter Glass, Bailey, "Cotton Ed" Smith, and Walter George were openly working with the Republican minority to strangle administration programs.[27] As a result of their work, no major piece of Roosevelt's legislation passed Congress between the court imbroglio and the bombing of Pearl Harbor, save for the creation of Social Security, resurrec-

[24]Judge Mark Dunahoo, oral history, 49, Russell Library.

[25]Fossett, "The Impact of the New Deal on Georgia Politics, 1933–1941," 278.

[26]Five states (Louisiana, Arkansas, Mississippi, Alabama, and Georgia) gave their electoral votes to third party presidential candidate George C. Wallace.

[27]Carlton and Coclanis, eds., *Confronting Southern Poverty in the Great Depression*, 14.

tion of the draft, and the Lend-Lease bill, which passed probably only because Walter George led the fight for it. With the gain of eighty-one seats for the Republicans in the House and eight in the Senate in the 1938 elections, the coalition became even stronger.[28] Disrupted by the wartime unity, during which little social legislation reached the halls of Congress anyway, this "unholy alliance" would last into the 1970s, when conservative Southern Democrats began to be replaced by candidates who ran as Republicans, not just Democrats that voted with them, and the abandonment of the Southern conservatives of the Democratic Party turned what remained into something politically like today's Democratic Party.[29]

The formation of this opposition would have been impossible for Roosevelt not to have notices, and having gotten his way since 1933 and having won in 1936 with the greatest presidential landslide in history, he did not take kindly to his defeats, especially since they came at the hands of members of his own party. Jim Farley, at one point his closest adviser who was playing both sides and had done his share of threatening conservative Democrats, recorded in his memoirs that he had advised Roosevelt "to bury party grudges," but as the defeats mounted up, Roosevelt fumed against members of his own party that he blamed for "his bucket of bitterness," and he began to drop hints to members of Congress that the traitors "would be sorry yet."[30] Out of his anger, Roosevelt's famous purge of conservative Democrats across the nation was born, and Walter F. George would receive the greatest blow of his attack

The prime motivation of the purge was most certainly revenge. These members of Roosevelt's own party had scuttled his program at a time when his powers seemed unassailable, and this *lese majesté* could not go unpunished. Roosevelt probably wished to make the Democratic party more liberal, especially since the Southern Democrats, who were generally more conservative, controlled the chairs of most of the committees that could block or weaken legislation. Since after 1936 many of these had begun to abandon the New Deal, it was essential to be rid of the conservative Southern Democrats. Roosevelt saw a purge as a means of preserving the New Deal since the Supreme Court, having seen a spate of resignations after 1937, turned

[28]Whereas non-Southern Democrats would frequently side with the coalition, it would be the Southern Democrats, usually conservative, who would be the core of the Democrats in it. See Patterson, "A Conservative Coalition," 758–59.

[29]Robertson, *Sly and Able*, 280.

[30]Farley, *Jim Farley's Story*, 93–96.

more favorably to his reforms.[31] The only opposition to him now, except for the weak Republican minority, lay in the renegade members of his own party.[32]

Nevertheless, the same polls showed that his interference would not help defeat the apostates, with only 20 percent stating that a Roosevelt endorsement would make them more inclined to vote for a candidate,[33] and an astounding 76 percent of Democrats nationally and 81 percent in the South opposed a purge in 1937.[34] Roosevelt must have ignored these numbers if he ever saw them, and Farley, who had his eye on the presidential nomination in 1940, and who would later change his tune, must have as well. He told a *New York Times* reporter in August 1937 that these anti-court senators will "have a lot of difficulty in explaining to the voters their opposition to the administration,"[35] a not too thinly veiled threat. Other party powers avoided any involvement, and when the time came, even Farley took off to Alaska, Ed Flynn secluded himself at Lake Tahoe, and Vice President Garner left Washington for his home in Uvalde, Texas, refusing to join Roosevelt when his train came through town.[36] Nevertheless, with Roosevelt's blessing, an "elimination committee" came into being composed of Harry Hopkins, James Roosevelt, Tom Corcoran, Benjamin Cohen, and Harold Ickes. These men encouraged Roosevelt to attempt an "Era of Vengeance," which court-packing opponents termed a "purge" after a term Joseph Stalin used for the cleansing of the Communist Party in Russia.[37]

Roosevelt had developed this attitude even before 1938. As early as on a fishing trip to Florida in 1937, Roosevelt spoke indiscreetly at a small dinner that he hosted about the possibility of "going out to defeat reactionary senators" next year, especially mentioning George and "Cotton Ed" Smith of South Carolina.[38] In frequent meetings and conferences early in 1938, Roosevelt often mentioned the senators that he wanted to see defeated.[39] Therefore, it is not surprising that as early as fall 1937, there were strong rumors that Roosevelt would try to purge those who had opposed his court-

[31]Hooper, "The Purge," 177.

[32]Coode, "Georgia Congressmen and the New Deal, 1933–1938," 230.

[33]Fagin, "Franklin D. Roosevelt", 179.

[34]Cantril, ed., *Gauging Public Opinion*, 933, cited in Hooper, "The Purge," 9.

[35]*New York Times*, 26 August 1937, cited in Fagin, "Franklin D. Roosevelt," 24.

[36]Fagin, "Franklin D. Roosevelt," 186.

[37]Stokes, *Chip Off My Shoulder*, 485–87.

[38]Pepper, *Eyewitness to a Century*, 66–67.

[39]Farley, *Jim Farley's Story*, 133. He reiterated to Pepper the need to defeat George in 1938 (Pepper, *Eyewitness to a Century*, 175).

packing plan, even before the "Conservative Manifesto" was published.

The defeat of the court bill due to the defection of Democrats fueled his desire to make the renegades pay, and in a statement of the court-packing failure, he openly denounced the treasonous Democrats.[40] A purge supporter, Senator Joseph Guffey of Pennsylvania, was not reeled in when he denounced the anti-court bill senators in a radio address as "ingrates" and made it plain that the administration was "bitterly angry at all deserters."[41] Roosevelt underscored his support by writing Guffey a note congratulating him "for saying vigorously things that needed to be said."[42] Two of his potential victims, Walter George and "Cotton Ed" Smith of South Carolina, could not have helped but notice that Georgia governor Ed Rivers and South Carolina governor Olin Johnston had lunched at the White House. Shortly afterward, Governor Johnston announced he would run against Smith. Governor Rivers, however, told the press he would decide what he would do by the first of June.[43]

Although Roosevelt had only openly mentioned Senator Joseph O'Mahoney of Wyoming in his denunciation of the renegade Democrats, it was not difficult to make a list of targets in the 1938 elections: Bennett Champ Clark of Missouri, Pat McCarran of Nevada, "Cotton Ed" Smith of South Carolina, Alva Adams of Colorado, Millard Tydings of Maryland, Guy Gillette of Iowa, Frederick Van Nuys of Indiana, Augustine Lonergan of Connecticut, and Walter George. All had opposed the court bill.[44] If Roosevelt could be able to defeat even a number of them, it would send a clear message to the others up for reelection in subsequent years, like Bailey of North Carolina, and Byrd and Glass of Virginia. Like any good politician, Roosevelt did not try to defeat those whom he believed he could not beat, and he did not try to defeat anyone in the spring primaries. He avoided a fight with Bennett Champ Clark, whose father's machine was still in full vigor, and when he had been unable to find a suitable challenger for Augus-

[40]Alsop and Catledge, *The 168 Days*, 168, 280, cited in Thomas, "Roosevelt vs. George," 9.

[41]*New York Times*, August 21, 1936, cited in Thomas, "Roosevelt vs. George," 11. On the Senate floor, Burton Wheeler, whom Guffey had mentioned, invited him to come to Montana and campaign against him (Fagin, "Franklin D. Roosevelt," 23).

[42]Roosevelt to Guffey, August 21, 1936, box 451, FDR Library, cited in Fagin, "Franklin D. Roosevelt," 23.

[43]*New York Times*, May 17, 1938, cited in Thomas, "Roosevelt vs. George," 26.

[44]Thomas, "Roosevelt vs. George," 14; Fagin, "Franklin D. Roosevelt," 39.

tine Lonergan of Connecticut, he gave up there.[45]

Roosevelt himself made his first preliminary salvo in a trip to the West in fall 1937, inviting certain "friends" to board his train, sending a strong message to those he did not. In passing through Nebraska, he blatantly snubbed Senator Edward Burke by not inviting him to join him, and in Wyoming, he had not invited O'Mahoney to join him either. The latter was in Chicago anyway, but rushed back in order to join a "Citizens' Welcoming Committee." With O'Mahoney present, he gave a foretaste to Walter George of what awaited him when he attacked those who paid lip service to the New Deal but not their votes.[46] In Montana, Roosevelt invited all sorts of politicians to join him except Burton Wheeler, who handled the insult by wiring a regret to the president for his inability to be there.[47] On returning to Washington, Roosevelt was mindful of what he had done. He had been warmly received everywhere, and he logically felt that the people would now join him in punishing his enemies.[48] He gloated to Farley, "They'll know I was there—let 'em begin eating their votes now."[49] Therefore, not surprisingly by January 1938, open stories, no longer rumors of an impending purge were sweeping Washington.[50] Not all were pleased, and one critic called it "high school girl revenge."[51] Petty or not, Walter George must have been aware that he was on the list for extinction.

In these early months of 1938, Roosevelt generally stayed in the background but allowed his minions to do the interfering, but late in March, the White House announced that Roosevelt's support in the coming primaries depended on loyalty to the New Deal[52] He was buoyed by the win of Phi Beta Kappa key-wearing New Deal supporting Congressman Lister Hill, who had announced his intention to run for the Senate by telegram from Paris, France. Hill buried by almost two to one a typical Southern demagogue, Thomas Heflin, for Hugo Black's seat when the later was appointed to the Supreme Court.[53] Roosevelt had given Hill some modest help, and

[45]Lonergan was nevertheless defeated in November by a Republican (Hooper, "The Purge," 21–24).

[46]Farley, *Jim Farley's Story*, 115–20.

[47]Wheeler, *Yankee from the West*, 342.

[48]Fagin, "Franklin D. Roosevelt," 41.

[49]Farley, *Jim Farley's Story*, 115–20.

[50]Timmons, *Garner of Texas*, 230, cited in Fagin, "Franklin D. Roosevelt," 96.

[51]Johnston, "President Tamer," 8.

[52]*New York Times*, March 25, 1938, cited in Thomas, "Roosevelt vs. George," 17.

[53] 88,401 to 48,467 (Hooper, "The Purge," 51; Coode, "Georgia Congressmen and the New Deal, 1933–1938," 230; Michie and Ryhlick, *Dixie Demagogues*, 153–56).

although Hill would probably have won anyway, Roosevelt attributed the win to his influence. This emboldened the president to stir in the Florida Senate primary in May where strong New Dealer Claude Pepper was opposing Congressman Mark Wilcox, a New Dealer himself but more conservative. Roosevelt authorized Tom Corcoran to use whatever federal government assistance possible to help him, and his son James Roosevelt publicly endorsed Pepper when visiting Joseph P. Kennedy's home in Palm Beach. Pepper crushed Wilcox without a runoff in a large turnout.[54] This victory was attributed to the release of the wage and hours bill from the committee where it had lain dormant.[55] That same month Farley endorsed New Deal governor and Senate candidate George Earle of Pennsylvania, and he won the primary.[56]

These victories gave Roosevelt an inflated notion of his influence in state politics, and merely encouraged his desire to punish the traitors.[57] Then the New Deal took several hits. Moderate Scott Lucas defeated the Democratic machine candidate in Illinois, and when Guy Gillette was renominated in Iowa without Roosevelt's interference, the president must have decided it was time to go public.[58] On June 24, Roosevelt openly declared war on the conservatives in his party in one of his fireside chats. He gave his listeners a lesson in political terms by defining "liberal" and "conservative," and he called the conservative Democrats "copperheads," who he said would "give up the fight *in the middle of the fight* [his italics]." He went on to say that he would give the liberals of his party any help possible, including speaking for liberals in the party primaries.[59] Roosevelt, however, either ignored or did not notice that there was a very negative public reaction to his proposed purge.[60] Roosevelt left on a train one might called the "Purge Special" on July 5, 1938, headed west. In California, he was to board a ship, fish in the Pacific, return through the Panama Canal, and land in Pensacola, Florida. From here, he would board a train for the journey to Washington, stopping briefly at the Little White House at Warm Springs, Georgia.[61] In what was billed as a vacation, Roosevelt's zigzag trip was designed to pass through

[54]*New York Times*, May 4, 1938, cited in Fagin, "Franklin D. Roosevelt," 134; Shannon, "Presidential Politics in the South, I," 151.

[55]"Aunt Mary's Applecart," 15.

[56]Fagin, "Franklin D. Roosevelt," 111. He went down to defeat in November.

[57]Pepper, *Eyewitness to a Century*, 73.

[58]Leuchtenburg, *Franklin Roosevelt and the New Deal*, 267

[59]F. D. Roosevelt papers, VII, 391, in Thomas, "Roosevelt vs. George," 42.

[60]*New York Times*, June 26, 1938, cited in Thomas, "Roosevelt vs. George," 43.

[61]For details, see, Patterson's, *Congressional Conservatism and the New Deal.*

various states where there were liberal-conservative primary contests in which he would pronounce his blessing on the candidate of his choice. He felt confident that his actions would reform the Democratic Party.

His first stop was Covington, Kentucky, where in a public setting, he gave a foretaste of his attack on Walter George. He first leaked a letter praising Alben Barkley, and then in the state he more openly endorsed Barkley by stating that although he considered Governor A. B. "Happy" Chandler "a friend of mine," he praised the New Deal supporter Barkley, telling Kentuckians that it would be "foolish to throw away his seniority." He further informed the voters that Chandler had been able to balance the state budget only because Barkley had brought home several million dollars of federal aid. Despite statements that he was not stirring in the primary, this thinly-veiled endorsement was supplemented in stops in Louisville and Bowling Green with references to "my old friend Alben Barkley."[62] Roosevelt then gave another casual endorsement to Senator Robert Buckley of Ohio over his opponent, former governor George White, before turning south to Arkansas, where he again casually endorsed the reelection of Senator Hattie Caraway, by calling her "a very old friend and a very good friend of yours" and shunning her opponent, Congressman John McClellan.[63] From a distance, he gave the nod to Jerry O'Connell in Montana against the Wheeler machine. In Oklahoma, with both Senator Elmer Thomas and his challenger Governor William Marland together with him, he praised Thomas for his extensive river projects. In Texas, where his own Vice President John Garner declined to board the Roosevelt train, he failed to recognize Senator Tom Connally when he cited the dignitaries on the train platform, and he took the opportunity to humiliate Connally by announcing the appointment of Governor James Allred to a federal judgeship, when everyone knew that Connally had been promoting someone else. Although he did not actually enter their districts, he praised Congressmen Lyndon Johnson, William McFarland, and ultra-liberal Maury Maverick, who had cast the sole Southern vote for the anti-lynching bill, and he snubbed Congressmen Hatton Summers, the chair of the House Judiciary Committee, and ultra-conservative Martin Dies.[64] Zigzagging through Colorado, where anti-New

[62]Not to be left out, the brassy Chandler pushed himself next to Roosevelt several times and accepted for himself applause that was intended for the president (Address of the president, 1938, Henry Kannee Official Reporter, PPF 1820, FDRL, cited in Fagin, "Franklin D. Roosevelt," 187; see also 205).

[63]Burns, *Roosevelt: The Lion and the Fox*, 361, cited in Hooper, "The Purge," 117.

[64]Fagin, "Franklin D. Roosevelt," 189–93; Byrnes, *Speaking Frankly*, 101; Hooper, "The Purge," 145–52.

Deal Democrat Alva Adams had weak opposition, Roosevelt declined to endorse his opponent, thus avoiding a defeat.[65] He likewise did little for pro-New Deal Albert Hilliard against popular anti-New Deal Senator Pat McCarran, feeling that he would be unable to help him much. In California, Roosevelt warmly embraced Senator William McAdoo, Woodrow Wilson's son-in-law, against Sherman Downey, a former Republican and big supporter of old-age pensions, who had switched parties and was making a serious challenge to the senator. In San Diego, Roosevelt boarded the *USS. Houston*, on which he would be at sea for three weeks during the primary season.

To some journalists, Roosevelt's "endorsement special" was a pale edition of what they were expecting. Former New Dealer Raymond Moley wrote in *Newsweek*, "What threatened to be a conquering march of a Tamerlane turned out to be the good-will trip of an Edward VIII."[66] Knowing he was returning through Georgia, pundits began speculation about what he might try there, but it is understandable that Walter George, who had often praised the president, would not expect Roosevelt to be too heavy-handed.[67] Fortunately for him, he was to get some warning in time to prepare.

So far, Roosevelt could rationalize that his score card was a good one. By the time that Roosevelt arrived in Pensacola, Barkley had defeated Chandler in Kentucky, Hattie Caraway edged out McClellan in Arkansas, Senator Thomas won in Oklahoma, and Senator Robert Buckley won renomination in Ohio.[68] However, none of those on whom he placed his blessing against incumbents was victorious, and incumbent Maury Maverick was defeated. So was Senator James Pope of Idaho, who had rejected Roosevelt's help. What is more, each of the victorious incumbents he endorsed would have probably won anyway (with the possible exception of Hattie Caraway), so Roosevelt's meddling had essentially no effect. In fact, it may have been counterproductive. In November, in Pennsylvania, Connecticut, Idaho, and Ohio, the Roosevelt-blessed Democratic nominees were defeated in November by Republicans.

George's role in the court fight, as well as his other opposition to more recent New Deal measurers, made George a certainty to be a victim of Roo-

[65]*Time*, 32/4 (July 25, 1938): 7, cited in Fagin, "Franklin D. Roosevelt,", 194–95.

[66]Raymond Moley, "Perspective," *Newsweek* 12/4 (July 25, 1938): 40, cited in Hooper, "The Purge," 152.

[67]Fagin, "Franklin D. Roosevelt," 200.

[68]Only to be defeated in November by Republican Robert Taft, son of the former president.

sevelt's "purge special." When the post of Collector of Internal Revenue for Georgia opened that year, George and Russell each submitted a different nominee, and Roosevelt picked Russell's.[69] "We've got to beat George, Jim," Roosevelt told Jim Farley in one of their conversations, because it would serve as "a lasting lesson" to the Southern bloc to get into line.[70] Farley claimed in his memoirs that he advised against taking on George because no one could beat him, but Roosevelt seemed adamant. He told Georgian Chip Robert of the need to defeat Georgia's senior senator, and when Robert asked why, Roosevelt replied, "It's as simple as this. Senator George's position in the Senate is such that anything he advocates, you can count on at least forty senators going with him. I can't pass legislation without him, and I cannot depend on him being with us," adding that "we've got to get someone who'll think our way."[71] George was later told as much by people in the administration. In writing a graduate student working on the purge in 1952, George told him that friends around Roosevelt felt that the New Deal "could not hope to accomplish certain so-called reforms" as long as George remained in the Senate.[72] By late spring 1938, rumor was rife all over the country that Roosevelt would go after George, for Roosevelt had openly told too many people of his intentions "to make it perfectly clear where I stand when I come through Georgia in August."[73] "I'm going to endorse someone [other than George] if I have to pick my tenant farmer, Moore," he told Farley with grim determination. Powerful Jimmy Byrnes, who wore many hats in his public career (senator, Supreme Court justice, secretary of state, governor), remembered that many knew of Roosevelt's desire to get George, adding, "I only regretted I could do so little to help George."[74] Apparently the stories got so bad that Senator Wheeler of Montana, with a keen sense of prophecy, told the *New York Times* that Roosevelt's interference in the Georgia senatorial primary was "a rule or ruin move that may lead to a divided party in 1940."[75]

One wonders why Roosevelt, who had clearly avoided tackling anti-New Deal Democrats whom he could not defeat, thought he could beat

[69]*Atlanta Constitution,* August 22, 1937, cited in Fossett, "The Impact of the New Deal on Georgia Politics, 1933–1941," 281.

[70]Farley, *Jim Farley's Story*, 122.

[71]Anderson, *Wild Man from Sugar Creek*, 174, cites his 1971 interview with Robert.

[72]George to Thomas, May 3, 1952, in Thomas, "Roosevelt vs. George," 51.

[73]Roosevelt to L. W. "Chip" Robert, June 13, 1938, cited in Fagin, "Franklin D. Roosevelt," 180.

[74]Byrnes, *All in One Lifetime*, 102.

[75]*New York Times*, June 2, 1938, cited in Thomas, "Roosevelt vs. George," 36.

George. Most certainly a major factor was the amount of time he had spent in Georgia at Warm Springs for treatment for his polio. He had even bought a farm there on which he had a home called "The Little White House." He had often reminded Georgians that he paid taxes in their state, and that Georgia was his second home. Georgia had early supported Roosevelt in 1932 at a rally in Atlanta in that campaign, which one historian has called "one of the wildest demonstrations ever witnessed in Georgia."[76] Moreover, he had carried Georgia in 1936 255,364 votes to 36,942 for Landon, taking 157 of the 159 counties.[77] In a "presidential" preference primary held in Seminole County, Georgia, by the local party organization on March 4, 1936, Roosevelt had won by six to one over all opposition.[78] Moreover, we have seen that George was very reserved for a Southern politician of his day. He had little sense of humor and rarely spoke in the Senate unless he had something to say.[79] Someone like that in the South with its usual flamboyant politicians, Roosevelt likely figured, should be easy pickings.

One might well ask just how openly guilty George was of being anti-New Deal. During the campaign, George said in a speech in Atlanta on August 20 that he had voted for 98 percent of the legislation passed by Congress since Roosevelt's inauguration in 1933,[80] and in Statesboro on September 1, he claimed that he had supported 95 percent of the New Deal legislation.[81] The former claim may well be correct, since much of what passes Congress is not particularly partisan, but the second claim is not. Whereas he had voted 100 percent for New Deal legislation in 1933, George had voted for only thirty-four of the forty-four pieces of "New Deal" legislation since then, most of the votes against coming after 1935 as he and other conservatives soured on the Roosevelt Revolution.[82] Among the latter were the Wagner Housing bill, the Wages and Hours bill, the government

[76]Coode, "Georgia Congressmen and the New Deal, 1933–1938," 13.

[77]*Kaltenborn 1940 Campaign Handout* (Chicago: Rand McNally, 1940), series 1, box 1, f. 19, Hardwick papers.

[78]Marion H. Allen to Marvin H. McIntyre, 3-4-36, DNC, OF 300, box 14, f. Ga., 1933–45, Roosevelt papers.

[79]Patterson, "A Conservative Coalition," 45, 188.

[80]George, *Addresses*, Atlanta, August 20, 1938, 10.

[81]Ibid., Statesboro, September 1, 1938, 19.

[82]Raymond Moley, "Perspective," *Newsweek* 12/4 (July 25, 1938) in Fossett, "The Impact of the New Deal on Georgia Politics, 1933–1941," 277; Zeigler, "Senator Walter George's 1938 Campaign," 333.

reorganization plan, and of course the Supreme Court plan.[83] George could argue that he had voted for New Deal legislation because he had voted for the bill in final form, but as we have seen, what he frequently did was support Republican amendments that weakened or gutted the legislation.[84] He had even opposed crop quotas for cotton and tobacco, which he freely admitted.[85] George, though, had used his influence to add $400 million dollars to the National Recovery Act to build roads in the US; he had voted for all liberal appointees to the Supreme Court; and he had supported the Farm Tenancy Act, which would help tenant farmers become farm owners. Roosevelt would accuse him of being a tool of the utilities and lacking sympathy for the common man, but he had voted for TVA, which the utilities had strongly opposed, the Social Security bill, and the Wagner Labor Relations Act. Moreover, he remained personally a strong supporter of FDR and had been one of the few politicians willing to defend him at the 1934 Georgia Democratic convention, when apostates criticized the president.[86]

Roosevelt's first choice as a candidate to oppose George, and by far the most powerful possibility, was Georgia governor Eurith Dickerson "Ed" Rivers, a strong New Dealer. As a matter of fact, he had seen the enactment of his own "little New Deal" in Georgia as governor, and when Roosevelt was in Gainesville, insulting Walter George by ignoring him in March, he asked Rivers to join him "for a confidential talk."[87] He suggested that he bring with him Clark Howell, the publisher of the *Atlanta Constitution*.[88] Four days of talks followed at Warm Springs, but Rivers left without making a commitment because Rivers feared that if he entered the race, Talmadge would pull out and support George.[89] He did, however, leave the door open for a possible run.

Roosevelt continued to court Rivers in Washington with the White House luncheon, where he was able to convince Governor Olin Johnson to take on conservative "Cotton Ed" Smith. Rivers still remained uncommitted though he did tell the press that he was not "shutting the door" on a race

---

[83]*New York Times*, August 12, 1938, in Thomas, "Roosevelt vs. George," 60.

[84]See a digest of George's voting record: OMG to Christie, August 12, 1938, f. 315, Gardner papers.

[85]George, *Addresses*, Vienna, July 4, 1938, 176-188.

[86]Ibid., Dublin, August 30, 1938, 14.

[87]Bernd, *Grass Roots Politics in Georgia*, 8.

[88]McIntyre to E. D. Rivers, March 21, 1938, FDR mss, Personal papers, f. 4966, cited in Hooper, "The Purge," 161.

[89]Rivers interview, *Atlanta Constitution*, 21 May 1938, 3, cited in Hooper, "The Purge," 173.

against George,[90] and that George "would have to give an accounting to the people."[91] He kept Roosevelt and the press guessing, thus preventing Roosevelt from encouraging other candidates.[92] Finally, a combination of factors ended the courtship. Roosevelt discovered that Rivers had Klan ties,[93] and Rivers's financial backers told him that they would back only George in the Senate race.[94] The *Atlanta Constitution* at the same time editorialized that the state's best interest would be served with the reelection of both Rivers as governor and George, "a brilliant spokesman for a large school of thought in Georgia," to the Senate. With a wide missing of the mark, the paper predicted that if a Rivers-George race did not occur, there would be a "quiet year in Georgia politics."[95] Faced with desertion on all sides, Rivers announced in conference on the elegant rooftop at Atlanta's Ansley Hotel on Saturday, May 28, that he would run for reelection as governor "and remain 100 per cent loyal to President Franklin D. Roosevelt."[96] Roosevelt's best potential candidate to defeat George had left the field with only seventy-two hours remaining to find a candidate before qualifying ended.

By this time political perennial Gene Talmadge had entered the race despite the fact that he had been crushed in a landslide two years before by Richard Russell. Roosevelt and other political operatives thought that a third candidate just might win because George and Talmadge would split the rural vote, thus enabling a candidate from either Rivers' machine or Russell's machine to win.[97] Roosevelt first tried to enlist Georgian Lawrence Wood "Chip" Robert Jr. to run. A prominent Atlanta businessman and former Georgia Tech football star who had been part of a Jewish and Catholic group that raised money for Roosevelt in 1932, Robert had been tapped to head the Wage and Price Administration. He was also the DNC Committeeman from Georgia. He was close to the Roosevelt family and a frequent visitor to Hyde Park.

Early in 1938, Roosevelt had invited him there and over breakfast said, "Chip, I've got a job for you to do. We've got to beat Senator George in

---

[90]*Atlanta Constitution*, April 1, 1938, cited in Thomas, "Roosevelt vs. George," 26.

[91]Ibid., cited in Fagin, "Franklin D. Roosevelt," 178.

[92]Thomas, "Roosevelt vs. George," 34.

[93]Farley, *Jim Farley's Story*, 133 34; *New York World Telegram*, 21 May 1938, cited in Hooper, "The Purge," 163; Cobb, "Not Gone, but Forgotten," 200.

[94]*Atlanta Constitution*, May 29, 1938, cited in Fagin, "Franklin D. Roosevelt," 178; Michie and Ryhlick, *Dixie Demagogues*, 190.

[95]*Atlanta Constitution*, May 17, 1938, cited in Thomas, "Roosevelt vs. George," 27.

[96]*Atlanta Constitution*, 29 May 1938, 1, cited in Hooper, "The Purge," 164.

[97]Ibid.

Georgia, and you're the logical one to run against him." In his memoirs, Herman Talmadge, who was not there, wrote that the stunned Robert acted as if "he had just been asked to...praise General Sherman's efforts on behalf of urban renewal."[98] Robert was one of George's friends and declined, adding that he "could not get elected dogcatcher in Georgia." Roosevelt laughed and then told him, "You're going to have to pick out the man to beat him." Robert felt he would have to accept this task for the president.[99]

Ultimately Robert was joined by Marvin McIntyre, Roosevelt's presidential secretary, who was going to Georgia to receive an honorary degree from the Atlanta Law School. Both men began contacting possible candidates. McIntyre spoke with a prominent lawyer in Atlanta and was rejected. On telling Roosevelt of his failure, Roosevelt said, "I don't want you to stop with him. My instructions are for you to get someone to run. I don't care if he isn't well-known," he said, then added with tremendous hubris, "I will elect him."[100] Robert did not have much better luck. Calling a number of prominent Roosevelt supporters, he was "summarily cursed, called a fool, laughed at, and hung up on."[101] Roosevelt also enlisted another prominent Georgian, Clark Foreman, the Harvard-educated, New Deal liaison with the black community and the nephew of Clark Howell.[102] Foreman warned Roosevelt that he had been away from Georgia for a long time and had few contacts, but he did suggest that the president publish a pamphlet on Southern poverty and what the New Deal had done for the South. Roosevelt liked the idea, feeling that "if the people got the facts...they will find their own remedies," Foreman remembered in 1948.[103]

Despite a dearth of contacts, Foreman headed to Atlanta and joined the search. Somehow, he and Robert settled on Lawrence Sabyllia Camp, who had served as Georgia's attorney general, the state Democratic Party Chair, and US District Attorney for North Georgia. Camp had also been a close associate of junior senator Richard Russell. The two men had served together in the legislature, and he had been both a finance chairman and campaign manager for Russell in several statewide races. He had a "fine record," according to Isaac Hay, his assistant, and "had dug up things [on crim-

---

[98]*New York Times*, August 21, 1938, sec. IV, 6, cited in Hooper, "The Purge," 160.

[99]Talmadge, *Talmadge: A Political Legacy*, 39.

[100]Ray Henle, *Pittsburgh Post Gazette*, quoted in the *Atlanta Constitution,* August 13, 1938, in Fossett, "The Impact of the New Deal on Georgia Politics, 1933–1941," 283.

[101]Anderson, *Wild Man from Sugar Creek*, 174, interview with Robert in 1971.

[102]Foreman also managed Henry Wallace's campaign for president (Egerton, *Speak Now against the Day*, 404–405).

[103]Carlton and Coclanis, eds., *Confronting Southern Poverty*, 14–15.

inals] that not even the FBI would think about."[104] He had presided over the Democratic convention that instructed Georgia delegates to support Roosevelt in 1932 and was himself a delegate and a member of the platform committee.[105] Soon Clark Foreman was able to report to the White House that he had been able to arouse "considerable support for a Camp candidacy."[106]

For all his credentials, Camp was "no ball of fire," wrote journalist G. Gould Lincoln in the *Washington Evening Star,* adding that he will need the help of Roosevelt and Rivers's machine to come close to being successful.[107] Another account called him "a dull, colorless man who read his speeches,"[108] a characteristic that was the kiss of death in Georgia politics of the time. Moreover, Camp had been reluctant to oppose George. He had written to congratulate George on his unopposed reelection in 1932, for which George wrote him a note of thanks, adding the curious handwritten sentence at the bottom of the letter, "I especially appreciate your willingness to cooperate with some of my friends. W. F. G."[109] Camp discussed the possibility of his running with some friends, but he seemed to have met with little enthusiasm. He apparently did not decide to run himself until Roosevelt himself called him early one morning at his home on the last day of qualifying.[110] That morning, June 2, he did not come into his office but called one of his aides to the Biltmore and handed him the entrance fee, telling him to file for him at the capitol.[111] According to the *New York Times,* Camp's filing fee reached its destination fifteen minutes before the deadline.[112] Two weeks later, Camp formally began his campaign by blasting George for being "the most subtle and adroit enemy of President Roosevelt and the Democratic party in the United States," calling him "the Senate leader for the forces of entrenched greed, big business and its millionaire owners in the country."[113]

---

[104]Isaac Hay, oral history, 45, Russell Library.

[105]Exhibit (2), Record of Lawrence S. Camp, attached to Clark Forman to Rudolf Foster, August 5, 1938, PSF, box 136, f. Ga. Campaign, 1938, Roosevelt papers.

[106]Interview with Ralph McGill, who had been told this by White House secretary Stephen Early in Thomas, "Roosevelt vs. George," 34.

[107]G. Gould Lincoln, "The Political Mill," June 21, 1938, *Washington Evening Star,* series VI-B, box 36, f. 2, Russell papers.

[108]Hooper, "The Purge," 165.

[109]WFG to Lawrence Camp, June 14, 1932, ibid., f. 4.

[110]Fossett cites a personal interview with someone in Camp's campaign who asked not to be identified ("The Impact of the New Deal on Georgia Politics, 1933–1941," 283).

[111]Ike (?) to Richard B. Russell, VI-B, box 63, f. "Pol. General 1938," RBR (Winder papers), Russell papers.

[112]*New York Times*, 2 June 1938, 1, cited in Hooper, "The Purge," 164.

[113]*Atlanta Journal*, June 16, 1938, in Anderson, *Wild Man from Sugar Creek*, 175.

He formally announced on July 4, the same day that George did, tearing into George as being "an ally with the Republicans to destroy Roosevelt and the Democratic party," thus "stabbing [Roosevelt] in the back." He enunciated the theme that Roosevelt himself would use against George, the charge that he was a tool of the "vested interests," which for some reason he thought were originally behind Talmadge but had shifted to George.[114]

In the Roosevelt Library in Hyde Park is an unsigned memo outlining the help Roosevelt could give Camp. It suggested that he use his "being a taxpayer in his adopted state of Georgia" as a reason to interfere. The memo stated that Roosevelt's association with George would also limit "outside influence and pressure" and concluded with the statement that "George can be defeated with the president's support." It also called for raising $10,000 for Camp.[115]

Under the guise of being made director of the National Emergency Council, a study group likened to various government agencies, Clark Foreman again returned to Georgia, but his real function was to manage Camp's campaign. In taking over his job, he forced out Erle Cocke, who was a George supporter.[116] Foreman went to work endeavoring to get endorsements, pressuring the Democratic Women's Clubs to remain neutral, and pressuring Rivers to endorse Camp.[117] He did secure the endorsement of *The Liberal Democrat* along with that of Mrs. Virginia Pohill Price, the Democratic National Committee chairwoman,[118] but he was not able to budge Governor Rivers, whose own campaign was not a sure thing.[119]

Camp's campaign was almost dead in the water from the beginning. Since he started so late, most of the state politicos had already sided with either George or Talmadge.[120] Moreover, it was late to begin raising money. Nevertheless, by August 1 Camp had received $15,000 from outside Georgia,[121] but this amount and what he was able to raise in-state would be

---

[114]*Atlanta Constitution*, July 5, 1938, cited in Zeigler, "Senator Walter George's 1938 Campaign," 336.

[115]"Notes of Senatorial Campaign in Georgia" from R. R. (?), n. d., PSF, box 136, f. Ga. Campaign: 1938, Roosevelt papers.

[116]U. S. Senate Investigation of Senatorial Campaign Expenditures, 2:33–35, cited in Hooper, "The Purge," 169.

[117]Hooper, "The Purge," 169.

[118]*The Liberal Democrat*, September 8, 1938, VI-B, box 68, f. Pol Gen. 1938, RBR (Winder), Russell papers.

[119]*New York Times*, June 2, 1938, 1, cited in Hooper, "The Purge," 164.

[120]Clapper, "Roosevelt Tries the Primaries," 18.

[121]Memo for the president, August 1, 1938, PSF, box 136, f. Ga. Campaign 1938, Roosevelt papers.

swamped by the avalanche of dollars that flowed into the George campaign from all over the country.[122]

As a plus, however, Roosevelt mobilized the full might of the federal government. He dispatched White House official Harlee Branch to Georgia to try to unseat George. Joseph B. Kenner was made the go-between for the White House and Atlanta, and Clark Foreman at the National Emergency Council, was told to corral federal workers for Camp. None of these shenanigans had been done too subtly, apparently, because they appeared in the Atlanta press.[123] Roosevelt had unabashedly poured federal money into the Kentucky race,[124] and he did not hesitate to do likewise in Georgia. Federal grants tumbled into the state in June, and in one day, six grants of $6.5 million was announced, and the next day came another one of a half a million.[125] Additional aid for school construction followed, and there were increases made to the Public Works Administration. Early in the election campaign itself, Georgia received the largest grant for roads it had ever received, and one week before the election, there was an additional allotment announced.[126] One historian has estimated that Roosevelt funneled perhaps as much as $54 million in federal money into Georgia during the campaign.[127] Furthermore, Miss Gay B. Shepperson, the WPA administrator for Georgia, was strong-armed to pressure WPA workers to vote as a bloc for Camp, both the *Atlanta Constitution* and the *New York Times* reported.[128] The president also went after George supporters in government jobs. We have already seen the removal of Erle Cocke. Others followed, but the firing of Gainesville lawyer Edgar B. Dunlap from his position as the Reconstruction Finance Corporation legal counsel proved to be Roosevelt's greatest mistake. Dunlap's ouster became a rallying cry for the George campaign, and Dunlap became one of George's major campaign managers. He traveled with George and was displayed at rallies as a symbol of outside meddling, always to great acclaim. When he was introduced at a rally in Macon, the press reported that it was as if "like a shock of electricity" went through the

[122]Edgar B. Dunlap, Jr. interview.

[123]*Atlanta Constitution*, August 13, 1938, in Thomas, "Roosevelt vs. George," 64.

[124]Thomas, "Roosevelt vs. George," 63.

[125]*Atlanta Constitution*, June 23, 1938 cited in Fossett, "The Impact of the New Deal on Georgia Politics, 1933–1941," 305.

[126]Fossett, "The Impact of the New Deal on Georgia Politics, 1933–1941," 307.

[127]*New York Times*, August 20, 1938, in Fossett, "The Impact of the New Deal on Georgia Politics, 1933–1941," 304.

[128]Fossett, "The Impact of the New Deal on Georgia Politics, 1933–1941," 307.

crowd. The crowd rose to its feet and cheered loudly.[129]

The race was made more unpredictable by Gene Talmadge's entry into it. This "wild man from Sugar Creek," if nothing else, made Georgia politics colorful, but he was usually so far beyond the pale that he could not win unless his opposition was split.[130] As commissioner of agriculture, he had engaged in all sorts of hijinks that appeared to help the farmer but were so outrageous that there was a move to impeach him in the state legislature. By his theatrics and demagoguery, the legislature not only impeached him but also invited him to address the body, the only non-governor ever to have been asked to do so.[131] In his first race for governor in 1932, he had promised to reduce the auto tag tax, reorganize the highway department (which was almost an autonomous government unto itself within the state), reduce utility and freight rates, and cut general taxes. He was ultimately successful in everything except reducing freight rates, and proving wildly popular as agriculture commissioner, he was reelected in a landslide in 1934, carrying 156 of Georgia's 159 counties.[132]

After his smashing victory, his ego got the better of him. In his second term he engaged in arrogant antics: he physically expelled the state treasurer from his office, used an acetylene torch to cut into the state safe, shipped Georgia hogs to Chicago at a disastrous cost to the state, and despite his claim to be the spokesman for the common man, he arrested textile workers after the textile bosses gave him a $20,000 contribution.[133] Worst of all, he attacked the New Deal, which he called a combination of "wet nursin', frenzied finance, and plain damn foolishness."[134] Despite the fact that he had his own "new deal" for Georgia,[135] he went so far in 1935 to imply that Roosevelt was a Communist.[136] Former governor Hardwick dismissed him as "the reckless and radical and dangerous demagogue, filling the air with fantastic promises."[137] As we have seen, Richard Russell buried him in 1936, and many thought that his political career was finished. It would not be the last

[129]"George has Ouster…," August 20 or 21 (date unclear), 1938, apparently a *New York Times* clipping, Edgar B. Dunlap Scrapbook, "We're For George," Gainesville, GA.

[130]Bernd, *Grass Roots Politics in Georgia*, 7.

[131]Gaillard, "Georgia at Last Has a Good Governor," 242.

[132]Ibid.

[133]Cobb, "Not Gone, but Forgotten," 198.

[134]Ibid.

[135]Hooper, "The Purge," 159.

[136]*Atlanta Constitution*, October 9, 1935, cited in Fossett, "The Impact of the New Deal on Georgia Politics, 1933–1941," 150.

[137]Hardwick remarks 1932, series 1(a), box 1, f. 13, Hardwick papers.

political obituary written on this colorful Georgian.

One historian has put it aptly when Talmadge qualified on May 13: "Once it became known that Gene would run against George, those who had questioned his good judgment in 1936 questioned his sanity in 1938."[138] In many ways, George might have been more vulnerable to a Talmadge campaign than Richard Russell, who was better at the political fray than was the stately dignified George. Although Talmadge was a bitter opponent of Roosevelt, his basic platform, whose focus was "free land for the unemployed," made Roosevelt look quite moderate. He used the argument of Roosevelt that George was a tool of big business, accusing him of having "spoken out of one side of his mouth and voted on the other."[139] He told Richard Russell's father that "this time I am running against a man in tailor-made clothes, full only of wind and broken promises."[140] Both Talmadge and George generally appealed to some of the same people, so Talmadge's entry was a serious threat to George if for no other reason than with the conservative vote split, Camp might win. On qualifying to run, Talmadge received thousands of telegrams asking him to leave the race.[141] George feared that there was a conspiracy between Talmadge and Roosevelt for Talmadge to run as an independent in the general election if the lost the primary.[142] Whatever he did, he would be a dangerous opponent if for no other reason than that he had long ago cornered the racist vote, a legacy he would pass on to his son. Both would use the tactic that "if-all-else-fails-blame-the-'niggers,'" to great effect in many a Georgia race.[143] With Talmadge in the race, it was not going to be a pretty election.

George's behavior clearly demonstrates that he was disturbed at Roosevelt's ill-disguised hostility, and he tried to make amends. In January 1938, George had promoted the president's birthday in Georgia, sending letters to all district and county chairs to recognize it. Ironically, Roosevelt's latest victim, Edgar Dunlap, was the organizer of the statewide effort.[144]

When Roosevelt did come on March 24, to Gainesville, George intro-

[138]Anderson, *Wild Man from Sugar Creek,* 170.

[139]Thomas, "Roosevelt vs. George," 29.

[140]*Atlanta Journal,* June 16, 1938, cited in Anderson, *Wild Man from Sugar Creek,* 176.

[141]Herman E. Talmadge to James Cobb, March 14, 1972, cited in Cobb, "Not Gone, but Forgotten," 206.

[142]WFG to Josiah Bailey, September 28, 1938, box 476, f. 1938, October–November, Bailey papers.

[143]Egerton, *Speak Now against the Day*, 109.

[144]WFG to McIntyre, January 5, 1938, box 2, f. 4, Presidential Alpha file, Roosevelt papers.

duced him and slathered on the praise rather thickly. Before a crowd of 50,000 people, George called Roosevelt "not only great leader of a great party but a great leader of a great people," adding that he was "the greatest leader among English-speaking peoples at this hour anywhere on earth."[145] Despite the slavish praise, Roosevelt completely ignored George and instead reminded the audience of the one million dollars of federal aid that had helped restore their community. He praised Governor Rivers and Congressman Frank Welchel for their liberal voting records, totally ignoring George, a slight that did not go unnoticed by the press.[146]

Probably still sensing Roosevelt's hostility and likely having by now heard many rumors, George wrote a letter to Roosevelt late in June 1938 to try to make peace. In a note written in his beautiful Spenserian script, George said, "I have learned indirectly that you felt that I had in public addresses…spoken in offensive terms regarding your good self," he wrote, probably having in mind the deleted reference in his anti-court speech the year before. "I hasten to assure you that I have never meant to be offensive to you. On the contrary I have had and still have for you the deepest personal affection," he wrote, almost petulantly. Then he in effect admitted some offense when he wrote, "I may have…too little self-control at times[,] but I am unwilling to have you think I have on any occasion…felt anything but deep affection for you." He signed it, "Cordially, Walter George." He asked the White House Secretary Marvin McIntyre to hand deliver the letter to the president.[147]

Roosevelt answered George's letter of June 27 rather promptly with a type-written letter. It was very warm and friendly and likely dismissed any gossip he had heard: "Mac has given me that mighty nice note of yours[,] and I want you to know that I appreciate it." He added that he had never been offended but that he "did feel that at the time of the court fight you were a bit emphatic that I had horrid designs on the judiciary." He mentioned that he had heard "cloakroom gossip" to which he never paid any attention, and he voiced his great "respect and affection," telling the senator, "You are a scholar and a gentleman." He then to some degree stuck in the knife by writing that he, Roosevelt, was a liberal and that George was a conservative, and that if George were from a Northern or Western state, he would most probably have been a Republican. He concluded rather disarm-

---

[145] *Atlanta Constitution,* March 24, 1938, cited in Thomas, "Roosevelt vs. George," 15.

[146] Ibid., 17.

[147] Attached to a letter to McIntyre, June 27, 1938, DNC, OF 300, f. 15, PS file, box 136, f. Ga. Campaign 1938, Roosevelt papers.

ingly that though they would always have differences, "that does not mean that our personal friendship will in anyway be affected by it."[148]

Despite the fact that Roosevelt had in effect called George a Republican, George could not have but been somewhat relieved at the president's affable response. It also left him unprepared for what followed. Given what Roosevelt had done across the country, George must have known that at least Roosevelt would call Camp "his good friend" and ignore George. In a letter to his friend Josiah Bailey on July 21, he rejoiced in the renomination of Indiana's Fred van Nuys, who had been on the Roosevelt hit list, and then turned to his own race. He noted that "unquestionably" one of his opponents was put in the race by the president, but felt confident that at this point his position was solid. He then noted that "the president will probably take pleasure in giving me a kick down stairs [*sic*] on his visit" but added that "Many of my friends are confident that the visit of the president will be deeply resented."[149] Nevertheless, when it became known that Roosevelt would be in Barnesville, Georgia, in August to inaugurate a rural electrification project, George in a public statement said, "I shall be pleased to welcome…that great and good man, President Roosevelt."[150]

George then did a curious thing. That same day, George called Marion Allen, one of Richard Russell's 1936 campaign managers, who was currently working with Russell in Washington, from the lobby of his hotel and invited him to lunch. Uncertain of what this meeting would entail, Allen told George that there were several people with him, and he would be unable to join. However, only Mark Dunahoo, a Winder native who had been Russell's driver in the 1930 gubernatorial campaign, was in the room. Not to be put off, George called Allen again several days later and asked him to come by his office. Allen again demurred, saying that he had not dressed all day but that he would be happy to have George visit him in his hotel room, a rather shabby way to treat the senior senator from Georgia. To Allen's utter amazement, George accepted. When George arrived, he was surprised to find Dunahoo there. With Dunahoo in the room, however, George apparently felt hesitant to discuss what he wanted, but he did have a "heart to heart conversation" with Allen. At some point, Allen must have followed George into the street because Dunahoo apparently was not privy to the conversation, nor did Allen tell Dunahoo all that had transpired. Exactly what George said, or wanted to say, is somewhat unclear, but he seems to

[148] Ibid., FDR to WFG, June 19, 1938.
[149] WFG to Josiah Bailey, July 21, 1938, box 476, f. 1938, June–August, Bailey papers.
[150] "Purges Resumed," 3.

have handled himself rather clumsily. Since Dunahoo is the source of the conversation, and he was not privy to all of it, we must extrapolate from what Dunahoo wrote Russell of the part of the conversation he did hear. George seemed to be warning Russell through Allen that Rivers was planning to run against Russell in 1942 and that it might be a good idea to destroy him now by countering his support for Roosevelt's chosen opponent to George.[151]

If George was trying to elicit Russell's support, he chose a strange, inept way to do it, and it seems especially odd that he did not go directly to Russell himself. George's actions indicate a certain panic that was not typical of him, and he must have assumed, as did Roosevelt, that the president had much more influence in Georgia politics than he had.

Journalist Arthur Krock incorrectly felt that Roosevelt knew enough to stay out of Georgia politics because to support someone against George would only propel voters to George.[152] Krock apparently was wrong. Roosevelt had misread his "successes." Those chosen candidates who had won (e.g., Barkley) would probably have won anyway, and for him to think that his interference had caused their victories was akin to the notion of a rooster thinking that his crowing brought up the sun, and this misguided notion led him to commit the error Krock had thought he would avoid. Roosevelt had not at this point directly opposed a strong, entrenched Democrat like George. When he arrived in Pensacola, Hopkins and others began pressing for an attack on George.[153] Moreover, he was told that if he did not intervene, George would win anyway, so he had nothing to lose.[154] He consulted with some delegations from Georgia and examined a study of George's voting record and "*attitude* [italics in original]" prepared by his staff. It stressed that George had consistently voted against the legislation for the working man and had never once introduced a bill to relieve any form of "human distress in the South." He had voted to weaken much legislation such as an amendment to the social security bill that would have eliminated half of the recipients.[155] Clark Foreman weighed in with a memo telling Roosevelt to stress Camp's career of service to the Democratic Party and to liberal ideas,

---

151Mark Dunahoo to Richard B. Russell, June 27, 1938 (per postmark; no date on the letter), VI-B, box 36, f. 2, Russell papers.

152*New York Times,* June 15, 1938, cited in Thomas, "Roosevelt vs. George," 9.

153Stokes, *Chip Off My Shoulder*, 496, cited in Thomas, "Roosevelt vs. George," 51.

154Alsop-Kintner column, *Atlanta Constitution,* August 15, 1938, cited in Thomas, "Roosevelt vs. George," 51.

155"Study of George's voting record and *attitude*," PSF, box 136, f. Ga. Campaign 1936, Roosevelt papers.

and since Richard Russell would be on the platform, Foreman told Roosevelt to make a comparison between Russell's support of the administration and George's lack of it. He noted that George has been making the point that a vote for Camp would be a vote for Talmadge and suggested that the president should point out that there was no difference between George and Talmadge, a monumental leap in logic by any rational observer.[156] Doubtlessly, a final reason for his open opposition to George was his feeling that his frequent visits to Georgia and his owning property there gave Georgians the perception that he, the president, was one of them. Whatever strange calculus catalyzed his subsequently actions, they led him to make one of the biggest political blunders of his life.

As for Roosevelt, he departed and by the time that he arrived in Warm Springs on August 10, his staff had leaked rumors that he might "crack down on George." A further indication was the presence of both Camp and Governor Rivers at luncheon when he arrived.[157] Elements of the press were already dubbing his visit "another march through Georgia," and at the very least, it was generally expected that Roosevelt would endorse Camp.[158] There, Roosevelt introduced Rivers to the press as "an old friend of ours," and then he dropped a bombshell: He introduced Camp as "the gentleman who I hope will be the next senator from this state."[159] Most felt that Roosevelt might obliquely support Camp, as he had others around the country, but no one expected anything like a direct endorsement. The remark was a stunning revelation to White House Secretary Steve Early, who rushed to the presidential press corps lounging outside on the railroad siding to tell them of the news.[160] It was at this time that the Roosevelt released Clark Foreman's aforementioned *Report on Southern Poverty*, which he would use in his attack against George the next day.[161]

Roosevelt then absented himself to his office in the "Little White House," supposedly to work on his speeches for the Barnesville meeting and for one at the University of Georgia, where he was receiving an honorary degree. In reality he met for two hours with Hopkins, who continued pres-

---

[156]Memo for the president by Clark Foreman, August 5, 1938, Ibid.

[157]Anderson, *Wild Man from Sugar Creek*, 176.

[158]Frank H. Quentin to McIntyre, July 11, 1938, PPF, box 107–117, f. 109, Roosevelt papers.

[159]Stevens, *Hi-Ya Neighbor*, 65–66; *Atlanta Constitution*, August 11, 1931, 1, cited in Hooper, "The Purge," 171.

[160]Thomas, "Roosevelt vs. George," 53.

[161]Burns, *Roosevelt: The Lion and the Fox*, 361–63, in Carlton and Coclanis, eds., *Confronting Southern Poverty*, 22.

suring him to go a step further and actually attack George.

Meanwhile, Camp, Rivers, and Joseph B. Keenar, a member of the White House staff who was on leave to work in the Camp campaign, met and decided to instruct Secretary of Agriculture Henry Wallace to increase Georgia's tobacco quotas to undermine further Talmadge's attacks and bolster Rivers' renomination and Camp's campaign.[162] Camp tried in the meeting to obtain Rivers' public endorsement, but the politically slick governor refused, saying that it was not necessary. By some accounts there were bitter recriminations between the two, but Rivers needed George supporters to win renomination, and he refused to enter the George-Camp fight.[163]

Roosevelt left by midnight by train for Athens for his appearance at the University of Georgia the next day, after which he would then travel to Barnesville to throw the switch to send electricity to 357 families in that county.[164] That night, Camp made a speech attacking George as "the Senate leader of entrenched greed, big business, and its millionaire owners of the country." Curiously he added the unlikely prediction that George's reelection would facilitate the Republican return to power.[165]

A number of people were puzzled that Roosevelt would have come to Barnesville to dedicate the REA unit there because it was one of the smallest in the US[166] In his pre-luncheon address, Roosevelt admitted that his visit was not in the works when he had been in Gainesville in March, the reason likely being that in March, he would not have seen his "successes" and had probably not thought he could defeat George.[167] Believing now that he could defeat George, Roosevelt had Marvin McIntyre arrange for his Barnesville appearance because REA was extremely popular in Georgia, and the podium would be filled with pro-Roosevelt figures.[168] Everyone knew that something was in the works for the appearance at Barnesville, especially since Roosevelt did not attack George in Athens. He certainly knew better than to criticize George in front of a university crowd, so everyone thought that some anti-George utterance would come in Barnesville. There was

---

[162]*Atlanta Constitution*, August 15, 1938, cited in Thomas, "Roosevelt vs. George," 52.

[163]Third Tom Corcoran interview, September 21, 1938; Alsop and Kintner, *Atlanta Constitution*, August 11, 1938, cited in Fagin, "Franklin D. Roosevelt," 224.

[164]Stevens, *Hi-Ya Neighbor*, 66.

[165]Mark Dunahoo oral history, 52, Russell Library.

[166]Stevens, *Hi-Ya Neighbor*, 183.

[167]Harlee Branch to McIntyre, June 15, 1938, M to B, June 20, 1938, OF 300, DNC, box 31, "Georgia, FDR Library," cited in Fagin, "Franklin D. Roosevelt," 180.

[168]"Judge Russell Hits Camp," *Washington Post* clipping, July 23, 1938, (?) f. G-biog., Box 337. Republican National Committee, Dwight David Eisinhower, Roosevelt papers.

much speculation, however, on exactly what he would say. Richard Russell's father, still smarting from his 1926 defeat at George's hands, had publicly called on Roosevelt to "speak out boldly" against George. In threatening tones, he told Roosevelt, "I am going to vote against Walter George," and unless Roosevelt really blasts George in Barnesville, "I might be forced to vote for another candidate [such as Talmadge]."

Walter George had not had a rough-and-tumble campaign since his race against Judge Russell in 1926. At best, he was out of practice. He certainly was unprepared for what finally happened. He was extremely lucky to have in his corner former North Carolina governor Max O. Gardner. After his term as governor, Gardner had become a very influential Washington lobbyist with close ties to the White House. Gardner like George also lived in the Mayflower, and the two had become close friends. George, who usually avoided the Washington social scene, would go to informal functions in Gardner's suite, and this friendship might well have saved George's career. A very shrewd operator, Gardner, who did not want to lose his access to the White House, began helping George secretly. Going to his home in Shelby, North Carolina, he wrote a memo after a conversation with George on the phone and sent it to George's secretary, Christie Bell Kennedy. In it, Gardner advised George, regardless of what Roosevelt said or did, at least to shake Roosevelt's hand enthusiastically.[169]

What resulted was a brilliant political coup. Had George reacted differently, it might have been a disaster. As events developed, it was Franklin Roosevelt who emerged the loser in the encounter. To quote Herman Talmadge many years later, "When Franklin D. Roosevelt's train rolled into Barnesville, Georgia, on August 11, 1938, the president was one of the most popular men in the state. When he left that same day, he was one of the least popular.... The minute Roosevelt attacked Senator George, he ceased to be the Great White Father in Washington and became just another Yankee carpetbagger."[170]

Mark Dunahoo states in his oral history contribution that "George knew absolutely nothing about it [Roosevelt's coming attack], had no inkling of anything of that nature." George himself wrote to a historian in 1952 that he did not learn that Roosevelt would make a personal attack until Au-

[169]Morrison, Joseph, *Governor O. Max Gardner*, 184, cites a memo in the Gardner papers.

[170]Talmadge, *Talmadge: A Political Legacy*, 39–40.

gust 10, the day before the appearance in Barnesville.[171] Neither of these statements is absolutely true. We have seen that George told Josiah Bailey early in August that he expected to be kicked "down stairs" when Roosevelt came. Journalist G. Gould Lincoln wrote openly about it as early as June 21, but adding that "no one knows just how far the president is prepared to go in an effort to dislodge the senator."[172] Moreover, George and Max Gardner had been for some time conversing over the phone on strategy.[173] One source states that Cully A. Cobb, a Georgia journalist and educator, received an advanced copy of Roosevelt's remarks and showed them to George, who was stunned that the president would do "such a dastardly thing."[174] Moreover, Roosevelt had frequently in the past referred to Georgia's politics as being "feudal" and once even equated it to a "the Fascist system."[175] It is probably after reading the draft of Roosevelt's remarks that George talked with Gardner and received the simple advice mentioned above. George had to know that something unpleasant would occur; he just did not know the severity of it.[176]

The invitation committee invited Roosevelt to speak "on any subject you may deem of interest to Georgians."[177] Locally a group of politicians, expecting Roosevelt to be partisan, met at the Lamar County Court House and passed a resolution condemning any political involvement during the president's visit.[178] Whether Roosevelt was informed or not of the attempts to limit his speaking topic is not known. If he had been told of the local interference, he clearly ignored it.

George had not originally been invited to Barnesville by the planning

---

[171]Judge Mark Dunahoo, oral history, 54, Russell Library. George himself wrote a historian in 1952 that he did not learn that Roosevelt would make a personal attack until August 10, the day before Roosevelt's appearance in Barnesville (George to Thomas, May 3, 1952, quoted in Thomas, "Roosevelt vs. George," 54).

[172]G. Gould Lincoln "The Political Mill," clipping, 21 June 1938, series VI-B, box 36, f. 2, Russell papers.

[173]Morrison, *Governor O. Max Gardner*, 184–85.

[174]Cully Cobb, COHP, 110, cited in Fagin, "Franklin D. Roosevelt," 237; Even Fagin feels in "Franklin D. Roosevelt," that given the warning he had gotten from Roosevelt's endorsement of Camp at Warm Springs it is hard to accept this account. This document must have been how George learned of the "personal attack" about which he wrote Thomas in 1952. Time does dim memories.

[175]*Atlanta Constitution*, 24 March 1938, cited in Zeigler, "Senator Walter George's 1938 Campaign," 334–35.

[176]*Atlanta Journal,* August 9, 1938, cited in Anderson, *Wild Man from Sugar Creek,* 176.

[177]Fossett, "The Impact of the New Deal on Georgia Politics, 1933–1941," 292n.

[178]Thomas, "Roosevelt vs. George," 50.

committee, which included Camp, but he was included among the group of dignitaries invited by Barnesville mayor J. A. Cason and some of George's local supporters. In his acceptance letter, George, at this point not knowing exactly what would follow, replied that "I shall be pleased to welcome that great and good man, President Roosevelt,"[179] and continued with praise of the TVA, the NLRA, and the REA, and a vow to support "liberal democracy."[180] It is therefore entirely possible that the president did not expect George to be there. Would he have planned things differently had that been the case? Some accounts also have Talmadge there, but he was not.[181] It is not clear whether Talmadge was invited (he most probably was not), but he told the press that he would listen to Roosevelt's remarks on Atlanta radio. He added humorously, "I don't know whether or not he will anoint Camp. I know [only] one thing: He will not anoint Gene Talmadge."[182]

On August 11, 1938, the city of Barnesville, population about 3,000, drew a crowd of 30,000, another account stated 50,000, to see the president.[183] The rally was to be held on the Summers Field Arena of Gordon Military College. On the podium was Governor Rivers, Senator Russell, Camp, Gary Sheppardson of the State WPA, Marion Allen of the IRS, and a Camp campaign manager, and oddly, Edgar Dunlap of the Reconstruction Finance Corporation (RFC), whom the *New York Times* (maybe the *Atlanta Constitution*) stated was working *sub rosa* for Camp, and of course, Walter George.[184] Somehow George was on the train with Roosevelt as he arrived in Barnesville from Athens, where the president had taken the opportunity to warm up for his attack on George by stating that Georgians did not believe in "demagoguery or feudalism even though they are dressed up in democratic clothes."[185] Only half the necessary cars appeared at the station to transport the dignitaries to the event, and George was left standing on the

---

[179] *Vienna News*, August 8, 1957, 5.

[180] *Atlanta Constitution*, July 23, 1938, cited in Zeigler, "Senator Walter George's 1938 Campaign," 337; *New York Times*, August 8, 1938 (the source states *July 8*), in Fossett, "The Impact of the New Deal on Georgia Politics, 1933–1941," 292n.

[181] Miller, *FDR*, 414; Thomas, "Roosevelt vs. George," 57.

[182] *Atlanta Journal*, August 9, 1938, cited in Anderson, *Wild Man from Sugar Creek*, 176.

[183] WFG, "My Party and Myself," 19. The *New York Times* estimated the crowd at 50,000 (August 12, 1938, cited in Fagin, "Franklin D. Roosevelt," 226). Both figures are unlikely

[184] *New York Times*, August 12, 1938 and the *Atlanta Constitution*, 12 August 1938, cited in Fagin, "Franklin D. Roosevelt," 226.

[185] Addresses of the president, 1938, August 11, 1938, cited in Fagin, "Franklin D. Roosevelt,", 225; "Purges Resumed," 13.

platform and had to hitch a ride to the arena.[186]

The day was brutally hot as only Deep South summer days can be. Ralph McGill of the *Atlanta Constitution* waxed poetic in his description: "The sun beat down. It was terribly hot. The sky was serene and beautiful. Great white clouds, assuming fantastic shapes, moved slowly about a canopy of blue."[187] Dr. Ross McIntyre, the president's physician, remembered that despite the heat and since it was rumored that the president would endorse Camp, "You could hear the ice forming as the [people] sat in angry silence."[188]

On the dais, George was seated next to Harry Hopkins, who had come to Barnesville for the speech.[189] George seemed cool in a white suit but stirred uneasily (another account states that he "stared motionlessly ahead") while candidate Camp sat "mouse-still."[190] Roosevelt arrived after all the others had, and he was introduced by Governor Rivers. When the president rose to speak, *Time* reported that "hanging in the air like a summer thunderstorm was the question: What would Franklin Roosevelt do now...."[191] In the words of one historian, what followed was "the most scorching indictment ever publicly leveled by Franklin D. Roosevelt against an important member of his own party."[192] His attack became known as the "Barnesville Manifesto."

Addressing his audience as "my neighbors in Georgia," Roosevelt began innocuously enough by telling the history of the REA, but then he added that examining the REA had made him address the economic conditions of the South. He had just issued a report on Southern poverty about the time he returned to the United States, and invited his audience to read it.[193] In it, he noted that Georgia's per capita income was fortieth in the nation

---

[186]Anderson, *Wild Man from Sugar Creek,* 177.

[187]*Atlanta Constitution*, August 12, 1938, cited in Thomas, "Roosevelt vs. George," 55.

[188]Ross T. McIntyre, *White House Physician* (New York: Putnam's Sons, 1946) 107, cited in Hooper, "The Purge," 171.

[189]Michie and Ryhlick, *Dixie Demagogues*, 193.

[190]WFG, "My Party and Myself," 20. A 1943 article mentions the white suit, but a photograph on the same page (supposedly taken in Barnesville) shows George wearing a dark suit ("Old Independent," 21).

[191]WFG, "My Party and Myself," 19.

[192]Hopper, "The Purge" 161. For this speech, see Roosevelt, *The Public Papers and Addresses of Franklin D. Roosevelt*, 463–70.

[193]See Egerton, *Speak Now against the Day*, 180; for the full report, see Carlton and Coclanis, eds., *Confronting Southern Poverty*, 22.

and only 57 percent of the national average.[194] He then contended that progress on this front was hindered by the anonymous conservative politician, "who says he is in favor of progress but whose record shows that he hinders or hampers new measurers." Only the most naive could not know of whom he was speaking. Roosevelt went on to say that the poverty problem was too complex to be handled by the states alone, so federal help was needed. He followed that by adding that it was incumbent upon the citizens of Georgia to elect representatives who would understand and support this idea.

Roosevelt then turned to the Georgia primary. Telling his listeners that the obvious fact that they have every right to choose whomever they want and that he had no idea of impairing that right, he said, "I feel no hesitation in telling you what I would do if I could vote here next month." He contended that he had been asked by many Georgians, including the "state's Supreme Court Chief Justice" (Richard Russell's father) to express his view on the September primary. Reminding them that he had endorsed Barkley over Chandler in Kentucky, where there was no clear-cut liberal-conservative divide, because of his experience, he opined that in Georgia there was "a liberal on one side and a dyed-in-the-wool conservative on the other." Then he began his attack on George, stating that in his view, "the senior senator cannot possibly...be classified as belonging to the liberal school of thought." People like George had "listened to the dictatorship of a small minority of individuals and corporations who opposed the objectives [of a liberal program.]," so his "seniority falls by the wayside." Feeling that his election in 1936 had given him a mandate, Roosevelt was going after members of Congress of his own party who "represented a small powerful minority." Mentioning his correspondence with George given above, he noted that he had told George that "he and I do not speak the same language."

Turning his attention from George, he praised the liberal Camp, whom he assured his listeners would make a fine senator despite his young thirty-nine years, and dismissed Talmadge, whose election, he felt, "would contribute little to practical government." He concluded with the news that if he lived in Georgia, he would "most assuredly cast my vote for Lawrence Camp."[195] Then as if to decriminalize his action, he added, "I hope that

[194]Calvin B. Hoover and B. U. Ratchford, *Economic Resources and Policies of the South* (New York: Macmillan, 1951) 50, cited in Fossett, "The Impact of the New Deal on Georgia Politics, 1933–1941," 5.

[195]Roosevelt papers, 7:463, cited in Thomas, "Roosevelt vs. George," 57; *New York Times*, August 12, 1938.

Senator George and I will always be good personal friends," but he then likened him unto most Republicans, a terrible insult to most Georgians of that day. It had been Roosevelt's most unequivocal attack on any Democratic candidate in the purge.[196] Walter George then rose and handed Roosevelt a written statement, which had been in effect written by Max Gardner, and then quoted it to him orally.[197] "Mr. President," he said, "I regret that you have taken this occasion to question my Democracy and to attack my public record. I want you to know that I accept the challenge."[198] The thunderous applause that followed easily equaled Roosevelt's when he had arrived.[199] Even the super-confident Roosevelt must have known that he had erred.

There seems to have been a delayed reaction to Roosevelt's attack. The crowd at first gave Roosevelt polite applause when he finished, but it was not enthusiastic. Frances Coley, a neighbor of the Georges in Vienna who was then living in Barnesville, was seated with Miss Lucy, Irma, and Heard. As the tenor of the speech became obvious, the four got up and left. Others began leaving as well.[200] When George accepted the challenge, the remaining crowd cheered their senator as loudly as they had cheered Roosevelt in the beginning. There were indeed cries of "Goodbye, Senator," but there were many cries of "Hurrah for Senator George."[201] Roosevelt seemed visibly disconcerted when George took his hand, and as evidence that he had become rattled, he left the arena without throwing the switch sending electricity to the rural area he had come to electrify. It was left to the project manager, Walter Audres, to start the electricity flowing five minutes later.[202] The general tension began to abate somewhat as George and Roosevelt slowly made their way through the crowd to the waiting cars, although with some in the crowd, the tension intensified. Mayor Cason was so incensed that he drove his car, carrying the president's one-time law partner, Basil O'Connor, and assistant to the attorney general, Joseph B. Keenan, like a wild man. The passengers became so agitated that the three nearly came to fisticuffs. Mrs. Cason was to drive White House secretaries Steve Early and Marvin McIntyre, but she flatly refused to do so.[203] Other members of the presidential party were also refused rides and had to trudge on foot to the

[196]Fagin, "Franklin D. Roosevelt," 226.

[197]Mellichamp, *Senators from Georgia*, 234.

[198]This statement is quoted many places (WFG, "My Party and Myself," 20).

[199]*Vienna News*, August 8, 1957, 5.

[200]Frances Coley interview.

[201]Anderson, *Wild Man from Sugar Creek,* 178; WFG, "My Party and Myself," 20.

[202]"Roosevelt forgets...," Unidentified newspaper clipping, f. Sen G (NC), VHPS.

[203]WFG, "My Party and Myself," 20.

waiting train. The sentiment of the majority of the crowd was summed up by the *Charlotte Observer* when it wrote, "The president struck with brass knucks a helpless and defenseless man in the household of his fathers who could do nothing but sit and take it."[204]

On his way north, Roosevelt stopped in Greenville, South Carolina, to boost the candidacy of Olin Johnson, who was opposing "Cotton Ed" Smith. His close friend Senator Jimmy Byrnes boarded the train and curiously got an immediate apology from McIntyre for the Georgia incident, who must have been only trying to soothe Byrnes's anger. Byrnes still went to Roosevelt's car, and obviously having already heard of the "Barnesville Manifesto" and very apprehensive of a similar occurrence happening in South Carolina, asked Roosevelt what he was going to say. Roosevelt replied, "I'll tell them about my fishing trip."[205] He did not endorse Johnson, who introduced him, but did take a swipe at Smith's previous remark that fifty cents a day was a decent wage.[206]

All Roosevelt had succeeded doing was turning Walter George into a martyr. A distressed Herman Talmadge, who was managing his father's campaign, felt that Roosevelt had undone much of the elder Talmadge's work to this point. "Here Papa had been trying to portray George as a Washington insider who had lost touch with the people, and the number one insider had just got done denouncing him."[207]

With the announcement of the "Barnesville Manifesto," George became overnight a hero across the country. The *Charlotte Observer* called George's response to Roosevelt "historic words spoken for all Americans in their struggle to stem the on-coming tide of centralized government.[208] National journalist Joseph Alsop called Roosevelt's attack "a rather sordid, slapstick comedy" and was incredulous that Roosevelt would risk electing Talmadge just to get his revenge on George.[209] The *New York Times* and the *Baltimore Sun* attacked Roosevelt and drew national attention to George. So did many papers in the Southeast.[210] *Time* likened Roosevelt's attack unto an

---

[204]"I Accept the Challenge," August 13, 1938, typescript memo to *Charlotte Observer*, f. 315, Gardner papers.

[205]Barclay, *That Reminds Me*, 103.

[206]Roosevelt, *The Public Papers and Addresses of Franklin D. Roosevelt*, 103. In September Roosevelt blasted Tydings of Maryland almost as vigorously as he had attacked George.

[207]Talmadge, *Talmadge: A Political Legacy*, 39–40.

[208]*Charlotte Observer* quoted in the *Atlanta Constitution*, August 19, 1938, cited in Thomas, "Roosevelt vs. George," 60.

[209]Anderson, *Wild Man from Sugar Creek*, 177.

[210]Cobb, "Not Gone, but Forgotten," 203.

excommunication, where "liberal" Roosevelt had denied the sacraments to "conservative" George "about as completely as any pope ever cut off from grace an unrepentant sinner."[211] Even ardent New Dealers like Senator Herbert Lehman of New York, a man who was a political enemy of Walter George, denounced the attempted purge, stating that "it deserved failure and would get it," adding that "an executive had no right to try to punish legislators for an honest difference of opinion."[212]

Roosevelt received only ten or fifteen letters supporting his action. George got thousands; Camp received only one.[213] In fact, George received such a flood of correspondence that his campaign ran days behind in their responses to it. One letter, although pro-Roosevelt, warned the president that Georgians felt that he was trying to dictate the election. "That impression will [re]elect Senator George just as sure as 2 & 2 are four."[214] Clearly Roosevelt had indeed blundered badly.

Locally within Georgia, the reaction was even stronger. "There was a lot of resentment to what Roosevelt did," Henry Woodward, the son of Walter George's law partners, remembered.[215] Congressman Steven Pace of Americus went even further, stating that all of Georgia became "utterly inflamed" at Roosevelt's meddling.[216] One Baptist minister weighed in with a campaign address titled, "Why Baptists Cannot Endorse President Roosevelt's Barnesville Address." Because Baptists had always fought for religious and civil rights, they could not tolerate anyone "including Roosevelt" telling the people of Georgia "how to vote."[217] This attack was clearly reflected in the state's press's reaction. The *Atlanta Constitution* accused Roosevelt of trying to turn the US Senate into "a gathering of Charlie McCarthies with himself as the sole Edgar Bergen to pull the strings and supply the vocalism."[218] The *Macon Telegraph* went so far as to inform its readers that the liberal Democrats "would subject the South to a return to the horrors of Re-

---

[211]WFG, "My Party and Myself," 19.

[212]Nevins, *Herbert A. Lehman and His Era*, 193.

[213]*New York Times*, August 17, 1938, and an interview with an anonymous Camp insider (cited in Fossett, "The Impact of the New Deal on Georgia Politics, 1933–1941," 311).

[214]Joseph E. Millwood to FDR, August 30, 1938, DNC, OF 300, box 15, f. K–M, Roosevelt papers.

[215]Woodward interview, August 11, 2003.

[216]Steven Pace interview, cited in Coode, "Georgia Congressmen and the New Deal, 1933–1938," 234.

[217]*Atlanta Constitution*, 15 August 1938, cited in Coode, "Georgia Congressmen and the New Deal, 1933–1938," 235.

[218]*Atlanta Constitution*, August 12, 1938, in Cobb, "Not Gone, but Forgotten," 203.

construction." Others likened it to Sherman's march through the state.[219] Moreover, many of the small county weeklies like the *Fitzgerald Herald,* the *Livonia Times,* the *Butler Herald,* and the *Dawson County Advertiser,* most of whom had endorsed Talmadge two years before, either endorsed George or remained silent.[220] The *Cairo Messenger* near the Florida line waxed punnish: "Are you a George-ian? We are!"[221]

Moreover, much of the state press further supported the embattled senator refusing to give his opposition any coverage. When Harry Brown, the assistant secretary of agriculture and a Georgian, came to Atlanta to make a radio speech for Camp, no newspapers would report that the speech was going to be made.[222] Georgian Max E. Land wrote McIntyre that journalists at the *Atlanta Journal* were "pressagenting for George" and were interviewing only "people who are on *his side* [emphasis original]."[223] Governor Gardner, with his shrewd political ear to the ground, wrote a friend, "My information is that the nerve center of the state has been struck and that the response for George has been favorable.... You may expect tremendous excitement in Georgia."[224] He might have added that one might expect "tremendous excitement" other places as well.

One historian studying the matter has written that by the time of the "Barnesville Manifesto," George had spent $100,000 and had another half million in the bank.[225] This amount is an overstatement, as we shall see, but the absence of money was not a problem in the campaign. "Money came from all over the country" after Roosevelt's attack, Ed Dunlap Jr. remembered.[226] Even Northern financial groups headed by Wendell Willkie, who already had his eye on the Republican nomination in 1940, sent a Washington publicist, Carlyle Bargeron, to Georgia with articles and editorials and money supporting George's reelection.[227] George collected so much money that he could afford to reject the support of the Georgia Power Company, whose support might make him vulnerable to Roosevelt's attacks, especially

[219]Caro, *The Years of Lyndon Johnson*, 64.

[220]Cobb, "Not Gone, but Forgotten," 203, 208.

[221]"We're for George," A scrapbook for Georgia," Dunlap scrapbook.

[222]Paul Appleby to Stephen Early, September 15, 1938, DNC, OF 300, f. Ga. 1933–45, Roosevelt papers.

[223]Max E. Land, March 17, 1938, DNC, OF 300, box 15, f. k-p, Roosevelt papers.

[224]O. N. G. to Fred Morrison, August 15, 1938, f. 315, Gardner papers.

[225]Fagin, "Franklin D. Roosevelt"?], 260.

[226]Edgar B. Dunlap interview.

[227]Carlyle Bargeron interview cited in Thomas, "Roosevelt vs. George," 46.

since Coca-Cola stepped in to take up the slack.[228]

More importantly, Roosevelt's speech jumpstarted George's campaign.[229] The attack energized George's supporters in a way nothing else could have. Moreover, it inadvertently derailed Talmadge's campaign strategy. Talmadge was planning to campaign on the accusation that George was a New Deal puppet, and the attack destroyed that ploy.[230] Governor Marvin Griffin, a major cog in the machine of Gene Talmadge's son in the 1950s, told an interviewer that if Roosevelt had not come to Georgia, "I think Gene Talmadge would definitely [have] been elected to the United States Senate."[231] A Talmadge victory was by no means ever that certain. He had been buried two years before, but without Roosevelt's attack, George could well have been forced into a runoff. It nearly happened as it was.

---

[228]Ibid.

[229]Tindall, *The Emergence*, 627; Anderson, *Wild Man from Sugar Creek,* 179.

[230]Coleman, et al., *A History of Georgia*, 317.

[231]Marvin Griffin, oral history, 14, Russell Library.

5

THE 1938 SENATE CAMPAIGN IN GEORGIA

The revivalists had come and gone. The converts had hit the sawdust trail. The question now becomes one of how long the converts will last and how many will inevitably back-slide.

—Ralph McGill[1]

George supported a whole galaxy of measurers sponsored by the president…I venture that no party in any democratic country ever expelled a member of this small degree of non-conformity. If a party did so, it would destroy itself, because honest-minded men would tell such a party to go to blazes.

—Raymond Moley[2]

Is he to go there pledged beforehand to vote as any one man shall direct…? No! You know we are not in any contest to elect a parrot; we are going to elect a United States Senator.

—General Walter Harris[3]

Roosevelt's attack was not enough. He had to go after George's friends whom he could reach. A government order of April 1, 1938, forbade political action of government employees in primaries and the fall elections.[4] We have seen how Roosevelt had fired Erle Cocke in July to make a place for Clark Forman as the Georgia Director of the National Emergency Council to have him in the state really to work for Camp while drawing a government salary.[5] Roosevelt's attention was now turned to Edgar B. Dunlap, counsel for the Reconstruction Finance Corporation (RFC), who had appeared in the press as a Camp supporter but who was really supporting George. A loyal Roosevelt man, Dunlap had even received in 1936 a letter from Jim Farley thanking him "for your outstanding contribution to the

[1]*Atlanta Constitution,* August 12, 1938, cited in Thomas, "Roosevelt vs. George," 61.

[2]R. Moley, "Perspective," *Newsweek* 12:40, July 25, 1938.

[3]George, *Addresses*, General Walter Harris introduction to Macon address, August 19, 1938, 3.

[4]Jesse Jones to manager of agency, August 1, 1938, Dunlap scrapbook.

[5]"Georgia MUST accept the challenge," unidentified clipping, Dunlap scrapbook.

[election] result."[6] The RFC director met with Dunlap on August 17 and ordered him to stop supporting George. Dunlap told his boss that he could not do that "with honor," and the director said he would discuss the matter with higher-ups. That day Dunlap wrote his wife that he suspected he would be fired.[7] That very day, Dunlap received a wire demanding his resignation, adding that his replacement would take over on August 20.[8] To add insult to injury, his successor was William J. Hobbs, a North Carolinian. The government allowed Camp to maintain his position as federal attorney while campaigning for George's seat, and he was in his office so rarely that most of the work fell on his assistant Isaac Hay.[9] Dunlap did, however, receive a silver tray to commemorate his service.

Edgar Dunlap's firing made national news and aroused the ire of a nation. Richard Russell, who usually stayed out of such matters, wrote Dunlap a note of confidence, adding that he would "take no part in the campaign for the Democratic nomination," and telling Dunlap, "You had a perfect right...to support him."[10] Russell even went public with his criticism. In an undated news release, Russell declared his public neutrality in the race but added, "I have no hesitation in saying...that I do not approve of the methods employed in discharging Edgar Dunlap from his position.... He had the perfect right to support Senator George with any penalty or punishment."[11] RFC officials in Washington had noted that it was usual policy to prohibit employees from political activity,[12] but if that was the case with Dunlap, why had it not been applied in Camp's and Clark Foreman's cases?[13]

Overnight Ed Dunlap became a national hero as a victim of Roosevelt's pedantry, and he received a flood of telegrams and letters from all over the country expressing support. One admirer wrote Dunlap, "The courage and patriotism as you displayed made and will save Georgia democracy."[14] Given his new status, he began traveling with George across the state, where he was introduced at rallies always to great acclaim. When called on to speak,

[6]Jim Farley to Edgar B. Dunlap, November 7, 1936, Dunlap scrapbook.

[7]Edgar B. Dunlap to Mrs. Ed Dunlap, August 17, 1938, Dunlap scrapbook.

[8]Claude Hamilton, RFC general counsel in Washington, to Edgar B. Dunlap, n. d., Dunlap scrapbook.

[9]Isaac Hay, oral history, 11, Russell Library.

[10]RR to Edgar B. Dunlap, August 22, 1938, Dunlap scrapbook.

[11]Undated news release, VI-B, box 36, f. 2, Russell papers.

[12]Jones, *Fifty Billion Dollars*, 91, cited in Thomas, "Roosevelt vs. George," 65.

[13]Roosevelt's vindictiveness did not stop there. Dunlap learned that Roosevelt blocked his award of the Distinguished Service Medal as well (Edgar B. Dunlap interview).

[14]JBG Logan to Edgar B. Dunlap, August 19, 1938, Dunlap scrapbook.

he would make statements such as the one he made in Macon shortly after his dismissal: "You can't scare Georgia."[15]

Dunlap was afterwards used by the George campaign as an anti-Roosevelt symbol. At a rally in Macon on August 20, General Walter Harris, a local historian and celebrity, introduced him by saying that on reading of Dunlap's dismissal, he did not know "whether I'm in Russia or Germany." Then Harris said to the roar of the crowd, "Stand up, Edgar!"[16] He also was used as an anti-Roosevelt symbol as he was used in the same day and even became George's campaign manager, or as one journalist called him, "the Generalissimo of the George campaign."[17]

As late as fall 1937, George did not expect any serious threat to his 1938 reelection. "Unless Gene Talmadge runs against me[,] I do not see any serious opposition," he wrote Josiah Bailey in October 1937. Even then he thought it possible that Roosevelt "may put his arms around our present governor [Ed Rivers] and persuade him," which George felt would not be a "difficult task," but he had heard both publicly and privately that Rivers wanted to succeed himself as governor.[18] Given his position as an ardent New Dealer, Rivers might have been a formidable threat, and the reader is aware that he certainly gave it some serious thought. By the last day of April, no serious opposition had appeared, and Scott Candler, a George supporter from Decatur, made public a telegram that gave the authority of a veterans' organization to pay George's senatorial qualifying fee, which it formally did on May 21, 1938.[19]

Congressional business detained George in Washington until into June, but his supporters opened his headquarters at the Henry Grady Hotel on June 3. On June 11, Heard George, who was at this point serving as his campaign manager, announced that he would formally launch his father's campaign with a radio address on June 25, followed by a formal kickoff rally in Vienna on July 4.[20] At that large rally, which included his eighty-seven-year-old father, Robert George, people from all over the state came to Vien-

---

[15]George, *Addresses*, Macon, August 19, 1938, 8.

[16]"Roosevelt has ousted…," *New York Times* (?), August 20 or 21, 1938, Dunlap scrapbook.

[17]Ralph Smith, "In Crackerland," Dunlap scrapbook; see also John Carlton, oral history, 14, Russell Library.

[18]WFG to J. W. Bailey, October 5, 1936, box 475, f. 1937, August–December, Bailey papers.

[19]Thomas, "Roosevelt vs. George," 30; *Atlanta Journal,* May 2, 13, 1938, cited in Cobb, "Not Gone, but Forgotten," 200; *Atlanta Constitution*, June 25, 1938.

[20]Thomas, "Roosevelt vs. George," 36.

na, where George made the first political speech he had made for himself in twelve years. He was stiff, erudite, and formal and kept his coat buttoned throughout the speech, despite the heat. Still, the Atlanta press gave him great coverage.[21] Stating that he represented "rich and poor alike," the *Atlanta Constitution* called him "a man of the people" and praised him for not lowering himself into demagoguery. The paper concluded its praise by advising its readers, "Georgia and the nation both need such a man in the doubtful years to come."[22]

As though he had anticipated Roosevelt's attack a month later, he spoke of his support for the New Deal but stressed his allegiance to "Georgia Democracy" which would always come before his allegiance to any man. He never mentioned the rumbling opposition from the White House.[23] Roosevelt's attack turned the campaign into one of the strangest in Georgia, with Governor Rivers subtly supporting Camp, while members of his organization supported George. Russell remained quiet while his large family openly took sides. Organized labor supported both George and Rivers.[24] Roosevelt's endorsement of Camp did little to help his candidacy, but one historian felt that it destroyed whatever chance Talmadge might have had by the promotion it gave George by martyring him.[25] We have noted what damage Herman Talmadge felt that it had done to his father's campaign. It also gave George's somewhat overconfident campaign a well-needed kick in the pants.

George's opposition, the liberal Camp and the demagogue Talmadge, offered something for everyone to vote for—or against—was joined by W. G. McRae, who called himself 100 percent New Dealer, but wanted the government's programs financed by a sales tax, which was an echo of the Townsend plan. In the campaign, George lashed back at Roosevelt, but on the advice of Max Gardner, he did not name him personally. After the attack at Barnesville, George returned to Atlanta, where a crowd had assembled to greet him at his headquarters at the Henry Grady Hotel. It filled the lobby of the hotel and spilled onto the sidewalk. There were also banners and a brass band, which indicates that George had put to use his forewarning of Roosevelt's attack. Shaking hands throughout the crowd, he ascended

[21]Anderson, *Wild Man from Sugar Creek,* 171.

[22]*Atlanta Constitution*, July 6, 1938, cited in Zeigler, "Senator Walter George's 1938 Campaign," 336.

[23]Thomas, "Roosevelt vs. George," 37.

[24]Fossett, "The Impact of the New Deal on Georgia Politics, 1933–1941," 316–17.

[25]Cobb, "Not Gone, but Forgotten," 197–209.

to the balcony from which he made his first real speech of the campaign. Beginning with John Paul Jones' famous cry, "I have just begun to fight," he lashed out at any notion that the Democratic Party was the party of one man but was in reality a party of "the rank and file." Then he sounded a theme he would repeat in many a campaign stop before the voting: "I am confident that the George people are ready to fight this thing through to the finish and prove we are capable and determined to run our own affairs."[26] Then waxing oratorical, he thundered in that voice for which he was famous, "Events have lifted this campaign above the level of other campaigns[;] they have lifted it to a struggle for human liberty."[27] To support George for reelection now became a cause that both the Left and the Right could embrace.

George in the next few weeks hammered on the questions of states' rights, which was not really the issue at hand but would play well with the people, and he stressed the separation of powers. He made frequent references to Tom Watson, and he resurrected his old isolationism. He defended his New Deal record and carefully defended each of his anti-New Deal votes. Most importantly, he shed the quiet dignified image of a statesman and morphed into a coatless, loose-tie-wearing candidate that Georgians of that era so loved, as he went on the counterattack. In that mode, he vowed that he would fight, using a curious metaphor, "to the last dying ditch."[28] Despite the mixed metaphors, his audiences loved it.

While George did not ever attack Roosevelt by name, he did attack those around him, "the little people near the throne, that little group of communists," he called them. He even included among the villains, for good measure, James Ford, the Communist Party's black nominee for president, who as far as this researcher can ascertain, never interfered in the Georgia race. His references were to Tom Corcoran, Benny Cohen, C. H. Foreman, and Marvin H. McIntyre, who had encouraged Roosevelt's course of action and who were in some cases already working against him in the state. "If my return [to the Senate] depends on [these four men], I don't want to go back. I will not mention them in the same breath with the president for whom I still have the utmost respect and admiration."[29] Blaming Roosevelt's attack

---

[26]*Atlanta Constitution*, August 12, 1938, cited in Fagin, "Franklin D. Roosevelt," 229–30.

[27]"Human Liberties are Endangered by FDR—George," *Atlanta Constitution*, n.d., Dunlap scrapbook.

[28]*Atlanta Journal*, August 15, 1928, cited in Anderson, *WIld Man from Sugar Creek*, 179.

[29]*New York Times*, August 16, 1938, cited in Fagin, "Franklin D. Roosevelt," 237.

on his circle (though no clear-thinking person would have thought that Roosevelt was controlled by these men) was the position he maintained throughout the campaign. When attacking Roosevelt's actions, he never mentioned him by name, and when he did invoke the president's name, it was always with the greatest respect. In the midst of the campaign in a speech in Decatur, he demonstrated this tone in clear language: "I do not tonight, and I will not at any time engaged [*sic*] in personalities and personal denunciation of the chief Executive of the Nation." The next day in Thompson, George told the crowd, "I know that here in this state we hold in the deepest respect the chief executive, and I do not seek to detract from the respect and confidence of our people in our national leadership. I merely seek to encourage you to assert your own right."[30] In Monroe several days earlier, he had voiced this theme but in a different way. "I have gone along 98 percent of the time with the president," he said, playing a little fast and loose with his percentages. "I will go along with the president whenever he is right 100 percent, and I will stand against the president when he is wrong 100 percent."[31]

Some students and one journalist of this election have said that George, in mentioning Cohen, was playing the bigotry card, since Corcoran was Catholic and Cohen was Jewish.[32] He may well have been, but few people noticed. Although George did mention that Ford was black, people in largely Protestant Georgia hardly knew that Corcoran was a Catholic. Georgia had recently had a US Senator named Cohen, the stand-in for Richard Russell, less than a decade before, and if Benny Cohen was Jewish, most Georgians were probably unaware of it, and those who sensed it would probably not have been swayed by it. If the references to these names were hatemongery, they were certainly mild for the language of that day. Moreover, as George defended his opposition to Roosevelt's anti-lynching bill, he peppered his speeches with such phrases as "our good colored friends."[33] One is hard-pressed to imagine Governor Clifford Walker or Gene Talmadge using such moderate language.

George's first campaign swing began in Waycross, Georgia, on August

---

[30]George, *Addresses*, Decatur, August 25, 1938, 21; Thomson, August 25, 1938, 23.

[31]George, *Addresses*, Monroe, August 22, 1938, 20.

[32]Ralph McGill, *Atlanta Constitution*, August 18, 1938, cited in Fossett, "The Impact of the New Deal on Georgia Politics, 1933–1941," 295; J. B. Shannon, "Presidential Politics in the South: 1938, I," *The Journal of Politics* 1/2 (May 1939): 146–170. Cited in Fossett, "The Impact of the New Deal on Georgia Politics, 1933–1941," 294; Egerton, *Speak Now against the Day*, 119.

[33]See George, *Addresses*, Passion.

15, and it was to be a tour through the tobacco and cotton belt, a part of the state that would have been "Talmadge Country." Two thousand people stood in 105-degree heat (a temperature so hot that the rose in George's lapel wilted[34]) to hear George's call for his reelection. It was easily the most impassioned and bitter speech of his political life, and its contents would be repeated in every campaign appearance until the day before the voting on September 14. It would essentially be Walter George's campaign brochure, which was circulated by the thousands around the state. It became known as the "Waycross Declaration."

In the sweltering heat, he pulled out all of his oratorical stops to a crowd of 1500 supporters. Nearly blinded by sweat running down his face, his voice choked with emotion, George began with, "I was born in poverty in the sand hills of Webster County, Georgia, the son of a tenant farmer.... I know what it is to long for things that I cannot have. Back there in the days when as a boy I plowed the white, sandy soil...[and his voice would choke with emotion] and I grew into manhood during a period of progressive hardship. I came along...when my native state...was still struggling under the backlash of Reconstruction."

Mentioning his desire for a college education, he said, "There were times when the halls of Mercer [College] were as distant in my dreams as the castles of Spain." He said, "I am a Georgia, bred and born. I am a full-time Georgian," he would add, taking a dig a Roosevelt's claim to be a part-time citizen of the state. Then he launched into a defense of democracy.

> I am a Democrat. I have fought the party's battles in Congress and upon the hustings. Just ten years ago I was called back to Georgia...to take part in a campaign in which [Georgia] democracy was at stake [in the 1928 presidential election]. Although I did not agree fully with some of the things advocated by the nominee of the Houston convention, I came back to do my part.... I was born in a Democratic family. I am no part-time Democrat. And I never scratched the party's ticket from constable to President—Never!

He denounced "outside influence in Georgia politics," and he drew a parallel between Roosevelt's actions and Sherman's "March to the Sea." He stressed over and over again that the people of Georgia could make their own decisions and would not tolerate outside interference.[35]

---

[34]Chandler, *Natural Superiority of Southern Politicians*, 325.

[35]For various versions of the speech, see George, *Addresses*, Passim 1–2; *New York Times*, August 16, 1938, cited in Fagin, "Franklin D. Roosevelt," 259–60; "Voice of the 84th," 23.

The crowd, many of them weeping, cheered loudly, so much so that he had trouble finishing his speech. When he did, the band erupted in a rousing rendition of "Dixie," which was almost drowned out by the roar of the crowd. From now to the end of the campaign, this pattern would be used for his rallies, and he would give the same speech about his poverty-ridden youth, which the reader will remember, was somewhat fictitious. How much of his performance was an act, we will never know. If indeed the tears were faked and the emotion was feigned, it was easily the greatest performance of his life.

In a speech in Thompson, Georgia, he spoke of his mother and how she used to look into his face with a look of deep concern. "I did not understand it then," he admitted, "but as I grew older I learned what a mortgage was, I knew that gave her concern.... I saw the plowshare of care cut deeper and deeper and the furrows of care in her sad and patient face.... I wanted to do what I could to help that class of people."[36] At times he used mild demagoguery, referring to Labor Secretary Frances Perkins as "Ma Perkins" and calling the anti-lynching bill "carpetbaggery glorified," but it remained tame compare to the bellowing of many other Southern politicians.

In the speeches that followed, he stressed that he was "a liberal Democrat within the American Constitution" and that he would be no president's puppet. Except for his tweak at Roosevelt for being a "part-time Georgian," he never made any references to him except to say, "I have nothing but the deepest and most profound respect." If the people of Georgia had never known of Cochran, Cohen, and McIntyre, "these Wall Street lawyers," as he villainized them, their names were well known throughout the state by the end of the campaign. He frequently said that he was on trial and that the people of Georgia were the jury. He often referred to Camp not by name but as the "anointed candidate" or the "hand-picked candidate."

After his first swing through tobacco country, he returned to Vienna for a brief rest. He had been encouraged by what he saw and heard, and he told a reporter that he felt that the president's intervention had helped him. It had brought some of his friends "militantly into the open," and had brought to his cause many men "who had not reached a final decision."[37] Resuming the campaign trail, he made a campaign speech almost every day except Sundays, sometimes with rather long drives between rallies on the Georgia roads of that day. He went from Monroe on August 22 to Canton,

[36]George, *Addresses*, Thomson, August 26, 1938, 10–11.

[37]"George is Given Edge," *Washington Star* clipping, August 18, 1938, G-1938, box 337, DDS, RNC papers.

north of Atlanta the next day. Then to Rome, then Decatur, then Thompson, then Atlanta, then over 150 miles south to Dublin the next day. The day after that found him in Thomasville near the Florida state line, then halfway up the state to Statesboro the next. He hit small towns like Trion and large ones like Atlanta. He ended with a rally in Vienna on Tuesday night, September 13 in Vienna, with the election the next day. He had driven 39,000 miles around the state, often driven by Erle Cocke, Jr., who had been a victim as had Edgar Dunlap.[38] When he caught a cold touring a cold storage plant in Waycross, he continued his speaking despite a hoarse voice.[39] As he barnstormed about the state, he became more and more aggressive and self-confident, obviously feeding on the adulation he was receiving. He also came to brag on himself more as well.[40] He always hammered most effectively on the theme that he was not indeed the "rich man's candidate" but the candidate of the common man. He also attacked the liberals for their intolerance. To a crowd in Commerce, Georgia, he thundered, "Everybody is a liberal who agrees with them [those around the president], and nobody is a liberal who does not agree with them. I am not going out of the Democratic Party, and I will fight…to prevent a little group of selfish men…from destroying the Democratic Party."[41] The theme carried well.

Showing a more far-reaching view of events, he spoke to women, something many candidates would not have done in the Georgia of that day. Early in the campaign he reminded voters of how he had stood aside to allow Mrs. Rebecca Felton to be sworn in as the first woman US Senator. "In honoring Mrs. Felton," he said, "we have honored womanhood everywhere, and reflected new glory upon our great state." The only place in which Miss Lucy was in evidence in the campaign was in the Macon rally, where she met with women workers after George's speech.[42] Men still thoroughly dominated Georgia politics, but George showed keen political savvy in reaching out to women.

Georgia historian Kenneth Coleman accused George of using the race card in the election, but if he did so, he did it so mildly that many would not have recognized it.[43] George was certainly not for a Second Reconstruction

---

[38]Erle Cocke, oral history, 8, Russell Library.

[39]George, *Addresses*, Waycross, August 15, 1938, 1.

[40]Ibid., *passim*.

[41]George, *Addresses*, Commerce, September 3, 1938, 188.

[42]Ibid., 1–2.

[43]Coleman, et al., *A History of Georgia*, 317.

that would finally come in the 1950s and 1960s, but his record on race and minority relations was never one of the harsh, bitter rantings of other Georgia politicians. Indeed he often spoke out in their interest. In October 1938, after he had won the primary and could gain no political advantage by doing so, he took the British to task for restricting Jewish immigration to Palestine, and was the only member of the Georgia delegation to do so.[44] When helping doing so could only have hurt him politically, he endorsed Rev. L. D. Watson, a black minister, for a federal job in 1937 for his work for the Democratic Party.[45] Indicative of his attitude was his inclusion of the "contribution of the Negro" to the history of Georgia in a speech made in 1948, a very racially charged year, and praised their "cultural independence in literature." In the same speech, he called Booker T. Washington, who "challenged Georgia, as well as the South in general, to a new and more hopeful and practical view of interracial relations."[46]

Coleman is likely referring to the anti-lynching bill. George did attack the Wagner Lynching bill despite the fact that there had been a recent lynching in Crisp County.[47] George opined that the bill "reflected on the South," and had been introduced only to gain black votes in New York and Pennsylvania, where it might tip the balance to a candidate.[48] George argued that the problem was not just Southern and that many lynching occurred out of the South, and indeed he was right. In 1933 in California, two white kidnapper-murderers were lynched in San Jose, and the governor of California had announced a message congratulating those who had lynched these two men.[49] George did seem, however, to wear as a badge the call for his defeat by vice-presidential candidate of the Communist Party, Jamie Ford (whom George always mentioned that he was "a negro" when he told his unsuspecting audiences).[50] To liken George to the Talmadges, the Smiths, the Bilbos, and the Vardamans is simply missing the mark.

Probably his largest rally of the campaign was held in the City Auditorium in Macon, the mid-state county seat of a six-unit vote county on August 19. George arrived in town by motorcade and was met by a local delegation. A police escort brought him into town. The program was emceed by local historian, general, and lawyer Walter Harris, who warmed up the

---

[44]See 700, October 27, 1938, box 2, f. 4, Pres. Alph. file, Roosevelt papers.

[45]Memo, July 15, 1936, box 2, file f, Pres. Alph. file, Roosevelt papers.

[46]*Exhibition Commemorating the Settlement of Georgia, 1733–1948*, 6.

[47]Cobb, "Not Gone, but Forgotten," 205.

[48]George, *Addresses*, Carrolton, 15.

[49]Freidel, *FDR and the South*, 84.

[50]See George, *Addresses*, Canton, August 23, 1938, 4 and Atlanta, August 27, 1938, 17.

crowd with a lecture on "What Are the Qualifications of a United States Senator?" These were, as he saw them, a "democrat," not a "follower of some strange -ism born in foreign lands," apparently not realizing that democracy had not been birthed in Georgia, nor was the Georgia electorate open to all citizens. He said that the senator must favor "equal rights for all and special privileges for none" and "someone who believes in the "constitution…and the Declaration of Independence."[51] He further excited the crowd by introducing Edgar Dunlap. When George himself spoke, he called on Georgians not to be bought by the flood of federal money that Roosevelt was sending into the state, noting that they would get it anyway: "But if you never get it, you cannot pay the price of self-respect that you will be asked to pay."[52]

Behind this campaign, one sees the fine, moderate hand of Governor Gardner, who had snooped around Washington and learned that Roosevelt even preferred Talmadge to George.[53] So subtle was Gardner's involvement that no historian of the purge has ever mentioned his role. With his help, George and his organization ended the campaign with great confidence. In June, George had written Senator Bailey, "I shall be wise as possible in this campaign. I will endeavor to make no serious mistake," adding, "I have no fear of the outcome unless the president can name the senator from the State."[54] By the time of his last rally in Vienna the night before the vote, he was confident of an overwhelming victory. As it turned out, he was to spend a long night on September 14–15 before his radio.

After the "Barnesville Manifesto," Camp became falsely confident about his chances, obviously believing, as did Roosevelt, that the president's anointment would be all that would be necessary to propel this rather obscure protégé of Richard Russell into the United States Senate.[55] His supporters at the very least believed that Roosevelt's blessing had turned the race into a contest between Camp and George, with Talmadge no longer a factor, since the blessing had turned the race into a question of New Deal support.[56] His campaign slogan became "If he's good enough for Franklin D. Roosevelt, he's good enough for me."[57] Wrapping himself from the beginning in the mantle of the New Deal, he supplied Roosevelt with a list of Georgian governmental figures who were not supporting him so that presi-

[51]Ibid., Macon, August 19, 1938, 3; UNC, n.d., Sen. Gardner (NC).

[52]Ibid., 26.

[53]Morrison, *Governor O. Max Gardner*, 184.

[54]WFG to Josiah Bailey, June 20, 1938, box 476, f. 1938, June–August, Bailey papers.

[55]Thomas, "Roosevelt vs. George," 70.

[56]Anderson, *Wild Man from Sugar Creek*, 178.

[57]*New York Times*, August 17, 1938, 12.

dential pressure could be brought to bear on them.[58] After Barnesville, his attacks became more vicious—and ridiculous. Shortly after the incident, Camp told a reporter that "If a hungry man asked Senator George for bread, he might be constrained to refuse, but at the drop of a hat…he will sing 'Dixie.'"[59] He overused several of Roosevelt's clichés such as "entrenched greed" and "tool of the wealthy" until they became monotonous, and in the *Atlanta Constitution* he ran an ad that was likely lost on most Georgians of that day. Called "Behold…Walter Saint George the George," it began,

> And it came to pass that they had an election in the Land of the Georgey-its…. They have reared a mighty idol before them[,] and they call him Walter St. George the George…. What's St. George the George ever done that we should bow down and worship him…? … When there is poverty among his people, [he]…introduceth a resolution…. Behold in all the sixteen years he hath…[been] amongst the Pharisees…he hath never adopted any other course to succor thee….

Informing his readers that the plutocrats, a term which would probably have been unknown to most Georgians in 1938, were paying George's bills, he asked the question, "And what shall we do?… Why do thou just as the Chief of the Democratic Party saith…. Get thee all in line behind that clean-cut, alert, patriotic and loyal candidate Lawrence S. Camp and elect him."[60] The only major Georgian to "get thee in line behind" him was Richard Russell's father, Judge Russell,[61] who was still smarting about his defeat at the hands of George in 1926, who called him "a mere servile tool of the great utilities' trust."[62]

Moreover, much of what Roosevelt tried to do behind the scenes either failed or backfired. Let us remember the utter failure of firing Edgar Dunlap. At the same time, Camp's efforts to get the president to obtain reversals

---

[58]Harley Branch to Marvin McIntyre, June 27, 1938, marked "confidential," O.F. 300, box 31, "Georgia," RDRL, cited in Fagin, "Franklin D. Roosevelt," 179.

[59]*Macon Telegraph*, August 15, 1938, and August 19, cited in Cobb, "Not Gone, but Forgotten," 204.

[60]Quoted in the *Atlanta Constitution*, clipping, September 6, 1938, f. 970, Gardner papers.

[61]Untitled *Atlanta Journal* clipping, Dunlap scrapbook.

[62]Coode, "Georgia Congressmen and the New Deal, 1933–1938," 235. See his announcement before Roosevelt had endorsed Camp that he would not vote for George. *Atlanta Constitution* clipping, July 23, 1938, DNC, OF 300, box 14, f. Ga. 1933–45, Roosevelt papers. His son Bob Russell, however, openly worked for George (Farley to McIntyre, 2 July 1938, OF 300, box 31, "Georgia," FDRL, cited in Fagin, "Franklin D. Roosevelt," 179–80).

of earlier union endorsements of George[63] did not result in one reversal. Efforts to use the WPA membership for Camp ran afoul of the redoubtable state director, Miss Gay Sheppardson, who out of fairness blocked any effort to use "her people" as they had been used in Kentucky.[64] In this case, 40 percent of the 53,000 WPA employees were black and therefore could not vote in the primary anyway. Many of the remainder failed the voter qualifications of having either forty acres or $5,000 worth of property or money.[65] Finally, a major detriment to Camp's campaign was former Georgian Clark H. Foreman, ostensibly sent, one will remember, into Georgia as National Emergency Council state director, but really to work for Camp. There is probably no bigger example of the clumsiness of Roosevelt's efforts than his involvement of this politically inept figure. Foreman had no greater understanding of Georgia politics than the people who had sent him. His ham-handed attempts to force the bureaucrats to Camp failed miserably, and he personally became a lightning rod because he had served on several interracial committees. A rumor circulated around the state that in Washington he had a black secretary and that he was part black himself. A Georgian wrote to a national journalist, "Whoever thought of sending Foreman to Georgia deserves a leather medal for stupidity."[66]

Other factors hindered his campaign. One that was detrimental for Camp, and to some degree for George as well, was the county unit system, in effect an electoral college for the Georgia counties, in which three counties with a handful of voters could nullify an opposing candidate's having carried Fulton County (Atlanta). Camp was definitely an urban candidate in an essentially rural state. The one dollar per year poll tax discouraged many people from voting who might otherwise have supported him. Another was the utter disorganization and ineptness of his campaign. We have noted the ad in the *Constitution* that would have at best puzzled many readers. With his nose in the text, Camp read prepared speeches that went over the heads of his listeners, mentioning groups like the Liberty Leaguers, of which most Georgians had never heard. He repeatedly used the statement that "Liberals were marching through Georgia," which no one in his campaign realized the General Sherman implication to most Georgians. He never even played a

---

[63] Hon. Harlee Branch to F.D.R., August 16, 1938, PPF, box 107–117, f. 109, Roosevelt papers.

[64] Clapper, "New Deal," *New York World Telegram*, 23 August 1938, 20, cited in Hooper, "The Purge," 168.

[65] Ralph South to R. Clapper, August 17, 20, 1938, Clapper papers, Library of Congress Manuscript Division, cited in Fagin, "Franklin D. Roosevelt," 265–66.

[66] Ralph South to R. Clapper, August 20, 1938, ibid., 264.

radio ad using the president's speech, so Roosevelt's endorsement availed him little good and did him much harm.[67] The one element that might have mattered was the federal government's fast-flowing spigot and the number of federal employees in Georgia, which outnumbered those in any state in the union, with only the District of Columbia having greater numbers. The tsunami of tax dollars started flowing in August and continued until the voting. Georgia received millions of dollars in highway grants that seem to be announced virtually every few days.[68] The last one, made public five days before the primary, would add 35,000 workers to the employment rolls. The next day arrived a four million grant of emergency loans to farmers.[69] This disgusting buying of votes with federal money failed for several reasons. For one, the crassness of it all alienated many people, and second, the grants were announced but the money would not be felt in the state before the voting. Moreover, many of the potential voters that were to be corralled would have difficulty voting because of Georgia's restrictive voting qualifications. The whole Camp "movement" was a lost cause from the beginning.

Talmadge, on the other hand, was a horse of a different color. A shrewd politician who was at the same time a colorful campaigner, he was a real threat to the dignified, aloof George. Although he had become damaged goods politically after his resounding defeat by Richard Russell in 1936, he had a large following and was a force with which to be reckoned. Many at the time thought he would win. Joe Alsop and Robert Kinter were in Atlanta for Roosevelt's speech, and they stopped by Talmadge's office. Noting that besides his talent for demagoguery, Alsop condescendingly observed that Talmadge was unsurpassed at hitting a spittoon no matter how great the distance, but concluded on leaving the interview that he felt that he had been talking to Georgia's next senator.[70] Former governor Marvin Griffin, a politician who had quite a heyday in Georgia politics until he was overtaken by the times, believed that had Roosevelt not attacked George, Talmadge "would definitely [have] been elected to the United States Senate."[71]

In the past, when Talmadge had won, it was always because of the bi-

---

[67]Fagin, "Franklin D. Roosevelt," 262.

[68]See *Atlanta Constitution*, August 13, 23, September 8, 9, 11, 12, 1938, cited in Fagin, "Franklin D. Roosevelt," 265.

[69]*New York Times*, September 11, 12, 1938, 12, and 2, cited in Hooper, "The Purge," 177.

[70]*Atlanta Constitution,* August 11 and 12, 1938, cited in Anderson, *Wild Man from Sugar Creek,* 177.

[71]Marvin Griffin, oral history, 14, Russell Library.

zarre alchemy of the county unit system, his popularity in rural areas, and the splitting of his opposition, which allowed him to carry a majority of the county unit votes with a mere plurality of the popular vote. If Georgia had had direct election of statewide politicians, he most probably would have always been an also-ran. In his final electoral victory in 1946, he trailed his opponent in the popular vote but still won. The county unit system was the reason he would supposedly always say (and his son denied that he ever said it) that he did not care whether or not he ever carried a Georgia county in which there was a streetcar. The 1938 election was ironically his only defeat where his opposition was divided.[72]

Roosevelt's curt dismissal of Talmadge "concerns me not at all," he said after the event.[73] The *Atlanta Constitution* and the *New York Times* both felt that Roosevelt's action really gave him a boost.[74] The historian James C. Cobb, however, agreed with son Herman's assessment in that he felt that Roosevelt's attack really destroyed Talmadge's chances of victory.[75] Talmadge, on the other hand, felt that it had damaged George badly and consequently helped him. At his first speech after Barnesville, delivered in Gainesville, Georgia, Talmadge told his audience that "The President reminded me of a bucking horse. He threw George clear over the Gordon Institute."[76]

Talmadge and his son, Herman, who managed his campaign, felt that Talmadge's biggest asset was George himself. George was a distinguished white-shirted gentleman who "looked like he had reached full maturity back when God was still a boy," Herman remembered in his memoirs.[77] Compared to his father, George was a "cold fish" as a campaigner, Talmadge remembered. Moreover, George's rallies were often attended by small groups of men in business suits to whom George would read a foreign policy speech, which "even managed to put those boys to sleep." His rallies were often preceded by motorcades from different sections of the state that would rendezvous at a given town, where George spoke to them, but these congregations reinforced the charge that George was the candidate of the wealthy when most of the cars of the attendees were Cadillacs.[78] At this point, George was nearly blind with cataracts, and Herman witnessed what he felt

[72]Bernd, "Corruption in Georgia Primaries and Elections, 1938–1950," 16.
[73]Anderson, *Wild Man from Sugar Creek*, 178.
[74]*Atlanta Constitution*, August 11, 1938; *New York Times*, August 13, 1938.
[75]Cobb, "Not Gone, but Forgotten," 197.
[76]*Atlanta Journal*, August 13, 14, 1938, cited in Anderson, **[which Anderson title?]** 179.
[77]Talmadge, *Talmadge: A Political Legacy*, 38–39.
[78]Ibid., 38.

was an unforgivable transgression for a politician.[79] A man at a rally tried to shake George's hand, and not seeing him, George turned away. The man tried a second time and was "snubbed" by the unseeing George. The third time he managed to connect. "When I saw that," Herman thought, "My God, this is going to be duck soup."[80] Talmadge's assault on Roosevelt and the New Deal in 1936 had not worked, so he changed his tactics to promote himself as a champion of the little man, dubbing George as a toady of the rich, thus following Roosevelt's same attacking point at Barnesville. Except for calling Camp "the 100 percent coattail rider," he largely ignored him. One of Talmadge's typical tricks was to drive into town on a wagon pulled by a mule team. It was always said that the team and wagon would be hauled by a truck to the outskirts of the intended destination, where Talmadge would meet it in a car. He often planted hecklers in the audience to lob soft attacks, which he would knock out of the oratorical ball park. In the campaign, he attacked George for "talking one way and voting another."[81] The moneyed interests had ignored Talmadge since his loss in 1936, so he stressed the support George had received from the wealthy, big business, and so forth. According to Talmadge, George made much of the money he had to spend from big business. Speaking in small towns, Talmadge always mentioned a local George supporter who controlled local funds and tell the crowd that they better be certain that they got their share.[82] In his usual fashion, he attacked George when Secretary of Agriculture Henry A. Wallace cut Georgia's tobacco quota by 25 percent from what the crop produced, because George had voted for the AAA, ignoring, of course, that what farmers received for their tobacco was much greater than it had been, thanks to the bill George had supported.[83]

Business Week reported after Roosevelt's speech that the White House had come to fear a Talmadge victory which was "even more unnerving" than a George win.[84] Although there seems to have been some idea that Roosevelt would have even preferred Talmadge's replacing George in the Senate, Talmadge's son correctly pointed out that such a change would be like trading "a fever blister for a skin cancer,"[85] given Talmadge's anti-New Deal po-

[79]Jarman, "Taxpayer's Senator," 41.

[80]Talmadge, *Talmadge: A Political Legacy*, 38–39.

[81]*The Statesman*, May 17, 1938, cited in Cobb, "Not Gone, but Forgotten," 200.

[82]Carlyle Bergeron interview in Thomas, "Roosevelt vs. George," 70.

[83]Thomas, "Roosevelt vs. George," 47.

[84]"Washington Bulletin," *Business Week* (August 13, 1938): 7, cited in Thomas, "Roosevelt vs. George," 70.

[85]Talmadge, *Talmadge: A Political Legacy*, 38.

sitions. "Ole Gene" would never make it to the Senate, no matter how badly he wanted to go. As one old Georgia political hand told a reporter for *Collier's*, "The people of Georgia were too ashamed of his carryings-on to send him up there."[86] Locally, he maintained some aura of respectability. He was, after all, elected governor twice more before he died. Lawrence Camp endorsed him in his successful race in 1940,[87] and Walter George attended his funeral in 1946.[88]

Faced with the exterior challenge, George's supporters began to emerge from the woodwork. They consisted of a broad and extensive galaxy of supporters, ranging from organized labor and federal employees to university professors and business leaders. Undergirding this broad strength was an all-important and almost total support from the press.[89] Business was a most important factor, for it would supply the necessary money, of which Talmadge was so jealous. This consisted, according to Joseph Alsop and Robert Kintner in their column "The Capitol Parade," of the utilities, the banks, railroads, and the large industries of the state. "In fact," the pair wrote, "you have to look twice to tell this group of Senator George's supporters from the fat cats of Pennsylvania politics."[90] When asked about it, George candidly admitted their support.[91]

Local courthouse politicians, elected officials, congressmen, and other political figures who favored the senator supported him in various degrees of openness. Members of Rivers's organization began secretly supporting George as well, despite the fact that Rivers himself was more or less for Camp. George's son Heard told an interviewer in 1972 that Russell supported his father, but if he did so, he did it very subtly, despite the fact that George had openly endorsed him two years before.[92] Mark Dunahoo mysteriously, and somewhat unclearly, implied in his oral history that Russell did not support George. He speaks of Russell's leaving a meeting with House Speaker Roy V. Harris, him, and Russell's brother Bob "and didn't come

---

[86]McMillan, "So Goes the South," 45.

[87]Stoney, "Georgia's Rotten Boroughs," 248.

[88]Talmadge, *Talmadge: A Political Legacy*, 81.

[89]*New York Times*, August 13 and 19, 1938, cited in Fossett, "The Impact of the New Deal on Georgia Politics, 1933–1941," 291.

[90]"The Capital Parade," *Atlanta Constitution*, August 11, 1938, cited in Fossett, "The Impact of the New Deal on Georgia Politics, 1933–1941," 290.

[91]Michie and Ryhlick, *Dixie Demagogues*, 190, cited in Zeigler, "Senator Walter George's 1938 Campaign," 334.

[92]Heard George, interview by Jane W. Herndon, March 14, 1972, cited in Cobb, "Not Gone, but Forgotten," 207.

back," adding "That's about all I'm going to say about that campaign [laughs]."[93] One local pol who did openly support George was Roy V. Harris, the ubiquitous politician and on and off speaker of the Georgia House. He was quite an asset. Ralph McGill called him "the best political organizer in the state" and "a most adept county unit politician." Wartime Governor Ellis Arnall, who probably shared few political views of the conservative Harris, called him "the best politician I have ever known."[94] Harris's major contribution was coordinating the pro-George Rivers supporters with George's organization.[95] In the same vein was the undercover work of Max Gardner, who summered that year in Highlands, North Carolina, on the Georgia line, instead of his home in Shelby, North Carolina, better to work on the George campaign. He had been secretly active since March. When summoned to Atlanta by Robert Woodruff on Coca-Cola business, Gardner told George, "I will keep my ear to the ground and my mouth shut, but if I hear anything that appears to be of importance to you, I will let you know."[96] Emory Bass, a prominent New Dealer, abandoned his own Congressional race in the 8th district to work full time for George. Abit Nix, and Athens political figure and gubernatorial candidate and Wiley Moore, a big Roosevelt supporter in 1936, both endorsed George.[97] One of the unkindest cuts of all for Roosevelt, if he ever learned of it, was the endorsement of George by Dr. Michael Hoke, the chief surgeon at Warm Springs.[98]

Interesting but not terribly valuable was George's rather broad organized labor support mentioned above. The number of members of organized labor in the state was very small, and labor's backing could sway only the closest of elections. Its sustenance, in other cases, could be detrimental to support in some other sectors, given the South's general anti-labor hostility. Moreover, within the labor movement, George's support was not solid. Whereas the American Federation of Labor (AFL) endorsed George, the Congress of Industrial Organization (CIO) endorsed Camp. In a grade of "A" to "F," the CIO's political instrument "Labors Non-Partisan League,"

---

[93]Mark Dunahoo, oral history, 57, Russell Library.

[94]Henderson, *The Politics of Change in Georgia*, 44.

[95]Roy V. Harris, oral history, 52, Russell Library. Rivers expressed official neutrality in the senate race, stating only, "I am for the New Deal and the president," *Atlanta Constitution*, August 11, 1938, cited in Fossett, "The Impact of the New Deal on Georgia Politics, 1933–1941," 297.

[96]O. M. Gardner to WFG, March 28, 1938, f. 299, Gardner papers.

[97]*Atlanta Constitution*, July 10, 1938, cited in Zeigler, "Senator Walter George's 1938 Campaign," 336.

[98]*New York Times*, September 12, 1938, cited in Fagin, "Franklin D. Roosevelt," 270.

gave George a grade of "D."[99] One of Georgia's leading labor publications, *Journal of Labor*, called George "one of the president's most able supporters." William Green of the AFL told Charles B. Gamling of the Georgia Federation of Labor in July before Roosevelt's speech that the national leadership was "behind George 100 percent."[100] These endorsements had come when only George and Talmadge were in the race. As the reader will recall, Camp tried to use Roosevelt's leverage to undo the endorsements, and many locals wanted to back Camp. Had the organized labor vote been of any size, these machinations might have been important, but given the paucity of their ranks, whatever labor did would be of little import.

Of greater importance in both numbers and financial support was the endorsement of George by the state Republican Party. Georgia National Committeeman James W. Arnold openly called on the state's Republican voters, which he stated consisted of the unlikely figure of 40,000 members, to vote for George "because we are at the crossroads of a great national crisis."[101] Landon had received 36,942 votes (12 percent) in Georgia in 1936, and if these swung behind George, it would be a valuable voting bloc indeed. George even received the endorsement of the North Carolina Young Republicans, whose influence would certainly be minimal.[102] Arnold, however, undermined whatever support this move would have given George because he included, in a widely-circulated letter, that the reelection of George and other conservative Democrats would split the Democratic Party, thus improving the party's chances of recapturing the White House in 1940. Camp had already charged that George was a Republican anyway, and this move gave credence to the charge. Roosevelt weighed in with the only public statement he made about the Georgia race after Barnesville with a condemnation in the *New York Times* of the Republican support.[103] When asked himself about the endorsement, George refused to make any comment, and his campaign ignored it.[104]

Help came from outside the state in the form of political endorsements.

---

[99]*Atlanta Constitution*, July 16, 1938, cited in Thomas, "Roosevelt vs. George," 48. Two days later, the *Atlanta Constitution* editorialized that to describe George in such lowly was "outrageous effrontery."

[100]Ibid.

[101]"The Purge Spreads," 9.

[102]Bennett Riddle, Jr. to J. W. Bailey, August 13, 1938, box 476, f. 1938, June–August, Bailey papers.

[103]*New York Times*, August 23, 1938, cited in Fagin, "Franklin D. Roosevelt," 268.

[104]*Washington Daily News*, August 23, 1938; *Atlanta Constitution*, 23 August 1938, in Michie and Rhylick, *Dixie Demagogues*, 198–99, cited in Fagin, "Franklin D. Roosevelt," 268.

As early as mid-July, Senator Bailey had already offered if George needed him "to come on down there" and campaign for him.[105] After Roosevelt's attack, Senator M. M. Logan (D-Kentucky) endorsed George,[106] and Gardner, in his own careful way, supported the senator by writing a congratulatory letter to Clark Howell of the *Constitution* for his pro-George editorial after the Roosevelt attack, calling it "a masterpiece."[107]

One potential source of help that remained silent was Richard Russell. Aside from the fact that he had not intervened in other races since his election to the Senate, he had good reasons for remaining on the sidelines. On one hand, George had endorsed him for reelection in 1936 against Talmadge. Moreover, if George was reelected to the Senate, working with him would be difficult if he had come out openly for Camp. On the other hand, he and Camp had been very close. They had both been elected to the House of Representatives in 1920. From that time on, Camp had been an important cog in the growing Russell machine. Camp had managed Russell's campaign for speaker pro-tem in 1923 and had supported him for speaker in 1927. He had managed Russell's campaign for governor in 1930, as well as his campaign for the Senate in 1932. Russell had made him Georgia attorney general when he was governor and, as a senator, had gotten Camp the appointment as US attorney for the northern district of Georgia. He had raised money for him in all his races, and in 1933 he had gone to Washington for his swearing in. When Russell ran for the full term in 1936, Camp had managed his campaign then, too, though he was on the federal payroll and used government employees to work part-time for him.[108] Roy V. Harris remembered, "Dick [Russell] had no brother that was [as] close to him as Lawrence."[109] Russell's failure to support Camp weighed heavily on the senator, given their closeness. He told Superior Court judge Mark Dunahoo, who served on his staff in his early days, that "there was nobody who had ever been any closer to him than Lawrence Camp." He noted, "Anything I had ever wanted, Lawrence has sponsored me and gotten behind me and pushed me." Russell was bothered by his own neutrality all the more because he always disliked "a person who was disloyal [and] untrustworthy."[110]

---

[105]J. W. Bailey to WFG, July 14, 1938, box 476, f. 1938, June–August, Bailey papers.

[106]*Rome News and Courier,* August 19, 1938, Dunlap scrapbook.

[107]O. M. Gardner to Major Clark Howell, August 15, 1938, f. 315, Gardner papers.

[108]Isaac Hay, oral history, 13, Russell Library.

[109]Roy V. Harris, oral history, 54, Russell Library.

[110]Mark Dunahoo, oral history, 65–66, Russell Library. For their relationship, see Fossett, "The Impact of the New Deal on Georgia Politics, 1933–1941," 42; Fagin, "Franklin D.

Russell's dilemma was aggravated by the close ties he had with the Roosevelt administration. He had been much more supportive of the New Deal than had Walter George.[111] Moreover, he greatly admired Roosevelt the man, wishing he could have the president's "balance and poise."[112] He had run as a strong New Dealer in 1936, and indeed his smashing victory might have induced Roosevelt to take on Walter George.[113]

In 1937, however, Russell had begun to distance himself from the New Deal for the same reasons that Walter George had done so, and his rightward movement could not have gone unnoticed by Roosevelt. This shift might have been part of the reason he avoided involvement in the race. If Roosevelt was successful in unseating George, Governor Gardner noted to Clark Howell that "it will be definite notice to Dick Russell to prepare for the guillotine."[114] There was also the consideration that Georgia had always geographically split its two senators. If one was elected from the southern part of the state, the other would represent the north. If Camp would be elected, he was also from the north, and this might not work well for Russell, when he was up for reelection in 1942.[115] Moreover, if George were defeated, given this division, George might return to run against him in 1942, when the geographic balance and the county unit system would be against him.[116] As Governor Griffin remembered, "He [Russell] could put his ear to the ground pretty good."[117] All in all, Russell found himself in a "pretty good spot," as Marvin Cox, who worked for several Georgia congressmen remembered,[118] but none of the political activists could remember Russell having ever done anything for either candidate.[119]

Despite Russell's aloofness, Roosevelt had early tried to draw Russell into the "Dump George" movement. In February 1938, the president sum-

---

Roosevelt," 181, Fite, *Richard B. Russell, Jr., Senator from Georgia*, 164; and *New York Times*, August 30, 1938, 3, in Hooper, "The Purge," 164.

[111]Fagin, "Franklin D. Roosevelt," 177.

[112]Richard B. Russell to Mother, March 10, 1938, V-1, f. parents, 1938, Russell papers (Winder).

[113]See Fossett, "The Impact of the New Deal on Georgia Politics, 1933–1941," specifically chapter 4, "The Senate Campaign of 1936," 120 ff.

[114]O. M Gardner to Clark Howell, August 15, 1938, f. 315, Gardner papers.

[115]Fagin, "Franklin D. Roosevelt," 278. Arthur Krock advanced this theory as well (*New York Times*, June 15, 1938, cited in Thomas, "Roosevelt vs. George," 35).

[116]Arthur Krock, "In the Nation," *New York Times*, June 15, 1938, 22, cited in Hooper, "The Purge," 161.

[117]Marvin Griffin, oral history, 14, Russell Library.

[118]Marvin Cox, oral history, 15, Russell Library.

[119]John Carlton, oral history, 39, Russell Library.

moned Russell to the White House, told him of his desire to beat George, asked him to pick a candidate and he, Roosevelt, would supply the money. The conversation caused Russell to break into a cold sweat, but he refused to be enlisted in the fight.[120] It is also of interest that he does not seem to have told George of the meeting. Many suspected that Roosevelt's tapping Camp to run was done as much to blackmail Russell to support his close friend.[121] Roosevelt later asked Chip Robert to tell Dick Russell that the president felt "he should commit himself definitely; that he should not align himself with the ultra-conservative group in the party."[122] In fact, it became well known that Roosevelt had pressured Russell "very vigorously" to do it.[123] It did not work, and Roosevelt learned while still at sea that Russell had not come around.[124] His attack on George would have to be his alone.

Russell's sister remembered that Roosevelt took umbrage at the way her brother did not help him depose George and felt that Roosevelt was probably angrier at him for not cooperating than he was at George.[125] Roosevelt did not speak to Russell for two years, Russell later wrote to a friend. When he attended a White House reception on January 17, 1939, he wrote to a friend "President cold."[126]

We might ask, What exactly then did Richard Russell do? Whereas Russell had voted with the New Deal more consistently than George had, he had opposed the court packing and Roosevelt had rejected a compromise that he had offered. One observer wrote that this was the point at which Russell began to "slide off the New Deal" bandwagon."[127] Governor Griffin, who was not around at the time, felt that Russell "did not like very much" Roosevelt's attempted purge.[128] In Russell's papers is an untitled, undated news release in which he reiterates that he is taking no part in the campaign and adds, "I do not approve of the methods employed in discharging Edgar Dunlap.... If he [Dunlap] believes Senator George is the best man...for the

---

[120]Fite, *Richard B. Russell, Jr., Senator from Georgia*, 163, cited in William B. Gateward, "Georgia Giant," *Georgia Historical Quarterly* Richard, 76(1), 13, 19.

[121]Roy V. Harris, oral history, 27, Russell Library.

[122]Richard B. Russell to "Chip" Roberts, June 13, 1938, PP 3061, cited in Fagin, "Franklin D. Roosevelt," 180.

[123]Ernest Vandiver, oral history, 80, Russell Library.

[124]Fagin, "Franklin D. Roosevelt," 213.

[125]Peterson/Russell interview, oral history, 47, Russell Library.

[126]Richard B. Russell to Charles Ewing, September 12, 1952, Russell Papers, cited in Fite, *Richard B. Russell, Jr., Senator from Georgia*, 164.

[127]Goldsmith, *Colleagues*, 11.

[128]Marvin Griffin, oral history, 14, Russell Library.

Senate…he had the perfect right to support Senator George." Still stressing his neutrality, he gave what could possibly be read as a mild endorsement of George: "My colleague was elected by the Democrats of Georgia as a Democrat and [has] served as an ambassador from this sovereign state…. No other power has any right to pass upon his Democracy than the Democrats of Georgia."[129] Moreover, a close associate had the "impression" that Russell had supported the senator.[130] His sister felt that he was for George "as far as I ever heard."[131] He wrote a letter of congratulation to "Cotton Ed" Smith, at whom, the reader will remember, Roosevelt had taken a whack while traversing South Carolina, when Smith was reelected.[132]

Where Russell remained publicly neutral, much of his machine worked for George.[133] Charles "Charley" Block of Macon was openly for George, as was Frank Foley in Columbus. Roy V. Harris added, "We can just name one right after the other all over the state. But as far as Dick, if he ever did anything, I never knew or heard of it."[134] Russell and Camp had obviously talked about Camp's entering the race,[135] and Roy V. Harris was fairly certain that Russell had not asked him to run.[136] Given their close association, it would have been unnatural if they had not. It is obvious from one piece of correspondence that Russell did not encourage Camp, if he did not outright discourage him. For the reasons stated above, he could not afford "to stir in the race," and he had told Camp that he would not before he entered the contest.[137] Camp probably did not expect Russell to help him after their conversations, but he probably felt that some of Russell's machine would support him, and the reader is aware, and as we have seen, little of it did. Moreover, except for Russell's father, most of his kin seemed to support George. The reader is aware, Bob Russell [Dick's brother] was a major figure in George's campaign, and this irked Camp. He was "extremely disappointed" that the Russell family did not help him, given the role he had

[129]Untitled, undated news release, VI-B, box 36, f. 2, Russell papers.

[130]Judge Linton Collins (a close friend of Russell), oral history, 9, Russell Library.

[131]Peterson/Russell interview, oral history, 54, Russell Library.

[132]E. D. Smith to Richard B. Russell, September 2, 1938, VI-B, f. 2, Russell papers.

[133]A. Krock, "In the Nation," *New York Times,* June 15, 1938, 22, cited in Hooper, "The Purge," 161.

[134]Roy V. Harris, oral history, 54, Russell Library.

[135]Richard B. Russell to Camp, August 12, 1942, series VI-B, box 34, f. 4, Russell papers.

[136]Roy V. Harris, oral history, 55, Russell Library.

[137]Richard B. Russell to Camp, August 12, 1942, series VI-B, box 34, f. 4, Russell papers.

played in Dick's campaigns.[138] Even Russell's brother-in-law delivered his congressional district for George.[139]

A few days after Barnesville, George was fired up and confident of victory on September 14, wiring his friend Senator Bailey that victory was certain, adding humorously, "unless government payroll greatly increases."[140] In a speech in Decatur, he thundered, clumsy syntax aside, "If I go back—and I will go back—because I know, I have heard the voice of the people of Georgia, the farmers, the soldiers, the teachers, the professional men, the workers, all of our people to [*sic*] often to mistake the determination of Georgia men and women to elect their own representatives." Then he promised that in returning he would "not disturb the judicial branch of the government; I will not destroy the Executive Branch of government…and I will make the last fight within me to retain unto the Congress that branch of government closest to the people—the powers rightly belonging to Congress."[141] Miss Lucy reflected the same feeling two days later when she wrote her friend Edith Bailey, wife of Senator Bailey: "Reports from every section in Georgia that we know are authentic, indicate victory unless some deviltry from Washington at the last minute has enough power…to upset everything."[142] Two weeks later, Miss Lucy wrote to Edith again with the same confidence, informing her that in winding down, the campaign had not been so strenuous in the past few days. She ended with, "We anticipate a great victory…."[143] Even Clark Howell of the *Constitution* predicted as early as August 18 that though there would likely be a runoff, George would win.[144]

The end of August gave George a boost when Roosevelt target "Cotton Ed" Smith was reelected, defeating Governor Olin Johnson, Roosevelt's hand-picked candidate. George had earlier endorsed Smith, and on hearing of his victory, he told a Thomasville audience that Georgians should "say to the good old state of South Carolina" that "We, too, know how to choose

---

[138]Isaac Hay, oral history, 46–47, Russell Library; Mark Dunahoo, oral history, 56, Russell Library.

[139]Peterson/Russell, oral history, 54, Russell Library.

[140]WFG to Josiah Bailey, August 13, 1938, box 476, f. 1932, June–August, Bailey papers.

[141]George, *Addresses*, Decatur, 25 July 1938, 23–24.

[142]Lucy Heard George to Mrs. Josiah (Edith) Bailey, August 27, 1938, box 476, f. 1938, September–October, Bailey papers.

[143]Lucy Heard George to Josiah W. Bailey, September 12, 1938, box 478, f. 1938, September–October, Bailey papers.

[144]Clark Howell to O. M. Gardner, August 1938, 1938, f. 316, Gardner papers.

our senators."[145] One George supporter felt Smith's win was worth an additional 25,000 votes on September 14.[146] Dunlap early ran radio ads announcing commanding leads in the polls when there were not any such polls (though the first polls early in September did indeed give George a commanding lead).[147] The first Gallop surveys gave George 51 percent to 28 percent for Camp to 19 percent for Talmadge. The second, a few days later, gave George the same 51 percent, with Talmadge and Camp receiving 25 percent each. The day before the election showed a five-point decline for George to 46 percent, with Talmadge moving into second place with 28 percent and Camp remaining at 25 percent.[148] The breakdown showed George running, not surprisingly, extremely well in urban areas and small towns (59 and 57 percent respectively), but beating Talmadge among farmers 44 percent to 34 percent. He was even defeating Talmadge and Camp among lower income voters, 39 percent to 30 percent and 31 percent, respectively.[149] The always-optimistic Dunlap predicted, probably for public consumption, a landslide of 60 percent in the final tally, based on informal and definitely unscientific polls. He further stated that George would carry an unlikely 140 of the 159 counties of the state.[150]

The last big rally was held in Atlanta at 8:00 p.m. in the city auditorium several days before the election. The crowd was composed of people assembled by from all over the state. George was introduced by Charles B. Gramling, president of the Georgia Federation of Labor.[151] As usual, at the end of his speech, members of the audience were in tears.[152]

George's last rally was on September 13 in his front yard in Vienna. In speaking to the crowd, he predicted complete victory. "I say good night," he told his friends and neighbors, "with the full confidence that the good men and women of our party throughout the state of Georgia will give to us, to our great cause, an overwhelming victory." He then invited the assembly to

[145]"Smith's Victory," *Savannah Morning News* clipping, September 1, 1938, box 1890, f. 1, Ellender papers.

[146]Clipping attached to interlude of M. H. McIntyre to Mrs. Elsie O'Neal, September 10, 1938, DNC, OF 300, box 15, f. N–R, Roosevelt papers

[147]Edgar B. Dunlap interview.

[148]*Atlanta Constitution*, September 4, 9, 13, 1938, cited in Bernd, "Corruption in Georgia Primaries and Elections, 1938–1950," 5.

[149]*Atlanta Constitution*, September 7, 1938, cited in Fagin, "Franklin D. Roosevelt," 269.

[150]"Dunlap predicts George…," n. d., *August Labor Review*, Dunlap scrapbook.

[151]*The Georgian* 2 (September 1938), VI-B, box 63, f. Political Ga., 1938, Russell Papers (Winder).

[152]*New York Times*, August 5, 1957, 21, RCB-5804, box 1998–1980A, f. WFG-GSA.

join him for a ham sandwich and a Coca-Cola, which had been put under an oak tree near the house. Then he asked that each say good night to him personally.[153] The judicial Townshenite candidate William G. McRae had just withdrawn and endorsed Camp, but George did not seem to think that his departure would make a difference. Nor would the most recent announcement of federal pork: $990,000 for highway construction by the WPA.[154] He went to bed certain of victory.

Dunlap returned home to Gainesville about 7:00 PM on election night and announced to his family, "Don't worry, we won!" Exhausted, he went to bed.[155] His early-to-bed move spared him some tense moments because George's victory was not certain for hours.

Talmadge, who had not bothered to vote ("Telfair [County] is for me anyway, so why go home [to McRae] to get one more vote?"), stayed in his Atlanta office in the William Oliver Building all day and greeted friends and well-wishers. He had bragged to a reporter the day before that he had received $400 in the mail on September 12, with no contributions more than five dollars. That large donation demonstrated, he said, his broad support across the state. "Tell 'em that Talmadge will be nominated in a landslide," he added to his analysis. "I know my Georgia and I know my politics. I am deceived by neither. On Wednesday, the Talmadge supporters, the so-called wool-hat boys will come to town."[156] As the votes began trickling in, he developed a commanding lead in the county unit vote, although George had a substantial lead in the popular vote. His prediction seemed to be correct; this early surge was because the first precincts to report results were the small rural precincts with fewer than a hundred votes in them. Many of those had closed at 2:00 p.m. and reported their returns before the larger precincts closed at 7:00 p.m. These rural votes, largely for Talmadge, gave him a lead in most counties and an early lead in the county unit vote. By 10:00 p.m., he led in almost a hundred counties, most of them two-vote units, giving him essentially a victory in the county unit vote.

At this point, he left his office and went to his campaign headquarters at the Ansley Hotel. An enthusiastic crowd awaited him in the ballroom there. Someone handed him a drink, but after taking a swig, he spit it out,

---

[153]George, *Addresses*, Vienna, September 13, 1938, 16.

[154]"Townshendite quits," September 13, 1938, *New York Times* clipping, box 337, f. Ga, 1938, RNC papers.

[155]Edgar B. Dunlap, Jr. interview.

[156]*Atlanta Constitution*, September 13, 1938, cited in Anderson, *Wild Man from Sugar Creek*, 180.

probably mindful of what he was doing in front of reporters. He shouted something to the effect that someone was trying to convince people he was the alcoholic that everyone said he was. Standing on a table, he shouted to his supporters, "I'm tired, I'm broke, and I'm happy." He was then carried out of the room on the shoulders of his ecstatic supporters. By 11:00 p.m., Talmadge had led for five hours, so he had a few (more?) drinks, and went to sleep, certain he had been elected to the US Senate.[157] It did indeed look bad for George. Josiah Bailey was in the hospital, and when he heard the early returns indicating a George loss, he had "something like a heart attack," he later wrote George.[158] As it turned out, when he awoke the next day, the state of Georgia had taught him a fresh lesson in political science.

After voting in Vienna and stating to the press for the umpteenth time that "the people of Georgia want a voice in the Senate, not an echo," George drove to Atlanta to await returns at his state headquarters, where his supporters' enthusiasm was decidedly restrained. Talmadge shortly lost his early popular vote lead and George pulled ahead, but Talmadge clung to his commanding lead in the unit votes. The first good news for George was the report of final returns from Liberty and McIntosh counties, two coastal counties where early returns had shown a Talmadge lead. George carried both of them. Also, though Talmadge had been leading in many of the rural counties, the larger towns and the county seats began reporting, and those votes pushed George ahead. As the evening progressed toward midnight, one by one the Talmadge counties continued tipping to George.[159] After midnight, George passed Talmadge in county unit votes, and at 1:00 a.m., the Associated Press gave George 204 unit votes, one short of the majority, to 188 for Talmadge. When WSB radio went off the air at 2:50 a.m., it gave George a majority of 220 county unit votes. He had won a majority of the unit vote and a sizable plurality of the popular vote.[160] George had his victory and Roosevelt his comeuppance.

Roosevelt's first open attempt to purge a sitting incumbent had failed. Camp had conceded before midnight and predicted that liberalism would

---

[157]Ibid.; Roy V. Harris, oral history, 53, Russell Library; Bernd, "Corruption in Georgia Primaries and Elections, 1938–1950," 1–3, citing various state newspapers; "George, Talmadge Run a Close Race," *New York Times* clipping, September 15, 1938, f. George, 1938, box 337, RNC papers.

[158]Josiah Bailey to WFC, September 24, 1938, box 476, f. 1938, September–October, Bailey papers.

[159]Ibid.; Bernd, "Corruption in Georgia Primaries and Elections, 1938–1950," 28.

[160]*Atlanta Constitution*, September 15, 16, 1938, cited in Bernd, "Corruption in Georgia Primaries and Elections 1938–1950," 7–8.

eventually triumph in Georgia. When Washington reporters asked White House officials what Roosevelt thought about George's victory, they received the reply that the president was too embroiled in administration affairs to comment on Georgia politics.[161] Actually, given the enormous financial advantage and the fact that he had the purge issue in his favor, George must have been somewhat disappointed in his performance. Of the 435,915 votes cast (an increase of 65,000 more than in the 1934 elections), George received only 44 percent of the popular vote for the 242 county-unit votes he won. Talmadge had garnered 31.7 percent with only 148 unit votes, and Camp received 24.3 percent and 20 unit votes.[162] George had beaten Talmadge by only 38,000 votes statewide, although the two together captured 76.1 percent of the vote, leaving an embarrassing 24.9 percent for Roosevelt's candidate.[163] George had carried five counties by fewer than 20 votes; Merriweather County (where Warm Springs is located) went for George by a suspicious margin of only one vote, and Camp came in third, having carried only the Warm Springs precinct. Talmadge carried four counties by fewer than twenty. A switch of 210 votes in the right counties would have given the race to Talmadge.[164] In some places, George had polled some impressive totals. In Atlanta, which Camp called home, George outpolled him by 41,000 votes, lacking only 196 votes of winning a county majority.[165] Twenty-nine counties gave George a total majority, with Chatham, Houston, and Richmond counties giving him more than 70 percent of their votes.[166]

Talmadge immediately cried foul. It must have been painful for him, after going to bed confident of a victory, to wake up and learn he had lost. In a radio address on the night of September 15, he announced that he was contesting the election. "The George backers went so far as to try to buy me out, and from the evidence I have, they went to the extreme limit—first, to buy the State of Georgia and when they failed, they tried violating the elec-

---

[161]Thomas, "Roosevelt vs. George," 72.

[162]Other tallies give slightly different results. See Fossett, "The Impact of the New Deal on Georgia Politics, 1933–1941," 307; Bernd, "Corruption in Georgia Primaries and Elections, 1938–1950," 25; Bonner, "Legislative Appointment and the County Unit System," 370.

[163]Heard and Strong, *Southern Primaries and Elections*, 64.

[164]Anderson, *Wild Man from Sugar Creek*, 181.

[165]Michie and Rhylick, *Dixie Demagogues*, 200–201; *Atlanta Constitution*, September 13, 14, 1938, cited in Fagin, "Franklin D. Roosevelt," 270.

[166]Heard and Strong, *Southern Primaries and Elections*, 64–65.

tion laws to claim the election."[167] He was flooded in the next few days with letters, calls, and a few sworn affidavits describing voting irregularities, vote buying, pre-marked ballots, payoffs, and the usual antics in stolen elections.[168]

On September 19, Talmadge filed a formal challenge, questioning the vote in thirty-four counties, all of which he lost by fewer than 100 votes. In thirteen counties, someone filed a challenge for him. One was filed in Baldwin County (Milledgeville), but it was withdrawn. By law, he had to make specific charges, but his complaints were more general, alleging stuffed ballot boxes, mistabulations, and illegal persons voting.[169]

The challenge fell flat. Thirty-two counties refused to recount their ballots, and the one county that did perform a recount, Evans County, George's vote fell from 429 to 426, with Talmadge's remaining at 425.[170] Coweta County blasted Talmadge back, saying that he had insulted their county and moreover, they were billing his campaign $76.50 for the trouble he had caused them.[171] Talmadge carried the challenge to the state Democratic Convention in Macon on October 5, but his challenge was soundly defeated.[172] Perhaps there was a bit of truth to Talmadge's accusations; there was simply too much smoke for there not to have been some fire. Talmadge cited such situations as Pike County, where almost twice the number of votes were cast in the Senate race as had been cast for governor. It appears that in some places, county leaders added Camp's totals to George's, with the rationalization that Camp's voters would not have voted for Talmadge anyway, if that had been the choice.[173]

In his study on corruption in Georgia politics, Joseph Bernd raises a pertinent point: If they had nothing to hide, the thirty-two counties that refused to recount should have simply done so to "*offer the best evidence of*

[167]*Atlanta Constitution*, September 16, 1938, cited in Bernd, "Corruption in Georgia Primaries and Elections, 1938–1950," 8.

[168]Anderson, *Wild Man from Sugar Creek*, 182.

[169]*Atlanta Constitution*, September 20, 1938, cited in Bernd, "Corruption in Georgia Primaries and Elections, 1938–1950," 11; see also *Report of the Special Committee to Investigate Senatorial Campaign Expenditures and the Use of Government Funds in 1938*, 76th Congress, 1st session, report no. 1, part 2 (Washington: U. S. Government Printing Office, 1939) 38–39, cited in Fossett, "The Impact of the New Deal on Georgia Politics, 1933–1941," 309.

[170]Bernd, "Corruption in Georgia Primaries and Elections, 1938–1950," 15.

[171]Anderson, *Wild Man from Sugar Creek*, 182. The account does not say whether or not they recounted the ballots.

[172]Anderson, *Wild Man from Sugar Creek*, 184.

[173]Bernd cites interviews he made ("Corruption in Georgia Primaries and Elections, 1938–1950," 9).

their honest intentions." If there were questions, an investigation would have cleared up suspicion. Bernd notes that the very absence of an investigation set a precedent to "handle" charges of corruption in future elections.[174] Bernd concludes, that there may have been some counties carried illegally for George, but not enough to change the election.[175] George did have a powerful statewide organization and strong ties with the courthouse crowd who counted the votes. He also had a mountain of utility money to spend.[176] Whatever cloud might hang over the election, or rationalization that since the county unit system was not democratic anyway, it is probably safe to say that in a head-to-head match between George and Talmadge, few of Camp's 76,000 votes would have gone to Talmadge, giving George a clear win. He had won a clear popular plurality, but there is certainly the unpleasant possibility that George returned to the Senate due to voter fraud.

It is less of a mystery as to why Camp did so poorly; his campaign was doomed from the beginning. He was unknown, had entered the race late when most of the state's politicians had already committed to Talmadge or George, had no statewide organization, and had no big name political support. He raised almost no money from Georgia, and sadly, he ended the campaign with debts that he had to pay from his resources. Georgia's voting rules were of no help. One had to be registered six months before the general election in order to vote, so he had entered too late to mobilize and register the 12,000–15,000 WPA workers. Of course, Roosevelt's endorsement likely hurt him more than it helped.

After his loss, Camp returned to the US attorney's office. His subordinate remembered that he had "found his experience quite trying, most expensive…and had gained some bitter experiences."[177] He now had a campaign debt to pay with little help from anyone. He expected to be rewarded with a federal judgeship or some governmental appointment, but nothing was forthcoming from the Roosevelt administration. It was assumed, however, that if some appointment came, George would use senatorial privilege to block it, and this fact may have explained why nothing came to him even though Russell continued to promote Camp for other government jobs.[178] Although he had been told that Russell would not support him, Camp be-

---

[174]Ibid., 18.

[175]Ibid. 28–29.

[176]Anderson, *Wild Man from Sugar Creek,* 181, cites interview with a Mr. Peters, a Talmadge man, June 12, 1970.

[177]Isaac Hay, oral history, 11, Russell Library.

[178]Ibid., 48.

came particularly bitter toward him after his humiliating defeat.[179] He felt that he had been double-crossed, "that Dick owed him."[180] He and his wife became very cool to the junior senator.[181]

In 1942, Russell nominated Camp for the position of special attorney. Around the same time, a journalist named James Myron (a *nom de plume*) in his weekly article called "The Capital Sideshow" had been attacking Russell, and Russell learned that Camp was associated with the distribution of this anti-Russell column in the state. He also learned that Camp had been saying in Georgia political circles that Russell could be beaten if the right person opposed him. On learning of Camp's perfidy, Russell wired Washington to withdraw the nomination for special attorney. Russell then wrote Camp a letter in which there is clearly pain at his protégé's *lese majesté*: "I thought that was a very strange statement for a friend to make," Russell wrote. He reminded Camp that he had told him before he had qualified to run against George that he could not expect his help, writing, "You certainly had no cause to hold any hard feelings toward me about your senatorial campaign in 1938, for I told you frankly before you qualified how I was situated."[182] Russell continued, "I would not do you any injury, but I prefer not to...approve the appointment of a man who feels toward me as you do."[183] We do not know if the two men ever spoke again. Camp died a few years later, probably bitter to the end. This entire imbroglio evokes President Harry Truman's famous remark, "If you want a friend [in politics], you'd better get a dog."

There was one overriding factor that helped vanquish both Talmadge and Camp: George had raised a large sum of money, mainly from the big interests. In addition, Republicans from all over the country sent him money as well.[184] There were smaller donations, of course, such as the Floyd County farmer (ironically, whose name was J. E. Camp) who donated his first

179Roy V. Harris, oral history, 28–28, Russell Library.

180Ibid.

181Peterson/Russell, oral history, 52–53, Russell Library. Camp wasn't the only one feeling bitter; liberals in the state were upset by the way Roosevelt abandoned Camp after pressuring him to carry the banner for the administration. Albert C. Leitch, editor of *Georgia Homestead*, a liberal weekly, criticized Roosevelt for his inaction in helping Camp, lamenting that now the Georgia liberal Democrats had no leadership, likened their position to "the citizens of Czechoslovakia," who had just been deserted by their allies in the West.

182Richard B. Russell to Camp, August 12, 1942, series VI-B, box 34, f. 4, Russell papers.

183Richard B. Russell to Camp, August 12, 1942, series VI-B, box 34, f. 4, Russell papers. Camp remained anonymous in Georgia and died at age forty-nine in 1947.

184Edgar B. Dunlap, Jr. interview.

bale of cotton to George.[185] Talmadge's newspaper *The Statesman* reported in October that he had spent $12,000, to Camp's $17,000 to George's $50,000, boasting that he had less money to spend than George had for postage.[186] Historian David Noland Thomas claims that George spent $500,000, much of it used as "walking around money" for his operatives to carry their counties, but whatever he had to spend, most probably it was money that made the difference.[187] George's campaign had in effect bought the election. Needless to say, he swamped his independent opponent, Charles A. Jiles, in the general election in November with 66,897 to 3,442, or more than 95 percent of the vote.[188] Congratulations poured in from friends and colleagues. Senator Bailey, whom the reader will recall, had "something like a heart attack" on hearing the early returns, wrote to say how "happy and relieved" he was and how "glad for you, and for Mrs. George and for our Party and our country and for myself."[189] Senator Carter Glass wired, "God Bless you, Walter. Likewise the sovereign state of Georgia."[190] One quick congratulatory telegram came from James Farley, Roosevelt's right-hand man. He had also felicitated with "Cotton Ed" Smith as well. Farley had opposed the purge, but he also wanted to make amends with the Southern conservatives, because he was planning his own race for the presidency in 1940.[191]

At the state Democratic convention in October, George pledged his continued loyalty to the Democratic Party. "I accept the nomination and pledge my continued loyalty to the Democratic Party," he told the delegates, and added that he would continue to support the administration "so long as it holds true to Democratic Party principles." Returning to his old campaign theme that the Democratic Party was a big tent, he added, "It is not intended that we all see alike any more than it was intended that we should all look alike."[192] He would not side with Roosevelt again until the war, and on domestic issues, he had in effect left the Democratic Party, except on one of his last acts in the Senate, for the rest of his life.

---

[185] *The Georgian* 2, September 3, 1938, VI-B, box 63, f. Pol. Gen, 1938, RBR papers (Winder).

[186] *The Statesman*, October 4, 11, 1938, cited in Cobb, "Not Gone, but Forgotten," 206.

[187] Thomas, "Roosevelt vs. George," 66.

[188] Dubin, *United States Congressional Elections*, 530.

[189] Josiah Bailey to WFG, September 16, 1938, box 476, f. 1938, September–October, Bailey papers.

[190] "God Bless You, Walter," clipping, September 16, 1938, box 336, f. RNC papers.

[191] Thomas, "Roosevelt vs. George," 25.

[192] Untitled speech by George, f. 970, Gardner papers.

Roosevelt's "purge" in other places had been notably unsuccessful as well, and he was spared further embarrassment because it was only after his landing in Pensacola that he went aggressively after incumbents.[193] A few incumbents he favored had won (Barkley, Elmer Thomas), but they probably would have won anyway. At first, he had avoided trying to defeat incumbents, and as we have seen, avoided tackling those he felt that he could not beat. Van Nuys was renominated in Indiana, and New Dealer James Pope of Idaho was beaten by a conservative young millionaire, D. Worth Clark, despite a flood of federal money into the state. Adams of Colorado and Bennett Clark both coasted to victory against New Dealers, and radical New Dealer Maury Maverick of Texas, on whom Roosevelt had specially given his blessing, lost by 546 votes. Conservative Democrat Howard Smith defeated William Dodd Jr. in Virginia in a rout that began Smith's thirty-year career in the House, and another Virginia New Dealer went down to defeat despite the fact that Roosevelt had flooded his district with $100,000,000 worth of pork.[194] His one congressional victory was the defeat of Rules Committee chairman John H. O'Connor, who, when learning of Roosevelt's efforts against him, said, "Like Senator George, I accept the challenge." He was one of the most effective obstructionists in the House and had led the fight against the reorganization bill.[195] He lost by about five hundred votes to James Fry, but running in the Republican primary as well, he defeated Allen Dulles by a thousand votes, thus winning the GOP nomination. He did, however, lose in November.[196]

A number of George's supporters crowed at his victory. Georgian Lucy Stanley McArthur wired Roosevelt, "We are returning our full time Georgian, Democrat, scholar, gentleman and statesman to Washington. We hope our part time Georgian and democrat will welcome our full time Georgian and democrat to the Senate as one shall be glad to welcome our part time Georgian and democrat back to Georgia."[197] A local Cordele, Georgia, businessman and George supporter Wiley Moore wired the president a mockingly "God bless you, Franklin."[198] Roosevelt had to bear a

[193]Tyndall, *The Emergence*, 627.

[194]Harry Byrd to Josiah Bailey, August 4, 1938, box 476, f. 1938, June–August, Bailey papers.

[195]"The Purge Spreads," 8.

[196]Hooper, "The Purge," 219; Farley, *Jim Farley's Story*, 139; Harold Ickes, *Inside Struggle*, 416, cited in Coode, "Georgia Congressmen and the New Deal, 1933–1938," 236.

[197]Lucy Stanley McArthur to FDR, September 15, 1938, DNC, OF 300, box 15, f. K–M, Roosevelt papers. I have retained her original punctuation and capitalization.

[198]Jake Gregory interview.

tweaking at the annual Gridiron Club skit when the curtain rose to reveal a cotton field titled "The New Deal's Cotton-pickin' Project no. 37." In the field were reporters dressed like senators Walter George, Pat Harrison, Millard Tydings, and "Cotton Ed" Smith.[199] They sang hurtful songs about New Deal failures, especially Roosevelt's inability to defeat these men.

One last footnote to the campaign occurred in New York, where one of George's young drivers had gone after the election for a vacation. On Broadway, he was stopped by a radio announcer, who was conducting a street contest of anyone who could make the best impromptu speech about their state. He went to the microphone and immediately launched into the speech he had heard dozens of times: "I was born the son of a poor tenant farmer...." He won the $10.00 prize.[200]

Roosevelt's meddling, along with his policies, had most certainly had a negative effect on his part in the November general elections. The Republicans gained more than eighty seats in the House and eight in the Senate, giving the GOP 170 seats in the House and 23 in the Senate. Since there were already 40 unreliable Democrats in the House and 20 in the Senate, the newly forged "Conservative Coalition" had a solid base from which to work; as a result, no major administration legislation passed Congress in the remainder of Roosevelt's second term.[201] Roosevelt had lost his grip on Congress. Walter George called the Republican gains "a danger signal from sober-minded American voters calling us back to common sense in legislation."[202] He seems to have taken great satisfaction at the great Republican victory.

As for George's relationship with Roosevelt, on the surface it appeared that all was forgiven. To his supporters in Atlanta on election night, George seemed prepared to let bygones be bygones. "The great Democrats will be quick to cast aside bitterness," he told his supporters after his victory, adding, "These differences are natural...within the party.... All great Democrats bow to the will of the people."[203] Over six decades later, George's law partner T. Hoyt Davis told this author that George did not feel vindictive,

---

[199] *Washington Post*, 18 December 1938, 1:2–3, cited in Robertson, *Sly and Able*, 277–78.

[200] Jarman, "Taxpayer's Senator," 42.

[201] Patterson, "A Conservative Coalition," 765; Plesur, "Republican Congressional Comeback of 1938," 543; Moore, "Public Office on Easy Payments," 206.

[202] *Atlanta Constitution*, November 13, 1938, 1, cited in Tindall, *The Emergence of the New South*, 630.

[203] "George promises to support Party," unknown newspaper clipping, September 17, 1938, box 337, f. George, 1938–, RNC papers.

for "he was not a vindictive man."[204]

An article in his hometown newspaper at the time of his death echoed these same sentiments. Journalists at the time noted that George voted about the same way as he had before Roosevelt's attack, but it must be remembered that he had for some time opposed what Roosevelt wanted to do, so his votes mean nothing.[205]

Journalist Frank C. Waldrip, in an article titled "No Southern Comfort," saw things differently, writing that "No one came back to Congress swearing stouter enmity [than George]."[206] In a conversation with Walter George, "Cotton Ed" Smith, also a survivor of the Roosevelt purges, opined that Roosevelt was his own worst enemy, to which George supposedly replied, "Not as long as I'm alive."[207] Intimates said that deep inside, he forever nursed a bitter resentment against Roosevelt.[208]

As for Roosevelt, he continued to trip up George whenever he could. In 1939, Roosevelt told Farley that he would not reappoint the collector of customs in Savannah because he had supported George. When Farley told him he was being foolish, Roosevelt stated emphatically, "I won't appoint him again."[209] When George and Russell had offered different men for a judgeship, Roosevelt appointed Russell's candidate.[210] Farley tried to bring the two men back together. In discussing the Georgia political situation in a letter to Roosevelt, he wrote, "Frankly, Mr. President, I think you are wrong about Walter George. I am of the impression that he wants to go along if given the opportunity. I think you should sit down and talk with him when the opportunity presents itself."[211] Roosevelt did send a memo to Corcoran four days later asking for a check on George's votes and utterances in the Senate for the past four or five years.[212] It's not known if anything came from this investigation, but when George entered the hospital for cataract surgery in August 1939, E. M. "Pa" Watson (someone around Roosevelt) sent a note to the president that George was "going blind" and suggested

[204]T. Hoyt Davis interview. An article in his hometown newspaper at the time of his death echoes the same sentiments (*Vienna News*, August 8, 1957, 5).

[205]Jarman, "Taxpayer's Senator," 42; *Vienna News*, August 8, 1957, 5.

[206]Frank C. Waldrip, "No Southern Comfort," unidentified clipping, box 28, f. WFG, Wallace papers.

[207]Byrnes, *All in One Lifetime*, 103.

[208]"One of the Greatest," *Newsweek*, 50(August 12, 1957), 35.

[209]Farley, *Jim Farley's Story*, 161.

[210]Roy V. Harris, oral history, 44, Russell Library.

[211]Farley to FDR, December 3, 1938, PPF, box 107–117, f. 109, Roosevelt papers.

[212]Attached to the Farley letter in note 1374.

that a letter to him might "work wonders." Steve Early wrote, "Okay with me" on the memo, and after George had had his surgery, Roosevelt wrote, "I have learned with genuine regret that your eyesight is giving you concern.... I hope that skillful treatment...will speedily remove all cause of apprehension.[213] Four months later, George requested on January 7, 1940, to meet with Roosevelt for five minutes, adding, "*Not on foreign relations* [italics original]."[214] What he wished to discuss with Roosevelt or what occurred in the meeting is unknown, but this encounter must have been the first since Barnesville a year and a half before. After this encounter, his next one was in August. After that, he seems to have gone to the White House every two or three months on foreign relations or finance committee business.

We do not know if the Barnesville Manifesto was ever discussed or if an apology was ever made. In one of the sessions during the war, however, when George was discussing the draft of a tax proposal, Roosevelt said in the conversation, "Walter, if I know anything at all about Georgia politics," and then he added sheepishly, "and certainly I don't," and then began laughing and finished his comment.[215] As far as we know, that is the only time that the question of the great unpleasantness was mentioned between the two men.

When George suffered the great loss of his son Marcus in 1943, Roosevelt wrote a condolence letter, which was curiously worded. "I cannot restrain [?] the impulse to let you know that I am thinking of you...[and to give my] assurances of deepest sympathy,"[216] the president wrote. Marcus, who had apparently not felt any animosity toward Roosevelt for his attack on his father, had asked for an autographed photo of the president in 1940, calling the acquisition his "one ambition in the world."[217] George replied to Roosevelt's letter from Vienna on September 2, 1943, where he and Miss Lucy must have remained. "If we do not hear from the boy again [,] I have the faith that to the end he measured up to the high standards and traditions of the Navy."[218]

Roosevelt must have overcome his animosity to George in time, and George to the president. When Roosevelt was reelected in 1944, George

[213]FDR to WFG, September 7, 1939, PPF, box 107–117, f. 109, Roosevelt papers.

[214]WFG to FDR, January 7, 1940, PPF, box 107–117, f. 109, Roosevelt papers.

[215]White, "Senator George, Monument Determined," 47; "Voice of the 84th," 24.

[216]FDR to WFG (no mention of Miss Lucy), August 30, 1943, PPF, box 107–117, f. 109, Roosevelt papers.

[217]E. M. Watson memo, PPF, November 10, 1941, PPF, box 107–117, f. 109, Roosevelt papers.

[218]WFG to FDR, September 2, 1943, PPF, box 107–117, f. 109, Roosevelt papers.

wrote a highly congratulatory letter and offered "every possible assistance...in meeting the high responsibilities resting on your administration." Roosevelt replied, "That was a mighty fine note you sent."[219] In an interview a decade later, George seemed to have forgiven Roosevelt although it was at a time when he could have been magnanimous. "Mr. Roosevelt...had a quite genuine gift for separating his personal feelings from his political feelings," he told a reporter. "He never mixed the two."[220] One of the last appointments Roosevelt ever made was his elevation of Walter George's law partner, T. Hoyt Davis Sr., to the federal bench in 1945.[221] Davis had "read the law" in George's office, and in rendering one of his first decisions, he ruled unconstitutional the all-white Democratic primary in Georgia. Roosevelt would have been pleased.

There was, however, one more political tangle between George and the president, but this one was not as personal: George was to clash with Roosevelt again on the eve of the war. Roosevelt wanted a third term, despite George Washington's admonitions about one, but he was not certain how a third term would be perceived. He knew that the conservatives in the party would not want it, and it seems he did not immediately decide to run himself. In late 1938, he wrote Josephus Daniels, "I think the idea is slowly getting through the heads of people like Tydings and George and Bennett Clark that even if they control the 1940 convention [and nominate someone other than me], they cannot elect their ticket without the support of this administration."[222]

By 1939, there was evidence that Roosevelt was trying to control the 1940 delegates, even if he were not competing for the nomination. George accused Roosevelt openly of using patronage to do so. "I know what is happening in Georgia," he told reporters, "and I understand that substantially the same thing is taking place in several other states."[223] By August 1939, it was evident that Roosevelt wanted a third term, but in his usual manner he was being very coy about it. George openly denounced a third term for Roosevelt "under any circumstances or conditions" and demanded that Roosevelt

[219]WFG to FDR, November 17, 1944 and FDR to WFG, November 22, 1944, PPF, box 107–117, f. 109, Roosevelt papers.

[220]White, "Senator George, Monument Determined," 47.

[221]Egerton, *Speak Now against the Day*, 406. His son, T. Hoyt Davis, Jr., granted me several interviews for this work and readily opened the files he had on the senator to me.

[222]Kilpatrick, ed. *Roosevelt and Daniels*, 178.

[223]"George Finds Jobs," unknown newspaper clipping, March 17, 1939, box 337, f. George, 1938–, RNC papers.

openly state his plans.[224] At the same time, he was trying to encourage Vice President Garner to run and openly backed him.[225] Not only did Roosevelt want to run, he feared that the New Deal might be dismantled if one of the conservative Democrats got elected. In a conversation with Farley, Roosevelt denounced Garner as a possible successor and noted that he was being promoted by about a dozen US senators including Byrnes, George, and Bankhead.[226]

In January 1940, George began openly trying to enlist the Georgia Democratic delegation behind Garner. His close associate Edgar B. Dunlap became his agent, and in that same month, he mailed a hundred thousand circulars throughout Georgia with both Garner's and George's picture on it. On it were written the words, "Give the People a Choice." In case that Garner would not run, the flier also supported Secretary of State Cordell Hull as a second draft choice.[227] Delegates, nevertheless, were already coming out for a third term. Alaska's delegate to Congress, Anthony J. Dimond, announced that Alaska's six delegates to the convention had pledged themselves to Roosevelt. "Cotton Ed" Smith joined George on the same day, decrying the notion of a third term as disastrous, warning that "Roosevelt may be nominated, but if he is—goodbye Democratic Party as it has been known all these years."[228]

George was never part of the inner circle of the Georgia power barons and had generally remained aloof from state politics, so he was easily outfoxed. Roosevelt supporter Ed Rivers left for Washington as George was promoting Garner in the state to a meeting of the Democratic National Executive Committee. On leaving, he announced that the Georgia delegation to the Democratic Convention would be an "uninstructed" one. When he returned, everyone expected him to convene the State Executive Committee and kill any notion of a preference primary, thus placing the delegation under his control.[229] Both George and Russell opposed Rivers's actions, and they were the two most powerful politicians in the state.[230] The fact that the two could not prevent this move is a strong indication of just how powerful governors were in their state parties.

Roosevelt, as always, played his cards closely to his chest. Wanting, of

---

[224]"George Calls on Roosevelt," unknown newspaper clipping, August 9, 1939, ibid.

[225]"George Backs Garner," *Washington Post* clipping, August 10, 1939, ibid.

[226]Farley, *Jim Farley's Story*, 184.

[227]*Atlanta Constitution*, February 3, 1940, 2:2.

[228]Ibid., February 2, 1940, 1:3.

[229]Ibid., 1:2.

[230]Ibid., February 5, 1940, 4:6.

course, a third term, he preferred that he be drafted. His longtime campaign manager, Jim Farley, had himself wanted to run and asked Roosevelt if he was going to run. If not, Farley would enter several primaries. Waiting for a draft so that he would not appear grasping, he told Farley to "go ahead," when he really did not want him to enter the race. Calvin Coolidge had played the same game when he made the famous remark, "I do not choose to run for president," only to stand by fuming as the Republicans took him at his word and nominated his Secretary of Commerce Herbert Hoover. George and countless others were not fooled. George wrote Governor Hardwick in February 1940, "On the whole, I do not think our friend [Roosevelt] wished Farley to enter."[231] The *Atlanta Constitution* posted headlines the next day: "Garner will Be a Candidate in Georgia if State Holds Presidential Primary." George had written the Vice President, asking the specific question, "Would you run?" and had gotten a reply in the affirmative. Meanwhile, Ed Dunlap announced that he was leading a statewide movement to force a primary. Other powerful figures joined the call, including Talmadge, Governor Hardwick, Richard Russell, Congressman Cox, and W. T. Anderson, publisher of the *Macon Telegraph*. When Rivers was asked if he would permit a primary, he replied, "no comment," but it was well known that Rivers and the party leaders had no intention of allowing one.[232] As members of the party stopped by Rivers's office for talks, the governor left no doubt that the committee would be ruled by him.[233] Seeing their effort to have a primary, in which Roosevelt would probably not have been victorious, slipping away, Dunlap pledged on February 3 to produce a rival delegation if Rivers continued with his plans.[234]

By April, the mask came off when Clark Howell, publisher of the *Atlanta Constitution*, called on Georgia to lead the move for a third term, using the headlines, "Stampede to Roosevelt Starts as State Committee Gathers," as members of the state Democratic Central Committee poured into Atlanta to choose the state's delegates to the Democratic convention that summer. Howell's argument showed he was not aware of Roosevelt's true actions when he wrote, "He knows how to keep us out of war," while Roosevelt was openly supporting Great Britain. Rivers and committee chair Jim Gillis echoed his sentiments. Roosevelt was at that time vacationing in Georgia as his Georgia bandwagon began to roll.

---

[231]WFG to T. Hardwick, February 19, 1940, series I, box 2, f. 7, Hardwick papers.
[232]*Atlanta Constitution*, February 3, 1940, 1:8, 2:3.
[233]Ibid., April 25, 1940, 4:2.
[234]Ibid., February 5, 1940, 1:7.

The meeting of the Executive Committee was a sham. The self-proclaimed "uninstructed delegation" elected Clark Howell as its chair and unanimously passed a resolution calling on Roosevelt to run for a third term. The seventy-two delegates were all from liberal factions of the state Democratic Party, the conservatives having been totally out maneuvered. It was signed by sixty-nine delegates, the other three not being present. Dunlap appeared with a petition, which he had filed a month before, on which he said were 22,000 signatures for a primary, but he was not allowed even to address the committee.[235]

The George forces caucused after the meeting and charged that "a dictatorship is being established in Georgia," adding that the committee had "stolen the…rights of Georgia Democrats and sold them down the river in the interest of politicians." It was a further slap in the face that neither George nor Russell were chosen as members of the Georgia delegation.[236] This incident was the first major time that George, who generally remained aloof of Georgia's local politics, was outmaneuvered by the folks back home. It would not be his last.

---

[235]Ibid., April 26, 1940, 1:8 and 2:3.

[236]*New York Times*, April 26, 1940, 22:2.

Sen. Walter F. George during a speech
with Gov. Eugene Talmadge, 1940s.

Copyright Atlanta Journal-Constitution. Courtesy of Georgia State University.

Sen. Walter F. George with Gov. Herman Talmadge, 1956.

Copyright Atlanta Journal-Constitution. Courtesy of Georgia State University.

Sen. Walter F. George welcomed home with wife Lucy, 1940s.

Copyright Atlanta Journal-Constitution. Courtesy of Georgia State University.

Sen. Walter F. George and Sen. Richard B. Russell Jr., 1930s.

Sen. Walter F. George listens to President Roosevelt
back his opponent at a campaign rally, 1938.

Copyright Atlanta Journal-Constitution. Courtesy of Georgia State University.

Sen. Walter F. George with wife Lucy
during a city celebration in his honor, 1956 .

Copyright Atlanta Journal-Constitution. Courtesy of Georgia State University.

Sen. Walter F. George campaigning for re-election, 1938.

Copyright Atlanta Journal-Constitution. Courtesy of Georgia State University.

Sen. Walter F. George being interviewed on WSB-TV, 1955.

Copyright Atlanta Journal-Constitution. Courtesy of Georgia State University.

Sen. Walter F. George reading over an Atlanta Constitution article on World War II in his home, 1940s.

Copyright Atlanta Journal-Constitution. Courtesy of Georgia State University.

Sen. Walter F. George preparing to go fishing
at his Vienna home, 1949.

Mourners pay their respects at Sen. Walter F. George's funeral at Vienna First Baptist Church, 1957.

Lucy George at the funeral for her husband, 1957.

6

THE FORGING OF A STATESMAN, 1938–1945

No well-informed person ever imputed inconsistency to another for simply changing his mind.
—Cicero[1]

I change my mind as I go along.... I am glad to do [so] because it is probably the only proof that I have that I am in existence.
—Senator Walter F. George[2]

I have never been an isolationist, nor have I been for intervention. I [simply] favor making the whole Western Hemisphere economically as well as militarily immune from attack.
—Senator Walter F. George[3]

Walter George first rose to national prominence when he became the victim of the "Barnesville Manifesto" in 1938, yet it would be the evolution of his world view of and leadership in foreign affairs on the eve and during the world war when George first rose to the status of "statesman." Once an avowed isolationist and a virulent opponent of the League of Nations, by the end of World War II, George was just as strong an internationalist and advocate of the United Nations as he had been an opponent to these ideals over two decades before. The change was no Damascus Road conversion, and we shall see that even as his ideas began to evolve toward a greater world view, elements of his old isolationism remained. Moreover, there was a logic the thread of isolationism that remained at least until Pearl Harbor. His transformation was aptly described in his alma mater's alumni magazine *The Mercerian* in a 1956 testimonial: "As the world shrank and the country grew, Senator George grew with it, and that's what makes a statesman."[4]

The first decade and a half that George served in the Senate, the

[1]Cockfield, "The Union Sacrée," 103.
[2]George, "Russia Will Lose Power as Germany and Japan Gain," 81.
[3]*Atlanta Constitution*, November 11, 1949, 9:5
[4]"Dinner for Senator George," *Mercerian 1956*, WFG-MU.

American people largely wallowed in a know-nothing isolationism. There were many reasons for this attitude. Many people felt the enormous American casualties of World War I (which were nowhere close in number to those suffered by France, England, and Russia) were needless as our soldiers were fighting Europe's fight. There was also the annoyance that Britain and France, both bankrupt, had failed to repay their war debts.[5]

The strong isolationists in the 1930s consisted as a constant minimum of 35 percent on the Senate foreign relations committee, and they continuously pounded the drum of avoiding Europe and Asia's problems.[6] Leading isolationists did well in the elections of 1934, 1936, and 1938. Six of the seven members of the old Senate Munitions Investigating Committee ran for reelection in 1938, and five of the six won, the lone exception being Senator Pope of Idaho, who was defeated in the Democratic primary by D. Worth Clark, who became an even stronger isolationist than Pope.[7] George's colleague Richard Russell digested the attitude of many isolationists in the country when he wrote his mother the year before the war erupted in Europe, "It seems that we cannot learn…that we have no business in other peoples' quarrels, most of which had been the subject of many wars…long before Columbus ever sailed."[8] The prevailing majority attitude of Americans on the eve of the war was either indifference or avoidance of Europeans' problems.

Walter George was largely with them. Whereas old Judge Russell attacked him in the 1926 campaign for supporting the League of Nations and the World Court,[9] George had done really little more than tolerate these institutions.[10] George supported the Neutrality Act of 1935, which called for mandatory arms embargoes and the refusal of protections to Americans who sailed on the ships of belligerents. He joined senators Nye and Clark, both strong isolationists, in supporting the formation of the Munitions Control Board to implement the act itself.[11] Both Nye and Vandenberg then intro-

---

[5]Clapper, *Watching the World,* 239.

[6]Glad, *Key Pittman*, 223.

[7]Wayne Cole, *Roswell and the Isolationists, 1932-1945* (Lincoln: Nebraska Press, 1983) 293.

[8]Russell to his mother Ida, October 2, 1938, V-I, box 41, f. Parents, 1938, RBR papers (Winder).

[9]Mann, *The Walls of Jericho*, 32.

[10]George expressed himself favorably to the World Court Protocols in January 1938, but he did not appear at the meeting of the Foreign Relations Committee when they were discussed. See Schewe, *Franklin Delano Roosevelt and Foreign Affairs*, 2:354.

[11]Glad, *Key Pittman*, 237, cites Connally, *My Name is Tom Connally*, 220.

duced a resolution demanding an investigation by the Foreign Relations Committee of the munitions industry, and Pittman, the Foreign Relations chair and a Democrat, named Nye, an isolationist Republican, to chair the committee.[12] George served on it as well. When in January 1936, Nye declared that President Wilson had lied to a Senate committee about secret agreements among Allies in 1919, George began to back off from these extremists. The committee eventually called for the nationalization of the armaments committee on a vote of 4–3, with George, Vandenberg, and Barbour in the minority. The three issued a minority report,[13] and George then resigned from the committee.[14]

The next year, George voted for Senate Joint Resolution 3, which refused "arms, ammunition, and implements of war" to Spain, and when the next year Roosevelt made an off-handed remark in April in Warm Springs that he would return to the Little White House "if we are not at war,"[15] George denounced the idea that war was impending. He told the press, "I will cast my vote against any participation in any war anywhere except on our soil."[16] Late in the 1938 campaign when Roosevelt had said in Canada that the United States would support and defend Canada from invasion, George tore into the president, who had just called for his defeat. He sternly reminded the voters,

> It takes not only the president, but it takes the vote of the US Senate to declare war and I will tell you now, tell the mothers of Floyd county…of all Georgia that whenever the president…asks me to vote for war, that before I will send…the boys of these mothers of Georgians to fight our battles or anybody else's battles on foreign soil, that I will permit this good right arm to be severed from my body.[17]

He broadened that statement in a speech in Savannah the next day by adding that he would not vote for war "merely at the behest of 'any president'…without sufficient reason."[18] A week later in Thomasville, he repeated essentially the same promise, although specifying fighting "again on the

[12]Connally, *My Name is Tom Connally*, 211–13.

[13]Cole, *Senator Gerald P. Nye*, 94-95 cites the committee's report.

[14]Connally, *My Name is Tom Connally*, 212.

[15]George's voting record, 1933–38, 17, box 245, f. campaign file, WFG, Corcoran papers.

[16]"New For. Rel. Chief," clipping, November 12, 1940, box 337, f. George…'38," RNC papers.

[17]George, *Addresses*, Rome, August 24, 1938, 21.

[18]"George blasts…," *Savannah Morning News* clipping, August 25, 1938, box 1390, f. 1, Ellender papers.

soil of Europe."[19] The next year he took Roosevelt to task for constantly predicting war, stating that if the president continued to predict war, it would in effect become a self-fulfilling prophecy.[20] He even went so far in the campaign to predict the plausibility of another European war. In Thomasville on August 31, 1938, he told his listeners,

> It takes no student of world affairs, it takes no prophet looking into a dim and distant future, to discuss movements in the great powers of Europe that are making unquestionable to an [*sic*] other world conflict. That conflict must be averted.... I contemplate the possibilities that the sons of the mothers of Georgia may be hurled into a death struggle on the soil of Europe.... I am moved to tell you that if you again trust me as your servant, I will permit the severance of this right arm before I will follow the dictates or command of any party leadership on the issue of peace and war.... I will stand in my tracks until the eve before I will send American boys, the sons of Georgia mothers, to fight again on the soil of Europe.[21]

Even after World War II had begun in Europe and he had begun to emerge from his cocoon of isolationism, he stayed between the Isolationists and the Interventionists. Both he and Pat Harrison led a middle-of-the-road faction that opposed giving Britain and France "federal credits" because they felt that to do so would increase taxes or raise the national debt, or perhaps both. They suggested instead giving agricultural subsidies to the Allies but no money or arms.[22]

George outlined his position, which remained consistent, rather clearly when he replied in May 1940 to Governor Thomas Hardwick, the man he had defeated when first elected to the Senate. Hardwick had written him criticizing the lack of neutrality of Roosevelt's actions, calling on the United States to "display some symptoms of actual neutrality."[23] "There is a difference between an isolationist and an interventionist," he wrote to his former foe. "It seems to me that America should occupy a strong and well-defined middle ground. I believe in thorough preparation," he continued, adding, "I do not see how we can maintain our neutrality unless we are strong enough in the present state of the world to defend it." He acknowledged, however, that America was facing a "move towards intervention." He wrote, "You

[19]"Smith's Victory," clipping, box 1390, f. 1, Ellender papers.

[20]Chandler, *Natural Superiority of Southern Politicians*, 325.

[21]George, *Addresses*, Thomasville, August 31, 1938, 7.

[22]Heinrichs, *Threshold of War*, 102–103, 109, cites Foreign Relations Committee hearings.

[23]Gov. T. W. Hardwick to WFG, May 20, 1940, series 1, box 2, f. 7, Hardwick papers.

know from experience what a difficult fight lies ahead," leaving his position in the fight unclear.[24] Journalist Arthur Krock, who felt that compared to past Georgia politicians George was a liberal, noted how he was sailing between the Scylla and Charybdis of the two extremes when he wrote, "George, while not accurately to be called an isolationist, is most accurately to be called a non-interventionist."[25] George himself had said at the time, "I have never been an isolationist, nor have I been for intervention [in the European war]. I favor making the whole Western Hemisphere militarily immune from attack."[26] These words were an honest summation of the man's position. He was not playing politics. He had never joined Burton K. Wheeler or Gerald Nyes. After Pearl Harbor, they all three would join Roosevelt.

Although he was hesitant to give help to belligerents in Europe, his isolationism did not hinder his desire for security at home. In June 1940, Roosevelt called for defense spending cuts as the Allied armies were crumbling before the German attack in the Battle of France, and George advocated an increase and called for a tax increase of about a billion dollars to pay for it, with increases falling on incomes between $12,500 and $160,000.[27] He also got the Senate to pass a bill extending retirement and disability pay to World War I officers who had lost their benefits under the 1933 Economy Act.[28]

In spring 1939, the European situation caused rumbling about the necessities of changing the nation's neutrality positions. Senator Key Pittman, chair of the Foreign Relations Committee, felt that he could get repeal of the arms embargo, and he also felt that he could get his good friend Walter George to support it. He named it the "Peace Act of 1939," but the bill failed mainly due to his poor leadership (he had a severe drinking problem). Roosevelt took over and had Congressman Bloom lead a movement in the House to repeal the embargo. It passed the House, and when it arrived in the Senate Foreign Relations Committee, George supported the isolationists' position of Senator Bennett Champ Clark of Missouri to delay discussion until 1940. With the Foreign Relations Committee containing a sizable minority of hard-core isolationists, the Clark amendment passed in the committee by a vote of 12–11, with George and Senator Gillette casting the

[24]Ibid., May 22, 1940.

[25]*New York Times*, November 12, 1940, 22. 5.

[26]Ibid., November 11, 1940, 12:3.

[27]*New York Times*, June 4, 1940, 13:3.

[28]Ibid., January 19, 1940, 3:3.

deciding votes for delay.[29] Delay was defeated on the floor of the Senate 60–33.[30]

A few days later George proposed military training for CCC enrollees although he stressed that it should be voluntary. This proposal was defeated the next day, but it had the effect of opening the discussion of the question of general conscription, which George stated that he would support.[31] When the Burke-Wadsworth Selective Service Bill was introduced, George spoke forcefully against it, feeling that this bill did everything but ask Congress "to declare war." He felt that it would turn the November election into a referendum on peace or war. "Do you hope to convince the American voter that you are not going to war?" he thundered at his colleagues and pounded his desk. He did not oppose training men, but this bill asked Congress "to do everything but actually declare war." He pointed out to his colleagues, "Do you have the faintest idea that you can conscript the manpower of the country…and then say, 'We are standing for peace'?" Warning his colleagues that in the November elections, the American people would vote against those who supported this bill, he concluded that "this country does not want to get into war and there is no occasion to go to war." He attacked the administration for fostering the attitude that the United States was going to war eventually and the American people might as well accept it.[32] Curiously, when the Burke-Wadsworth Selective Service Bill passed later that day by a vote of 58–31, George voted with the "ayes."[33] Why George seems to have changed his position we do not know, but perhaps after much soul searching, George must have decided that perhaps a selective service bill, while appearing to prepare for war, would actually best protect the Western Hemisphere if there were to be one.

His notion of the limited use of the armed forces was expressed in a debate in spring 1941, after he had shepherded the Lend-Lease Bill through the Senate, a bill which would create a way to provide military aid to other countries during World War II. Again we see his view of protecting our shores: "[I have not held] the view that American armed forces…could be

[29]Both had been intended victims of the purge the year before (Glad, *Key Pittman*, 246–48; Langer and Gleason, *Challenge to Isolationism*, 143, 183).

[30]Manfred Jonas, *Isolationism in America, 1935–41* (Ithaca: Cornell University Press, 1966), cited in Porter, *The Seventy-sixth Congress and World War II*, 75. Porter contends that Clark had used Roosevelt's purge attempt to sway George, but there is no real evidence that this statement is true. George at this point was still very isolationist.

[31]*New York Times*, June 13, 1940, 11:1–2, 13:2.

[32]Ibid., August 29, 1940, 10:4.

[33]Ibid., 10:7.

sent anywhere in the world for any purpose," he told his colleagues, and he agreed that "generally speaking, the president may send the army and navy to protect American rights, American property, and the lives of American citizens" because such use of the military was "primarily defensive action." He admitted that sometimes offensive action must be taken "in order to make the defense perfect and complete, but that is the exception." Noting that in peacetime an American president could legally send troops to protect American citizens and property, he added that we "have never conceived that he had any right…to send the army or the navy for offensive purposes any place on earth."[34] When in the summer, Roosevelt wanted to extend the term of service of men in the armed service, George opposed it. First, he felt that a new law was necessary, but he felt that extension should be voluntary and brought about by inducements "such as pay increases."[35] It passed largely as the administration wanted it, and in August, the House passed what was essentially the Senate version with several weakening amendments by the smallest of margins, 203–202.[36] George was still of the position that we should be well prepared to defend our shores, but offensive action was out of the question.

Roosevelt is probably the greatest president of the twentieth century, and his greatness is evident in the fact that he took a country where it should go but did not want to. Roosevelt's greatness as a leader was his dragging a reluctant nation from isolationism to preparedness. Seemingly motivated by a hatred of the Japanese and German totalitarian systems, Roosevelt wanted them not merely contained but destroyed, and he was willing to risk war to do so. Indeed, it is arguable that he hoped to bring the might of the United States on the side of the democracies. Many have accused him of intentionally provoking the dictatorships into attacking us. He early called for changes in America's neutrality laws "to keep us out of war,"[37] but even without the changes, he violated the Neutrality Acts that he himself had signed, positioning America into not even a thinly disguised assistance to France and Britain. He refused to mediate an end to the war at the request of both Belgium and Germany in fall 1939.[38]

Roosevelt then moved for the repeal, or at least revision of the Neutrality Act of 1937. In summer 1939, Roosevelt wanted the repeal of the

[34]*CR*, 77/1, 2857.

[35]*New York Times*, July 13, 1941, 1:1.

[36]Ibid., August 13, 1941, 1:8.

[37]Dallek, *Franklin D. Roosevelt and American Foreign Policy, 1932–1945*, 199–200.

[38]Ibid.

arms embargo provisions and asked to be given the power to identify the aggressor in foreign wars. Clark of Missouri moved that any consideration should be delayed until the Second Session of Congress in January 1940. It passed the committee by a vote of 12–11, with the hardcore isolationists being joined by George and Gillette. Four of the five Democrats had been opposed by Roosevelt for renomination in his 1938 purge, and it was thought at the time that their votes were swayed by his actions the previous year.[39] In George's case there is no evidence of this motivation. He was still hostile to active assistance to the Allies at this point, and both he and Connally had warned Roosevelt that the isolationists would tie up the Senate with a filibuster on neutrality.[40] Cordell Hull, the secretary of state, worked on both George and Gillette in July 1939 to swing their votes, and he made some progress on softening them.[41]

On September 1, 1939, the entire playing field changed when the Nazi war machine slammed into Poland, followed by France and Great Britain's declaration of war on Germany two days later. A special session of Congress was convened in September, and Walter George was among the leaders of repeal, a total reversal of his position two months before.[42]

When George had entered the hospital for a cataract operation in 1939, Roosevelt, ever the politician, worked on him by sending him the personally signed get-well card described earlier.[43] The eruption of war brought to Roosevelt's side many of the conservative Democrats who had opposed him in July, joined by the Republican Vandenberg, in time to be called part of "the most faithful of rubber stamps."[44] George defended Roosevelt through the neutrality debate, not infrequently getting the worst of it in exchanges with Wheeler and Taft, but indeed, he and his close friend Senator Pittman led the fight to repeal the arms embargo.[45]

George's transition was much more studied than it seems. In the fall of 1939 the Neutrality Act was amended. It maintained the basic framework of the previous act but now allowed war materials to be sold to belligerents—provided that the sale was made in the United States and that the goods were shipped from US ports in non-American ships. The law even provided

---

[39]Cole, *Roosevelt and the Isolationists, 1932–45*, 316–17.

[40]Dallek, *Franklin D. Roosevelt and American Foreign Policy, 1932–1945*, 290.

[41]Porter, *The Seventy-sixth Congress and World War II*, 49.

[42]Jarman, "Taxpayer's Senator," 44.

[43]Thompson, *Time for War*, 187.

[44]Vandenberg diary, October 27, 1939, cited in Heinrichs, *Threshold of War*, 76.

[45]See *CR*, 77/1, 1240, 1279, 1427, 1470; *New York Times*, November 25, 1940, 16:2; Glad, *Key Pittman*, 206.

short-term credits for the buyers. George challenged the legality of the loans during the debate, pointing out that even these types of loans were prohibited to both individuals and corporations.[46] The Senate passed it anyway, of course, with George's vote, on October 27, 1939, by a lopsided 63–30. Dallek felt that had the war in Europe not erupted the month before, it would not have passed, and he is probably right.[47] It certainly would not have had George's vote.

George did not go over fully to the administration's position. Senator Pittman had introduced a bill to require Senate ratification of reciprocal trade agreements. Roosevelt, always eager to bypass the niceties of cooperation with Congress, wanted to negotiate reciprocal trade agreements without Senate interference, and George and Senator Harrison of Mississippi met with Hull to suggest that any agreements be submitted to the Senate for ratification. George later told the press that he had told Hull that there would "likely to be a great deal of force behind amendments calling for ratification," but Hull retained his position. He did accept a certain time limit on the duration of the treaties but felt that the president needed this "emergency grant of power."[48]

George supported the Pittman position—but not on the grounds that they were treaties and required Senate ratification. He supported the Pittman position because the Constitution gave the Senate the power to regulate commerce with foreign nations. In its defense, he gave a long, erudite speech on the Senate floor in its defense, citing legal decisions and authorities. When in April, the isolationists introduced in Congress a resolution forbidding the use of American vessels or aircraft to transport supplies to belligerents, George did not immediately support the administration on this question either, but he did ask Hull's advice. Hull opposed its passage, writing on April 29 to George that such action would discourage the Allies and encourage the Axis, but he put it more diplomatically by simply stating that "its passage would be misunderstood abroad."[49]

In August 1940, Richard Russell introduced to a bill an amendment that would authorize the secretary of war and navy to expropriate any factory that was having labor problems for war production. Because the workers would then *ipso facto* become federal government employees and lose the

---

[46]*CR*, 76/2, LXXXV, October 27, 1939, p 1017–18.

[47]Dallek, *Franklin D. Roosevelt and American Foreign Policy*, 205; see also Davis, *FDR: Into the Storm, 1937–40*, 453 ff.

[48]*New York Times*, January 5, 1940, 9:2.

[49]Hull, *The Memoirs of Cordell Hull*, 2:949, 944.

right to strike, George strongly opposed it, but added that if such "conscription of [civilian] manpower is resorted to…the inevitable next step is the conscription of labor." He stressed that to do so in peace time would only mean that the government is planning to go to war. Such an action could only bring the country one step closer to entering one.[50]

When Roosevelt the next year asked for authoritarian powers by passage of the Merchant Shipping Priorities bill, George publicly denounced his "totalitarian methods," and opposed the piece of legislation. It was George's first public criticism of the administration since he had assumed the chairmanship of the Foreign Relations Committee and long after he had done Roosevelt's bidding for the important Lend-Lease bill. He eagerly used the opportunity to call for the avoidance of entering the war. "I profoundly hope that this country will not become an active participant in the present war…," he told national reporters. "I have not accepted the fatalistic doctrine that our actual military…participation is inevitable," as Roosevelt was trying to give the impression, and he found it "a bit discouraging that a great many things that we are doing have not any proper connection with any legitimate defense program."[51] In April 1941, George introduced a bill for Roosevelt to amend the Neutrality Act of 1939 to permit the transport in American ships "articles and materials" to certain naval and air bases leased by the US, presumably with the ultimate destination Great Britain. He would continue to support several changes.[52] By the end of the year, just a month before the sword was forced into America's hand, George gave a radio address in which he noted that in the past, neutrality was natural since we were "separated by the broad oceans from so much of the civilized world." Noting that Lend-Lease had not propelled the United States into war, as its critics had predicted, but he admitted what anyone knew, that with its passage, America "threw over the whole concept of neutrality," and he called on Americans to present a unified front to discourage aggression on the part of the Axis powers. "If Hitler knows that all America is speaking when Mr. Roosevelt is speaking," he admonished, "there is less danger of a conflict."[53]

A casual look at his actions belie the general belief by December 1940

---

[50]WFG, "Speech Opposing the Russell Amendment," 277–78.

[51]*New York Times,* June 29, 1941, 23:1.

[52]*CR*, 77/1, 2951.

[53]The *Washington Post* seized on his choice of words and twisted them somewhat in an echo call for support of the president (*CR*, 77/1, A4992; 4950–51).

that he was "in line" with FDR's foreign policy.[54] Once again George was stressing the theme that ran through his pre-Pearl Harbor actions: Everything for defense but strict avoidance on any involvement that was not directly in America's interest; support our friends in the fight but keep us out of the actual fighting. His position remained consistent, even after the war ended, and we had entered the Cold War with the Russians. His support of foreign aid in the late 1940s and 1950s would be motivated by the same objective.

Throughout, George had maintained the distinction between "internationalism" and "intervention." When moves were made by the administration to increase the Export-Import Bank's authority to loan money to Finland to buy agricultural surpluses, George opposed it, asking rhetorically, "Are we trying to shape our foreign policies to fit the needs...of the American people, or are we trying to serve the ends of others...as being our...interests?"[55] George noted that if the US lifted the restrictions by the Neutrality Act on credits for any foreign nation, "It is easy to see that we have destroyed the Neutrality Act," and he argued that if the restrictions were relaxed for Finland, pressure would "be doubled and redoubled" to loan money to Great Britain. Allowing these violations would be no different "than if we sent an American battleship to Finland," telling Congress that if it wished to send aid to Finland, then do it, and adding "Let's stop whipping the Devil around the stump and take the responsibility for it."[56] A month later, when the Senate passed (49–27) the Finnish Aid Bill, which also gave aid to China, George warned in the debate that the bill might be America's first step toward involvement with the Soviet Union. "No country, and particularly, no free country goes to war in one stride," he reminded his colleagues. "It goes stage by stage until one day we find ourselves in a position from which we cannot turn back."[57]

George's analysis was correct. The enemy was Germany, but many did not see it that way because of their sympathy for tiny Finland. Whereas France and Britain were formally at war with the Third Reich, their political leaders were criticized for not helping Finland in the "Winter War" when neither of them was in war with the Soviet Union. Indeed, Daladier's gov-

[54]"New Foreign Policy Chief," clipping, November 12, 1940, box 337, f. George, July 1938–, RNC papers.

[55]Carlton, "The Record," 3, cites *CR*, July 31, 1939 (1940?), foreign relations file, WFG VHPS.

[56]*Atlanta Constitution*, January 17, 1940, 8:2.

[57]*New York Times*, February 14, 1940, 1:5.

ernment in effect fell over the question of his not sending aid to that country when he was not fighting the Germans on his own borders.

Where Great Britain was concerned, George was more generous because he correctly saw the United Kingdom as the sole bulwark against Hitler. When he opposed Roosevelt's exchange of old destroyers for British bases, he did so only because the president had taken "on the most momentous obligations in the nation's history without giving Congress an opportunity to express its wishes on the matter," not because it jeopardized America's neutral position.[58] He seems not to have cared in November when the US released to Britain forty-six Grant bombers, which had a range great enough to bomb the Skoda munitions factories in Bohemia.[59] And although he thought it "impractical and somewhat premature" to act immediately on British loans, he expressed a willingness to hold hearings on the Johnson Act amendments, which would have permitted loans to Great Britain even though Britain had yet to repay all of their World War I loans.[60] After meeting with Hull, Roosevelt, and the Marquess of Lothian, the British ambassador to Washington, on November 26, however, George expressed "general agreement" with them on the question.[61] He had expressed to the three, however, that passage of the Johnson amendment would be difficult in this session of Congress due to the problem of acquiring quorums in December and predicted any action would come in the new year.[62] Following his leadership, the Foreign Relations committee unanimously voted to delay action until early in the next session "unless an occasion would arise which demanded immediate steps." He also seemed to hedge on the question of loans when he told reporters that he felt that aid should be given, but "it is a technical question what kind of aid."[63]

In December George chastised the American people for "not seem[ing] to sense the growing need for even greater or faster production," and he said that the US should "get rid of anything and everything that gets in the way of stepping up the program."[64] He continued to stress in January 1941 his view that we should avoid direct military involvement. Helping Britain "short of war" was not just a "catch-penny phrase" with him. He wanted to

---

[58]Ibid., September 11, 1940, 11:1. George was careful to make the point that it would have passed Congress anyway.

[59]*Atlanta Constitution*, November 21, 1940, 8-B.

[60]Ibid. November 27, 1940, 1:5.

[61]Ibid.

[62]Ibid.

[63]*New York Times*, November 28, 1940, 1:3.

[64]*Atlanta Constitution*, December 5, 1940, 1:1.

"give aid to England" but short of bringing retaliatory measures on the United States from Great Britain's enemies. He expressed the curious opinion that American avoidance of war might help Britain more, since if we entered, we would have to devote much of what might go to Britain to our own defense.[65]

George's concern about Britain continued to intensify, probably heightened by the Lend-Lease fight, and by midsummer, George was almost to the point of calling on the US to enter the war. When the Germans took Crete in the Mediterranean from the air, he felt that this move proved how vulnerable Britain was and believed the easy occupation of Crete proved that warships could not protect narrow waters like the English Channel.[66] At a meeting of the English-Speaking Union on May 14, 1941, he eulogized the Anglo-American Union of World War I, which "preserved the rule of law and social justice among nations." He noted that since "over the free France of Lafayette and Foch waves the swastika," it was all the more necessary for strong Anglo-American cooperation. In his mind, George already had America in the war when he said to his Senate colleagues, "We are engaged in the greatest struggle in history to preserve freedom in the modern world."[67]

When the Germans invaded Russia in late June 1941 and Churchill astounded his people by offering an alliance to his avowed enemy, Communist Russia, George defended Churchill's actions, calling them "a logical and necessary evolution under the circumstances." He stopped short of recommending aid to Russia but said that to give greater aid to Britain "so that she can redouble her blows against Germany" was to give in effect aid to Russia.[68] Where Germany was concerned, George does not seem to have had much vitriol, despite the fact that he had abandoned his isolationism due to German aggression in Europe. As for Germany, its leaders did not feel that America would enter any European conflict. Joachim von Ribbentrop, the German foreign minister, had stated even as early as 1939 that the isolationist sentiment in America was so great that Germany need not fear American intervention.[69] By 1939, George had been so bothered by cataracts that he had to turn his head sideways to read a bill, and when Nazi Germa-

[65]Sen. George says Aid Short of War," January 1, 1941, *Herald Tribune*, box 337, f. George 1938–, RNC papers

[66]*New York Times*, June 1, 1941, 4:5.

[67]*CR*, 77/1, A2962–63.

[68]*New York Times*, July 14, 1941, 3:1.

[69]Clapper, *Watching the World*, 174–75.

ny invaded Poland on September 1, 1939, George was in a New York hospital having surgery on them.[70] Not wanting to excite him, Miss Lucy did not tell him about the beginning of war, and even went so far as to remove newspapers and the radio from his room to isolate him from the news. He only discovered the war's outbreak when a deputation from the administration came to him to ask his advice on a special session of Congress to consider the repeal of the Neutrality Act of 1937. He strongly urged it.[71] As we have seen, the Pittman Resolution to revise the neutrality legislation had gone nowhere, so Roosevelt had turned to the House to begin the repeal process, arguing that the US would more likely remain at peace if the arms embargo was repealed that if the act stayed in its present form.[72] It was in the days that followed than George came to decide fully that he had been mistaken about the League of Nations all these years, and he then joined the administration, the reader will remember, in calling for revision of the act.

This position was still part of George's "keep the fight over there" mentality. George had continued to stress that America should not entered the conflict as late as July 3, 1941, when an editorial outlining his views appeared in the *Washington News.* "I profoundly hope that this country will not become an active participant in the present war, or any other war," he told a reporter, adding, "I have not yet accepted the fatalistic doctrine than our...participation [in the war] is inevitable." The newspaper opined, "We are thankful that Chairman [of the Foreign Relations Committee] George is in that position of great responsibility." His position was so pacifist that Rep. Jeanette Rankin, the only member of Congress to vote against American entrance into both world wars, asked that the editorial be placed in the *Congressional Record.*[73] When Russia invaded the Soviet Union in June of that year, George blasted Germany, stating that the invasion was proof that "no credence whatsoever can be given to any of Germany's pretentions and promises," although he felt that German military involvement in Eastern Europe would be good for both the British and the Americans because it meant that Germany could not now threaten either of these powers and it would give the United States extra time for preparedness.[74] The next day the *Atlanta Constitution* reported that Hitler's reason for attack was military. He hoped to prevent attacks coming on his eastern flank, rather widely missing

[70]Mark Dunahoo, oral history, 55, Russell Library.
[71]Jarman, "Taxpayer's Senator," 40.
[72]Thompson, *A Time for War*, 187.
[73]*CR*, 77/1, A3287–88.
[74]*New York Times,* June 22, 1941, 8:1.

the mark on Germany's motives.[75] At the same time, he feared the attack might derail America's preparedness program because people will feel that preparedness is no longer necessary.[76] When in August Marshall Philippe Pétain, leader of the defeated French government, caved to German demands to use French African ports, thus giving them a embarkation point to attack Brazil, George even suggested that this action might necessitate that the US would have to occupy Martinique to prevent German activities in the Caribbean.[77] Germans had already in May sunk the American ship, the *Robin Moor*, in the South Atlantic where Germany had designated a war zone. They had allowed the crew to leave on life boats, hundreds of miles from land.[78] After sinking the *Robin Moor*, the Germans torpedoed two American destroyers in late 1941, and these events seem to have been George's tipping point. He echoed Roosevelt's notion that "convoys meant shooting and shooting meant war," and he was taken to task by the isolationists. "If we are convoying half-way across the Atlantic[,] we have the right to convoy. Where an American merchantman may rightfully go on the high seas, there may go the whole navy. The doctrine of freedom of the seas would be meaningless if that were not true." When Senator Taft pointed out that this view was inconsistent with George's position six months earlier, George replied, "But at that time the free right to sail on the high seas had not been challenged by Germany.[79] German aggression changed him, and within a month he would shed the last of his isolationism.

Curiously, George's attitude toward Japan, the other totalitarian regime, was at once more optimistic and less belligerent than his attitude toward Germany. Since we have only his public statements on which to rely, it is sometimes difficult to divine why he viewed them differently. What one journalist called "the gangster of the Orient"[80] had already displayed a much more brutal face in the war in China since 1937 than the Germans ever did, even if we include the horrors of the Holocaust. Whereas public figures spoke of inevitable war with Japan, George seems to feel that an Asian war was less likely.[81] As early as March 1931, Senator George predicted that the Japanese would not attack Singapore because they would not misjudge the

[75]*Atlanta Constitution*, June 23, 1941, 3:4.
[76]*New York Times*, June 23, 1941, 1:4.
[77]Ibid., August 13, 1941, 5:4.
[78]Hull, *Memoirs of Cordell Hull*, 2:944–45.
[79]Lash, *Roosevelt and Churchill*, 428–29.
[80]Clapper, *Watching the World*, 287.
[81]Ibid., 285.

war for being a short one as the Italians had.[82] In August 1941, he again missed the mark when he predicted that the Japanese would not attack the Philippines. He reasoned that since they had not completely overrun China, they did not have the resources to strike as far as the Philippines, although he did feel that they would be able to occupy all of French Indo-China and Thailand. On August 1, 1941, the US had partially embargoed selling aviation gasoline to the Japanese and had frozen credits, and George stressed the partial nature of the restrictions, feeling that "following a period of readjustment and assuring there is no further Japanese aggression, limited commerce...might be resumed." Moreover, he argued against complete severance of relations with the Japanese Empire.[83]

In July he had been hopeful that a shakeup in the Japanese cabinet would lead to better US-Japanese relations, pointing out that the US State Department "manifested a desire to keep upon our approaches to Japan" and that with the new cabinet, "the way is open for the creation of more amicable relations...and can be regarded as a more hopeful sign."[84] Roosevelt's Japanese policy became more hostile when that same month, ten Japanese ships were not allowed to pass through the Panama Canal.[85] George did not join him in his anti-Japanese turn, as he had in the conflict between Britain and Germany. The very next month in a press conference, George predicted that if the Japanese would curtail their aggression, US-Japanese trade might resume, and he feared that the current direction of trade relations "seem to be moving...in the general direction of a complete severance of trade relations." He added that sanctions would not have stopped the invasion of Indo-China. What we had done had already damaged the American silk industry. Gerald Nye had underscored George's point more unequivocally by stating that "we should be very careful in depriving ourselves of needed commodities and at the same time moving closer to war."[86]

By September, George, from his seat as chair of the Foreign Relations Committee, was reassuring the Chungking government of Chiang Kai-shek that any negotiations would not result in our abandonment of "free China" and that China could continue to rely on the flow of aid coming over the Burma Road.[87] This statement was the most anti-Japanese one he had made

---

[82]*New York Times*, March 30, 1941, 12:3.

[83]*Atlanta Constitution*, August 3, 1941, 8A:6.

[84]*New York Times*, July 19, 1941, 4:8.

[85]*Atlanta Constitution*, July 21, 1941, 1:7.

[86]*New York Times*, August 3, 1941, 21:1.

[87]"US will Stand by China," clipping, September 14, 1941, box 337, f. George, July 1938–, RNC papers.

all year, but he still had not become as hostile as he had toward the Germans.

It is difficult to understand why George was less hostile to the "gangster of the Orient." Quite probably it was distance and simple interest. China and Japan were half a world away from the shores of Georgia, which George had repeatedly stated that he wished to protect. He seems to have had a natural affinity for Great Britain, which had, when seeming all was lost, continued to fight on. China was a distant mystical land.

When the Japanese finally attacked Pearl Harbor in December 1951, George, as chair of the Foreign Relations committee, was invited to a closed-door briefing of major figures in the government and the military.[88] George seemed to have no illusions of the crisis in which America had become involved. A *chargé d'affaires* of the German Embassy reported to Berlin that the surprise attack had hit America like a "bolt of lightning" (*Blitzschlag*) and that no one seemed to think that a war with the Japanese Empire would be a "piece of cake" (*Spaziergand*). George proved even more pessimistic; in his opinion, the conflict with Japan would be at least a two- or three-year war.[89] Even here his optimism got the better of him; the war with Japan would last just short of four years.

What placed Walter George firmly on the stage of history was his shepherding the aforementioned Lend-Lease Act through the US Senate. One journal described his appearance at the time as that of the stereotypical image of a Senator: "a tall, dignified man of sixty-two with fast graying hair," yet it more intimately spoke of his speaking ability, stating, "He makes few speeches but can be persuasive orator when he gets started."[90] It would be this latter quality in his abilities that would be needed so badly. Chairing the Foreign Relations Committee by itself designated him the man to lead the fight for passage, but President Roosevelt was indeed lucky to have this particular man at its head. The amiable Senator Pittman could probably not have done it.

Americans generally supported the principles of Lend-Lease, but it emphatically wanted no part of the European war.[91] The bill in effect stated that manufacturers could make war materiel vital to the defense of the United States, and it gave the president of the United States the authority "to lease, lend or otherwise dispose of" these materiel to any state (i.e., Great

[88]Bloom, *The Autobiography of Sol Bloom*, 259.
[89]Weintraub, *Journey into War*, 571–72.
[90]"Back in the Fold," 16.
[91]Clapper, *Watching the World*, 270.

Britain and China) "whose defense the president deems vital to the defense of the United States" and he could accept any foreign repayment he felt satisfactory toward for the then-hefty price tag of $7,000,000,000.[92] Powerful and influential Senator Burton K. Wheeler would lead the fight against it with such stinging rhetoric as calling Lend-lease the "Triple A Bill, because it would plow under every fourth American boy."[93]

Henry Stimpson first suggested Lend-Lease to Roosevelt, who first proposed it to his staff through Morgenthau in December 1940. Roosevelt began warming the country up for the Lend-Lease legislation in a statement on December 31, 1940, when he somewhat overstated his case by declaring that "Never before since Jamestown and Plymouth Rock has our American civilization been in such danger." Describing the war in Europe, he added additional hyperbole by noting that the Atlantic Ocean was not so wide that German planes could not cross it, overlooking the fact that if they did cross, the planes of the day would not have been able to return. Using the theme that Walter George had used, that supporting Great Britain was the best way to defend our shores, he intoned, "We are planning our own defence [*sic*] with the utmost urgency…[and to do so] we must integrate the war needs of Britain and the other free nations."[94] When British gold reserves were depleted the next month, he further violated American "neutrality" by sending the USS *Louisville* to South Africa to ship a load of gold to the US to bolster British purchasing power.[95]

Roosevelt announced his plans for Lend-Lease in his annual message to Congress on January 6, 1941, calling for "total aid to England," which led a member of a British firm in American to state that "on Monday, January 6, 1941, I dare to predict the second world war has been decided."[96]

Walter George, as chair of the Foreign Relations Committee, had to carry the ball for the administration, would remember Lend-Lease at the end of his career as "my toughest political scrap."[97] George told Roosevelt that if he was lucky, the bill would pass by a couple of votes, and Roosevelt thought that too close. George then suggested that the bill be introduced in both houses at the same time by the majority leaders, both of whom were, of

[92]Connally, *My Name is Tom Connally*, 243.

[93]Caro, *The Years of Lyndon Johnson*, 72.

[94]*Daily Telegraph*, December 31, 1940, FO 371/26149, America (The United States), British National Archives.

[95]North Whitehead, cypher telegram, 3 January 1941, FO 371/28791, 241–42, British National Archives.

[96]Dispatch 150, January 9, 1941, 112, FO 371/27149, British National Archives.

[97]"People of the Week," *US News & World Report* 41 (July 27, 1956): 20.

course, Democrats, instead of the traditional committee chairmen, to give the bill more punch. This technique would also avoid a conflict in both houses as to which committee the bill should be sent for discussion.[98] Therefore, on January 10, the hypocritically titled "Act to Further Promote the Defense of the United States and for Other Purposes" was introduced into the House by majority leader John McCormick and in the Senate by majority leader Alben W. Barkley.[99] In the House, it had the ironic number of HR 1776. With this piece of legislation, America abandoned any pretense whatsoever of neutrality in the European conflict.

The isolationists immediately swung into action. Roosevelt's biographer Cole wrote that "not since the repeal of the arms embargo of 1939 had interventionists worked so hard to defeat an administration proposal."[100] Many felt that it would in effect be a shadow declaration of war against Germany, which in effect it was, with a real declaration of war to follow. Bennett Clark of Missouri called it "a bill to authorize the president to declare war."[101] Others called it giving Roosevelt a "blank check" and dictatorial powers. It would give Roosevelt more power than any peacetime president had ever had and make the United States a *de facto* ally of Great Britain. Within twenty-four hours of its introduction, Thomas Dewey, a rapidly rising star in the Republican Party, issued a statement that the bill was "an attempt to abolish free government in the United States."[102] Vandenberg led the opposition, which contained the old isolation stalwarts, Wheeler and Nye, with Southerners such as Louisiana's Allen Ellender and North Carolina's Robert Reynolds.[103] The discussion often took an anti-British hue, and opponents frequently cited George Washington's letter to Henry Laurens on April 20, 1778, in which he spoke of "the injuries we have received from Great Britain can never be forgotten," stressing "her love of tyranny" and how she would no doubt "attempt again to bend our necks to the yoke of

[98]Kimball, *The Most Unsordid Act*, 147.

[99]Dallek, *Franklin D. Roosevelt and American Foreign Policy, 1932–1945*, 258; for a copy, see Ellender papers, box 596, f. 9, September 25, 1944; see also box 1390, f. 1, Baker, *Wheeling and Dealing*, 77.

[100]Cole, *Roosevelt and the Isolationists, 1932–45*, 414.

[101]"The Battle of HR 1776," 5.

[102]Clapper, *Watching the World*, 168.

[103]A story circulated for years that Senator Reynolds received a German medal, the Iron Cross, for his opposition to Lend-lease (See Egerton, *Speak Now against the Day*, 220), but his current biographer, Julian Pleasants, strongly asserts that the story is not true and that it was fabricated by his political enemies in later campaigns as he tried to regain his Senate seat. Julian Pleasants, "Buncombe Bob," (Chapel Hill, N.C.; UNC Press, 2009), 244.

slavery."[104] A little more crudely, Congressman Martin Sweeney, described by the historian Kimball as a "professional Irishman" read into the *Congressional Record* new lyrics to "God Bless America":

> God Save America from British Rule.
> Stand beside her and guide her
> From the Schemers who would make of her a fool.
> From Lexington to Yorktown,
> From blood-stained Valley Forge,
> God Save America
> From a king named George.[105]

The House Foreign Affairs Committee began hearings on January 15, and fourteen days later reported out the bill favorably 17–8. General debate began in the House on February 3, and the House passed it five days later by a vote of 260–165.

Meanwhile, in the Senate, George led the fight for Lend-Lease since he had just assumed the chair of Foreign Relations since Pittman had just died.[106] He was also present for the many strategy sessions at the White House. He suggested that it would be wise to bring some Republicans on board, and on January 26, the Democratic leadership and George met with both Representative Joe Martin (R-Massachusetts) and Senator Charles McNary (R-Oregon).[107] Roosevelt expressed a willingness to "accept any amendments that were desirable," whatever that meant, and George suggested three that had been discussed earlier in Democratic discussion groups. One was a time limit to Roosevelt's powers. A second denied Roosevelt as commander-in-chief the power to order American ships to convoy belligerents' transports. The third required the president to make periodic reports to Congress on what he was doing with the materials he was sending.[108] Roosevelt had used his usual gambit by calling it the best way to keep us out of war. Arthur Vandenberg sarcastically called it "Peace through war

---

[104]Copy of George Washington to Henry Laurens, 20 April 1778, box 1331, f. 9, Ellender papers.

[105]*CR*, 77/1, vol. 87, pt. 12, June 1941, A2941, cited in Kimball, *The Most Unsordid Act*, 186–87.

[106]Stettinius, *Lend-Lease*, 68.

[107]Martin eventually voted against the bill on its first reading.

[108]Warren F. Kimball cites *New York Times,* January 28, 29, 1941 (*The Most Unsordid Act*, 199); Langer and Gleason, *The Undeclared War*, 273.

by proxy."[109] Vandenberg felt that Congress was "less than enthusiastic," with even the Democrats showing no enthusiasm. Of course, few Republicans applauded it at all.[110]

George had hoped to begin Senate committee hearings after the bill had passed the House on February 8, but the hearings and debate dragged on such that George started hearings on January 31. He conducted them fairly, allowing opponents to be heard. The Democratic leadership chose senators Jimmy Byrnes and Carter Glass to fill two vacancies in the committee to insure its passage.[111] Senator Connally remembered that the committee hearings were so packed one could hardly breathe. The pro-witnesses were Secretary of State Hull, Henry Morgenthau, Secretary of War Stimson and Wendell Willkie, who had opposed Roosevelt for reelection just a few months before and who made an "excellent witness," the British thought.[112] The America-Firsters pushed Charles Lindbergh front and center and even hired hecklers. Some opponents on the committee even answered for the witnesses.

With the Capitol abuzz over Lend-Lease, Edward Frederick Lindley Wood, Viscount Halifax, the new British ambassador to Washington, paid a visit to both Walter George and Congressman Bloom, chair of the House Foreign Relations Committee. Certain newspapers in the country reported that he was "lobbying" for passage of the bill, which his mere presence indeed suggested to some extent, but Secretary of State Hull issued a statement that the meetings were no more than "courtesy calls." Halifax, who had been a strong candidate and rival of Churchill for British prime minister when Neville Chamberlain resigned in 1940, denied that he had tried to influence the debate. Writing that it was "only natural that the Lend-Lease bill came up" and he had inquired about the parliamentary process for passage, he had expressed no opinion as to the merits of the bill and "said nothing which could possibly be interpreted as an attempt to influence either chairman." Knowing the criticism coming from the isolationists, he felt that in most circles little important could "be attached to the obvious attempt by the opponents of the Bill [*sic*] to make bricks with so little straw."[113]

George opened the debate for the Senate with a radio address on January 27. He spoke of international law for peace yet noted that "three of the

[109]Vandenberg, *The Private Papers of Senator Vandenberg*, 8.
[110]Ibid.
[111]Connally, *My Name Is Tom Connally*, 243.
[112]Departmental no. 2, 13 February 1941, 104, FO 371/26149, FO-BNA.
[113]Halifax to Foreign Office, 5 February 1941, FO 371/26149, 101, FO-BNA.

most powerful nations of the world have chosen an aggressive path." He repeatedly stressed that the bill was a defensive measure, designed to keep war away from our shores by supporting "those friendly nations whose continued independence existence is necessary for our vital defense." He also warned against "emasculating amendments" to the bill that would "block the achievement of its great purposes." He harped on the fact that the Germans and Italians had both violated the Kellogg-Briand pact, an international treaty that had "outlawed war" in 1929, and by so doing had forfeited American neutrality.[114]

On February 13, the Senate Foreign Relations committee reported the Lend-Lease bill out favorably 15–8, with one Republican vote in favor.[115] George had crafted it so that it was identical to the one that had passed the House. Debate on the floor of the Senate started four days later with Walter George at center stage.

In February and March, even as the debate was raging in Congress, George attended many strategy sessions in the White House with Hull, Morgenthau, and Stimson planning strategy to gain for Roosevelt the freedom of action in the bill that he wanted. Roosevelt wanted to see that the original bill, giving the president highly discretionary powers, would be kept intact, while Taft and Vandenberg wanted Congress to authorize every appropriation.[116] Speeches opposing the bill seemed endless, and there was some fear of a filibuster. Those favoring the bill had spoken eighteen hours. Those against had logged in forty-four hours. Nye himself had held the Senate floor for a total of twelve hours.[117] The administration leaders were in a quandary. They hesitated to leave the attacks unanswered, but if they answered them, they would prolong the debate and delay final passage.[118] The threat of a direct invasion of the United Kingdom had abated somewhat, but matters were heating up in North Africa. Aid was necessary. Moreover, George had to be brought on board to retain the measurers that gave him the freest of hands in doling out the material. Roosevelt had to be ever mindful of handling George because of the incident in Barnesville two and a half years before. He knew that George had not forgotten, nor probably forgiven him, and he might be inclined to tweak Roosevelt by tying his hands.

---

[114]Reprinted in the *CR*, 77/1, Appendix 280–81.

[115]Connally, *My Name Is Tom Connally*, 249. He states all Republicans on the committee voted "no."

[116]Kimball, *The Most Unsordid Act*, 212–13.

[117]Connally, *My Name Is Tom Connally*, 243–44.

[118]Lord Halifax to Anthony Eden, March 26, 1941, 47, FO 371/26150, FO-BNA.

On Tuesday, February 25, George was included for the first time in a meeting of the "Big Four," i.e., Vice President Henry Wallace, Alben Barkley, Sam Rayburn, and John McCormack. Roosevelt was disturbed that there were reports that passage of the bill might be stymied, but both George and Barkley expressed confidence to the president that the Senate would pass the bill by Saturday, March 1, without changes. George told Roosevelt that voting on amendments would begin on Thursday but he anticipated no problem.[119] The bill did not pass by Saturday, and on March 1, George met again with Roosevelt, who was in bed with a cold, and then again on March 4.

In the debate on the bill, George went toe-to-toe with the bill's opponents. Throughout the debate, George swayed and sidestepped, parried and thrusted, and at times he made arguments that he must have known were fallacious. In a number of cases in the debate, George became customarily rude and even insulting. When Senator Clark of Missouri read to George on the Senate floor a part of one of George's speeches from 1939 calling strongly for our non-involvement in the European conflict, George candidly admitted, "I am perfectly frank to admit that I was mistaken then," but then nastily added, "The difficulty with the senator from Missouri is that he never knows when he is mistaken although everyone else clearly recognizes it."[120] In a tangle with Senator Nye, George told the senator that he, George, understood that the senator favored aid to Great Britain "to the extent of at least enabling her to survive," to which Nye replied, "That is correct," to which George patronizingly replied, "Very well. We can [at least] agree upon that." At that point Nye felt compelled to add, "If we can go through steps that are short of war." To this addition George added, "How many more 'ifs' does the senator want to attach to it?... Each time the senator attaches another 'if.'"[121] He even told Nye that no one could convince him "of anything with respect of the bill, even the plainest and most palpable truth written all over its face."[122] When Burton K. Wheeler himself said he could not see how any lawyer "could stand on the floor of the Senate" and state that the bill was not contradictory, George went after him. "The Senator from Montana asked no question; he is...merely dogmatically

[119]"Senator Talks...," *Atlanta Constitution*, February 26, 1941, RCB-5804, box 15, f. WFG-GSA.

[120]Ibid., 1631.

[121]Ibid., 1427.

[122]Ibid., 1426–27.

stating as fact a thing which is not a fact."[123]

The isolationists introduced amendment after amendment. The whole tilt was the fear, as Viscount Halifax told his government, of the superpowers that the bill gave the president.[124] Senator Allen Ellender had introduced an amendment in committee that stated nothing in the bill gave the president the authority to commit ground troops on any foreign soil. It had been defeated there, so he tried to reintroduce it on the Senate floor. George told reporters that the bill did not affect the president's powers but the amendment, if passed, would have a "moral effect" on the bill, giving the appearance that Congress did not have confidence in the president and give the Japanese especially a "go ahead" sign.[125] George restated on the Senate floor the premise that the bill did not "as it stands" authorize the president to make military commitments but only to dispose "of a certain quantity of defense articles."[126] On March 4, George met with Hull to tell him that the opposition was going to argue that if the bill did not give the president the power to send troops, why object to saying so?[127] Eventually the amendment was watered down with Ellender and the president working together, and the weaker version passed 65–24, despite the efforts of Senator Robert Taft to strengthen it.[128]

Senator Taft introduced an amendment of his own, which included aid only to Britain, whereas the Lend-Lease bill gave aid to any opponent of Hitler. It would give, Senator Vandenberg said, "direct and immediate aid to Britain" without any of the "trimmings." Eighty-nine out of ninety-five senators voted for either HR 1776 or the Taft Amendment, and even those who voted against both expressed publicly on the Senate floor that they wished for a British victory.[129] Still the bill too was defeated. As all of this debate raged, Roosevelt continued as though the bill had passed. In February, Roosevelt transferred fifty US destroyers to the British navy at Halifax, Nova Scotia.[130]

---

[123]Ibid., 1240.

[124]Lord Halifax to Anthony Eden, March 27, 1941, FO 371/26150, 47, FO-BNA.

[125]*New York Times*, February 23, 26, 1941, in Kimball, *The Most Unsordid Act*, 214.

[126]*CR*, 77/1, 1428.

[127]Hopkins papers, box 302, "Book III: Background of Lend-lease," cited in Kimball, *The Most Unsordid Act*, 215.

[128]*CR*, 77/1, March 6, 7, 1941, 1884–1901, 1948–60, 1975, 1984, vol. 87, cited in Kimball, *The Most Unsordid Act*, 216.

[129]Vandenberg, *The Private Papers of Senator Vandenberg*, 9–10.

[130]Britain expressed thanks and Sumner Wells replied (February 27, 1941, FO 371/26149, FO-BNA).

Recognizing a filibuster, George called on March 3 for limiting the debate on the Lend-Lease bill.[131] Three days later he chided the opposition's informal filibuster: "But if we want to carry the debate over from one week to another, week after week, the American people have the right to ask whether or not we mean it when we say we are in favor of aid to Britain."[132] As was often the case, George had the last word that day. In a rather lengthy speech, he stressed that Lend-Lease was a blow against those who would end freedom of the seas, stressing that we must assist any foes of Hitler and the Japanese Empire: "And here is a bill. It is not a perfect bill. It may grant powers that many of us would think are too great.... Whatever may be the shortcomings of Great Britain, one this ought to be made clear.... Every [bit of our legal system that guarantees our freedoms] came out of English common law."[133] He continued to stress how the bill would not get us into war. He thundered as only he could: "A mighty impulse is stirring at the soul of America...put weapons into the hands of the single nation which stands in the way of the group of aggressors to which I have referred."[134]

Lend-lease passed on Saturday March 8 by 60–31, with four senators paring with each other.[135] On March 11, the House of Representatives adopted the Senate version, and Roosevelt signed it the same day. George received a pen with which the bill was signed.[136] A gleeful unknown author of a memo titled "Note on the Future of Anglo-American relations," observed, "Washington appears to be in a resolute mood now that the lend-lease [*sic*] bill has become law. Isolationism is buried."[137] Reporting the debate to Anthony Eden, Lord Halifax described the three-weeks' debate as having "generated more heat than light [?]"[138] but gave credit for its passage to "pro-public opinion."[139] Curiously he does not mention nor give Walter George credit for passage in any of his dispatches, but thanks Secretary of the Treasury Morgenthau for Lend-Lease.[140] In fact, except for his early

[131]*CR*, 77/1, 1640.

[132]Ibid., 1889.

[133]Ibid., 1893.

[134]Ibid., 1887–95.

[135]Ibid., 2097.

[136]"George Given Pen," *Atlanta Constitution* clipping, March 13, 1941, RCB-5804, box 15, f. WFG-GSA.

[137]"Note on the Future of Anglo-American Relations," April 5, 1941, FO 371/26149, 147, FO-BNA.

[138]Halifax to Eden, March 26, 1941, FO 371/26150, 47, FO-BNA.

[139]Ibid.

[140]See FO 371/26149, 121–22, FO-BNA.

meeting with George, he never mentions his name again in his dispatches.

The passage of Lend-Lease did not end the opposition to it. It even came under criticism long after Pearl Harbor, yet George continued to defend the act to all of its critics. In 1943, when the Lend-Lease appropriation for the year was debated, and critics were harping on the waste and mismanagement that was obvious in the program, George, a strong foe of waste, continued to defend the bill. Listening to the debate on the question, he tried to stay out of it but eventually could stand it no longer. Admitting that since its passage there had been "waste, mismanagement and incompetency" in its management, because of the bill, "We are at least half a year, if not a full year farther toward the final conclusion of the war.... If lend-lease did nothing more than shorten the war by twelve months...it would pay back in dollars and cents considerably more than the entire appropriation made for lend-lease, to say nothing of the blood of our men which will be saved."[141] Even in 1945, when the defeat of Nazi Germany was only days away, George was discussing on the Senate floor the impact of the act. Admitting that no one could say for certain by how much Lend-Lease shortened the war, he added, "If the war has been shortened one hour, and one single American life has been saved, I shall never be an apologist for the passage of the Lend-Lease Act."[142]

George later always referred to the Lend-lease act as "one of the most important acts of my time." He felt that not only was England saved by it, it had put America's industrial machinery into high gear, making America's recovery from the Pearl Harbor attack much easier than it might have been. He called it "the greatest single piece of legislation from those years," and he always said that he was "proud to have been one of its architects."[143] The *Atlanta Journal*'s Ralph Smith's opinion that no one else but George could have gotten the bill through the Senate[144] is certainly an overstatement, given the wide margin by which it passed, but his leadership probably made it easier. He genuinely saw the bill as a defensive action, not as an abandonment of neutrality, which it clearly was, or an offensive action, as Roosevelt probably meant it to be. "I do not want to go into any war," he told his Senate colleagues in the beginning of the debate, "and I support the bill because I believe it to be the one means...of providing against the danger of in-

[141]*CR*, 78/1, 5371.

[142]Ibid., 79/1, 3245.

[143]Gene Methvin, "Statesmanship," *Vienna News*, August 8, 1957, RCB-5804, box 15, f. WFG-GSA.

[144]*Atlanta Journal*, December 20, 2007, 6-B

volvement in the war, [i.e.] by the strengthening primarily of our own defenses."[145] His support of the bill was seen as abandoning his old isolationism, but it was merely a move to the middle; he never became the interventionist he was accused of becoming. Edward Stettinius remembered in March 1943 that George had made another related truism that was undeniable. "The historians of the future will recognize that the date of the signing of the Lend-Lease bill was the day on which the Axis Powers were defeated."[146]

Between the signing of Lend-Lease and America's entry into the war nine months later, Walter George continued on his consistent path of nonintervention but equally consistent fortification of the Western Hemisphere. On March 10, the day before Lend-Lease was signed, George introduced a resolution in the Senate that passed unanimously to the effect that the United States would not recognize the transfer of any territory in the Western Hemisphere from one non-American power to another. It was derived from the fear that Vichy France would be forced to give Martinique or Guadeloupe to Germany. This question was not new and had been discussed at the Inter-American Conferences of 1936, 1938, and 1939 proclaiming inter-American solidarity against foreign intervention. His resolution read, "If such transfer or attempt to transfer should appear likely, the United States shall in addition to other measurers, immediately consult with the other American republics to determine upon the steps which should be taken to safeguard their common interests."[147] Two months later, George introduced Senate bill 1544 providing for the cooperation with the Central American republics for the construction of an Inter-American highway, which would be primarily used for defense of this portion of the hemisphere. The Senate conferred it to the Foreign Relations Committee.[148] In speaking at a banquet given in his honor in Cordele, Georgia, in April, George sounded this theme again, although a little more belligerently. He praised the aid that the US had given Britain in 1940, before Lend-Lease, and pledged that America would continue "to aid and assist all democracies…in their struggle against aggressor nations." He actually seemed to predict war. "We will soon come to a forking of the roads, and we must make our decision as to which road we will take." He even predicted that the fork would come in sixty to

[145] *CR*, 77/1, 1427.
[146] Stettinius, *Lend-Lease*, 328.
[147] *New York Times*, March 11, 1941, 10:7.
[148] *CR*, 77/1, 4239, 4357.

ninety days, adding that "We will defend the Western Hemisphere."[149] He said nothing more specifically and was probably thinking about the possible transfer of the French West Indies to Germany, which he had pledged to prevent.

He continued to balk on direct involvement overseas. When Senator Charles W. Tobey of New Hampshire introduced a resolution to prohibit "the use of American armed forces, vessels, and aircraft [i.e., convoys] for transporting, delivering or conveying articles or materials to belligerent countries, he favored it. Almost everyone had denounced such action during the Lend-Lease debate, including Roosevelt, who had once said, "Convoying means shooting, and shooting means war." There was often in the preparedness debate a chasm between what Roosevelt said and what he truly believed. Barkley's interest in the resolution indicates this, and he inquired of George, to whose committee he had sent it, about the committee's action on it. He would not say when the committee would act, but he made his position plain to the majority leader: "We are not going to convoy. We are not going to deliver arms...on the other side of the ocean in areas of danger."[150] George was concerned enough on the question to consult his friend Secretary of State Hull on the questions. Hull, in the usual language of the Roosevelt administration, told George that he did not feel it was time to revise the Neutrality Act, but he did not want Congress to pass such a resolution now. Letting his true feelings out, he wrote to George on April 29, "It would discourage the Allies, [and] encourage the Axis," adding that its passage would "be misunderstood abroad."[151] George remained opposed to the use of convoys.[152]

After Roosevelt, in one of his famous "fireside chats," stated that Germany was bent on world domination, Senator Claude Pepper of Florida introduced a resolution in the House endorsing Roosevelt's policies. Representative Woodruff of Michigan called the speech "a declaration of war," and even the Russians, who had not yet been attacked by the Germans, printed it for distribution in Russia. George opposed Pepper's resolution because it would highlight the lack of unity in the country behind the president and would generate "an unnecessary and most regrettable debate at this time," most assuredly not his real motive for his position.[153] A month later,

[149] *Vienna News*, April 24, 1941, 1.
[150] *CR*, 77/1, 2854–55, 2857.
[151] Hull, *Memoirs of Cordell Hull*, 2:944.
[152] Israel, ed., *The War Diary of Breckenridge Long*, 200.
[153] *New York Times*, May 30, 1941, 7:1.

on June 28, George denounced the "totalitarian methods" employed by Roosevelt to forge a national unity. If and when Americans find themselves in the line of fire, "the American people themselves will have some opportunity to pass upon the question…[after] a few days or even a week or so of debate…. The people themselves have the real right to make the decisions…under the machinery [i.e., the Constitution] which they have adopted for their use."[154] Although he noted several times that Roosevelt had a "personal devotion to democratic methods," he called his actions "totalitarian." Stressing that the country is "not at war," he thundered, "I have not yet accepted the fatalistic doctrine that our actual military or naval participation is inevitable" and he complained that what Roosevelt was doing was not compatible with "any legitimate defense program."[155]

George's speech had a "smashing impact," one journalist wrote, because this criticism had come from a "presidential confidant," not from one of the isolationists. Many thought that this oration might be his "valedictory speech" and he would leave foreign relations over Roosevelt's highhandedness and move to finance, which was an option, since Pat Harrison had passed away.[156] As it turns out, he would for a while chair both.

For the remainder of the summer and into the fall, George continued to oppose the president most stridently. George opposed the next month the arming of merchant ships, which Roosevelt wanted, although his opposition was more measured. He and Connally warned the president that the Selective Service extension, which was at that time being considered by the Senate, might be subject to a filibuster by the isolationists if he persisted in this policy.[157] In August he attacked the administration for the manner it was directing raw materials to defense industry. Larger concerns were receiving most of the materials and this method of allocation was causing many small concerns to close down for want of materials. George told the press that he had received "floods" of complaints and called for a centralized office to allocate these materials.[158] In the fall there were numerous strikes in the defense industries which George felt "cannot be defended," and he called on Roosevelt to end the strikes, which Roosevelt was not willing to do because of the Democratic Party's ties to labor. "Full operation of all industry is now vitally

---

[154]*CR*, no page given, in Carlton, *The Record…*," 12, GFR-VHPS.

[155]"George Criticizes Roosevelt's Policy," June 29, 1941, f. George, July 1938–, box 337, RNC papers.

[156]"Sen George Demands Curb," June 29, 1941, f. George, July 1938–, box 337, RNC papers.

[157]Dallek, *Franklin D. Roosevelt and American Foreign Policy, 1932–1945*, 290.

[158]*New York Times*, August 25, 1941, 27:8.

necessary…, he announced to reporters in November, adding, "the only sacrifice worth mentioning is made by the young men who have been drafted into the military and naval service."[159] While supporting Roosevelt on Lend-Lease as a defensive measure, he now opposed both the methods and goals which seemed to him too interventionist, having maintained a consistent policy throughout as war clouds gathered.

On December 8, 1941, Roosevelt called a joint session of Congress to ask for a declaration of war against the Japanese Empire. Mark Dunahoo, then an assistant to Senator Richard Russell, remembered George was coming to the Senate that Monday morning and meeting with a group of senators in the reading room. He came over to Richard Russell, who was conferring with Dunahoo. "Well, boys," George said, "I know how you feel…. My country's at war…just as quickly as I can get an appointment, I'm going to the White House and I'm going to pledge my wholehearted support and coordinated effort to the president of the United States." He then turned around and walked away. Dick Russell said, "My God, did you hear that, Mark? ...How could he do that after he tried to unseat him?" Obviously, Russell would not have. Dunahoo replied, "Well, Dick, he's quite a man…. It takes a man to do that." A skeptical Russell said, "I'll have to see it."[160]

George's visit to the White House made the newscasts that night. On entering the president's office, George reportedly said, "Mr. President, my country and your country are at war. I've come down here for the sole purpose of promising and pledging to you my unequivocal support, and I intend to lay all political affiliations aside and hope we can get this man's war over at the earliest possible date." Roosevelt said, "Come in, Walter," and then hugged him and added, "God bless you. I'll always love you for this."[161]

On Monday morning, August 8, 1943, the war came home to Walter George: He received a call from his daughter-in-law Mary Senate George, who was then living in Brooklyn, that her husband, Joseph Marcus "Blackie" George, who had been stationed at Floyd Bennett Field, had gone missing over the waters off Long Island. Early in August, a German submarine had shot down several planes off Long Island, and on August 6, an SOS came into Floyd Wright field from a Navy plane on anti-submarine patrol.

---

[159]"Sen. George Insists," November 17, 1943(?), f. George, July 1938–, f. 337, RNC papers.

[160]Mark Dunahoo, oral history, 56, Russell Library.

[161]Ibid. The leading isolationists Wheeler and Nye also publicly rallied to the president. Charles Lindbergh, however, remained silent.

George was not supposed to be flying, but there was no one else to be sent, so he borrowed a PV-1 and went to the rescue of the troubled pilot. He never returned, and the last words from his plane was his voice saying, "On station." An oil slick on the ocean indicated his fate.[162]

The Georges, who had returned to Georgia in July when Congress took its first wartime vacation, left at noon that same day for Washington. George had been scheduled to speak to the Atlanta Civic Clubs the next day, and Governor Arnold filled in for him.[163] Both of the Georges' sons were serving in the military at this point. Lt. Heard F. George was in the Army Air Corps stationed at Wright Field in Dayton, Ohio, at the time.

Nothing much has survived about George's thoughts at the time of his son's death. He seems to have borne his grief in stoic silence, although a reference to that loss is the only personal part of his Congressional Directory autobiography.[164] Many people have believed that Marcus's death made George an internationalist, and it has been said that his moving speech calling for the adoption of the UN Charter in 1945 was his epiphany.[165] George had begun to recognize that the world at large could not be ignored well before his son's death, and his role in the creation of the United Nations began well before the ratification of the charter. George became involved indirectly when Senator Elbert D. Thomas (D-Utah) introduced a resolution in the Senate to authorize the Foreign Relations Committee, which George still chaired, to make a full study of all matters pertaining to the establishment of a lasting peace throughout the world, but on June 7, 1941, Cordell Hull wrote George that the State Department was working in the direction of the ideas of Senator Thomas.[166] George soon transferred to the Finance Committee but was drawn into the debate in January 1943 by Hull, who, in an effort to diminish Sumner Wells's influence on the UN advisory committee he had established earlier, moved to broaden congressional participation by inviting George to join the advisory committee. He also added Senator Thomas, representatives Sol Bloom of New York, Luther Johnson of Texas, and a few Republicans to join as well.[167]

---

[162]Marcus George folder, VHPS.

[163]"Sen. George's son…," misc. clipping in the Marcus George file, VHPS.

[164]D. W. Brogan, "A Portrait of Senator George," *London Calling*, August 25, 1955, scrapbook, LHG-VHPS.

[165]"Personalities in Years Past," 6, WFG-MU; "Voice of the 84th," 24; Mellichamp, *Senators from Georgia*, 236.

[166]Hull, *Memoirs of Cordell Hull*, 2:1630.

[167]Divine, *Eisenhower and the Cold War*, 83. Divine states that George was the only member not also a member of a foreign relations committee in Congress, but that statement

The next month, Senator Guy Gillette introduced his bill mentioned above to form a world organization for peace along the lines promoted by Hull and proposed that its basis be the wartime alliance. In March Republican senator Joseph H. Ball of Minnesota, Harold Barton of Ohio, Democrats Carl A. Hatch of New Mexico and Lister Hill of Alabama and others introduced a stronger bill which would authorize the president to summon a meeting of the Allied members (by then calling themselves "the United Nations") to form an organization to provide economic aid and assistance and to create an international police force. The Foreign Relations Committee created a subcommittee that included in its membership Walter George. The subcommittee did not immediately warm to the Ball proposal, which it sarcastically dubbed "B2H2."[168] Eventually this proposal was scrapped after much wrangling, and Roosevelt himself weighed in with a vaguely worded resolution, and that document became the focal point of the U. N. Charter.[169]

Meanwhile, Vandenberg, who had emerged from his isolationist past, introduced a similar resolution, and Hull suggested that he get bipartisan support. Walter George was the first person he approached. George refused to support it, probably because he was already involved in the State Department-Roosevelt movement, and Vandenberg, stymied, retreated temporarily.[170] In the mix a smaller committee including George and Vandenberg was created and scrapped, but the movement could not now be stopped. Another committee, formed by Hull, called the Committee of Eight, including Walter George, was at some point active as well. From these clumsy beginnings came the Dumbarton Oaks Conference in 1944, where the United States, Great Britain, and the Soviet Union announced plans for an organization called the United Nations. In April 1945, a conference of fifty nations meeting in San Francisco wrote the UN Charter.[171]

One of the greatest concerns of the sceptics was the formation of the International Organization to Secure the Peace, which many feared might drag the United States into war. George favored the military arm, but he was "a little off the reservation," in that he wanted to see "what kind of a

---

is not accurate. George had remained chair for a while on the Foreign Relations Committee after he had become chair of the Finance Committee.

[168]Cole, *Roosevelt and the Isolationists, 1932–45*, 520.

[169]Divine, *Eisenhower and the Cold War*, 95–96.

[170]Tomkins, *Senator Arthur H. Vandenberg*, 203.

[171]Chandler, *Natural Superiority of Southern Politicians*, 327–28; see also Mazuzan, *Warren R. Austin at the UN*, 57.

peace we have to enforce."[172] On the question, Hull tried to counter by saying that the president would always "consult" Congress on the dispatching of troops into action spots, but there was a growing movement in Congress, led by Vandenberg, to require congressional approval before dispatching troops. George, who had his doubts about Vandenberg's position, sided with the internationalists and even lobbied for them.[173] Breckinridge Long was not certain where George stood on the question. "We were fearful he would not accept our position—completely," he remembered. The internationalists wanted to see if he would lead the floor fight for it. They approached him cautiously—and were eventually surprised to find him entirely in accord and willing to assume an active part in the possible (probable) debate on the Senate floor. George agreed to lead it.[174]

George did not feel that the charter should be rammed through the Senate simply because they had the votes. He felt for the public good it should be widely discussed and debated in and out of Congress. "I think it would be regarded throughout the world as a flippant act if the Senate of the United States were to vote its ratification...without very thorough consideration," he told his colleagues. "Not in the history of the Republic has any proposal of this kind, with all its vast implications, even been submitted to Congress...[and] this is one of the most important steps the United States Senate has ever been called upon to take."[175] Indeed, George was a key figure, along with other Southern senators Hill, Pepper, and William Fulbright, in molding opinion in both the public sector and the congressional caucus.[176]

The UN Charter was submitted to the Senate in July 1945. The high-water mark in the Senate discussion was Walter George's speech at the end of the debate on July 27, 1945. He did not directly mention Marcus's death, but everyone knew of what he spoke when he said, "Our best men have died on the earth; the blue waters have swallowed them up; from the flaming skies they have gone down to death—to win this war and to make possible a better world for another generation of Americans." All knew, of course, that this was a reference to the manner in which his son had died. "The opportunity for world peace lies in the charter now before us for ratification. We

---

[172]Israel, ed., *The War Diary of Breckenridge Long*, 346–47.

[173]Divine, *Eisenhower and the Cold War*, 223.

[174]Israel, *The War Diary of Breckenridge Long*, 377.

[175]*CR*, 79/1, 6918.

[176]Howards, "The Influence of Southern Senators," 63–71, cited in Hero, *The Southerner in World Affairs*, 6.

promised them something. I am sure that every member of the Senate means to keep that promise and go all out in an effort to make that promise good.... We should now do all in our power to see to it that these honored dead should not have died in vain." Then he waxed poetic:

When I think of the great host of American youths who had been taken from our midst over this land, I can think only in terms of the beautiful words—

They shall not grow old as we that are left to grow old.
Age shall not weary them, not the years condemn.
At the going down of the sun and in the morning
We shall remember them.[177]

After George finished his speech, Senator Tobey rose to praise him for it. Observing that it was inappropriate to applaud a Senate speech, he asked all to stand in silent tribute to the speech and to the speaker. Everyone stood without waiting for Tobey to place this in the form of a motion and stood in silence for a few moments. Afterwards George's colleagues made their way to him in the front row of the chamber to congratulate him. The Senate honored the dead by a vote of 89–2.

It had been a complete reversal of his position in 1922 when he had opposed the League of Nations, and from this point until the end of his life, he would remain an internationalist. He could not have known it at the time, but he had crossed the threshold into statesmanship and even greater days were to come when he would make an even greater mark. As a major force in the foreign policy of President Dwight Eisenhower ten years after his work on the creation of the United Nations, George summed up a refutation of his own past in a speech to the Society of Newspaper Editors when he warned, "This is no time to turn away from our international obligations; whatever those obligations are[,] it is not time for us in the present...to grow soft in our ability to carry out and execute those programs that we regard as vital."[178] He had come to see that the United States had an obligation to lead on the world stage and could not abdicate that leadership to the dark forces competing for that place. This position would ultimately help end his Senate career.

---

[177]Donovan, "Senator George," 34; *Atlanta Constitution*, July 28, 1945, 1:6.
[178]"Donovan, "Senator George," 34.

7

SENATOR GEORGE AT WAR, 1941–1945

Hitler and Japan have chosen to live by the sword, and by the sword they shall perish.
—Senator Tom Connally[1]

I had an engagement tonight with Walter George, Senator of Georgia. He is probably the ablest man in the Senate. His judgment, reason, praise and experience, together with his character and acumen, have combined to create a reputation for solidarity and ability which he richly deserves. He has the confidence of the Senate, as no other member has.
—Senator Breckinridge Long[2]

Senator George of Georgia...is one of the most responsible and patriotic members of Congress.
—Arthur Krock[3]

It was during the war years that Walter George first began to appear as one of the lions of the Senate. He had always been respected, of course, but it was his work on war questions and his expert handing of financial matters that earned him a seat among the giants. The *New York Sun* told its readers, "His colleagues have high regard for this Southerner with graying hair and the aristocratic manner. None would dare slap his back, however, and few call him Walter. Even his wife refers to him as 'Mr. George.'"[4] His speaking style in the Senate had an Olympian air about it; he would begin with a promise to be brief and a promise not to detain the Senate very long. Then he would speak for at least an hour. When he spoke, the cloakrooms emptied, and the Senate chamber filled unlike it did for other senators. Walter Jenkins, who later served Lyndon Johnson, remembered that "he really was [an orator] when he got unwound. It was not a spellbinding type of oratory,

[1]*New York Times*, January 1, 1942, 18:1

[2]Israel, ed., *The War Diary of Breckenridge Long*, 377.

[3]*New York Times*, June 30, 1942, 20:5.

[4]"Who's News Today," June 17, 1943, box 337, f. George, RNC papers.

but it was very convincing."[5] His leadership of the committees he chaired was rather autocratic. White, in his memoir *Citadel*, remembered that when confronted with an "unsuitable" committee proposal, George would simply "stare…with a kind of wary and incredulous distaste, simply refusing to recognize them at all."[6] He had come to the status of a giant.

George, of course, continued to go to bat for Georgia. Throughout the 1930s, he had funneled pork into the state at every opportunity, be it tornado relief at Cordele, a levee for Augusta, or a new bridge over the Savannah river at Sylvania.[7] Even as he had advocated strong defense buildup on the eve of the war, he diverted 3,600,000 gallons of asphalt from Eglin Air Force Base in Florida to a Georgia project.[8] Shortly after the war broke out, he was vigorously lobbying for a bomber plant for Atlanta.[9]

Though he made short trips back to Georgia, George and Miss Lucy spent the war largely in Washington, foregoing their usual three- or four-month annual stay in Vienna. His work was in the nation's capital, but he did not forget or take for granted the people of his native state.

George threw himself vigorously into the war work. His first major action was an appearance at the Defense Rally at the Municipal Auditorium in Atlanta on February 22, 1942, organized by the famous Baptist preacher Louis B. Newton, known affectionately as "the Bishop of Druid Hills." The date was chosen because it was a commemoration of George Washington's birthday. George and Miss Lucy arrived at the Brookwood Station in Atlanta at 9:10 a.m. after an all-night train ride from Washington. They were greeted at the station by Col. Lindley W. Camp of the State National Guard and Mrs. E. D. Richardson Jr., who headed the Red Cross Motor Corporation, and were immediately taken to their hotel suite to freshen up and then on to the governor's mansion to have lunch with Governor Talmadge and his wife, Mattie, who would appear on the podium with the senator. Talmadge was to introduce George, while Robert B. Troutman, chairman of the Citizens' Defense Committee, presided. George, the keynote speaker, spoke on "The Financial Aspects of National Defense," hardly a topic that would rouse patriotism but one on which George was superbly qualified to speak.[10]

---

[5]Walter Jenkins, oral history, VI:2, Johnson Library.

[6]White, *Citadel*, 191.

[7]*CR*, 74/2, 6252, 7297, 8593–94.

[8]*Atlanta Constitution*, June 25, 1941, 5:2.

[9]Memo from M. D. Taylor, January 21, 1942, PPF, box 107–117, f. 109, Roosevelt papers.

[10]*Atlanta Constitution*, February 22, 1942, 21:1.

The speech itself spoke of matters other than finance. Indeed, it was a ringing call to rally American patriotism. In his stentorian voice, George called for "the elimination of incompetents from the Nation's war effort," without mentioning any names, adding, "If the best leadership is not provided, we will pay for it with the blood of our men in uniform." While denouncing their political system, George praised the efforts of the Russians, who he said had found good leaders. Given the cataclysmic defeats that the Russians had sustained in their eight months of war to that point, mainly caused by poor leadership, one wonders to which leaders he was referring. Using this question of good leadership, nevertheless, George warned that "America must find them as well." He called for the sacrifice of both labor and management to unite to provide war material for the army. "There must be neither lockouts nor strikes," he warned, "because the battle line is made up of sons of workers, of farmers, of doctors, of lawyers, of every field and avocation."[11] In this case, it would seem that he was foreseeing the coming labor struggles that would in time hinder the war effort.

Miss Lucy did her bit as well. In the last months of peace, she christened the ship *Surprise* launched on September 27, 1941, in the Sun Shipbuilding Co.'s shipyards. It was the first of fourteen to enter water that day in various shipyards across America in an orchestrated launching[12] performed to get the attention of the Germans and the Japanese. A little over a year later, she also christened the USS *James Oglethorpe*.[13]

Georgians did not forget the Georges in the war years either. On a quick trip home in December 1944, George spent the night in Atlanta on the return trip to Washington. When he left the hotel for the station in the morning, he noticed he was being followed by a number of bellboys carrying boxes and parcels. When he asked what this trail was about, he was told that the hotel management had learned that Christmas-type food was somewhat scarce in Washington and that the hotel was sending the makings of Christmas dinner back with him. There was so much food in his compartment that there was hardly room for the senator, and he slept that night with two twenty-pound dressed turkeys. When he arrived in Washington the next morning, he was looking "rumpled and disheveled" and eyeing helplessly the compartment of Christmas groceries. Friends who were sent to meet him remembered that it was the only time they had ever seen

[11] *New York Times*, February 23, 1942, 14:3.

[12] Ibid., September 21, 1941, 46:5.

[13] "Part of the throng…," *Savannah Morning News*, November 21, 1942, LHG-VHPS.

George lose his dignity.[14]

In the last year before America formally entered the war, George was chairing the Foreign Relations Committee when Senator Key Pittman of Nevada died just days after his reelection. He had failed to appear at one of his own rallies on Monday, November 4, 1940, the day before the election, because he had entered a hospital in Reno with chest pains. He died five days later. His Republican opponent Sam Platt firmly believed that Pittman had really died before the election and that the body had been kept on ice until five days after the election, when his death was announced.[15]

Senators George, Connally, and Green went to Nevada for Pittman's funeral, and on the return trip to Washington, there were naturally discussions about Pittman's successor. George was second in line to chair either the Finance or Foreign Relations Committee. Pat Harrison was just ahead of him on both committees and could choose to chair either one he wanted. Connally was next in line after George. Connally remembered that George, as ranking member on Finance, told him on the train ride back, "I'd like to see you succeed to the position of [chair of] Foreign Relations."[16] On returning to Washington, George told reporters that he would be happy to serve under Harrison on Foreign Relations as he had on Finance, somewhat muddying the waters from what he had told Connally.[17] Then he chose to chair Foreign Relations when Pat Harrison chose to stay on Finance. Had Harrison moved to Foreign Relations, George would have taken over as chair as the ranking Democrat under Harrison, since Senator William King, Democrat of Utah, had been defeated on November 5.[18] Connally wryly noted in his memoirs that although George had every right to do what he did, he had obviously "changed his mind."[19] We do not know if he received any encouragement from the administration or not. He was personally close to Cordell Hull, and, as we have seen, generally supported Roosevelt's interventionist foreign policy, so he might have been so encouraged. He probably did not need much encouragement; it would be rare indeed for a US Senator to refuse a chairmanship to remain second banana on another committee. The *New York Times* reported on November 11, "Georgian, Roosevelt Supporter in Foreign Affairs, due to get Chairmanship."[20] George's first state-

[14]Jarman, "Taxpayer's Senator," 44.
[15]Glad, *Key Pittman* 307.
[16]Connally, *My Name Is Tom Connally*, 241.
[17]*New York Times*, November 11, 1940, 12:3.
[18]*Atlanta Constitution*, November 11, 1940, 1:3, 9:5.
[19]Connally, *My Name Is Tom Connally*, 241.
[20]*New York Times*, November 11, 1940, 12:3.

ment indicated that he was what Roosevelt wanted: "My policy will be to work in close harmony with the State Department." Although Sam Rayburn told members of Congress to go home as there would be no important legislation before the two houses, George stayed and the next day began work on the US-Dominican Republic Trade Bill.[21] Most certainly Roosevelt must have stirred in it to some degree. Whatever Byzantine transactions transpired, George became chair of the Foreign Relations Committee on November 25, 1940, and immediately began his work revising the Neutrality Act and preparing for the famous Lend-Lease legislation to come.[22]

The *New York Times* editorialized that George "seems likely to lend the chairmanship weight, dignity and intelligence," something they must have seen lacking in the leadership of Key Pittman, who they felt "had embarrassed it with bellicose statements."[23] Breckinridge Long, a figure in Missouri politics and one time American ambassador to Italy, seemed to think that because of the purge attempt in 1938 and his perceived opposition to entering the European conflict, George would be "more difficult to deal with than Pittman" for the White House. He added in his diary, "However, he [George] is a man of fine honor and a very able citizen. He is an excellent lawyer and a high type of American."[24] George did indeed make it plain that he was making "no blanket commitment on administration proposals but will consider each proposal as it appears."[25] If Roosevelt had indeed encouraged George to assume the Foreign Relations chair, he likewise must have had pause because of these very points. George also quickly made it perfectly clear that he would "give all sides their day in court," and that as well could not have pleased Roosevelt.[26]

As if an act of providence, after George had chaired the Foreign Relations Committee for seven crucial months and had secured passage one of the most important wartime acts, Pat "Old Fox" Harrison died on June 22, 1941, at age fifty-nine, after an operation. George praised him highly at his death, stating that "he devoted his entire life unstintingly and unselfishly to the welfare of his country," calling him "one of the most able and useful men in public life," adding that his death was "a great personal loss to every

[21]Ibid., November 24, 1940, 42:1.

[22]"Old Independent," 21.

[23]*New York Times*, November 25, 1940, 16:2.

[24]Israel, ed., *The War Diary of Breckenridge Long*, 151.

[25]"Senator George will be Chairman," clipping, November 25, 1940, box 337, f. George-bio., RNC papers.

[26]Cole, *Senator Gerald P. Nye*, 168.

member of the Senate."[27]

George now had a choice to chair two committees. The Democrats wanted him in both places, at least until the tax committee could write the 1941 budget, and he had been such a strong supporter of Roosevelt's foreign policies that they also wanted him to chair that committee as well.[28] Connally, heir presumptive on Foreign Relations, returned from Harrison's funeral in Mississippi to find that George's indecision had produced the odd situation where he was chairing two committees. Actually, it was not just George's "indecision" but the Roosevelt administration's desire for George to shepherd through the administration's 1941 tax bill. Moreover, if George stayed on Foreign Relations, Massachusetts isolationist senator David Ignatius Walsh would take over Finance, and the Naval Affairs chair would go to anti-New Deal Senator Tydings.[29] The administration pressured George to move to Finance, which would place Connally, a strong administration supporter, over Foreign Relations.

George admitted publicly that he had been pressured by both President Roosevelt and Alben Barkley, and he would switch only reluctantly. He finally chose Finance. "I am relinquishing the chairmanship of the Foreign Relations Committee with great regret," he told reporters, "because I have found the work most pleasant and agreeable…." George had already directed as a ranking member the $3.5 billion tax bill through Finance anyway, so he would as chair merely finish what he had begun.[30] At the time it was rumored that George had gone to Finance to prevent the Coca-Cola Company from having a tax on its drinks and products, but that reason never figured into the mix.[31] George also felt with the war clouds gathering, Roosevelt would dominate foreign affairs anyway, leaving the Foreign Relations Committee in his shadow. Also, Finance required fewer social obligations, which George hated. Others thought it was because he just liked working with figures.[32] Whatever complicated thoughts and actions molded his actions, in his choice, the Administration received what it had largely wanted: Walsh and Tydings stayed where they were.[33] As in most of what he did in these days, George received encomiums from many quarters. Jour-

---

[27]*Atlanta Constitution*, June 23, 1941, 2:5.

[28]*New York Times*, June 28, 1941, 13:4.

[29]"New Team," 15.

[30]*Atlanta Constitution*, July 31, 1941, 12:3.

[31]Darrell St. Claire, oral history, 137, Library of Congress.

[32]Jarman, "Taxpayer's Senator," 23.

[33]"George Yields," *Atlanta Constitution*, July 31, 1941, RCB 5804, box 15, f. WFG-GSA.

nalist Arthur Krock, always in George's corner, praised him highly in his "difficult choice." Already thinking of war almost six months before the US entered it, Krock noted that George would not be in a "great place to eventually shift America to peace," adding that his decision was "patriotic, constructive, and wise." His chairing the Finance Committee would "preserve the American economic system…and Mr. George was especially fitted by view point, experience, and ability to bear it." He added a thought that many probably had overlooked: George would remain as a ranking member on Foreign Relations, where he will "wield great influence."[34] Indeed, joining with Elbert Thomas of Utah and Connally, George made the Foreign Relations committee a "Council of State" or an "executive council" that played a major role in American foreign policy, anyway.[35] The *Atlanta Constitution* added its praise (and a prediction) that "the nation's economic structure will be builded [sic] the more soundly because of his presence on this important committee." It further added that "George proudly promises the nation it may expect from the distinguished son another distinguished service in the field of taxation and finance."[36]

Walter George had always fought waste of government money, and he naturally continued to do so as chair of the Finance Committee. Moreover, he further attacked waste because of his membership on Senator Harry Byrd's Joint Committee on Reduction of Non-essential Federal Expenditures, which he joined in September 1941. It consisted of such conservative penny-pinchers as Carter Glass of Virginia, Senator Kenneth McKellar of Tennessee, and Gerald Nye of North Dakota. The purpose of the committee was to rout around in the budget to find unnecessary spending, although Senator Byrd personally saw it as a committee to dismantle the New Deal.[37] One of many examples of George's watchdog behavior was his opposition in 1943 to the resurrection of the Regional Agricultural Credit Corporation (RACC), a government agency created in the deepest part of the Depression to provide credit to the livestock producers and other farmers because banks had closed everywhere. It was an institution that would have been of some benefit to Georgia farmers had it been brought back, but George opposed it because it would have wasted money. "Our debt is high enough; our obligation is already heavy enough; and at this time there is no possible reason for

[34]*New York Times*, July 31, 1941, 16:5.

[35]Chandler, *Natural Superiority of Southern Politicians*, 320.

[36]"Well done, Thou Good and faithful Servant," *Atlanta Constitution*, July 31, 1941, RCB-5804, box 15, f. WFG-GSA.

[37]Heinemann, *Harry Byrd of Virginia*, 219.

the revival of this corporation," he told his colleagues. George made a reference to a statement of Senator Homer Bone of Washington, who had said that the apple growers of his state can be cared for by the RACC, by adding, "I have no doubt that they can be cared for without the language [I have] proposed to be stricken out." This fight was one that George lost by a vote of 41–31, with his colleague Richard Russell voting with the majority.[38]

Hand in hand with his conservative management of money went his strong support of capitalism. Even before the war, he championed business. In December 1938, in a speech to the American Association of Textile Chemists and Colorers in the Atlanta Athletic Club, he thundered that "Business and free enterprise can put people back to work…and alone offers the way out [of the Depression]." The seven hundred delegates roared with approval.[39] He championed and supported Roosevelt when in his state of the union address in January 1940 Roosevelt had called for a freer trade policy. "The message was a very strong plea for liberal trade policies," he told reporters, "upon which the prosperity and peace of this nation depends [*sic*]." This praise of Roosevelt came less than two years after the Barnesville Manifesto, but it was one of Roosevelt's few pro-business statements, and George felt he should support him on it.[40] When in summer 1941 the administration allowed the Maritime Commission to control trade, George opposed this excessive invasion of free enterprise. Already half the ships of one company in Savannah had been confiscated, and this move had occurred six months before we entered the war. Stressing his position that the country should prepare for war while seeking peace, he noted that he opposed regulation of shipping and price controls which have hurt cotton producers. "Does national defense call for that?" he asked rhetorically.[41]

His general conservatism on both taxation and business continued into the war. When critics decried the lower taxes on business when citizens shouldered "the back-breaking and unbearable rates which are placed upon individuals in the United States," implying that corporations were not paying their fair share, George rose to defend the corporations by pointing out that the personal income taxes in both Great Britain and Canada were twice as high as those in America.[42] George again supported giving Roosevelt

[38]*CR*, 78/1, 5694–5700.

[39]*Atlanta Constitution*, December 4, 1938, misc. clipping, box 245, Walter F. George campaign file, Corcoran papers.

[40]*Atlanta Constitution* January 4, 1940, 10:1.

[41]Ibid., June 28, 1941.

[42]*CR*, 77/2, 8412–13.

power for three years to negotiate lower tariffs by as much as 50 percent with reciprocity from the country whose goods were being less taxed. This provision would enable the quick reduction of tariffs rather than the usual cumbersome path through the legislative process. When Senator Joseph O'Mahoney of Wyoming felt that giving the president such power was "a grave threat to Democracy," George saw it as "an essential weapon to preserve the free enterprise system," reminding the senator that the last tariff revision, Hawley-Smoot, had taken thirty months to become law. He pointed out that tariff revision with this addition could be immediate.[43]

In 1943, when Roosevelt proposed a six-point plan to aid returning veterans with social security, George called for caution, noting, "We will proceed slowly to expand any program which is dependent on a capital levy," adding his usual support for business. "Any social security program must depend on prosperous business," he opined, reminding all that "If we have prosperous businesses, we don't need to make people dependent on government."[44] That same year he supported a House bill that allowed business relief from excessive or discriminatory excess-profits tax.[45] At the same time, he tried to prevent inequities that gave benefits to higher-income individuals.[46] He introduced an amendment to a tax bill that allowed authors who had worked on a book for years and who received 80 percent of the royalties the first year be allowed to spread the income over a number of years so the royalties the author earned would not be taxed so heavily. It passed.[47]

George's pro-business stance, coupled with his belief that the country should make a unified, single effort for the war, led him to side against the strikes that were to plague the war effort from time to time. Even before we entered the war, he and Senator Barkley were named to the Senate committee on the coal strike in April 1941. Bituminous coal miners in the South had gone on strike for a wage increase of a dollar a day, and the industry had countered that they would have to close their mines if they gave such a raise.[48] The committee called on Roosevelt to ask him to refer this strike to the National Defense Mediation Board. Roosevelt does seem to have appealed to the American labor leader John Lewis with no permanent result.

[43]*New York Times*, June 13, 1945, 33:5. This bill was another one George lost. On July 19, Senate voted 47–33 to return the bill to committee. See *New York Times*, June 20, 1941, 1:6.

[44]*Atlanta Constitution*, August 1, 1943, 4B:7.

[45]*CR*, 78/1, 2329 ff.

[46]Ibid., 1268.

[47]Ibid.

[48]*New York Times*, April 17, 1941, 18:3.

When strikes intensified in fall 1941, George, in a statement issued from Vienna, Georgia, called on Roosevelt to the end of strikes in the defense industries and mines. In a prepared statement, he wrote, "Strikes in the defense industries cannot be defended. Full operation of all industry is now vitally necessary; hence strikes generally should cease in this emergency." Expressing the belief that the majority of the workers opposed such strikes, he opined that they were brought on by "selfish dictators in positions of leadership." Being an ardent capitalist, he opposed, he said, the government's takeover of mines and factories, as some around Roosevelt were advocating, and he added that "milk-and-water laws," which called for a cooling off period, were likewise not the answer. He admitted that all strikes could not be prevented, but he felt that "a strong executive course of action," a jab at Roosevelt's dillydallying, given his union support, would have prevented a majority of them.[49]

Ten days later, George called for troops to protect miners who wanted to return to work. He felt, and it was probably untrue, that most miners wanted to work, but that they feared for their lives if they did so. With troops there to protect them, they would return.[50] On November 19, a few weeks before America would enter World War II, he restated his call for an end to strikes, again from Vienna, with the same language he had used a month before, calling again for a show of "executive leadership" (read: FDR), adding that with such a show, Congress would be ready to pass such legislation, if Roosevelt led.[51] After the war began, George continued to come down on the side of business in the area of war work. Congressman Howard Smith of Virginia had introduced in April a bill calling for the abolition of overtime pay for more than forty hours of work.[52] George felt that "drastic legislation" was not necessary but advocated a voluntary extension to a forty-eight-hour workweek, calling an extra workday "War Day" or "Victory Day." Such voluntary work would eliminate the need for business to pay overtime, but in either case, management would not have to pay overtime to its workers.[53] In the grip of a major coal strike in spring 1943, George called on the union and the industry to settle to prevent more stringent legislation from being passed. He then warned labor that "if the wages and price dam

---

[49]Ibid., November 19, 1941, 17:2.

[50]Ibid., October 29, 1941, 15:7; *Atlanta Constitution*, October 29, 1941, 1:8.

[51]*Atlanta Constitution*, November 19, 1941, 1:5; 4:4.

[52]*New York Times*, April 5, 1942, 34:3.

[53]Ibid.

broke, the worst sufferers would be the wage and salary workers."[54]

Senator Lister Hill introduced a bill in fall 1943 to begin federal aid to medicine, feeling that such a move was the answer to help poor states that did not have excess money to spend on medical education. As Hill argued, "the educational level of the people of the United States is not a state problem alone; it is a national problem." On October 15, 1943, George argued against the bill because he thought it would lead to the federal control of education, an argument that would be used by Southern solons into the 1960s. Hill countered, "I believe that we are over-exaggerating the possibility of undue and improper federal control over…our school system." George seems to have changed his mind somewhat and come to favor the aid to medical schools even though he had received more mail against it than for it. It died, however, because many felt the expenditure, $300,000,000 was "not consistent with an all-out war effort."[55] The battle would be fought many times over the following two decades. George had no qualms of promoting his old favorite, vocational education, which the reader will remember was one of his career-long chief interests, during the war. A monument to him for his efforts stands today in the town square of Vienna, Georgia.

George's greatest expertise was in the arcane, boring area of tax law. George could give the Senate a twenty-minute explanation of a complicated tax bill after only one reading, and then hours later he could repeat the same explanation "word for word, comma for comma, and period for period," one journalist noted. George had always believed that taxation should be low enough to encourage growth and never so high as to stifle it. He believed that there was always a golden mean. He repeated his belief that "a government can confiscate only once, but it can tax forever, provided it preserves free enterprise and the American way of life."[56] As a representative of his generation, George abhorred debt, and like the citizens of his time, avoided debt, especially needless debt. There might be good debt, money borrowed for an investment, to buy a farm, or to defend one's country, but debt for consumer items was an abomination. In short, what he wanted was a shift from a peacetime effort to a wartime economy a full year before the United States entered the war, and he called, as we have seen, for an end to "anything and everything" that would impede this goal, i.e., the current labor

[54] Ibid., March 22, 1943, 20:3.

[55] *Congressional Digest*, 23:52–53.

[56] Jarman, "Taxpayer's Senator," 44.

troubles.[57]

As Americans began to rearm for any coming fight with the Axis Powers (in George's view, the reader is aware, it was to keep war from the Western Hemisphere), George favored tax increases to pay for it rather than the floating of bonds. In December 1940, he predicted corporate taxes in America should rise from the present 24 percent to 30 percent and called for an increase in personal income taxes,[58] a prediction he repeated the next month.[59] George always insisted that "somewhere, sometime, some place, there must be a limit to war spending" as well, not because he was tightfisted, but because, as one writer noted, he was "a man of solid sense, who was raised to respect plain arithmetic." War or no war, George never accepted the notion of "a dream world of frenzied finance."[60] Continually raising taxes, George realized, hindered growth, but he believed that politicians responsible for higher taxes became "easy targets for the political hokum of unscrupulous and irresponsible opponents."[61]

As noted, the American mentality of the time was more nearly "pay as you go," but when Roosevelt, who always paid lip service to "cash and carry" financing, asked Congress for $650,000,000 for defense in June 1940, the House of Representatives gave him a billion and voted to increase the national debt from $45 billion to $49 billion, the excess to be used if necessary.[62]

Caution remained George's byword. When Senator Pat Harrison, chair of the Senate Finance committee, rushed through a bill on excess profits tax on business without even holding hearings, George openly objected to the haste, and he called for a study of the entire tax system and for the creation of a permanent program.[63] George recognized the need for an excess profits tax, but he wanted that tax to be "reasonable," a term he frequently used. When a reporter asked him what percentage of profit would be proper, George replied, "I think about 8 percent would be re-e-easonable," he said, dragging out the word. "Maybe 6 percent. Possibly as high as 10 percent.

[57]*New York Times* praised George as "a statesman who recognizes clearly that the battle for greater production is now the decisive battle for the world" (December 6, 1940, 22:1).

[58]"Corporation Income Taxes," clipping, December 2, 1940, box 337, f. George, July 1938–, RNC papers.

[59]*Atlanta Constitution*, January 5, 1941, 11A.

[60]"Old Independent," 21.

[61]Clapper, *Watching the World*, 230.

[62]*Atlanta Constitution*, June 5, 1940, 1:6.

[63]*New York Times*, August 31, 1940, 24:2.

But 8 percent is probably the most re-eeasonable."[64]

Roosevelt had called for an excess profits tax bill in late summer 1940, an election year when the major issue was his running for a third term. He did not want to give the Republicans much additional ammunition, but at the same time, he wanted to tell his base that he was preventing the fatcat industrialists for making vast profits from rearmament. He told his secretary of the treasury Henry Morgenthau, "I want a tax bill; I want one damn quick; I don't care what is in it; I don't want to know."[65] He let Walter George play the major roll in writing it, and it was a very mild bill in line with George's thinking on taxation. The radical leftist Senator Bob La Follette was appalled at the weak bill that emerged and was further shocked at how little interest the committee members (other than George and Harrison) had in writing one. La Follette called the bill "a slap on the wrist" and a "sham," and he accused Walter George for "trying to help the high profit, low capitalization companies."[66] In a letter to his family, he accused George and Harrison of discrediting "the whole idea of excess profits taxation and thus pave the way to slip the whole burden on the people by a sales tax in the end."[67]

Surprisingly, George himself was not pleased with his feeble bill even though he was one of the conferees with the House version, which had lowered the tax rate by five more percentage points. Although Roosevelt had signed the bill, he called it "a rank injustice against normal business earnings. There is no possible justification in an excess profits tax bill for taxing earnings which are clearly normal."[68] George, torn as always between paying one's bills and spending necessary money for necessary projects as soon as possible, stated in December that taxes in the long term might need to be increased because there was no alternative, but he feared, as always, the harm increases in corporate taxes might do to business.[69] The year 1941 was not an election year, and the seriousness of the war in Europe, including Hitler's invasion of the Soviet Union in June 1941, changed matters. In September 1941, George shepherded a tax bill through Congress which included an excess profits tax, but it also added 4,930,000 new taxpayers to the

[64]"Voice of the 84th," 22.

[65]John M. Blum, *Years of Urgency, 1938–1941* (Boston: Houghton Mifflin, 1965) 289–92, cited in Maney, *Young Bob La Follette*, 236–37.

[66]Maney, *Young Bob La Follette*, 237.

[67]RML to family, 12 August, 7 September 1940, box 47-1, La Follette family papers, cited in Maney, *Young Bob La Follette*, 237.

[68]*New York Times*, October 2, 1941, 8:3.

[69]Ibid., December 2, 1940, 13:3.

rolls of personal income tax payers by reducing the personal exemption from $2,000 to $1,500 for married couples and for singles from $800.00 to $750.00.[70] That same month, however, George locked horns with Morgenthau when the secretary of the treasury proposed a tax plan to limit corporation profits to 6 percent. Denouncing the proposal, George opined that such a move "would not only crush small businesses" but would "result in incalculable hardship to legitimate business, disrupt production vital to national defense, and confiscate normal profits essential to the survival of free enterprise." Then he rebuked Morgenthau by adding that "it would be wise to let the ink dry" on the most recent tax bill passed just weeks earlier "before upsetting every one [*sic*] with objectives that the country cannot and will not accept." As he would his entire life, he defended the capitalist system. Calling for "a fair return on capital measured by the risks involved," he noted that Congress would be willing to impose taxes on "true excess profits," but it should be done by "first laying down a fair yardstick for measuring normal profits."[71]

On December 3, 1941, George announced that the tax ceiling had been reached "without weakening the whole economy" and that the rest of the defense program would have to be borrowed and paid off over two to three generations.[72] Events four days later would blow that prediction to bits, of course. At the beginning of World War I, the American national debt had been a billion dollars. On December 7, 1941, it was $55 billion. By November 1943, the debt would be a staggering $175 billion, and with all the generations since that time, the debt has not been paid off.[73] At best, subsequent governments have been able to balance some annual budgets, or at best run small surpluses, but except for the money raised by the tax system (a system that resulted in paying more than 40 percent of the war's cost on a cash and carry basis and that George helped create during the war), the American people have not paid the debt. Indeed, they have greatly added to it. The tax ceiling that George noted on the eve of Pearl Harbor was breached well before the end of the war. A married man with two dependents with an income of $4,000 paid an annual tax of $12.00. By February 1944, that same person paid $484.97 on the same income. In 1944–1945, that same person with the same income would pay $532.22 because of built

[70]Ibid., September 18, 1941, 20:4.

[71]Ibid., September 28, 1941, 43:1; "George Opposes Profit Limit," clipping September 28, 1941, box 337, f. George, RNC papers.

[72]*New York Times*, December 4, 1941, 21:3.

[73]Clapper, *Watching the World*, 232.

in changes.[74]

Whether George had been influenced by him or not, economist David McCord Wright wrote George just days before Pearl Harbor to suggest taxation as a means of fighting inflation. Using a rather callous logic, he lectured George that taxation was a means "to keep the poor from spending." Noting that there are only two ways to suppress consumption, either taxation or by the concealed tax of inflation, Wright warned that the latter is by far the worse. Once prices start to rise, "labor will demand higher wages," thus creating a "vicious cycle." The only way to stop the cycle once it has begun, is by "taxing the purchasing power of the masses, especially labor, for they do most of the consuming." Inflation, moreover, will result in the "poor will be made more miserable, the middle class will be destroyed, while a group of clever speculators and a few predatory labor unions will succeed in exploiting the general misery."[75] This economist also suggested to George the "taxing of small incomes" by means of forcing the purchase of bonds in small denominations that would be redeemed after the war, adding "the borrowing from small incomes necessarily curtails private spending."[76] Whether George was influenced by Wright or not is impossible to say, but in one form or another, George was to implement Wrights suggestions.

Throughout the war, George was, however, frequently at odds with the administration on taxation. He, for example, favored a sales tax at one point, which Roosevelt opposed. He favored compulsory savings, which Morgenthau opposed. He objected to price ceilings, arguing instead for increases in the production of civilian consumer goods to dampen inflation through the regularity of supply-and-demand economics. He called for capping war spending, which Roosevelt could not accept. He carefully watched wartime expenses because, as *Time* magazine told its readers, he was a man "who was raised to respect arithmetic."[77] When he had stated that the country had "reached the limit" of the tax burden it could bear, he readily after the Pearl Harbor attack supported a bill to raise another four for five billion more.[78]

Frequently an issue would become the excess profits made by industry off of the war contracts. Calls for taxing industry heavily made good political points back home, but George, ever on the side of business, generally opposed excess profits tax bills. In the debate on the issue at one point, George

[74]WFG, "New Methods," 274.

[75]D. M. Wright to WFG, December 4, 1941, box 4, fr. 27, D.M Wright papers.

[76]Ibid.

[77]"Old Independent," 21.

[78]*New York Times*, December 13, 1941, 11:4.

came down against it, using an emotional argument. Observing that a 40 percent normal tax and a 90 percent excess profits tax would hold business profits down to 6 percent, he wistfully noted that if these were applied, "There will not be any millionaires made." But then he added, "I am not sure that I would not rather see the man escape with a million dollars which he had stolen rather than see our boys in Australia and in Africa and elsewhere about the earth die because they had not the machines and arms with which to fight."[79] To George, businessmen had to be guaranteed their profits in order to induce them to produce war materiel, but he readily called for no salary raises for federal employees. Here he had another motive. High government salaries, he felt, were making it difficult to recruit labor on the farms. He warned that it was already depleted because of salaries being what they currently were. Using another emotional argument, he said he doubted if even 75 percent of that year's crop could be harvested because of the labor shortage—a highly unlikely prediction since most civil service jobs and agricultural work would not compete for the same type of worker.[80]

Just as he opposed trimming profits from businesses, he also opposed any kind of laws that limited the prices of farm products unless the cost of what the farmer needed were also controlled.[81] Before the United States had been involved in the war six months, George did endorse "forced savings," or "draft dollars," as it was sometimes called, that is, requiring citizens to buy bonds that would not be redeemable until after the war. Drawing this money out of the money supply, George felt, would both help control inflation and help finance the war.[82] *New York Times* columnists also condemned this approach, arguing that a 10 percent forced savings for the "upper classes" would require them "to dismiss some of their servants who have grown old working for them [!!]"[83] Loss of servants or not, George until the end of the war supported this peculiar form of "temporary taxation" to pay the bills. Spending bills are supposed to originate in the House, but everyone knew that whatever tax legislation passed through Congress was essentially written by Walter George, and the legislation always called on Americans to pay

---

[79]*CR*, 77/2, 3399.

[80]Ibid., 6526.

[81]Ibid., 6528.

[82]Ibid., 7650–51. At the same time, George opposed wage and price controls as a means to stymie inflation, which was increasing due to the rise of employment, because "that program will not work," but he ultimately voted for them despite his belief that they were useless. The reader is aware that George no infrequently opposed something and then voted for its passage. See p. 7650.

[83]*New York Times*, May 14, 1942, 18:5.

their bills. Since Roosevelt generally favored a "pay-as-you-go" approach to war financing (at least half taxation and half by borrowing), George could work with him.[84] Even with all the additional taxation, George saw the need to increase the debt limit for additional borrowing. On January 25, 1943, he introduced a bill to increase the debt limit to $210 billion, and the amount would be the national debt limit at the end of fiscal year 1943–1944 (July 1, 1944).

The 1942 tax legislation was high, raising $26 billion, which almost equaled the total national income in 1932. The bill was highly detailed with facts and figures, but George added a "Victory Tax," a 5 percent levy on all incomes over the curious figure of $624.00 per annum.[85] It was to begin in January 1943. About a third of the tax, however, was to be returned after the war. The tax bill also added an additional 18.5 million taxpayers to the federal rolls. The total number of tax payers rose from 27,000,000 to 46,000,000. George preferred this approach to a much-discussed sales tax, which would be regressive. Nevertheless, in order to spare the corporations a greater tax burden, he preferred to "reach down into the lower-income groups" in order to "raise the large amount of additional revenue."[86]

In November 1942, he moved to abolish tariffs, another financial change favored by Roosevelt. Admitting that it should come from the House of Representatives, he added, "But I am offering the bill, and I ask that it be referred to the Committee on Finance,"[87] in strict violation of the Constitution. His unconstitutional actions did not go unnoticed by the media. In mid-1943, *Time* stated, "Though the House is constitutionally supposed to initiate tax legislation, of late years it is the Senate's bill that is most likely to become law. One substantial reason for this procedure is Senator George himself."[88] These increases, coming about in 1943, were rather stiff for the times. In an article George wrote for *American Magazine* that year, he explained the new taxation scale. If a man was single without dependents and made $1200 per year, he would pay the government $150 in taxes, or six weeks' salary. If a citizen makes $2,000, he would pay $450, or nine weeks' pay a year. This reform would hit hardest those who spend everything and those who have a smaller income than in 1942. Withholding tax had not yet been conceived, so George advised taxpayers to save the money "through

[84]Clapper, *Watching the World*, 232.
[85]*CR*, 77/2, 7793 ff.
[86]Ibid., 7797.
[87]Ibid., 8704.
[88]"Old Independent," 20.

careful budgeting and saving" so that each tax payer would "have his tax money ready when due." Recognizing that most people could not be this thrifty, George floated the idea of withholding.[89] It was later that year that withholding would become law.[90]

Despite the fact that Americans were more responsible about saving and paying their bills at the time than they are now, George added a caveat to those who might complain about enduring "the heaviest burden of taxes we have ever known." Paying these taxes will "involve hard work, saving, scrimping, economizing, [and] self-denial." Predicting that some might whine "that the sacrifice is too great to bear," he admonished them "not [to] complain too loudly" because "certain young Americans in the Solomons or in Africa…might hear them and be ashamed of the people at home."[91] At this point, George himself had yet to pay the supreme sacrifice for the war.

Having opposed a national sales tax the year before, he had been converted to the idea by the gigantic cost of the war. By 1943 he called for a 10 percent sales tax on all items "with no exceptions for even food or clothing" because he felt that if any exceptions are made, "it will simply create pressure for further exceptions." Knowing the argument of how sales taxes are the greatest burden on the poor, he asked the rhetorical question in response: "In this war is there any class which can be exempt from additional burdens, exempt from the necessity of working a little harder and economizing more carefully?" He also argued, as he did on many of many tax increases, that the sales tax would dampen inflation.[92]

In debate on the new budget for 1944, George made a speech on NBC radio for additional taxes in the new budget. He informed the radio audience that in December 1943 alone, the government had spent $7.5 billion, and that sum was $36 million for each working hour. More than 90 percent of it had gone to the war effort, and he warned that war costs in 1944 would be 20 percent higher still. In the current fiscal year, George informed his listeners, the government would spend $57 billion more than it will receive in taxes, bringing the total national debt to $200 billion, i.e., $1500 for every man woman and child. Admitting that taxes had increased 600 percent since 1940, he opined that they were necessary "to fight the enemies of mankind or lose our freedom." He, therefore, called for additional taxes to pay the country's bills, with the burden being placed on individuals. With George's

---

[89]WFG, "Your $100,000,000,000 Tax Bill," 33.
[90]Ibid., 32–33.
[91]Ibid.
[92]Ibid.

usual desire to protect business, he would not bring the finance committee to follow the government's recommendation to raise taxes on corporations. He intoned his listeners to buck up, for "each stands ready and willing to meet your share of the cost of this costliest of wars."[93] Despite his efforts, the new tax bite raised rates on individuals and corporations, increased excise taxes and postal rates, all for an income increase of about $2.3 billion dollars. There was no formal rate increase on the tax scales for individuals, but each had to pay a 3 percent "victory tax." Moreover, earned income credit was disallowed, and certain deductions were abolished, changes George euphemistically tried to soften by saying that "income tax computations will be considerably simplified."[94]

George and Morgenthau had collided as early as December on the proposed tax bill. The secretary of the treasury had particularly opposed the provision of the bill that allowed the renegotiation of war contracts. He publicly stated that the bill as it now stands was "worse than no bill at all, and the renegotiation provision would lead to extortionate profits" and hold the "seed for a national scandal." Blasting the secretary, George stated that Morgenthau "knew nothing about renegotiation and less about administration of the existing act." Moreover, his criticism had come, George felt, "with extremely bad grace."[95]

Roosevelt and Morgenthau had asked for $10 billion more in tax revenues. Wendell Wilkie, Roosevelt's opponent in 1940 and who was campaigning hard for the Republican nomination for 1944, had been critical of the management of the war. Alben Barkley felt that Wilkie's needling had pushed Roosevelt to ask for so much, and even he, the Democratic Senate leader, had supported George's bill. Moreover, Roosevelt had suggested an increase in Social Security taxes to use, illegally, for the war effort. He did not win that ploy either. Roosevelt vetoed the resulting bill, saying that he had asked Congress for "a loaf of bread," but had gotten only "a small piece of crust, which contained many extraneous and inedible matters." George responded strongly to Roosevelt's veto, but Roosevelt could not hurt him. Barkley felt, however, that his support of the modest George tax measure cost him a place on the Democratic ticket in 1944.[96]

In 1945, with the end of the war in sight, George suggested huge tax cuts on corporate tax liabilities in the form of $5.9 billion, and at the same

[93]WFG, "New Methods," 273–75.

[94]Ibid., 274–75.

[95]Ibid.

[96]Barkley, *That Reminds Me*, 170, 173.

time, he blasted deficit spending.[97] "We have got to get away from deficit spending," he warned in July 1945. "We are taking a great risk in continuing it for it might raise a question in people's minds as to the soundness of our money." He must have been thinking about personal income taxes on individuals, for he warned, "It would be putting the cart before the horse to fix a budget first, and then draw up a tax program."[98] One would think that it would be a tax program first and then, knowing revenues, draw up a budget. George never seemed to be inclined to lower individual taxes. In 1945, at the end of the war, he predicted that taxes would remain at the present level for the first couple of years after the war, and only then, drastically reduced to a level that "will cause business to be stimulated."[99] At the same time, however, he called in July 1945 for the writing of a tax code that would cut taxes in half a year after Japan's defeat, and he forecast a complete revision of the tax code which would reduce taxes from $18 to $27 billion a year after the war ended.[100]

By fall 1945, after Japan had been defeated, George, ignoring the taxing power of the House, introduced the Revenue Bill of 1945, which called for steep tax cuts. "It is a pleasure to present [to the Senate]," he told his colleagues as he fielded their questions, "a bill which will afford some relief to our taxpayers from the burdensome taxation made necessary by the war." He did warn that America still had serious financial obligations with demobilization and occupation, and therefore he felt that Congress must proceed with caution "in reducing the tax burden." By the end of 1946, he predicted that the deficit would be $30 billion and $5–8 billion for the fiscal year 1947, these rates coming with the reduction of excess profits tax to 60 percent to go in place in January 1, 1947, and the abolition of excise taxes on automobiles and boats.[101] Again, he does not seem to have planned much relief for the individual. Senator Chapman Rivercomb asked if there would be a general tax cut in 1946 because of sharp cuts in appropriations. George replied in the negative, noting that they were still predicting deficits until 1948, but he hoped by that year, the country might have a balanced budget, and then there could be a further reduction of taxes.[102] Budget surpluses did follow after the war, based on George's wartime tax codes. From the crea-

[97] *CR*, 79/1, 10258–59.

[98] *Atlanta Constitution*, July 28, 1945, 3:8.

[99] Jarman, "Taxpayer's Senator," 44.

[100] *Atlanta Constitution*, July 28, 1945, 3:7.

[101] *CR*, 70/1, 9946–56; 9979, 9981, 9982, 9985.

[102] Ibid., 10829.

tion of the income tax before World War I, tax revenues into the Federal Treasury have averaged 18.5 percent of the Gross Domestic Product (GDP) while spending has been somewhere between 18 and 20 percent. Only two times in American history has tax income into the treasury exceeded 21 percent: In 1945 and 1998 when the dot-com explosion created a massive revenue inflow. Both times led to budget surpluses.[103] As a result of George's tax policies and his insistence on maintaining war taxation to cover peacetime demobilization, the tax bill for 1946 was able to remove 12,000,000 persons from the tax rolls.[104] More than 40 percent of the gigantic cost of the war had been paid for, but it was done in a way that did not crush business, which could shift after 1945 to production of consumer goods to fulfill the desires of a population long starved for a peacetime economy.

Meanwhile, back in Georgia, politics continued as usual. One victory which George could claim to have assisted in victory was the wartime election of Governor Ellis Arnall, probably the most liberal governor Georgia had in the twentieth century. Arnall was being opposed by the incumbent governor Talmadge, and by a major state Baptist celebrity, Columbus Roberts, for whom a chair is named in Mercer University's Christianity Department. George came out strongly for Arnall, describing him as a man "with eyes forward but feet on the ground," adding that "when led by men like him…we can contemplate the future with confidence." George teamed up with Roosevelt to lure Columbus Roberts out of the governor's race with a federal appointment,[105] and Arnall became a widely respected governor.[106]

Due to Arnall's popularity, it was believed by some that he might challenge George in 1944. In an effort to squelch any such notions, Arnall declared himself "very enthusiastic" for George, and speculation then focused on Georgia's agriculture commissioner, Tom Linder, as a George opponent. Linder had briefly entered the race against Richard Russell in 1942, only to withdraw.[107] In the final wash, George's only opposition was John W. Goolsby, an unknown forty-six-year-old Washington County farmer and appliance salesman, who based his campaign on an expanded agricultural

[103] *The Telegraph*, August 5, 2011, 61.

[104] *CR*, 70/1, 9953.

[105] Henderson, *The Politics of Change in Georgia*, 62.

[106] Charles C. McGehee to FDR, February 25, 1942, DNC, OF 300, box 15, f. K-M, Roosevelt papers.

[107] "George to Get State Support," August 4, 1943, box 337, f. George, July 1938–, RNC papers.

marketing system.[108] George carried every county, winning statewide by about six to one (211,081–34,465).[109]

George's popularity and great esteem led to his being seriously mentioned as a vice-presidential candidate in 1944, at least by conservative senators Connally, McKellar, and his close friend Josiah Bailey. There were some rumblings that the Deep South was about to jump the traces and vote Republican, and George's presence on the ticket would help hold these states in line. Roosevelt, for whatever reason, was contemplating abandoning Wallace, who was a liability in the South, and George's name began to come forward. George had even implied that he would overlook the 1938 purge attempt and join Roosevelt on the ticket. Journalist Frank C. Waldrip, however, summed up liberal opinion on this issue when he wrote of George in this bizarre alliance as more suitable to run "with the late William McKinley," who had been dead for over four decades, than with Roosevelt, sarcastically calling him "the absolutely essential White Knight" to ride to the rescue "if the terrified maiden Southern Democracy is to be saved from the buzz saw in 1944."[110]

Smart money, however, was on Supreme Court Justice Jimmy Byrnes, who had often been called "the assistant president" because of his close association with Roosevelt. Roosevelt, who had apparently indicated to Byrnes that he would be his choice, however, began to get pressure from labor and civil rights groups. In his usual way of handling such matters and trying to give the impression that he was not involved, he remained aloof in California while the convention nominated Harry Truman. The irony is that Byrnes had asked Truman to make his nominating speech, and Truman had already written it. Truman was nominated, and the rest is history. Byrnes had to settle for being, briefly, Truman's secretary of state. Walter George would never be mentioned again for national office.

George and Arnall did fall out in 1945 over Arnall's friendship with former vice president Henry A. Wallace. Deprived of his place on the ticket with Roosevelt in 1944, Wallace's consolation prize was, as we have seen, the nomination to be secretary of commerce. By this time Wallace's leftward leanings had earned him a great deal of enmity in Congress, especially among Southern conservatives. George led the attempt to reduce the power

[108]*New York Times* and *Washington Star*, clipping, April 29, 1944, box 337, f. George, 1938–, RNC papers.

[109]Heard and Strong, *Southern Primaries and Elections*, 66–67.

[110]Frank C. Waldrip, "No Southern Comfort," unidentified clipping, July (?) 1944, box 28, f. WFG, Wallace papers.

of the commerce secretary in his lending functions, given that Wallace would now be heading the office. Wallace had become close friends with Arnall, whom Wallace had called an example of "an emerging constructive liberal leadership in the South" and "a pillar of the new liberalism in the South."[111] When Wallace was nominated as secretary of commerce, Arnall endorsed him, calling on both Georgia senators to support him. Despite Arnall's plea, George's efforts to strip Wallace of some of his power passed Congress, with only fourteen dissenting votes and the support of the entire Georgia delegation.[112] George's relationship with Arnall would never be the same. Further, Wallace's call for friendship with the Soviet Union as the Russians were clamping down on Eastern Europe hurt the reputation of both men. Two decades later Ellis Arnall would still be regarded as a wild-eyed radical by Georgia voters, so much so that clown-like figure Lester Maddox defeated him in the Democratic primary in 1966, with some Republican help. Maddox went on to lose the popular vote to Republican Bo Callaway, with Arnall running as a write-in. Callaway won a plurality of the vote, but since no candidate received a majority, the state legislature chose the governor from among the top two. Being overwhelming controlled by the Democrats, Maddox was elected governor.

One other question on which George and Arnall did not agree was on the issue of voting rights for soldiers. It is well known that Georgia was the first state to give eighteen-year-olds the right to vote under the logic that if the country should draft eighteen-year-olds to fight and die for their country, it should certainly give them the right to vote, and it was Ellis Arnall's first administration that gave them the right to do so. Georgia had supported the war enthusiastically, with 320,000 men and women, about 10 percent of the population, serving.[113] A bill was introduced in Congress in fall 1942 requiring states to provide absentee ballots for all soldiers. Georgia had an absentee ballot act in 1942, a rarity in Southern states at the time, but George opposed the federal mandate because he feared the next step would be federal legislation determining the qualification of electors. "Once the Congress embarks upon the course of fixing the qualifications of electors in the several States, even for soldiers in wartime," he warned his colleagues, "it has opened the door for all kinds of future legislation along that line. There is no doubt that...the bill...would subject the elections in every state...to

[111]Henderson, *The Politics of Change in Georgia*, 156.

[112]Ibid., 156–57.

[113]Coleman, et al., *A History of Georgia*, 340. Coleman notes that the physical rejection rate for Georgia volunteers and draftees was higher than the national average.

absolute federal control. Federal authorities would go into every remote precinct...to see that the absentee ballots were handled just as Congress [has designated] that they should be handled."

When his friend Senator Theodore Green of Rhode Island pointed out that the bill only allowed federal agents to distribute the applications for ballots, George replied "I know that," but went on to warn that even in allowing this move, Congress "has taken jurisdiction of the whole field." Calling the pending bill "not an innocent step for the good purpose of permitting soldiers to vote," but a bill with "attendant possibilities...of very great evil and of very great abuse." Extending federal control over elections would "be a dangerous thing to do in this country. I do not know a better way of creating a dictatorship."[114] George moved for a delay "to study and print the bill," and on August 20, 1942, he expressed the opinion that if Congress did not pass this bill before the fall elections, "by the time that the next general election comes around, every state...will have provided for the casting of ballots by their absented soldiers."[115] Again he warned that if the bill passed, it would start a process where other groups would claim that "there are certain obnoxious things going on in a state which we would like to eliminate."[116] Such actions would lead to placing a state's election machinery in wartime "under federal regulation and control."[117]

When Senator Carl Hatch of New Mexico and Senator Warren Austin of Vermont promoted a suspension of the poll tax in states that had it, expressing that it was unconstitutional, both agreed that war gave members of Congress the right to vote for bills that were unconstitutional. George quickly interrupted. "Mr. President, I should like to make an observation, in view of the extraordinary turn the debate has taken.... In my judgment there is no power in the Constitution...to do anything in wartime that cannot be done...[in peacetime]. War does not suspend the Constitution." Then, he intoned with some sarcasm, "I think the whole argument might well be summarized by a suggestion that we amend the oath we take...by saying that we will support the Constitution except in wartime."[118]

Here, George exemplified for probably the first time in the struggle for blacks' voting rights the language used by Southern politicians who opposed their voting. Even George himself brought into the debate the question of

[114]*CR,* 77/2, 6864.
[115]Ibid., 6896.
[116]Ibid., 6899.
[117]Ibid.,
[118]Ibid., 9818.

Georgia's poll tax, which was hardly germane to the topic at hand, but it showed where his fears really lay.[119] The Senate finally passed a bill that "recommended" that states permit military personnel to vote in federal and state elections, but did not require them to do so. George immediately wrote Governor Arnall, urging him to prod the state legislature to implement the Senate's recommendation. Arnall, always eager to try to move Georgia out of what he considered the Dark Ages, replied that he would be delighted "to blaze a trail" on this question. On January 1, 1944, he called a special session of the legislature to consider a soldiers' voting law.[120] George must have felt that the South had dodged a bullet, and it would indeed be more than twenty years before federal legislation would intervene and guarantee voting rights for blacks.

George frequently championed soldiers' rights and benefits. On January 17, 1944, he introduced a bill for expediting soldiers' ballots. His bill, S.1655 to amend the Second War Powers Act, permitted any registration credentials or absentee ballots sent by members of the military to be transmitted by airmail, free of postage. Georgia had done the same for soldiers from that state, and George probably got the idea from this action. He later suggested that this change include ballots in primary elections as well.[121] He was active, as a member of the Finance Committee, in passing the famous GI Bill of Rights, and he included the concerns of housing for veterans returning to school, given the problems of overcrowding.[122] Since the war was winding down, he joined New York's Senator Wagner in supporting his bill, which allowed soldiers to receive payments into their Social Security accounts for their time in service as though they had been paying into Social Security in private business all that time. Moreover, it was made retroactive to the curious date of September 7, 1939.[123]

With the war in Europe having ended and the war in the Far East winding down, on June 1945, George called for "tax freedom" for all servicemen up to and including the rank of major who had no income other than their pay. "I believe all men in the services, especially enlisted men, should be relieved of making all tax returns from 1941 on," he told a reviewer with the International News Service. His justification: "I don't see how

[119]Ibid., 6937.

[120]George's letter is printed in the *Atlanta Journal*, December 12, 1943, cited in Henderson, *The Politics of Change in Georgia*, 74.

[121]*CR*, 78/2, 1054.

[122]*CR*, 79/1, 10508–10.

[123]Ibid., April 18, 1945, 40:6.

boys in the foxhole can keep in mind little matters like taxation," and he called for the implementation of this proposal as an amendment to the GI Bill of Rights.[124] He became indignant after the war's end that troops were being left "on lonely Pacific outposts" while shipping was being diverted to transport merchandise to other countries. Such action, he told his colleagues, was "inexcusable, unpardonable, and even criminal."[125] Since vocational education was always one of George's favorite issues, it is not surprising that he rekindled it in favor of veterans. He sponsored in 1945 a vocational education bill designed to aid "hundreds of thousands of demobilized war production workers to prepare them for civilian pursuits," but more importantly, "to train large numbers of veterans." This bill focused on giving assistance to local communities to train veterans returning to civilian pursuits.[126] As a result of his action on vocational education for veterans, thousands of young men, drafted into the armed forces at eighteen before they had been able to begin a career, were now given a chance to train for one or to continue the education they had received in the military.

In the beginning of the war, George held no illusions about its difficulty. When Senator Connally predicted that the Philippines would fall because they were indefensible, George echoed his sentiments, saying that if they fell to the Japanese, its recapture would be "incidental" to achieving victory. He added that it would probably be a year before America's war economy "would hit full stride." He would also make one of his many correct predictions about the war when he prophesied that "when Hitler is crushed, the war will be practically over," although he could hardly have known at that point the real reason why. He felt that with Hitler defeated, Japan "will negotiate and try to maintain some of her gains." He felt that America should not go this route but demand "unconditional surrender."[127]

It early became US-British policy to win the war in Europe first, then turn their attention to the Far East, and some Chinese groups expressed concern that the British-American alliance would only fight defensively in the Orient. Both George and Connally tried to assure the Chinese that "events will demonstrate that we will withhold nothing to crush Japanese aggression and to assist China,"[128] and the Doolittle Raid, the Battle of the Coral Sea, and the stunning victories at Midway and the Solomons Cam-

[124]*Atlanta Constitution*, June 7, 1945, 1:1.
[125]*New York Times*, October 30, 1945, 5:3.
[126]*CR*, 79/1, 1411.
[127]*New York Times*, January 1, 1942, 1:4.
[128]Ibid., January 20, 1942, 10:2.

paign in the subsequent months must have somewhat allayed their fears. In 1943 when British secretary of state for foreign affairs Anthony Eden championed the cause of China and praised that nation's contribution to the war effort, George echoed his sentiments and moved that his speech be added to the *Congressional Record.* In his introduction of the speech, he expressed his support for China by saying, "I think it would be difficult for any responsible leader in this country to visualize the termination of this war except in complete and final victory for China." Making a reference to the large military contribution "made by China, her magnificent leaders and her brave people," he expressed a certainty that in any "edifice to repair against future world war, China must be one of the great pillars upon which that edifice shall rest."[129]

When in May 1942 some politicians in both Britain and America called for meetings to discuss post-war planning, George felt that they would be pointless and reminiscent of the last war. "We haven't won the war yet," he warned the government, "and we must come near the end before we can discuss any peace plans." He also added that if only the US and Britain met, the other allies (the Soviet Union, Canada, etc.) might feel that their contribution to the war effort was being ignored.[130] George did agree to attend as a US Senate representative the Canada Branch of the Empire Parliamental Association meeting late in June 1943 along with senators Connally, Austin of Vermont, and Burton of Ohio, but this action would not have been misconstrued by the other Allies as being exclusive.[131]

One area where George swam against the tide in America was in his support of Soviet Russia and his recognition of Russia's contribution to the war effort. In both world wars, Americans were either ignorant or dismissive of Russia's war contribution. Americans either ignored or did not know that Russia suffered more casualties in the Battle of Stalingrad than the Americans, British, and French had in all the rest of the war in all theaters. Half of Russia's housing was destroyed by the fighting (not just in the occupied areas but in the entire country), and the general estimate today is that Russia lost 26,000,000 people, civilian and military, in the conflict. The Russian Revolution and civil war two decades earlier had left a hostile impression in the capitalist West, where the Communist confiscation of private property and the clamp down on religion had produced complete disgust. There was general talk in the army during the war that the Allies should let the Ger-

[129]*CR*, 78/1, 2737–38.

[130]*New York Times*, May 24, 1942, 32:3.

[131]*CR*, 78/1, 6306.

mans kill as many Russians as they could because that would mean that many fewer we would have to kill later.[132] Walter George, nevertheless, supported the Russians during the war. He promoted Cordell Hull's participation in the Foreign Ministers' Conference in Moscow in October-November 1943, where the Allies discussed issues such as the surrender of Italy and Russian intervention in the war with Japan. George was delighted that so much more came of the Moscow Foreign Ministers' Conference than had been expected, and he attributed the success to "the patience, persistence and wisdom" of his friend Secretary of State Cordell Hull. "I think he has demonstrated his sterling worth and value as a public servant," he told his Senate colleagues, and then taking a slap at other administration figures, he added, "attributes so sadly and so seriously needed at this time of crisis in our history and the history of the world."[133]

George was given an honorary doctorate by Columbia University at its spring commencement in 1945. He made two speeches that day, both dealing with Russia's contribution to the war effort, and praising a Russo-American union. At an alumni meeting before commencement, George told his listeners, "Russia and the US standing together could constitute the most powerful force for an enduring peace in the world," and he warned those who would criticize Russian actions, which had not at this time become as hostile as they would become, that "to stress the differences would be one of the most certain ways of bringing about international disagreement and ultimately war.... America should be very slow to give expression to that kind of thought."[134] We will see George change his attitude toward the Communist world in general and Russia in particular in the years that followed, when the Cold War deepened, but at the time, he was one of the lone voices calling for cooperation with the Soviet behemoth.

By late 1943, it was clear that the Axis Powers were going to lose the war eventually, and Roosevelt began calling for a program of demobilization. George criticized the president for making such plans, for he feared that doing so would give the false impression that the war would soon be over; his belief was that there would be two more years of war, if not more. Its end would come only after "a long, hard pull," and though we should be ready for anything, we should not give the impression of the need for

---

[132]My father, who served in the U. S. Army Dental Corps, told me that such was the general scuttlebutt during the war. If it circulated in the Dental Corps, it circulated all over, and given the Russian network of spies, such hostility must have been known to the Russians.

[133]*CR*, 78/1, 8923.

[134]*New York Times*, June 6, 1945, 14:5; see also *Atlanta Constitution*, June 11, 1945, 6:6.

"speedy action."[135] A year later, however, the end was clearly in sight, and George began making suggestions and plans for the peace conference, which he felt would come soon after the end of the war. Speaking in Augusta in October 1944, he made the novel suggestion for female representation at the peace talks because "they will accept no compromise in the way of peace." He further opined, "I can't think of anything as big as world peace without women having a voice in it" because "they make the greatest sacrifice when they give up their sons to war."[136] In summer 1945, he expressed the certainty that any peace delegation should include several US senators—who had been excluded from the delegation to Paris in 1919.[137]

November 1944 found George fighting Sol Bloom's suggestion of a constitutional amendment that would allow for treaties to be ratified by a majority of both houses of Congress instead of the two-thirds of the Senate. Bloom was probably fearful that any peace conference treaty would die in the Senate just as the Treaty of Versailles had died after World War I. "There isn't the slightest justification for a change in the fundamental constitution system at a time when we are trying to work out far-reaching international agreements," he told reporters on November 15, 1944. On November 27, he predicted that the Senate would "stand firmly" against any such change, as would the American people after "sober second thought." George feared that "more drastic things might be done with the approval of a bare majority—things that we might regret later." He dismissed the whole notion that anything like this proposal could even get a majority of the Senate, must less the necessary two-thirds.[138]

In late 1944, Secretary of State Hull turned seriously ill, and though he did not resign, he told Roosevelt that his illness would prevent his "returning to his desk." Needless to say, speculation on Hull's eventual successor began making the Washington rounds. George told reporters that if Hull did depart, it would be "one of the great losses, not merely to the US but to all the peace-loving nations of the world." He did note that should a successor be needed, US Supreme Court Justice Jimmy Byrnes, George's old friend, would be a good replacement "who could hold the position in shape [better] than anyone else."[139] When Hull did resign, he was replaced by Edward Stettinius, who after the famous Yalta conference of 1945 became ra-

[135]Ibid., November 29, 1943, 13:5.
[136]Ibid., October 25, 1944, 24:8.
[137]Ibid., July 30, 1945, 19:1.
[138]Ibid., November 28, 1944, 5:5.
[139]Ibid., November 27, 1944, 10:6.

ther unpopular. George had frequently been mentioned to go to Treasury because of his enormous experience and knowledge of tax matters, but by summer 1945, he was now being mentioned as Stettinius's replacement at the State Department.[140] After President Roosevelt's death in March 1945, President Truman named Byrnes instead, which pleased George, who probably would not have taken the position had it been offered.

We have seen George deviate from his isolationism in the past, but his final step came with his support for the United Nations. He had run for the Senate in 1922 as a strict isolationist and opponent of membership in the League of Nations, but over time, George slowly emerged from his isolationist past. Steps were being made in summer 1941, before America entered the war, for what Hull called "a post-war organization," and on June 7, 1941, he appraised George about it since George chaired at the time the Foreign Relations Committee.[141] Hull took a formal step on February 12, 1942, in the dark shadow of Pearl Harbor, to form an advisory committee on post-war foreign policy focusing on the formation of a United Nations-type organization. Hull wanted it broadly non-partisan to avoid the partisanship that wrecked the Versailles treaty in the Senate. On May 27, he invited Connally as well as Senator Warren Austin, who later became the US Representative to the UN, and of course Walter George. Ultimately the committee had forty-five members from Congress, the war and navy departments, and even the Library of Congress.[142]

The reader will remember that in March 1943, Guy Gillette introduced a resolution, prepared by the State Department, calling for American involvement in any such post-war international organization. The resolution was brief and consisted of only two paragraphs. The first called for complete and unlimited prosecution of the world conflict until victory; the second that the Senate advocates "participation by the United States in the creation and maintenance of an international organization to insure permanent peace." On March 22, Hull read and discussed the text with Connally, George, Vanderbilt, and Gillette.[143] A little over a year later, Connally met with the Foreign Relations Committee and suggested the creation of a subcommittee of "two or three Democrats and two or three Republicans" to discuss these matters formally. He then formed a committee of eight outstanding senators (George, Connally, Barkley, Gillette, Vandenberg, La

---

[140]*Atlanta Constitution*, June 12, 1945, 6:6.
[141]Hull, *Memoirs of Cordell Hull*, 2:1630.
[142]Ibid., 1635.
[143]Ibid., 1261–62.

Follette, White, and Austin (dubbed "the Committee of Eight" by the press), who would confer with Hull on the question, with Connally serving as chair.[144] They all supported "the creation of a security organization in the most enthusiastic spirit."[145]

The committee first met in Hull's office on April 25, 1944. Here he gave the members in confidence a draft of the State Department's plan for the UN organization. They met again on May 2 after all had had time to read and digest it.[146] After these preliminary discussions, the committee did not meet again until August 1944, by which time new proposals had been presented, such as the inclusion of France as one of the permanent members of the NATO security council. Meanwhile the Dumbarton Oaks discussions in Washington were underway, at which time senators raised any objections. Hull stressed the need for the American public to appear strongly behind the organization, if only for the sake of the Allies.[147]

By the time the debate reached the Senate floor in July 1945, George was supporting the inclusion of US troops in the UN forces. Debate ran for five days but was concluded with a stirring speech by George on July 27 in which he gave his all. He admitted that he had not examined the bill for "microscopic defects," but he had considered instead "the broad positive effects it would bring." Then he made his reference to the blue waters yielding their dead. He made no direct reference to his son, but everyone understood. Had there been some organization in the inter-war years, the war might have been prevented and his son would have lived. Noting that in the 3500 years of recorded (sic) history, there had only been three hundred years of peace. There had been a decline in war, but a slow one. The rules of the Senate do not permit applause of a speech, but the senators on the floor showed their respect by rising when George finished as a testimonial to his actions. That day the Senate ratified the charter by a vote of 89–2, with only William Langer of North Dakota and Henrik Shipstead of Minnesota voting "no."[148] It was clearly George's finest hour in the Senate.

With the exception of the financial guidance he gave the nation during World War II, George's greatest work came in his efforts to stave off a post-war depression. The government began to wind down spending, and thousands of soldiers were being demobilized, many of whom had been drafted

[144]Divine, *Eisenhower and the Cold War*, 195.

[145]Ibid.; Hull, *Memoirs of Cordell Hull*, 2:1658–59.

[146]Hull, *Memoirs of Cordell Hull*, 2:1658–59.

[147]Ibid., 1697.

[148]*New York Times*, June 28, 1945, 1:1.

before they could become establish careers. A deep recession had followed the Great War of 1914–1918, and Roosevelt wanted to prevent another such financial crisis. In a private conversation with Walter George, Roosevelt told him that the president would "exercise due vigilance" over demobilization and that post-war life would not quickly become normal once hostilities would end.[149] Perhaps prompted by this conversation, in February 1943 George asked the Senate to form a special committee to study possible post-war economic problems. In March, Roosevelt threw his weight behind the idea, and the Senate with SR 102 created the committee and made George the chair. It was hereafter called "the George Committee," and it included Democrats Barkley, Carl Hayden, Joseph C. O'Mahoney of Wyoming, Scott Lucas of Illinois, and Claude Pepper of Florida. The Republicans were McNarey, Vandenberg, Austin, and Taft.[150] The charge to the committee read, "It shall be the duty of the special committee to investigate all matters relating to post-war economic policy and problems; to gather information, plans and suggestions from informed sources with respect to such problems; [and] to study the plans and suggestions received.... It is intended that full authority to accomplish this general purpose shall be granted by this resolution."[151] Vandenberg wrote, with enthusiasm, in his diary, "I think this may be the most important committee in the history of the Senate." His embellishments aside, he did later note with more logic that the committee did good work and was a good example of bipartisan cooperation.[152]

George's work began by hosting a luncheon in May for Sir William Beveridge, Britain's most famous social security expert and author of the famous Beveridge Plan, a cradle-to-grave social system. The entire "Committee of Eight" were guests. One wonders why George, given his politics, would treat Beveridge with such friendship, and it was probably because Beveridge stressed that state management of an economy should "complement," not replace, George's "human initiative." Moreover, Beveridge felt that it was "imperative that a people plan to keep their liberties and also provide work and a subsistence security."[153]

In a speech to the War Council of the US Chamber of Commerce in

---

[149]Garson, *The Democratic Party*, 135.

[150]*New York Times*, February 15, 27, and March 13, 1943, in Wonderlin, *Papers of Robert A. Taft*, 2:425; see also *CR*, 78/1, 1929.

[151]*CR*, 78/1, 900.

[152]Vandenberg, *The Private Papers of Senator Vandenberg*, 34.

[153]"Senate Gives George Top War Spot," *Atlanta Constitution*, May 22, 1943, clipping, RCB-5804, box 15, f. WFG-GSA.

April 1943, George outlined what would be his theme for the remainder of his work on this question: It would be business, free enterprise, and capitalism that would provide the jobs that would prevent the post-war recession from becoming a reality. Noting to the group that despite the fact that many of the wartime employed would now voluntarily leave their work (women returning to be homemakers, etc.), there would still be a need for 56,000,000 jobs after the war. The transition might be rough, and he called for temporary unemployment support for returning service men and women to help make the adjustment to peacetime. He likewise called for one of the Great Depression's public works projects to help curb unemployment, but he stressed that these measures would be temporary and expressed the fear that borrowing money to keep the economy up "is too widely accepted." He noted that such action would encourage the American people to turn to government "as the chief employer." Then he continued to express his belief that "free enterprise in the post-war years" would supply employment if we implement "public policies which will increase jobs in the private sector."[154]

George's formula to achieve a job increase has a very modern ring and sounds like the rhetoric of Republican politics of today as these words are written. He felt that there should be no increase of corporate or personal income taxes, and no increase and possibly a cut in capital gains levies. There should absolutely be a termination of the excess profits tax. Industry profits should be taxed only once. He reminded his Chamber of Commerce audience, as if this group needed reminding, that "all the large pages in human history have been written by men and races who were willing to fight for economic freedom."[155]

In November, he praised his friend Jimmy Byrnes and others who were already working on a plan to convert war surpluses for peacetime use.[156] With all of his heartfelt rhetoric, he joined Senator Wagner that same month in introducing a program of fifty-two weeks of unemployment insurance.[157] However, when Roosevelt, during his January 1944 inaugural address, called for an "Economic Bill of Rights" for every American, George felt that he had gone too far.[158] As he often had, especially after 1938, George tried to take power out of the Roosevelt Administration's hands. Less than a month after the inaugural address, he and Senator Philip Mur-

---

[154]*CR*, appendix, 78/1, A2071.

[155]Ibid.

[156]Ibid., November 7, 1943, 7:4.

[157]Roosevelt, *FDR: His Personal Letters*, 1928–1945, 1462.

[158]Huthmacher, *Senator Robert F. Wagner*, 29.

ray promoted the George-Murray Omnibus Contract Settlement Bill, which would create the Office of Contract Settlements with a director appointed by the president. In the design of the bill, Congress would have some oversight rather than only an executive agency, which would have only executive controls. Presidential adviser and famous financier Bernard Baruch had suggested allowing the Office of War Mobilization to handle contracts, but neither George nor Murray wanted its interference. George wrote a bill to create the Office of Demobilization to be completely separate from the Office of War Mobilization, which was controlled by the executive branch, with power over contract settlement and surplus property. Many cosponsors joined, and it was introduced on February 22, 1944.[159] This action was merely one of George's many pinpricks at the Roosevelt administration. Meanwhile, George had formed an alliance on his committee with Senator Vandenberg, the prominent Republican and also a Roosevelt nemesis, and the Michigan senator worked with George and Murray to enact the George-Murray contracts settlement legislation.[160] Meanwhile, Senator Harley Kilgore of West Virginia, probably acting as the administration's catspaw, produced a bill to replace George-Murray on March 29, 1944. It created the Office of War Mobilization and Adjustment "to facilitate the reconversion of an economy without violent declines in production or decreases in employment." As the *New York Times* described it, it proposed a very "Keynsian approach." Senators Warren Austin of Vermont and Chapman Rivercomb of West Virginia opposed the Kilgore bill in committee somewhat in the manner of a filibuster, analyzing it word for word, to give George the chance to muster forces. At first its demise looked doubtful, especially when Murray deserted George and began to support the Kilgore bill, which now had become the Murray-Kilgore Bill. Somehow the Kilgore bill was also introduced into the Military Affairs Committee as well, and it was passed by a vote of 10–7.[161] Both bills were recommended to the Senate floor. The major difference between the bills was that George's bill gave federal unemployment compensation under state standards for federal works while Kilgore's bill called for federal standards everywhere with two years of unemployment compensation for a full two years after the war's end.[162]

---

[159]Stephen Bailey, *Congress Makes a Law* (New York: Columbia University Press, 1950) 30–32, cited in Maddox, *The Senatorial Career of Harley Martin Kilgore*, 141.

[160]Tomkins, *Senator Arthur H. Vandenberg*, 234.

[161]*Wall Street Journal,* August 5, 1944 cited in Maddox, *The Senatorial Career of Harley Martin Kilgore*, 148.

[162]Tomkins, *Senator Arthur H. Vandenberg*, 234.

When Harley Kilgore's bill reached the Senate floor first, "all hell broke loose," the *Washington Post* told its readers as the Southern Democratic-Republican coalition "rolled out its heaviest guns for a devastating attack."[163] Labor lined up behind Kilgore and Murray. The president attacked "the feeble synthetic George bill" in a telegram to Barkley and called for the enactment of the Kilgore bill.[164] This telegram probably at least resulted in the desertion of Barkley, who had voted for the bill in committee.[165]

On August 1, George introduced his version, which had "a modest states' rights" flair and was passed by the Finance Committee the next day. The *Washington Post* called George's bill "utterly inadequate."[166] The working man's journal *Labor* attacked George as leading "an alliance of Southern Tory Democrats and anti-labor Northern Republicans," which it felt represented the views of "the National Association of Manufacturers and other selfish groups."[167] In the fight that followed, strange alliances were made and friends deserted friends. At one point George introduced amendments to the Kilgore bill that in effect turned Kilgore's bill into George's bill. Vandenberg at one point criticized the Kilgore bill solution to the problem as a man's "trying to drink himself sober,"[168] which to Senate insiders might have appeared as a jab at Kilgore's well-known drinking problem. Outside the Senate, George told reporters that Kilgore's bill "would upset Veterans' Administration jurisdiction over returning soldiers and upset state unemployment systems."[169] After an eight-hour non-stop debate, the Senate passed the George version by a vote of 55–19, with 60 percent of the Democrats and 97 percent of the Republicans supporting George's version.[170] The George-led Conservative Coalition of Republicans and Southern Democrats, forged in the fires of the New Deal in the 1930s, was victorious again. The *New York Times* reported it concisely: "Senator George, a conservative southern Democrat, shrewdly out maneuvered the Murray-Kilgore forc-

---

[163]*Washington Post*, August 7, 1944, cited in Maddox, *The Senatorial Career of Harley Martin Kilgore*, 149. In his book, *All in One Lifetime*, Jimmy Byrnes states that George and Senator Kilgore co-sponsored a bill, which could not have been farther from the truth. 213.

[164]Kilgore release, August 2, 1944, in Rosenberg papers, cited in Maddox, *The Senatorial Career of Harley Martin Kilgore*, 146.

[165]Maddox, *The Senatorial Career of Harley Martin Kilgore*, 151.

[166]*Washington Post*, August 4, 1944, in Maddox, *The Senatorial Career of Harley Martin Kilgore*, 146.

[167]Maddox, *The Senatorial Career of Harley Martin Kilgore*, 146.

[168]*CR*, 78/2, 6824.

[169]Maddox, *The Senatorial Career of Harley Martin Kilgore*, 152.

[170]*CR*, 78/2, 6917. Maddox states that it was August 11 (*The Senatorial Career of Harley Martin Kilgore*, 153).

es."[171]

We do not know if Senator Kilgore was embittered in defeat or if he held any animus against Walter George, but he told the gossip columnist Allen Drury before the vote, "George has the votes, but he won't talk to me."[172] If Kilgore did have any hard feelings toward George, he would pay him back handsomely a decade later.

As a coda to George's war work, he was placed on the "Pearl Harbor Committee," the congressional committee composed of members of both houses to investigate the Pearl Harbor disaster to determine how such a thing could happen.[173] The joint congressional committee was named in early fall 1945, and from the Senate, George was made a member along with Alben Barkley, Scott Lucas, Owen Brewster of Maine, and Homer Ferguson of Michigan.[174] The House appointed from its members Jere Cooper (D-Tennessee), J. Bayard Clark (D-North Carolina), John W. Murphy (D-Pennsylvania), Bertrand Gearhart (R-California), and Frank B. Keebe (R-Wisconsin).[175] The committee, therefore, consisted of five senators and five representatives (three Democrats and two Republicans from each house), so the administration to be investigated had a 6–4 party alignment in its favor. The majority could also pick the counsel, and it chose Democrat William D. Mitchell, who had served under Stimson in Hoover's cabinet. He served without salary.[176] As for Walter George, he tried to be excused for serving on it when named but was for some unknown reason his request was not granted.[177]

Trouble developed immediately when it became known that Roosevelt had issued an order on August 28, 1944, that sealed some of the Pearl Harbor evidence even before the committee was created. Moreover, the committee voted in executive session, along a party line vote, to rely on the committee counsel to sort through the files for pertinent information. Sena-

---

[171]*New York Times*, August 11, 1944, cited in Maddox, *The Senatorial Career of Harley Martin Kilgore*, 153.

[172]Drury, *Senate Journal*, 238–39.

[173]Bartlett (*Cover-up*) and Toland (*Infamy: Pearl Harbor and Its Aftermath*) are two authors who examine the question thoroughly. Both works, as seen by their titles, point to a cover up of Roosevelt administration's negligence and perhaps worse, and both make a good case that the Roosevelt administration knew more than it gave to the men on the ground in Hawaii about a coming attack. Admiral Kimmel and General Short have never been cleared or pardoned for negligence on their part by the United States government.

[174]*CR*, 79/1, 8583.

[175]Bartlett, *Cover-up*, 90.

[176]Toland, *Infamy*, 157–58.

[177]*CR*, 70/1, 10354.

tors Ferguson and Brewster demanded that individual senators be allowed to examine the files because they feared the Democratic counsel would not go as far as they would in searching the evidence. They were voted down in a 5–3 vote, with George in the majority.[178] Both senators then took their argument to the Senate floor. Brewster spoke first, complaining that the committee members would not be allowed to pursue records, and Senator Ferguson joined him, adding, "It is absolutely impossible for the Committee to function properly and to cross examine witnesses, if we don't have the records. The fact that files are necessary…is material to the investigation."[179] Barkley, apparently from the chair in the Senate, defended his committee's actions, saying that the Democrats were only trying to direct the committee to act as one and to prevent "general cruising," not having individual members acting as "private detectives."[180]

At this point George rose to defend the Democratic majority's actions. Employing the skills he had demonstrated almost half a century before on the debate team at Mercer, he adroitly muddied the water by implying the Republicans had committed some untoward act. Asking Senator Ferguson to yield, in his disarming manner, George referred to the senator from Michigan as being "irrepressible," "delightful," and "charming," and then asked, "Has the senator ever advised any member of the committee that counsel had reached some decision contrary to what he thinks should have been done?" He then went on to add, "What the senator is now saying seems to be very highly prejudicial to a correct understanding of the situation." He then inaccurately said that this transaction was never brought up in the committee, adding again inaccurately, "I never heard of it before today," when he had voted not to allow individual senators to do their own research. He then waxed indignant that the committee's affairs had been aired in this manner and asked if there was ever any evidence of "the disinclination of counsel to go into certain matters." George went on to say that had it been brought to the attention of the committee, the committee would have taken action. Then, totally twisting the issue, he added, "There never has been an understanding that the counsel should have final authority to determine what is to be put into the record." Noting that the hour was late, he then moved for adjournment.[181]

The Republicans had, of course, never accused the counsel of selective

[178]Ibid., 10356.
[179]Ibid., 10345.
[180]*New York Times*, November 3, 1945, 5:6.
[181]*CR*, 70/1, 10344–45.

research or hiding materials that might incriminate Roosevelt nor said that counsel would have sovereign authority to determine what would be in the report. They had only implied that it might happen by insisting that they be allowed to do their own research. In his shrewd way, George turned the issue on them, implying that they had impugned the integrity of the counsel. From the beginning to the end, George sided with the Democrats to stifle the Republican attempts to throw light on the matter, thus contributing if nothing else to the appearance that something was hidden. President Truman did eventually allow the disclosure of some additional materials in what must have been an attempt to mute any charges of a cover-up, but the Republicans were never satisfied.

The hearings began on November 15, 1945, in the Senate Office Building's caucus room, where many government scandals, Tea Pot Dome for example, had been exposed. Kimmel and Short were both in attendance. Just as Senator Barkley brought down the opening gavel, the lights in the room went out. Counsel Mitchell made the opening remarks, which began the sixty-seven days and three nights of public hearings involving thirty-nine witnesses and 14,000 pages of testimony.[182] From the beginning, however, it was obvious that the committee would have both a majority and minority report.[183] That George never played a prominent role in the hearings is not surprising since he had tried to avoid service on the committee, but he did always side with the Democratic majority. John Toland in his work on the affair states that George had converted to Roosevelt's interventionist policy[184] (which we know now is not completely accurate), so he was unlikely to join the Republicans "in attacking a policy he had come to accept."[185] In the absence of any evidence, one can only surmise that George's actions were molded by his loyalty to the Democratic administrations under which he had served. He rarely seems to have taken much of a role in the debates. When the ailing Cordell Hull appeared with his statement, which was 22,000 words long, George tried to spare his friend the burden of having to read it since they all had been given a copy, but Senator Brewster insisted that Hull read it.[186] George said little after that except when General George Marshall had been strongly criticized by the Republicans, he attacked their methods: "Of course, I recognize the right of all members of the committee

[182]Toland, *Infamy*, 244.
[183]Ibid., 162.
[184]Ibid., 165.
[185]Ibid.
[186]Ibid.

to cross-examine witnesses at any length, but I have wondered whether or not we were confusing the issue rather than arriving at any answers in which the public could have any confidence."[187] As many had predicted, in March 1946 two reports came from the committee, one Republican, one Democratic. Seth Richardson, the final chief counsel of the committee, wrote a long draft stating that "Washington must bear a large share of the burden of what occurred on December 7, 1941." His assistant, Sam Kaufman, wrote a report that blamed the local Hawaiian command.[188] The issue of guilt is still debated to this day.

---

[187]Ibid., 194.
[188]Ibid., 246.

8

THE SOUTH'S AMBASSADOR TO THE NATION, 1945–1955

Walter George was a powerful patron and a dangerous opponent.
—Secretary of State Dean Acheson[1]

On numerous occasions, my illustrious predecessor Carter Glass told me that the senior senator from Georgia was the ablest man in the Senate, as well as one of the finest, and I have since had the opportunity to learn how very right he was.
—Senator A. Willis Robertson (D-Virginia)[2]

He [Walter F. George] was a very wise and far-seeing man.
—Harold Stassen[3]

In his book *Sketches*, US Secretary of State Dean Acheson wrote that during the postwar Truman years, the three giants in the US Senate were Alben Barkley, soon to be vice president, Tom Connally, and Walter F. George. George had first achieved national prominence when Franklin Roosevelt tried to purge him in 1938, but he began building his reputation as a senator as he assisted Roosevelt in overcoming the isolationist mood of the country to lead the US toward preparedness. He finally abandoned the last vestiges of his own personal isolationism when he helped form the United Nations. His monumental work on the nation's finances, while more arcane and less showy, burnished his image further among the powers in Washington and was a solid contribution to the war effort. As early as 1941, the *Atlanta Constitution* had called George "a statesman, instead of a mere politician," whose career had undone much of the "extremely bad advertising, which some prominent politicians have given this state [e.g., Gene Talmadge]."[4]

By 1945 George was beginning to achieve the legendary status that would reach its summit by 1956. Journalist Sylvia F. Porter wrote in the

---

[1]Acheson, *Sketches from Life of Men I Have Known*, 142.

[2]*CR*, 80/2, 3163; A. Willis Robertson to WFG, August 14, 1952, Correspondence f. General G, A. W. Robertson Papers.

[3]Harold Strassen, oral history, 34, Eisenhower Library.

[4]"They All Advise Him," *Atlanta Constitution*, September 9, 1941, in WFG-GSA.

New York Post after Franklin Roosevelt died, "Out of the flood of rumors about changes under the Truman administration, the name Senator Walter F. George is emerging with significant frequency. There is no doubt that this veteran senator from Georgia is destined to be a powerful figure on the American scene in the next several years."[5] Porter's prediction was certainly borne out. By 1950 *Time* included George among "The Senate's Most Valuable Ten" while omitting Richard Russell. Calling George "the ablest of the Southern Conservatives,"[6] *US News and World Report* almost a decade later told its readers that George was the "conscience of the Senate." Describing him as "a kindly Georgian of impressive personal dignity and reserve," the journal touted him as "a respected elder statesman of staunch integrity," adding that "leaders of both parties...often look to Senator George for guidance."[7] Secretary of State Dean Acheson remembered him as one of the types of men who are "apt to dominate a male organization." He included George with Barkley and Vandenberg as "the *beaux idéals*" of what he wrote.[8] As early as 1945, the *Saturday Evening Post* noted that George was regarded by his colleagues "as the most powerful Senator."[9] *US News* told its readers four years later that "in many battles with the White House, Senator George seems to have a Senate majority on his side."[10] His seniority added to this power. In 1947 there were only two senators who had been there longer than George, and with the 1950 elections and the defeat of a number of Democrats, most prominently Democratic leader Senator Scott Lucas (D-Illinois) and Senator Millard Tydings (D-Maryland), George's seniority was further enhanced. In short, as his colleague Senator George Smathers told an oral historian, "Nothing occurred [in Washington] that he didn't know about."[11] For all the laudatory remarks, his tireless work for Georgia led him to be jokingly called, surely behind his back, "The Senator from Coca-Cola."

His physical appearance was not overbearing. *Time* described him as a

---

[5]"Key Man in Capital," clipping, April 28, 1945, *New York Post,* box 337, f. George biog., RNC papers.

[6]*Time*, April 31, 1950, 20.

[7]"How a Democrat Guides Republican Tax Policy," 60.

[8]Acheson, *Sketches from Life of Men I Have Known*, 132. Curiously, though, Acheson did not seem to like George, writing once that George "contributed very little to political thought and leadership in the United States," a statement on which there is ample evidence to the contrary (Acheson, *Sketches from Life of Men I Have Known*, 141–42).

[9]Jarman, "Taxpayer's Senator," 22.

[10]"Senator George, Who Is Saying 'No' to President on Tax Rise," 42.

[11]George Smathers, oral history, 108, Russell Library.

"thin-lipped, medium-sized man without a paunch." Several spoke of his "dignified dress" (dark gray double-breasted suits) and his perfectly combed white hair, "parted on the left." Although he has been termed a "typical Southern aristocrat," the word "austere" is frequently used in the description, and George was certainly not a glad-handing, baby-kissing politician, generally a negative image for a Southern politician of that era. He had what one associate called "character."[12] *US News* characterized his power by noting that both Republicans and Democrats "yield to his judgement. Senator George is the pivot man in almost every turn the Senate takes."[13] This popularity led to his being recommended by a group of Georgians in Atlanta for the Supreme Court seat of Justice Harlan Stone in 1946. State Senator Abit H. Nix was chairman of the group, and Governor M. E. Thompson was the secretary.[14] George had been mentioned before, as the reader is aware, for a seat on the Supreme Court, but he had always discouraged such moves, preferring to remain in the Senate. He was always frequently mentioned for the position of majority leader, but in 1952 he turned that down as well, paving the way for Lyndon Johnson's career in that office.[15]

Although he was respected throughout the chamber, the Southern representatives were his base. In the post-war years, he was clearly the Dean of the Southern Delegation. When the twenty-two senators of the Old Confederacy caucused, usually in Dick Russell's office, George would preside over the meeting. They would agree on a position, and then they would walk *en famille* to the Senate chamber, entering together through the large central doors, with George in the lead. Usually someone in the press gallery would note, "Well, the South has arrived."[16] By the late 1940s, George was also recognized as "the South's greatest orator,"[17] although we have seen that his oratorical talents had been recognized well before 1945. While one author described him as being "quiet-spoken," like "maybe a corporation lawyer or a Harvard professor of literature," others usually mention his thundering oratory. One who worked around him told an interviewer for an oral history project that he did not have a commanding presence, "but he did have a commanding voice. When Walter George spoke, senators listened. They came onto the floor to see what he had to say."[18] Moreover, George

[12]Pat Holt, oral history, 96, Library of Congress.

[13]"Senator George, Who Is Saying 'No' to President on Tax Rise," 39.

[14]No title, April 25, 1945, general file, f. WFG, Truman Papers.

[15]Caro, *The Years of Lyndon Johnson*, 361.

[16]Donovan, "Senator George," 34.

[17]"Voice of the 84th," 22.

[18]Valeo, oral history, 162, Library of Congress; Caro, *The Years of Lyndon Johnson*, 855.

did not speak unless he had something to say, although often he spoke longer than others when he did finally address the body. "It has not been my habit to fill the *Congressional Record* with speeches," he once said, "…unless I had a real conviction…. If I have any influence in the Senate today, it is because the Senate has generally credited me with being sincere."[19]

"I do not intend to discuss this question at great length at this time," he said in his typical style in 1949 when a cloture motion was being debated,[20] but he obviously forgot his own habit when he added in the midst of this speech of several pages the dubious information, "I have never made lengthy speeches in this body."[21] Still, people listened. When he made a speech on the Formosa Question in 1953, James Enlo Smith, an assistant to Senator Karl Mundt, remembered, "Every seat was taken, and you could hear a pin drop."[22] One of the most remarkable talents he had in speaking was inspiring listeners to change their votes. Rarely do speeches on the floor of the US Senate change senators' minds. George was one of the few who could change votes by his oratory. Senator Ralph Flanders of Vermont noted that the only time he even changed his mind because of a speech of a Senator on the floor of the Senate was during one of George's speeches. *Newsweek* noted, "When he talks, the Senate not only listens; it seriously considers what he has to say…. He has…the ability to marshal facts into powerful arguments, and a sharp tongue which he can use like a lash."[23]

Another such occasion occurred in 1950 concerning a matter connected to a question on post-war Germany. The Senate leadership was hoping just to get a simple majority. Then George took the floor and spoke for forty-five minutes while the Senate remained deathly silent. It was apparent that the mood of the Senate was shifting, because Senator Richard Nixon, who was presiding over the chamber, leaned over and said to someone, "There goes one of the last men that when he speaks, he changes the points of view of senators." When the roll was called on the question, not only was the hoped-for majority in favor, the tally was 92–2.[24]

In give and take debate, George was rarely bested. Usually when a senator spoke in debate, he had an aide sits beside him passing him notes with statistics and facts. George usually went alone. During one debate on a

---

[19]Solberg, *Hubert Humphrey*, 161.
[20]Caro, *The Years of Lyndon Johnson*, 96.
[21]Ibid., 786.
[22]Carl Marcy, oral history, 69, Library of Congress; "Old Independent," 20.
[23]Mellichamp, *Senators from Georgia*, 236.
[24]*CR*, 81/1, p 1606–08.

reciprocal tax treaty with Canada, Carl Marcy, George's staff director, was observed sitting in the back of the Senate chamber. When asked why he was not with George, he replied, "Hell, he knows more about the treaty than I do. Why should I be there?"[25] George participated, acting alone, rendering statistics and debate points without help from anyone.[26] One Harvard economics student who observed the committee hearings on a topic he had studied spoke of George's "great intelligence and experience" in his questioning, noting that George was one of only two senators who asked intelligent questions "that got to the heart of the matter."[27]

Moreover, Walter George usually got the last word usually because he was conceded by everyone to be the last person to speak. Senator Clinton Anderson (D-New Mexico) summed it up: "Walter George…was expected to be the last speaker in any debate, bringing to bear his accumulated wisdom on some given question."[28] Sometime this "last word" manifested itself by his gently correcting one of his colleagues. Frequently his correction would begin with a compliment such as "the senator is entirely correct" or "I am in total agreement with the senator" although then there would follow a "but" after which he would politely say that his colleague was "a bit confused," and then correct the senator's error.[29]

In private conversations George was quite the speaker as well, usually dominating the conversation with anyone. Once when he was a guest at Robert Woodruff's plantation Ichauway in South Georgia, with his friend former North Carolina governor Max Gardner, he held forth for an hour on his acquaintance with the late senator John Sharp Williams of Mississippi. The next morning at breakfast, Gardner playfully said, "Senator, last night at dinner you touched upon the edges of your experiences with John Sharp Williams. Would you mind giving us now the details of the story?"[30]

Frequently George could be found in the afternoons seated in one of the leather chairs in the Senate cloakroom holding court before younger senators telling old Senate stories to admiring colleagues, with even Lyndon Johnson frequently sitting in attendance.[31] It was out of the public eye that

---

[25]Ibid., 1607.

[26]James Enlo Smith, personal interview with author.

[27]"George of Georgia: Ike's Friend in Need," 29; these words were plagiarized in the *Atlanta Constitution* article, "When Georgia's Sen. George Speaks Out," *Atlanta Journal-Constitution*, misc. clippings, undated, scrapbook, LHG-VIIPS.

[28]Floyd Riddeck, oral history, 243, Library of Congress.

[29]Carl Marcy, oral history, 70–71; see also Riddeck, oral history, 244.

[30]Riddick, oral history, 244.

[31]*Vienna News*, 8 August 1957, 5.

George's humor, not part of his public persona, would emerge. George once told his secretary to call Jake Carlton, an administrative assistant to Senator Smathers, to tell him to come over to his office, if he was not busy. "What do you want me to tell him if he is busy?" she asked. George replied, "Why, tell him to come anyhow."[32]

His management of legislation on the Senate floor reflected this same courtesy. He would always submit the bill to his colleagues several weeks before he would call it up for debate. He would get the bill in draft stage and then announce to the Senate that the finance committee had concluded the hearings on it. "It's now being printed, and a copy of it will be available for all senators tomorrow," he would inform his colleagues, but then he would add, "but we have decided to wait until a certain date [to bring it up]." That date would always be at least two weeks away in order to give senators a chance to study the bill thoroughly, and he would allow plenty of time for discussion of it.[33] In management of legislation, he could be quite crafty. Once Senate leader Mike Mansfield (D-Montana) came to George to ask how he wanted people to vote on a certain bill. "Well, Mike," the senator replied, "I going to have to vote 'aye,' but I hope it's defeated." Mansfield instructed the Democrats not to follow George's lead and vote "no." The bill was defeated.[34]

Though George collaborated closely with a number of senators, he seems to have been closest to Harry Byrd (D-Virginia). Byrd was always a penny-pincher on budgetary matters, as was George. Both men felt that the government should pay its bills and not waste money. Moreover, he and Byrd were key figures in the so-called Conservative Coalition after the war.[35] Byrd had been a newspaper editor, but his great wealth came from his apple orchards. He was the largest individual apple grower in the nation, raising a million bushels a year, 1 percent of total US production.[36] To trim spending, the two men worked not only with each other but also with the Republicans to cut spending. Since often there were several liberal northern Republicans who would vote against spending cuts, the Republican leadership needed the fifteen or so Southern Democrats that Byrd and George could sway.[37] In general, George, Byrd, Eugene Milliken of Colorado, and Taft of Ohio,

[32]Anderson, *Outsider in the Senate*, 98.

[33]For an example, see *CR*, 80/2, 875.

[34]R. B. Troutman, Sr. to Morrison, July 1, 1968, in Morrison, *Governor O. Max Gardner*, 189.

[35]Caro, *The Years of Lyndon Johnson*, 148–49.

[36]Donovan, "Senator George," 33.

[37]Mark Dunahoo, oral history, 55, Russell Library.

frequently joined by Tom Connally, were the "core of most of the opposition" to Truman's Fair Deal.[38] Their ties to Byrd are manifested in the fact that when the Republicans regained control of the Senate, they asked Byrd, a nominal Democrat, to remain as chair of the special committee to watch non-essential spending.[39]

George liaised with the Republicans, but Georgia's Dick Russell was regarded as the leader of the Southern bloc, which was cynically called "Dick Russell's Dixieland Band." It is well known that the Southern states wielded undue influence because in the absence of the two-party system in the South, the same people continued to be returned and hence had the seniority to dominate committee chairmanships. In 1957, although the South had only 28 percent of the population, a large portion of which was black and had little or no say in politics, Southerners chaired eight of the fifteen standing Senate committees and twelve of the nineteen in the House.[40] On the Finance Committee, which George chaired, four of the six top members were Southern Democrats, as were four of the six Democratic members of the Agriculture Committee. The Southerners usually were able to determine the assignments within the party.[41]

George remained basically a loyal Democrat, and he always supported the national ticket even if he did not always vote with its senators. He campaigned for the national ticket in every election, even though he generally opposed many aspects of the candidates' program. When in 1956 John Bell Timmerman, governor of South Carolina, made noises about forming a third party after the Democratic Convention, George wrote to him to say that such things would be "suicidal." He added, "We certainly cannot expect to have a persuasive voice in the party if we withdraw therefrom.... Such a course seems to be unwise...as has been demonstrated in the past."[42] He did, however, place what he considered the good of the country over that of the Democratic Party, but when the Republicans tried to strengthen the Taft-Hartley Act in 1954, he united the Democrats against the Republican amendments, for which the party was grateful, since it needed a victory out of the Republican Congress.[43] Many of his actions seemed to smack of *lèse majesté.* George expressed pleasure at the Republican gains in the 1950 elec-

---

[38]Carl Marcy, oral history, 68–69.

[39]U. S. News, June 6, 1947, 50–52, cited in Wilkinson, *Harry Byrd and the Changing Face of Virginia Politics*, 65.

[40]"Senators Byrd and George," 51.

[41]Ibid.

[42]"Senator George, Who Is Saying 'No' to President on Tax Rise," 42.

[43]"Senators Byrd and George," 50.

tions because he felt these victories "will serve to check the unnecessary spending by the administration."[44] In his Jefferson-Jackson Day speech, delivered, of course, to a solid Democratic audience, he praised President Dwight Eisenhower as "a man of great industry and patience."[45] When majority leader Scott Lucas publicly criticized the Southern Democrats for not doing more to support Truman, George as the "Southern Dean, with a hoarse and shaking voice," rose to "repel this outrageous and unprovoked attack," which he called "cruel" and "without provocation."[46]

It is not surprising that, just as George mentored young lawyers on the front porch of his home in Vienna, he guided young senators when they entered the body. Mike Mansfield told a reporter that George "treats the newest of us just like his old friends," and to become his protégé was worth a king's ransom.[47] Two senators who later made great marks in American history owed much of their early success to George's patronage: Mike Mansfield and Hubert Humphrey.

Mansfield, a soft-spoken former college professor, came to the Senate in 1952, and with George's help moved up quickly. For example, George saw that the rookie was given a place in the US delegation to the SEATO (Southeast Asia Collective Defense Treaty) Conference,[48] and one of the major reasons that Mansfield was chosen Senate whip in 1957 was George's influence, or so he thought.[49]

The brash, egotistical Hubert Humphrey of Minnesota owed him even more. Humphrey, formerly a mayor of Minneapolis, had been elected to the Senate in 1948 after he had split the Democratic Party by securing passage at the convention that year of a strong civil rights plank. Never at a loss for self-confidence and always believing that he was right and everyone else was wrong, Humphrey came to the Senate assuming that he would upend the establishment and pass his left-wing agenda on everything from civil rights to socialized medicine. He once debated Senator Homer Capehart (R-Ind.)

---

[44]"The Influence of the South," Sir Harold Caccia to Selyn Lloyd, January 21, 1952, no. 15, 2, FO 371/126675, FO-BNA.

[45]Douglas, *In the Fullness of Time*, 208.

[46]"George Flays Third Party Move," clipping from the *Washington Post-Herald*, June 19, 1956, f. George, RNC papers.

[47]"George of Georgia: Ike's Friend in Need," 29.

[48]"GOP Victory to Help US, George says," *Los Angeles Times* (?), clipping, November 9, 1950, F. George, W. F., July 22, 1938 to January 1, 1955, box 331, A65-12, Eisenhower papers.

[49]*Providence Journal*, December 3, 1953, clipping, F. George, July 1922–1957, box 337, Eisenhower papers.

on the radio when Truman had fired McArthur, and was so insulting that Capehart tried to take a swing at him. He was prevented from doing so only by an aide who grabbed his arm.[50]

A greater mistake of Humphrey's early career, was a public attack on venerable Senator Harry Byrd, who chaired the sub-committee on Reduction of Non-essential Federal Expenditures. In his speech, Humphrey accused the straight-laced Virginia senator of everything from hypocrisy to nepotism. Byrd was not there to reply, which was, in itself, a serious Senate discourtesy, but other senators quickly responded, though, the first being Walter George. Rising from his front row desk and staring directly at Humphrey, the senator from Georgia told Humphrey that Byrd's committee should not be abolished because it was doing a "magnificent job," and he called the attack on him "the height of reckless irresponsibility."[51] For four hours, member after member followed George's example, walking out after attacking Humphrey, until the Minnesota senator was sitting in an essentially empty chamber.[52] Six days later Byrd spoke to defend himself and carefully and convincingly dissected Humphrey's argument, proving that much of it was based on allegations and short on truth.[53] After this mammoth indiscretion, Humphrey became a pariah. Even Vice President Barkley referred to him as "Minnesota's goddam ass."[54] For days, the president of the Senate refused to recognize Humphrey, no matter what he did.[55]

At some point after this episode, we cannot say exactly when, George and Humphrey had a conversation in which the elder senator advised him to learn to compromise. At the same time that Humphrey entered the Senate, so did Paul Douglas of Illinois. His political and economic views were similar to those of Humphrey, maybe farther to the left. He, too, wanted to see the immediate implementation of the socialist millennium, and like Humphrey, lost battles. Hubert (George pronounced it "Hoobert") Humphrey did learn from George to compromise and began winning battles; Douglas went on losing them.[56]

Humphrey afterwards openly showed great humility toward Walter George. In August 1950, he tried to close what he had considered loopholes for the wealthy in George's tax bill for that year, issuing twelve amendments

[50]White, *Citadel*, 77.

[51]Caro, *The Years of Lyndon Johnson*, 449.

[52]Ibid.

[53]Stolberg, "Buzz Windrip, Governor of Georgia," 143.

[54]Ibid., 161.

[55]Ryskind, *Hubert*, 167–68.

[56]"Humphrey and Walter George," *Parade Magazine,* August 3, 1964, 6.

that he had written after studying tax law for ten days. In an almost groveling manner, he humbly praised the senator from Georgia as "the very distinguished and able chairman of the [Finance] Committee," and then he admitted that he was no authority on tax law and that to amend a tax bill "is a new experience for me."[57] George and Milliken, the ranking Republican, interrupted him, their voices showing a touch of sarcasm; at one point, Humphrey even made Milliken laugh. All of Humphrey's amendments were defeated. A meeting between him and George after the tax bill passed unamended forever changed their relationship. George walked up the aisle from his front desk to Humphrey's back row desk, and the two men shook hands and became friends.[58] Their understanding was strengthened when George came to realize that his and Humphrey's views on world affairs were almost identical.[59] Civil rights was another matter. Once when Humphrey was holding forth on civil rights on the Senate floor, Max Kampelman, a close friend of Humphrey's, overheard Walter George in the Democratic cloakroom of the Senate talking to someone on the phone. His voice boomed out in his usual stentorian fashion: "That fellow, Hubert, Hubert Humphrey? That young fellow *really believes* what he's doing with that civil rights stuff."[60]

In 1953, Humphrey wrote a letter apologizing for not having been able to attend a birthday celebration for George because of the flu. "I know you must have a great sense of satisfaction when you look back over the many years of service you have given our country," he wrote, and then he added, "I just want you to know that I am honored at your friendship and feel privileged to be able to serve with you." George replied, "It isn't a question of agreeing on all problems: It's a question of being honest with one another and the striving toward a common end."[61]

In 1953, after Humphrey's amendments strengthened Maryland Republican senator John Butler's anti-Communist bill, which drew opposition from the ACLU, Americans for Democratic Action, and the NAACP, their

[57]Griffith, *Humphrey: A Candid Biography*, 197. Humphrey himself wrote in his book, *The Education of a Public Man*, 107, that this incident took place in 1951.

[58]Solberg, *Hubert Humphrey*, 146–47.

[59]Mann, *The Walls of Jericho*, 144.

[60]This account is a combination of the incident as Kampelman reported it in two interviews to different historians: Mann, *The Walls of Jericho*, 117, and Garrettson, *Hubert H. Humphrey*, 121–22.

[61]Quoted from the correspondence in the Humphrey papers cited in Garrettson, *Hubert H. Humphrey*, 121.

friendship was sealed.[62] George readily accepted Humphrey on the Foreign Relations Committee, with a little pushing from Lyndon Johnson.[63] By the time the Senate passed Humphrey's 1953 Agriculture Trade Development and Assistance Act, which dumped surplus crops in government storage outside domestic markets, George and he were good friends. Ever a supporter of agriculture, George wrote to Humphrey, saying, "You are certainly entitled to great credit for initiating this program."[64] The next year, George, at Lyndon Johnson's request, wrote to the *Minneapolis Star* a letter of endorsement for Humphrey's reelection.[65] George even offered to campaign for Humphrey although *Time* told its readers that he had declined the offer because Humphrey wanted a "Minnesotans campaign."[66] In 1956, he promoted Humphrey for the vice-presidential spot, along with senators Sparkman, Hill, Russell, Johnson, and Rayburn; George had even left a meeting with Stevenson thinking that he had the nomination sewed up for Humphrey, but Stevenson instead opened it to the convention to decide.[67]

The colleague with whom George was naturally associated and for whom he had enormous respect was his colleague, Richard Russell. We have already seen hints that Russell never entirely forgot George's campaign against his father in the 1926 Senate race. Of the two, George, immediately after the war, was probably the more respected and more widely known. Richard Russell was not well known outside the South, but to many Southerners, he was a mini-messiah and would become more so after his nomination for president in 1948 and especially 1952, when he actually launched a national campaign for the job. To some, George was more of a distant god-like figure to be admired from afar and outside of Georgia.[68] A story is told

---

[62]Robert Sherrill and Harry Ernst, Drugstore Liberal, (NY: Gressman, 1968), 86-90.

[63]Caro, *The Years of Lyndon Johnson*, 497; Griffith, *Humphrey: A Candid Biography*, 213.

[64]George to Humphrey, July 11, 1953, box 94, Humphrey papers, cited in Solberg, *Hubert Humphrey*, 165.

[65]Solberg, *Hubert Humphrey*, 168.

[66]"Voice of the 84th," 22. There is some indication that he may indeed have campaigned for Humphrey in Minnesota anyway. In doing so, he praised him for his moderation. Sherrill and Ernst, 93.

[67]Stevenson later claimed that he had made no such commitment to George or Humphrey (Solberg, *Hubert Humphrey*, 174–75). See Humphrey, *The Education of a Public Man*, 137 and Mann, *The Walls of Jericho*, 177.

[68]Mrs. Gladys Giddens, a daughter of a Mercer University professor, told me that when in high school in the late 1940s, she visited Washington and shook Walter George's hand. She felt that she could never again wash it. Russell inspired awe but was not regarded as a deity. Professor Ben Tate, a retired Macon State University professor, told me that when he was a student at the University of Georgia, he had to escort Russell to a speaking engage-

that someone from Vienna came to Russell at his home in Winder to get help with a problem. When asked by Russell why he did not go to his neighbor, Walter George, Russell said, "Well, I wouldn't dare bother the senator with a problem like this. After all, he is *the* senator, and you didn't bother *the* senator with something as minor as that."[69]

Senate colleagues and people outside the Senate seemed to agree that no state was better represented than Georgia. Senator John McClellan of Arkansas had said repeatedly at home and even on the Senate floor how Georgia was "the most represented state" there.[70] When he was being interviewed on Russell, Senator James Eastland praised George by saying, "I think that when Dick was here that Georgia was the best represented state in the union with both George and Senator Talmadge."[71] Francis Wilcox considered the George-Russell pair "the best team in the Senate."[72] There are many such expressions of high confidence in the Georgia senatorial team.

Both men were often mentioned as candidates for majority leader. Senator A. Willis Robertson suggested to George that he run for the job, adding that if he would not do so, it should go to Richard Russell. George made it plain, as he had in the past, that he would not accept the position; in a formal letter he encouraged Russell to be a candidate. In another letter to Russell in 1948, he suggested that his colleague be put forward for the position of Democratic leader now that Alben Barkley was ascending to the vice presidency. "I am suggesting that all of us from the South ought to give most careful consideration to the Senate," George wrote, "in view of issues which we certainly know will face us [he is probably speaking of civil rights]."[73] Willis Robertson, a great admirer of both men, wrote to Russell the day before George did to suggest Russell's candidacy, but at the same time seeming to defer to George. Expressing the admiration he held for Russell, he said that for majority leader, he would be for Russell "first, last, and always, if you want the position." He added, however, "Both of us, of course, would be for Senator George, if he wanted the honor…."[74]

The job of majority leader ultimately went to Senator Scott Lucas of Il-

---

ment. Russell arrived in a car driven by a woman in hair curlers (his sister). Russell exited the vehicle and approached Tate, who told me, "I knew I was in the presence of greatness."

[69]Glen and Marie Wilson, oral history, 11, Johnson Library.

[70]*CR*, 84/1, 12574.

[71]James O. Eastland, oral history, 7, Russell Library.

[72]Francis Wilcox, oral history, 123, Eisenhower Library.

[73]WFG to Russell, November 5, 1948, VI-B, box 33, f. 8, Russell papers.

[74]A. Willis Robertson, November 4, 1948, VI-B, box 33, f. 8, Russell papers.

linois. Noting that Richard Russell was the leader of the Conservative Coalition, Humphrey recalled that even though Senator Lucas, who acted as though he were in charge, "always checked any important or controversial question with Russell, or in his absence, with Walter George."[75] Lucas's habit merely underscores the power of both men.[76]

Regarding Georgia, both senators worked together for things for the South in general and Georgia in particular. *US News* told its readers in 1954 that in matters that concerned their region, George "largely makes policy," which is usually "translated into action by his Georgia colleague, Senator Richard Russell, an aggressive and resourceful parliamentary tactician."[77] Neither of them liked Harry Truman, but they did not hesitate to go to the White House, hat in hand, to ask for favors for Georgia.[78] George went in July 1946 over the question of a river and harbors bill,[79] but he and Russell went together many times on other matters.[80] Sometimes they disagreed on some matters, such as judgeships, but often they blindly endorsed the work of the other.[81] Once George, very busy with his own legislation, heard that Russell had some important bill coming up for a vote. He went over to Russell on the Senate floor and said, "Dick, they tell me you've got a little bill coming up this afternoon. Now tell me about it." The "little bill" was a $750 million pay raise for servicemen. Russell gave a two-minute synopsis of it, and on that alone, George agreed to support it.[82] One bit of cooperation between the two men was to have national implications: Their promotion of the career of Senator Lyndon Johnson. Because of the support of these two giants, Johnson moved up quickly in the Senate hierarchy. Two years after entering the upper chamber, Johnson became the majority whip, largely because of the support of George and Russell. They supported Johnson, and

---

[75]Humphrey, *The Education of a Public Man,* 93.

[76]Jean Daridan, the chargé d'affaires at the French embassy in Washington, wrote the ministry of foreign affairs in Paris in 1953 that Richard Russell, as leader of the conservative Southern Democrats, was the dominant personality among them (Daridan to Schuman, June 8, 1953, Etats Unis: politique intérieure, Within Amérique: Dossier Générale: Rélations Franco-Américaine [America: General File: Franco-America Relations], 1952–1963, 170, AMAE.

[77]"How a Democrat Guides Republican Tax Policy," 63.

[78]Roy V. Harris, oral history, 31, Russell Library.

[79]See memo Dr. John R. Steelman to WFG, November 29, 1946, f. WFG, general file, Truman papers.

[80]See requests to see the president, January 19,1948, box 537, f. PPF 1913, Truman papers.

[81]S. Ernest Vandiver, oral history, 76, Russell Library.

[82]Chandler, *Natural Superiority of Southern Politicians*, 329.

he became minority leader in 1953 and then majority leader in 1954. In the Senate, Johnson's desk and George's desk were side by side; immediately behind George was Richard Russell. Their promotion of Johnson became solid when he organized the defeat of Leland Olds, the chairman of the Federal Power Commission, early in his Senate career. Using smear tactics worthy of Senator Joseph McCarthy, Johnson implied that Olds was a communist. Since most of the Senate liberals were boycotting Johnson's speech, "the two giants from Georgia," George and Russell, looked at each other and without speaking left the chamber to corral a number of senators to produce a crowd. After Johnson finished his oration, George approached him and said, "I've never heard a more masterful speech against a nomination." The partnership of the triumvirate was sealed.[83]

Their support would lead to the presidency for Johnson. Given their conservative views, neither Russell nor George could have become the first Southern president, but both men saw that Johnson might. Johnson, in effect, used both men shamelessly. Later, George was on his deathbed when Lyndon Johnson was walking a pathetically weak civil rights act through the Senate to boost his credentials on that issue. Russell had acquiesced, in part, because the bill was so insipid that to the South it meant little danger. Although voting against it, Russell helped behind the scenes to get it through, thinking that Johnson would be an anti-civil rights president in the White House.[84] Feeling really deceived after Johnson was in the White House and was pushing civil rights, Russell pointedly refused to campaign for him in 1964.

What there was of a George-Russell friendship continued to be somewhat one-sided. In January 1951, George presided over a dinner of Georgia quail and wild rice, hosted by Governor Herman Talmadge in the Mayflower Hotel, to honor Russell's elevation to the chair of the Armed Services Committee.[85] That same year, George endorsed Russell for president and was one of the major Southern leaders to support him and encourage him to make a run.[86] George further supported him when he spoke at a luncheon of fifty or sixty people urging Russell to run. Spence Grayson was there and called it "one of the most beautiful speeches…that I ever heard in my life."[87]

---

[83]Caro, *The Years of Lyndon Johnson*, 248–303.

[84]Thurmond, oral history, cited in Goldsmith, *Colleagues*, 45.

[85]H. Talmadge to Hon. Hugh Peterson, January 10, 1951, f. "Talmadge, Herman (governor and senator) and Mrs. Talmadge, 1949–1950," Peterson papers, Russell Library.

[86]*New York Times*, June 28, 1951, 24, cited in Potenziani, "Look to the Past," 36.

[87]Spence Grayson, oral history, 33, Russell Library.

George also helped raise money outside the South for Russell's candidacy.[88]

The greatest service that he performed for Russell's campaign was making his nominating speech at the 1952 Democratic Convention. Russell went to Chicago thinking that he still had a chance in spite of the cool reception he had encountered everywhere outside of the South. Texas governor John Connally recalled, "They thought that Walter George could work a miracle." George tried to make Russell seem much like a mainstream liberal Democrat. Over the din on the floor of the convention in the International Amphitheater near the Chicago stockyards, George called Russell "a president who believes in equal opportunity for all, equal education opportunity, equal economic opportunity, [and] equal political opportunity." Anyone who had the vaguest knowledge of Russell's position on race could probably not maintain a straight face as George spoke. He also asserted that his Georgia colleague believed in "the common brotherhood of man."[89] Yet George's stentorian voice could not be heard over the buzz of the delegates as they talked inattentively with each other.

Following George's nominating speech, here was a twenty-minute demonstration composed only of Southern delegates and Lyndon Johnson, but Stevenson had already won the nomination, and Russell received only five more delegates (268) than he had won in 1948, when he had just allowed his name to be placed in nomination.[90] On the second ballot, there began a stampede for Stevenson, and it was all over. If Russell ever had any serious yearning for the presidency, this failure ended it. He was always going to be regarded as a regional candidate, although Senator Robertson of Virginia felt that the good that had come out of the candidacy was the driving of Truman out of the race. In a letter to Walter George, he said that Russell's effort was "needed to convince Mr. Truman that he should not run," and that was "a major contribution to what I hope will now be a definite trend to the right."[91]

Both George and Russell sulked in their tents during the campaign. In a meeting with Russell, the nominee had left him with the impression that he opposed the change of the cloture rule in the Senate, the major tactic the

---

[88]Ibid., 35.

[89]In the Winder files of Russell's papers is a copy of the speech inscribed to "Mrs. Ina Dillard Russell—the great mother of a great son, Senator Dick Russell—great in victory—great in defeat. He will always bring pride to you. Sincerely, Walter F. George." Goldsmith felt that George's speech signaled the end of the discord over the 1926 election, but it is not clear that that is the case (*Colleagues*, 28).

[90]Fite, *Richard B. Russell, Jr., Senator from Georgia*, 294–95.

[91]Robertson to WFG, August 14, 1952, General Correspondence, Robertson papers.

South had to stop civil rights legislation. When Stevenson had spoken to accept the Liberal Party nomination in New York, he had publically said otherwise, so Russell would not campaign for him. He believed that Stevenson would win the election, and therefore the question of cloture would come up immediately in the Senate in 1953. He wrote Macon journalist Joe Parham in October that his not campaigning would leave him "in a stronger position" to defeat efforts to modify the rule.[92] The *Union-Register* in Milledgeville took both senators to task for not supporting the national candidate. In an article titled, "Georgia Senators Should Back Party," the editors praised Representative Carl Vinson for speaking for Stevenson, but it concluded by saying, "We wish Senator Russell, especially, and Senator George, too, had stood by the party that has made them great."[93] Even without their help, Stevenson carried Georgia with the biggest percentage he received in any state. It would be two more presidential elections before the "Ma-daddy-was-a-Democrat" crowd would either die out or begin to switch their political allegiance, and Georgia would vote for a Republican presidential candidate.

In the postwar years, Walter George remained firmly at the helm of the nation's finances as he had during the war, recognized as "an outstanding expert on taxation," as his colleague Senator Edward Martin of Pennsylvania called him.[94] Encomia came from everywhere. Virginia Senator Robertson called him "the ablest man in the Senate"[95] regarding tax law. When Henry Morgenthau, Jr., left his post as secretary of the treasury in 1945, George was seriously considered, but the desire to have George as treasury secretary was not, however, by any means universal.[96] Even the Detroit Post Veterans of WW II requested that he not be named.[97]

George was always looking for ways to reduce the budget and cut waste from it, because he felt that only when budgets were cut could taxes be cut, and he always favored both measures. With the end of the war and its gigantic cost, he thought that taxes could then be cut as well. Indeed, after the

---

[92]Russell to Joe Parham, October 10, 1952, Series VI, G1, box 153, f. 6, Russell papers.

[93]"Georgia Senators Should Back Party," n. d., clipping, Series VI, box 152, file 2, Russell papers.

[94]*CR*, 81/1, 5941.

[95]Ibid., 80/1, 3163.

[96]"Senators Byrd and George," 52.

[97]Letters, April 21, 1945, 66, f. WFG, general file, Truman papers. In the file, there were letters of support but other letters were in opposition. One, from one H. B. Shafer stated that "it would be a crime to appoint Senator Walter George as treasury secretary of state [*sic*]" (H. B. Shafer to President Truman, June 7, 1945, f. WFG, general file, Truman papers.

Germans surrendered, but the Japanese were still fighting, George called for an immediate reduction, reflecting the reduced need for revenue. Even his great friend and supporter, Senator Robertson, recoiled at the prospect and wrote President Truman asking that the wartime rates be maintained.[98] As late as 1954, George was even willing to cut appropriations to NATO, which he called "a vast expenditure."[99] He had expressed the view in the late 1940s that only a one-term president could successfully cut spending, something he would discover not to be true in election year 1956.[100] In August 1946, he said that the present rates on personal income and corporation taxes would continue because "the budget is very high—entirely too high—and we must therefore raise as much revenue as we possibly can raise," and it would probably be 1948 before a tax bill "of a constructive nature" could be passed. The only event that could throw his predictions "out of kilter" would be for a number of tax cutters to be elected in November 1946. That might result in a "quickie" bill to be enacted by mid-1947.[101] As it turned out, the Republicans gained control of Congress in the elections that fall, and in 1947 the Republican Congress, after talking about a 20 percent across-the-board cut, finally passed a 30 percent tax cut for incomes under $1,000, with gradual lessening reductions to 10 percent on incomes above $302,000.[102] George supported the bill, and his support made its passage certain, but when it reached President Truman's desk, he vetoed it.[103] Everyone expected a budgetary surplus by 1948, so the Republicans tried again in late 1947. The bill had George's general support, but ever cautious, he warned his colleagues that it would be unwise to act until they knew definitely what the expected surplus would be. Generally acknowledging that to sustain the economy, tax rates must be greatly reduced, but he argued that it was unwise to do as the Republicans wished until it was known how much the surplus would be. Congress would be making a great mistake, he pointed out to cut taxes blindly, "knowing that it will not be able to restore the old rates whatever happens."[104] George, who, as the reader is aware, favored paying the nation's bills and who had even advocated during the war a federal sales tax

[98]A. Willis Robertson to Harry S Truman, May 17, 1945, Gen. File, f. WFG, Truman papers.

[99]*CR*, 83/2, 13036.

[100]*Washington News* clipping, May 25, 1948, f. George, July 22, 1938–, box 337, RNC papers.

[101]*New York Times*, August 5, 1946, 12:5.

[102]Hartman, *Truman and the 80th Congress*, 75–76.

[103]Ibid.

[104]*CR, 80/1, 5593.*

so that the 9,000,000 untaxed Americans would pay something toward its cost, told the press that it would be unwise to cut taxes until it was "obvious that the budget can warrant such action."[105] When the Republicans introduced a bill providing for $4.5 billion budget cuts, George supported it, telling his colleagues, "I would enthusiastically support a larger cut...if I believed it were possible."[106]

In fall 1947, the government was indeed running a surplus, and the Republicans' second tax bill passed the House by a whopping 302–112, a veto-proof majority. George, Byrd, and Johnson of Colorado supported the bill, and it passed the Senate by 60–32, with twelve Democrats siding with the Republicans. Truman vetoed it as he had promised, and the veto was sustained with 57 to override to 32 against it.[107]

In spring 1948, George again worked in tandem with the Republicans to lower taxes. The budget of 1948–1949 included a cut, which George supported. Senator Robertson, who as a member of the House had served on the Ways and Means Committee, asked George on the floor of the Senate if "we could take care of the essential functions of government and make the tax reduction proposed in the 1948–49 budget?" George replied in the affirmative. "In my opinion we can," he told his colleague. "I do not believe there is any question regarding a surplus in the fiscal year 1948 and in the fiscal year 1949, so that we could make out obligations," and expressing opinion characteristically heard from politicians only when the public seemed inclined toward fiscal responsibility, he added, "if a shortfall seemed eminent, I would advocate a tax increase to maintain a balanced budget if things warranted it. I am committed to that course."[108] He also advocated removing from the tax rolls some seven or eight million people.[109]

Reinstatement of the wartime excess profits tax as a revenue measure was advocated in 1948 by left-leaning politicians, who saw corporations making vast profits from the consumer spending that had been pent up during the war, when there was nothing to buy. George had led its repeal in 1945 at the war's end, and now George fought its reinstatement.[110] The reader is aware that he always championed business, especially small business, and a restoration of this tax would, he felt, cripple business in general.

---

[105]"Senators Byrd and George," 50–52.
[106]*CR*, 80/1, 1425.
[107]Hartman, *Truman and the 80th Congress*, 96.
[108]*CR*, 80/2, 3163.
[109]Ibid., 3162.
[110]Ibid.

"Corporations cannot be made to earn profits in peacetime, if the profits are all to be taken from them in taxes," he told his colleagues. Postwar growth, which had been phenomenal, was indeed due to the repeal of the excess profits tax in 1945.[111] If profits were to be taken from business, he argued, corporations would find some other way to waste its income rather than "turn the money over to the tax collector."[112] When the Democrats took the Senate in 1948, George resumed his chairmanship on the Finance Committee, and any restoration of the excess profits tax was doomed.[113] In August 1950, when the excess profits tax measure reared its head again during the Korean War, George did not oppose it but did his best to soften its blow. He criticized it as "double taxation," which he felt was "fundamentally wrong." The bill he saw through committee provided that one half of the excess profits would be taxed normally.[114] He shared the view of Senator Flanders, who believed that taxing excess profits was "one of those bright, shining liberal tags which appeals to the ordinary voter."[115] When the excess profits tax was repealed at the end of the Korean War in 1953, George gave a summary of his view on all taxes in reply to Senator John Williams of Delaware, who wanted to eliminate it only for small businesses. On excess profits, he thundered at his colleagues, "The excess profits tax never has been a good tax; it is not a good tax now, and we cannot make it an equitable tax, try as hard as we may.... Who is being hurt by heavy taxes?" he asked his colleagues rhetorically. "Is he [*sic*] not the individual? Is he not the little men? Unreasonable high taxes do but one thing: They crucify the middle class. The excess profits tax does but one thing: It tends to crucify small businesses organized in corporate form." He argued, however, that relief must first be given the small taxpayer. The corporations would simply "have to wait until we can also do something for the small taxpayer, for the little individual."[116]

By 1949 George concluded that the recipe for a balanced budget was cutting spending, and he recommended a cut of 5 percent in both domestic and foreign-aid appropriations. Domestically, the cut would come from administrative costs, and a price decline permitted a cut of 5 percent in foreign operations. Truman wanted to balance the budget by raising taxes and pro-

---

[111]Ibid., 3159.
[112]Ibid., 3162–63.
[113]Abels, *Out of the Jaws of Victory*, 282.
[114]*CR*, 81/2, 13943.
[115]Ibid., 16807.
[116]Ibid., 83/1, 8871–72.

posed a tax increase in fiscal 1949; George wanted to balance it by cutting spending. As *US News* explained, "The George-Truman argument is this: The president wanted to spend much and tax much; Mr. George wants to spend less and tax less."[117] George was convinced that a tax increase at that time, when inflation was abating, would give deflationary forces a heavy impetus.[118]

In January, when Truman had first proposed a tax increase, and had been unclear about just what brackets to raise, George had suggested, that if they must be raised, half of the increase should be derived from corporate tax increases.[119] By February 1949, however, George moved to a hardline position against any tax increase, noting that the business boom of the past four years was cooling, and a tax increase at that point might push the country into a recession. He advocated waiting into fall the fiscal year to see how much was needed. In contrast, Speaker Sam Rayburn called for one at that moment because "we must keep out of the red."[120] By April, George was giving the president a flat "no" on a tax increase.[121] The economy had slowed so much by late summer that George was calling for tax cuts in all areas in the tax work in 1950, mainly by giving reductions in the lower brackets. Such a cut would increase incentives and "would, I think, result in an expansion of business." Furthermore, he advocated increasing corporate taxes while eliminating the tax on dividends, which he saw as double taxation. He also advocated accelerated depreciation and a tax credit for salaried income. He wanted the wartime excise taxes repealed at once, not piecemeal, and a reduction in the holding period for capital gains. He did advocate the increase of social security taxes from 1 percent to 2.5 percent by January 1952.[122]

The year 1950 saw George leading a broad campaign to lower the corporate tax. Total tax on individuals in 1950 was $22 billion, while corporation taxes netted $19 billion. If the present expansion of corporate taxes continued through 1951, he argued corporations would be paying more than individuals, even after the cutting of the 95 percent World War II rate back to 72 percent. George called this level "extremely high,"[123] and demanded its reduction. In August 1950, he also attacked the capital gains tax, noting that

[117]"Senator George, Who Is Saying 'No' to President on Tax Rise," 42.
[118]Ibid., 39, 42.
[119]*New York Times,* January 14, 1949, 1:6.
[120]Ibid., February 15, 1949, 1:7, 2:6.
[121]"Senator George, Who Is Saying 'No' to President on Tax Rise," 39.
[122]WFG, "Why Taxes Must Be Cut," 32–35.
[123]*CR*, 81/2, 16807.

it was producing little revenue because "people could not afford to sell." When the length of maturity was cut for the first time in years, revenue began coming in from capital gains tax.[124]

Much of George's work, though, was undone by the Korean Conflict. The war started in summer 1950, and President Truman called on George and the Congress to increase taxes to cover the increase in military appropriations. He also urged George to rescind the tax cuts he had approved.[125] Later that year, Truman called for the reinstatement of the wartime excess profits taxes, a request to which George was receptive.[126] In January 1951, George endorsed the pay-as-you-go approach, which he called an "absolute necessity." The fighting in Korea and needed rearmament should be paid, he felt, "as far as possible," out of incoming revenues, "and that means increasing taxes," he told reporters, adding, "Any other course [i.e., borrowing the money] would be extremely dangerous." As usual, he asked for a proportional increase on all taxpayers, regardless of income.[127]

On January 9, 1951, he proposed a new bill to increase taxes to finance the war. The proposal had been born in a meeting of Walter George, House Ways and Means chairman Robert Doughton (D-North Carolina), and John Snyder, secretary of the treasury. Amazingly, they did not know for how much Truman would ask, but their best guess was $7 billion. Doughton hoped to begin work on the bill itself on February 1. George told the press that taxes would be raised all along the line, adding, "Even a sales tax at the manufacturing level is on the table." This proposed tax would probably not be included in the bill, he added, but it was brought into discussion so that the staff would have data available should it be seriously considered. Apparently, Truman had made the very unpolitic statement that the situation required "taxing until it hurts."[128]

So, when in February 1951, Truman called for a $10 billion increase, with an additional $6 billion request likely later in the year, George balked. George questioned the advisability of passing two tax bills in one session, since there would not be time to discuss the possibilities of cutting nondefense spending. The next day the House demanded a detailed hearing, which would delay an increase for months. Meanwhile, there were biparti-

---

[124]Ibid., 13684.

[125]Harry S Truman to WFG, July 25, 1950, box 700, f. Of 137, Truman Papers.

[126]WFG to Harry S Truman, November 17, 1950, and Harry S Truman to Robert Doughton, November 14, 1950, copy to WFG, box 700, f. OF 137, Truman papers.

[127]*New York Times*, January 4, 1951, 1:3, 24:1.

[128]Ibid., January 10, 1951, 1:2.

san efforts to cut non-defense spending by $9 billion.[129] A third bill was coming, the third since the conflict had begun, that would provide for moneys exceeding by $21.5 billion, the highest revenue collected in any one year of World War II. George became severely alarmed. “I am concerned that we have already reached the point of diminishing returns,” he told his Senate colleagues. “I believe “that any further increase in income tax would not only discourage the taxpayer…but will also encourage business to become extravagant, wasteful, and inefficient.”[130] In September 1951, George shepherded Truman’s third tax bill through the Senate, providing for an increase of $5.5 billion (which got trimmed to $5.4 billion). It would be George’s last, and he clearly was not pleased with himself. He told reporters that the Truman administration was using the measure of higher taxes to fight inflation.[131]

In January 1952, George, feeling that the American people had had enough, stated publicly that they would “accept no excuse if the new administration had not balanced the budget in a manner by enacting reductions in taxes.”[132] In an article in *Look* in January 1952 titled “Higher Income Taxes will destroy a Large Segment of our Free Society,” George opined that “higher taxes would impair our productive strength and add to inflationary pressure.” Usually higher taxes dampen inflation, as he himself had noted, so it is unclear what he was thinking. He observed, “It is the highest tax burden in our history, and it is considerably higher than economists believe can be carried by a private enterprise economy.” Citing Britain as “a tragic example,” he said that the British economic decline is what happens when the middle classes are ignored in authorities’ “scramble for taxes to support swollen government.” He stressed the importance of giving individuals incentive, noting that is “how we have always done it.”[133] He introduced this theme in an article for the *St. Louis Post Dispatch* in which he told a reporter: “I believe that we have reached the safe limit of our taxable capacity and that

[129]Ibid., February 4, 1951, 27:3.

[130]*CR*, 82/1, 115970. Mathew Wall, chair of the Committee on Taxation of the American Federation of Labor, wrote Truman (and sent a copy to WFG) that the committee considered the tax increases “inadequate, inequitable, and poorly considered in view of the current economic situation” (Mathew Wall to Truman, March 5, 1951, f. WFG, general file, Truman papers).

[131]*Los Angeles Times*, clipping, September 20, 1951, f. WFG, July 22, 1938–, box 337, RNC papers.

[132]Daridan to MFA, 9 January 1953, Etats Unis: politques intérieure, 177, AMAE.

[133]*CR*, 82/2, appendix, 368.

higher income taxes will destroy a large segment of our free society."[134] Since the Republicans gained control of Congress in the 1952 elections, George again lost his chairmanship on Finance. In an interview with the newspaper in Vienna in December 1952, he expressed confidence that there would be tax relief "in the next year or two." At the very least, he felt, the Korean War tax increases would be repealed. He favored lowering the corporate taxes and the planned-expiration of the excess profits tax, but keeping current rates for all categories, individuals included. Later individual tax cuts should be done in such a way as "to equalize and readjust those tax rates so that they will be fair and equitable on all classes." As always, he called for the reduction of expenditures.[135]

By the following summer, he wanted to do something for the individual income tax payer in 1954. He noted to the press that the 11 percent increase at the start of the Korean War was due to expire in January 1954, but the Eisenhower administration was running a deficit with the current tax rates and that the Republican Congress would offer "considerable opposition" to raising the debt ceiling. George supported a continuation of the excess profits tax, which he had opposed in the past, as a way of making up the difference.[136]

By February 1954, however, as the economy continued to slide into a recession, and with the steel industry operating at only 65 percent capacity, George introduced a tax cut in the form of an increase in the personal exemption and for dependents to $800.00 for the 1954 tax year. Then he called for the reduction or even elimination of excise taxes. Colin Clark, a noted economist, had expressed the opinion that to avoid a depression, Congress must reduce taxes by $20 billion.[137] By March, when it was known that the Republican tax bill did not call for a cut to put more buying power in the hands of individuals, he proposed to raise the figure of $800 to $1,000.00 deductible.[138] In 1955, when House Speaker Sam Rayburn forced through the House a $20/head income tax cut, George opposed it as being too much, and all of Lyndon Johnson's legislative prowess could not save it. In what *Time* called a "humiliating defeat in the Senate," it lost by six votes because of George's opposition.[139]

---

[134] *St. Louis Post Dispatch*, clipping, February 6, 1952, f. George, July 22, 1938–, box 337, RNC papers.

[135] "Sen. George, Finance," 34–36.

[136] *Vienna News*, July 30, 1953.

[137] *CR*, 83/2, 2039.

[138] *Vienna News*, March 18, 1954, 1.

[139] "Voice of the 84th," 22.

With the Democrats' regaining control of Congress in the 1954 elections and George's resumption of the chairmanship of the Foreign Relations Committee, this *démarche* was Walter George's swan song on finances. He had always maintained the position that a "government can confiscate [only] once," but it could tax forever if it provided a financial climate to foster the growth of business, which meant an increase in employment, hence an increase in tax revenue. This position was always coupled with the idea that a government had an obligation to pay its bills without going into debt during ordinary times; hence he occasionally called for tax increases to cover deficits. How different that mentality is today as these lines are written.

George's tax policies always reflected his strong support of business because he had always felt that, if business prospered, so would everyone else. There would be jobs and money to spend. This attitude has had its ups and downs since George's time and is generally belittled by the those who assert that too many CEOs do not reinvest in employees or in creating new jobs but instead reward themselves with more pay. He feared the potential postwar economic slump that he knew would come when the government stopped spending money. We have seen that he especially feared the national debt that the war had brought. Moreover, there would be the veterans who would have to be cared for, the largest number in American history, and he told reporters that two generations would pass before the peak of the burden would be felt.[140] He would not know, of course, that in addition to Korea, there would be Vietnam, Iraq, and Afghanistan. A prosperous business community would be the only way to finance it all, and for the rest of his career, he continued to press for the pro-business legislation that he had supported all of his life. When Ohio's senator Robert Taft, "Mr. Republican," immediately started trying to dismantle the government controls that had been imposed in wartime, and he had the enthusiastic support of Walter George and other Southern conservatives.[141]

One of George's first acts at war's end in 1945 was to try to curtail the power of the newly appointed secretary of commerce, former vice president Henry A. Wallace. Roosevelt had not retained him on the ticket in 1944, but as a consolation prize, Wallace was given the cabinet post. Wallace was a well-known anti-business radical leftist idealist, and the *Baltimore Sun* called his appointment "a heavy blow at business confidence." As part of his job, Wallace would have the responsibility of liquidating billions of dollars of industrial property. He had, as secretary of agriculture, initiated the policy

---

[140]*Vienna News*, August 16, 1945, 3.
[141]Patterson, *Mr. Republican*, 260.

of getting farmers to plow under alternate rows of cotton and corn to try to raise prices. Now the *Sun* said he was going to "plow under quite a substantial amount of private enterprise."[142] Business interests especially did not want Wallace's controlling the lending powers of the Department of Commerce.

George immediately swung into action. He introduced a bill that separated the Commerce Department and the Federal Loan Administration to take lending out of Wallace's hands. George testified before the Commerce Committee on his bill and received a standing ovation. George's bill passed the House by a whopping 400–2 and the Senate 74–12, both veto-proof majorities. As it turned out, George's bill probably saved Wallace's candidacy because the Commerce Committee voted 15–5 against Wallace's nomination. Without his controlling the money, the Senate then confirmed him by a vote of 56–32 on March 1, 1945.[143] Wallace remained as the secretary of commerce until Truman fired him in 1947.

In January 1947, George lost a lot of his influence because, as we know, the GOP had gained control of the Senate in the 1946 elections, and he lost the Finance chairmanship. This change was made all the worse because Georgia lost four other chairmanships, including Russell's chair of the Immigration Committee and Carl Vinson's chair of Naval Affairs, which he had held longer than any other man.[144] George and the others regained them after the upset 1948 elections, and George resumed wielding his enormous influence on the government's business policies. He was active in promotion of foreign trade.[145] He argued that in order for other countries to buy our products, we had to buy theirs, so that they would have the dollars to purchase American goods. In a Senate speech in September 1949, however, he made a curious argument, noting that we were selling twice the amount of goods abroad than we were purchasing, a favorable balance of trade which had been unknown to the United States for decades.[146] "In order to sell, we must buy," he told the Senate, arguing that in order to discontinue gifts to Europe, we had to give Europe the power to buy by purchasing their goods. His logic seems a little shaky, especially when he attacked those who were calling for tariffs at a time when we were selling more than we

[142]Timmons, *Jesse H. Jones*, 360.
[143]Ibid.; Littell, *My Roosevelt Years*, 363n.
[144]*Vienna News*, November 7, 1946, 1.
[145]*CR*, 81/1, 12618 ff.
[146]Ibid., 12616.

were importing.[147]

The postwar years saw George continuing to help constituents with the smallest requests, even forwarding unopened letters to the White House, but he also did services for corporations, such as helping Eastern Airlines get flights into Mexico.[148] He led delegations to the White House for various objectives and promoted the Clark Hill Dam on the Savannah River. Starting in 1947, he began working for an appropriation for it, increasing the funding from $40 million to more than $68 million.[149] Calling it "a defense project," since it would service the "one of the largest hydrogen bomb plants in the world being constructed in the Savannah Valley."[150] George was mistaken when he said it made hydrogen bombs. It merely made heavy water, but it was good for his constituents, whatever it manufactured. When his reelection was looming in 1956, he continued to harass the White House to try to jump-start the project.[151] When visiting the White House in February 1955 to discuss the question of routes for Eastern Airlines, he lobbied for it again.[152] In the same time but of smaller importance, he joined Herman Talmadge in dedicating the Savannah Electric and Power Company's riverside power station in 1949.[153]

George also joined Richard Russell and Carl Vinson in bringing in military money for Georgia, and in his position on the Finance committee, he always championed military spending in general, with as much as possible being funneled into Georgia. He also used an argument for this spending that he would use again and again: Namely, that the US should support its allies with arms because it was cheaper to have them do much of the fighting abroad in the Cold War. As always, he was the vets' champion. When General Omar Bradley wanted to deny the GI Bill to farmers, George was in the midst of the fray. George made "an impassioned plea" to prevent Bradley's view from prevailing, and farmers were included. In an address, Congressman Pace gave George the credit: But for the skilled and effective work of Senator George, it is doubtful that this training would have continued for farm veterans."[154]

[147]Ibid.

[148]J. J. Parlo to President and leaders of the U. S. A., August 17, 1949, 1949, Truman papers.

[149]*CR*, 81/1, 14763.

[150]Ibid., 82/2, 9711.

[151]Eisenhower, *The Eisenhower Diaries*, 292.

[152]Ibid., 295.

[153]Unidentified clipping, October 8, 1949, f. WFG, Peterson papers.

[154]Addresses of Congressman S. Pace, 4, RCB-5804, box 14, f. WFG-GSA.

As always, George did whatever he could for Georgia farmers in particular. In the tight demand days after the end of the war, when there was often a desperate struggle to obtain consumer goods due, George and his friend Congressman Pace had lobbied and gotten in August 1946 for Georgia peanut farmers nine additional carloads of nails. Both President Truman and the Secretary of Agriculture had promised them to Georgia before George left Washington after the end of the congressional session, and after he arrived in Georgia, he kept their feet to the fire, seeing to it that the farmers would get them.[155] He championed rural telephone service at the end of the 1940s the way he had worked to establish the REA during the New Deal.[156] In 1950 George was pushing for the abolition of the penalty on a farmer for exceeding his peanut allotment. Excesses beyond the allotment were used for making peanut oil; any other use resulted in a stiff penalty. Since the oil sold for only 14 cents a pound, however, it was not worth it to sell one's allotment to be crushed for the oil. A profit for the farmer, because of the penalty, could be made only if the excess was sold at the market price.[157] Then in 1952, serious drought plagued thirty-five Georgia counties, George championed assistance, mainly in the form of hay for cattle, and Truman declared these counties a disaster area.[158] In 1954, when farm prices were declining and Ezra Taft Benson, the secretary of agriculture (and someone, like George, who advocated laissez-faire) was doing little, George joined others in calling the farmers a "neglected" group.[159]

George was active in a minor way in the momentous Taft-Hartley Act of 1947. The Wagner Act of 1935 had been responsible for, among other things, the so-called "closed shop," which required a worker to be a member of a union in order to be hired for a job. Strikes by unions during the war created a strong anti-union sentiment throughout the country, and it propelled the strong anti-union bill sponsored by Senator Robert Taft of Ohio. The bill abolished the "closed shop" and made legal the union shop, one in which someone did not have to be a union member to be employed but a new employee had to join soon after employment. Moreover, it did include a provision that in a secret ballot the union shop could be voted out in favor of the open shop. It also allowed states to pass "right to work laws," which stat-

[155] *Vienna News*, August 15, 1946, 1.

[156] *CR*, 81/1, 13869.

[157] Ibid., 2119, 2379.

[158] WFG telegram to Harry S Truman, August 25, 1952. Truman declared these counties a distressed area (Matthew J. Connelly to WFG, August 28, 1952, box 1286, OF 431, Truman papers).

[159] Parmet, *Eisenhower and the American Crusade*, 323.

ed that a worker did not have ever to join a union to work for a "unionized" company.

George joined his friend Harry Byrd to try to toughen Taft's bill. His efforts would be one of his few defeats in the Senate. He introduced an amendment to ban totally the union shop; it was defeated 57–21. He introduced an amendment to place limits on industry-wide bargaining. That failed 44–43.[160] He tried to pass an amendment to allow private individuals the right to seek injunctions against secondary boycotts and jurisdictional strikes, but his efforts here failed as well.[161] Truman vetoed the bill but curiously did not make a strong effort to have his veto sustained. He simply stated his reason for opposition to it and asked for no commitments from members of Congress.[162]

One of the Democrats to vote to override was, of course, Walter George. In June 1947, just before the vote, George addressed his colleagues. "Mr. President," he told the chamber, "I voted for this legislation when it came before the Senate. I voted for the conference report, and I shall have to vote to override the president's veto." He reminded the Senate that he had voted for the Wagner Act of 1935, so he was not casting an anti-labor vote, but he felt that the current bill eliminated some of the abuses of the Wagner Act. "I do assert that if there is to be any labor legislation in America, if we are to bring about any degree of balance in the unbalanced condition which has existed for almost twelve years, now is the time to act," he said. He might have added that at this point the mood of the country was anti-union, but that mood might not last. He also might have included the fact that there was a substantial Republican majority in Congress, and such corrective legislation could never be passed by a democratically controlled one. He made it a choice of whether the people of the United States would be allowed to function through lawmaking bodies or "whether organized minorities are to control and dictate the legislation which we must now have." He tried to argue this legislation was not anti-labor, a definite stretch of the imagination, but was designed "to break the stranglehold of labor bosses."[163] The override of the bill passed the Senate by a 68–25 vote, in which 48 Republicans and 20 Democrats (17 from the South, two from Maryland, and one from New Mexico) opposed 22 Democrats joined by 3 Republicans (William Langer of North Dakota, Wayne Morse of Oregon, and George

---

[160]Heinemann, *Harry Byrd of Virginia*, 254.

[161]Hartman, *Truman and the 80th Congress*, 85.

[162]Ibid., 89.

[163]*CR*, 80/1, 7536.

W. Malone of Nevada).[164]

The Democrats regained control of Congress in the elections the next year, and Truman not surprisingly tried to repeal Taft-Hartley. When queried on the matter, George told a reporter, "I certainly will never vote the law off the books. I am, [however], perfectly willing to entertain *reasonable* [his italics] constructive comments, but repeal—no." He stated that Taft-Hartley had "done a great service" and that "it certainly has not hurt labor," again another stretch of the imagination, and he added that going back to the Wagner Act, as Truman wanted, would be a "bad mistake."[165]

The late forties saw a continuous flood of awards, honors, and praise come George's way. In 1949 he received the Distinguished Service Award of the American Legion. Because of Marcus's death, he was already a Gold Star father, but this medal was quite an honor because it was rarely given. The commander of the American Legion praised George as "a tried true and trusted friend of every righteous cause to which the American Legion has dedicated its efforts," and the reader is certainly aware of George's work on behalf of veterans from his first arrival in the Senate in the 1920s.[166] He likewise received a number of honorary degrees from prominent universities such as Emory, Brown, Columbia and Georgetown, plus several from his own *alma mater*, Mercer College.

Truman's first administration, or rather the large fragment remaining after Roosevelt died, was generally a disaster from a number of standpoints, and many Democrats hoped to replace him with a more electable candidate in 1948. The Republicans were generally licking their chops at the prospect of winning the presidency for the first time in twenty years. Many Southern Democrats wanted to remove Truman for his civil rights stands, and there were already rumblings of a third-party movement that eventually blossomed into the so-called Dixiecrat movement. Ironically, there was even a move among the Democrats to draft Eisenhower, but he refused largely because Truman as his commander-in-chief told him to stay out.[167] One name that came to be mentioned as a candidate, especially among Southern Democrats, was Walter George.[168] Certainly by today's standards he would probably be thought too old at seventy, his age in 1948, but age was not as great

[164]Hartman, *Truman and the 80th Congress*, 90.

[165]*Vienna News*, January 20, 1949, 1; Congress did repeal the electoral provisions of the Union shop in 1951.

[166]Address of Congressman S. Pace, 5, RCB-5804, box 15, f. WFG-GSA

[167]Clark Clifford actually drafted his refusal (Egerton, *Speak Now against the Day*, 479).

[168]*Atlanta Constitution*, August 5, 1957, in RCB-5804, box 1998–1980 A, f. WFG-GSA.

a factor in presidential elections then as it would be today. Strangely, given Talmadge's opposition within a decade, Herman Talmadge asked George in March 1948 to permit his name to be placed in nomination at the Democratic Convention, but George declined twice. Although he was later to have doubts, he felt that Truman's renomination was assured at the same time, but he unquestionably felt that Truman would be defeated in November.[169]

George's relations with Truman had been formally polite, but they were not by any means warm. In September 1945, Truman had written in his diary an echo of Roosevelt's re-alignment efforts of 1938, that "there should be a real liberal party in this country[,] and I don't mean a crackpot professional liberal one." He felt that the conservatives in the Democratic Party should "openly join together in real opposition," and he included Walter George among those who should get out and join Taft and his like.[170] When George's father died in 1948, Truman expressed his condolences on the death of Mr. George, "rich alike in years and honor."[171] On a dinner cruise the previous year aboard Secretary of Defense James Forrestal's yacht, the *Sequoia*, George expressed his warm personal feeling toward the president and regretted openly that Truman was not closer to his old colleagues in the Senate.[172] In 1948, however, George and Russell were among the most vocal calling for Truman not to run.[173]

The Dixiecrat movement began in the spring, appearing at first to be a tectonic political shift that would destroy the Democratic Party in the South.[174] Although none of the US senators from the South attended the Dixiecrat convention in Jackson, Mississippi, George was mentioned as a possible presidential candidate several days before the States' Rights Convention in May 1948.[175] Mississippi governor Fielding Wright, a prime figure behind the movement and its eventual vice-presidential candidate, announced that if they did not extract concessions on the question of civil rights from the Democratic Party, he would support either Walter F.

---

[169]"Senator George Will Be Willing," March 29, 1948, f. George, July 22, 1938–, box 337, RNC papers.

[170]Truman, *Off the Record*, 68.

[171]Harry S Truman to WFG, June 18, 1948, PPF, box 537, f. PPF 1913, Truman papers; WFG's reply of June 22, 1948, appears in the same place.

[172]Duffield, ed., *The Forrestal Dairies*, 292–93.

[173]Egerton, *Speak Now against the Day*, 479.

[174]For the best work on the Dixiecrats, see Frederickson, *The Dixiecrat Revolt and the End of the Solid South*.

[175]Abels, *Out of the Jaws of Victory*, 99.

George or Governor Strom Thurmond of South Carolina for the presidency.[176] When the convention assembled in Jackson on May 10, there was still talk of George, Byrd, and Russell, but the Georgia delegation withdrew and remained only as observers.[177]

George avoided the rebellion. He suggested, however, that the Georgia Democratic Party should withhold Georgia's electoral votes in a "ransom account" to extract concessions from the national party.[178] In fact, in January 1949, after Truman's victory, rumors flew about in January 1949 that both George and Byrd would withhold their respective states' votes unless Truman capitulated on civil rights. Byrd came out to say that these talks were only rumors and that he opposed any such measures because it violated "honor and good faith."[179] In fact, the whole movement had little strong support from any quarter of Congress. Claude Pepper stated that he knew of no senator who identified with the movement or admitted that he had voted for Thurmond.[180] As for George, he opposed the whole Dixiecrat mentality. He felt that Wallace's candidacy would insure the defeat of Truman and the party regulars, so all the South had to do after the election was to step in a take over the party, forcing on it "sound principles and good government."[181] Moreover, George had some sort of visceral dislike of Republican presidential candidate Thomas Dewey. In a letter to Russell, he stated that Dewey's election would present "a problem for us all," without saying exactly what that problem was. He felt that if he was elected, "We must have a strong, militant minority party,"[182] apparently already conceding the reelection of the Republican majorities in both houses.

Meanwhile, Richard Russell suggested a more active role for George late in June when he proposed publicly that Georgia should nominate George as a favorite son. George replied to Russell's suggestion by letter: "I appreciated your public statement regarding the presentation of my name to the Democratic National Convention. In my personal [*sic*], I do not think my name should be presented."[183] George did not say why, and his demurring was certainly far from being Shermanesque. The *Atlanta Journal* had

[176]Cohodas, *Strom Thurmond and the Politics of Southern Change*, 144.

[177]Abels, *Out of the Jaws of Victory*, 87.

[178]Egerton, *Speak Now against the Day*, 500.

[179]Heinemann, *Harry Byrd of Virginia*, 264.

[180]Claude Pepper, *Eyewitness to a Century*, (San Diego: Harcourt, Brace, 1989), 129

[181]Abels, *Out of the Jaws of Victory*, 25. Russell pointedly would not support the Dixiecrats (Roy V. Harris. oral history, 30, Russell Library).

[182]WFG to Richard B. Russell, June 25, 1948, VI-B, box 33, f. 8, Russell papers.

[183]Ibid.

suggested George even before Russell did in headlines announcing, "George for President."[184] This tentative draft, of course, went nowhere, and George even campaigned for Truman as the nominee.[185]

Although Thurmond received a hundred thousand votes in Georgia in 1948, Truman carried the state, which could not bring itself to vote Republican. George sent a congratulatory telegram to Truman. "Heartiest congratulations upon your most magnificent victory even against great odds," he wired from Vienna, adding, "Cordial good wishes for a most successful administration."[186] On returning to Washington in December, George made a request for a White House visit to "pay his respects" to Truman and to ask for an appointment.[187]

Soon into Truman's first full term, George and Russell virulently opposed Truman's nomination to run again in 1952, and a major reason was disagreement over civil rights. When Congress convened in 1949, there was rumbling that states that had gone for Thurmond would be punished by having choice committee assignments taken from their representatives. Such a move would be tricky because, in many cases, the second- and third-ranking Democrats were from the Deep South, and reaching that deeply into the committees could cause chaos. Nothing came of the tentative move because, George felt, both sides "wanted to forget the whole unhappy incident [the Dixiecrat revolt]." He thought the Democratic victory would only whet the liberal Democrats'—and many Republicans'—desires to push civil rights legislation. George felt that unless there was a change in Senate rules, mainly on cloture, there was no possibility for the passage of a civil rights program, with the exception of an anti-poll tax measure or an anti-lynching law.[188]

To these fears of liberal initiatives was added the annoyance of Truman's ham-handed appointment of Neil Andrews as interim federal judge in the northern district of Georgia without consulting either George or Russell. They got their revenge in August 1950 when the Senate turned down the nomination in a voice vote because Truman had violated "senatorial

---

[184]*Atlanta Journal*, June 13, 1948.

[185]Kirkendall, "The Presidential Election of 1948," 417–18.

[186]WFG to Harry S Truman, from Vienna, November 3, 1948, box 203, f. PPS 200, Truman papers.

[187]Requests to see the president, December 9, 1948, box 537, PPF 1913, Truman papers.

[188]"George is Doubtful of Income Tax Cut," November 19, 1948, f. George, July 22, 1938–, box 337, RNC papers.

courtesy."[189] Truman further stirred in Georgia politics when he made wartime governor, Ellis Arnall, director of the Office of Price Stabilization in an effort to blunt Talmadge's patronage control.[190] By 1952, an anti-Truman revolt was in full swing. South Carolina governor Jimmy Byrnes even joined Harry Byrd in speaking of a third party.[191] The main reason for opposition was Truman's civil rights program, but a further irritant was the high taxing and spending of his administration. George, Byrd, Byrnes, and Russell led the group of Democrats who wanted Truman gone and would oppose him if he would run again. Unlike the Dixiecrat revolutionaries of 1948, these dissenters were well known throughout the country. They had unenthusiastically supported Truman in 1948 because they thought he would lose. Now they were prepared to attack Truman within the Democratic Party. Their displeasure, one journalist wrote, could be "a controlling factor" on whether Truman ran or not, and their opposition had a "rule or ruin air to it."[192] As one of the "quiet bulwarks of the stop-Truman campaign," George was especially peeved with Truman on taxing and spending, but he was saying little publicly late in 1951.[193] By 1952, however, one historian points out, George was among "the most conspicuous" anti-Trumanites, and in March 1952, George criticized publicly Truman's ability to choose good people for his administration.[194] George pointed out to the Senate on March 7 that two of Truman's appointments as collectors of revenue in Missouri and Massachusetts were on trial for corruption. Truman had sent a letter to Congress asking it to approve his reorganization plan to prevent this sort of thing, and George said that his letter "is a plain confession that he is not capable of appointing clean, decent, and honorable men to fill high public office."[195]

To oppose Truman in 1952, the rebels tapped Richard Russell to make a formal campaign for president. Senator Claude Pepper called it a "protest candidacy,"[196] but Russell and his supporters did not see it that way. To Russell, it was a national campaign. He even chose Senator Edwin Johnson of Colorado as his campaign manager to make it appear not just a Southern movement. Russell had allowed his name to be placed in nomination in 1948 as a protest and had received three hundred votes at the Democratic

[189]McCoy and Ruetten, *Quest and Response*, 183.
[190]Roy V. Harris, oral history, 42, Russell Library.
[191]Pepper, *Eyewitness to a Century*, 133.
[192]"Big Guns of Southern Revolt," 46–47.
[193]Ibid., 49.
[194]Egerton, *Speak Now against the Day*, 479.
[195]*CR*, 82/2, 1984.
[196]Pepper, *Eyewitness to a Century*, 130.

National Convention, all from the eleven states of the Old Confederacy. When he waged a real campaign in 1952, he received only seven more delegates than in 1948. When Russell agreed to support the Democratic nominee after the convention, Governor Talmadge was "shocked," and Allen Ellender and others said that if Russell would not lead a third-party movement, they would find someone who would.[197]

George gave only a tepid endorsement of Adlai Stevenson, the eventual 1952 nominee, but he did raise $25,000 in Georgia for the national party.[198] George said his contribution to the Stevenson-Sparkman campaign would just be his vote; he would not campaign for Stevenson. "I do not know Governor Stevenson.... Some of his recent statements I do not agree with. But I think that on the whole I will support the ticket."[199] Eisenhower won in a landslide, bringing in a Republican Congress with him. On election night, George and his son attended a squirrel purlieu dinner in a backyard in Vienna. All were listening to returns by radio, and when it became obvious that the Republicans could control the Senate, someone asked George if this would affect his committee chairmanship. "I'll wire my resignation in the morning," he said strongly.[200] George may have been in his cups. He certainly knew that he would not have to wire in his resignation; the new Republican Senate would handle that for him.

Foreign policy was always one of George's great loves, developed in the many years he served on the Foreign Relations Committee. He had begun to make his mark in the field when he championed the formation of the United Nations, but it was in the last decade of his Senate career that he became the giant in this area, which became his legacy.[201] The *New York Times* extolled him in the late 1940s as one of the "Molders of [American] Foreign Policy." Although the paper named Vandenberg "the undisputed leader of [American] foreign affairs," it listed George as well, with Tom Connally, Alben Barkley, and Alexander Wiley. All were recognized leaders in the field.[202] It was often noted that George had never left the United

[197]Ibid. 132.

[198]"Viewing the South from Washington," 2, Series, VI-B, box 33, f. 1, Russell papers.

[199]It should be noted that even Herman Talmadge had warmly welcomed Eisenhower in Atlanta (*Washington Times*, September 6, 1942, clipping, box 337 f. George, July 22, 1938–, Eisenhower papers.

[200]Jake Gregory interview.

[201]Valeo dismissed George as not know "much about foreign policy" (Valeo, oral history, 761).

[202]*New York Times*, March 14, 1952, VI, 7:3, as evidence of the lack of his foreign policy expertise.

States, and unlike many in the field he did not go often, these junkets were rarely more than government-paid vacations for members of Congress, but his lack of foreign travel certainly did not hurt George's perception of foreign policy.[203]

George saw domestic and foreign policy as linked. "Our domestic stability is vital and cannot...be separated from our aims in the international relations field," he told the graduates of the University of South Carolina in a commencement address on June 2, 1953. America could no longer ignore the world, he observed, as George himself had advocated in the early years of his career. "It is in the field of foreign policy that we are called upon to make our most...irrevocable decisions." Noting that a half century before, America was concerned with "manifest destiny," "Today," he added, "Americans are concerned with mankind's destiny."[204] In an article on foreign policy, he expanded on this theme. Stating that American foreign policy must be positive and flexible, he insisted that "it must never be negative," or limited only to "anti-communism." To follow such a policy would leave the initiative to the communists. Potential allies must be treated as equals. "Our course of action must be positive in that it must be framed to treat other nations as partners, not pawns, in man's struggle for freedom."[205] In the early days after the war, George wrote to Truman that he generally supported his foreign policy, "as expressed by Secretary [Jimmy] Byrnes."[206] This view would change as a result of numerous Truman blunders, and not only in foreign policy. By March 1952, George would tell his Senate colleagues that Truman "is the poorest advocate of a cause, good or bad, or indifferent, that the world has ever produced," yet he continued to support the good of bipartisanship as Vandenberg had conceived it during the war and coined the term.[207] The *New York Times*, by no means a sympathizer with George's domestic agenda, wrote in 1955, "He is not merely a partner in bipartisanship but its abundant embodiment.[208] To George, foreign policy should be

---

[203]George did visit Europe in April–May 1945, but nothing is known about his trip (WFG to Harry S Truman, October 14, 1946; Truman to WFG, October 9, 1946, box 772, f. OF 204-misc., Truman papers). There is some evidence that WFG once went to Cuba in the 1930s.

[204]*CR*, 83/1, 5872.

[205]"Comments on Foreign Aid," GFR-VHPS.

[206]WFG to Harry S Truman, September 20, 1946, box 30, official file, OF 3, misc., Truman papers.

[207]*CR*, 82/2, 2163.

[208]A cynical junior Democrat sarcastically called him "the rich man's Arthur Vandenberg" (White, "Senator George, Monument Determined," 12).

directed without partisan rancor, and he was particularly proud of the way his Foreign Relations Committee conducted foreign policy in that manner. He proudly told his senate associates, on the eve of his departure from the body, "The committee on Foreign Relations displayed no partisanship."[209]

The principal foreign policy issue in the last decade of Walter George's Senate tenure was US relations with the Soviet Union. Any prescient observer of the actions of Soviet Russia during the last year of the war could have foreseen that it would cause trouble with the Allies after the end of the conflict. President Roosevelt was oblivious to this threat; Churchill was much more aware of the possibility of conflict. There was, of course, immediate absence of agreement as the Russians dismantled pro-Western governments in the Eastern European countries and replaced them with pro-Soviet puppets. Moreover, they unilaterally redrew the boundaries of Eastern Europe. The most outrageous defiance came with the Berlin blockade beginning in 1948.

Walter George, owing to his role on the Foreign Relations Committee, was immediately thrown into the struggle called the "Cold War." From the beginning, he was in favor of facing down the Russians. He agreed with Senator Vandenberg that "appeasement" of Russia was "surrender on the installment plan."[210] It would be inaccurate to label George a "Cold Warrior," however, but he felt that Russian aggression should be resisted and contained wherever possible. In 1947, he told his Senate colleagues, "We wholly misconceived the aims of Soviet Russia. Having been associated with Soviet Russia in a high military exercise[,] we naturally assumed that she shared somewhat our democratic ideas.... Events have very clearly demonstrated that...we were in error, grievously in error."

In part because of the friction between the US and the USSR, no universal peace treaty with vanquished German or Japan had ever been signed. In August of 1948, George called on the United States to sign separate treaties with the two defeated powers, ignoring Russian opposition. In a speech to the summer graduates of the University of Georgia, George predicted that Russian obstructionism would continue to block cooperation among world powers. He proposed several changes of policy. He noted that the division of Germany and Korea and the occupation of Manchuria must be considered as accomplished and irreversible facts. That being so, America should hasten to sign foreign treaties with its former enemies. The American, British, and French zones should be returned to full peacetime status so

---

[209] *CR*, 84/2, 13409.

[210] Vandenberg, *The Private Papers of Senator Vandenberg*, xiii.

that needed food, clothing, and medicines could be imported. Furthermore, it should be understood that there would be no further demands for reparations from the defeated nations. He stressed that America would help the defeated powers, but he added that Europe had to help share the burden. He expressed the view that the Soviets neither desired nor were prepared for war with the West, for America had a nuclear monopoly. He ominously suggested that if a break came between the Western Democracies and the Communist states, "we will be forced to make the supreme military effort of all time." It would be costly, but a "cost we should bear without delay." He further advocated the "rehabilitation," clearly a euphemism for rearmament, of both Germany and Japan. The productive capabilities of both peoples would prevent leaving them "as vacuums to be filled by any dynamic power within reach of them."[211] It was a clear message to the Russians from a powerful member of Congress that at least this American would stand up to Russian imperialism. By 1953, George's fear of the Russians led him to call for the rearming of Germany. He told his fellow senators that "there would be no ultimate hope without Germany of building a military force in Europe that could withstand a determined aggressive movement by the Soviet Union."[212]

In October 1947, George sounded almost bellicose in a speech to a meeting of B'nai B'rith. On the question of what America must do if the Russians left the United Nations, he said that the US must "take immediate military action [he did not specify what] on the widest scope it has even known," and he called on President Truman to call a special session of Congress to vote "stop-gap aid" for any country in Europe that was threatened by communism. While stating that America would not wish to meddle in the internal affairs of any European nation, including the Soviet Union, he felt that the United States should always be prepared "in the atomic age" to move in a defensive manner "to conserve policies to preserve freedom and peace."[213]

George seems to have been swept along, as were many others, in the Red Scare of the late 1940s and early 1950s, where people saw communists under every bush. Senator Pat McCarran of Nevada even called for the expulsion of the Russians from the UN.[214] Senator Joseph McCarthy was

[211]*New York Times*, August 31, 1947, 13:1.

[212]*CR*, 83/1, 7788.

[213]*Vienna News*, *October* 23, 1947, 1.

[214]Clipping with LBJ to Oran M. Heath, August 11, 1951, LBJ subject file, for. rel., LBJHA collection, box 68, Johnson papers.

making a career of "exposing" communists in the State Department. This hysteria was fanned by the Korean War, and when the Republicans gained control of the government in the 1952 elections, they released the "Yalta Papers," a collection of documents revealing some of the seamy aspects of the Yalta agreements, where Roosevelt seemed to sell Eastern Europe down the river. The papers were given to certain members of Congress with the admonition not to reveal their contents, a definite invitation to do so. George refused, however, to accept the copies sent to him, so that he could not be accused of being the leaker.[215] It was indeed a grim time for America; reputations were ruined, and good men remained silent. George was never one of the more rabid anti-communists, and it would be one of the many ironies of history that he would be a major actor in the twilight of his Senate career in instigating the process of detente that would be completed by the Nixon Administration.

In 1947 President Truman advanced what was called "the Truman Doctrine," a policy of supporting democratic governments threatened by Russian or other communist takeovers. The nation in most imminent danger in 1947 was Greece, locked in a civil war between the forces of democracy and the communism. Walter George became a strong advocate of the policy. On the Finance Committee, he had already supported aid to Greece and Turkey for reconstructive purposes, but he changed the reason for support to political ones. Under his leadership, the Senate Foreign Relations Committee voted 13–0 for a $400 million assistance bill, sending it to the Senate. "I deliberately place my support of this bill on the belief that it is vital to us to check Russian expansionism now," he told reporters. "If unchecked," he warned, "Russia will eventually overrun Europe, extend herself into Asia, and perhaps South America," which would be getting too close for comfort. As George saw the issue, we had a choice between "action or non-action." In the case of Greece, he warned that if Greece fell to the communists, "all the Balkan Peninsula would be under Russian control and so would the eastern Mediterranean."[216] George added a caveat: Annoyed with the British for evacuating Greece without careful consideration and creating thus a full-blown crisis that needed immediate action, he reserved for himself the right to amend the bill when it reached the Senate to postpone implementation of it for sixty days, during which time the United Na-

[215]"George's Plain-talk, a Lesson for Ike," unidentified clipping, n. d., scrapbook, LHG-VHPS.

[216]*New York Times*, April 5, 1947, 1:4.

tions could be given time to act.[217]

On March 6, however, George, the ever-vigilant financial watchdog, demanded more detail about how the money would be spent. He told a reporter that the Economic Cooperation Administration, which would manage the money, had been too vague "about where it intends to spend the dollars."[218] George must have been satisfied by what he heard because on March 13 of the next year, he supported a bill for $5.3 billion in European aid.[219]

Devised at the same time was the European Recovery Plan, more widely known after its creator, Secretary of State George Marshall, as the Marshall Plan, which President Truman signed the authorization on May 31, 1947. It called for $350 million in relief for liberated countries (Italy, Greece, Hungary, Austria, Poland, China, and the Free Territory of Trieste) to steady their economies against totalitarian takeover from either the Left or the Right. Eventually other countries such as France would join the recipients. George told the press that he did not foresee any other long-range foreign aid programs passed in that session of Congress, nor would President Truman ask for any. Vandenberg strongly supported the plan, but strangely, Tom Connally, George's close friend on Foreign Relations Committee, was not enthusiastic.[220] Tied closely to foreign aid was George's philosophy of keeping the fight "over there," the theme he would repeat endlessly. It made him a strong supporter of the NATO alliance. "If the Iron Curtain ever falls upon the shores of the Atlantic," he told his colleagues for what must have been the umpteenth time, "then the difficulties in America will be immensely increased," adding, "the safety and economic independence of our people will be very gravely threatened and circumscribed."[221] Given his place on the Foreign Relations Committee, George was a major figure in drafting the treaty, which was signed on April 5. The covenant of the treaty outlined a defensive alliance of twelve nations, with an article pledging that an attack on one would be an attack on all. This aspect of the agreement disturbed a number of important members. Some senators feared that that particular clause would draw the United States into a war that was not declared by Congress.

[217]Duffield, ed., *The Forrestal Dairies*, 260–61.

[218]*New York Times*, March 7, 1949, 7:1.

[219]Ibid., March 14, 1948, 53:4.

[220]Johnson, *Congress in the Cold War*, 22. George opposed Spain's being a recipient of Marshall Plan funds, but in the following year, he supported a loan to Spain to buy Georgia cotton (Smith, *Dean Acheson*, 16:369).

[221]*CR*, 83/1, 7789.

Having been ill, George missed a number of days of the debate. When he returned to the committee hearings, he allayed his colleagues' fears. He made it perfectly clear that the American president could not commit American military forces without the approval of Congress. George added Article 11, which stated that any assistance would be made "in accordance with the constitutional process of the countries involved." Some thought that it weakened the treaty and showed a lack of resolve, but without George's additions, the treaty probably would not have passed.[222] George, Connally, and Vandenberg held a two-hour meeting with Ernest Gross, assistant secretary of state, to smoothe out the rough spots. Vandenberg, the old isolationist turned internationalist, had opposed Article 5, but George brought him around by adding a compromise that the treaty "would neither increase nor decrease the presidential authority to use troops without congressional approval."[223] George's addition to the NATO treaty has ever since been a standard clause in all America mutual defense treaties.[224]

Funding proved a different matter. Truman asked for a very expensive military assistance program for NATO, as well as for Greece, Turkey, Iran, the Philippines, and Korea. Conservatives balked at the expense, adding to the already-costly Marshall Plan. The House voted to cut the appropriation in half, and the Senate opposition was more trouble because Senator Taft was leading the fight there. He was joined by Walter George and Harry Byrd. George felt that surplus arms from World War II would be sufficient for arming the NATO partners,[225] but Truman eventually got much that he wanted.[226] Subsequently, George reversed his position on arming NATO. Whereas he had been stingy at its founding, he became by 1952 a strong supporter of generous funding. Truman had tried to obtain a $7 billion appropriation for Western Europe in general and NATO in particular because he felt that America needed to show the Russians that it was firmly behind its allies. The House had reduced the appropriation to $6 billion. Then, General Eisenhower, the head of NATO, said that any further cuts would "cripple" the alliance. Isolationists such as Taft argued that such funding was like "'throwing money down a rat hole,' a familiar metaphor we will hear after." There followed several amendments to cut the appropriation. Many

---

[222]*New York Times,* June 3, 1949, *4:2;* Frances O. Wilcox, oral history, 219, Eisenhower Library.

[223]*New York Times,* June 5, 1949, 13:3.

[224]Donovan, "Senator George," 34.

[225]Senator George, Who Is Saying 'No' to President on Tax Rise," 42.

[226]Donovan, *Tumultuous Years,* 52.

Democrats were out of town, and George, almost alone, stood like Horatius at the bridge fighting to retain the appropriations. "Nothing less is involved in this," he told his colleagues, "than the will of free men, especially in Western Europe, to stand up and integrate themselves in a federation which is the hope of the free world." He added, "If we over cut here, it would discourage the very people in Europe we hope to encourage at the time of their greatest need." Lyndon Johnson finally came to his assistance, and the cuts were killed.[227]

George became such a strong advocate of NATO that he supported Senator Estes Kefauver's call in 1950 for it to be converted into a Free Federal Union, which would create a united federal government to which Eisenhower could report.[228] The proposal eventually drew the support of nineteen Senate co-sponsors, including a young senator named Richard Nixon.[229]

There was also much concern about American foreign policy in the Far East. Of first importance in 1945 was the future of Japan. George did not favor a "Carthagenian peace" with the hated enemy, but he also did not favor a treaty with "soft terms." Aware that the Germans were willing to fight another world war because they were not convinced they had lost the previous one, George felt that "we must make it impossible for Japan to feel that she was not conquered" and that their "military was not defeated."[230] At the same time, and probably in view of the fact that the Russians had become a menace in both Europe and Asia, he thought that it would be a "great mistake" to cripple totally Japan and Germany, with the result that they would not become once again "great producing nations."[231] When John Foster Dulles, who at that point was special assistant to Secretary of State Dean Acheson, went to Japan in 1951 to begin treaty talks with the Japanese, he made a point of meeting in secret with the Far Eastern Sub-committee, of which George was a member, to gain insight from that bipartisan congressional group. The meeting lasted for three hours. No one would state what occurred, but since by that time, the Korean Conflict had demonstrated considerable instability in the Far East, one can be certain that George's position on a resurrected Japan remained firm.[232]

---

[227]Caro, *The Years of Lyndon Johnson*, 398–400.
[228]*New York Times*, January 16, 1951, 14:2.
[229]Fontenay, *Estes Kefauver*, 329; Gorman, *Kefauver*, 72 ff.
[230]*Vienna News*, August 16, 1945, 3.
[231]Carlton, "The Record...," 6, GFR-VHPS.
[232]*New York Times*, January 13, 1951, 2:2.

The eruption of the Korean War in 1950 (the Korean Conflict, in Truman's explanation) redirected all American foreign policy goals in the Far East. Korea had been divided, along the 38th parallel, into two occupation zones, each of which became essentially a separate entity. In the south, the occupants instituted the Republic of Korea, and in the north, the People's Democratic Republic of Korea was created under a communist government. On June 25, 1950, the North Koreans attacked the South, beginning the "Korean Conflict" which eventually embroiled the United States in a war with Communist China before an armistice was reached in 1953.

As a member of both the Finance and Foreign Relations committees, George was *ipso facto* in the middle of the formation of war policy, and within a few days after North Korea's attack on South Korea, he was one of many congressional leaders invited to the White House for a briefing.[233] Immediately the White House planned to issue a National Emergency Proclamation on the Korean struggle, calling for all Americans to rally to the cause. Opinion was still divided in Congress on what to do, and given that division, George felt that the differences should be reconciled before any proclamation should be approved. He also foresaw a protracted struggle although the UN sent forces from fifteen nations to help. He believed that economic limits and a new program of taxation should be put in place to pay for the new demands on the budget, just as just as during the Second World War.[234] He hoped to keep inflation in check as far as possible and follow a pay-as-you-go policy to pay for the war. America's mentality at the time was one of "pay your bills," so the administration and Congress following his thinking on taxes.

In the postwar years, George continued to champion his policy of keeping war "over there," and one of his methods was to follow the policy of "containment" of Communist aggression. In the above-mentioned commencement address at the University of South Carolina in 1953, he gave reasons for supporting the US action there. "Had the Communists been permitted to get away with their aggression in Korea," he told the graduates, "the psychological, political, and strategic conditions for aggressive advances elsewhere would have been created. Had we not acted as we did, the Communists would have taken a vital step toward global domination." American action had encouraged "other free peoples to stand up to communist aggression." Otherwise, they "might well have concluded that there was no percentage in fighting Communist subversives…or standing up to Communist

---

[233]Truman, *Memoirs*, 2:338.

[234]Ibid., 2:425.

threats from abroad." The Communists would have then, he felt, been in the position "to tear the Free World apart, bit by bit." What would have followed would have been a "global war on their terms," and America might have found itself "fighting a battle for survival...and [perhaps] fighting it on our own soil."[235]

In January 1954, however, when the Eisenhower administration proposed a Mutual Assistance Pack with South Korea, George insisted that it be made clear to South Korea that American support was in no way intended to encourage adventurism in regard to the North. Moreover, he wished that it to be understood that the United States was not required to support South Korea if it were the aggressor. He did not offer a "formal reservation" to the treaty but instead "a purely interpretive clause" to be presented on the question. John Foster Dulles, by then secretary of state, noted that the Eisenhower administration had made it "perfectly clear [to the South Koreans] on this point" and felt that it was appropriate for the Senate to "make itself equally understood." George's insistence was the only impediment to the speedy ratification of the pact.[236]

Communist activity in Southeast Asia led to the creation of the Asian equivalent of NATO. Called at first "the Manilla Pact," in early September 1954, Dulles assembled representatives from Australia, France, New Zealand, Pakistan, the Philippines, Thailand, the United Kingdom, and the United States to form an alliance to oppose aggression "by armed attack...to meet the common danger."[237] Senator Alexander Wiley, who had lost the Foreign Relations chair when the Republicans lost control of the Senate in 1954, called for public hearings by the lame-duck Congress on November 11, 1954. After the beginning of the year, George assumed the chair on January 13, 1955, conducting first executive sessions. Open hearings were held on January 19, and on January 21, the committee voted 14–1 to report the treaty to the Senate for final action, and SEATO (Southeast Asia Collective Defense Treaty) was born.[238] Impetus to the treaty was the dramatic fall of French Indo-China (today Vietnam, Cambodia, and Laos) to communist aggression. In July 1953, George had expressed his general opposition to intervention, while acknowledging that if France were to withdraw, Indo-

[235]*CR*, 83/1, 5872–73.

[236]*New York Times*, January 14, 1954, 3.5.

[237]Address by J. F. Dulles, September 15, 1954, Asia, 1952–1963, Etats Unis, relations—Asie, f. 414, 90, AMAE.

[238]Southeast Asia Collective Defense Treaty: Report of the Committee on Foreign Relations, January 25, 1955, 3–4, Am. 1952–1963, Etats Unis, Asie, f. 414, 150–51, AMAE.

China might "fall victim to Red China," but he recognized that if the US encouraged France to stay, it might cause NATO "to fall apart."[239] Within seven months, however, when Eisenhower was publicly saying that he "could conceive of no greater tragedy than for the United States to become involved in an all-out war in Indo-China," and senators Russell and John Stennis of Mississippi advising that the US should avoid involvement there, George had become a militant hawk. In February 1954, he said publicly "that if the situation in Indo-China becomes very much worse, the US will have no alternative but to send troops." Two months later Dien Bien Phu fell to the communists.[240] He agreed with Eisenhower's fear of "danger," but he believed that if the French departed, the Chinese would enter in force. The only action that could prevent this disaster would be for America to send a "sizable number of men over there," but in a masterpiece of understatement, he added that to do so "would bring on real trouble."[241] Although noting in February that Eisenhower did not have the right to send troops into Vietnam, George and Senator Wiley called for US help to prevent the absorption of Southeast Asia "into the Communist Empire."[242] George called it a "turning point in the history of collective security against communist aggression.[243] What followed is a well-known story. The French left and we replaced them, slowly but surely.

George's greatest concern and interest, however, lay with America's closest ally, Great Britain, and in general, the English-speaking nations. They would, he thought, be the cornerstone to the world's security in the post-war future. In a 1945 speech praising the United Nations, he said, "The great English-speaking peoples…certainly have a great contribution to make in the setting up of the political machinery, the organization to which the world may confidently look for a better day."[244] These "English" nations would be the linchpin that would hold the UN together. He was, though, concerned chiefly for Great Britain itself. The war had wrecked the British economy, and in the austerity that followed, Britain struggled to survive. In championing economic support for the UK, he told his Senate colleagues, "If Britain goes down, we will go down, too, in a matter of months…. If

[239]*CR*, 83/1, 7788–89.

[240]Fren. Wasl to Foreign Office, February 13, 1954, no. 78, FO 371/109100, FO-BNA, British National Archives.

[241]*New York Times*, February 11, 1954, 6:4.

[242]Bonnet to MFA Georges Bidault, 3 February 1954, Amérique, 1952–1963, relations Ex. Avec Asie, f. 414, 11–12, AMAE.

[243]Ibid., May 20, 1954, 50.

[244]WFG, "International Law," 688.

sterling takes a real decline...perhaps it will not be Britain alone that will decline. It will be other countries as well."[245]

In December 1945, Secretary of State Jimmy Byrnes held a dinner party to discuss British financial problems in general and a loan to Britain in particular. In addition to cabinet members such as Dean Acheson, he invited senators George, Connally, Kenneth McKellar, Henry A. Wallace, Vandenberg, Wagner, and others. Senator Connally was convinced that if the US lent money to England, it must loan money to Russia as well; to do otherwise would mean war with Russia. Moreover, he noted that England could not repay the loan, so any money "loaned" would in reality be a gift. George, whom Wallace felt was "a little tight," vehemently and harshly disagreed with Connally but urged not only a loan but also one larger than planned. Probably the fact that he had drunk too much led George to be uncharacteristically brutal with his colleague, but it demonstrates his sympathies for the British. Acheson told someone after the party that he "never saw such a stupendous ignorance in his life as that displayed by the assembled senators."[246]

George's support of Great Britain did not include support of the Israeli state, which was, immediately after the war, a British problem, one of which they would quickly rid themselves. In a letter to President Truman in 1946, George cautioned against becoming involved in the Palestinian question and the formation of a Jewish homeland. "I seriously question the advisability of American intervention in the Palestine picture," he told the president. He then suggested that the "problem is one for the United Nations Organization."[247] In an attached letter, Truman wrote to George, "I have no intention of attempting to assume the British responsibility in Palestine."[248]

By 1949, however, George had cooled in his enthusiasm for direct aid such as loans. In 1945, the British had elected a socialist government, an economic philosophy which was condemned by the senator. In a speech to graduates of the University of Georgia, he said, "If the British people expect aid from America, they must be willing to dig coal. Austerity is not a substitute for production."[249] In these oblique criticisms of the British, George seems to be objecting to the British government's socialist policies. The Labour (i.e., Socialist) Party had gained power in 1945 and had implemented

[245] *CR*, 81/1, 12617.

[246] Blum, *The Price of Vision*, 526–27.

[247] WFG to Harry S Truman, October 14, 1946, box 772, f. OT 204-misc., Truman papers.

[248] Ibid., October 17, 1946.

[249] *Vienna News*, September 4, 1947, 1.

socialist welfare programs as well as the nationalization of British coal and much of its big industry. George felt that most of these programs paid the workers not to work, and that that sort of economics was an anathema to Walter George.[250]

Britain was still in a bad financial state, a condition caused, he believed by its being "a high cost producing country," and it had "steadily...had priced herself out of the world's markets in which she formerly played a heavy hand." Socialism was not his only complaint. Observing that its colonies were "a heavy drain now," the cost of empire was a factor, he thought that "she had got to bring costs down; no one else can do it [for England]." He felt that "charitable aid," one presumes loans that we knew that the British could not repay, would be "to the English people themselves a decided disservice."[251] More acceptable would be legislation such as the Trade Agreements Act, which would increase British foreign trade."[252]

George's earlier support for Britain does not seem to have gained him much lasting favor with the British leaders, just as his shepherding Lend-Lease through the Senate did not gain him any recognition from the British diplomats and Whitehall. Neither did his post-war efforts in their behalf gain him much recognition. His *volte face* on the British certainly did not do anything to improve his standing with them. In January 1953, he was invited to the British Embassy for "a late cup of tea" with Prime Minister Churchill, but he was joined by all of the congressional leaders of both parties. Later that evening, when Churchill hosted a dinner for President Truman and the wartime leaders, George was not on the guest list.[253]

In those years, the job of a Senator or congressman was still considered only a part-time job, so the Georges often spent a large part of the year back in Vienna. This change did not always mean a relaxation of his pace; in fact, for George, who generally avoided the Washington social scene, it meant an increase in social activity. In 1946, the Georges returned to Vienna in April, after having stopped off in Atlanta for a few days for George to get a physical examination. It showed nothing wrong of "a serious nature." From there, he planned a trip to go fishing in Florida.[254] For Mrs. George, returning to Vienna meant a whirl of parties and teas like the one thrown for her by Mrs.

---

[250]Ibid.

[251]*CR*, 81/1, 12763.

[252]Ibid., 12615.

[253]*New York Times*, January 8, 1953, 3:4.

[254]*Vienna News*, April 18, 1946, 1.

G. N. Guest in May 1946.[255]

For George, it was usually a sequence of local speaking invitations. When he came home after the adjournment of the 80th Congress in July 1947, he had Heard came home as well, presumably preceded by Mrs. George. The Senator told the local press that he hoped "to get as much rest as possible," but he had already accepted a number of speaking invitations around the state, most important to him being to address the summer graduates of the University of Georgia on August 30. He had refused an invitation to attend the Inter-American Conference in Rio de Janeiro because he wanted to spend the time in Georgia "studying questions of interest to the state." Like all politicians, George reminded the people at all of these engagements of the bacon he was bringing home, as in his legislation aiding forestry interests and various dam and waterway proposals, including a Brunswick harbor project. He gave generously the Republican majority credit for "their cooperation," which helped make these appropriations possible.[256]

George often spoke to relatively small groups that many politicians would be reluctant to address, and he tried to bring big names to small town events as well.[257] He invited Clinton Anderson, the US secretary of agriculture, to Vienna's Lupine Festival. Anderson did not come owing to "pressing business," the standard reply when a politician does not want to go somewhere; he sent Norris Dodd, the under-secretary of agriculture.[258] Moreover, he used personal events to broadcast his political message.

On his seventy-fifth birthday in January 1953, he used the occasion to send a message to the nation. He expressed the view that the country was then in "semi-darkness" because of Korea; but as usual, he added a positive, optimistic note to his observations. For instance, he stressed the opportunity of making peace with the Soviet Union, an initiative he had hoped to see before the end of his present term. He noted that Eisenhower could use his first state of the union address to outline a policy for the new administration in regard to the Far Eastern conflict. He knew that all would be looking for clues on how the president would "shorten the war [in Korea]" as he had promised in the 1952 election campaign, noting that "communist groups" are in a "state of concern" about what his administration would do.[259]

---

[255]Ibid., May 9, 1946, n.

[256]Ibid., July 31, 1947, 1.

[257]E.g., the Irwin County Pioneer Families' meeting (ibid., September 28, 1950, 1).

[258]Ibid., March 23, 1947, 1.

[259]*New York Times*, January 30, 1953, 11:2.

Honors from his home state continued to be numerous. Saturday, June 10, 1950, was designated in Vienna as Walter F. George Day, when the bust of him was unveiled in the town square in honor for his work on vocational education.[260] In 1949 the local Legionnaires gave him the Legion Service Award[261] although he had never served in the military. When honors were bestowed on his deceased son, they were instead a tribute to George himself. The Vienna American Legion Post was named for Lt. Joseph Marcus George, and the University of Georgia designated a building "George Hall" in honor of Marcus.[262] Eisenhower wrote Senator George a warm letter stating that the naming of the building must be "a great consolation for you," opining that the naming "will recall to many thousands of US Navy men his service and his sacrifice for [his] country."[263] As before, there were recommendations that George be nominated for the Supreme Court.[264] He was also named to for the board of the Smithsonian Institution.[265]

The greatest honor given Senator George in that period, however, was naming Mercer College's (today Mercer University) law school the Walter F. George School of Law. Since his days on the Georgia Supreme Court, he had maintained an interest in his alma mater, and in October 1921 he joined trustees T. E. Ryals and E. T. Holmes to formulate a program for university development. Their work resulted in a plan for raising $250,000 for a college dining room for 500 students and for refurbishing the library, chapel, and heating plant.[266] Although the information about his later efforts for the college is skimpy, it seems he maintained a keen interest in the college during his years in the Senate, and the reader will remember his fond references to it in his campaign speech that he gave over and over in the 1938 race. His loyalty was rewarded when a committee, which included his fishing buddy T. Baldwin Martin, approached him in 1946 about naming the law school in his honor. He was reluctant at first but finally agreed when he was told that it would make raising money for the school easier. The announcement was to be accompanied by the launching of a $1 million fundraising cam-

---

[260] *Vienna News*, June 15 and June 22, 1950, 1.

[261] Ibid., December 8, 1949, 8.

[262] Ibid., October 23, 1952, 1.

[263] D. D. Eisenhower to WFG, December 16, 1954, box 943, f. 347, central files, PPF, 343, Eisenhower papers. In 1947, Richard Russell and Congressman Pace introduced a bill to name the Americus veterans' hospital for Marcus (*Vienna News*, January 9, 1947, 1).

[264] Emory F. Dean to D. D. Eisenhower, October 25, 1954, box 76, f. 4-A-2, central files, George, Walter, Eisenhower papers.

[265] *CR*, 82/1, 437.

[266] Dowell, *A History of Mercer University*, 271.

paign, to which a number of George's wealthy supporters would be encouraged to subscribe.[267] Robert W. Woodruff and Hughes Spalding, with a few others, raised almost half of the sum themselves.[268]

The trustees announced the name change formally on April 8, 1947, before a large gathering in the Willingham Chapel. Federal Judge T. Hoyt Davis read the resolution to the crowd, which included a number of Georgia's congressmen, with the most distinguished guest being US Supreme Court Justice Frederick Moore Vinson, who was given an Honorary Doctor of Laws degree.[269] The school would be housed in the newly built Ryals Building, still standing on the campus today.[270] Mrs. Spright Dowell hosted a reception after the ceremony, and the Macon Bar Association held a dinner that evening at which Walter George was the featured speaker.[271]

The next year, he was the principal speaker at the First Law Day, and five years later, a $2 million law center was planned as an adjunct to the school, to be called the Southeastern Law Center.[272] Its purpose was to improve "law, government, and administration of Justice," particularly at the local level, to promote research for marketing in the southeast, and to offer lectures and law seminars. The foundation to support it was incorporated by a former student, Charlton Ogburn, of New York City, with Judge T. Hoyt Davis, Walter F. George, and of course T. Baldwin Martin as permanent trustees.[273] The institution never materialized. One of the oldest living members of the law faculty only faintly remembers having heard something about it, and T. Baldwin Martin's son had only hazy recollections of having heard about it. That amount of money would have been hard to raise in 1952, and the institution apparently just did not gain adequate support.[274]

This postwar decade also saw Walter George's last election. The county unit system was still in full vigor and would still be for five years after his

---

267Ibid., 353.

268Woodruff continued to be generous with the law school, at one point giving the sum of $15,000,000.

269*New York Times*, April 18, 1947, 22:3.

270*The Mercer Cluster*, April 18, 1956, 3.

271*Vienna News*, April 12, 1947, 1.

272Dublin attorney Jules Greene, himself a graduate of the law school and editor of *The Cluster* in his undergraduate years, told me recently that he ran an editorial cartoon in the paper of President Dowell (with dollar marks for eyes) watching the sign with the new name of the school being placed on the building. I was unable to find it.

273*Vienna News*, June 12, 1952, 1.

274Email conversation with Mercer law professor Joseph Claxton, December 2014, and a phone conversation with T. Baldwin Martin, Jr.

death.[275] Moreover, not all the counties had the secret ballot because each county had the option to use a secret ballot or not, and only about 80 of the 159 counties chose it. When a poll manager was asked if he favored a secret ballot, his reply was, "Why, hell no! I think you oughta know how some of these lying sonsabitches voted."[276] In 1948 only Fulton County (Atlanta) had voting machines, and it was estimated that in 1948, 30–40 percent of all votes in the state were bought. (One observer noted, "Why, those people can make more money selling votes than they can farming."[277]) When the county units system was challenged in the courts in 1950, the Northern Georgia Federal District court ruled 2–1 affirming the system. George was pleased with the decision, telling a reporter that the court found "the only logical conclusion that could have been reached."[278]

Then there was an issue of the poll tax. At this time, North Carolina, South Carolina, Georgia, Florida, Louisiana, and Tennessee had abolished it, leaving Texas, Alabama, Mississippi, Arkansas, and Virginia as the only states that maintained the tax. When in 1953 ten Southern Democratic senators surprisingly sponsored an amendment calling for the abolition of the poll tax in federal elections, Walter George was one of the ten who supported it. Richard Russell, who remained hostile to black advancement to the end of his life, was not one of the sponsors. Senator Spessard Holland had led the drive to abolish the tax and would have done so sooner, but with so many Southerners were on the judicial committee, he felt that it would be impossible to get it through. With the Republicans controlling Congress in 1953, Southerners' power was reduced, and he felt that they could not stop it.[279] Unfortunately, however, it would be another decade before it would pass.

George indicated in September 1949 that he would again be a candidate for Senate. The announcement was intended to squelch the rumors going around the state that he would not run, but his statement had a certain weakness to it. He said in a letter to the United Press that he would "likely" seek reelection "if his health remains good." He added that he would make a formal declaration at the end of the next Congress. It had been reported in the *Macon Telegraph and News* less than two weeks earlier that "a

[275]The eight most populous counties contained slightly over a million votes (a third of the state's population) but had only 11.7 percent of the voting power (Kytle, "A Long, Dark Night for Georgia?" 57).

[276]Ibid., 59.

[277]Ibid.

[278]*New York Times*, April 18, 1950, 1:5.

[279]*New York Times*, January 24, 1953, 1:5 and 10:8.

source high in state politics" had said that Governor Talmadge would seek George's Senate seat in 1950.[280] George's announcement stopped the rumors, and if Governor Talmadge had planned to run, it stopped his campaign as well. George won in a landslide in June 1950.[281] His election in 1956 would have the eerie feel of these events with a different outcome.

The decade after World War II saw the extensive American involvement in "foreign aid," such as the Marshall Plan, mentioned above. George's advocacy of it in time would be a major factor in his undoing. As John Carlton remembered, "[George] has not—and never has been— 'for' or 'against' foreign aid as such. He has been—and is—for foreign aid when it is directly and specifically designed to accomplish an objective which he conceives to be in the national interest." Then he added, "He has been...against foreign aid when it appears not to have been carefully thought through...[or only] roughly defined."[282] When the Republicans regained control of Congress in 1946, they made cutting foreign aid one of their cost-saving measures. Both George and Harry Byrd sided with the Republicans, but he was on the losing side, and he eventually voted to pass the bill.[283]

Whereas he supported the Marshall Plan, he felt that military aid to much of Western Europe would be a waste of money. Such peoples would be unable to resist Russian invasions, so the weapons would ultimately fall to the Russians. The only way rearmament would be safe would be to arm West Germany because it could resist Russian aggression, but arming the Germans would be "provocative" toward Russia. He did favor the $500 million in weapons pledged to NATO but no other, and he made a distinct difference between military aid and the Marshall Plan, opposing Truman's attempts to cut it.[284]

George did, however, support Truman's notion of "peace through disarmament," as he expressed it in a speech to the UN General Assembly in October 1950, and he joined a number of his Senate colleagues, most of them liberals, to ask Truman for some "definite proposals."[285] When in 1951, a movement started to allow the military greater choice in determining its troops size, Senator Wayne Morse moved to stop it. George strongly

---

[280]*Vienna News*, September 8, 1949, 1. See also the article in *Vienna News* on November 24, 1949, 1.

[281]For details, see *Vienna News*, June 29, 1950.

[282]Carlton, "The Record...," GFR VIIPS.

[283]Hartman, *Truman and the 80th Congress*, 119.

[284]*New York Times*, March 20, 1950, 3:5.

[285]Harry S Truman to Senator Flanders, February 26, 1951, General File, f. WFG, Truman papers.

supported Morse not because he feared military aggrandizement but because such action would give military authorities a blank check. As Finance chair, he did not want to fund military expansion that Congress had not approved: "If [in matters of military size] the Congress is not to assert some authority, then I think we have arrived at a tragic point in our history."[286]

By 1952 George seemed to be inconsistent in his views on foreign aid and associated subjects and was losing his enthusiasm for all foreign "giveaways." Senator Paul Douglas moved for a blanket cut in foreign aid of 12.5 percent because much of the previous appropriation had not been spent, and George moved in May 1952 to cut a further billion dollars from the foreign aid bill though he favored allowing the president to shift aid around if appropriations had been unspent. George observed, "However, when there is flexibility, and 10 percent can be taken from one item and applied to another...I think the objection to an overall cut is overcome to some extent," he argued to his colleagues. He felt that cutting foreign aid would send a bad message and "discourage the people in Europe whom we hope to encourage at the time of their greatest possible need."[287] That same year Taft and the Republicans, led by Senator Herman Welker of Idaho, proposed similarly to take seemingly indiscriminant whacks at the foreign aid budget, though many believed the US had "already poured...dollars down a rat hole and [we] still are losing people by the millions to communism." George rose in the Senate to oppose the cuts, which he did, as historian Robert Caro wrote, "saying in majestic, organ-like tones," that "if we over cut here, it would discourage the very people in Europe we hope to encourage at the time of their greatest need."[288]

By 1953, however, George seemed to have cooled on all foreign aid, telling President Eisenhower that he had "voted for the last time for foreign aid," a threat he never did carry out, but he did work for hard cuts.[289] Later in the year, he opposed additional mutual security assistance when the current bill would expire in July 1954. He stressed that he would not necessarily be opposed to "some foreign aid," but he felt, and seemed to argue against his argument of the previous year, i.e., that European nations knew that the current act expires and would therefore should not be disturbed by it. He said, "I am only serving notice...that in so far as I am concerned, the law will not be extended after the fiscal year which begins today." He felt that "if

[286]*CR*, 82/1, 1992–93.

[287]Ibid., 82/2, 6025.

[288]Caro, *The Years of Lyndon Johnson*, 398.

[289]*Vienna News*, August 8, 1957, 8.

after seven years of large appropriations...from the United States they are not on their feet, they never will be."[290] In the eleven years after the end of World War II, we had spent $52 billion for such funding as aid to Greece. He noted in 1956 that we had given $41 billion in gifts and $11 billion in loans, of which $3 billion had already been paid back with interest. This amount has cost every American $30.00 per year.[291] These facts seem to bother him, and it is curious that they did, since his alleged support for foreign aid largely contributed to costing him his Senate seat in 1956.

In the 1940s and early 1950s, George's own electoral successes are little more than footnotes. He had won easily in 1944, with 100 percent of the vote in the general election (272,541 votes with no opposition).[292] This scenario was almost the same case in 1950 when he garnered 261,290 votes.[293] This figure was 82.5 percent of the vote in the primary against two unknown opponents, one of which was the perennial candidate, Albert Cobb of Savannah, whose only campaign issue was that George had made "a Republican speech" when dedicating the Savannah electric power plant.[294]

The presidential election in 1952 brought no surprise in Georgia, which gave Adlai Stevenson the highest vote percentage he received in any state. The election had, however, cracked the Solid South, whose blind allegiance to the Democratic Party, regardless of the issues, had more than once saved America's liberal party and would so again as late as 1960. Perhaps the Southern states that had "deserted" to Eisenhower had forgotten Reconstruction, but in these states, important local Democratic leaders endorsed, or at least sent signals, for Eisenhower (Jimmy Byrnes in South Carolina, Allan Shivers of Texas, and Harry Byrd of Virginia, by pointedly not endorsing Stevenson).[295] It is, however, highly unlikely that even an open endorsement of Eisenhower by both George and Russell, which would never have happened, would have lured Georgia in that day from its Democratic moorings. Georgia would not leave the Solid South for another decade.

---

[290] *CR*, 83/1, 7768.

[291] WFG to Edward H. Reynolds, March 21, 1956, GFR-VHPS.

[292] Dubin, *United States Congressional Elections*, 558.

[293] Ibid., 586.

[294] Clipping, December (?) 1949, in George, Sen W. F., 1949–57, Petersen Papers. I was generously permitted access to these papers before they had been completely sorted by the archivist of the Russell Library, Ms. Tuten, so some of the documentation may differ. Bartley and Graham state the total as being 569,624 (Bartley and Graham, *Southern Elections*, 94).

[295] "Myrick cites reasons for Ike Victory," unidentified clipping, n. d., series VI-B, box 33, f.1, Russell papers.

In 1954, the GOP lost control of both houses of Congress, introducing only the third time in forty years that the party in the White House did not have control of Congress.[296] Sir Roger Makins, the British ambassador, reported to his government that ten of the fourteen chairmanships in the Senate and fourteen of the nineteen in the House have gone to "conservative Southern Democrats." He opined that "their conservatism is as reactionary and their foreign policy more international than those of the men they have supplanted."[297]

What Senator Hubert Humphrey had called the "unholy alliance" (the Conservative Coalition) gave Eisenhower the support he needed, with Walter George being one of the more pronounced heretics to the liberal Democrats. *US News* told its readers in spring 1954 that "Senator George is hardly…a party man…. In fact, he has opposed official Democratic policy more often than he has supported it."[298] In early 1955 Eisenhower and George formed a partnership that would last until George left the Senate two years later. In December 1954, Ike wrote to a friend of the "splendid Southern senators" with whom he would be able to work. Among the list was Byrd, Stennis, Russell, and Holland, but he named George first among equals.[299] In writing to a friend in 1954 on the question of "greatness," he said that of Americans he had known "personally," George Marshall as possessed "more of the qualities of greatness than has any other," adding that Senator Vandenberg "came close." Then he said of Walter George "*in his prime* [my emphasis] I think that Senator George likewise did so."[300]

Although George became a major player in Eisenhower's first term, there are indications that the two men never became that personally close. Bob Woodruff, the Coca-Cola king, who had a great deal of influence with George, frequently went to George at Eisenhower's request; Ike did not go directly to the senator.[301] At times when George planned to support the administration, the president does not seem to have known it in advance.[302]

The decade after World War II saw the full-blown emergence of an issue that was to be a dominate factor in American politics for decades to come: civil rights. In one sense, the civil rights issues for black Americans

---

[296]The other times had been 1918–1920 and 1946–1948.

[297]Makins to Foreign Office, January 15, 1955, FO 371/114350, FO-BNA.

[298]"How a Democrat Guides Republican Tax Policy," 60.

[299]Eisenhower, *Ike's Letters to a Friend*, 137.

[300]Ibid., 140.

[301]Eisenhower, *Diaries*, 310, 322, 323, and *passim.*

[302]Ibid.

began, one historian noted, around 1831. The South assumed a no-retreat position from the beginning, and its "generals" in the battle would extend from John C. Calhoun and Jeff Davis to Walter George, Strom Thurmond, John Stennis, Sam Ervin, to their last, Richard Russell.[303] The emancipation of the slaves was the first major defeat, but the newly freed slaves found themselves, even in freedom, second-class citizens. For a while after Reconstruction, the blacks could vote, but gradually that right was taken away, and black disfranchisement in Georgia became law in 1908.[304] That year the last black congressman left the legislature, and the Democrats made Georgia a one-party state. For most of the early years, blacks comprised a majority of the Republican Party in Georgia. In 1927, the GOP national committeeman in Georgia was Benjamin Jefferson Davis, the black editor of *The Atlanta Independent,* and a majority of the GOP Central Committee was black.[305] The black vote was not to become a factor in Georgia elections until February 1945, when the blacks caused a machine candidate for Congress, Tom Camp, to lose to Mrs. Helen Mankin.[306]

Racial separation in Georgia was most rigid. In restaurants, blacks and whites were served in separate rooms, if blacks were allowed to eat inside at all, and whether they were in a park, bleachers at a sporting event, theater, or auditorium, blacks and whites had separate sections. In 1931, a law was passed making it illegal for a black citizen to inhabit a house whose former resident was white if the house was within fifteen city blocks of a public school. Curiously, reading rooms of public libraries were not segregated because no one had ever thought to pass a law mandating it.[307] The first case involving rights and race on education before the US Supreme Court came in 1938 in *Missouri ex rel. Gaines v. Canada*, in which the court ruled, with former Ku Klux Klan member Hugo Black voting with the majority, that the University of Missouri must offer equal opportunity in the university for a black applicant, Lloyd Gaines.[308]

Race could be an issue in any Southern election because politicians could always insert it into the contest. Their rhetoric varied. It would have

---

[303]Chandler, *Natural Superiority of Southern Politicians*, 132.

[304]Grantham, *Hoke Smith and the Politics of the New South*, 143; Georgia Laws 1908, 2731, cited in Bonner, "Legislative Appointment and the County Unit System," 365; Woodward, *Tom Watson*, 370–71.

[305]Davis had a son who had graduated from Amherst and was in the Harvard Law School and a daughter at Radcliffe (Moore, "Public Office on Easy Payments," 203).

[306]Reid, "Georgia's Negro Vote," 13.

[307]Moore, *Senator Josiah William Bailey of North Carolina*, 558-60.

[308]Egerton, *Speak Now against the Day*, 113.

been hard to "out-nigger" Tom Watson in his heyday, as it would have been difficult to better the Talmadges at it at a later time. Where was Walter George on this issue? In 1943, *Time* wrote that "to the few rampant New Dealers left in Washington, Walter Franklin George is a black reactionary. He would never let an anti-lynching or anti-poll tax bill come to a vote in the Senate."[309] The statement was rather unfair to Senator George. George was not, of course, an integrationist, nor did he probably favor true equality, politically or socially, of America's blacks, but he was not a racist, put in the context of his time.

In fact, Walter George was of a totally different hue from the basic Southern politician. Ralph McGill noted in 1955 that George never "played on prejudices of race or religion."[310] While the statement is not totally correct, race was never a central theme in any of his campaigns, however desperately he may have been in trouble. As early as the 1920s, he spoke openly of the manner in which the South had treated its black citizens. "Why apologize or evade?" he said. "We [Southerners] have been very careful to obey the letter of the Federal Constitution [regarding the rights of racial minorities]—but we have been very diligent in violating the spirit of such amendments and such statutes as would have a Negro to believe himself the equal of a white man."[311] As for his personal association, he said on the floor of the Senate in the late 1940s, "I was reared with a Negro, and partly by him. I never had any prejudice against the Negro race as a race."[312] Despite the fact that the statement has the air of "Some-of-my-best-friends...," etc., it rings true and is partially supported by George's record. One observer of his life, and there are many such statements about him, said in the 1950s, "And the senator himself proved that to be successful[,] one does not necessarily have to be the provincial peddler of prejudice."[313] There are many such statements about him. His law partner, T. Hoyt Davis, who certainly knew him well, told this author, "He never was a [racial] rabble rouser. I never heard him say anything that was demeaning [to a member of a racial minority]. He was an Old Time Southerner, but I never heard him make a racial slur."[314] In 1935, when a petition against slum clearance signed by hundreds of blacks in Macon, Georgia, was sent to Senator George, he dutifully forwarded it on

---

[309]"Old Independent," 20.
[310]"Political Test," 33.
[311]Tyndall, *Emergence*, 160–61.
[312]*CR*, 78/2, 4251.
[313]*"Tributes to George,"* n. d., clipping, f. Sen. George (NC), VHPS.
[314]T. Hoyt Davis interview.

to the White House.[315] In the 1950s, not long after the *Brown v. Board of Education* decision, there was a black secretary, Thomasene Smith, who worked on the foreign relations committee. Walter George had no problem with her.[316]

When the Vienna Historic Preservation Society held a memorial on the fiftieth anniversary of George's death, Sally May Childs, a ninety-nine-year-old black woman, came and asked if she could speak. She had been one of Walter George's nurses in the last months of his life. She told of an incident when she was helping George down the stairs into the back yard, and the two had fallen on the steps. She quickly checked him out to make sure nothing was broken, rubbing his elbow on which he had fallen. Then he said, "Now, I'll rub your elbow," and then playfully did so.[317] True, there are signs that George was not so enlightened on these matters in his early years as later. In the 1938 campaign, he championed the all-white primary. "It would be a great mistake," he told a crowd in Greenville, Georgia, "to place back again our primary elections in the hands of members of both races."[318] He also played on the theme of "white democracy" in a speech in Waycross, where he said, "I am persuaded that this generation of White Democrats will not let Democracy down in our beloved state." The band broke out into "Dixie," and many in the audience had tears in their eyes.[319]

George was never so rabid about the issue as his opponent Talmadge; but in running against Talmadge, he had to pay court to the Georgian attitudes of the day on race. In 1945, it was his friend and law partner, T. Hoyt Davis, whom he had sponsored to be a federal judge, who struck down the all-white primary.[320] When an education bill was being debated in 1943, Senator William Langer (R-North Dakota), introduced an amendment that passed 40–37; it read, "That there shall be no discrimination in the administration of the benefits...made under the respective provisions of this act...on account of race, creed or color." George had favored the bill before the amendment, but when Senator Taft, who did not support the bill, moved that it be returned to the Education and Labor Committee, George rose to attack the amended bill, but from a different angle. He accused Langer of introducing the amendment to drive Southern senators to oppose

[315]Letter to Secret Service, November 5, 1935, PPF, box 107–117, f. 109, Roosevelt papers.

[316]Valeo, oral history, 339.

[317]I spoke with her at the service and then again by telephone.

[318]George, *Addresses*, Greenville, September 2, 1938, 13.

[319]"Old Independent," 21.

[320]Egerton, *Speak Now against the Day*, 407.

it. "Senators who voted for the amendment have definitely done a disservice to the Negro in the South," he lectured his colleagues. "Negroes are very intelligent, they know that the bill would have helped them.... To undertake to control the schools of the South [is] definitely a disservice, and harm is being done [to them,] to the cause of public education in the South."[321] When Edgar Kobak of the Mutual Broadcasting Co. ran a series of episodes titled "To Serve These Rights" on the civil rights issue, George was one of the many Southern senators who signed a protest demanding equal time.[322]

The unlimited debate in the Senate gave the South one powerful weapon in the civil rights fight, the filibuster. They could literally talk a bill to death, and George was a strong supporter of the filibuster. In 1949, he and then-Republican Senator Wayne Morse tangled over the issue. Truman had called for relaxing cloture rules ending a filibuster, and Morse praised him from the floor. Morse and Truman wanted to be able to close debate with a simple majority. George rose to oppose the proposal noting that had the members voted to limit debate in the Constitutional Convention in 1787, it would have dissolved the convention. George told Morse that weakening the cloture requirement was a way of limiting the powers of the states and that states' rights were guaranteed by the Constitution.[323] Filibuster was "a check and control of the actions of a majority," he argued to his colleagues.[324] Later in the debate, George argued, "If the hands of the minority are not constantly strengthened, we are headed toward a form of government under which minorities will not have any rights.... Any Administration with a majority back of it can work its will."[325] George may have unknowingly saved the cloture rule that year by his simple existence. Senator Paul Douglas (D-Illinois), one of the most liberal men in the body at the time, was a strong champion of civil rights, and he realized early that in order to get any civil rights legislation passed in the Senate, the 2/3 cloture rule had to be changed. It could of course itself be filibustered when the change was debated. One way to obtain the change was to hold the Senate in continuous debate. Majority leader Scott Lucas (D-Illinois) refused to take this route because he feared it might kill some elderly senators, like Walter George, who was thought to have a weak heart, so he stopped the

---

[321] *CR*, 78/1, 8466.
[322] US Senators to Edgar Kobak, March 5, 1948, VI-B, box 34, f. 1-B, Russell Papers.
[323] *CR*, 81/1, 2144.
[324] Ibid., 2266.
[325] Ibid., 2268.

debate after 10:00 p.m. so the older Southerners could recuperate.[326]

One civil rights issue that the blacks were winning as the war ended was the abolition of the poll tax. Only eight states still had it, and South Carolina, among others, which had not yet abolished it, did not even collect it as early as the 1940 primaries.[327] Walter George opposed the tax, but he did not want it abolished by the federal government. When the issue arose in 1944, he spoke against it on the Senate floor. Beginning, as he often did, by saying that he would be brief, which he rarely was, he said that the issue here was not race and that he hoped that the Senate would not consider the poll tax on the false issue of "alleged discrimination." He accused those who were doing so were "creating prejudice through which to control the votes of members of the Senate." He noted that he had supported the abolition of the poll tax in his own state and that it should be abolished everywhere, but he added, "It should be abolished by the only sovereignty that has a right to create it…namely the states. The federal government has nothing whatsoever to do with it." He stressed that he had no quarrel with the fight against it and predicted that in time it would be abolished everywhere, but he denounced "the reckless leaders of some well-meaning persons" who argued that the Fourteenth Amendment, which made blacks citizens, gave everyone the unhindered right to vote. Only the Fifteenth and the Nineteenth amendments did that. He restated that in time the poll tax would be abolished everywhere, but it should not be done by the federal government.[328]

On January 16, 1946, however, George sought a five-minute meeting with President Truman for a committee on religious liberty representing the Baptist Church National, a group that was both black and white. Among them was Rev. W. S. Abernathy, father of leading civil rights leader Ralph Abernathy.[329] A wild-eyed racist would not have made this effort. Indeed, he would never have been asked to do so. On the issue of the lynching bill, George continued to hold forth. In 1949, for instance, he asserted: "With all the vigor in my soul, I deplore mob violence in any form; I have stood against it all my life, even when it hurt. But the federal government cannot be given power to prevent the commission of crime by mob violence in the States, unless it is asserted that the federal government possesses total and absolute police power."[330] He argued, furthermore, that the bill was not

[326]Douglas, *In the Fullness of Time*, 268.
[327]Stoney, "Georgia's Rotten Boroughs," 249.
[328]*CR*, 78/2, 451–55.
[329]Memo, F. January 13, 1946, General file, WFG file, Truman papers.
[330]*CR*, 81/1, 1607.

needed since lynching was down dramatically, and indeed it was. The year 1952 was the first year in post-Reconstruction America that no lynchings were recorded.[331] Lynchings continued for more than two decades, however, not just of blacks but of gays as well.

Another civil rights initiative associated with the anti-lynching movement was the issue of the Fair Employment Practice Committee (FEPC), usually called the Fair Practice Committee. It had been created by executive order by President Roosevelt in 1941 to ban racial discrimination in plants employing defense workers. In June 1944, George called to defund it in a speech that was sheer demagoguery. He was up for reelection that year, and there had been talk that Gene Talmadge would oppose him, and those circumstances probably led to his excessive language. Unlike the Talmadges, however, he founded his opposition on claims that the legislation was inspired by class hatred. Making a somewhat unrelated point, he wrote, "This country cannot survive if the class hatreds, class distinctions, and class division, which have made such remarkable progress in the past several years are hurried along to their final conclusion." He went on to attack in a rather incoherent speech those who would "communise America."[332] In showing Georgian moderation, he said, "Let me repeat, I would be ashamed of myself as an American citizen and as a member of this body if I did not positively favor the payment of equal wages and salaries for equal work by whites and blacks alike."[333]

In January 1946 at a time when most senators were absent, Senator Denis Chavez introduced a bill, supported by President Truman, to make the FEPC a permanent part of the federal bureaucracy. In the ensuing furor, George told the press, "If this is all Harry Truman has to offer, God help the Democratic Party in 1946 and 1948."[334] A filibuster followed, led by Walter George. The opponents of the bill met in his office to plan strategy, and as is often the case in these sensitive matters, people did more talking than they did thinking. Some said that the bill would lead to miscegenation, and there were even slurs on Senator Chavez's Catholicism. George, in one of his most uncharacteristically extreme statements of his career, spoke of the events by saying, "We are called up to go Nazi."[335] There were moves to

[331] *Washington Post*, December 31, 1952, 7(?).

[332] *CR*, 78/2, 6255–56.

[333] Ibid., 6254.

[334] *Atlanta Constitution*, January 18, 1946, cited in Garson; Tindall, *Emergence,* 551–53, cited in Potenziani, "Look to the Past," 52.

[335] Stone, "Swastika over the Senate," 158–59.

close debate, of course, at which Senator Tydings of Maryland intoned, "It was cloture that crucified Christ on the cross." One caustic witness wrote, "For one breathless moment one wondered if he would go on to accuse Pontius Pilate of being a Republican."[336] As was often the case, the FEPC was killed by filibuster that lasted late into January. George defended the endless debate. Denouncing the bill as "a tyrannical abuse of government power," he asked rhetorically, "Who shall put limits on freedom?"[337]

The issue never really went away. In May 1950, the Fair Employment Practices bill once again came before the Senate. On May 16, Walter George threw his considerable political weight and oratorical skills on the scales against passage. Behaving in a demagogic manner, which he rarely displayed, he thundered on for pages in the *Congressional Record* that day. "Not in all the wildest dreams of Charles Sumner or Thaddeus Stevens...was there any concept of a Fair Employment Practice Commission.... The situation now is that both parties cater to and both are seeking to take the credit for it." He noted that it had its origins from neither but from the Communist Party. "Do not rob the Communists of their just credit," he sarcastically enjoined his colleagues. "Let the commies have it [the credit]. Let them keep it." Bigotry is a "common trait among mankind," he lectured his colleagues, "[but] I do not believe that the government has any power to enter this field and undertake to control likes and dislikes." Government did not have the power to "make a man be a good Christian or tolerant ... If government undertakes to do so, it becomes a tyranny." He emphasized that the bill would be divisive in American society at a time "when nation unity is essential at home and abroad.... Everyone knows the highly explosive character of this proposal."[338]

During the debate, Senator Bob Smith of New Jersey had stressed the need for equality of opportunity. George agreed with him. "I agree with the senator [Smith of New Jersey] that it is the duty of government to provide equality of economic opportunity and educational opportunity.... In all our states we must provide equality of opportunity in education," something that Georgia was not providing at the time. He then went off the track, expressing the fear of all white Southerners that any bill that favored black rights would lead to integration of the races. Then George added, going far afield of the subject, "We do not mean by that that we favor the mingling of the races in the schools and colleges," a question which in no way dealt with the

[336]Ibid.

[337]*New York Times,* January 30, 1946, 15:2.

[338]For the whole speech, see *CR,* 81/2, 7068–72.

bill before the Senate. When asked if he would join his fellow senators in seeking equality of opportunity for all, George replied, "Not only would I be willing to join with them, but I would be willing to do all I can as I have tried all my life to bring out equality of opportunity for all our people. In that I thoroughly and basically believe."[339] His antagonist Senator Smith then thanked "the senator from Georgia for his splendid exposition, which is very enlightening."[340] It is difficult to tell today from the sterile ink of the *Congressional Record,* and by the elapsed time of over six decades, whether or not the senator from New Jersey was serious in his praise or simply being sarcastic.

Of course, the most momentous civil rights issue in this crucial decade was the *Brown vs Board of Education of Topeka* decision of 1954, which decreed the end to racial segregation in American public schools. What followed in the South was called "massive resistance" to school integration. In a biography of Strom Thurmond, the author quotes Talmadge on the decision ("the high court has reduced our Constitution to a scrap of paper") and Richard Russell (the court is "a pliant tool of the executive branch"), but there is no well-known remark from Senator George.[341] Ultra-liberal Senator Paul Douglas himself believed that George was on race "a moderate," but being challenged by a younger rival Herman Talmadge, had to appear strongly opposed to integration and therefore assumed a backbench leadership of the opposition. None of the major recent works on Southern opposition even mention, or mention only in passing, Senator George.[342] One may be certain that George did not approve of *Brown*, but there is no evidence that he harbored toward it any of the hostility of the more rabid Southerners, perhaps because he had a longstanding respect for the judiciary from his time serving as a judge. Whatever caused his moderation, in May 1956, in a conversation with President Eisenhower, he expressed great concern about the race relations in the South and called for "moderates on both sides working on the problem." If they did not work together, he argued "We will get in a pretty sorry mess." He noted that if he retired in 1956, "his successor would only be an extremist on the racial problem."[343] He could only be speaking of Talmadge.

[339]Ibid., 7071–72.

[340]Ibid.

[341]Cohodas, *Strom Thurmond and the Politics of Southern Change*, 254.

[342]Douglas, *The Fullness of Time*, 280–81. On massive resistance to integration, see Lewis, *Massive Resistance*; Webb, *Massive Resistance*; Roberts and Klibanoff, *The Race Beat*; Winant, *The World Is a Ghetto*; and Wilhoit, *The Politics of Massive Resistance*.

[343]Eisenhower, *Eisenhower Diaries*, 322.

By 1956, Strom Thurmond and Harry Byrd had created a plan to resist the *Brown* decision and demanded a meeting of the Southern Caucus. George, as the senior Southern senator, convened it on February 8. The result was a document called "The Declaration of Constitutional Principles," less charitably known as the "Southern Manifesto." Because he was a senior member of the group and for political reasons, George was asked to read it into the *Congressional Record* on March 12, 1956.[344] Nineteen of the twenty-two senators of the states that made up the Old Confederacy signed it, as had eighty-one members of the House. Richard Russell had worked on the final draft, but George does not seem to have had any role at all in actually writing it.[345]

The author of a biography of Senator William Fulbright (D-Arkansas) quotes someone named Erickson in an oral history of saying that many moderate Southerners were induced into supporting the manifesto because to do so would "save [Walter] George's seat."[346] George had definitely been pushed front and center on the issue, and he could not have had Talmadge's shadow far from his mind. Through the entire race issue, still, George's moderation, at least in comparison to the more raw-meat segregationists, is evident. In the end of his career, many publications at the time, and many historians since, have called him a racial moderate and even "soft on integration."[347] In an interview on his seventy-ninth birthday in 1957, George stated that the race question would best be handled locally.[348] He doubtlessly knew that meant little handling at all. When in 1956, Georgia Governor Marvin Griffin induced the state legislature to pass a resolution declaring the Brown decision "null and void and of no effect," George remained silent when other national legislators supported it.[349] This moderation was one of the major factors that ended his political career.

Since in the 83rd Congress (1953–1955) Walter George's party was in the minority and he had, of course, lost his chairmanship, he was not in the news as much. The one issue on which he nevertheless played a pivotal, well-advertised role, however, was in the fight over the famous "Bricker

[344]Cohodas, *Strom Thurmond and the Politics of Southern Change*, 284–86; Heinemann, *Harry Byrd of Virginia*, 335.

[345]Potenziani, "Look to the Past," 132.

[346]Woods, *Fulbright*, 208.

[347]"Voice of the 84th," 22; Hero, *The Southerner and World Affairs*, 131; "Georgia Loses," 23; "When Senator George Steps Out," 46; "Senator and Senator to Be," 37.

[348]"Sen. George hailed….," U. N. C., n.d., f. Sen. G(NC), VHPS.

[349]Cook, *Carl Vinson*, 273.

Amendment." Roosevelt had made a number of agreements with the British and the Russians in conferences during the war that had the flavor and were, in effect, treaties. According to an agreement Roosevelt made with the Russians at Yalta, they were to enter the war against the Japanese Empire three months after the war in Europe had ended. He agreed to the redrawing of Poland's boundaries, as well as the plans to occupy Germany. According to the American constitution, treaties have to be ratified by the US Senate, but these understandings, clearly a form of treaty, were never ratified by the Senate. Even Roosevelt never intended these understandings as an invitation to the Russians to invade Manchuria, Korea, and Eastern Europe, to the detriment of these places. Furthermore, there was fear of some American leaders that international treaties and laws would override American state and national laws. John Foster Dulles, briefly a US Senator and by 1953 Eisenhower's secretary of state, had stated as much in April 1952 in a speech in Louisville, Kentucky, when he said that treaties "become the supreme law of the land" and that they are "more supreme than ordinary laws," adding that "treaty law can override the Constitution."[350]

By the 1950s these areas into which the Russian army had been invited, basically on Roosevelt's invitation, had "gone communist" owing to the Russian presence. In an effort to preclude such unratified treaties in the future, Senator John Bricker of Ohio introduced in September 1951 his famous "Bricker Amendment" to the Constitution, limiting the treaty-making powers of the president and stressing that international law could not override federal and state laws. The amendment at first languished in the Senate Foreign Relations Committee, but by the opening of the 83rd Congress in January 1953, it had sixty-three sponsors (forty-four Republicans and nineteen Democrats). It delineated definite limits on the president's power to enter into international agreements and stressed that no international treaty could superseded federal or state laws. Proponents feared that treaties might be signed to establish the United Nations as a super-government overriding American laws. Some even feared that Americans might become victims of international court trials on vague charges.[351] Many thought that the unfortunate consequences of Yalta and Potsdam might have been avoided if congressional consideration might have been mandatory.[352] Although the Brick-

[350]Eisenhower, *Mandate for Change*, 279–80; Bonnet to Bidault, 8 April 1953, Etats Unis: Politique intérieure, f. 480, 407, AMAE.

[351]"The ABC's of the Bricker Amendment," 37–38; Makins to Eden, March 15, 1954, no. 118, FO 371/109105, FO-BNA.

[352]Ibid.

er proposal was endorsed by the American Bar Association, its most prominent supporters were extreme right-wing elements such as the DAR, the Hearst and McCormick papers, and prominent racist and anti-Semite, Gerald L. K. Smith. Other organizations blossomed for the cause such as the certainly indomitable "Vigilant Women for the Bricker Amendment." On the opponents' side was the fear of the great limitations that would be placed on a president to conduct foreign policy, as well as a fear that each state might be required to ratify any treaty negotiated by a president. Among these opponents was Walter George himself.

The greatest irritant to the amendment's critics was the famous "Which Clause," which William S. White called, "the famous clause which nobody could understand."[353] The sentence with the clause read: "A treaty shall become effective as internal law in the United States only through legislation *which would be valid in the absence of [such] a treaty* [emphasis added]." Many interpreted this clause to mean that after a treaty or international law was ratified, Congress would then have to pass, and the president sign, a bill making it the law of the land internally. As a pamphlet distributed by the Committee for the Defense of the Constitution put it, "This provision would make our proceedings for carrying out our treaty obligations the most cumbersome in the world."[354] The most extreme interpretation held that even the forty-eight state legislatures would have to pass similar legislation as well, or at least all of them would have to ratify the treaty, giving one of the forty-eight the right to block it.[355] George Reedy, a journalist and Congress watcher, told an interviewer in 1954 that in his sixteen years of working around Congress, he did not know of any single thing that "has aroused such intense emotion."[356]

The debate on "Bricker" (SJ Res. 1) was to last for five weeks and would see various "amendments," which were really different versions offered by Bricker himself, most importantly those of Senator Bill Knowland, the Republican Senate leader, and of course Senator Walter George,[357] who would play a pivotal role.[358] Regarded as an outstanding constitutional scholar, George was thrown into the fray, and indeed, Senator Willis Smith

[353]William S. White, oral history, interview III, 20, Johnson Library.

[354]Eisenhower, *Mandate for Change*, 283–84.

[355]*New York Times*, January 28, 1954, 1:1.

[356]George Reedy, oral history, 16, Johnson Library.

[357]Tananbaum, *The Bricker Amendment Controversy*, 154–55.

[358]For a statement of the amendment, see Dole, *Historical Almanac of the United States*, 262; for an account of George in the Bricker debate, see Caro, *The Years of Lyndon Johnson*, 532 ff.

of North Carolina had suggested to Bricker that he bring George on board from the beginning. Knowland had warned Eisenhower that George would be one of the "key men" on any bipartisan amendment that might evolve from Bricker.[359]

Because of its implications, George seems to have been opposed to the concept of the Bricker amendment as early as 1943, when he told his Senate colleagues, "I should not want to vote...for an amendment which was predicated even upon the thought or fear that under our Constitution a president...by any mere executive agreement, could bind this country to any such international authority."[360] He added, "[Yet] when we consider an amendment which provides that a president must do that [only] by treaty, it is tantamount to conceding that he might do it by executive agreement."[361] Did Yalta change his mind? By 1948 George told the Senate, "When a solemn agreement is entered into by the president with Country X, the agreement becomes binding only when ratified by the Senate."[362] He decided that he preferred not to tinker with the president's treaty-making ability.[363] In February 1954, he announced that he was not supporting Bricker "solely because it includes treaties," [and] because he did not think it "necessary to disturb the treaty-making power."[364] Still, executive agreements disturbed him, and Knowland and Bricker warned Eisenhower as early as February 1, 1954, that George would insist that on Section 3 of Bricker include executive agreements.[365] Even before the debate started, Senator Knowland called the Bricker Amendment a "festering sore" that must be "closed out of the Senate."[366] Eisenhower was just as emphatic.

Eisenhower told Press Secretary Hagerty that if it was true that when a person dies, things that bother them the most are engraved on their skull, he said, "I am sure I'll have there the mud and dirt of France...and the name of

[359]Tananbaum, *The Bricker Amendment Controversy*, 144–45, citing numerous sets of senatorial papers.

[360]George is referring to the "Pink Case," when Louis Pink, New York State insurance commissioner, sued to block Roosevelt's executive agreement with Maxim Litvinov, then the Soviet foreign minister, to give the Soviets the assets of a Russian insurance company in New York (Tananbaum, *The Bricker Amendment Controversy*, 169–72).

[361]Carlton, "Record...." 13, GFR-VHPS.

[362]*CR*, 80/2, 874.

[363]Tananbaum, *The Bricker Amendment Controversy*, 160.

[364]*CR*, 83/2, 2204.

[365]Memo for Mr. Dodge, February 1, 1954, box 1, f. Legislative meetings, 1951 (Whitman file), Eisenhower papers.

[366]Ibid., meeting on January 11, 1954, f. Leg. Meetings-01951 (1), box 1, Whitman file, Eisenhower papers.

Senator Bricker."[367] George opposed the undermining of presidential authority and said that Frank Holman, president of the American Bar Association and supporter of the amendment, "was trying to save the United States from Eleanor Roosevelt." When the Judicial Committee reported it out favorably, Ike announced that he was solidly against it. In a letter to Senator Knowland, he wrote, "I am unilaterally opposed to the Bricker Amendment as reported.... It would impair our hopes and plans for peace."[368]

Eisenhower turned to George on January 20, 1954, to obtain a less objectionable amendment to replace the Bricker proposal, since it seemed that it might pass. He instructed Dulles to approach George, with whom he was close, to draft a bipartisan substitute that would be weaker. Dulles met with George that day, and on January 25, George came to the White House with a draft of an amendment that was more palatable to the administration.[369] Eisenhower at first liked the substitute better but was openly noncommittal. When George was asked later that day by the press if the president supported it, he replied that he had not specifically endorsed it. Privately, Ike told Bedell Smith, the under-secretary of state, that he "had no objection to it" and even went so far as to state that George's substitute would protect Americans' rights but not hamstring a president's power to direct America's foreign policy.[370] Although Dulles liked the amendment "very well," some of his staff were not so enthusiastic and felt that it would still require congressional passage of executive agreements. Ike did then agree to withhold his endorsement until it would be studied further. Brownell conferred with John W. Davis, a great constitutional lawyer, the 1924 Democratic presidential candidate, and the lead lawyer for the South in the *Brown v Board of Education*. Both concluded that it would severely limit presidential authority.[371]

There were other opponents to the amendment. Then Senator Knowland introduced his own version, which was similar to George's. It eliminated the "which" clause and added that any treaty that ran counter to the Constitution would be nullified automatically.[372] On January 22, 1954,

[367]Hagerty, *The Diary of James C. Hagerty*, 1 and 2 February 1954, 141, cited in Tananbaum, *The Bricker Amendment Controversy*, 151.

[368]Adams, *Firsthand Report*, 108–109.

[369]Tananbaum, *The Bricker Amendment Controversy*, 144. Dallek states that LBJ got George to introduce the amendment. He clearly did support it, but it does not appear that he was the instigator of George's amendment (*Lone Star Rising*, [page?]).

[370]Tananbaum, *The Bricker Amendment Controversy*, 147.

[371]Ibid., 148.

[372]Eisenhower, *Mandate for Change*, 282–83.

Senator Prescott Bush of Connecticut, the father and grandfather of two presidents, came out in total opposition to Bricker's original version. That day, James Hagerty wrote in his diary, "Sure we can beat the isolationists on it.... Plan is to get bipartisan sponsorship of [a] substitute amendment.... Senator George probably will help."[373] Six days later he wrote, "Our GOP boys still trying to compromise with Bricker isolationists. George and Democrats now got [the] jump on them with a simple George amendment." He opined that the best that the administration could do was arrive at a bipartisan agreement, "a compromise giving Democrats credit for saving the Constitution. Now [we] have to confer with George, in addition to Bricker. How dumb can we get?"[374]

Eisenhower's attorney general, Herbert Brownell, then began trying to rewrite George's draft. In conjunction with Herman Phlegler, a state department legal advisor, the administration moved to make George's amendment as narrow as possible and suggested to George that he add a clause stating expressly that the amendment would not limit the authority of the president in the realm of foreign affairs. This change would have in effect totally nullified his amendment.[375] With this move, all cooperation between George and the administration ended. George further separated himself from the Eisenhower camp by blasting Brownell as "a very odd attorney general" and belittled him further by stating that a Brownell memo on the constitutionality of Bricker "had undoubtedly been written by some clerk in the Justice Department."[376]

Into this struggle entered Lyndon Johnson. We have seen that various associates of the future president claimed that it was Johnson who had apparently encouraged George to lead the fight against Bricker by producing his own substitute, but it has been seen that Johnson had not been party to the negotiations from the very beginning.[377] It is not implausible, however, that given his personality and his ambition to be president, he had stirred in it early. He clearly did later. Robert Caro, Johnson's most prominent biographer, believed that Johnson's actions were motivated by more than one goal. By supporting the George substitute, he wished to give the impression that he was saving the president from the isolationists of his own party; nev-

---

[373]Hagerty, *Diary of James C. Hagerty*, 9.

[374]Ibid., 10–11.

[375]*New York Times*, February 3, 1954, 1, 10, cited in Tananbaum, *The Bricker Amendment Controversy*, 149.

[376]White, *Citadel*, 10–11.

[377]Gerald Siegel, III, oral history, 5; William S. White, oral history, 21, Johnson Library.

ertheless, at the same time he himself wanted the George amendment defeated, but narrowly, so that it would not be an embarrassment to Senator George, whose support he wanted for his own political career. By arm twisting, he changed three liberal votes: senators Lister Hill of Alabama, Warren Magnuson of Washington, and Henry Jackson of Washington.[378]

In a meeting between Johnson and George, Gerald Siegel, a member of Johnson's Senate staff, was present and described in an oral history how Johnson gave George the "Johnson Treatment." Calling it a "stellar performance of persuasion," Siegel remembered, "I sat there and watched Johnson…talk to the substance of the issue and persuade Walter George that he should not lead a massive fight in favor of the Bricker Amendment…. I know it was a rapid-fire almost uninterrupted monologue…. I'm sure he probably went back and talked about how Walter George's mother and father might feel."[379] George Reedy claims that the Democratic Policy Committee then began assisting Senator George in writing and rewriting the amendment, "working long hours over the wording—to help Senator George word the substitute."[380] Walter Jenkins, an administrative assistant in Johnson's office, was not as certain of Johnson's role in the affair. He remembered in an oral history only that "he [Johnson] talked with George a lot and met with George a lot…. I wouldn't want to say that he was the moving presence behind the George compromise, but I know he was involved."[381] Probably Johnson's role shadowed George's contacts with the administration. At any rate, George's amendment pushed Bricker off the front pages, and George's efforts became, as *US News* stated it, "a fresh start" on the issue of congressional control of "executive agreements with foreign powers."[382] As historian Richard Rovere put it, "The Bricker amendment…evolved gradually and against the will of its author into the 'George Amendment.'"[383]

George's amendment, introduced on February 2, 1954, read, "Section 1. A provision of a treaty or other international agreement which conflicts with the Constitution shall not be of any force or effect." Section 2 focused on executive agreements: "An international agreement other than a treaty shall become effective as international law in the United States only by an

[378]Caro, *The Years of Lyndon Johnson*, 533.
[379]Gerald Siegel, oral history, 8–9, Johnson Library.
[380]George Reedy, oral history, tape 1, 17, Johnson Library.
[381]Walter Jenkins, oral history, 15, Johnson Library.
[382]"People of the Week," (February 12, 1954), 12.
[383]Rovere, *The Eisenhower Years*, 207.

act of Congress."[384] On February 5, George stressed the focus of his amendment. "I have suggested that if we are going to preserve the right of individuals and of the states, we must do so by saying that executive agreements, which can override laws of the states…must not be made merely by one man but must be submitted to the Congress."[385] Later in the debate, he restated his position to his colleagues. "My proposal simply is this, and nothing but this: That with respect to executive agreements which Congress has no part in shaping or fomenting, such executive agreements shall not become internal or domestic law of the United States unless Congress, by an act, shall so provide."[386] In subsequent debate, George stressed that his amendment was not for limiting treaty-making powers of the executive but rather agreements "other than a treaty."[387] Except for the "which clause," which some interpreted would give an individual state the power to block a Washington-negotiated treaty, one is hard pressed to see much difference in George's substitute. The *New York Times* called it "a softer approach than Bricker's," which it was, but otherwise there was not much difference.[388] Knowland immediately postponed his proposal, which had been made largely to remove the stigma of the GOP's having been saved from itself, and Lyndon Johnson had gotten what he wanted.

Until this point, the debate had been largely between pro-Bricker and pro-administration Republicans. Now the Democrats, led by Walter George (with Johnson pulling strings in the background), had hijacked the issue.[389] Essentially, Bricker's amendment made necessary legislative action for both treaties and executive agreements. George's amendment, on the other hand, stressed the need for legislation for only executive agreements.[390] Now the Republican leaders, who had, as we have seen, encouraged George, backed off in their support for the George Amendment because they did not want to give the impression that the Democrats were saving Eisenhower from the isolationists of his own party.[391] Then, Attorney General Brownell entered with his confusing contribution, which was destroyed on the Senate floor by

[384] *CR*, 83/2, 1103.

[385] Ibid., 1404.

[386] Ibid., 1402.

[387] Ibid., 1664; The French were watching this debate most closely. See Bonnet to Bidault, 11 February 1954, Amérique, 1952–63, E-U: politique intérieure, f. 481, 320, AMAE.

[388] *New York Times*, January 28, 1954, 1:1.

[389] Ibid., 10:4.

[390] Arthur Perry to Paul Daugherty, April 4, 1955, box 121, Subject file: Treaties, Bricker Amendment, 1955, Johnson Papers.

[391] Tananbaum, *The Bricker Amendment Controversy*, 150–51.

Walter George, as noted above. The *New York Times* reported that had Brownell been there, he "would hardly have known what had hit him."[392] When the George amendment superseded the Bricker proposal, George Reedy remembered, "suddenly all of the steam went out of the Bricker drive.... As a result nothing became law."[393] Results of the various votes was bizarre, and one can see the machinations of Lyndon Johnson in the murkiness. On February 17, the Senate eliminated the "which clause," 44–43. On February 25, Bricker's version was rejected by a surprisingly large margin (50–42), given that it had originally had more than sixty sponsors.[394] The next day, the Senate voted to substitute George's amendment for Knowland's by a vote of 61–30.[395] On February 27, George called for a vote on his amendment, warning his colleagues, "Mark my words, now, Gentlemen: You are going to [pass] a constitutional amendment.... You will do it now, or you will do it later. This is the best amendment that can be worked out." At this point Bricker saluted George on the Senate floor and George saluted back. Vice President Nixon then called for a vote.[396] There occurred the usual switches. Knowland, Carlson of Kansas, Robert Hendrickson of New Jersey, and Milliken of Colorado voted with Bricker and George, but Ralph Flanders switched, as did Lister Hill, Henry Jackson, and Warren Magnuson, all of whom had voted for the measure previously as a substitute.[397] When the voting stopped, it had passed with the necessary two-thirds vote: 60–30.

Suddenly and unexpectedly, into the Senate chamber stumbled an inebriated Senator Harley Kilgore of West Virginia. It was explained later that he had had flu and had been asleep in his office; less charitable were rumors that he was sleeping off a drunk or had been drunk in a nearby bar. His name was called and a "nay" was heard, with the result that the Senate, no longer with a two-thirds majority, defeated the amendment by 60–31.[398] If Kilgore still held any animus toward George because of his mistreatment in the readjustment imbroglio at the end of the war, the West Virginian got his revenge that day. Lyndon Johnson, who, of course, had not wanted it to pass, voted for it but was prepared to switch and had several switches lined

---

[392] White, "Senator George, Monument Determined," 42.

[393] George Reedy, oral history, tape 1, 16–17, Johnson Library.

[394] In his book *Mandate for Change*, Eisenhower states that it was defeated 42–50 (Eisenhower, *Mandate for Change*, 284).

[395] Tananbaum, *The Bricker Amendment Controversy*, 175.

[396] Caro, *The Years of Lyndon Johnson*, 538–39.

[397] Tananbaum, *The Bricker Amendment Controversy*, 179–80.

[398] Brownell, *Advising Ike*, 270; Maddox, 180; *Time*, 63(March 8, 1954), 27.

up. As a coda, Bricker praised George for his effort, but a number of Bricker supporters were defeated in 1954, thus in effect ending any serious chance of passage of the amendment.[399] To paraphrase Benjamin Disraeli, the Bricker amendment was "not only dead but damned."

The Bricker amendment did sputter again a time or two. Bricker reintroduced his amendment in January 1955, to George's surprise, and Eisenhower summoned George to the White House to discuss it. Eisenhower left a cabinet meeting to see George and asked him to see if he could derail Bricker's *démarche.* George feared that a majority of the Foreign Relations Committee might bring it out and asked the president if he could personally dissuade Bricker. George agreed to talk to him as well. Ike told George that he would always be available to him on the telephone or in his office on the matter.[400]

Once more, the amendment raised its head in 1956 as Bricker tried to resurrect his proposal, with the assistance of the oleaginous Senator Everett McKinley Dirksen of Illinois.[401] Dirksen's role in the resurrection was, as was often with this senator, self-serving. Dirksen had been an uncompromising isolationist who had recently adopted "a more statesman-like attitude," supporting the Eisenhower Administration on foreign aid.[402] Nothing came of this move, and then Bricker was defeated for reelection in 1958, ending the matter altogether. Ironically, the liberals who opposed it in 1954 were later to wish in the Vietnam-war era that they had had something like this amendment to curtail Lyndon Johnson's unrestrained free-wheeling Southeast Asian foreign policy.

In the 1954 elections, the Republicans narrowly lost control of the Senate, and George once again could move into a prominent chairmanship. What followed, and his choices from it, were to be very positively important for American foreign policy but detrimental to George's Senate career.

---

[399] *CR*, 83/2, 2374.

[400] Conversation with Senator George, 1/7/55, box 4, f. ACW diary, (Whitman file), Eisenhower papers.

[401] See "Personal and Confidential," March 20, 1956, box 2, f. "Leg. Leaders meetings," 1956, (2), Whitman file, A75–22, Eisenhower papers.

[402] "He's now swinging back," Child to Foreign Office and *New York Times* clipping, FO 371/120324, FO-BNA. The *New York Times* had called it the "step brainchild."

9

EISENHOWER'S FAVORITE DEMOCRAT, 1955–1957

Disagreeing with [Walter F.] George would seem almost sacrilegious, like questioning Moses on the authority of the Ten Commandments.
—Arthur Edson[1]

May I...express the earned hope that when evening comes and the shadows fall.... You drop on your knees and thank our Gracious God for Walter George, for his continued strength of body and mind.
—Congressman Stephen Pace[2]

No foreign policy will receive any respect unless the people who put it forth have the strength and the will to carry it to execution.
—Walter F. George[3]

Keep an eye on Senator Walter F. George of Georgia. Ike and his advisors are courting him assiduously in hopes of making him into a Democratic counterpart of the late Senator Vandenberg. Ike's aides see George, one of the most powerful men in the Senate, as crucial in preserving bipartisan foreign policy
—*Atlanta Journal*[4]

George had never seemed to be a man overly driven by ambition, or if he had, he certainly hid it well. Still, by 1955, Walter George was everywhere recognized as one of the most powerful men in the United States. National news publications were giving full coverage to almost anything he said. *Life* called him "one of the most distinguished legislators of his time and the most revered man in the Senate."[5] One historian wrote that at the height of his power with "a nod from him, half a million dollars would be spent. Treaties would be signed or rejected. Foreign trade could be expanded

[1]*Atlanta Constitution,* August 6, 1957, 17, RCB 5804, box 15, f. WFG-GSA.
[2]"Address of Congressman Pace...., 8, ibid.
[3]WFG, "Russia Will Lose," 81.
[4]"Senator George: A Potent Voice," n. d., misc. clipping, scrapbook, LHG-VHPS.
[5]"Sentimental Send-off," 95.

or shut off.... The president courted him, and the secretary of state was his 50–50 partner. He was, without competition, the most important man in Congress."[6]

As early as 1949, the *New York Times* had already named him one of the twelve key members of Congress, and by 1955, he was probably the most powerful. In May 1955, *Collier's* told its readers, "Seldom in the history of the United States Senate has any member reached the pinnacle of power, respect and influence that is occupied today by Walter Franklin George, the solemn, dignified, and well-nigh unassailable senior senator from Georgia."[7] Journalist White wrote in 1955 that on almost any issue George could muster at least twenty-five Senate votes, and in the field of foreign affairs, "Whatever George decides...is very nearly final with nearly all the Democratic rank and file and with a good number of Republicans as well.... His positions become dogma to many like teachings of an 'established church,'" adding that when the Democrats get into a bind, they ask one another, "Shouldn't George go in now?—that means go onto the floor and do his stuff."[8] *Time* simply stated on what most agreed: "the 84th Congress's most influential figure is Georgia's Democratic Senator Walter Franklin George."[9] Due to the defeat of Senator Kenneth McKellor of Tennessee in 1952, George had become the Dean of the Senate, and when he "laboriously" ascended the dais to accept the gavel to lead the chamber, an admiring reporter in the press gallery muttered, "Save your Confederate money, boys. The South is rising again."[10]

George usually exercised his power quietly. At meetings, he usually said little, but his power was felt everywhere. When he supported anything, it usually passed. When he opposed something, it was usually defeated. When in 1955 Senator Albert Gore of Tennessee introduced an amendment allowing the federal government to control advertising rights on both sides of the highway, George opposed it on the Senate floor, probably as a favor to Coca-Cola. "Evidently he defeated it right on the spot," Gerald Siegel remembered. "They immediately took it out [of the bill] when he launched against this. He had tremendous clout."[11] His leading areas of expertise were constitutional questions and taxes. His Senate colleagues regarded him as the Sen-

[6]Chandler, *Natural Superiority of Southern Politicians*, 329–30.

[7]Donovan, "Senator George," 32.

[8]White, "Senator George, Monument Determined," 44.

[9]"Voice of the 84th," 22.

[10]Caro, *The Years of Lyndon Johnson*, 562.

[11]Gerald Siegel, oral history, III, 23, Johnson Library.

ate's leading constitutional authority, and all regarded him as one of the two senators who knew most about taxes, the other being Senator Eugene Milliken of Colorado.[12] Given the range of his authority, William Allen White wrote in the *New York Times*, "Very grown men dread his frown and fear his displeasure." When he was challenged, he showed enormous patience with the person who had questioned one of his positions, but then with his "magnificent basso-profundo, admonishing voice" he would "patiently correct the person who has been mistaken." In the exchange, the Senate would come to "a most respectful halt. The air is filled with Jovian bolts and rolls of thunder, and members not remotely involved in the cause of his distress will nevertheless look a bit guilty and apologetic that matters have come to such a sorry point."[13]

His command of those around him extended to those beyond the Senate. Once when a group of annoyed farmers came to Washington to remonstrate with George on a piece of farm legislation he had sponsored, George spoke to them, and in no time, one account had it, "had the rafters ringing." By the time he finished, the fight had gone out of those assembled. These men had been accompanied by Georgia's very powerful congressman Carl Vinson. When they left, tail between legs, a reporter said to Vinson, "I thought you were going to put a blister on the senator," to which Vinson replied, "Heck, he's a sleeping lion, the old senator. I don't want to get tangled up with him."[14]

By 1955, he was affectionately known in Washington as "the Old Man," and his mere presence brought pages running. People rushed to open doors for him. On entering the Senate cloakroom, he would remove his hat and merely hold it out for someone to take it, knowing that someone always would. He remained as always aloof. No one would ever dare to call him "Walter" (and, as the reader knows, that included his wife) or slap him on the back. No one would ever dare to try to make a deal with him.[15] There were two men in Washington with whom George of the 1950s would have great contact. One was the new president, Dwight D. Eisenhower. The other was the Senate majority leader, Lyndon B. Johnson. Eisenhower had won in a landslide in 1952, dragging in with him a Republican Congress. Lyndon Johnson had just been reelected in 1954 to a second term and had already in his short tenure, due to the defeats of two majority leaders in two

[12]"George of Georgia: Ike's Friend in Need," 29.
[13]White, "Senator George, Monument Determined," 12.
[14]Donovan, "Senator George," 35.
[15]"George of Georgia: Ike's Friend in Need," 29.

elections, become the majority leader by 1955. The leader of the Democratic Party in the Senate had never been a very powerful post until he assumed it and turned it into one. George would work closely with Eisenhower on foreign policy and with Lyndon Johnson on domestic and political issues. He had already joined Richard Russell in promoting Johnson as the first "Southern" president, and George became a major force in the majority leader's future career.

In 1955, President Dwight D. Eisenhower was at a peak in his career. He had ended the Korean conflict, avoided involvement in Indo-China, defused the Formosa crisis, reduced defense spending, had essentially balanced the budget, presided over a 1 percent inflation rate, and had kept the Republican Right from repealing the New and Fair Deals. Even Jawaharlal Nehru, the president of India and a frequent critic of America, termed Ike, "the greatest force for peace in the world today."[16] Moreover, 1955 was a boom year economically. Eisenhower had extended Social Security and unemployment benefits to millions of previously without coverage and had raised the minimum wage from $.75 to $1.00 per hour. The county was in a boom without inflation. Car sales, always a crucial part of the American economy, soared, and by 1955, 70 percent of all American families owned a car.[17]

Ike would in time have his detractors. By the late fifties, millions of homes in America had televisions, and the news showed lots of footage of Eisenhower either fishing or on a golf course, and the jokes came accordingly. Senator Wayne Morse, who as a Republican had endorsed Eisenhower for the Republican nomination in 1952, but who became an independent, said sarcastically on Ike's return from a vacation, "Glad to note that our foreign policy has finally moved off the golf course and Georgia hunting grounds and back to the White House." A prominent Philadelphia Republican quipped, "Wouldn't it be terrible if Sherman Adams [Eisenhower's chief of staff] died and Ike took over?"[18]

After 1952, George and Eisenhower developed a close bond. Ike had nothing but praise for the wisdom of Senator George,[19] and by May 1955, only four months after George's taking the chair of the Foreign Relations Committee, it could be said that every single foreign policy measure Eisen-

[16]Ambrose, *Eisenhower*, 2:253.

[17]Ibid., 2:249–50.

[18]These jokes were dutifully reported to the British Foreign Office (Sir H. Caccia to Foreign Office, April 1, 1957, no. 172, FO 371/126677, FO-BNA).

[19]Rovere, *The Eisenhower Years*, 365.

hower had submitted to Congress had George's mark on it.[20] *The New Republic* termed George's control of the Foreign Relations Committee as his "autocracy" and his work "false bipartisanship,"[21] but his power was most valuable to Eisenhower in his battle with the isolationists of his own party. One journalist summed it up nicely: "The man [Walter George] is not a part of the administration—yet he is vital to it. Some claim he had made a captive of it; others…say he has provided the ballast any successful administration needs." He wrote that George was "the man most responsible for our course in foreign affairs."[22]

George and Eisenhower were personally close as well. Eisenhower would often relax with drinks and hors d'oeuvres after 5:00 p.m. in the White House with important members of Congress, and very frequently, Walter George would be there.[23] When Eisenhower went to the Master's in Augusta, as he did every year, Miss Lucy, George, and T. Hoyt Davis, his law partner, would drive over and stay in "Mamie's Cottage."[24] Once while there, George made a TV speech on US foreign policy in which he took Eisenhower's side in a disagreement with Adlai Stevenson.[25] On his seventy-seventh birthday in January 1955, the president gave George a surprise birthday party at which Mamie kissed him.[26]

George, however, was not a blind Eisenhower automaton. When the administration tried to strengthen the Taft-Hartley Act in 1954, George used his power to kill the move, giving the Democrats a much needed victory and morale booster.[27] In 1956, George would actively and stridently call for Eisenhower's defeat.

George's relationship with Lyndon Johnson, then the Democratic Senate leader, was different from his with Eisenhower, but so was that of most senators. During his entire career, Lyndon Johnson catered to anyone who might be of use to him, and on arriving in the Senate, he immediately became a sycophant to the Southern power brokers who could move his career. George was certainly one of them.[28] As Senator George Smathers remem-

---

[20]Donovan, "Senator George," 32.

[21]"George of Georgia," *New Republic* 134 (May 21, 1956): 5.

[22]*Personalities in Your Government,* June 26, 1955, WFG-MU.

[23]Adams, *Firsthand Report*, 86.

[24]T. Hoyt Davis interview.

[25]"Voice of the 84th," 25.

[26]"Can Talmadge Beat George in Georgia?" 37.

[27]"When Georgia's Senator Speaks Out," *Atlanta Journal-Constitution*, n. d., scrapbook, LHG-VHPS.

[28]Dallek, *Lone Star Rising*, 366.

bered, "He cultivated them and he got them to go along."[29] He instilled in them the belief that he was the only chance a Southerner had of winning the presidency, and they became his greatest supporters.[30] Johnson did anything for them he could, whether it was kissing Sam Rayburn of the top of his bald head or regularly taking Richard Russell home to a home-cooked meal at his house. He occasionally managed Walter George's bills on the Senate floor, and would even step between George and reporters when the "Old Man" was leaving an important meeting.[31] Nevertheless, as Hubert Humphrey remembered, while using the Southern Bulls to promote himself, Johnson was always careful not to be labeled a Southerner.[32]

The Southern Democratic titans were willing to allow Johnson some mildly liberal moves, such as putting Wayne Morse, whom George and Russell both disliked, on the Foreign Relations Committee, and backing out of the Southern Caucus on more liberal issues such as efforts to limit Rule 22 (the filibuster rule). Yet generally, Johnson marched with "Dick Russell and his Dixieland Band."[33] None seem to have any idea how they were being taken.

To George, whom he treated like a father figure, Johnson gushed at every opportunity. On George's seventy-fifth birthday, Johnson was absolutely fawning. "I doubt if there is a member of this body for whom any of us have more admiration or greater respect and affection," he stated at the celebration.[34] In a letter to George in 1954, as Johnson was still getting his sea legs as a legislative leader, he wrote Walter George, "I would like to make this one observation. I don't know of a member of the Senate who has made a sounder contribution to this session than Walter George," he said. Then in pure Johnsonian hypocrisy, he added, "Frankly I do not know how I could have gotten through many of the trying days without your wise counsel and your unselfish help." Then he spread it on even thicker, "I will never forget your many kindnesses and your generosity [,] and I hope someday I will...be able to repay the tremendous debt that we [imperial "we"?] owe you."[35]

Johnson eventually repaid the Southern giants in worthless currency as

---

[29]Senator George Smathers, oral history, 128, Russell Library.

[30]Caro, *The Years of Lyndon Johnson*, 514–15.

[31]Ibid., 561.

[32]Humphrey, *Education*, 116.

[33]Caro, *The Years of Lyndon Johnson*, 599.

[34]*Atlanta Constitution*, August 5, 1957, RCB-8504, box 1998–1980 A, f. WFG-GSA.

[35]Lyndon Baines Johnson to WFG, April 19, 1954, f. Geo-Gid 96, box 67, "Master file," index, Johnson papers, Johnson Library.

president.

He did often call upon George for advice. Walter Jenkins, his long-time assistant, replied, when asked if he turned to George for help, "Yes, very much.... It's Walter George that he looked to.... He had tremendous respect for Walter George."[36] In the early fall 1955, he asked George's permission to release some of George's correspondence on the farm issue. Beginning with his usual flattery, "Please let me hear from you again as there is no other person who gives me such a feeling of confidence that the course I am following is right for our country."[37] His flattery also took physical forms. Several days before he had his heart attack, when he himself felt very bad, Johnson stopped by the hospital on July 2, 1955, to visit Walter George, who was himself in the hospital with a pulmonary infection, and conferred with him on some issue.[38] Nevertheless, there is some evidence that he did genuinely admire George and that at times, George had some control over him, or at any rate certainly never feared him. Glen Wilson, who served on Johnson's staff, remembered that Johnson had "remarkable admiration" for Walter George.[39] Johnson would call his office speech writer Horace "Bugs" Busby to observe a senator who sounded "senatorial," presumably so that he could model his speeches for Johnson after these men. He thereafter paid special attention to George's speeches.[40] Once when Truman had complained that the Democratic congressional leaders were kissing Eisenhower on both cheeks, Johnson blew up about it in the presence of George. With his familiar voice that must have gone well beyond those in the immediate conversation, George said patronizingly, "Now, Lyndon, I wouldn't get too upset. Knowing Harry, it's lucky he didn't say he was tired of your kissing both cheeks of Eisenhower's ass."[41]

When, shortly after arriving in the Senate, freshman Johnson importuned George to obtain for him better offices and positions on the more powerful committees. George told him calmly that it would be "inappropriate" for a new senator to try to bypass the seniority system. Johnson apparently became insistent, a tactic later known among his Senate colleagues as

[36]Lyndon Baines Johnson, interview VI, 2, Johnson Library.

[37]Lyndon Baines Johnson to WFG, September 9, 1955, box 67, f. Geo-Gid 96, master file, Johnson Papers.

[38]Senator George Smathers, oral history, 20; Glen Wilson, who worked for Johnson, oral history, II, 29, Johnson Library. Johnson biographer Robert Caro says that he visited him in the Mayflower, not in the hospital (Caro, *The Years of Lyndon Johnson*, 621).

[39]Glen Wilson, oral history, II, 11, Johnson Library.

[40]Caro, *The Years of Lyndon Johnson*, 151.

[41]William S. White, oral history, III, 9, Johnson Library.

"The Johnson Treatment," at which point George simply showed him the door.[42] When George died, however, Johnson attended the funeral in Vienna. He no longer had to play politics with George, so we can assume that his letter to Miss Lucy in the days following was sincere, when he told her, "I left some part of me in Vienna the other day." In his memoirs written fourteen years after George's death, Lyndon Johnson did not mention Walter George even once.[43]

Johnson never tried to bully George, as he did others, but he did manipulate him. He wanted to get freshman senator Mike Mansfield on the Foreign Relations Committee, though Lehman of New York, whom George did not like, was next in line. Using a version of the "Don't throw me in the briar patch" technique, Johnson said, "George, I'm sure you would like to have Lehman on the [Foreign Relations] Committee." George, as Johnson suspected that he would, hit the ceiling and suggested Mansfield, who was Johnson's choice anyway.[44] In another incident, Senator Wayne Morse, a Republican-turned-independent-turned-Democrat in the Senate, wanted a seat on the Foreign Relations Committee, and he knew that George did not want him, but in a conversation, Johnson pointed out that it might bring Morse over to become a Democrat, so George went along with it.[45] He also promoted a rapprochement between George and Hubert Humphrey, whom Johnson was trying to promote. Johnson would tell George things like, "Senator Hubert Humphrey isn't such a bad fellow, you know," and when Humphrey entered the cloakroom, Johnson would bring him over to George, who was usually holding court there. For once, the loquacious Humphrey listened, and the two developed a mutual respect for one another. George actually came to like him, and even campaigned for his reelection in 1954.[46]

Walter George's greatest contribution to the Eisenhower years was in foreign policy since he chaired the Foreign Relations Committee. Still, having been for decades on the Finance Committee and many years its chair, he could hardly have totally left that work. Next to the chairman, who was, of course, a Democrat, George remained the second-ranking Democrat since he chose to chair the Foreign Relations committee. Every tax bill since 1936

[42]Caro, *The Years of Lyndon Johnson*, 135.

[43]Johnson, *Vantage Point.*

[44]Chandler, *Natural Superiority of Southern Politicians*, 329.

[45]Caro, *The Years of Lyndon Johnson*, 557.

[46]Ibid., 460.

"has borne the stamp of the senator from Georgia," *US News* told its readers in 1956.[47] Senator Paul Douglas (D-Illinois), who self-righteously wore a halo resembling a crown of thorns as champion of the poor, wrote that George had "lost his popular sympathies" (one is hard-pressed to see when he had had them) and called George among "the sharpest-tonged and most knowledgeable member of the Senate." Douglas remembered that in dealing with George and his cronies, he and Hubert Humphrey felt like they were "leaving the catacombs to enter the coliseum, with its man-eating lions."[48]

The *New York Times* summed up Walter George's views on the federal budget: "Few public men feel, in principle, deeper pain at the size of the public debt [than does Walter George]."[49] Unlike our politicians today, George did not shy away from raising taxes to pay for deficits, even in a declining economy. When in 1953 the Democrats in the House passed a tax cut, getting enough Republican votes to pass it in the Republican chamber, hoping either to gain credit for it or to try to embarrass the Republicans when they opposed it, George was the first Democrat to break ranks and oppose the Democratic tax cut. He became the key to the opposition, robbing the Democrats of a partisan victory. Fiscal conservative Harry Byrd followed him, as did other Southern Democrats, and the Senate swung against it. The House then reversed itself, and the *Atlanta Journal* called it a "triumph for a few individuals like Senator George who took a stand for the best interests of the nation."[50]

In spring 1954, when the deficit had tightened, the budget appeared to be balanced, and the economy was improving, George favored a tax cut and became its champion.[51] In any cut, he looked after Big Business, as he always had. He supported the administration's proposals for reducing income dividend tax and easing depreciation allowances, as well as a "slight" corporation tax cut.[52] He wanted to increase consumer purchasing power and proposed the individual exemption increase from $600.00 to $800.00 this year and to a $1000.00 the next. A couple with two children would in 1955 get a $4,000 exemption instead of the $2400 today. In George's plan, ten million people would be removed completely from the tax rolls. These changes would reduce revenues, George admitted, but it would prevent unemploy-

[47]"When Senator George Steps Out," 46.

[48]Douglas, *The Fullness of Time*, 425–26.

[49]White, "Senator George, Monument Determined," 42.

[50]"Victory for Senator George," *Atlanta Journal*, n. d., scrapbook, LHG-VHPS.

[51]"How a Democrat Guides Republican Tax Policy," 62–63.

[52]Ibid. 62.

ment from rising, which would cost more. George saw this action as "a forward-looking step before the economy falls on its face."[53] Some pundits saw his reductions as a political move in an election year, but *Newsweek* recognized it for what it was: An attempt to head off an economic slump, noting that his long record of fiscal conservatism defended him against charges of politicking. *Newsweek* further reminded its readers, "His policy of giving the consumer more money is supported by many eminent economists." Moreover, a number of Republican conservatives favored it as well.[54]

His move was a departure from George's past support of business first, believing that if business prospered, so would "the little man." George argued that individual amounts might be small, but the cumulative effect would be great.[55] The Republicans were dragged along with this logic because they had more to fear from a declining economy that increased deficit spending. Moreover, if the economy did not improve, deficits would be worse anyway.[56]

Eisenhower was as a strong fiscal conservative as Walter George, and regardless of George's position on the committee, George still ruled it. After the Republicans won the congressional election in 1952, Gene Milliken, a Republican, assumed the chair, and George reverted to the ranking minority member, one could not tell any difference in tax policy: George still led the committee, and the GOP was happy to let him do so. George's and Eisenhower's monetary policies, all agreed, would "leave more money in people's pockets."[57] As *US News* explained it, "When Senator George talks taxes, Congress listens."[58] When tax receipts began to decline in the first months of the Eisenhower administration, Eisenhower called for the rescinding of a number of tax cuts that had been passed in the last year of the Truman administration including the corporate and excise rates.[59] George was in agreement.

Early in 1955, the House passed a tax cut of $20.00 per person, proposed by Sam Rayburn, the speaker, and John McCormack, the Democratic leader. It would cost the government $2.3 billion a year. Efforts to defeat this proposal lost 210–205. It was, however, stopped cold in the Senate Fi-

[53]"High Bid for Favor," 19.

[54]Lindley, "Way to Win an Election?" 26.

[55]"How a Democrat Guides Republican Tax Policy," 60.

[56]Ibid.

[57]WFG, "Democratic Tax Proposals," 118–19.

[58]"How a Democrat Guides Republican Tax Policy," 6.

[59]"Legislative Achievements of the 83rd Congress," December 1, 1954, 3, FO 361/109109, FO-BNA.

nance Committee by a vote of 9–6.[60] George was joined by Harry Byrd in killing it.[61] Byrd pointed out that the cut would get each taxpayer only about six cents a day, and George's opposition in the Senate made the defeat "all but certain." It lost by a vote of 50–44, with five Southern Democrats joining the solid no-vote by the Republicans. George's opposition stemmed from the fact that with the budget so out of whack and with business now "booming," it was not necessary. Moreover, the cuts would not go into effect for sixteen months.[62] George, however, left a way open for a compromise with the House, which had just voted itself a 50 percent pay raise, ($15,000 to $22,500) and handed the GOP a nice election issue for 1956.[63]

In December 1955, George was again championing a tax cut, which puzzled Eisenhower. He and Hagerty were on his front porch in Gettysburg, and George and Sam Rayburn, whose tax cut George had helped defeat earlier in the year, announced a tax cut. Ike had said that he "expected nothing but politics from Mr. Sam," but he was surprised that George himself had done a flip-flop. Hagerty opined that on the eve of an election year in which he faced a tough reelection against the probably candidacy of Herman Talmadge, George had changed his tune.[64] Talmadge's candidacy ultimately made George change his mind on a number of issues. In his proposals of December 1955, George made the point that relief must be given to lower- and middle-income groups, and he predicted that in spring 1956, individuals would be given "quite substantial tax reductions," and he suggested this change in the form of raised tax exemptions, what he had championed and what had failed in 1954.[65] Soon George's political problems would eclipse any benefit that he might have gained for posing as a tax reformer.

There are some small indications that Walter George might have been a bit anti-Semitic, despite the fact that he had a Jewish law partner in Vienna. He manifested a strong dislike for Senator Herbert Lehman of New York. Some of it might well have been just politics, for Lehman was one of the most liberal members of the Senate and, therefore, to George might have seemed fiscally reckless. Moreover, Lehman had defeated Senator John Foster Dulles, whom George came to admire greatly in his short, appointed

---

[60]Dallek, *Lone Star Rising*, 469.

[61]Heinemann, *Harry Byrd of Virginia*, 364–405.

[62]"George of Georgia: Ike's Friend in Need," 29.

[63]Makins to Foreign Office, March 5, 1955, weekly political survey, no. 145, 3, FO 361/114350, FO BNA.

[64]Hagerty, *The Diary of James C. Hagerty*, 243.

[65]WFG, "Who Needs Tax Relief Most?" 46.

term in the Senate, and that must have caused some bitterness. George had made an intemperate attack on Lehman when he was governor of New York in 1938, for which he apologized to Roosevelt saying, "I may have…too little self-control at times." (He was at this time becoming a potential victim of Roosevelt's 1938 purges.) Not long after Lehman entered the Senate, he and George tangled over the Humphrey-Lehman bill (S. 2842), legislation that would expand immigration. George denounced the legislation, stating that it would open the doors "to a hoard of people—of foreigners," and that it would bring harm to American labor. Moreover, he implied that any supporters of the bill were "pink," i.e., communists. He then left the Senate floor. For Walter George, it was a rude and intemperate outburst. [66]

Lehman immediately denounced George's statement as "bitter remarks" and "one of the most remarkable, one of the most disturbing statements I have heard on the floor of the Senate." He expressed the view that senators should "speak strongly" on the Senate floor but "not bitterly…and in good temper." Lehman went on, "I am the son of an immigrant. I am proud of it.…I believe that my record is that of a good American.… I am the only member of the Senate who has the Distinguished Service Medal given for service in the First World War." Noting that all of his children, including a daughter, had served in World War II, and that one of them had not returned, he added, "to hear a member of the Senate imply that those who oppose this bill are less patriotic than he.… I believe is a libel on the patriotism…and the Americanism [of the Humphrey-Lehman bill's supporters]."[67]

The two had also tangled over several financial issues. One was Lehman's proposal to extend Social Security to the Virgin Islands, and later Puerto Rico.[68] That same year they had sparred over the Revenue Act of 1951. Lehman, Paul Douglas, and Humphrey had proposed stiffer rates. George infuriated Lehman by accusing him of a "soak-the-rich" tax plan that was politically motivated. An intemperate exchange took place on the Senate floor with George's interrupting Lehman in a very uncharacteristically rude way when Lehman had the floor and would not yield. When Lehman pointed out that the bill favored men of higher incomes over men of small and moderate incomes," George exploded. "Mr. President," he exclaimed. "I resent the statement, and no man worthy of a seat in the Senate

[66]Ibid.

[67]"A reply to Senator George (from the *CR*), May 21, 1952, special files, 484, Lehman papers.

[68]H. H. Lehman to WFG, March 7, 1950, file 483, Lehman papers.

will make that statement," leading to raucous disorder in the Senate galleries, which had been packed with the bill's opponents.[69] George's uncharacteristic remarks seem to be driven by more than simple collegial disagreement.

Whatever had motivated George's rudeness, any lingering animosity on Lehman's part had dissipated by 1954 when another Social Security bill, which would have adversely affected immigrants had Chairman Milliken and Walter George stricken Lehman's changes from the bill. Thanking George, he wrote, "I want to thank you most sincerely for the consideration you showed in this matter. I think the action taken by your committee was a highly enlightened one. I know it was due in large measure to the sympathetic consideration you gave to the [my?] objections which were made to these provisions. I have been told of the leadership you furnished in this matter."[70]

For all of the impact that George had in his Senate career, the effect that he had on foreign affairs in the last two years of his Senate tenure was his greatest. His passage of the Lend-Lease bill, his work on the wartime alliances, his contributions in building the United Nations, and his support of the Truman Doctrine and the Marshall Plan were themselves giant strides to America's security, but his work in his last two years in the Senate were all enormous steps on the world stage. The entire focus of his efforts was for peace, but peace through strength, and the avoidance of any fighting that would ever take place on American soil. His actions in foreign policy were always designed to serve American interests. George's support of foreign aid, a position that was to give him so much political trouble in 1956, was adopted as a measure for enhanced US security, in order "to promote the foreign policy, security and general welfare of the United States."[71]

To him, the foreign policy of our nation should be directed by the White House, as long as the administration was acting "with proper responsibility" and with proper deference to the Senate,"[72] and in his efforts in 1955–57, he fought to put it firmly in Eisenhower's hands. Moreover, he felt that no nation's foreign policy will be respected unless the administration who presents it has the strength and the will to carry it to execution. In the atomic age, in which America had arrived by 1955, such a position

[69]Nevins, *Herbert A. Lehman and His Era*, 325–26.

[70]Lehman to WFG, July 21, 1954, Special Files, f. 485, Lehman papers.

[71]"What is Foreign Policy?" 1, attached to a letter by Carl Marcy to WFG, November 28, 1955, WFG-VHPS.

[72]White, "Senator George, Monument Determined," 44.

meant remaining militarily strong with a willingness to flex one's military muscle.[73] An aggressive foreign policy such as the one he favored meant receiving continued opposition in the Senate. The Senate of the 83rd Congress was more reactionary than the Congress he had fought in 1937 when he had helped Roosevelt drag the country toward preparedness.

The reader is aware that George had entered the Senate in 1922 as a confirmed isolationist, and he had campaigned as a strong opponent of the League of Nations. He shared the isolationist view that we are protected by two vast oceans and the British navy. We have seen how his views had changed during the pre-war and war years. His change of opinion came, he told the American Society of Newspaper Editors in 1955, when he saw that isolationism led to the disappearance of American markets, and "Americans of all walks of life began to realize that every important public action committed on the other side of the globe directly affected the welfare...of the American people."[74] To the Rotary Club of Thomasville, Georgia, he went so far that same year as to express puzzlement at the attitudes of the isolationists: "I cannot understand how some Americans can be paralyzed by the thought of assuming full leadership of the world. I do not understand why so many Americans are so skeptical of our ability to meet the world's problems."[75] His aggressive attitude led Congressman Stewart L. Udall to call him, "the quarterback for the State Department." He told his House colleagues, "From crisis to crisis he has been out ahead of the secretary of state and the president, and the country is better for it."[76] Eisenhower became in these years dependent on Walter George when, as the French Ambassador to the United States wrote the French foreign ministry, he had to "reduce to silence his own party and depend on the Democrats, notably Senator George."[77] Adlai Stevenson seemed, nevertheless, to be annoyed by George's new role in the Eisenhower administration. Planning to run for the presidency again in 1956, Stevenson seemed to regret the help that George had given his former and future opponent. To his diary, he confided that George was "by no means 'illiterate' on foreign policy," but he felt that he was "too content to let them [the Eisenhower administration] lead the way" in international matters.[78]

---

[73]*CR*, 84/1, 5262–63.

[74]WFG, "Russians Will Lose," 78.

[75]"Political Test," 32.

[76]*CR*, 84/1, 5262.

[77]Ambassador of France to Pinay, 6 October 1955, Amérique, 1952–63, EU: politiques intéreure, f. 482, 370, AMAE.

[78]Martin, *Adlai Stevenson and the World*, 176, quoting a Stevenson diary.

Generally speaking, the Democrats were rather silent on Ike's foreign policy by 1955.[79] Indeed they had given him generally more support than his own party had in foreign issues. Roger Makins, the British ambassador, informed the Foreign Office that even in the new Democratic congress, Eisenhower "will have more trouble with his own party...than with the Democrats." Now that the Democrats had a small majority, the president will now achieve "the liberal and progressive policies set out last year but since ignored or refused him [by the Republican Congress]."[80] Where Ike had the most opposition was indeed with the Taft wing of his party. Taft was dead but the isolationist "Taftites" were still very much alive. To forge his foreign policy, he had to rely on a bizarre coalition of the Democrats and the minority of liberal Republicans.[81] In this alliance, however, the Democrats would be the centerpiece with George leading the coalition.[82]

Walter George's seniority on both Finance and Foreign Relations could make him the chair of either one he chose, but Dr. Francis O. Wilcox, at one time the chief of staff of Foreign Relations, remembered that Eisenhower lobbied George to take Foreign Relations. If he had not, the ancient Rhode Island senator Theodore Green would have become the chair, and he would not have the vigor to help as George, who was ten years younger, could.[83] Moreover, Secretary of State John Foster Dulles had very good relations with Walter George, and George's power in the Senate, his leadership skills, and his grasp of foreign matters, Dulles felt was greater. Moreover, the two men respected each other.[84]

In December 1954, when George was at the White House on another matter, Eisenhower "tactfully intimated to him that he would like to see him assume the chair over Foreign Relations [Committee]."[85] George was more interested in taxes than he had been in foreign policy and really did not want the chairmanship of Foreign Relations Committee, but he finally took it, partly to keep the aged Senator Theodore Green out and partly to help Ei-

[79]Graebner, *New Isolationism*, 203–204.

[80]Minutes of Ch. Tickell, for Makins, 8 January 1955, FO 371/114350, FO-BNA, British National Archive.

[81]Caro, *The Years of Lyndon Johnson*, 522.

[82]According to historian Stephen Ambrose, Eisenhower even gave some thought to running in 1956 as a Democrat since he feared that his victory might bring in a lopsided Republican majority, and he would have such reactionaries as Knowland as committee chairmen (Ambrose, *Nixon*, 1:386, 405).

[83]Francis O. Wilcox, oral history, Eisenhower Library, 147.

[84]Ibid., 146.

[85]"Pusca [illegible] in your Government, 7, WFG-MU.

senhower.[86]

As further encouragement, his good friend, Harry Byrd of Virginia, a strong fiscal conservative, could achieve his life-long ambition of becoming the Finance chair. Moreover, George would remain on the committee as a member.[87] George did remain as a member of the Finance Committee, and generally speaking, he exercised over Finance power as great as though he were chair.[88] On the down side, Foreign Relations would not have for him politically the certain support of financial backers, which journalist Doris Fleeson noted, "No amount of statesmanship can attract."[89] George was not aware, nor probably anyone else for that matter, that he had driven the final nail in his own political coffin.

George replaced Republican Senator Alexander Wiley, who, Valeo remembered, "was not a profound man and he knew it. He did not make any pretense of being other than a nice guy from a small town in Wisconsin."[90] Wiley, however, wrote George in February 1955 a very warm letter offering his full cooperation in the transition, adding, "I shall be not only happy, but honored, to 'hold up your hand at all times.'"[91] George took over foreign relations work like the proverbial duck to water, but one Washington observer described his manner as "gentle but almost dictatorial control of the Foreign Relations Committee."[92] Immediately George and Dulles became a well-oiled team. Every Thursday, George and Dulles met in George's apartment in the Mayflower for breakfast, and Miss Lucy cooked eggs, bacon, and grits for them. At the meetings, Dulles briefed George on the latest foreign policy developments and suggested a strategy on how to meet them.[93] The two men had formed a warm relationship in Dulles's short term in the Senate, and this deep respect flourished into a confident and comfortably informal working relationship.[94] Curiously, they never left these meetings and talked [publicly] about what was said.[95] Eisenhower came to rely on

[86]White, "Senator George, Monument Determined," 47.
[87]"George of Georgia: Ike's Friend in Need," 29.
[88]Donovan, "Senator George," 33.
[89]Doris Fleeson, "Ike's Pillar of Strength," WFG-VHPS.
[90]Valeo, oral history, 161.
[91]Alexander Wiley to WFG, February 1, 1955, WFG-VHPS.
[92]Stone, *The Haunted Fifties*, 92.
[93]"Voice of the 84th," 24.
[94]Donovan, "Senator George," 32.
[95]Pat Holt, oral history, 81. Holt remembered that the meetings always took place on Wednesdays.

George as "a second Senator Vandenberg,"[96] and he even used George to deal with the Democratic majority, bypassing Lyndon Johnson and many of the Republican leaders.[97] His importance was noted by *Time*, which said of the association, "He is hand-in-glove with Secretary of State Dulles and the president, though sometimes his is the hand and theirs is the glove."[98]

In this high-profile role, *Newsweek* told its readers that George was immediately recognized as "the most powerful spokesman in Congress in the field of foreign policy."[99] One of his major strengths as far as all sides were concerned was his devotion to bipartisan foreign policy. His position, as one journalist noted, "is probably setting an all-time high for intimate cooperation between representatives of the two parties in peacetime in dealing with issues beyond the water's edge."[100] Everyone saw George as the inheritor of Vandenberg's mantle of bipartisanship.[101] Vandenberg had become a proponent of bipartisan diplomacy in 1941 when HR 1776 had passed, and although he did not like it, he had to make it work. He felt that unity at home was essential in the looming world crisis, so there began the idea of nonpartisan foreign policy.[102]

On this question, George became more Catholic than the pope. In an address to the American Society of Newspaper Editors in April 1953, George outline the reason for it. "A bipartisan policy is something more than the non-partisan conduct of our foreign affairs," he told the audience. "Wherever possible we should seek out areas of agreement and act within those areas. Otherwise, in the face of a threat from aggressor nations…we will present a divided opposition to aggression." Noting that the real purpose of American foreign policy must be both peace and security, he pledged that "the Democrats will loyally support policies which will promote this purpose."[103] As early as 1946, George had proposed a bill to promote the military cooperation of the American states of the Western Hemisphere,[104] and his position landed him a position on the Joint Committee on Foreign Economic Cooperation in 1949.[105] By the time Eisenhower was in the

---

[96]"Personalities in Your Government," June 26, 1955, 3, WFG-MU.

[97]Chandler, *Natural Superiority of Southern Politicians*, 329.

[98]Ibid.

[99]WFG, interview, "But No Neutral Zone," 22.

[100]Donovan, "Senator George," 32.

[101]McPherson, *A Political Education*, 35. McPherson was an assistant to LBJ.

[102]Vandenberg, *The Private Papers of Senator Vandenberg*, 12.

[103]*CR*, 83/1, appendix A1979–80.

[104]*CR*, 70/2, 3368–69.

[105]*CR*, 81/1, 670.

White House, George even had Stevenson assuring Ike of Democratic support.[106] In this position, George's non-partisan support cut both ways. He once proclaimed that he was not concerned which party was making the nation's foreign policy; he would be for it if it was "workable," adding that "it makes no difference whether it is put forward by a Democratic or a Republican president."[107] Shortly after assuming the chairmanship of Foreign Relations, he stressed that a chair must be "inherently non-partisan," and adding that chair who "kept himself at a partisan level would be doomed to failure."[108] To cement the two parties together on these issues, George held bipartisan congressional luncheons, which usually were reports more than dialogues, during which George, as was customary at such things, said little.[109]

The Democrats had so thoroughly supported the administration's foreign policy that was difficult to make that an issue in the 1956 presidential campaign, although that did not stop individual Democrats like Hubert Humphrey from attacking Secretary of State Dulles. However, Walter George and Mike Mansfield, both powerful men, generally maintained a moderate course in the 1956 race.[110] Dulles had suggested to George that there were "one or two questions" that would be off-limits as campaign issues, the State of Israel probably being one of them, but the press was never notified what they were.[111] In general, George, Eisenhower, and Nixon agreed to eliminate foreign policy as an issue in 1956 "in order to preserve bipartisanship," and this strategy worked until the Middle East and Hungary blew up in the midst of the campaign.[112] In a speech to the annual forum of the *New York Herald Tribune*, Nixon generously thanked Walter George and Lyndon Johnson for their "magnificent" support of the administration's foreign policy.[113]

During George's two-year tenure as chair of Foreign Relations, the committee produced the greatest volume of business of any Congress since

---

[106]Stone, *The Haunted Fifties*, 93.

[107]"Personalities in your Government," 26 June 1955, 8, WFG-MU.

[108]*Washington Daily News*, February 16, 1955, cited in Carlton, "The Record...," 13, WFG-VHPS.

[109]Bipartisan Congressional Luncheon, March 31, 1955, f. Legislative meetings 1955(2), legislative meetings series, Eisenhower papers.

[110]Ambassadeur de France to Pinay, January 27, 1956, Amérique, 1952–63, Etats Unis: Politique intéreure, f. 483, 30, AMAE.

[111]Telegram, January 26, 1956, ibid.

[112]*US: Annual Review*, 1955, cited in Parmet, *Eisenhower and the American Crusade*, 422.

[113]*New York Times*, October 1955, cited in Parmet, *Eisenhower and the American Crusade*, 422.

the committee had kept records. George called it "one of the heaviest foreign policy schedules that I have ever experienced."[114] The committee reported out and the Senate approved thirty-two treaties, thirty-four bills and joint resolutions, and thirty Senate and concurrent resolutions. The work included two Mutual Security acts (1955 and 1956), the Formosa Resolution, the Southeast Asia Collective Defense Treaty (SEATO), Mutual Defense Treaty with the Republic of China, the termination of the formal occupation of Germany by the western powers, the admission of Germany to NATO, and many other minor events.[115]

Although Germany had rearmed and joined NATO, Europe cooled somewhat in importance. The French ambassador Maurice Couve de Murville noted soon after Walter George's assuming the chair of Foreign Relations of the "increasing influence exercised by Senator George on the Congress and on the administration in the domain of foreign policy." He cautioned his government that what George had to say "merited attention," and that he "without any doubt [is] a determinant element in the present orientation of American foreign policy."[116] As for the direction of American foreign policy, the French ambassador noted Walter George's power, but dubbed him "more conservative" than "Democratic."[117]

When the former French president Vincent Auriol visited the United States, George hosted a luncheon for him and fifteen important senators.[118] While in the US, the former French president suggested a meeting of the "Big Four" in San Francisco at some future date.[119] His suggestion was perhaps the instigator of a later *démarche* by Senator George.

George's position on America's arch European enemy in World War II ran contrary to the position of most Americans, and it was probably in the mid-1950s that he did a turnaround. In a speech in May 1955 to the American Society of Newspaper Editors, he said, "I think it may now be said…that we made a great mistake in insisting upon the complete destruction of the great producing nation in Europe—Germany. Then after Japan came in…we again insisted upon its destruction…." Noting that we were right in destroying the military governments of both, he observed that "in

[114]Statement of WFG, chairman, foreign relations committee, n. d., GFR-VHPS.

[115]For details, see *CR*, 84/2, 13409.

[116]Couve de Murville to Pinay, 6 May 1955, Amérique, 1952–1963, Etats Unis: Asie, f. 414, 210, AMAE.

[117]Ibid., March 17, 1955, f. 482, 274.

[118]Ibid., May 27, 1955, f. 350, 384527.

[119]*Chicago Daily News*, clipping, May 31, 1955, Rel. F-A, f. 350 (384527), Ibid.

the process America created economic and political vacuums,"[120] into which Russia might enter. With quite a prescient observation, he predicted that we "will see the day when our Russian friends will go back to their ancient borders."[121] Few would have agreed with him at the time.

Partially to counter the Russian Cold War threat, the United States had agreed to the rearmament of Germany in the Accords of Paris, which were discussed in late 1954 to early 1955. They had understandably made many in France ill at ease, a feeling that was shared in other quarters, the British ambassador reported to the British Foreign Office.[122] Curiously, Pierre Mendès-France, prime minister and a politician who had sided with the Free French in World War II, had encouraged German rearmament. He was a strong anticommunist, who, one journalist opined, will "look reality in the face."[123] When his government fell in February 1955, even *New York Times* called it "a shadow of unease on the plans of Western defense."[124] When the government of Mendès-France fell, Walter George echoed the idea, saying that the fall of the French government "delivers a very severe blow to the contribution of Germany to the defense [of Europe]." He feared that the Soviets would take advantage of the French political crisis to intensify their efforts in France and Germany against German rearmament.[125] The American press trumpeted Mendès-France's replacement, Edgar Faure, as one who would support the ratification of the Paris Accords, and George's and others' fears were unfounded. Faure announced before the end of February that he would call for the ratification of German rearmament "*avec rapidité*" (quickly) because it was essential "to the survival of the West."[126]

In April, George introduced to the Senate a protocol, signed by Germany, the United Kingdom, and France, calling for the de-occupation of Germany and the admission of Germany to NATO. Praising Germany's progress over the past ten years since "the unconditional surrender of Nazi Germany," the German nation "had become a land of prosperity with a well-established democratic government." George felt that if nothing else, Germany's geographical location should make it "an integral part of the

---

[120]George, "Russia Will Lose," 78–79.

[121]Ibid.

[122]Makins to Foreign Office, January 3, 1955, FO 301/114350, FO-BNA.

[123]Bonnet to MFA, Etats-Unis, June 15, 1954, f. 7USA-France, 111, AMAE.

[124]Couve de Murville to MFA, February 7, 1955, Rélations Franco-Russe, f. 350 (now 384527), AMAE.

[125]Ibid.

[126]Ibid., February 25, 1955.

North American Community" and moreover, "the difficulty...of defending Western Europe without Germany has long been obvious."[127] Germany then joined NATO, and the Warsaw Pact, NATO's Communist counterpart, created by the Soviets. Peace, as uneasy as it was, was maintained until the Iron Curtain collapsed in the 1980s. The Soviets had called in May for the "neutralization" of Germany, much as Finland had been neutralized in its foreign policy. George felt that the idea "was very seductive" but "very dangerous and one which ought not be discussed." As usual few people in Congress opposed George's view on the question.[128] George was, of course, proved right in his prediction to the American Society of Newspaper Editors in April 1955 when he said, "The coming back of West Germany will not be immediate but ultimately it will mean the organization of all Western Europe and the retreat of the Soviets back to their ancient boundaries."[129] In the late 1980s, the wall came down and the Russian troops returned home.

Latin America and the Middle East did not hold the importance that both would have at a later time, but George had activities in both areas. In December 1955, George helped ratify Puerto Rico's constitution, and in a speech at the national banquet of the Exchange Club in Puerto Rico, he warmly addressed Puerto Ricans as "my fellow citizens."[130] He led the admission of Greece and Turkey into NATO in January 1952. The Foreign Relations Committee had passed it unanimously, and Senator Connally, then the chair, had asked George to guide it through the Senate, which he easily did.[131] The Middle East in general was plagued with "appalling poverty and high population growth," which worsened the former. These problems were worsened by rising nationalism, anti-colonialism, and anti-Westernism. Not having had to face these threats before, America had no clear objectives in the area.[132] These problems manifested themselves in rumblings throughout 1956, and George and Dulles met to discuss the questions. The issue exploded in the Suez Crisis in fall 1956, when France and Britain moved unilaterally to prevent the Egyptian takeover of the canal.

George, who had by that time been nominated to be Eisenhower's representative to NATO and was already leaving the Senate, told reporters that he felt the joint Anglo-France action had given "a death blow to NATO"

---

[127]*CR*, 84/1, 4207.

[128]Makins to Foreign Office, Wkly Pol. Sim, no. 295, 2, FO 371/114350, FO-BNA.

[129]Quoted with no source from Carlton, "The Retreat," 10, GFR-VHPS.

[130]George, "World at Peace," The Exchange, December 1955, scrapbook, LHG-VHPS.

[131]*CR*, 82/2, 587.

[132]C. Marcy to WFG, February 2, 1956, GFR-VHPS.

and that the whole imbroglio was "one of the meanest pictures in world affairs we have had in some time." Serious though it was, he added that he did not feel that the Russians would intervene.[133] He compared Gamal Nasser to Mussolini and felt that he had been strengthened in his political position by the Anglo-French action.[134] He strongly supported Eisenhower's and Dulles's policy of non-intervention and conciliation.[135] He met with the president at the White House on November 16, and on leaving the meeting, he told the press that no one need be "unduly alarmed," nor did the president need to reconvene Congress.[136] When Senator William Fulbright demanded a statement of specific policies on Suez and the recent Hungarian uprising, George dismissed his request in effect by adjourning the meeting early. He promised a brief statement and observed that Eisenhower's witnesses from the State Department had essentially answered these two questions.[137] George had done one more favor for Eisenhower, although by this time he had essentially exited forever from American politics and diplomacy.

American activity in the Far East had been for a decade a major problem for American diplomats because the "fall" of China to the Communists and the subsequent Korean War had led to a seismic disruption of the area. George's work on the overall Far Eastern problem resulted in the Formosa Resolution and the Southeast Asia Treaty Organization. Although he did not chair Foreign Relations in the 83rd Congress, he played a role in the 1954 Paris agreements on Indo-China. These three successes resulted in the stabilization of this sector of the world for a decade.[138] In the whole question of Far Eastern troubles, George, on resuming the chair of Foreign Relations in 1955, had in effect replaced Senator Knowland of California, who lacked enthusiasm for some of Eisenhower's Far Eastern progress. The *Atlanta Journal* pointed out to its readers that with George "in the commanding position that he occupies…the administration, in exploring avenues of peace, can look to Congress with the confidence it could not muster if it had to rely on Senator Knowland."[139]

Journalists jokingly called Senator Knowland, "the senator from Formosa" because of his unrelenting efforts to curb Red China and indeed even

---

[133]"People of the Week," *Newsweek* (November 9, 1956), 20.

[134]Ibid.

[135]Kingseed, *Eisenhower and the Suez Crisis*, 70.

[136]Ibid.

[137]Ibid., 137–38.

[138]Chandler, *Natural Superiority of Southern Politicians*, 329.

[139]Thomas L. Stokes, "George of Georgia…," n. d., *Atlanta Journal*, scrapbook, LHG-VHPS.

restore Chiang Kai-shek to power on the mainland. George, on the other hand, had called for an open dialogue with Communist China and raised even broader questions with the Communist giant on Far Eastern problems. He did not believe in the imminence of armed conflict with the Communists but instead thought a working relationship would create a certain equilibrium among the nations of China on the one hand and India and Japan on the other. Japan would play the role of the counterweight on the continent, with India representing the center of "fixed convictions." George had been concerned for some time with the alleviation of "the tensions of the world" but had wanted to avoid "unilateral decisions." Instead, the United States should incorporate "the views of their friends on the problems" in the Far East. He stressed economic aid, noting that assisting nations economically trumps military aid to them.[140] Connected with this idea was George's support of Dulles's belief that Sigmund Rhee, the president of South Korea, should never be encouraged to "break the armistice" with the North. He felt that Eisenhower's hand would be strengthened on this point if Congress made it abundantly clear that we would not support Rhee in an aggressive move.[141]

Moreover, George favored allowing the Japanese to trade with Red China. In an appearance on *Meet the Press* in June 1955, he made this point, especially in the trade of textile goods. He felt that this exchange would help the American textile industry from "cutthroat competition" with Japanese goods. The China market would absorb cheap Japanese textiles, and they could not then be available to flood the American market now that tariffs had been lowered.[142] He likewise committed what the right-wing Republicans called the ultimate heresy by advocating trade with potential enemies. He called it a "fantastic theory" that we had to have normal relations with a country in order to trade with it. "We do not necessarily [have to] recognize them or approve of their governments…[to reap] the advantage that comes from fuller trade with all nations," he said.[143]

The problem of Vietnam was beginning to loom on the horizon, and Eisenhower had asked majority leader Johnson to test the Democrats' view of sending troops there. In an impromptu meeting of the Democratic Policy

[140]Couve de Murville to Pinay, 6 May 1955, Amérique 1952 1963, Etats-Unis en Asie, f. 414, 209–10 and 244, AMAE.

[141]Bipartisan legislative meeting, January 5, 1945, f. Leg. Meetings-1954 (1), box 1, Whitman file, Eisenhower papers.

[142]Carlton, "The Record," 10, GFR-VHPS.

[143]*Meet the Press*, July 24, 1955, in Carlton and Coclanis, eds., *Confronting Southern Poverty in the Great Depression*, 11.

Committee, George, who was not a member but who came on Johnson's request to act as a "Devil's advocate" for sending troops, recommended sending American forces there. George Reedy remembered violent objections, and Johnson, who would a decade later get America mired in the country, reported back that there was "little support" for intervention among the Democrats.[144]

As part of American general policy of the "containment" of Communism, the United States signed the agreement founding SEATO, an alliance of a number of nations in the Far East designed to contain the spread of Communism. Dulles had felt that if both a Republican and a Democratic senator signed the treaty, it would have a better chance of passing the Senate. In August 1954, Dulles asked Senator Wiley, then chair of Foreign Relations, to sign for the Republicans, and Wiley recommended that Mike Mansfield sign for the Democrats. Dulles then called George, who would have been the likely Democratic signatory, to ask his opinion. George, who had only once (or possibly twice) ventured out of the United States, warmly endorsed Mansfield, adding that he "would be good, he is developing, and will be a great fellow in the Senate."[145] The United States signed the Southeast Asia Collective Defense Treaty on September 8, 1954, and the Foreign Relations Committee under George's chairmanship reported it out favorably on January 21, 1955. It was introduced in the Senate in February 1955. In defending it, George admitted that it was not "regarded as a definitive solution to the Pacific defense problem," but was, however, "a more comprehensive, collective security system" in view of the division of Indo-China. "It is our purpose," he told his colleagues, "to give advance notice to any Communist nation contemplating aggressive action in that area that they will have to reckon with the United States." He felt that any "potential aggressor" may be deterred from reckless conduct by a clear-cut declaration of our intentions."[146] Under his guidance, it was, of course, quickly passed.

There were, however, two major international developments that occurred during George's watch in the 84th Congress. The first was the Formosa Crisis that happened shortly after he assumed the chairmanship of the Foreign Relations Committee, and it gave the appearance that it would bring war between the United States and Red China. Ever since the Nationalist Chinese had fled to Formosa after their fall in 1949, it seemed inevita-

---

[144]Goldsmith, *Colleagues*, 39.

[145]Oberdorfer, *Senator Mansfield*, 123.

[146]"Southeast Asia Collective Defense Treaty Statement of Mr. George," 2 (unnumbered), February 1, 1955, GFR-VHPS.

ble the Chinese Communists would one day attempt to cross the Formosan Straits and take the island. By January 1955, the Communists had built an airfield on the mainland opposite Formosa, giving them air superiority over two Nationalist-controlled islands near the Chinese coast, Quemoy and Matsu. On January 10, Red planes bombed the Tachen Islands north of Quemoy and Matsu, and on January 17, 4,000 Chinese soldiers seized the small island of Ichiang, two hundred miles northwest of Formosa and seven miles north of the Tachen Islands, threatening 15,000 Nationalist troops. As Eisenhower wrote in his diary, "The time had come to draw the line."[147] The Mutual Defense Treaty with Taiwan was still pending before the Senate, so Eisenhower felt that he needed something from Congress to authorize what he was doing.[148] He knew that Walter George's support was crucial. However, the point at which he made the decision to ask Congress for a resolution, George, by some accounts, was not yet back in Washington. Assistant secretary of state for Far Eastern affairs, Walter S. Robertson, flew to Georgia expressly to "consult" with George on the Formosa treaty before the beginning of Congress, so George was already committed when the debate started.[149] Robertson's "few days attendance" in Vienna resulted in "the practical elimination of opposition to any real debate of the Formosa Treaty and Resolution."[150] From this point on, George was consulted every step of the way, and his support contributed to its bipartisan passage.[151] His position, however, was more moderate than that of the right-wing GOP, which wanted "dynamic liberation." George's position was instead, as we shall see, "static containment."

On January 19, Eisenhower and Dulles asked Congress for a resolution authorizing the defense of Nationalist China. On January 20, Walter George (who must have returned quickly to DC) and other leaders were summoned to the State Department for a briefing by Dulles and Admiral Arthur W. Radford, chairman of the joint chiefs of staff. At this meeting, George first learned of the Formosa Resolution, and from that point on, George was in the thick of the crisis. On Sunday, January 23, Mr. and Mrs. Dulles stopped by George's apartment in the Mayflower with a revised draft of the resolution for George's opinion and revisions. The president sought

[147]Eisenhower, *Mandate for Change*, 467.

[148]Weiler and Simons, *The United States and the United Nations*, 352.

[149]Cater, "Foreign Policy: Default of the Democrats," 23.

[150]Acheson, *Sketches from Life of Men I Have Known*, 142. The dates do not exactly fit, but there is too much evidence that the administration sent Robertson to Georgia to woo George for something like this action for it not to have happened.

[151]"Personalities in your Government," June 26, 1955, 8, WFG-MU.

this resolution "to clearly and publicly establish authority of the president as commander-in-chief to employ the armed forces of this nation promptly and effectively for the purpose indicated if in his judgment it became necessary." It was unclear whether Eisenhower meant to defend Quemoy and Matsu, for Eisenhower had decided to wait and see. If they attacked these islands, the president would decide at that point what to do.[152] George later stated that when he had to make a decision, "he will get the best info from the Joint Chiefs, and if I do not mistake the man, he will then go into his closet, and face to face with his Maker, he will make his own decision."[153] Eisenhower technically already had the authority as commander-in-chief, and he had also opposed the Bricker Amendment. He was acting, however, as though it had gone into effect.[154] He wanted to avoid making Truman's mistake of sending troops to Korea without asking Congress. He wanted specific authorization to defend Formosa.[155]

On Monday, President Eisenhower sent his historical message to Congress calling for authority to defend Formosa and the islands it controlled. He stated that Formosa and the Pescadores were "the backbone of [US] security in the [Pacific] Ocean. We have a mutual defense treaty with Formosa and that treaty is before us now," he told the nation. "The Reds are making every sign of attacking. In the interests of peace, the US must remove any doubt regarding our readiness to fight...to preserve the vital stake of the free world in a free Formosa."[156] On January 26, after the House approved it by a vote of 410–3,[157] the Senate Armed Services Committee and the Foreign Relations Committee both approved it and sent it to the Senate floor.[158] As chair of the Foreign Relations Committee, George now assumed command.

George used the premise that America must stand firm in facing the Chinese. "God, keep us out of war," was his plea, but he felt that "if war must come, let us not draw a line and say that beyond that line is a sanctuary...behind which we may retreat."[159] George insisted and had a concrete agreement with this point with Dulles that nothing in the resolution and

---

[152]Ambrose, *Eisenhower*, 2:233; Adams, *Firsthand Report*, 130.

[153]WFG, "Russia Will Lose," 80.

[154]Rovere, *The Eisenhower Years*, 251.

[155]Walter Robertson, oral history, 120, Eisenhower Library. Robertson was US ambassador to Taiwan and had handled lend-lease to Australia.

[156]Eisenhower, "Situation in the Formosa Straits," 1026–27.

[157]Eisenhower, *Mandate for Change*, 468.

[158]Donovan, "Senator George," 35.

[159]Graebner, *New Isolation*, 201–202.

any subsequent treaty would go beyond "*defending* [italics in original] the Pescadores and Formosa." George made certain that this agreement was no understanding to let the Nationalists Chinese take the offensive or for the administration to "fish in troubled waters."[160] He did privately have reservations about the resolution and treaty and the authority it gave the president, but he felt strongly that a stand must be made, for the Reds had forced the issue. He therefore fought for the resolution and a treaty on the question.[161] He realized that the vital national interests of the United States would be endangered if Formosa and the Pescadores were to fall into "unfriendly hands." The president felt, and George strongly supported him, that if the Americans made it unequivocally clear to all that they were prepared to use force in the crisis, it will be less likely that America would have to use it. In passing the resolution, Congress would make it unlikely that the Communist world would misjudge American intentions to defend Formosa. As George stated publicly the day before the vote, "There comes a time in the life of every nation when it must make its position unequivocally known. This resolution does that."[162]

There was indeed opposition to the resolution, and several senators had tried to weaken it. Hubert Humphrey had introduced an amendment in the committee to limit defense solely to Taiwan and the Pescadores, but the committee defeated it. On the Senate floor, Senator Lehman, George's nemesis at the time, sought to draw a defense line in the straits excluding Quemoy and Matsu. It was defeated 74–13 after three days of debate.[163] George led the defeat of the Lehman Amendment because he had argued that to abandon these two islands would create "a disintegration…swift, quick, speedy and final of the entire free-China position."[164]

Adlai Stevenson, thinking ahead to 1956, was advised by Democratic diplomat Chet Bowles to make the whole imbroglio an issue for 1956 by making the Formosa Resolution an example of a bankrupt policy. The fact that Lyndon Johnson and George had both supported Formosa led Stevenson to give the speech to both men for clearance before he used delievered it. Neither man seemed interested, but he sent it to Johnson and let him decide who else would see it. It is unclear whether or not George saw the speech,

[160]Makins to Foreign Office, weekly political summary, no. 99, February 12, 1955, 1 and 3, FO 371/114350.

[161]Donovan, "Senator George," 35.

[162]Statement from George on Formosa, January 27, 1955, GFR-VHPS.

[163]Ambrose, *Eisenhower*, 2:234.

[164]Hoopes, *The Devil and John Foster Dulles*, 274–75.

but at a $100/plate dinner in honor of Sam Rayburn to raise money for the Democratic Party, Stevenson had the misfortune of having to sit next to Walter George.[165] Apparently the speech was never given.

Criticism came from both Republicans and Democrats. The liberals opposing it were not unified. They met on Sunday, January 23, to plan a strategy, but when they failed to arrive at any unified plan of action, they had no coherent defense when the resolution reached the Senate floor.[166] Senator Ralph Flanders (R-Vermont) criticized the treaty as "preventive war." Wayne Morse, who had by now ended his political schizophrenia and gone over unalloyed to the Democrats, opined that it was a "predatory authorization" and would give Chiang Kai-shek the power to drag the United States into another world war. Estes Kefauver suggested that the whole issue be given to the UN, with Eisenhower's having the power to act only until the UN took over. He also felt that the whole purpose of the resolution was to get the Democrats to share any blame for what he could do without Congressional approval, i.e., protect American troops.[167] Even Bobby Baker, the secretary of the Democratic organization whose day of fame was almost a decade away, told George, on being asked his opinion, "Senator, I can tell you this. I for one haven't lost a damn thing on Quemoy or Matsu."[168]

To prevent additional restricting amendments, Eisenhower decided to issue a statement that he alone would retain power to send American forces into action. George at first asked him to hold off, but by November 27, the critics were making so much noise that George suggested he should issue a statement. Dulles read a draft to George in a phone call, and George approved its tone. The White House then authorized it and George went to work in the Senate.[169]

There accompanied the resolution, a few days later, the Mutual Defense Treaty with the Republic of China, almost as an afterthought. The United States had already signed mutual defense treaties with Japan, Korea, the Philippines, New Zealand, and Australia but had delayed signing one with Nationalist China, the object of the current tension, because "we might want to trade Formosa and the Pescadores to Red China as part of an overall settlement in the Far East," George said publicly at the time. Approval of such a treaty "will dispel any clouds of doubt that may exist on this point,"

---

[165]Martin, *My First Fifty Years in Politics*, 176.
[166]Cater, "Foreign Policy," 23.
[167]Eisenhower, *Mandate for Change*, 468.
[168]White, *Citadel*, 211.
[169]Donovan, "Senator George," 35.

he said.[170]

Why some Democrats did not make more of an issue of the fear of war is probably due in part to the manner in which George managed the resolution. First, he stifled amendments in the Foreign Relations Committee. Then he refused to permit much debate on the question on the Senate floor.[171] Still, his greatest action that muted the opposition was what *Newsweek* called the "power of his oratory" on the Senate floor.[172] Here George's resounding voice laid waste to the resolution's opponents in a verbal carpet bombing. As one journalist put it, "In less than five minutes...he demolished opposition to the resolution giving President Eisenhower a blank check in the Formosa Strait."[173] It was one of the greatest speeches of his career.

George began by stating that the resolution did not need lengthy discussion and would in any case have greater impact if acted on promptly and not "crippled with trifling amendments," or descending "to the level of partisan politics, thus placing all opponents on the defensive." He praised Eisenhower for coming to Congress for approval, although he did not have to ask for "the moral support of the American people." He then warned that those who vote against the resolution "will have to answer to the American people." He further blamed those who had said that the administration's policy was a plan for war as "playing right down the line of Communist propaganda." He stressed the point that Eisenhower would be the one making the military decisions, not "any line officer...in some remote part of the world." He reiterated that the resolution did not authorize a preemptive strike, and all US forces would be under American control. "What does it say?" he asked rhetorically. "It says that Chiang Kai-shek will not make the decision."

Turning to military strategy, he pointed out that if Formosa fell, "it would be with the greatest difficulty that we could defend...the whole of Southeast Asia."[174] He criticized those who wanted the president to enumerate which islands he would and would not defend, stating correctly that in

---

[170]Statement of Senator George in support of the Mutual Defense Treaty with the Republic of China, n. d. (probably February 1955), GRF-VHPS. By a vote of 11–2, the Foreign Relations Committee favorably reported it out to the Senate, and it passed several days after the Formosa Resolution with only six hours of debate (Graebner, *New Imperialism*, 203).

[171]Melanson, *Reevaluating Eisenhower*, 74.

[172]"George of Georgia: Ike's Friend in Need," 29.

[173]Thomas O'Neil, "Politics and People," unidentified clipping, scrapbook, LHG-VHPS.

[174]*CR*, 84/1, 1029.

doing so would be to give the Chinese an invitation "to come and get some of those islands." To those who might want us to intervene only when the Communist actually "put his foot on the shore of Formosa," he blasted, "that suggestion cannot be seriously advanced anywhere."

In concluding, he rehashed his arguments about the problems caused by delay and the need to give the president moral support, adding, "I hope no Democrat will be heard to say that because the president...came to Congress, he is thereby subject to [reckless] criticism. The president chose a courageous course which would be taken only by a prudent, patient man, who knows the...horrors of war."[175] In this one speech, he skillfully painted any opponent of the resolution, without exactly saying so, as being either a coward, unpatriotic, or, to use a phrase at the time, "soft on Communism." The chamber fell silent, the resolution's opponents totally cowed. It passed with a crushing vote of 85–3. Eisenhower signed it on Saturday morning, June 29, in the presidential apartments in the White House.[176]

Several months later in a television speech given in Augusta, Georgia, George lamented that it was unfortunate that there is a disposition that hinged all Far Eastern policy on what the president might do about Quemoy and Matsu. "If that would advance the cause of peace," he told his listeners, "I would be happy for the president to declare his policy. But how could it advance the cause of peace to inform the enemy of what we intend to do? No one can say that it would advance the cause of peace to invite Red China to take more land held by Free China."[177]

At this point, Walter George faltered as though a painful memory had come to him. It was the same type of hesitation that had occurred when he called for the establishment of the United Nations in the last days of World War II. Both times he was clearly thinking of the son he had lost in that titanic struggle. Regaining his composure, he resumed, "If we do fulfill our high...destiny, it will be because we have resolved to do our dead level best to advance peace, to advance security, to shore up a shaky world. Only by doing that can we vindicate to sacrifice of those who died on land and sea, and fulfill the hopes of men and women in every free land."[178]

Praise for Walter George came from everywhere. Eisenhower wrote stating that George had done a "superb" job, and later telephoned additional

---

[175]WFG, "Joint Resolution on Formosa," 1028–31; see also *CR*, 84/1, 820–21.

[176]Pres.'s appointments, January 29, 1955, box 4, f. A.C. Whitman diary, January 1955, (1), Whitman file, Eisenhower papers.

[177]"Voice of the 84th," 25.

[178]Ibid.

congratulations. Dulles personally came by the Mayflower to escort George to the White House for the signing of the resolution.[179] Walter Robertson called his defense "one of the most powerful speeches made by anybody," and it "swings this into a bipartisan resolution."[180] Senator Smith of New Jersey on the Sunday TV show *The Leading Question* resoundingly gave George credit saying the 85–3 vote was due to "the masterly leadership of my chairman."[181] Sir Roger Makins wired London that "the most effective speech in defence of the resolution was delivered by Senator George...the respected elder statesman who is the chairman of the Foreign Relations Committee," adding that the lopsided vote demonstrates the "confidence which most members of both parties have in the military judgement of President Eisenhower."[182] Now the Democrats were equally responsible for any action taken in the Formosa Strait.

The nation's journalists chimed in. *Time* told its readers, "When he [George] arose to speak on the Formosa resolution one January day, there were worried, even hostile, faces in the chamber. Nearly a score of Democrats was ready for a last-ditch fight against the resolution, and several Republicans had grave doubts. By the time he sat down...the opposition had been shattered."[183] Conservative journalist David Lawrence wrote, "Seldom in the history of the United States Senate has there been an address of statesmanship comparable to that delivered by Senator Walter George of Georgia...as he upheld President Eisenhower's request for unrestricted authority to use armed force to defend Formosa." He added a lesson from history: If such a joint resolution had been issued "before 1914 and 1939 [it might] have prevented two world wars."[184]

The Chinese backed down, and in April at the Bandung Conference of twenty-nine African and Asian nations in Indonesia to promote cultural and economic issues, Chou En-lai, the foreign minister of Communist China, publicly stated that his country would only try to "liberate" Formosa by "peaceful means," and his statement went a long way toward easing ten-

[179]Ibid., 22.

[180]Walter Robertson, oral history, 120–21, Eisenhower Library.

[181]CBS, "The Leading Question," January 30, 1955, 19, GFR-VHPS.

[182]Makins to Foreign Office, weekly political summary, no. 58 (?), January 29, 1955, FO 371/114350, FO-BNA.

[183]"Voice of the 84th," 22.

[184]David Lawrence, "George of Georgia," *Atlanta Constitution*, n. d., scrapbook, LHG-VHPS.

sion.[185] Moreover, he added that China did not want war with the US and was willing to have talks to bring a "relaxation of tensions."[186]

George was receptive to this approach, in part because he had some respect for Chou (he told Pat Holt that Chou was the "ablest living Communist"[187]), and he felt that since the US was seen to have just won a great diplomatic victory, it would be a good time to converse from a position of strength. There were those who opposed any sort of intercourse with China, the Republican Right, for example, whom George had to convince. He felt that talk was cheap and could do no harm. He liked to tell the story of a long-ago litigation, where he approached a witness on the other side who refused to talk with him because "You are on the other side." George replied, "Of course, I am on the other side.... I can't learn anything...unless I can talk to the men who are on the other side of this problem." When the witness still would not talk, George asked him, "Are you afraid that you will tell me the truth or that you will tell me a lie?" To his critics, George said that he did not know how sincere Chou was, but we should be "'big enough' to talk to him."[188] The State Department insisted, however, that any talks with mainland China should include Chiang Kai-shek, but George felt that to include him would make the Red Chinese refuse to talk. To their argument he countered that there were "wide areas for negotiations without China's Nationalist leader." Within a few days, the administration reversed itself and agreed with George.[189] In speaking again to the American Society of Newspaper Editors in April, he urged a Far Eastern Conference with Peking without Chiang's regime, repeating his oft-quoted phrase, "This nation should be big enough...to talk to him." He warned Dulles that he would be unable to please anyone at home and still maintain leadership of the Free World, so he might as well not try.[190] The liberal wing of the GOP, however, immediately joined in one voice to support the move.[191] George did add the caveat that any agreements with Red China should not be detrimental to Nationalist China.[192] He did in that spring urge the administration to think

---

[185]Makins to Selwyn Lloyd, "US: Annual Review for 1955," February 21, 1956, 2, FO 371/120310, FO-BNA.

[186]Graebner, *New Isolationism*, 205.

[187]Pat Holt, oral history, 96, Library of Congress.

[188]*CR*, 84/2, 4227–28.

[189]"Sen. George Plays a Key Role...," article from McClatchey Newspapers (Sacramento, California), n. d., scrapbook, LHG-VHPS.

[190]Melanson, *Reevaluating Eisenhower*, 76.

[191]Graebner, *New Isolationism*, 206–207.

[192]"What Senator George said about...Red China," 80.

of more normal relations with Communist China, especially in regard to trade relations with the US. A leftist journalist praised George's tactics as being those of a "shrewd sell of a veteran political strategist," avoiding "such emotion-soaked issues" and concentrating instead "on the practical questions of trade."[193]

At this point, the Eisenhower Administration, with George also playing a major role, was preparing for talks in Geneva with the Russians, and George felt that time for talks with China was not "ripe." The US should wait until after the Russian talks. When Eisenhower returned from Geneva, reporters asked George if the time was now "ripe" for Chinese talks. George replied, "It is approaching." He then added, "It is difficult to mark a definite date on the calendar" and suggested that matters should be initiated at the foreign minister level. He cautioned that whatever that they do, they should do it within six months while there is quiet in the Formosa Straits. If we show genuine concern, there would be some sort of "flare-up" in the area.[194] He did call for the US and China to name ambassadors for the beginning talks. George's work on this question was seen by the British ambassador, "despite his role of elder-statesman," of being willing to "break the ice for the administration on occasions," adding that he was "not averse to stealing a little Republican thunder."[195]

One aspect of the China imbroglio that turned nasty came with an encounter with Senator Joseph McCarthy. McCarthy had been censured the year before and had few supporters in the Senate, but he argued in the Senate that any talks with mainland China should include Taiwan and not to do so would be tantamount to the sellout of Czechoslovakia in 1938. He introduced a resolution that Chiang be represented at the talks, and he more or less ordered that George bring the whole question up for discussion immediately. George replied that it would be brought up at its allotted time, at which McCarthy accused George of being hostile to the resolution and that he wanted to have the discussions without the participation of our allies. At this suggestion, George became quite angry and replied, "The Senator from Wisconsin has never found an utterance of mine to the effect that any question affecting our allies should be decided without full representation of our allies," i.e., the Nationalist Chinese. From that point, the discussion turned very ugly and personal, and finally George said, "I care not what the senator

[193]Freedman, "Washington in Focus," 280.

[194]"Meet the Press," transcript, July 24, 1955, GFR-VHPS.

[195]Makins to Foreign Office, weekly political summary, July 30, 1955, FO 371/114351, FO-BNA.

from Wisconsin may think of the senator from Georgia." McCarthy replied, "I think he is a good senator. I have always said that," apparently realizing it was not wise to incur George's wrath. To this George replied uncharacteristically insultingly, "Very well. I wish I could reciprocate the compliment, Mr. President, but I shall not perjure myself."[196] The two men calmed down somewhat, but the exchange showed that George was still quick on his feet.

Several months later, the Chinese Communists announced that they would release forty-one American civilians they had detained, and George stated that their action was "significant." Furthermore, he used this action to suggest a meeting between the US and China "later this year" to discuss Formosa.[197] George felt that the Chinese lessening of tension proved "that the Geneva Conference [with Russia] is worthwhile."[198] George returned to the question of trade with China "in peaceful goods" as an advantage that would come with trade with all nations.[199]

In August, Eisenhower and Dulles agreed to ambassadorial talks with China, and the British ambassador reported to London that "These, surprisingly, aroused surprisingly little opposition."[200] What little criticism that occurred puzzled George. "I have very little understanding for any American who is afraid for representatives of his gov't [sic] to talk with anybody on the peace of the world." Then he became a little insulting, "What do these timerous [*sic*] nit-wits think we are?"[201]

George himself eventually came to take a tougher stance on China. In July he openly opposed giving China a seat in the UN because to do so "would mean in effect a recognition of Red China," and that would create a position whereby we would "not be wholly in the clear in asserting…[the maintenance] of at least bases, naval and air, on Formosa as a safeguard against further aggression coming out of China."[202] In October 1955, he suggested that for there to be a "Chinese Geneva," the Chinese Communist must renounce the use of force. This change was a sharp reversal from when he had earlier called for an "unconditional meeting."[203] He had earlier stated

---

[196]*CR*, 84/1, 10185–87.

[197]United Press interview, September 11, 1955, cited in Carlton, "The Record," 9, GFR-VHPS.

[198]Makins to Foreign Office, weekly political summary, 1, FO 371/114351, FO-BNA.

[199]Frances O. Wilcox to Robert C. Fernley, August 26, 1955, GFR-VHPS.

[200]Makins to Lloyd, February 21, 1956, 2, FO 371/120310, FO-BNA.

[201]UP release, September 19, 1955, in Carlton, "The Record," GFR-VHPS.

[202]"Meet the Press," transcript, July 24, 1955, 6, GFR-VHPS.

[203]Makins to Foreign Office, weekly political summary, October 22, 1955, FO 371/114351, FO-BNA.

that he did not favor permitting China to enter the UN, and he retained that position in the midst of the discussions for the potential talks.[204] He would not even consider China's entrance into the world body until they had demonstrated "further evidence to their peaceful means on the Formosa Question."[205]

There is no evidence explaining why George took a markedly harder position. Perhaps he was getting criticism from home. He was facing a fight against the Talmadge machine the next year, so perhaps he felt that he had to take a tougher stance. Whatever his motives or later actions, his efforts produced the first cracks in the rigid hostility between the United States and China that would be the first step to full recognition between the two countries under President Richard Nixon seventeen years later.

The second monumental accomplishment in George's last term was even greater than the *démarche* toward China. It was his work that produced the Big-Four Geneva Accords of 1955, the first meeting of the Americans, British, and the French with the Russians since the Potsdam Conference in 1945. The Cold War had begun to rage in the years after the world war over a number of incidents, and the Korean War of the early fifties, where NATO fought the North Koreans and the Chinese Communists (openly backed by the Soviet Union), made the tension even worse. Minor incidents such as Russian jambing of landing gears of American planes flying into Berlin and the firing on American planes in the Bering Sea aggravated the already high tension.There were responsible voices who predicted war between the Russians and the West. There were others who actually called for it.

As often happened, cooler heads prevailed, one of whom was that of English prime minister Winston Churchill, who several months after Stalin's death in March 1953, suggested a meeting among the Big Four "without long delay." Even his own foreign office was skeptical, but Churchill approached Eisenhower to enter the picture. Eisenhower sent a firm statement that he and Dulles opposed his going to any such meeting under the tense prevailing conditions. The Russians, he felt, would have to indicate "a genuine readiness to negotiate constructively."[206] Churchill went public anyway with a proposal on May 11, 1953.[207] He was supported in July by Joseph Laniel, the French prime minister, who expressed readiness for "improving

[204]Ibid., February 5, 1955, FO 371/114350.
[205]*Atlanta Journal and Constitution Magazine*, September 11, 1955, 17.
[206]Eisenhower, *Mandate for Change*, 505.
[207]Williamson, *Separate Agendas*, 19–29.

the climate of international relations" and to talk with any interlocutor "who has given tangible evidence of his good will."[208] By 1955 other nations expressed interest in a meeting.[209]

Walter George in November 1954 had expressed enthusiastic support for Eisenhower's strong stand against the Russians, adding that "we can only deal with the Russians from strength."[210] Several months later, even in the midst of preliminary feelers for meeting with the Russians, George stated, "We made a supreme mistake...in assuming that because we fought side by side with our Russian friends...that they must be...people with aims...very much similar to our very own.... We, of course, [now] know that Russia is still associated [?] [*sic*] with the old Russian imperialism, plus the Communist ideologies of the 1917 Revolution."[211] In his same speech, nevertheless, George left the door open for conversations with the Russians and the Chinese, stating strongly that to talk "is not appeasement" for a strong power to agree to state that "we are willing to sit down and talk about the problems that concern you and concern the world."[212]

George genuinely felt that the Russians might be willing to talk at this point. Stalin's death had made major internal changes, most of which were not yet obvious, but at least had resulted in an enormous vacuum. Russian Premier Georgy Malenkov, had fallen from power in March, leaving internal politics unsettled. The Russians had reduced their armed forces by 640,000, reduced military appropriations (obviously from financial necessity), agreed to an evacuation and peace treaty with Austria, and surrendered their last Finnish military base, Porkkala. The Germans were rearming and making open moves to join NATO, which they did in May 1955. Moreover, the Chinese seem to be getting too frisky, and if they entered a shooting war with the West, Russia, who itself had food and hardware shortages, would be at least required to assist them with material aid that they did not have. The Russians were clearly hurting.[213]

In a television interview on *Meet the Press* on March 20, 1955, George

---

[208]Gov't of Laniel (service de press), July ?, 1953, Amérique, 1952–63, dossier général: France et Etats Unis, f. 348, 3, AMAE.

[209]Bipartisan meeting, March 31, 1955, f. Leg. Leaders meeting 1955, box 2, A75–22, Whitman file, Eisenhower papers.

[210]"George Backs Ike's Policy," *Washington Post* (?), November 25, 1954, box 337, f. George, W. F., July 22, 1938–, RNC papers.

[211]WFG, "Russia Will Lose," 79.

[212]Ibid.

[213]Ralph McGill, "Sen George Makes Sense," *Atlanta Constitution*, n. d., scrapbook, LHG-VHPS.

casually suggested talks with the Russians. "We've reached a stage in our international relations…when the real hope of avoiding war is through some high level conferences between the leading powers," George told his viewers.[214] George added, however, that the United States should abandon its stance, i.e., that of the right-wing Republicans, who felt that such a meeting would appear as appeasement, that the Soviet Union should meet certain conditions before such a conference could occur.[215] He suggested that the US should pursue the talks "even if the Russians show no concrete evidence in advance that it wants world peace," and he advised against "superimposing any conditions" or "raking up old matters." To do so might destroy any chance for fruitful talks.[216]

His surprise move made headlines all over the world and attracted the attention of diplomats in every capital.[217] *US News* credited the attention that it got to Senator George himself. "George…is listened to attentively when he speaks," the journal told its readers, adding that both Churchill's and Mendès-France's approach fell on "deaf ears" in Washington, but when Walter George suggested it, "Ears opened wide." When George advocates something in his rare speeches, "the Senate seldom rejects [it]," *US News* noted, adding, "The mere fact that it is George of Georgia, and not someone else who is urging a top-level conference, makes a conference more likely to be held."[218]

George had called for the talks without consulting any members of the Foreign Relations Committee or any of the major figures in the Democratic Party, but it is a tribute to the man that the Democrats at once rallied to his call. It gave Eisenhower a signal that he could act against the wishes of his own party, especially his minority leader Senator Knowland. The British ambassador Roger Makins informed London that George had been generally given credit for "clearing the space to manoeuver around the president" and in so doing had freed the president "from the grip of Knowland, who had rejected the George proposal out of fear of appeasement."[219] As for George himself, he could never be accused of being soft on Communism.

[214]Carlton, "The Record….," 6, GFR-VHPS.

[215]Makins to Foreign Office, weekly political summary, #180, 2, March 26, 1955, FO 371/114350, FO-BNA.

[216]"Big Power Talks," clipping, *Cleveland Plain Dealer*, March 22, 1955, box 338, f. G, January 1, 1955, RNC papers.

[217]Donovan, "Senator George," 32.

[218]"People of the Week," (April 1, 1955): 14.

[219]Makins to Foreign Office, weekly political summary, no. 180, March 26, 1955, 2, FO 371/114350, FO-BNA.

"There could be no more impeccable sponsor of a Big Four Conference than Senator George," *Nation* chimed in. "In addition to the fact that he is an implacable foe of Communism, George could never be accused of wanting to attend such a meeting for his personal glory. If he does decide to go, it will be from a sense of duty, not vanity."[220] Moreover, George did not believe that Russia and the West could immediately become friends, but he felt that it was impossible for the West to keep arming itself with nuclear weapons without negotiating. "Otherwise, the famous slogan about 'negotiation from strength' becomes a mockery."[221]

Sir Roger Makins also had other ideas. He wired London that although George was "an elder statesman," he was also a shrewd party politician and saw the move as a chance to seize the peace initiative for the Democratic Party and lay the groundwork for a Democratic peace program. Noting that the last three wars occurred during Democratic presidencies, the Democrats are most anxious to "prevent President Eisenhower from acquiring a monopoly of peaceful solutions."[222] The proposal did indeed quickly become a "rallying cry" for the Democrats even though George had not informed them beforehand.[223] It perhaps was in the back of George's mind that this move might help the Democrats in 1956, but partisan politics had never been a factor in George's actions. He definitely in his career had opposed his party too often, giving the Republican much grist for their mill.

Some people at the time felt that George and the president had had a meeting of the minds on the question before George had ever proposed it. It is true that Eisenhower and Dulles had considered such an action, but they had backed off because of "considerable opposition to it abroad." Nevertheless, Hagerty in his diary wrote that Eisenhower had never discussed the Big-Four meeting with George before the senator went on television.[224] Actually, Eisenhower was initially rather cool to the whole idea and told a legislative leadership meeting that he and Dulles had talked about it frequently but "always considered that it was not desirable," that is, "that there were more disadvantages than advantages." Obviously with an ear to the political ground of his own party, the president assured Senator Styles Bridges (R-New Hampshire) and Knowland that they would "be the first to know if

[220]Freeman, "Washington," 279.

[221]Ibid.

[222]Makins to Foreign Office, weekly political summary, no. 180, 22, March 26, 1955, FO 371/114350, FO-BNA.

[223]"Voice of the 84th," 22.

[224]Hagerty, *Diary of James C. Hagerty*, 215.

should there come an affirmative decision on this."[225]

Based on this conversation in the White House, Knowland announced that Ike was not sympathetic with George's plan. When a State Department proclamation said otherwise, he must have felt betrayed, and on March 23, Eisenhower held a press conference on the question in which he, not completely truthfully, noted that he and his advisers had talked "time and again" of the value of a conference. He suggested that lower level talks begin immediately and that he would not oppose a "non-agenda conference."[226] This *volte face* on the part of the president appeared to have jerked the rug from under the minority leader, so James Hagerty issued a public statement that Knowland had correctly reported the president's thoughts at the time but added that he saw no difference between the administration's ideas and those of George, a clear misrepresentation of the facts that gave the appearance of an administration in a bit of chaos.[227]

The confusion was clear bumbling, but Eisenhower saw in George's statements the assurance that he could "cut the diplomatic price for such a meeting" without fear of Senate repudiation.[228] He would have the support of at least some of the Republicans and almost all of the Democrats. He did, however, express the desire for the Russians to show "some act of good faith" before he moved on the issue, although George had suggested that he go ahead without it.[229] Eisenhower was slowly edging his own leadership out of the loop. Two days after George made his proposal, Eisenhower made a point in a press conference that was in line with George's statement: "There is no place on this earth to which I would not travel...no chore I would not undertake to promote the cause of peace," but he did add that there should first be exploratory talks at the lower level before the "Big Four" met.[230] These "exploratory talks" were a possible meeting point to his earlier notion that he wanted some Russian concessions. What else would "exploratory talks" achieve? He did indeed say that he no longer had "a list of concessions

---

[225]Legislative leadership meeting, March 22, 1955, Whitman file, f. Leg. Leadership Meetings, 1955, box 2, Eisenhower papers.

[226]Makins to Foreign Office, weekly political summary, no. 180, 2, March 26, 1955, FO 371/114350, FO-BNA.

[227]"George Plain-talk a Lesson for Ike," unidentified clipping, n. d., scrapbook, LHG-VHPS.

[228]Thomas O'Neill, "Politics and People," unidentified clipping, scrapbook, LHG-VHPS.

[229]"President's Party Never Hears Him," n. d., unidentified clipping, ibid.

[230]"For Talk of Peace," 24.

that the Soviets would have to make."[231]

As the Geneva Four Power Summit became more and more of a reality, George seemed more and more to assume the duties of a secretary of state. In mid-May, however, he somewhat tried to dampen hopes of some major breakthrough, and he refused publicly to predict "glorious success" or "dismal failure." In an article that he wrote for the International News Service, appearing in papers on May 15, 1955, George wrote, "I do not see how we can escape the conclusion that it is better to talk [if we accomplish nothing more]...than to go to war...when there is hope...of coming to some degree of understanding. We have nothing to lose by engaging in such talks. The United States of America must be big enough...to risk its prestige in conferences even with our potential enemies."[232] In an interview five days later, George speculated on what the Russians might want. He expected that they might want a "neutral zone" in Europe, but their primary purpose on agreeing to meet was to reverse the rearming of Germany, which they had so far failed to do. In neutralization, they had been more successful with the Austrian treaty, which all the interested powers had signed, and they had been successful in neutralizing Finland earlier. They now would like, George postulated, to neutralize Italy and Yugoslavia. "Will the Soviet effort get anywhere?" he asked rhetorically. "No, it will fail," he said, answering his own question. He added, "The efforts we have made to strengthen the free world are beginning to pay off." He felt that there would be general agreements on national self-determination of nations (one is hard pressed to accept the idea that he really believed that the Russians would genuinely concede this point in Eastern Europe) and the right to be free of the threat of military force, which had a greater possibility, since Russia could never win an arms race with the West. There might be some understanding on German reunification, yet in all cases, "the details or implementation will have to be worked out later." The most important outcome, he stressed to the public, will be the setting of a course "to lead us out of the present tensions."[233]

There was predictably a storm from the hard Right. Conservative columnist David Lawrence blasted all the major powers for being willing to talk to the Soviets: "The spectacle presented by the governments at Paris, London, and Washington in seeking a conference with...Soviet Russia is that of a hungry suppliant begging for almost any crumbs from the table of

---

[231]Ibid.

[232]International News Service article (untitled), May 15, 1955, in Carlton, "The Record...," 7, GFR-VHPS.

[233]WFG (interview), "But No Neutral Zone," 22.

the absolute monarch," he shrieked to his readers. "[The Russians are a people who are] the enemies of our civilization.... For it is written in the blood-covered pages of history that in the periods preceding the outbreak of World War I and World War II...vacillation and cringing fear on our side encouraged the aggressors."[234] As Eisenhower was about to leave for Geneva, Senator Joseph McCarthy introduced a Senate resolution to force him into a disruptive conflict with the USSR over "the captive nations of Eastern Europe." The Senate defeated it 77–4.[235] In another statement McCarthy accused Eisenhower of "betraying the trust of the American people."[236] George answered these isolationist critics by noting that they were in a minority, but he added that their opposition was still disturbing "since we must continue to strive for national unity as in wartime." Blasting their belief that 3,000 miles of ocean divorces the US from European problems, George accused them for "simply not [having] come to grips with the facts...[that we cannot] entertain notions of isolation. We have arrived at the age when to hold back from action is surrender, when to do nothing is fatal."[237] There were those who suggested to Ike that George accompany the delegation to Geneva, and Congressman Joe L. Evins (R-Tennessee), wrote the president to suggest it, so that "his voice might be heard by the leaders of the participating nations and that he might speak with authority as a representative of our government." As it was, Eisenhower had already considered taking George but he had rejected the idea. "No one could have greater admiration for Senator George than I," he said at a press conference but added that he and George had discussed it and were in "complete agreement that he should not go." He noted that the purpose was to highlight the problems between the two nations, not solve them, adding that "Congress will be employed [and therefore so will be George] when there is the actual working out of the detailed problems."[238]

Before leaving for Geneva, Eisenhower spoke to the nation on the upcoming conference. When he left that White House broadcast room and returned to Mamie and a group of friends in the living quarters, he received "to my delight," he wrote in his memoirs, "a call from the statesman who had put so much of himself behind the idea of the summit meeting, Senator

[234]Lawrence, "Four-Power Fantasy," 136.

[235]Wicker, *Shooting Star*, 183–84.

[236]*US: Annual Review for 1955*, 13, February 21, 1956, FO 371/120310, FO-BNA.

[237]Statement by Senator Walter F. George regarding the Meeting of Big Four, May 15, 1955, GFR-VHPS.

[238]*CR*, 84/1, 7669.

Walter George of Georgia." He recorded that George was "full of emotion and his congratulations and good wishes were heartwarming."[239] Without George's work, it is probably safe to say that the meeting, as and when it happened, would not have taken place.

The meeting in Geneva between Eisenhower and Bulganin proved quite cordial. Ike even made the Russians a vague offer of disarmament. Nothing was settled in any case, but Eisenhower described the meeting as "only a beginning in a renewed effort that may last a generation."[240] He told Bulganin that "The United States will never take part in an aggressive war," to which Bulganin replied, "We believe that statement."[241] He wrote Bulganin after the conference, "Now that the Four Power Conference has become a part of history, I want you to know how deeply I believe that our combined efforts…produced a result that will benefit the world."[242] Bulganin responded that he took "a positive attitude" toward the American president's ideas. Both seemed to be relaxing. In the past, the Russians had claimed that German rearmament would block such a meeting. It had not. Moreover, the Russians had always insisted on the inclusion of Red China in any such talks, but they did not in this case.[243] Bulganin even suggested the agreement of a US-Soviet treaty of friendship and cooperation.[244] George, who had played such a prominent role in the historic meeting, was asked by Jack Bell on *Meet the Press* what had been accomplished by the Eisenhower-Bulganin encounter. "Actually what was accomplished was the development of a spirit of friendliness or tolerance of view," George replied, "which is greater and more pronounced than it has been in any conference since World War II." George had made a safe statement since there had not been any such conferences since the Second World War, but he added that "it gave assurances to the people of the United States who have been willing to tax themselves to support a very heavy foreign aid program…that we had something more to offer…than merely vote money. [Second], it gave us a better understanding of how our friends in the free world were thinking and…how they were receiving our own position on more controversial points." After this somewhat

---

[239]Eisenhower, *Mandate for Change*, 510.

[240]*US: Annual Review for 1955*, 10, February 31, 1956, FO 371/120310, FO-BNA.

[241]Graebner, *New Isolationism*, 221–22.

[242]Eisenhower to Bulganin, July 25, 1955, Eyes-only basis to Sec. of State, f. USSR, 1953–55(1), box 49, Whitman file, Eisenhower papers.

[243]"For Talk of Peace," 24.

[244]Eisenhower to Bulganin, 28 January 1956, to Eisenhower (copy), Amérique, 1952–1963, Etats-Unis, relations avec l'Europe, USSR et pays satelites, 104–114, f.URSS, no. 381, AMAE.

incoherent reply, George added more meat: "Finally, I think that it did promote a more tolerant attitude, a more friendly relationship, which is bound to bear some fruits [*sic*] in the future."[245] Since Eisenhower had stolen a march on the Democrats with the help of their own partisan, there was some grumbling among Democrats going into the election year of 1956 that they had not been consulted, when in reality they had supported Ike's international efforts more than some members of his own party. In January 1956, George replied to them and in the process defended Eisenhower. "The letter of President Eisenhower is a perfect example of moderation and sincerity," he replied to the president's critics. He has not responded to the proposition of Bulganin by a refusal to meet.

Several months later, in a more coherent fashion, George told the press, "One of the great things that came about of the Summit Conference was the fact that…our purposes are peaceful. I think that we are very near a reasonable period of peace."[246] In another statement, he announced, "The letter of the president…is an excellent public document. It is our own expression of hope of the American people to see the establishment of an honorable and just peace…and extends the hand of friendship to all those who want to grasp it."[247] The Eisenhower-Bulganin meeting was followed by a conference of the participants' foreign ministers in October, and Walter George expressed optimism over this gathering as well, especially in a final solution of German rearmament and reunification.[248] George dampened expectations in a statement he wrote when he outlined what these men were to discuss, but said, "If wishful thinking will not solve these problems, neither will callous cynicism," taking a swipe at the naysayers who had ridiculed the whole process. "It would be idle to pretend that the problems which had been dealt with at Geneva lend themselves to ready solutions. It is [also] idle to assume that they are beyond solution." He expressed the belief that both the US and its allies were big and farsighted enough to "accommodate the legitimate security needs of the Soviet Union." He concluded with, "I pray [to] God that this meeting at Geneva will move us…toward peace."[249] George held no naive ideas of an easy fix. The foreign ministers' meeting showed that there would be no reunification of German except on Russian

[245]"Meet the Press" (transcript), July 24, 1955, 2–3, scrapbook, LHC VHPS, Carlton, "The Record…," 7, GFR-VHPS.

[246]*Atlanta Journal* and *Constitution Magazine*, September 11, 1955, 17.

[247]Couve de Murville to MFA, January 31, 1956, 117, Amérique: 1952–63, USSR, for. 381, AMAE.

[248]"Meet the Press" (transcript), July 24, 1955, 3, GFR-VHPS.

[249]WFG, "On the Eve of the Foreign Ministers' Conference," GFR-VHPS.

terms, and he felt that it meant that NATO must be strengthened.[250] He observed in January 1956, however, that there was no likelihood of a military conflict with Russia "in the immediate future," but he pointed out that the Russians were making loans to neutral countries, which would then be followed by Russian engineers and technicians. Foreign trade with these countries would follow, and they would be drawn into the Russian sphere.[251] Observing what the Russians were doing in what was to become known as the Third World was to push George further into supporting foreign aid, a position that would prove lethal to George back home.

Vice President Richard Nixon, whose diplomacy would eventually end the Cold War during his own presidency, spoke of the "Spirit of Geneva" in fall 1955. He truthfully stated (though it was probably not so apparent at the time) that we were "entering an era of peaceful exchange when war must be renounced as an instrument of national policy."[252] It had broken what two writers called "the dangerous silence that had characterized East-West relations since…the Korean War. The future would see plenty of formal…East-West Conferences that…slowly led to the build-up of a more trusting [East-West] relationship."[253]

As for the United States in 1955, it held the most powerful position it had ever held on the world stage. George, displaying his frequent modesty, stressed that the US was now indeed the leader of the world, but added that we had not sought this role and that a nation does not acquire such a position by striving for it. "World leadership comes to a nation…because of the superb and supreme heroism of its people, because of their devotion to duty…with tireless energy to bring it about…to rise to the challenge of stirring times."[254] Although he did not say it then, Walter George of Georgia had played a major role in getting the United States there.

---

[250]*New York Times*, January 11, 1956, cited in Carlton, "The Record…," 9, GFR-VHPS.

[251]AP release, January 27, 1956, cited in ibid.

[252]*US: Annual Review for 1955*, 16–17, February 21, 1956, FO 371/120310, FO-BNA.

[253]Klaus and Osgood, *The Cold War after Stalin's Death*, 150.

[254]WFG, "Russia Will Lose," 81.

IO

POLITICAL *PAS DE DEUX*: THE PHANTOM SENATE CAMPAIGN OF 1956

In Washington and abroad, Senator George has been looked upon as one of the nation's leading statesmen. His name rides high in headlines of big-city newspapers. National magazines print articles about him. He appears on television and radio programs. In the Senate, he is president *pro tempore*, entitled as such, to a free limousine and chauffeur.... It is this position of prominence which is credited with giving the senator trouble now.

—*US News*[1]

While distinguished men elsewhere ask the Nobel Peace award for Senator George, the *Savannah Morning News* asks that the senator meekly step aside....

—*Atlanta Journal*[2]

The senior senator from Georgia is not only an outstanding member of the Senate[,] he is outstanding throughout the United States. He is outstanding among the leaders of international affairs throughout the world.... No other person in this country...has made a deeper imprint on our foreign policy.... No one has served the cause of world peace with greater devotion.

—Senator Earle Clements[3]

I will vote for Herman [Talmadge,] but I sure will hate to see Senator George out of office.

—South Georgia farmer[4]

[1]"Famous Senator in Trouble with Voters," 32.

[2]The *Atlanta Journal* sums up the Savannah article, August 26, 1955, unnumbered clipping in WFG-DCPL.

[3]*CR*, 84/1, 12573.

[4]Asa W. Candler to Herman Talmadge, March 19, 1956, VI, A-1, box 1, f. 27, Talmadge papers.

By January 1956, Walter F. George had served in the United States Senate for more than thirty-three continuous years, a period that had seen America transcend more serious crises in its history than any other time except for the Civil War or perhaps the War of 1812. He had entered the Senate when Warren G. Harding was president and seemed poised to stay beyond Eisenhower's second term. Having served on fourteen committees and chaired five, George was generally recognized as the most powerful and respected US Senator in that august body.[5] His Senate colleagues sang his praises, echoed by editors all over the country. In 1955, articles titled "Senator George Is Most Powerful Single Solon," "Senator George: Monumental, Determined," and "Senator George: Preeminent Senator of 1955" appeared in the country's greatest journals.[6] Prominent journalist Roscoe Drummond told his readers that a majority of the Washington Press Corps felt strongly that George was "the single most powerful, most influential person" in the Congress. He was "a more positive force than any of the preeminent senators of the last quarter century," adding that he is "the second most powerful man in Washington—second only to the president himself."[7] Even his colleague Richard B. Russell, who had generally been reticent to speak for or against George, called him in May 1956 "the most distinguished Georgian who is alive today."[8]

On any issue, all sought his opinion. As one journalist put it, "Involved in every…field of legislative business—from reciprocal trade to the slapping down of Joe McCarthy—one question dominates among pre-debate dopesters: 'Where does Walter George stand?'"[9] By 1956, he held the longest Senate tenure of any serving member.

George had achieved great power not by wheeling and dealing and trading votes but by standing up for what he felt was right, almost always bringing the Senate along with him.[10] Moreover, he had always maintained, the *New York Times* had stated, a "characteristic of rugged independence. He always made up his mind on issues, and when he found reasons to change it, he unhesitantly did so."[11] John Temple Graves, a leading voice of the South, joined the general chorus of praise for Georgia's greatest statesman, noting that in him was "a grandeur of maturity," and adding, "the Georgia state

[5]Note to Editors, n. d., GFR-VHPS.

[6]See CR, 84/1, p 1426, 2841, and 5355.

[7]Ibid., 5355–56.

[8]*Atlanta Constitution*, May 4, 1956, 3.

[9]*CR*, 84/1, A1426.

[10]My interview with Senator George Smathers.

[11]*New York Times*, quoted in *Vienna News*, August 8, 1957, 5.

motto is 'Wisdom, Justice, and Moderation,...' [of which] he is the epitome."[12] Georgia state senator Spence M. Grayson, a close ally of Senator Richard Russell, joined the chorus of praise in calling Walter F. George "the greatest statesman the state of Georgia has ever produced."[13] With perhaps a nod to Jimmy Carter, that statement remains true to this day.

In 1956, however, Walter George's Senate seat was up for reelection, and he was in trouble, largely because of his national and international fame. There was a general feeling among some of the state's citizens that George, while walking on the world stage, had lost touch with the folks back home. It is not surprising that in Georgia, steeped in the "What-have-you-done-for-me-lately?" political mentality, some segments of the population wouldn't appreciate his many contributions. As one Georgian told a national journalist, "Sure, the senator is a great statesman. He is doing a good job for the nation. But what is he doing for Georgia? So far as Georgia is concerned, he might as well be from Connecticut."[14] One banker in a middle Georgia county not a hundred miles from Vienna noted that George had not been in his community in eighteen years, adding that he would not know three men in the county "if he met them face to face."[15] *US News* opined that his reputation outside of the state would do him no good at home, adding a stinging insult to Georgians by stating that his favorable press outside of the state would "cause him to be regarded with suspicion.... They think he had gone high-hat, or turned Yankee and forgotten their problems."[16] One Georgia publisher noted disdainfully that Georgians had a choice of either voting "for a representative of Georgia or of the nation."[17] An Atlanta businessman summed up this attitude in a letter to Herman Talmadge, "Which do we need most at this time? A national statesman or someone tending to Georgia's local needs?"[18] The *New Republic* stated it more eloquently, noting that in George's predicament there is "a touch of tragedy associated with Shakespeare's Wolsey. Had Senator George served the mass of his constituents with half the zeal he gave to other interests, he would not have been left naked to his enemy....[and] forced to give up to an egregious Johnny-come-lately....the seat he has held long enough to bask in

[12]Salute to Senator George by J. T. Graves, unidentified clipping, n. d., scrapbook, LHG-VHPS.

[13]Spence Grayson, oral history, 27, Russell Library.

[14]"Famous Senator in Trouble with Voters," 32.

[15]Ibid.

[16]Ibid.

[17]Cater, "Regression vs. Conservatism in Georgia," 14.

[18]John Harland to H. T., February 20, 1956, VI, A-1, box 1, f. 3, Talmadge papers.

the radiance of a 'George of Georgia.'"[19]

His problem was also exacerbated by his age. At seventy-eight (and at a time when medicine had not yet lengthened life expectancy much beyond his current age), he was still outwardly robust and basically in good health, but polls showed that a majority of Georgians believed that he would not live through another term if reelected.[20] Since Eisenhower had entered office in 1953, forty members of Congress had suffered heart attacks, with eight senators and two representatives not surviving.[21] Furthermore, George's physical appearance underscored his age: his white hair and extremely thick glasses (the result of the cataract surgery he had had in 1939) made less difference to the public before the days of television. By 1956, thousands of Georgians had televisions, and the contrast between the aging George with his "Coke bottle" glasses and a younger opponent portrayed on black-and-white television screens would have highlighted the age difference. Even his campaign brochure "Georgians for George" gave the impression that his return to Washington would be temporary; it explained that "for the present" the senator felt "obligated to remain at his post of duty," adding somewhat doubtfully that the "people of Georgia concur in that decision, I'm sure."[22]

In George's mind, there was no age issue. He felt good. Moreover, he came from long-lived stock. The story circulated that some visitor to his Washington office tactfully asked George during his last Senate term if he planned to retire. Before the senator could answer, a spry elderly man stepped into the room from a side door, and George turned to the inquiring visitor and said, "I'd like to have you meet my papa," referring to the elderly gentleman.[23] His father lived to be ninety-eight.[24] Moreover, if he left the Senate, his replacement as chair of the Foreign Relations Committee, Senator Theodore Green of Rhode Island, was ten years his senior. Given these circumstances, one can easily understand why questions about his age puzzled the senator.[25]

George, to be certain, had his supporters, and they were legion, but not

[19]"George of Georgia," *New Republic*, 5.

[20]Gould Lincoln, "Political Mill," in RCB-5804, box 15, f. WFG-GSA.

[21]*Parade* with the *Telegraph and News*, April 15, 1956, 4.

[22]*Georgians for George*, WFG brochure, WFG-MU.

[23]Donovan, "Senator George," 34.

[24]Thomas O'Neil, "Politics and People," clipping, n. d., scrapbook, LHG-VHPS, states that his father lived to be ninety-four.

[25]Bert Struby of the *Macon Telegraph* (Struby, "George Gaining the Younger Vote," March 5, 1956, unidentified clipping in House papers.

having had a serious race in eighteen years, he had not kept in place the political machines that Senator Russell and Governor Herman Talmadge had constructed. With the exception of Richard Russell's campaign against Gene Talmadge in 1936, George had stayed out of other campaigns, seemingly above the fray, while others had compiled political debts from various local political warlords. One outside political observer described George's political following as more "a broad social circle than a machine," and it was composed largely of personal friendships forged on fishing trips and quail shoots with powerful local public figures such Macon's T. Baldwin Martin.[26] To the lower-level politicians in the trenches back home in Georgia, he was a "lone wolf" who had stayed out of other races, unlike his likely opponent Herman Talmadge, whose machine and endorsement had elected many political figures, not least of all the current governor Marvin Griffin. Moreover, George's aloofness was real. In 1955, a local politician estimated that George had not made an appearance in at least a hundred of Georgia's 159 counties since his race in 1938.[27] With his age, such detachment was likewise hurting him.

"Georgians for George," the closest thing George had to a political machine, was founded only on February 28, 1956, and headquartered in the Henry Grady Hotel in Atlanta under the leadership of his close friend, the former congressman Steve Pace of Americus. Pace had been on the payroll of the Foreign Relations Subcommittee, and his job had expired in January 31, 1956.[28] One of the components of the organization was the "new voters division," headed by the youngest state legislator, State Representative John W. Love Jr., of Catoosa County.[29] This organization likewise had a "women's division," led by Mrs. Orville Tyler Schaefer of Toccoa, the wife of Stephens County surgeon Bruce Schaefer. Whereas his probable opponent Governor Herman Talmadge had summoned professionals to direct his still unannounced candidacy, George had no one in his inner circle who had had the experience of running a statewide campaign.[30] By March 1956, the group had done little but distribute by mail 30,000 pamphlets and 28,000 letters to Georgians calling for support and volunteers.[31] There was no organized fundraising or plans for a media campaign, so the whole operation had

[26]See the Martin memoir, n.p.

[27]Cater, "Regression vs Conservatism in Georgia," 14.

[28]"Matters to take up with the Chairman," 2, GFR VHPS.

[29]See *Georgians for George*, a campaign brochure in WFG-MU.

[30]M. L. St. John, "The Senate Race," *Atlanta Constitution*, May 9, 1956, 6, RCB-5804, box 15, f. WFG-GSA.

[31]Unidentified clipping, probably the *Washington Star*, WFG-GSA.

an "amateur night in Dixie" air about it.

What George did have going for him was a very broad and deep rank-and-file devotion of thousands of Georgians who revered and respected their great homegrown statesman. Ms. Gladys Giddens, wife of one of the leading Baptist leaders in the state, remembered going to Washington in high school and meeting Walter George, who came off the Senate floor to meet her class. "I didn't want to wash my hand after shaking his," she remembered.[32] Her attitude was typical among his longtime supporters.

In addition to this broad base, there were numerous groups within the state that were fanatically devoted to him. Curiously a core of his support came from young people, especially those who had at least a high school diploma, and since Georgians could vote at the age of eighteen, whole civics classes marched to their local courthouses to register to vote for him. Moreover, Georgia had 55,000 students of voting age in 1956, and these enthusiastic voters were solidly in his corner.[33] The reason for his popularity with the young centered on a number of factors. Few had forgotten Herman's father's conflicts with the University of Georgia during his terms as governor. Also, the college-educated were more internationally minded and were more aware of the world beyond the Savannah and Chattahoochee rivers. Moreover, these young people, the males of whom were of draft age, recognized the important role that George played in international affairs and George's efforts to insure peace.[34] These young people, it would seem, would be a solid and enthusiastic base for his campaign.

His efforts, moreover, to maintain a lasting peace made him very popular with Georgian women.[35] Bert Struby of the *Macon Telegraph* wrote in March 1956 that "it is fairly well conceded that Senator George will have the preponderance of the women's vote in any test with Talmadge."[36] His efforts for peace resonated well with them, and many had not forgotten that in 1922 George had delayed his own swearing-in so Rebecca Felton, the first woman ever to sit in the Senate, could take her appointed seat for at least one day. George's leadership role in vocational education for the past three decades garnered him support there; that students in vocational schools led the voter registration among the newly registered high school

[32]Conversation with Mrs. Giddens.

[33]*Mercer Cluster*, May 6, 1956, 2.

[34]*Macon Telegraph*, April 19, 1956, 4.

[35]"Famous Senator in Trouble with Voters," 34.

[36]Struby, "George Gaining…." March 5, 1956, *Macon Telegraph*, House papers.

students.[37] Moreover, the black vote in Georgia was not small, and it would go solidly for George in any contest with Talmadge. What George had going for him—and it was enormously powerful—was a deep and broad-based love and support of many in the state and their delight in the pleasant national attention he had brought to the state.

With his long seniority, he could chair either of two powerful committees, Finance and Foreign Relations, and if he retired, his replacement would begin at the bottom of the seniority pile. Moreover, if he left the Senate, the South would lose one of its nine committee chairmanships in Congress. Whereas the chairs of these committees were supposedly only the chief clerk of the committees, no one disputed the enormous power they held, power they could use to deliver for their state. Endorsing George for reelection, the *Macon Telegraph* told its readers, "We do not believe that the people of Georgia will want to deprive themselves of the benefits which accrue to them through the committee chairmanships which Senator George has attained only by many years of service."[38] It was an enormously important card to be able to play.

In 1952, *Fortune* described George's chances, stating that his seat was safe until 1957 but then adding "and probably for as long after that as George desires."[39] By 1956, though, success was not so certain. What's more, Talmadge forces around the state, possibly not without some element of truth, spread the word that George had said he would retire at the end of his term and that he hoped that Talmadge would replace him.[40] Gossip columnist Drew Pearson, whose articles often had a tabloid quality to them, had written early in 1956 that in 1950 George had told Georgia state comptroller general Zack Cravey the he would step aside in 1956 for Talmadge and that he had told a Georgia delegation caucus at the 1952 Democratic Convention that he would not run again in 1956. Pearson also claimed that in 1954, George had told Talmadge in a meeting in Miami that he would not run again, adding, "I'll be happy to take the stump for you if you want to run."[41]

Throughout 1955 and 1956, however, George dismissed these stories at every chance, caustically telling one reporter that "Drew is about as right as he frequently is," informing the press that he had never discussed his can-

[37]*Macon Telegraph*, April 17, 1956, 6.
[38]Ibid., April 14, 1956, 4.
[39]"The Southern Delegation," 87.
[40]"Can Talmadge Beat George in Georgia?" 39.
[41]*Macon Telegraph*, April 17, 1956, 18.

didacy with Cravey, and that the only time he had been in Miami in the past decade was a brief stopover on a return trip from Puerto Rico. His only speech to the caucus of the Georgia delegation in 1952 had been on the question of the "loyalty oath" that national Democratic leaders wanted to impose on the Southern delegations, not his political future.[42] Many in Georgia thought, however, that given his age, George should retire, that he should see the proverbial "handwriting on the wall" and give in gracefully to Talmadge.[43] Even the *Savannah Morning News*, a paper that had always supported George in the past, called on George to retire gracefully. AP picked it up and asked George about it. The senator quipped that those calling for him to quit "must be in their dotage," a reference to the fact that the newspaper's chairman was several years older than George himself.[44] *Newsweek* told its readers as late as March 1955 that his plan for retirement "is a secret he shares with no one."[45]

On *Meet the Press* in March 1955, George said that he would decide in the next spring if he would run again. Three days afterward, however, he informally semi-announced his candidacy for reelection. In his statement, he wrote, "I decided to make the statement now...because of the many rumors that are going around.... I felt it only fair to my friends to let them know before any commitments are made." He stressed that "too many things might happen between now and campaign time,"[46] but he left no doubt that he was planning to offer for reelection. At the same time, he reinforced his intention of running when he told a *Time* reporter, "I think I'm capable of doing some good work yet. I would like to be useful up to the end."[47]

There was speculation at the time that he had announced so early to discourage Talmadge from whatever plans he had and to stop the rumors, circulated mainly by the Talmadge machine, that his age and health were such that he would even be forced to retire early, allowing Governor Griffin to appoint Talmadge to the seat.[48] When pressed by a reporter on the same program in July, he side-stepped the question, adding that he would not "make any positive or definite statement until we approach the beginning of

[42]Ibid.

[43]Ibid. Talmadge himself felt that George would do so (correspondence between Re Ray Hill of Tennessee Legislature and Herman Talmadge before his death. Conversation between Hill and the author.

[44]Cater, "Regression vs Conservatism in Georgia," 13.

[45]"George of Georgia: Ike's Friend in Need," 29.

[46]*Vienna News, April 14,* 1955, 1.

[47]"Voice of the 84th," 25.

[48]Purcell, "George of Georgia: The Talmadge Threat," 115.

another year."[49]

The formal announcement came eight months later, five days before Christmas, in a news release at noon from Vienna. Reminding the readers that he had promised earlier in the year to "make a positive statement," he then announced, "I will be a candidate for nomination in the Democratic primary for the office of United States Senator next year." He went on to say that "matters of importance" will have to be considered in the second session of Congress, thereby delaying his campaign, but he rationalized that the "people of Georgia will expect me to give first attention to their business in Washington," specifying an agriculture bill, highway construction legislation, tax reductions, and foreign policy issues "for the avoidance of war." He had, he felt, to be in Washington for these matters. He concluded with, "As soon as the public business will permit, I will return to the state. In the mean time I shall depend on my friends in Georgia."[50]

A close associate of Talmadge's, Robert Troutman Jr., remembered that Talmadge was shocked at the announcement because he thought he had made an informal but genuine deal with George through intermediaries in 1950 that if Talmadge would not run against George in 1950, George would retire before the end of his term so that the governor could appoint Talmadge.[51] Such a scenario is unlikely and Troutman was probably mistaken, but Talmadge recorded in his memoirs that at the 1952 Democratic Convention, George had told him that he probably would not run again in 1956 and suggested that Talmadge run for his seat,[52] a scenario that Senator George's Vienna law partner, T. Hoyt Davis Jr., hotly denied.[53] Talmadge believed that the reason for George's decision to run again lay with Eisenhower and Dulles. Without having been privy to any conversation on the matter, Talmadge wrote that both men had convinced George that "the weight of the world lay on his shoulders" as chair of the Foreign Relations Committee, so he was prepared to change his mind and run though he was seventy-eight years old and in poor health.

As for Talmadge, the young former governor felt that he had raised too much money and was too far ahead in the polls to back out now.[54] Talmadge's contention that he was far ahead is questionable. Moreover, a

---

[49]"Meet the Press," transcript, July 24, 1955, 10, GFR-VHPS.

[50]Announcement of his candidacy, (no title), December 20, 1955, GFR-VHPS.

[51]Robert Troutman, Jr., oral history, 15, Russell Library.

[52]Talmadge, *Talmadge: A Political Legacy*, 169.

[53]Interview with T. Hoyt Davis.

[54]Talmadge, *Talmadge: A Political Legacy*, 169.

good campaign on George's part could have erased the lead. Curiously, a third factor began to loom in the race: Former liberal governor Ellis Arnall began to eye the Senate seat. With both Talmadge and George splitting the conservative vote, he might be able to win with the liberal minority, carrying enough counties with a plurality to give him a majority of the county unit votes, and throughout 1955, sources close to Arnall said that if such a race developed, he would jump in as a liberal alternative.[55] From this point until George's withdrawal, however, there occurred a curious political *pas de deux*, in which both George and undeclared Talmadge feinted, shadowboxed, and postured, both hoping that the other would bow out, with neither man formally attacking the other. Both repeatedly denied that a conflict existed, but both hoped to create a show of strength so great that the other would gracefully leave the political battlefield.[56] In fall 1955, however, George made no show of doing so. After Congress adjourned, he began traveling the state, making speeches to any organization that would have him, he said, "to learn if my friends want me [to run again.]"[57] He spoke a number of places, touting his role in the Eisenhower foreign policy. He accepted all speaking invitations possible. When he was invited to make the keynote address at the opening of the Emory Institute of Citizenship in October 1955, a date that would have to be nailed down well in advance by the hosts, he left them hanging rather than decline, in hopes that he could be there.[58] Typical was his speech to two hundred citizens at a luncheon in Thomasville, sponsored by the Thomasville Rotary Club and the local chapter of the League of Women Voters. George polished off a large lunch of ham, turnips, potatoes, apple sauce, and cornbread "with gusto," someone observed, and after the meal lit up a filter-tipped cigarette. When he rose to give his address, "the entire room rose with him in a thunderous ovation," *Newsweek* reported, and one woman in the audience told a reporter, "It thrills me that I'm sitting only a few feet away from one of the outstanding statesmen in the world."[59]

Likewise in Gainesville, where Roosevelt had snubbed him almost twenty years before, eleven service clubs hosted an occasion for him on November 28, 1955, billed "Senator George Day." Although noting that Senator George had not been in Gainesville for quite a while, the local paper *The*

[55]"Can Talmadge Beat George in Georgia?" 38. Since the George-Talmadge race never materialized, neither did Arnall's candidacy.

[56]Cater, "Regression vs Conservatism in Georgia," 13.

[57]"Political Test," 33.

[58]Cullen B. Besnell to WFG, *Newsweek* clipping, July 7, 1955, box 2, f. 3; WFG to Cullen B. Besnell, July 11, 1955, box 2, f. 3, Besnell papers.

[59]Ibid.

Daily Times, told its readers, "Such a tribute would certainly warm the heart of this longtime public servant and at the same time express what must be a common emotion in the hearts of all of us."[60] Gainesville was not through praising the senator, however, and honored him again in May the next year at a luncheon of the Fourth Annual Georgia Poultry Festival, sponsored by the Gainesville-Hall County Chamber of Commerce.[61] All of the praise and his speech-giving must have done some good; a poll commissioned by the *Macon Telegraph* just prior to his December announcement that he would run showed George receiving 57 percent to 34 percent for Talmadge, with 9 percent undecided. George was ahead in urban counties by a 2 to 1 margin and surprisingly holding a "significant edge" in rural ones.[62]

In the early days of 1956, George began to don the cloak of a politician rather than a statesman.[63] In some cases, his speeches became demagogic, and he said things that those who knew him well knew that he did not believe himself. For the first time, he began to be somewhat critical of foreign aid, for which he had been a leading champion, trying to blunt Talmadge's criticism of "foreign giveaways," and he openly opposed Eisenhower's proposal for a long-range foreign aid program,[64] citing specifically the construction of the Egyptian Aswan Dam[65] as a prime example, a "giveaway" of which Talmadge had been especially critical. By mid-April, he had secured a promise from Secretary of State John Foster Dulles to examine further the idea of loans to foreign countries as opposed to outright gifts,[66] and there followed on April 28 a big splash announcement that George, Eisenhower, and Dulles would have talks for a "sweeping review of the entire US foreign aid program."[67] After a White House meeting of congressional leaders the next day, George announced that the Democrats had been given "a better picture" of the situation, but George, a leading champion of foreign aid, added that the White House should expect cuts in the program.[68]

---

[60]Clipping from *Gainesville (GA) Daily Times*, November 8, 1955, scrapbook, LHG-VHPS.

[61]Brochure on the luncheon, LHG-VHPS.

[62]Congressional Report of the National Committee for an Effective Congress, 4, GFR-VHPS.

[63]"New Post Means Chance to Relax," *Ft. Worth Star-Telegram*, clipping, May 10, 1956, RCB-5804, box 15, f. WFG-GSA.

[64]Lubell, *The Revolt of the Moderates*, 224.

[65]*Macon Telegraph*, April 30, 1956, 1; *Atlanta Constitution*, April 28, 1956, 1, 3.

[66]*Atlanta Constitution*, April 18, 1956, 6.

[67]*Macon Telegraph*, April 29, 1956, 1.

[68]Ibid., May 1, 1956, 1. Much of this position has the air of posturing, and there seems to be a hint of White House assistance to George in the matter.

Although he had been largely responsible for the "Big Four" meeting in 1955, George started urging caution in dealing with the Soviet Union. On April 23, he stated that "the supreme mistake" at the end of World War II was the assumption that because we had fought side by side with "our Russian friends" that they must be people with "aims and aspirations much or very similar to our very own."[69] Furthermore, the Russian proposal for an arms embargo in the Middle East gave the senator a great chance to underscore this point.[70]

On the domestic front, Senator George also began to champion the small taxpayer against the corporations, and he announced his support for a costly large-scale aid bill for farmers. He arranged, probably with the help of his colleagues, a highly publicized Congressional meeting in Macon in November 1955 for the purpose of drawing up a new farm program, at which he was paid glowing tribute.[71] With the help of his Southern colleagues, he had already positioned himself as leader of the "massive resistance" to school integration, reading himself word-for-word the so-called "Southern Manifesto" into the *Congressional Record* in an effort to blunt Talmadge's leading position on opposition to school integration.[72] By April 1956, George was even calling for the defeat in November of his close friend President Eisenhower because of his veto of the 1956 farm bill, which had included great support for farmers. Speaking at a rally on a flag-festooned platform at Agricultural Day in Dawson in Terrell County, George announced that he would lead a fight in the Senate for 100 percent parity support for farm crops in the Senate, explaining, however, that it would have to be next year when he did so, presumably after his reelection. He received loud applause to his remarks at Dawson when he asked rhetorically, "Why is it wrong to pay the farmer a subsidy when everyone else is subsidized?"[73]

Even before this statement, Eisenhower was becoming disturbed at George's distancing himself from his former positions which had been so helpful to the Eisenhower administration. Eisenhower had recently eaten both dinner and breakfast with George Woodruff, the Coca-Cola magnate and prominent George-backer of many years, who told Ike that he was doing his best to prevent George's "partisan" drift and "to see that [he] oper-

---

[69]Speech to American Society of Newspaper Editors, Washington, DC, April 23, 1955, cited in Carlton, "The Record," GFR-VHPS.

[70]*Macon Telegraph*, April 30, 1956, 1.

[71]*Congressional Report* of the National Committee for an Effective Congress, 3, GFR, file, VHPS.

[72]"Famous Senator in Trouble with Voters," 32.

[73]*Macon Telegraph*, April 19, 1956, 1.

ates as a statesman rather than as a politician." He claimed that he had stressed to the senator that his "political strength in Georgia is based on the assumption that he is always a statesman first and a politician second." Eisenhower himself had scheduled an appointment with George several days later, presumably to hammer home the same theme.[74]

If the Eisenhower-George meeting took place in January 1956, as he had told Woodruff, the president did not mention it in his diary. The next meeting that he did record did not occur until March 23, during which George several times mentioned being "tired." As Eisenhower recorded the conversation, George was clearly fishing for encouragement to make another Senate race. George repeatedly stressed to Ike his desire to support him, obviously referring to foreign policy and making the case that his opponent probably would not. "The senator seemed to be waiting for me to express an opinion about the wisdom of running again," Eisenhower recorded after the meeting, "but I was careful to say nothing beyond the fact that I had always admired the firmness with which he stood for bipartisanship in foreign relations and for moderation in human progress." George seemed to be pleased with this, at most, tepid endorsement. When Eisenhower added that if he should retire, though, he would want to call on George for advice or maybe even appoint him as some sort of ambassador-at-large to represent him, George made it plain that he would not be interested. "No, if I retire," he told the president, "I want to stay home and rest. I am really tired." He did add that he might be available for small tasks occasionally, but the senator was making the message clear that if Eisenhower wanted his help, it would have to be as a member of the Senate.[75]

Perhaps the two incidents were unrelated, but within a week at a news conference, Eisenhower praised Senator George to the skies for his contributions to bipartisan foreign policy, for which he has been "working as hard as he can." Then the president denounced mudslinging, which was building up in this election year, adding curiously that he did not want "to say anything against a party which had in it a man like Senator George."[76] Eisenhower certainly could and should have been a great help to Walter George in any race against Talmadge, but his help would have had to have been very subtle, such as quietly alerting his financial backers to come to George's rescue. Anything overt could have given Talmadge the weapon that "outside meddlers" were stirring in the race, and a Republican at that. It had not

[74]Eisenhower, *Eisenhower Diaries, 310.*
[75]Ibid., 323.
[76]"George Given Praise," *Atlanta Journal*, March 30, 1956, scrapbook, LHG-VHPS.

worked in 1938 when a Democratic president tried it; it most certainly would have blown up in Eisenhower's face in 1956 for a Republican president to have attempted it, especially in a state where Eisenhower had made his worst showing of the forty-eight in 1952.

In 1956 it may have taken more than "encouragement" for the "Eisenhower Democrats" to have rallied to George, for they were the banking interests and big business.[77] They had done so in 1938, the last time George had had serious opposition, but by 1956, there was a different factor to consider: the question of George's longevity.

George had lots of support, nevertheless, starting with his US Senate colleagues. At a reference on the Senate floor to the Formosa Resolution, there had been a volcanic eruption of praise among his Senate colleagues.[78] When George entered the hospital in June 1955 for treatment of a bronchial infection, even his convalescence catalyzed an explosion of praise for the infirm solon, with the likes of Hubert Humphrey, Alexander Wiley, Lyndon Johnson, and the Republican leader William Knowland going out of their way to laud him, send him well wishes, and trumpet his many accomplishments.[79] Referring to his most recent success, the formulation of the Big-Four meeting, Senator Mike Mansfield used the metaphor "icebreaker in foreign policy" as a tribute to George.[80]

In August 1955, as the congressional session came to an end, there occurred what could only have been a staged endorsement of his reelection in the form of a "spontaneous" tribute to Senator George from colleagues, both Democrats and Republicans.[81] George had asked the day before final adjournment to be granted a leave of absence from his Senate duties (for health reasons) on the final day though he was "loathe to make the request."[82] There followed what was a clearly staged eruption of laudatory speeches, which were to appear off the cuff but some of which had obviously been prepared well beforehand. Senators from both sides of the aisle, more liberals than conservatives, stepped forward to sing the senator's praises: Wayne Morse of Oregon; Prescott Bush, the father and grandfather of two presidents and a governor; Bob Smith of New Jersey; Alexander Wiley of Wisconsin; Clinton Anderson of New Mexico; John McClellan of Arkan-

[77]Purcell, "George of Georgia: The Talmadge Threat," 116.
[78]*CR*, 84/1, 2031–32.
[79]Ibid., 7302.
[80]Ibid.
[81]"People of the Week," *US News*, 39(August 12, 1955), 12.
[82]*CR*, 84/1, 12572.

sas; Hubert Humphrey; and many others.[83] Mike Mansfield of Montana said, "We know that in the preceding months he has made a magnificent contribution not only to the welfare of this country, but...to the entire world." He added, "We see in him the traits and characteristics which we would like to see in ourselves."[84] Young George Smathers of Florida extolled, "One of the great privileges of my life has been to know...this truly great man."[85] The prolix Humphrey's "spontaneous" tribute was the longest and definitely had the air of pre-delivery preparation:

> The senator from Georgia is to the United States Senate a bulwark of strength. He has represented the finest traditions of this great deliberative body.... He is a profound and effective statesman.... When some of us felt too timid to speak up, this brave man spoke up. Even a short absence from the Senate by the senator from Georgia leaves a great vacuum in our midst.[86]

Proving that the whole thing had been staged was a tribute read into the record by Senator Smathers for Lyndon Johnson, who was recuperating from a heart attack at Bethesda Naval Hospital. It strains credulity to believe that in the course of about an hour, Johnson learned of the impromptu tributes and dictated one from himself to Lady Bird, who then rushed it to Smathers. At any rate, in it he wrote of how George's imprint "is indelibly impressed upon our times."[87]

The next day, Senator Knowland of California introduced a formal resolution, which, of course, passed the Senate unanimously: "Resolved, that the thanks of the Senate are hereby tendered to Senator Walter F. George...for the courteous, dignified, and impartial manner with which he has presided over its deliberations during the 1st session of the 84th Congress." Referring to the praise of the previous day, he told his colleagues that it was "one of the most touching and significant days of my 10 [*sic*] years in the Senate," and he praised, as so many others had done, George's efforts "to keep together the two great political parties in facing whatever common dangers may come from abroad."[88] Others praised George that day for his "vision and courage" in working with Eisenhower and Dulles, and they all

---

[83]Ibid., 12572–76.

[84]Ibid., 12572.

[85]Ibid., 12573. In a telephone interview, Senator Smathers told this author that George was the colleague he most respected of all he had known in the Senate.

[86]Ibid., 12575.

[87]Ibid., 12576.

[88]Ibid., 12916.

wished him many more years in the Senate.[89]

Oddly, the display had the aura of valedictory praise and many made references to his health, but since George had another year and a half in his Senate term left, this outburst could only have been a calculated, staged attempt to help spook Talmadge out of the race and to jump-start George's next campaign. What would be the reason to ask for a leave of absence when there was only one more day left in the session? Moreover, to ask would give the Talmadge forces evidence of his waning vigor, and George certainly knew that. He could have been absent "for reasons of business." The whole scenario with its testimonials had to have been planned to assist his reelection by a large segment, mostly liberal, of the Senate, who dreaded the appearance of the tobacco-chewing, race-baiting Herman Talmadge.

George, however, was to undermine much of the good this did in the same way seventy-nine-year-old Senator A. Willis Robertson of Virginia was to help doom his 1966 reelection campaign by inadvertently calling attention to his age. Speaking of being "wearied by his exacting duties...and weakened by recent illness," George told his colleagues that he was looking forward to a rest, adding, "I hope I shall come back."[90] Many of the senators undercut their own arguments by making references to George's health.[91] Asking to leave for reasons of health would have been the only legitimate reason for asking for a leave of absence at such a time, thus giving the excuse for the string of encomia.

There was one senator, however, who did not step forward to praise George: His Georgia colleague Richard B. Russell. Russell had a history of non-involvement in Georgia politics beyond his own campaigns, and the fact that he did not join in the praise of his senior colleague probably gives further proof that the performance was designed to promote George's reelection. At a 1955 Talmadge testimonial dinner, which was part of the warm-up for the 1956 Senate campaign, Russell, the leading speaker, had spoken most favorably in general terms toward Talmadge to the 2,000 assembled guests.[92]

In 1956, Russell seemed indifferent about George's race. John Carlton, a Georgian who was on the staff of Senator George Smathers, had been encouraged by Edgar Dunlap, George's 1938 campaign manager, to return to

---

[89]"People of the Week," (August 12, 1955), 12.

[90]Ibid. This sentence does not appear in the *CR* and must have been said to a *US News* reporter.

[91]*CR*, 84/1, 12573 ff.

[92]"New Voice for the South in Congress," 85.

Georgia and work full time in George's campaign. He encountered Russell in the courtyard of the Senate Office Building and talked with him for about thirty minutes about whether he should join George's reelection effort. Carlton made it plain that he would not do it unless Russell would recommend it. "You know," he remembered Russell saying, "He—he may just make it.... You've got nothing to lose.... Why don't you go ahead and take it." To this lukewarm encouragement, Carlton replied, "By George, I will."[93] Beyond that, Russell did nothing to help George.

If anything, Russell did things that would have hurt, if only personally. In 1956, while George was still in the race, he, Russell and David W. Brooks, chair of the board of Gold Kist Co., were eating breakfast together. All three had ordered eggs and ham. When George started eating, Russell said jokingly something that could only have been painful: "Well now, Senator George, I don't believe you better eat that ham; that's probably Talmadge ham and it'll probably give you indigestion!" George "sort of laughed," Brooks remembered.[94] Even after George's death, Russell made a few oblique swipes at him. At a Talmadge event even after George's passing, Russell backhandedly slammed George somewhat by his praise of Talmadge: "In my time, no man," he later publicly stated, "has ever come into the Senate, taken over and handled so aptly such difficult assignments normally given to veterans as has Herman Talmadge."[95] This sort of remark could only have been painful to Walter George, had he been alive to hear it.

There also occurred a number of honors obviously designed to bolster his campaign. In November 1955, Senator Robertson of Virginia nominated George as "Man of the South" for 1956.[96] In February 1956, the other senator from Virginia, Harry Byrd, presented him with the George Washington Award at a dinner at the Stadtler Hotel in Washington. In presenting the award, Byrd described George's "sterling character and his genius in statecraft which has won for him a place among the great men who have served in the United States Senate."[97] The next month in Washington, the Amvets gave George the National Peace Award for his "outstanding contribution to world peace." They cited him for "initiating bipartisan foreign policy," his work on the Formosa question, the Geneva Summit Conference, and the

[93]John Carlton, oral history, 22, Russell Library.

[94]David W. Brooks, oral history, 44, Russell Library. This explains the Talmadge's ham business.

[95]Cook, *The Governors of Georgia*, 269.

[96]"U. S. Senator WFG is nominated..." General Corres: Golden, November 9, 1955, Robertson papers.

[97]"Humphrey and George," *Evening Star*, February 23, 1956, scrapbook, LHG-VHPS.

Red China Conference, which resulted in the freeing of eleven American fliers held by the Chinese. In replying to their praise, George said that he hoped that the United States "moves toward peace and measurers up to its responsibilities."[98]

That same month, George presided over the Senate for the hundredth time since he had arrived. Ralph McGill wrote a brilliant editorial on George in August 1955, just as George was leaving for Georgia to begin his first campaign swing, praising the importance of the Geneva conference and George's role in it. Pleased, George wrote McGill a letter of thanks "for the splendid editorial support you have given my effort in recent days," adding that McGill shared a "special understanding of the objectives I had in mind for the Geneva conferences." "I do want you to know," he said in conclusion, "that I appreciate everything that you have done to keep people of Georgia enlightened on these vital issues."[99] In the last days of his campaign, on May 1956, the 8th Armored Division named him "Man of the Year for 1956" because of his efforts to ensure world peace. Also nominated were Richard Nixon, John Foster Dulles, Harry Truman and Hubert Hoover, and Henry Cabot Lodge.[100]

All of this gratuitous praise and shower of awards coming at the time they did could only have been coordinated and designed to assist his campaign and remind the people of Georgia that greatness resided in their midst. They also helped draw the sharp contrast to the insular and unsophisticated Governor Talmadge. How much of an impression this outside help made is impossible to measure, but it could only have helped if in no other way but to help wean away those who were for George in their devotion but were emotionally with Talmadge.

George must have found the political waters inviting, for in December 1955, Walter F. George was prepared to announce formally that he would be a candidate for reelection to the United States Senate in 1956. He made this move despite the fact that a number of his closest financial advisers remained at best lukewarm about his running. A number of them frankly told him that he would lose.[101] He had asked Robert Troutman Jr., a curious choice since he was a Talmadge supporter, to sound out twenty former supporters to see if he should make the race. Troutman reported that nineteen

[98]"Amvets Cite Sen. George," *Jessup Sentinel,* March 29, 1956, scrapbook, LHG-VHPS.

[99]WFG to Ralph McGill, n. d., box 6, f. 2, McGill papers.

[100]*CR*, 84/2, 10935–36.

[101]"Senator and Senator to Be," 37.

of the twenty did not want him to, only Senator Abit Nix of Athens, a figure in Georgia politics and president of the University of Georgia Alumni Association, was positive. When Troutman told him the bad news, the old senator was "sadly disheartened," Troutman remembered, and Troutman said that witnessing his dejection was "one of the saddest experiences of my life."[102] President Eisenhower reported in his diary on March 23, 1956, that in a meeting with him about another matter, George "talked like a man who was ready to quit but who would really like to be urged to stay." Eisenhower also remembered that George seemed "bewildered" that there was not a "practically unanimous" chorus that he run again.[103] Many continued to tell him that his ranking as a great statesman would not pull him through the Democratic primary in September and that Talmadge, who had not even announced, was pulling ahead. Then there were those supporters of his who wanted him to run even if he lost. "Dammit," one of his longtime financial backers told a reporter, "I have been stewing for weeks about the possibility that he might lose. But I think he should run. If he has to go down[,] it would be less humiliating to go down fighting."[104]

Much of this logic was written after George had withdrawn or was remembered years later. Troutman's recollection of his survey was flawed at best and dishonest at worst, as we shall see.[105] Granted, there was not overwhelming enthusiasm for George's running because of his age, and there was indeed a strong danger that he would lose, given the county unit system.[106] Politics in those 119 counties was often dominated by the redneck vote, which would go overwhelmingly for Talmadge, and herein lay George's biggest hurdle to reelection.[107]

Herman Talmadge's decision to run for George's seat was based on, beyond raw ambition, the above-mentioned conversation that he says took

[102]Robert Troutman, oral history, 7, Russell Library.

[103]Eisenhower, *Eisenhower Diaries,* 323.

[104]Congressional Report of the National Committee for an Effective Congress, 3, GFR-VHPS.

[105]Troutman was a close associate of Talmadge, whether George knew it or not, and late in April 1956, Talmadge used some heavy-handed tactics to try to force the acceptance of Troutman's candidacy as President of the UGA Alumni Association. See *Macon Telegraph*, April 28, 1956, 1.

[106]"Famous Senator in Trouble with Voters," 34; Belvin, "The Georgia Gubernatorial Primary of 1946," 44. Belvin incorrectly states that 121 counties had two votes each. In 1958, longtime Atlanta mayor William B. Hartsfield took the system to the federal courts, and Talmadge protegé Governor Marvin Griffin called him a "renegade and a traitor to our Georgia way of life" for his efforts ("Treachery?" 24).

[107]"George of Georgia," *The New Republic*, 4.

place between him and George at the 1952 Democratic National Convention[108] (a contention that T. Hoyt Davis refused to believe). There was also the fact that George had beaten his father in 1938, made all the worse because Gene Talmadge had gone to bed on election night thinking he had won and then later believed, not without some reason, that the race had been stolen.[109] His son probably still shared that view. Just as Richard Russell never seems to have forgiven George for trouncing his father in 1926, Talmadge never accepted the 1938 defeat at the hands of what Talmadge called "our stuff-shirt United States Senator Walter George."[110] To Herman Talmadge, George personified the bourbon South of the past, while he represented the South of the future.[111] Even before any campaign had formally begun, Talmadge's men had begun to give George a taste of the viciousness he could expect; they circulated rumors of George's senility and failing health, spread the fiction that he had to be led in and out of the Senate, and so forth.[112] His campaign focus was the one that the Talmadges had used in every campaign: country vs. city, American vs. foreigner, and of course "raking the segregation issue with demagogic fire," as one journalist put it. Another editor called it "McCarthyism with a Southern exposure."[113] It was going to be a bitter campaign even by the standard of Georgia, where politics had always been a favorite blood sport.

By late spring, however, there were indications that Talmadge was having second thoughts about running. By February 1956, most of his supporters felt that if he were running, he should have announced by now. The *LaGrange Daily News* opined that perhaps he was planning to avoid the race, observing that Talmadge's speeches the previous fall "sounded more like a candidate's than they do now."[114] Although he had been conducting an unannounced campaign since he left the governor's office early in 1955, Talmadge dispatched a mass mailing to friends and supporters in February 1956, asking their opinion of his candidacy against George.[115] In the letter,

[108]Talmadge, *Talmadge: A Political Legacy*, 169.

[109]Interview with T. Hoyt Davis. He contends that George's reason eventually for not running was that he had lost his "hard core base" and his health.

[110]Talmadge, *Talmadge: A Political Legacy*, 38.

[111]McMillan, "So Goes the South," 43.

[112]Ibid.

[113]Congressional Report of National Committee for an Effective Congress, 3, GRF file, VHPS.

[114]"Talmadge May Not Face George," *La Grange Daily News*, February 28, 1956, copy in the House papers.

[115]See Series VI-A-1, box 1, f. 1–6, Talmadge papers.

he speaks of "considering a race" and how he plans "to weigh carefully all of the factors," adding that "many of my friends throughout the state have urged me to run." He replied with courtesy to these those who answered, even to those who discouraged a campaign against George. He always ended his replies to their advice with an invitation to "come by to see me" if they are ever in either Lovejoy or Atlanta.[116]

In Senator Talmadge's papers on the 1956 race, letters on the campaign are labeled "Favorable" and "Unfavorable," with the former, i.e. those who wanted him to run, yet being far greater than the latter roughly a fifth favorable to George's support makes Troutman's assessment of his polling appear unlikely.

Many of the responders stated that any election between the Talmadge and George would be a close one.[117] C. A. Sirmans of Adel told Talmadge that it was "a big question mark who would win.... Senator George is a strong man[,] and I feel will be hard to beat." Sirmans added, "I feel sure he will carry [south Georgia's] Cook County."[118] Many of the responders mention the pride Georgians have in George's international stature. Georgia politician Carl L. Kelly believed that although the race would be close, he "was inclined to think that the senator would edge in, purely on account of his prestige and seniority...and not on purely political grounds."[119] Leary businessman Harvey Jordan did not feel that Talmadge would carry his rural community, supposedly an area where Talmadge would have run strong. In his county, there was a consensus, he told the former governor, of "Stick with George." He concluded his letter with, "I hate to be the bearer of bad news, but...remember, you asked for it."[120]

A great number of respondents praised Talmadge and stated that they would be willing to support him in any race—except one with George. One Columbus supporter felt that a fight between Talmadge and George "would [not] bring any credit to our great State of Georgia."[121] Some said that they think that Talmadge would win but would vote for George anyway. Many felt that he would be making a mistake in taking on George, suggesting that if he just bided his time, he would eventually get into the Senate anyway, either as an appointee or by being elected.[122] The aforementioned Carl L.

[116]Box labeled "Unfavorable," *passim*, series VI-A-1, box 1, Talmadge papers.
[117]Ibid., f. 1, 2.
[118]C. A. Sirmans to Herman Talmadge (HT), April 28, 1956, ibid.
[119]Hon. Carl L. Kelly to HT, March 17, 1956, f. 2, ibid.
[120]Harvey Jordan to HT, February 2, 1956, f. 3, ibid.
[121]Hon. John W. Sheffield (Sheffield Hardware) to HT, March 29, 1956, ibid.
[122]See for example the letter of Henry S. Cohen to HT, April 6, 1956, f. 1, ibid.

Kelly stressed this theme. George, he wrote, would not be able to finish his six years "if reelected," and that Talmadge would be the one appointed to finish the term. "You would in this instance emerge on top politically, with the full support of both his supporters and yours."[123] A few even suggested that he wait and run against Richard Russell in 1960, which presumably would be an easier target.[124] One former Talmadge supporter simply returned the governor's request letter with his response scrawled on the bottom: "Dear Governor, I am committed to Senator George and will support him. Cordially Sam [N. Matthews]."[125] Mrs. W. E. Hewitt of Douglasville wrote saying that while she felt that Talmadge was capable of "filling the office of senator," she was certain that he was "too wise to think that you can fill Senator George's place. His wisdom as a statesman and his influence as a world citizen are only gained by years of experience," she lectured the former governor. Then she added, "I am only a homemaker[,] and this does not require an answer."[126]

There were those responders who felt that Talmadge would win or carry their county, but they would still support Senator George. Madison attorney Kay Tipton predicted that Talmadge would carry Morgan County "against any reliable opposition," but then added that he personally "would be obliged to vote for Senator George."[127] Many felt that Talmadge could not win. Hudson Malone, the executive director of the Albany Housing Authority, reminded Talmadge that "in the hey-day of his popularity," Franklin Roosevelt had not been able to defeat Walter George, and to lose the election now would "be a blow to you politically." He suggested that he issue a statement to the effect that because of George's "long tenure of office and service," that he would not run against him, but "when the office is available, you will ask the people of Georgia elect him to fill it. That will be the most diplomatic thing to do," he added, and opined that such a shrewd approach would "win for you the future support of Senator George's many friends" as well as "strengthen the friendship with the people who would vote for you." When the office would become open, he would win, Mr. Malone felt, without opposition and would remain in the Senate for the rest of his life.[128]

In the considerable number from Bibb County (Macon), there is not

[123]Carl Kelly to HT, March 17, 1956, box 1, f. 2, ibid.

[124]Ibid.; Troutman interview, oral history, 6, Russell Library.

[125]Hon. Sam N. Matthews to HT, April 11, 1956, series VI-A-1, box 1, f. 1, Talmadge papers.

[126]Mrs. W. E. Hewitt to HT, April 28, 1956, ibid.

[127]Kay Tipton to HT, February 23, 1956, f. 2, ibid.

[128]Hudson Malone to HT, n. d. February 1956, f. 3, ibid.

one that seems to be a favorable response to the February inquiry, and almost all "favorable" were written after the election, congratulating him on his landslide victory against M. E. Thompson. Maconite Cecil Flick ran an informal poll and found Talmadge's support very weak in Bibb County. "I have talked with a maintenance man at the Terminal Railroad Station here, a carpenter, a farmer, a businessman, numerous housewives, teachers, teachers [sic], a doctor, a member of the UDC, the League of Women Voters, the Junior League, and a minister of the church. With only one exception these people said they would vote for Mr. George." His age was the only mitigating factor that any interviewees ever mentioned.[129] Flick's wife weighed in with a separate a letter of her own to add that her husband had visited "a small prosperous town sixty miles from here" for a Masonic meeting and found that a consensus of "a number of influential, wealthy men" was that Talmadge would lose.[130] Local Bibb county attorney and state legislative candidate John Maddox also predicted a George win in Bibb, adding that even some of Talmadge's friends "would work actively on behalf of Senator George,"[131] as did local businessman Linton Baggs, who felt it "extremely doubtful" that there would be a Talmadge victory in Macon because "Mr. George has been extremely active with Mercer University."[132]

One anonymous critic from Valdosta suggested that Talmadge would bring "shame and disgrace" on the state and that he was not "the type Georgia needs to represent her," adding, "You don't have the qualities to live up to the standard Senator George has set."[133] A religiously inclined anonymous critic called on Talmadge to read 1 Kings 12, in which Rehoboam, son of King Solomon, comes to grief because he does not take the advice of elders but listens instead to younger men.[134] The most ironic letter came from Nina McDuffie Pate of Hawkinsville, who informed the former governor, "I have never voted for you because you drank," but "However, since you have quit drinking….[!]"[135]

Forty-two-year-old Herman Talmadge was, of course, the son of one of Georgia's most colorful political figures, although the Georgia in which

[129]Cecil Flick to HT, n. d., ibid.

[130]Mrs. Cecil Flick to HT, February 28, 1956, ibid.

[131]John Maddox to HT, February 15, 1956, and March 28, 1956, f. 2, ibid.

[132]Linton Baggs to HT, April 23, 1956, f. 1, ibid.

[133]Unsigned and undated letter, f. 1, ibid. Another anonymous person referred to his running as "an evil deed."

[134]Unsigned and undated letter, f. 1, ibid.

[135]Nina McDuffie Pate to HT, April 18, 1956, series VI-A-1, box 1, f. 1, Talmadge papers.

his father had been running had changed. Herman, however, had changed with it. *Newsweek* had called him "Gene Talmadge with a University of Georgia degree."[136] His accent was "back-country" when talking with farmers, and he wore his father's red galleoses.[137] Talmadge, though, could move comfortably in the most polished elements of Atlanta society. One secret he kept from his wool-hat supporters was that he was a classical pianist.[138] His father had also perfected this dual image. Few of his supporters knew that Gene Talmadge himself was a second- generation college graduate, although he projected the aura of a functional illiterate, when speaking in rural Georgia, at any rate. When invited to speak to a big-city Rotary Club, "Old Gene" could appear in a suit and tie, giving a polished address that would rival any other.[139]

Herman had been the salutatorian of his high school senior class, and had been a member of the University of Georgia's law school honor court. He had served in the navy for fifty-three months, thirty-two of which were in the Pacific, where he had participated in the Guadalcanal operation.[140] His entré into real politics was his management of his father's 1938 senatorial campaign against Walter George and his father's successful campaign for governor in 1940. Released from naval duty at the war's end, he managed his father's successful gubernatorial campaign in 1946, and when his father died before assuming office, did himself no credit by trying to have himself seated as governor. In 1948 and 1950, however, he was elected in his own right.[141]

As governor, he built 10,000 miles of highways and many schools and hospitals on a 3 percent sales tax he had run against but then persuaded the legislature to pass. By the end of his four-year term, he was so powerful that he could essentially name his successor, Marvin Griffin, who catered to the same redneck, racist instincts of the rural Georgia of that day, and over 2,000 people attended a testimonial dinner when he left the governor's office.[142] Talmadge chewed tobacco when necessary, but generally smoked ten cigars a day.[143] By one account, he could call on encounter the names of

[136]"Senator and Senator-to-Be," 37.

[137]Ibid.

[138]Interview with Lyniece Talmadge, the senator's daughter-in-law.

[139]Conversation with Arthur Griffiths, a Bibb County Democratic Party activist. On Gene, see Cater, "Regression vs Conservatism in Georgia," 14.

[140]"Famous Senator in Trouble with Voters," 34.

[141]Varney, "Meet Senator Talmadge," 9.

[142]"New Voice for the South in Congress," 85.

[143]"Georgia Loses," 23.

15,000 Georgians,[144] 30,000 by another account.[145] Where the newer generation of Georgians could not say that they had ever seen Walter George, they all knew Talmadge and called him "Herman."[146]

Along the way, he had managed his father's business interests and expanded them. He continued with his father's newspaper *The Statesman*, built up a law practice in Atlanta, developed real estate and insurance interests, and founded a ham-curing enterprise.[147] He ran two farms totaling 4,000 acres and lived on one of them in Lovejoy, thirty minutes outside of Atlanta, in a white-columned mansion that had somehow been overlooked by Sherman's troops.[148]

Talmadge was a frequent speaker all over the state, making at one point forty-nine speeches over a fifty-week period, and he hosted a weekly television show.[149] Talmadge developed two main issues for the campaign: anti-foreign aid (in effect a neo-isolationism) and segregation vs. integration. Of the two, the latter was more on Georgians' minds in the immediate years after the *Brown vs. Board of Education* decision of 1954. The Supreme Court desegregation decision was a godsend to him politically, and he bore down hard on talk of integration, which was in sharp contrast to George, who was viewed as a racial moderate.[150] However, the race issue was foremost to Georgia voters in 1956. An Atlanta attorney told *US News*, "All they [Georgia citizens] can talk about is the race problem,"[151] and when it came to the question of race, no one in the state of Georgia had made greater use of the issue than had the Talmadges. In his 1950 gubernatorial campaign, Talmadge pledged to the voters that "negro and white children will not attend the same school" if he were elected governor. In 1950, the *Vienna News*, perhaps anticipating a future race between Talmadge and George, told its readers, "He injects into the campaign the race issues which would not be an issue at all except for his making them such."[152] Talmadge had circulated a pamphlet, complete with blacks and whites dancing, implying that his opponents had favored interracial socializing, which was based on

[144]McMillan, "So Goes the South," 43.

[145]"Can Talmadge Beat George in Georgia?" 38.

[146]"Famous Senator in Trouble with Voters," 32, 34.

[147]Ibid., 34.

[148]"New Voice for the South in Congress," 82.

[149]Cater, "Regression vs Conservatism in Georgia," 13.

[150]George never strongly attacked the 1954 Supreme Court decision.

[151]"Famous Senator in Trouble with Voters," 34.

[152]"Your Duty to Vote," *Vienna News*, January 22, 1950, RCB-5804, box 15, f. WFG-GSA.

nothing anyone else had said or done.[153] The Talmadges had built up the myth that they had saved Georgia "from the nigger," one observer wrote, yet he noted, "Of course, George will be for segregation too…so it will not be a matter of pro- and con-; it will be a matter of who can shout the loudest."[154]

While Talmadge had been quick to react to the *Brown* decision, George had remained relatively quiet. George had been a Georgia Supreme Court judge, and courts were part of government to be thoroughly respected. Talmadge did not have that hang-up; he made it the cornerstone of every speech he gave and stressed "his determination to maintain segregation in Georgia." *Newsweek* made the observation in contrasting the two that George favored segregation as well, but added, "He doesn't talk about it much."[155]

Talmadge immediately blasted the court as having lowered itself "to the level of common politics" and that "Georgians…will not accept a bald political decree."[156] He had also already gotten a constitutional amendment passed making public moneys payable to private schools in the event that any school district was so foolish as to integrate.[157] In a speech in Camilla, Mitchell County, population 4,000, and home of arch-conservative Congressman Eugene Cox, Talmadge denounced the court as "a little group of politicians [who have] not had enough experience to handle one chicken thief in Mitchell County." He promised that in the Senate he would reverse the *Brown* decision and generally limit the court's power.[158] On a more comical note, when he tired of calls from the Northern press to his home in Lovejoy, he refused to take any more of them, instructing his wife to tell all reporters that he was out in the field, drilling Confederate troops.[159]

It was on this issue that Senator George was most disadvantaged. No civil rights bill had passed Congress since 1875. Five of them had passed the House by 1956, but they had always been killed in the Senate with the filibuster.[160] To many Georgians terrified of the prospect of integration, it seemed essential to send Talmadge to the Senate to stop any future erosion

---

[153]Cater, "Regression vs Conservatism in Georgia," 15.

[154]Purcell, "George of Georgia: The Talmadge Threat," 116.

[155]"Political Test," 32–34.

[156]Bolster, "The Civil Rights Movements in Twentieth Century Georgia," 135.

[157]*Southern School News*, September 3, 1954, 5, and *New York Times*, November 17, 1953, **[both?]** cited in Bolster, "The Civil Rights Movements in Twentieth Century Georgia," 136; Caro, *The Years of Lyndon Johnson*, 847.

[158]"Georgia Loses," 23.

[159]A familiar story that circulates in Georgia.

[160]Caro, *The Years of Lyndon Johnson*, 852.

of white rights. Although George had been positioned as the titular head of the "massive resistance," he had clearly been outdistanced by Talmadge on this issue. One political observer of the Georgia scene noted that if George had just once come out against the Supreme Court on the *Brown* decision, he would have been home-free in 1956. He had not, and the issue had hurt him. Talmadge's position on segregation made him a major figure, and he had developed a distinct reputation in the South and had even been invited to address the Alabama legislature.[161]

Equally effectively used by Talmadge were his attacks on "foreign give-aways," which was his terminology for America's program of foreign aid to challenge Russian expansion in parts of the world. There is some question as to whether Talmadge really opposed foreign aid, but he certainly played on America's growing opposition to it, knowing it would play well in insular Georgia.[162] As early as 1953, Talmadge had publicly stated that the American people "are fast coming to the realization" that it was impossible to buy "lasting friendship from other nations," adding that "even the most foolhardy must now realize that there is a limit as to how much we can drain from our national resources."[163] In May 1955, he dubbed foreign aid "a global WPA," and denounced the construction of grain elevators in Pakistan when they were needed in Georgia. "Why, that's 12,500 miles from Georgia," he said, with *Time* calling the figure "for the wool hats," since Karachi was really only 8,700 miles from Atlanta.[164] In November 1955 in a speech to the Macon Real Estate Board, he called foreign aid "a big giveaway," pointing out the apparent foolishness of rebuilding the Japanese textile industry with its thirteen cents per hour wage compared to our $1.30/hour.[165] "We have been subsidizing nations all over the face of the earth," he thundered, and the seeds of doubt he cast about fell on fertile ground.[166] On *Meet the Press* in April 1956 he replied to the question that he was not opposed to all foreign aid if it strengthened the military position of the United States, but he condemned "such projects as the Aswan Dam," which would provide water for the Egyptians to grow cotton while farmers in Georgia were being

[161] Varney, "Meet Senator Talmadge," 8.

[162] In spring 1956, while George was still in the race, Congress refused Eisenhower's request for a long-term continuation of foreign aid (*Congressional Digest*, 35:257)

[163] Varney, "Meet Senator Talmadge," 8.

[164] "Georgia Loses," 23.

[165] In 1955, minimum wage in the United States was just rising to $1.00/hour.

[166] "Political Test," 33.

forced to reduce their cultivated acreage.[167] In every speech Talmadge gave his listeners the impression that when he got to Washington, he would put an end to such programs.[168] Talmadge hammered on this theme throughout Georgia in fall 1955 and spring 1956, never mentioning George by name, but it was obvious whom he was criticizing. The outcome of the probable George-Talmadge race concerned the French ambassador enough to send a memo to the French foreign office on the race, noting that "Senator George must confront the ambitions of the former Governor Talmadge, representing the most conservative Democratic faction" and pointing out how George was particularly being criticized for his support of foreign aid.[169]

George answered the oblique charges of his unannounced opponent as he spoke in both Georgia and Washington, but never so well as he did in promoting the foreign aid bill late in June 1956, after he had withdrawn from the Senate race. Not mentioning Talmadge by name, he condemned those who termed foreign aid "a giveaway" and "foreign rat holes," arguing how the severest critics of foreign aid were those most concerned by the "Communist threat." "How that conclusion can be entirely logical is a bit beyond me…because a large share of the funds are for the purpose of building military forces which oppose communism," George reasoned to the critics of foreign aid. He pointed out how in Turkey on the Soviet border, foreign aid helped maintain more divisions than the United States had at home, adding that the situation was the same in Korea, Formosa, and Pakistan. "We give them help," he continued, "because if we did not, there would be a standing invitation to the Communists to move into these defenseless vacuums that would exist." Stating his belief that war with the Soviet Union was not inevitable, especially due to the previous year's summit, which he had been instrumental in constructing, he added that the danger of war would not be averted "if we begin to liquidate the military strength of the free world." American actions had given notice to the world that Soviet aggression around the Earth "cannot lead to victory." Then he asked the question, "If we do not hold the torch of leadership and carry it forward, into whose hands will it fall? What other free nation is in a position to assume the burden?" Believing that Americans would not shirk their destiny, he warned, "I know that if the free people of this globe lose confidence in us,

---

[167]"New Voice for the South in Congress," 86; Parmet, *Eisenhower and the American Crusade*, 481.

[168]McMillan, "So Goes the South," 43.

[169]French ambassador to Antoine Pinay, December 28, 1955, Amérique 1952–1967, Etats Unis: politique intéreure, f. 482, 433–34, AMAE.

we shall disappoint the best hopes of mankind."[170]

There were those who worked behind the scenes to convince Talmadge not to run, using the argument which we have already seen: That after having been reelected, George would serve only a few years and resign, allowing Herman to be appointed to his seat. They warned him that given George's popularity in the Senate, Talmadge would be *persona non-grata* when he arrived after beating him. He would find it tough going in that body, where favors and political alliances were important. Talmadge's response was that he did not expect many senators to like him anyway and refused to step aside. The powers then tried to find George a face-saving exit. They proposed to Talmadge that he announce that he would not run, given George's great service to the state, and then George would himself withdraw and Talmadge would then run for the open seat. In this scenario, it would not seem that George had been pushed. Talmadge apparently agreed to the deal if George would personally come and request it, yet none of the plotters had the courage to suggest the deal to George. George was clearly intent on running, so nothing came of it.[171]

Despite any of the negatives, Walter George, still without formal opposition, came to Atlanta by train on Sunday, April 15, 1956, to begin his campaign, and he met with reporters in his suite at the Henry Grady Hotel, where his statewide headquarters was located. The focus of his press conference was agriculture, and he strongly urged Eisenhower to approve the omnibus farm bill that Congress had passed. The next day he formally launched his campaign for reelection against the still undeclared Talmadge, with newsmen and campaign workers in Atlanta at a breakfast, at which he announced that he would meet Friday with the Altamaha River Developmental Association to discuss making rivers navigable from the sea to Macon and Milledgeville.[172] This project would not only be a positive thing for these cities, but it would also create many jobs for the peoples of these river valleys, rivers that coincidentally fanned through an area expected to be pro-Talmadge. He then made an appearance on television at station WSB-TV sponsored by "Georgians for George," with his campaign manager former congressman Steven Pace of Americus, who flatly predicted he would win. In his television performance, George, who had helped Eisenhower block a

[170] *Congressional Digest*, 35:273–79.

[171] Congressional Report by the National Committee for an Effective Congress, November 10, 1955, GFR-VHPS. This organization had among its membership Eleanor Roosevelt.

[172] *Macon Telegraph*, April 17, 1956, 1.

tax cut the previous year because of its budgetary shortfalls, called for his own tax cut for the middle and lower incomes.[173] Moreover, he stated that the two main points of his campaign would be peace, which he would best be able to preserve, and the plight of the American farmer. He announced a campaign swing that would include appearances in Griffin, Dawson, Macon, and Baxley, adding that he would return to Washington the next week to work on congressional matters but would return in six weeks when Congress had adjourned to "campaign as much as necessary" for the senatorial nomination. He recognized that it would be "politically expedient" to remain in the state, but he placed "duty above his personal desires."[174]

His first full campaign address came the second day in Griffin to the Women's Society of Christian Service, a Methodist women's group, and its subject was foreign affairs, peace, and foreign aid, an area where his record was least popular with Georgians. On this issue he did not shift gears and lashed out at his critics. Noting that Russia was "the chief proponent of foreign aid," he told his audience, "I had rather spend money to keep war away from our shores" than to have America invaded. To an enthusiastic audience, he forcefully said, "I do not regret any money we have spent that is moving us away from war!"[175] He denounced the unfairness, exploitation [and] denials of human dignity around the world, injustices that were "storing up the Grapes of Wrath," and called for help for the teaming multitudes, which the Women's Society was promoting.[176] When he finished his speech, the entire audience rose to their feet in an ovation.

From Griffin, George went on Wednesday, May 18, to Agriculture Day in Dawson, Georgia, with its day of festivities that included a parade and a greased pig-catching contest.[177] Here he was introduced by Erle Cocke, Jr., now a Delta executive and former national commander of the American Legion, who called the senator "the greatest living Georgian and one of American's greatest statesmen of all time."[178] By this time, Eisenhower had vetoed the agriculture bill, and George unleashed on the administration's farm policy calling it "one of the greatest curses of the era" and demanding 100 percent of parity as part of a long-range farm program so that farmers could share in the nation's prosperity. He would, he said, vote to

[173]Ibid.
[174]*Atlanta Constitution*, April 17, 1956, 10.
[175]*Macon Telegraph*, April 18, 1956, 1.
[176]*Atlanta Constitution*, April 18, 1956, 1.
[177]*Macon Telegraph*, April 18, 1956, 18.
[178]*Atlanta Constitution*, April 19, 1956, 21.

override the veto, and he called for Eisenhower's defeat in the autumn elections.[179]

His next move was to center on youth. Mercer law students Mitchell House and Frank McKinney were already heading up a drive to form "Young Georgians for George" chapters on college campuses across Georgia. House, who would later serve in the Georgia legislature, became the president of the organization, and he and McKinney made a number of trips throughout South Georgia organizing chapters at various colleges.[180] They planned a statewide rally of the chapters in the Willingham Auditorium at Mercer campus, the president of which, Dr. Spright Dowell, headed a statewide "Older Georgians for George." Under the direction of House and McKinney, Mercer students laid the groundwork for the Mercer chapter in March, but the organization had been formally created at a meeting on April 3 under the co-presidency of Doe Brown and Ray Patterson. Also active in the Mercer effort was Jane Carol Adams, also a law student from Waynesboro, Georgia, and she became the state secretary. John Carlton, who had taken Richard Russell's advice and joined the campaign as Pace's assistant, was on hand.[181] Motorcades were to come from all over the state with the leaders converging on Macon, where they would meet at four o'clock at the Pinebrook Inn for a work session, followed by dinner at six. Then the group would relocate to Willingham Chapel on the Mercer campus, where the waiting crowd would have been warmed up by music, supplied by the Wesleyan Washboard Band.

The *Macon Telegraph* reported "a wildly enthusiastic crowd" of 800 students (the *Augusta Herald* stated 1,000) representing twenty-five colleges, and in the audience there was a sprinkling of signs.[182] Mitchell House presided. Student speakers led off, with Tab Joiner, a University of Georgia student from Griffin, giving the keynote address. Noting that the senator "has dedicated his entire life to serving the state and is now at the height of his influence and effectiveness," Joiner added that "the most powerful political machine ever organized in the state and [an unnamed] Richmond County kingmaker"[183] were plotting his removal. Referring to the state's "national representation" as a "brilliant galaxy," Joiner expressed the view that "[The

[179]Ibid., April 19, 1 and April 19, 1956, 23.

[180]Interviews with both Mitchell House and Frank McKinney.

[181]*Mercer Cluster* 18, (March 30, 1956): 1.

[182]Clipping from the *Augusta Herald*, n. d., copy to me from Ms. Jane Carol Adams-Finn, Adams-Finn papers (also on deposit with the VHPS).

[183]He is probably referring to Roy V. Harris.

People] will rise up and with resounding voice and with their ballots say that this shall not come to pass."[184] The senator was introduced by Bill Hendrix, president of the University of Georgia "Georgians for George," and Jane Adams, who told the audience that "no newcomer could apply the long experience and wisdom gained through his long career."[185] She reminded the audience that no one could make young George "cry uncle" when he wrestled as a boy, and "now a political upstart can't."[186] She also noted, "In our lifetime, Senator George has been one of the very few public servants who has never had a single question raised about his honesty, integrity, and steadfastness."[187] When George spoke, he began by saying that "consulting my own feelings, [I] would be happy to return to my little farm home...but I owe something to a great political party and to the strong men in both parties in Washington who are entering on a period of problems...to try to souls of men."[188] When George spoke, Homer Drake, now a judge in Newnan, remembered that the senator became very emotional, especially when he reminisced about his ties to Mercer. He told the young audience that although the "world outlook was brighter, there was still the possibility of war, and he pledged, "the best I have in me to prevent any hostile bomb [from] falling within the shores of Georgia." He also attacked Eisenhower's veto of the farm bill, now a major theme of his campaign. He was often interrupted by applause. The group proclaimed itself "a convention" and Bill Hendricks informed the senator that he had been "nominated." The *Telegraph* reported that George was "deeply touched and moved."[189] With George's nomination, the rally ended. George later thanked both Adams and House (and most probably the others) for the rally,[190] and House dispatched a letter to his fellow Mercerians, calling on them to campaign for George since he was tied up with work in Washington.[191]

---

[184]"George Pledges Effort or [sic] Peace," clipping, n. d., *Augusta Herald*, Adams-Finn papers.

[185]*Macon Telegraph*, April 19, 1956, 1.

[186]Interview by phone with Jane Adams-Finn. She had been at the Pinebrook Inn meeting and felt the senator seemed "old." She introduced him to the others, none of whom he knew (undated newspapers clipping from the House papers gives a slightly different version).

[187]*Atlanta Constitution*, April 20, 1956, 26.

[188]"George Pledge Efforts for Peace," Macon *News*, copy of Jane Adams-Finn to author.

[189]*Macon Telegraph*, April 20, 1956, 1.

[190]WFG to Adams-Finn and House, in both of their respective collections (Adams-Finn papers and House papers) in the Tarver Library.

[191]House to Mercerians, n. d., House papers.

Perhaps the *Telegraph* wished to color the event in George's favor, but Dr. Malcolm Lester, then a member of the Mercer faculty, attended the rally as a George supporter, and he called the rally "a most pathetic thing." Instead of the howling mob of 800, as the *Macon Telegraph* had reported, the event was more sparsely attended, he remembered. "Oh, we howled alright," Professor Lester said, "trying to make a noise." The group just was not as the *Telegraph* reported. "If there had been 800 people there, the auditorium would have been packed to the gills," he added, calling the whole event "very demoralizing." When George entered the hall, Dr. Lester remembered, "You could see him visibly wilt" at the poor turnout.[192] Some participants in the event agreed with Professor Lester,[193] but others, including Jane Adams, Mitchell House, and Judge Homer Drake of Newnan, remembered "a full house," which gave George "a roaring standing ovation."[194] Perhaps more realistically, Frank McKinney remembered that the crowd was "fairly decent" and "not embarrassing," but he felt that it was "disappointing considering the effort" they had made to assemble one. He sensed that when George looked up and saw so many empty seats in the balcony, he knew that the game was up.[195]

George continued with his campaign swing on to Baxley, where he predicted that the plans for the development of the Altamaha River Valley "have a good chance of finally gaining the necessary backing." George made a comparison with the time it took to develop the Chattahoochee and Savannah River valleys, but noted that had finally been completed because of "men of vision" had seen it through. He warned that the Altamaha project "might take a year or so," but predicted it would eventually come to pass.[196] Alas, the most crucial problems that George was having to face was the desertion of his big financial backers, what one journalist called "the Coca-Cola crowd": the Atlanta banks, the cotton mill concerns, Georgia Power, Coca-Cola, etc. All of his career Walter F. George had fought for Big Business, not because he was their tool, as Roosevelt had charged in 1938, but because he believed, as did Senator Albert Beveridge, that "America's Business is Business." If business prospers, then it makes jobs and people make money. Then both can be taxed to pay for the programs people need. All

[192]Telephone interview with Dr. Malcolm Lester, February 4, 2007. Frank McKinney felt that the *Telegraph* had padded the crowd.

[193] Interview with attendee Sid Johnson, who said that there may have been seventy-five there.

[194] Telephone interview with Judge Homer Drake.

[195]Frank McKinney interview.

[196]"George: Altamaha Plan's Chances Good," n.d., unidentified clipping, House papers.

large political contributions, nevertheless, are investments, and given George's age, the those with money did not want to spend what it would take to reelect George, only to have him retire or die in a year or so. Moreover, forty-two-year-old "Hummon" was pressing them.[197] He had courted them assiduously. Georgia Power, the most powerful state economic force since World War II, quietly shifted to Talmadge.[198] Some shifted not too quietly. Mills B. Lane, President of the C&S Bank, the largest in the southeastern United States, told a reporter, "I'm for Herman Talmadge and you can quote me."[199] As the *New Republic* put it, "The bloc which had always backed him [George] chose a younger mouthpiece."[200] The transition was simply political logic. As one businessman remarked, "An investment in George would have to have been amortized over a very short period," he told a *Collier's* reporter, but investment in young Talmadge was "as good...as a warehouse full of cotton when the price is right."[201]

At some point during this campaign trip, probably on Saturday or Sunday, April 21 or 22, George, Miss Lucy, and Heard George met with some of his old financial backers, a number of Atlanta money men, which probably included Woodruff, and they bluntly told George that they would not supply the money necessary for his campaign. George least expected the desertion of these money interests, and without them, he was vulnerable. He had not previously needed a political machine; his enormous works and his prestige had always been sufficient. He had spent a half a million dollars in 1938; it would take much more in 1956 since television was now reaching hundreds of thousands of Georgians. George could have raised a lot of money, but it would have been harder than before, and he had never before done it himself.

At one point, and it is unclear when, his good friend Robert W. Woodruff of Coca-Cola supposedly suggested "as a loyal friend" that Senator George "retire gracefully,"[202] and it is obvious from the Eisenhower diaries that Bob Woodruff had enormous influence in both Georgia and the White House.[203] When Talmadge asked Woodruff if he should run, the

---

[197]"George of Georgia," *The New Republic*, 4.

[198]"The Majority Loses," 92.

[199]McMillan, "So Goes the South," 43.

[200]Ibid.

[201]McMillan, "So Goes the South," 43. Local Macon attorney Frank Horne, himself a former legislator, stated it the same way in an interview with the author: "Business is business and politics is business." Phone interview with Frank Horne.

[202]Cater, "Regression vs Conservatism in Georgia," 16.

[203]Eisenhower, *Eisenhower Diaries*, 322, 323, 310.

Coca-Cola magnate remained non-committal, praising both men. Talking of his lack of political experience, which was a bad joke, Woodruff wrote Talmadge, "I just simply don't know what to advise you to do."[204]

Carlton was waiting for George and his family when they came down in the elevator from the meeting.[205] Methvin had been told of this meeting by John "Jake" Carlton, who claimed that he was present. Carlton, however, does not mention the meeting in his oral history.[206] The three looked very grim. On his departure for Washington by train on Sunday, however, George continued to play the role of Candidate Santa Claus, expressing hope that there would be in the present Congress expansion of Social Security, saying to reporters as he boarded the train, "I am hoping [as ranking member of the Finance Committee] we can get some action before the end of the month." He also put in another plug for the enormous project of making Macon and Milledgeville river ports.[207] He announced that he would return to the state on May 19 to introduce Vice President Alben Barkley, who was to address the Georgia Poultrymen's Convention in Gainesville.[208] George could not have known when his train departed for Washington that he would not return to introduce Barkley, although he must have by now been wondering if he would ever return to resume his senatorial campaign.

By chance, at this point, George's campaign received additional bad luck. The next day, Monday, April 23, 1956, the United States Supreme Court handed his opponent a monumental campaign issue: In a unanimous vote, the court outlawed segregation on public transportation, both inter- and intrastate.[209] It was grist for Talmadge's mill, and he immediately seized on it. Then, one week later, George's friend and former vice president Alben Barkley collapsed and died of a massive heart attack while giving a keynote address at a mock Democratic convention at Washington and Lee University in Virginia.[210] He was only two months older than Walter George. It was not only a personal blow, but it was also a stark reminder to everyone of George's age. At seventy-four in 1952, Barkley had tried to win the Demo-

---

[204]George Woodruff to HT, February 16, 1956, VI, A-1, box 1, f. 1, Talmadge papers.

[205]From a conversation between the author and Gene Methvin, son of the editor of *Vienna News* and an editor and reporter for *Readers' Digest*.

[206]See John Carlton, oral history, Russell Library.

[207]*Macon Telegraph*, April 22, 1956, 1.

[208]*Atlanta Constitution*, April 23, 1956, 1.

[209]Ibid., April 24, 1956; *Macon Telegraph*, 24, 1956, 1.

[210]*Macon Telegraph*, May 1, 1956, 1.

cratic nomination, but he had not gotten anywhere because of his age.[211] Had he gotten it and won, he would not have lived out his term. Asked to comment, George called Barkley "one of the most extraordinary man of our times. His passing is a great loss to the nation."[212] When asked if Barkley's death would have any effect on his thoughts on running, George had said that it would not, because physically there was "no similarity" between the two "except one of age."[213] Still, everyone drew the parallel, especially George's family.

After Barkley's death, George's family began pressing him not to take on the fight, and on Tuesday night, May 8, 1956, he decided to withdraw. He called Erle Cocke, who had only a few weeks before shared a podium in Dawson with George and endorsed his reelection, to come to Washington from New York and help him write his withdrawal statement.[214] In a hastily called news conference on the early afternoon of May 9, 1956, with a grim Miss Lucy at his side, Walter George told the state and nation that although he had said that he would run, he was going back on his promise.[215] With George's permission, his physician Dr. Worth B. Daniel first issued a statement that he had advised him not to run because he had a "mild" heart condition and "mild" diabetes, adding that the senator "needs to take care of himself."[216] The *Constitution* reported that when Eisenhower heard George was retiring, he called to see if it was true, adding that he seemed genuinely stunned that the senator had withdrawn.[217] Gene Methvin wrote that Eisenhower asked George to reconsider his decision.[218] At his announcement the next afternoon, he had a letter he read from Eisenhower, offering him a job. The news conference was delayed an hour and a half from the announced time to give the White House the chance to get the NATO offer to George. The president expressed in writing his "good hope that you would continue on in the Senate" where you "have been able to make so great a contribution to peace." Noting that he would now be free of his Senate duties, Eisenhower said, "I earnestly hope that you will be willing to act

[211]*Atlanta Constitution*, May 1, 1956, 14.

[212]Ibid., 1.

[213]M. L. St. John, "Senate Race," *Atlanta Constitution*, May 9, 1956, RCB-5804, box 15, f. WFG-GSA.

[214]*Atlanta Constitution*, May 10, 1956, RCB-5804, box 15, f. WFG-GSA.

[215]*Congressional Digest*, 35:161.

[216]*Atlanta Journal*, May 9, 1956, RCB-5804, box 15, f. WFG-GSA.

[217]Ibid.

[218]Gene Methvin, "Statesmanship," *Vienna News*, August 8, 1957, RCB-5804, box 15, f. WFG-GSA.

for this nation [as a representative to NATO]...to serve the cause of international peace...and freedom."[219]

The whole sequence—the resignation, the letter, the NATO offer—occurred too quickly and smoothly, and there certainly must have been several conversations between George and the White House to have produced such apparently "spontaneous" development of events. There are no records, so exactly what happened is lost to history. Moreover, his decision to quit was apparently not shared with his campaign staff, who were caught "flat-footed," the *Washington Star* reported, as inconceivable as it may seem.[220] Mitchell House and Frank McKinney first heard about it when "we read it in the press," McKinney remembered, adding that House "was green at the gills" at the news.[221] Jane Adams recalled that she did receive a call from someone after the event and received a letter of thanks.[222] Moreover, Adams received a call from the Talmadge campaign offering her a job. She refused the offer, telling the caller that she was not working so much for George as she was working against Talmadge.[223] George had at that point the longest service of any member than in the Senate.

George then announced that given the hellish weather in Georgia during the campaign season of July, August, and September, he had decided to withdraw.[224] He produced Eisenhower's letter at the press conference as well, reading it as part of his announcement. It is evident that great care was being taken to make the reason for his withdrawal one of health, not that he thought he would lose, or that he was being bullied, with the ability of continued government service in the cause of peace an option. The decision not to run was clearly not a decision that he wished to make. Moreover, he made it plain that he would serve out the remainder of his term; he would not vacate his seat so that Governor Griffin could appoint Talmadge early. "I would not shirk my duty...whatever I may do in the future may begin in January," he said, a message to Talmadge as much as anybody, yet he began his work with NATO without leaving the Senate.[225] Early in 1967, Virginia Senator A. Willis Robertson, defeated at seventy-nine by 600 votes by a younger William Spong, resigned his seat several days early so that the man

---

[219]The letter quoted in the *Atlanta Constitution*, May 10, 1956, 1, 16, ibid.

[220]Unidentified clipping, probably *Washington Star*, ibid.

[221]Interview with both Mitchell House and McKinney.

[222]Adams-Finn interview.

[223]Ibid.

[224]His wife later told a reporter that he did not run "because of his health and the heat and all that." "Miss Lucy Wants to Rock," unidentified clipping, LHG-VHPS.

[225]*Vienna News*, May 9, 1956, 1, RCB-5804, box 15, f. WFG-GSA.

who had beaten him could be appointed, giving him a few days of seniority advantage over the others elected that year. If anyone was about to suggest such an action, George was making it plain to all concerned that it was not going to happen. Talmadge would have to wait six more months to become a senator.

When asked by reporters as to why he was withdrawing, he would only say, "For good and sufficient reasons" and would not elaborate.[226] In a letter to Jane Adams, he wrote, "I was not physically able to make the race.... And solidly for that reason I was compelled to decline to formally enter [?] the race."[227]

Thus the long and mighty career of Georgia's greatest statesman ended, as T. S. Eliot had written, "Not with a bang but a whimper." President Eisenhower's immediate naming of George as his personal ambassador to NATO, apparently at the instigation of General Lucius Clay, himself a Georgian, could have done little to relieve the burning disappointment of the desertion of people he thought were friends.[228] As George was withdrawing "for good and sufficient reasons which I will not elaborate," a mile away Eisenhower was holding his own news conference, praising George as "one of the wisest and most [personally] disinterested" of men in his "efforts to promote peace and bipartisanship in international affairs."[229]

There followed a blast of praise in the press and the Senate that would have been befitting an emperor. One journal expressed the certainty that the United States Senate "will sorely miss this distinguished senator, who has consistently placed the great power of the United States within a context of great world responsibility."[230] Doris Fleeson of the *Washington Star* noted that the Democrats were losing "Wise counsel, vast experience, and a friend that found it possible to be loved for his personal qualities."[231] The *Baltimore Evening Sun* lamented George's passing, adding a most savage attack on the man who had ended his career: "Few men could step into Senator George's

---

[226]*Atlanta Journal*, May 9, 1956, ibid.

[227]WFG to Jane C. Adams, November 5, 1956, copy in Jane C. Adams-Finn papers. George had eventually written both House and Adams a form letter after his withdrawal, thanking them for their help (letters to House and Adams, dated May 18, 1956, in which he expressed that nothing could be "more heartening than to have the confidence of the young people of my state").

[228]"George of Georgia," *The New Republic*, 5.

[229]*Macon Telegraph*, May 10, 1956, 1.

[230]"Senator George," *Commonweal*, 410.

[231]Unidentified clipping of Fleeson article, probably in the *Washington Star*, RCB-5804, box 15, f. WFG-GSA.

shoes. Mr. Talmadge couldn't even shine them."[232]

Senate reaction bore these opinions out. No one could remember such an outpouring of respect and devotion to a colleague. One senator after another rose to praise this senator who had served since the presidency of Warren Harding. Prescott Bush, who had so praised George the year before to boost his campaign, said that he only hoped that he "might someday command the kind of respect that prompted George's wife always to call him 'Mr. George.'"[233] Albert Gore, who had also praised him highly the year before, called him a "Senator's Senator." Wheelchair-bound Republican senator Eugene Milliken was pushed onto the Senate floor, where he wept as he read a tribute in a voice few could hear.[234] Florida's George Smathers called him "the symbol of the Senate," adding that he "walked in the tradition of men who are remembered for achievement long after the partisan issues of the day are forgotten." Senator Stuart Symington called him "the greatest man I ever knew." Lyndon Johnson used the metaphors "a mighty oak" and "a national figure"[235] to describe him and said, correctly, "Without him, I do not believe I would have done as well as I have."[236] Johnson was at the time making one of his own half-in half-out campaigns for the presidency, and he told the retiring George, "I'm going to have first call on you to be my secretary of state."[237] To Smith of New Jersey, he was "a bulwark of strength," to Fulbright, "a fine public servant," to John Stennis of Mississippi, "a senatorial father."[238] Liberal Wayne Morse, probably more concerned at who would replace George, announced that he was "heartbroken over your decision." His longtime friend Harry Byrd told his colleagues, "No one can be associated with Senator George without forming for him a rare kind of love and admiration which seldom occurs in human relationships. His association is "one of the finest memories of my life."[239] The Senate Foreign Relations Committee, in which George had produced his greatest works, passed a resolution that summed it up: After "whereasing" all of his service and accomplishments, it "resolved" that the committee "expresses its warm affection for the senator and its deep appreciation for his devotion to duty and for the outstanding service which he had rendered to the Committee,

232 *Baltimore Sun*, quoted in "Georgia Loses," 23.
233 Ibid.
234 Ibid.
235 *CR*, 84/2, 6967.
236 Ibid.
237 Dallek, *Lone Star Rising*, 500
238 *CR*, 84/2, 6968–70.
239 Ibid.

the Senate, to the United States, and to the entire free world." The *Atlanta Constitution* saw in this enormous praise that "All Georgia Is Honored,"[240] with one of their journalists opining, "It is unlikely that any senator for years to come will command the respect, the influence and the genuine affection of his colleagues [that Walter George has]."[241] *Collier's* told its readers that the Senate "never comes closer to being the world's most august deliberative body than when...Walter F. George...takes the floor." Noting that it was one of the great ironies of politics that "Walter George, whose opinions are marked attentively in all the world's capitals, should this year have found his career eclipsed in the back-road counties of his native Georgia."[242] One person who seems to have said nothing was Richard Russell.

Many of George's neighbors bitterly lamented his departure. Locals in Vienna were devastated and did not believe the first accounts of his withdrawal. Vienna citizens gathered in small groups about the town that evening to "discuss and speculate." The first official word came, however, when former mayor L. N. Mobley received a call from Heard George at 9:30 a.m. on May 10, telling the former mayor that his father had made the decision on Tuesday, May 8.[243] "Gosh, we've lost something," said local caning operator Ed White. "It's a serious blow. It's a disgrace that Talmadge thought of forcing a race." Claude Harvey, a local service station operator, turned his anger on Talmadge: "We'll be the laughing stock of the nation again when Talmadge gets up there."[244] Other Georgians were relieved. Lieutenant Governor Ernest Vandiver expressed the belief that many in the state felt when he told the press, "No Georgian looked forward to a campaign between the senator [George] and former Governor Talmadge," he told the press.[245] The fear of a race was now over.

In the stand-down, George had blinked first. Talmadge, who had still never formally announced, was in Jacksonville, Florida, at the time that George withdrew, and he issued a laudatory statement from there to the effect that Senator George could "still render valuable service to the nation and to his state."[246] He told reporters that he would have a statement sometime that month but then announced the next day that he would run. He immediately scrapped the announcement speech, which was critical of

[240]*Atlanta Constitution*, July 21, 1956, clipping in scrapbook, LHG-VHPS.
[241]*Atlanta Constitution* (?), n. d., unidentified clipping, WFG-DCPL.
[242]McMillan, "So Goes the South," 42.
[243]*Vienna News*, May 10, 1956, 1.
[244]Ibid.
[245]*Macon Telegraph*, May 10, 1956, 1.
[246]Ibid.

George, and rewrote one praising the senator for his service to the state, adding that he would be frequently seeking his advice.[247] The next day, the *Atlanta Constitution's* headlines screamed out the news of the fallen giant: "TALMADGE ANNOUNCES FOR SENATOR/ RETIRING GEORGE OFFERED NATO JOB."[248] Already in the headlines George's name was appearing second. Any details of what George thought or felt have not survived. Mourning his departure, the *Constitution* noted, "Whatever measure of sorrow...[he felt], he did not say. It was locked in his breast and no biographer will ever be able to unlock it."[249]

Now the field was open for Talmadge, and although his old nemesis, M. E. Thompson, jumped into the race, Talmadge was elected in a landslide with 80 percent of the vote.[250] With virtually every paper in the state's endorsing him, he carried all 159 counties.[251] Despite his awesome victory, George's old supporters continued to snipe at Talmadge. McMullan of *Collier's* lamented that George and Russell "will be the last gentlemen from Georgia to sit in the US Senate,"[252] which could only be interpreted as a slap at George's replacement. Ralph McGill of the *Constitution* told his readers that Talmadge was "not the last Southern demagogue, but only the first of a new and shrewd breed."[253] Talmadge was received coolly when he did finally take his seat in the Senate itself; the only senator to greet him warmly was Lyndon Johnson, whose every action was a political one.[254] In 1960 when Richard Russell was up for reelection, the new boy-wonder of Georgia politics, Carl Sanders, gave some thought to running against Russell, thinking he might spook him out of the race as Talmadge had done George. When this scenario was presented to Russell by Governor Vandiver, Russell told

[247]*Atlanta Constitution*, May 11, 1956, 1; "Georgia Loses," 22–23.

[248]The evening *Atlanta Journal* had been the first to announce George's retirement the day before (*Atlanta Constitution*, May 10, 1956, 1).

[249]Ibid, August 5, 1957, 1.

[250]Coleman, et al., *A History of Georgia*, 396.

[251]Varney, "Meet Senator Talmadge," 10. Thompson's sister-in-law Elizabeth Newton told me over the telephone that WFG secretly supported her brother-in-law. "I can't prove it with documentation," she told me, "but then I'm ninety-six, there's no one left who can prove me wrong."

[252]McMillan, "So Goes the South," 43.

[253]Ibid., 47. Surprisingly, the *New Republic* dismissed WFG with no regret, noting that "one can be sorry for...George, as one is sorry for anyone slain in the house of his friends." Then with the lone voice of dissent on George's career, it opined, "It is maudlin to speak of him as a great or even superior statesman.... His record shows little of the large-mindedness or the creative leadership attributed to him" ("George of Georgia," *New Republic*, 4).

[254]Talmadge, *Talmadge: A Political Legacy*, 169.

the governor, "There are two things that are important [about that scenario]. I'm not Walter George, and he's not Herman Talmadge."[255]

Georgia journalist William M. Bates attended what must have been George's last press conference, one given before his departure for Paris in August after the Senate adjournment for his NATO post. The retiring senator was questioned on a wide number of world issues, and he handled himself expertly. "Not once did he babble—although he was tossed some tough ones.... His replies...were precise and to the point."[256] There was in the old Senator's performance none of the mental slowness or feebleness that had been rumored by the Talmadge people. He was still strong and mentally alert and could have continued to serve Georgia well for some time to come.

"What if" or "hypothetical" or "counterfactual" history has enjoyed a certain currency in recent years, and it is too tempting not to speculate on what might have happened in a real George-Talmadge race, for it is far from certain that George would have lost. Talmadge may indeed have defeated him; his chances were very good. He was popular, he was young, he had cornered the most important issue—race—and he had big money. Rural registration saw a great increase early in 1956, and most of that increase would most probably have gone to Talmadge.[257] In October 1955, the betting odds in Atlanta were that Talmadge would defeat George.[258] George's age was certainly a factor in Talmadge's favor. So was the county unit system, which was still in place in 1956. Moreover, a number of local politicians had begun to endorse Talmadge. The Georgia Association of County Commissioners as openly supported Talmadge, and the Georgia Association of Justices of the Peace had run some sort of poll, which showed that Talmadge would carry 118 counties with 300 county unit votes, with George's taking only sixteen counties with forty votes. Twenty-five counties were toss-ups.[259] This lopsided result was highly unlikely, but clearly George would have had his work cut out for him.

George, on the other hand, had many positives in his corner, the most important being his enormous prestige and popularity. He still had thousands of influential friends both in Georgia and across the country who could have raised large amounts of money for him from smaller sources. He had enormous support from the educated, more sophisticated elements of

[255]S. Ernest Vandiver, oral history, 26, Russell Library.

[256]Bates, "Newsmen hold...," 36.

[257]Ibid., May 9, 1956, 6.

[258]Cater, "Regression vs Conservatism in Georgia," 13.

[259]*Macon Telegraph*, April 17, 1956, 4.

the state. Half of all Georgian families had televisions in 1956, and this medium not only opened the world to them, but it daily drove home how important a man their senior senator was.[260] Moreover, the courthouse politicians across rural Georgia had begun to fear that if a man of George's stature was defeated by the county unit system, it might help bring its end. Reelecting Senator George, for whatever was left of his life, would be worth it to preserve this undemocratic electoral method, which gave the small counties control of state politics.[261] A Talmadge victory was by no means a proverbial "slam-dunk," and the race in any case, even in the county unit vote, would have been close.

Moreover, the age issue might not have proved so important. In 1956, the youth culture of the post-Kennedy era had not yet emerged, and age was still revered in America. In the last third of the twentieth century, a number of aged senators ran and won. Strom Thurmond was reelected at the age of ninety-four, and Senator McClelland of Arkansas was reelected in his upper seventies. Eighty-nine-year-old Theodore Green, George's friend on the Foreign Relations Committee and his replacement, was reelected in his eighties. Eighty-one-year-old Senator Allen Ellender died in 1972 in the midst of a campaign that killed him, but for weeks before his death he maintained a pace that would have exhausted a younger man.[262] He was ahead in the polls when he died. Seventy-nine-year-old Senator A. Willis Robertson of Virginia was defeated in 1966 by only 611 votes statewide.[263] Still, when the campaign was over, however, Robertson still had $300,000 of unspent campaign money in the bank, which properly used could have certainly insured his victory.[264] George's age was definitely not an insuperable factor.

What is frequently cited as George's most serious Achilles' heel, however, was the dominance of the rural elements in Georgia because of the county unit system, formally established by the Neill Act of 1917, by which three small South Georgia counties with a few hundred votes could neutral-

[260]Congressional Report of the National Committee for an Effective Congress, 3, GFR-VHPS.

[261]Ibid.

[262]Becnel, *Senator Allen Ellender of Louisiana*, 275–78.

[263]Wilkinson's study of the Byrd Machine.

[264]I was told this information in Washington in summer 1966 by a legislative assistant to Senator Strom Thurmond.

ize the thousands of votes cast in Atlanta's Fulton County.[265]

Talmadge's strength lay of course in rural, wool-hat Georgia, and many felt that in the county unit system, George's defeat was sealed. Roy Harris of Augusta, speaker of the house and perennial mover and shaker of Georgia politics, stressed the logic that a candidate beginning with the largest number of unit votes in "safe" counties could then concentrate on the marginal counties to win with less effort.[266] Talmadge had a solid base of county unit votes, but then George had a lock on the six-and four-vote counties, giving him 168 votes.

What gave George a lock on the large and medium size counties was Georgia's ever-growing black vote of which Talmadge would have gotten little. Black voter registration in Georgia had increased from 600 in 1936 to about 150,000 by 1956.[267] Moreover, Georgia led the South in black voter registration.[268] As early as 1948, 25 percent of Dougherty County's 12,723 registered voters were black.[269] This black vote was largely urban; that is, in the six-and four-vote counties, and would have solidified George's already strong position in these urban areas. As early as ten years before, the blacks who had voted did so with little opposition, despite Gene Talmadge's anti-black threats that year.[270] Against George, Talmadge would most probably not have carried one of these counties. George would need only nineteen of the 121 two-vote counties to win, certainly not an impossible goal. George himself was from a rural county. Various reports to Talmadge from supporters in the smaller counties indicates far less than solid support. Harley Langdale Jr., son of the Georgia Supreme Court justice, wrote Talmadge in 1956 of his prospects in South Georgia: "I doubt that you will be able to carry Lowndes County and probably not Lanier and Clinch counties," he

---

[265]Belvin, "The Georgia Gubernatorial Primary of 1946," 44. *US News* give the number of eight with six, thirty-two with four, and 119 with two votes. See "Famous Senator in Trouble with Voters," 34. That number still gives rural counties a majority.

[266]Roy Harris interview in the *Augusta Courier*, August 15, 1949, and September 27, 1954, cited in Bernd, "Corruption in Georgia Primaries and Elections, 1938–1950," 108.

[267]Bolster, "The Civil Rights Movements in Twentieth Century Georgia," 85. Grantham places the figure at 163,000 (Grantham, *The Democratic South*, 83). In the 1948 gubernatorial race, between 65,000 and 75, 000 blacks voted (Key, *Southern Politics*, 520). By 1956, it is conceivable that around 100,000 would have cast votes, almost all of which would have gone to WFG, thus securing the six-vote counties and probably all of the four-vote counties as well.

[268]*Albany Herald*, clipping (title unclear), September 7, 1948, DOC2–37, f. 4, (1948 election), Eugene Cox papers, GSA.

[269]Cater, "Regression vs Conservatism in Georgia," 15.

[270]Belvin, "The Georgia Gubernatorial Primary of 1946," 48.

wrote, sharing his political wisdom. "I think that your chances would be better in...Brooks, Cook, and Echols." Then he added his view that could hardly have been encouraging to the senator, "I believe you would carry all these counties against anyone other than Senator George."[271]

The Talmadge base had always been the wool-hat vote, and both Gene and Herman had played the race card with them. "If I get a negro vote," Gene Talmadge bragged in 1946, "it will be an accident."[272] Son Herman had carried on the family tradition. In 1955, he had strengthened his racist credentials by writing *You and Segregation*—a Georgia bestseller.[273] Results in Macon/Bibb County in 1956 in his race against M. E. Thompson show that of the 2,555 black votes cast in the county, Talmadge received only 181, a proportion (7 percent) that was typical around the state.[274] One of Talmadge's less politically astute Macon supporters wrote him, "I cant understand the negro, voting against you the way they did. You have always been their friend and did a lot for them when your were governor, in fact [I] thought that you did too much.... Of course I know why they voted for Thompson, following NAACP's orders."[275] What is more, the black voters were turning out. One supporter from Fort Valley (in largely rural Peach County) wrote Talmadge in February 1956 that there had been "a large black vote" in the recent municipal elections, "larger than ever before."[276]

Added to these totals were the votes of 150,000 AFL-CIO members and Georgia's liberals, who were ironically rallying, if unenthusiastically, to conservative George.[277] Whereas neither group would have been enamored with the incumbent senator and their support for him would have at best been lukewarm, they would have hardly voted in any great numbers for Talmadge.[278]

Moreover, Talmadge had some serious ballast, and the Talmadge machine was not invincible. The Talmadge vote in recent previous elections had been hardly overwhelming. Liberal Ellis Arnall, who had publicly referred to "the moth-eaten doctrine of States' Rights," had decisively defeated

---

[271]Harley Langdale, Jr. to HT, February 27, 1956, VI, A-1, box, f. 1, Talmadge papers.

[272]*Savannah Morning News*, June 21, 1946, 16.

[273]"New Voice for the South in Congress," 85.

[274]Charles Bloch to HT, September 14, 1956, VI, A-1, box 4, f. 5, Talmadge papers.

[275]Bill Miller to HT, September 22, 1956, box 1, f. 2, ibid. I have preserved the original grammar and punctuation.

[276]Homer J. Avera to HT, February 27, 1956, ibid.

[277]Cater, "Regression vs Conservatism in Georgia," 16.

[278]McMillan, "So Goes the South," 46. One labor leader told a journalist, "All in all, it might be smart to sit the thing out" (Cater, "Regression vs Conservatism in Georgia," 16).

Old Gene in the 1942 primary, and even in victory in 1946, the organization had shown weakness. Herman's father had won only because he was in a "three-cornered race," one with two other candidates to split the anti-Talmadge vote.[279] He had defeated former governor E. D. Rivers, who had run third, and Ellis Arnall's thirty-six-year-old hand-picked candidate, the relatively unknown James V. Carmichael, whose political career had consisted only of two terms in the legislature. Carmichael's greatest claim to fame was his cutting, as the manager of the Bell Bomber Plant in Marietta, the cost of producing B-29 bombers by 50 percent. The army had openly expressed the opinion that his plant had shortened the war by at least six months.[280]

To win, Gene Talmadge had to pull out all the race-baiting stops against Carmichael. He had distributed false Carmichael circulars over the state, advertising a "Big Carmichael Rally" in which "Mr. Carmichael especially invites his colored friends." Talmadge people moved Carmichael's campaign signs into black neighborhoods, and a Carmichael lookalike traveled about the state in a car full of blacks.[281] Even with this campaign, which son Herman was managing, Carmichael still outpolled Talmadge by 16,000 popular votes statewide, losing the race only in the county unit system.[282] The *Atlanta Journal* opined that 90 percent of E. D. Rivers's vote would have gone to Carmichael in a two-man race.[283] Moreover, Carmichael had made a good showing in the rural areas, carrying thirty-three of the counties that were more than 50 percent rural.[284] It is most likely that even against Herman, Walter George would have carried at least that many.

Moreover, in 1948, with a vigorous campaign to discourage black voting, Herman Talmadge received only 51.1 percent of the total state vote to Governor M. E. Thompson's 45.1 percent (357,865–312,005), and would not have received a majority had the blacks' votes been cast in the numbers that they had only two years earlier.[285] Running again against Thompson in 1950, Talmadge had failed to win a majority of the popular vote, receiving only 49.3 percent to Thompson's 47.9 percent, but had won 72 percent of

---

279 "The Majority Loses," 92.
280 Belvin, "The Georgia Gubernatorial Primary of 1946," 38.
281 Ibid., 46.
282 Bernd, "A Study of Primary Elections in Georgia," 22, 107.
283 Ibid., 70 ff.
284 Belvin, "The Georgia Gubernatorial Primary of 1946," 49.
285 Bernd, "A Study of Primary Elections in Georgia," 287.

the county unit vote, less than the 76.1 percent he had received in 1948.[286]

Talmadge was much more popular by the end of his term in 1954, however, primarily because of his ranting about the *Brown v Board of Education* decision of May of that year. His hand-picked successor, Marvin Griffin, had crushed M. E. Thompson with 75 percent of the county unit vote but with only 36 percent of the popular vote. Roy Harris saw Griffin's victory as the end of the anti-Talmadge faction of Rivers-Arnall-Thompson, but Talmadge's amendment to extend the county unit system in 1952, put to a non-binding popular vote, had been trounced despite a $300,000 budget versus the opponents' $15,000 and the use of opponents "every conceivable technique to pass it."[287] His segregation amendment, for which he had strongly campaigned in 1954 when it was a hot issue, received only 54 percent of the total vote. Moreover, state newspapers had come out four to one against it.[288] Therefore, what *US News* called the Talmadge name "a magical one with votes"[289] is not exactly a myth, but it was not absolutely true.

In addition, although Talmadge made his image more dignified by 1956, he had some vulnerabilities. He had introduced a 3 percent sales tax even though he had campaigned in 1950 against it.[290] In spite of bragging that he left the governorship with a surplus, the programs that he had started had thrown the state into a $61 million deficit by 1955, and the state had, as a result of Talmadge's financial mismanagement, accumulated a bonded indebtedness of $250 million.[291] Also, Marvin Griffin was proving unpopular, and the three men he had defeated (collectively receiving almost 65 percent of the vote), would have been in George's corner. Moreover, Griffin's floor leader, Macon attorney and veteran legislator Denmark Grover was defeated by Mercer law professor Ed Wilson.[292]

What is more telling about Talmadge's support, which created a great deal more light than heat, was an informal poll made by a journalist. He traveled through the Georgia backwoods, what one might call "Talmadge country," from Atlanta to Macon, asking people how they would vote. Unscientific as it was, it is somewhat revealing: Twelve responders were for George, while only seven were for Talmadge. He got frequent comments

[286]Ibid., 25; Talmadge had received 287,637 votes to Thompson's 279, 137 (Bartley and Graham, *Southern Elections*, 99).

[287]Bernd, *Grass Roots Politics in Georgia*, 309.

[288]Bolster, "The Civil Rights Movements in Twentieth Century Georgia," 137–38.

[289]"Famous Senator in Trouble with Voters," 32.

[290]Purcell, "George of Georgia: The Talmadge Threat," 116.

[291]Cater, "Regression vs Conservatism in Georgia," 15.

[292]Ibid., 16.

like "George is the biggest man in Washington today" and "George will keep us out of war."[293] In a straw vote at the University of Georgia, Talmadge's alma mater, the senator trounced Talmadge 611 to 225, almost three to one.[294]

The race, therefore, was not a given for Talmadge, yet there were other possibilities. Had he won, he likely would have won it only by the county unit system and lost the popular vote as his father and Governor Griffin had done. There is also a chance that he would have won it by default if Senator George had not survived what would have been a rough campaign in the Georgia summer heat at a time when cars and buildings were not air conditioned. Jane Adams recalled that as she introduced George around in Macon he seemed "old,"[295] and in the preceding year George frequently had commented that he was "tired." George lived only seven months after leaving the Senate. He might not have survived the campaign.

In the fall of 1956, although a lame duck, George was not finished with legislating. The first was the passage, against strong opposition, of Eisenhower's $4,457,575,000 foreign aid bill, called the Mutual Security Bill of 1957, which had appeared dead in the water since the spring. George himself had campaigned against elements in it, as we have seen. Large cuts had been made in the House, and George, back in Washington and free of his campaign, wrote Senator Carl Hayden, chair of the Senate Appropriations Committee, that making substantial cuts in the foreign relations budget "would be misunderstood abroad and might well have serious foreign policy implications." The U.S.-Soviet meetings were taking place in Geneva were taking place, and George felt it was "particularly important that the Senate take no action which might be construed as weakening our approach to foreign policy or as failure to support fully the president during these important negotiations."[296] When Walter George then rose to support it in a Senate with packed galleries, all was silent as a tomb. "Every senator was in his chair, and you could hear a pin drop," remembered James Enlo Smith, Senator Karl Mundt's administrative assistant, who was on the Senate floor

---

[293]Ibid.

[294]"Senator George Favored," unidentified clipping, May 9, 1956, RCB-5804, box 15, f. WFG-GSA. All the college vote was not locked up for WFG. At Mercer, there appeared a Talmadge-for-Senator Club, the president of which was Jim Green, a student in the Walter F. George School of Law, and the vice president, Earl Jones, who was vice president of the students of the College of Liberal Arts (*Macon Telegraph*, April 19, 1956, 7).

[295]Adams-Finn interview.

[296]WFG to Carl Hayden, July 18, 1955, GFR-VHPS.

at the time.[297] One more time George's magnificent oratory worked its magic. After speaking on the subject at length, he abandoned his notes, and as one journalist put it, "spoke from his soul." His eyes were wet with tears, probably not so much for the subject of his cause but because he knew this speech was probably his last, great Senate battle. "Whatever happens in the future," he told his colleagues, "I know that the American people are not going to step backwards. They may change administrations....methods... and...programs, but they are not going backward because I cannot think that the Divine Providence...which has permitted us to become the responsible leaders of the World, would do so only to bring that home." He noted that if the free people on earth were to lose confidence in America, America would "disappoint the best hopes of mankind" and in so doing would "utterly fail to justify the sacrifices of our heroic dead, whose bodies rest now in the blue waters of nearly every ocean around the world."[298] At this point his voice broke and he could not continue. He collapsed into his Senate chair.

George was overwhelmed by a number of emotions, no doubt. His Senate career was over, and his days in that chamber were numbered. His reference to "heroic dead" resting now "in the blue waters" was a paraphrase of the words he had made when he endorsed the UN Charter, when he referred to the loss of his son Marcus at sea in 1943. His speech had once again worked its magic. As a journalist with *Business Weekly* reported, "When George sat down, the bill was assured of Senate passage." The author of those words felt that it was not George's words that had changed their mind. It was their devotion and love for him that a bill meant so much to him led them to pass it by a vote of 54 to 25.[299] Their respect for George was a major factor, but his oratory had produced this sort of turnaround too many times in his career to dismiss their votes as devotion to him alone. Whatever combination of motives worked here, the passage by a more than two-to-one majority was another tribute to "George of Georgia."

Senator George was still not retiring his history pen just yet in what was the dusk of his career. He would have one more mark to make on American history, one that was very uncharacteristic of his long career and possibly done with a bit of vengeance. In the last days of his last session in the US Senate, Walter F. George announced his support of, and thereby guaranteed passage of, an amendment to the Social Security Act, which gave

---

[297]James Enlo Smith interview.

[298]"Parting Moment," 30.

[299]"George of Georgia," *Business Weekly*, 144; a copy of this article is also in a scrapbook, LHG-VHPS.

disabled people benefits under Social Security. The White House, the business community, Secretary of the Treasury George M. Humphrey, and George's old friend Harry Byrd, chair of the Senate Finance Committee all bitterly opposed the amendment. They felt that it would bankrupt the Social Security fund, and the bill was something that thrifty Walter George normally would not have supported. As in many other things, however, his support became crucial. He had tried late in April to obtain eligibility for women at sixty-two and for disabled children over eighteen who had parents on Social Security themselves.[300]

Disability benefits had been removed from HR 7225, and George acted to restore it. Calling it "the most important question I have ever presented to the American people,"[301] one of his rare exaggerations, he added that "If I can get this through, then I am ready to go away from the Senate."[302] He made one of his famous vote-swaying speeches, after which the Senate voted 47–46 to allow totally disabled persons to receive benefits at age fifty, giving about a quarter of a million disabled Americans an average $75.00/month in the first year.[303] Saying that it was "not pleasant" to differ with his long-time friend Harry Byrd, with whom he had fought on the same side in so many battles, George pointed out that it offered "protection that will be valued and appreciated not only by the thousands…who would receive payment," but also by the millions of Americans to whom the change "would have added a sense of security."[304] Senator Russell Long of Louisiana gave George full credit for its Senate passage, adding, "I don't believe anyone else could have done it."[305] He was right, since the switch of George's vote to "no" would have produced a tie, which would have been broken with a defeat with the vice president's voting against it. Without George's support, the amendment would never had gotten the forty-six votes to which his added vote made a difference.[306] The amendment had been opposed by the wealthy business interests, the American Medical Association, and other establishment groups, whose positions could usually count on George's support.

[300]*Atlanta Constitution,* April 23, 1956, 4.

[301]*New York Times*, August 5, 1956, 21.

[302]Cover of *National Welfare Advocate*, August 1956, scrapbook, LHG-VHPS.

[303]"Democrats Hail George," *Atlanta Journal*, July 18, 1956, 1.

[304]Ibid.

[305]Ibid.

[306]In his Senate memoir, Senator Clinton Anderson gives him and Senator Robert Kerr of Oklahoma credit for convincing WFG at a luncheon that adding the disability clause would not break the Social Security bill, and implying that the whole thing was George's idea (Anderson, *Outsider in the Senate*, 263–64).

Here, George's actions belied the notion that George was a tool of the corporate interests, but Paul Douglas of Illinois, one of the most liberal members of the Senate (and who had earlier run for local offices in Illinois as a Socialist), expressed amazement in his memoirs that George, a "faithful ally" of the Establishment for a third of a century, and in whose career Douglas could find "no record of any action to help the poor and disinherited, from whom he had sprung," became his ally in this matter. Since the moneyed interests had deserted him, Douglas assumed that George had decided "to break with precedent and do something for the class he had neglected for so long."[307] Because he had led, many Southern conservatives had followed, and members of the GOP did as well, because they owed him so many favors. Douglas was probably right: This parthian volley to his Senate career may have been motivated not so much by conviction but by some sense of revenge against the big interests who had deserted him for Talmadge. At any rate, Senator Paul Douglas thought that George took pleasure in it, remembering, "Once [after the vote] he even smiled when he met me—an unprecedented occurrence."[308] Douglas felt that the "breach in the wall helped pave the way for the Forand bill," which was one of the early forerunners of Medicare.[309] If revenge was his motive, he must have thoroughly enjoyed it.

---

[307]Douglas, *The Fullness of Time*, 391.

[308]Ibid., 391–92. Lyndon Johnson had also encouraged WFG to support the program because he said that it would give the Democrats a good issue in the fall elections (Dallek, *Lone Star Rising*, 495).

[309]Douglas, *The Fullness of Time*, 391–92.

EPILOGUE

A worn-out politician and a worn-out watch are very much alike. Neither is any good when they get so they don't run well.
—*Vienna News*[1]

I sometimes doubt that his own state fully appreciates the enormously important position he [Senator George] holds in the senate [*sic*] and the confidence he enjoys, the prestige he possesses.
—Ralph McGill, journalist[2]

The Senate will not be the same without Walter George, as it has not been the same without Henry Clay, Daniel Webster, and Robert A. Taft.
—George E. Sokolsky, journalist[3]

Although still retaining his Senate seat while working in NATO, George withdrew from politics and quietly went into "that good night." His departure was symbolized by the removal of a portrait of his son Marcus, which had hung over the fireplace in his office since the war years. It was shipped to Vienna, where it now hangs in the museum dedicated to his memory. *Newsweek* opined that "By that gesture he marked the end of a distinguished career."[4] As the Talmadge juggernaut that seemed to be hesitant to take on George cranked up for its inevitable landslide against Melvin Thompson, George was asked whom he supported. "I haven't taken any sides and I don't expect to," he snapped to a reporter.[5] After Talmadge won the nomination in August 1956, there were calls for George's resignation to give Talmadge a seniority advantage. George pointedly ignored them.

On the announcement of his departure, the Georges were feted all over both Washington and Georgia. On June 3, Senator and Mrs. Allen Frear of Delaware gave a farewell dinner at the Congressional Club, attended by over a hundred Senate officers and their wives. Nine senators gave two to five

---

[1]October 3, 1903.

[2]"Senate Gives George…," *Atlanta Constitution*, May 22, 1943, RCB-5804, box 1998–1980A, f. WFG-GSA.

[3]George E. Sokolsky, "Senator George—the Old Order Passeth," *Thomasville Times-Enterpriser*, May 18, 1956, scrapbook, LHG-VHPS

[4]"Parting Moment," 30

[5]*Atlanta Journal-Constitution*, June 24, 1956; Melvin Thomson's sister-in-law, however, remembered in a telephone conversation with the author that her brother-in-law received some covert help from George supporters.

minute talks on George. "All praised him for unerring wisdom and unfailing stature," the *Washington Star* reported.[6] The Mercer College Washington Alumni Chapter honored George with another dinner the next day at the Mayflower, and here, Richard Russell finally praised George as a "loyal, lovable, tolerant man" who is "the most distinguished Georgian alive today."[7] Later in the month, Mr. Corneal Mack, vice president and general manager of the Mayflower Hotel, and his wife gave a huge reception and buffet supper in the hotel's Chinese Room. More than half the Senate came, including Lyndon Johnson, and from the administration appeared presidential chief of staff Sherman Adams, Attorney General Herbert Brownell, and an assortment of judges and ambassadors.[8]

Just before Christmas, the Georgia congressional declaration hosted an event outside of Albany, Georgia, at the Radium Springs Casino. Present were senators Smathers and Russell, Senator-elect Herman Talmadge, and Secretary of State Ben Fortson. President Eisenhower was invited but declined.[9] The menu, written in a frightful mixture of French and South Georgian, boasted "Le Florida Pomplemousse [*sic*] à basquet [?] à anisette with Fresh leaf of mint, broiled beef tournedos on toast, baked Idaho potatoe [*sic*] stuffed with jambon et aux ciboulettes, salade panache chiffonade, les petit pain assorted, and charlotte russe à la creme [*sic*] Fouettee [*sic*] chantilly.[10] Senator Smathers emceed the event, and Richard Russell delivered the major address. In his talk, Russell opined, "What an ornament he would have made as chief justice of the United States."[11] In a less lofty demonstration of appreciation, friends gave George and Miss Lucy a Chrysler New Yorker with a pushbutton gear shift.[12]

The biggest farewell dinner held for George, however, was a fundraiser hosted at the Mayflower Hotel by the Democratic Party. Lyndon Johnson was the honorary chairman, and the invitation told the party faithful that George's reasons for allowing his testimonial to be used as a Democratic fundraiser were "his affection for his colleagues" and "his desire to see the

---

[6]"Senator Honored," *Evening Star*, June 4, 1956, scrapbook, LHG-VHPS.

[7]"Tributes Shared on Senator George," *Washington Post Herald*, May 4, 1956, ibid.

[8]Ev Peyton Gordon, "Senator George and Miss Lucy," *Washington Daily News*, June 15, 1956, ibid.

[9]Box 943, f. 347, PPF, RNC papers.

[10]"Testimonial Dinner for Senator and Mrs. Walter F. George," (program from dinner) RCB-5804, box 1998–1980 A, f. WFG-GSA.

[11]*The Evening Star*, December 18, 1956, box 1160, alpha beta file, f. 1, Eisenhower papers.

[12]Interview with Grace Slade Crovett.

Democrats continue Senate control."[13] Whatever George may have thought or wanted, the party hierarchy wanted to steal Eisenhower's thunder for appointing George ambassador to NATO. A friend wrote Johnson, reporting a conversation between Booth Mooney and Arthur Krock, "The Democrats were just renewing the lien on George, no matter what the president had done for him."[14] There was also a lot of political jockeying. A number of the major figures there were presidential candidates, who took the occasion to make self-serving remarks, and Kefauver pointedly left the hall in the middle of Stevenson's speech. It was supposedly at this event that Stevenson told Hubert Humphrey that he wanted him as his vice-presidential candidate, but then threw the nomination open to the convention.[15] Never at a loss for showmanship, Happy Chandler, with tears in his eyes, praised George but called him "Walter," which no one ever did. Then he hugged a startled George, which few people had ever done either.[16]

At the fundraiser, 1350 people paid a $100.00 a plate to eat tenderloin with George's favorite "magic wheat au gratin." The event was "garnished" by a cake on which was spelled "W-A-L-T-E-R. F. G E O R G E," with each letter given as one of his virtues (W for "warmhearted," A for "Accomplished," L for "Loyal," etc.)[17] The Georges were given a silver service on the tray of which were the engraved signatures of all of the US senators.

The spectacle was the largest assembly of Democrats since the 1952 convention. Most of the greats were there—Adlai Stevenson, Averell Harriman, Estes Kefauver, George Smathers, Happy Chandler, Sam Rayburn, and most of the Democratic senators and congressmen. Lyndon Johnson was the event's honorary chairman. Harry Truman, who was in Independence, Missouri preparing for a European tour, sent his regrets and a check for $200.00. Hubert Humphrey, whom the reader will recall had come to regard George as a mentor, stopped by the George's fifth-floor apartment before the event to chat.

In addition to the Washington notables, sixty Georgians attended. M. E Thompson, who was running for George's seat, appeared, but Herman Talmadge, who at first considered going, finally begged off, claiming campaign commitments.[18] Talmadge was probably fearful of the reception he

---

[13]LBJ formal letter invitation, July 3, 1956, f. George, Walter F., box 44, Johnson papers.

[14]Dorothy Blount to LBJ, July 20, 1956, ibid.

[15]Ryskin, *Hubert*, 211.

[16]"George Dinner," *The Evening Star*, July 20, 1956, scrapbook, LHG-VHPS.

[17]"Sentimental Send-off," 96.

[18]"Sixty Georgians," *Atlanta Journal*, July 17, 1956, scrapbook, LHG-VHPS.

would receive. One journalist lamented the departure of George, and Senator Milliken, whom the journalist described as "representing Conservatism at its best," noted that George was being replaced by "one of these radical conservatives."[19] The only Republican to come was Representative William C. Cramer of Florida.[20]

The irony was that since it was a Democratic Party fund raiser, a lot of the speeches were partisan, often blasting Eisenhower's foreign policy, much of which George had helped direct.[21] Averell Harriman criticized what he felt showed Eisenhower's ungratefulness to Senator George for not having sent a representative to the dinner, or coming himself. When returning to his seat, he passed George, who tapped him on his arm as if to say "thank you."[22] Estes Kefauver, however, tried to smooth things over by noting "all the good things" of Eisenhower's foreign policy came from George's influence.[23] Richard Russell sat in the back of the hall blocking an entrance and as usual said nothing.[24]

All the plaudits were not for George alone. The Senior Congress Club, which had been formed about a decade earlier by Supreme Court Justice Fred Vinson and his wife, feted Miss Lucy with a luncheon at the Chevy Chase Club. Along with a number of congressional and senatorial wives, President Wilson's wife, Edith Wilson, was present, and Mamie Eisenhower returned to Washington from Gettysburg just for the luncheon. An orchestra played many of Miss Lucy's favorite songs. In speeches, she was lionized as "America's secret weapon" to NATO, and to remember the event, she was given a gold charm bracelet. Usually not a woman to show much emotion, Miss Lucy teared up frequently throughout the festivities.[25] A friend, Leigh Wade, gave her another luncheon at the Sulgrave Club, where she was awarded a rhinestone-encrusted alarm clock,[26] and Mary Agnes Holland, wife of Spessard Holland (D-Florida), feted her at the Sheraton Park Hotel.[27] Mamie Eisenhower also held a luncheon for her at the White

[19]"We'll Miss Them," 4.

[20]"Sidelights," *The Evening Star*, July 20, 1956, scrapbook, LHG-VHPS.

[21]"George Dinner," *Evening Star*, July 20, 1956, scrapbook, LHG-VHPS.

[22]"Stevenson Salutes George," *Atlanta Constitution*, July 20, 1956, ibid.

[23]"Sidelights," *Evening Star*, July 20, 1956, ibid.

[24]"The Georges to Say Goodbyes," *Washington Post,* n. d., ibid.

[25]"Farewells for the Georges," unidentified clipping, ibid.

[26]"Mrs. George Get a Clock," *Washington Post*, "Mrs. George Honored," July 3, 1956, ibid.

[27]Ibid.

House.[28]

Lyndon Johnson, who seems to have genuinely liked George, called him "the most beloved man in public life today," adding that his "contribution to the cause of world peace leaves us all in his debt."[29] George returned the favor by in effect endorsing Johnson for president, calling him "a man of great strength," adding that he was "capable of taking on added and even higher responsibilities" than that of majority leader. Realizing that this statement could be taken as an insult to the other hopefuls, he quickly noted that this statement was in no way a slap at their ability.[30] The reader will remember that both George and Russell had for a long time promoted Johnson as the South's best chance to elect a president, but unlike Russell, George would not live to be disappointed when Johnson became the nation's chief executive.

George's departure created the usual political scramble to fill the void. Estes Kefauver, who had lost the Democratic nomination to Adlai Stevenson that year, wanted George's seat on the Foreign Relations Committee, feeling that it would give him a great deal of national exposure for a presidential run in 1960. John Kennedy wanted the seat for the same reason.[31] Lyndon Johnson, who controlled these matters, also had his eye on 1960, but apparently feeling Kefauver the greater threat to his candidacy, gave George's seat to the less-senior Kennedy.[32] Historian Ted Sorensen contends in his work on Kennedy that Johnson's action established a friendly relationship between the two that led later to Kennedy's selection of Johnson as vice president in 1960.[33]

George's departure didn't simply leave a void in terms of who would fill what roles; it would also have a broad detrimental effect in foreign policy. No one, certainly not Theodore Green, could maintain the bipartisanship in foreign policy that George had championed. *US News* feared as much, not-

---

[28]Invitation to the White House, May 8, 1956, scrapbook, LHG-VHPS.

[29]"Honored Dean," *Washington Daily News*, July 19, 1956, ibid.

[30]Kevin McCarran to Lee, December 29, 1956, box 1160, f. 1, and Cross reference sheet, Woehrle, Alexander J., December 29, 1956, Eisenhower papers.

[31]Rostow, *Eisenhower, Kennedy, and Foreign Aid*, 64.

[32]Sorensen, *Kennedy*, 164, in Fontenay, *Estes Kefauver*, 321–22.

[33]Caro, *The Years of Lyndon Johnson*, 123–40. Johnson's move might well have established some sort of friendly relations with Kennedy, but it is widely believed today that Kennedy never wanted Johnson on the ticket with him and only offered him the post for party unity, never expecting him to take it. In fact, after Johnson accepted, the Kennedy people tried to remove him. Robert Caro, Johnson's most recent biographer, states otherwise. He contends that Kennedy knew exactly what he was doing.

ing that bipartisanship would be "under a greater strain." As early as February 1957, Senator Clifford Case (R-New Jersey) sent a memo to Sherman Adams lamenting the "disastrous disintegration of bipartisanship in our foreign policy, particularly since Sen[.] Walter George left."[34] The astounding loss of so many conservative Senate Republicans in the 1958 elections might have eased matters for the more moderate Eisenhower, but without George at the foreign policy rudder, bipartisanship became a thing of the past.

Awards and honors continued to roll in even after he had formally left the Senate. George was awarded "Man of the South" in December and another group named him "the American who contributed the most to peace in 1956."[35] Eisenhower invited him and Miss Lucy to sit with him on the reviewing stand at the January 1957 Inauguration.[36] In February, George was called on to speak at the VFW Annual Dinner on February 5, 1957, and he was surprised when they likewise awarded him the Gold Citizenship Medal.[37] Mercer, his old alma mater, gave him a Doctor of Humane Letters degree at the June graduation to go with the Doctor of Law Degree it had given him in 1920, and with the two he had earned in 1900 and 1901.[38]

George turned seventy-nine shortly after leaving the Senate, but he made little fuss over the birthday. He worked at the State Department until noon that day and went home to his apartment on the fifth floor of the Mayflower, where a few old friends had a luncheon for him. Afterwards, he smoked a cigar and gave an interview to a reporter, during which he reminisced about his career and described past colleagues. George termed William Borah of Idaho the greatest advocate with whom he had ever served. James Reed of Missouri was the greatest debater, quite a compliment coming from someone of George's record in that field. John Sharp Williams of Mississippi and Henry Cabot Lodge, Sr., were the two most distinguished scholars.[39] Reminiscing must have pained him, given the fact that he had not wanted his Senate career to be in his past.

It has been written that "Diplomacy is the art of letting the other fellow have your way." If that is the case, then George, as a skillful politician, was an expert in diplomacy. Although he could be most useful to the Republican administration, his appointment as acting special ambassador to NATO had

---

[34]"Sentimental Send-off," 95.

[35]D. Eisenhower to WFG, January 5, 1957, ibid.

[36]"It came to me as a Surprise," George wrote LBJ, WFG to LBJ, February 4, 1957, LBJA Con. File: George, Walter F., Johnson papers.

[37]Ibid.

[38]*Mercer Cluster* 16 (March 29, 1957): 1.

[39]"Senator George Hailed…," n. d., unidentified clipping, Sen G (NC) folder, VHPS.

clearly been salve to ease the pain of his forced retirement. Eisenhower had hoped that in his new capacity, George would help continue the bipartisan nature of the foreign policy he had been so instrumental in forming. *US News* questioned quite legitimately if he could be as effective in his post outside the Senate as he was in it.[40]

There are indications that George did not really want this position. Miss Lucy had told the press that she did not want him to accept it and had been looking forward to "sitting and rocking" on their screen porch in Vienna. Still, George had felt that if his help was needed, he would not "shirk."[41] He could rationalize that he was important work at NATO though it is doubtful that he ever believed that himself. Explaining his position at one of his many testimonials, he said early in June, "I will confess I would like to go home. I am making a great sacrifice [by taking the NATO position]." Then he tried to make light of it all by saying that his wife had always complained that she had never been to Europe and that every woman wanted to go to Paris, so "I will make the sacrifice and I hope I do a little good."[42] He likely had few illusions that he would accomplish much if anything.[43]

George left for Europe the last week of August 1956 to investigate his new duties, but he planned to return to Washington in October to complete some of his Senate work. From this point until he returned to Vienna an ill man in spring 1957, it is amazing how few times he is mentioned in documents and in NATO information and correspondence. This absence underscores the unimportant nature of his new job.[44]

On arriving in Great Britain, George attended a luncheon hosted by former prime minister Winston Churchill. Though he spent his time in Paris, he does not seem to have had much to do and was rather ignored.[45] George did intercede and ask Douglas Dillon of the American embassy in Paris to arrange a meeting between Guy Mollet, the French prime minister,

---

[40]"When Senator George Steps Out," 48.

[41]"One of the Greatest," 35.

[42]"Senator Honored, "*Evening Star*, June 4, 1956.

[43]His appointment was hardly public when he was besieged by job-seekers (WFG to LBJ, June 7, 1956, box 44, f. LBJA cong. file: George, Walter F., Johnson papers).

[44]In the 1980s, one other defeated U. S. Senator from Georgia, Mack Mattingly, was made US Representative to NATO.

[45]Miss Lucy did go shopping for her friends. Returning early in November to Washington, she brought with her perfume for Lady Bird and a bracelet for Lucy Johnson. There was no mention of anything for Linda Johnson. She gave LBJ an Eiffel Tower tie (LBJ to Lucy Heard George, November 10, 1956, box 67, f. Geo-Grid 96, Master File, Johnson papers).

and Lyndon Johnson when Johnson came to a NATO convocation later in November.[46] When an official in the French diplomatic corps advised the ministry of foreign affairs about who was important among the congressional delegation that was coming, he mentioned Theodore Green, who would become the new chair of the Committee on Foreign Affairs in the Senate because the position had been "released by the departure of Senator George,"[47] but nothing of George's role in NATO or his continuing chairmanship of the Foreign Relations Committee.[48] Apparently unhappy in general, George casually added in a report on the Middle East that same month in November 1956 that he might leave his NATO post, but he did stay on.[49]

When his Senate term ended in January 1957, there seems to have developed a problem with a continued NATO appointment. In a memo to the president, Dulles wrote in December that he would like to give George an appointment in the Department of State, but to do so would raise some question about his senatorial retirement, which could not be cleared without special legislation (Dulles called trying to pass that legislation "unwise"). Dulles suggested to Eisenhower that "Senator George be appointed special assistant to the president with personal rank of ambassador and with duties…to advise the president and the secretary of state as regards the general development and implementation of bipartisan foreign policy." Using this ploy, George would be able to receive both his $12,000 Senate retirement and the $20,000 salary that went with the position of special assistant.[50] This salary, enormous in that time, was paid from the appropriation "Executive Office of the President, special projects."

On January 4, 1957, as the new Congress was convening, Hagerty, Eisenhower's presidential secretary, announced that "Walter F. George of Vienna, Georgia" would be the special assistant to the president of the United States with the personal rank of ambassador.[51] George did continue to be

---

[46]Douglas Dillon to LBJ, November 14, 1956, LBJ. Subject file: 2nd NATO Parl. Conf., box 121 LBJA subject file, ibid.

[47]Alphan to MFA, November 13, 1956, Amérique, 1952–1960: dossier general: relations F-A, folder 351, 58, AMAE.

[48]Ibid.

[49]"People of the Week," (November 9, 1956): 20.

[50]Memo for the president (signed by J. F. Dulles), December 20, 1956, box 287, f. 72-A-2, George, Walter F., Central files, official files, Eisenhower papers.

[51]Date "Jan 4, 1957," is scratched out with a pencil attached to memo for Governor Adams, January 2, 1957, box 287, f. 72-A-2, Walter F. George, Central files, official files, Eisenhower papers.

somewhat active in NATO affairs, at least enough so that the general press and public did not notice the change. When his name did not appear in a list of dignitaries attending the NATO council meeting in May, the press finally raised questions. In reply, the government issued a report that since January 4, George had not been NATO ambassador but instead Eisenhower's special assistant in bipartisan affairs. Another report attributed the change to Miss Lucy's ill health. Richard J. Kerry, George's assistant, said cryptically that the first of the reports was partially true and the second was wholly true.[52] That his change in roles had gone unnoticed for five months.

George's last diplomatic role was his appearance at the Bermuda Conference between Eisenhower and British Prime Minister Harold Macmillan in 1956. Anglo-American relations remained strained because of Eisenhower's lack of support of the British and the French in the Suez Crisis the previous fall, and the meeting was essentially to ease tensions. Also on the agenda were discussions of NATO troop reduction and Red China, which explained George's attendance. "Walter George is highly regarded by the British," reported *Newsweek* because he is "a resolute internationalist and champion of foreign aid" and had "consistently...maintained that the bulwark of Western defense and world freedom is the Anglo-US alliance."[53] It is curious that *Newsweek* did not mention Lend-Lease. If *Newsweek* respected George's talents and contributions to Anglo-American relations, the sarcastic, arrogant Brutish ambassador to the US, Sir Roger Makins, did not. In a report on the meeting, he said of the legislative godfather of Lend-Lease that George was "a shining example of the American disposition to venerate the aged and respect their wisdom. He is past the point of absorbing any but the most general ideas and propositions. He represents a kind of traveling benediction for everything that may happen at the meeting."[54]

Walter George had his first coronary occlusion in April 1957. He developed chest pains and shortness of breath. Then, early in June he had what must have been a heart attack in his Washington office and was brought to the Emory Hospital on June 12. He was deluged with calls from well-

[52]"George NATO Role Changes," clipping, May 4, 1957, F. George, May 10, 1956, box 338, f. George, RNC papers.

[53]"Face to Face by the Blue Bermudian Sea," 33.

[54]Roger Makins, "Bermuda Conference," 25 March 1957, FO 371/126690, FO-BNA. Makins is generally derogatory toward the Americans at the conference: "Carl McCardle was 'Dr. Watson' to Mr. Dulles' Sherlock Holmes." Referring to Henry Cabot Lodge, Jr., he wrote, "His ambition outstrips his abilities." Another congressman with the group was "a vain, elderly, obstinate and reactionary congressman from South Carolina," etc.

wishers, including Eisenhower, who expressed delight that from what he had read in the newspaper, he would "within a few days...be on your way to Vienna."[55] Indeed, within a few days, his pain was gone and his appetite had improved. Feeling much improved, George begged to go home, and he was finally allowed to return to Vienna although his doctors still considered him to be in "serious condition."[56] His health condition was "hush-hush," neighbor and long-time friend Frances Coley remembered in an interview in September 2006: "Neighbors were instructed to say he was fine."[57] When he felt good, he would sit on the screen porch he so loved, where the wind could come from three of the four sides, watching the cattle in the nearby pasture. He read and watched television. Sometimes he would sit in the yard, assisted by his nurse, Sally Mae Childs.[58]

After he left Emory, Emory came to him in the form of Dr. Willis Hurst, who shuttled between Atlanta and Vienna, driven by longtime Vienna mayor Lewis N. Mobley, called by one of Vienna's citizens, "a one-man Red Cross unit."[59] He had a few visitors, among them his formal secretary, the inimitable iron magnolia Christie Bell Meade, *née* Kennedy, who traveled from Greenville, South Carolina, where she operated a radio station.[60] Lyndon Johnson, who generally did not waste time with anyone who could not be of value to him, had stayed in touch with George after he had left the Senate with birthday greetings and other correspondence, indicating that his constant, almost nauseating praise of George was indeed sincere.[61] He generally seems to have loved the man. In reply to one of Johnson's letters, George gave him encouraging news in mid-July. "I feel that I am greatly improved," he wrote his protégé, "and get now more around the house. It is a slow process, but I am recovering.[62] Indeed, he seemed to have improved

---

[55]Eisenhower to WFG, June 17, 1957, box 943, f. 347, PPF 343, Eisenhower papers.

[56]"Senator George Grows Weaker," clipping, *New York Herald Tribune*, July 30, 1957, box 338, f. George, RNC papers; untitled newspaper clipping, August 5, 1956, f. "Senator George," VHPS.

[57]Frances Coley interview.

[58]Interview in person and by phone with Sally Mae Childs. At age ninety-nine, she appeared at the fiftieth anniversary celebration of the death of Walter George in 2007 in Vienna and made an impromptu speech at which she regaled the crowd with this story. I later spoke with her in detail by phone.

[59]C. Sibley, "A One Man...," unidentified, undated clipping, RCB-5804, box 15, f. WFG-GSA.

[60]*Vienna News,* 8 August 1957, 2.

[61]See LBJA Congressional file: George, W. F. in box 44, LBJA cong. files, Johnson Papers.

[62]WFG to LBJ, July 13, 1957, ibid.

and even took a short ride around his Dooly County farm. He did not know it would be his last.

On July 16, three days after writing Johnson, George wrote Eisenhower what was probably the last letter he wrote in his life.

> Dear Mr. President:
>
> I am getting much better but I am still rigidly restricted by my Doctors. They insist that I should not write a letter or do anything. However I am writing to say to you that I greatly appreciated your letter which I received some time ago [June 17] and I wish you to know that I sincerely appreciate the great confidence you have placed in me. With great respect, I am
>
> Most sincerely,
> Walter F. George.[63]

Six days later, George had a major coronary occlusion, which severely damaged his heart, and he began a severe decline. As he worsened, Dr. Hurst would give him a shot, and he would perk up. When he would slip again into pain and gasp for breath, the devoted housekeeper, Ada, would say, "Give him more of that life water!"[64] Eisenhower and Mamie tried to call Vienna to inquire about him, but were unable to get through.[65] The *Vienna News* editor, Madge Methvin, who had handled many of George's past news releases including the one that announced his withdrawal from the Senate race the year before, issued reports to the outside press stationed in Vienna. *Atlanta Constitution* journalist Celestine Sibley stayed as a guest in her house during the wait, and when Ralph McGill attended George's funeral, he remembered that Sibley "saved my life with some food and buttermilk."[66] When the funeral finally took place, this remarkable woman even played the organ for the service.[67]

On Friday, August 2, George of Georgia lapsed into a "state of unawareness."[68] He died at 1:52 on Sunday morning August 4, propped up on pillows in the hospital bed installed in the modest bungalow that had been his home for decades. In attendance were two doctors, two nurses, Heard

---

[63]WFG to DDE, July 16, 1957, box 943, f. 347, PPF 323, Eisenhower papers. Curiously, George signed his name in full, indicating a lack of closeness with Eisenhower. The letter retains his original punctuation and capitalization.

[64]Frances Coley interview.

[65]DDE to "Miss Lucy," July 26, 1956, box 943, f. 347, PPF 323, Eisenhower papers.

[66]Ralph McGill to Mrs. C. M. Methvin, August 7, 1957, box 6, f. 9, Ralph McGill papers.

[67]Celestine Sibley, "A Week's Memories," 58, WFG-GSA.

[68]*Vienna News*, August 8, 1957, 1.

and Irma, and his pastor Rev. L. C. Cutts. Miss Lucy, his wife of fifty-four years, held his hand at his bedside. In describing this scene in the end of his life, the *Vienna News*, a paper whose professionalism had for decades stood much above the average Georgia rural weekly, told its readers, "It was as if he went to sleep, to awake in the realm of the immortals."[69] The next day, Heard George issued a statement announcing his father's death.

When Vienna awoke to the news the next day, the town went into a state of shock, although there had been ample warning. Citizens of this town of 2,000 wandered by the small frame house in which he had lived and died, and many gathered in the town square and stared at the statue of their greatest citizen. Mayor J. T. DeLiesseline ordered a state of mourning and that all stores would be closed at 2 p.m. the day of his funeral.[70]

George was honored in death as he had been in life. President Eisenhower ordered flags on all federal buildings to be flown at half-mast. "I have lost a good friend and the nation has lost an outstanding American," the president wrote Miss Lucy, adding, "Your husband will be greatly missed."[71] In his old home, the US Senate, thirty members rose to pay him tribute: Lyndon Johnson called him "a truly great man who is going to be remembered long after the rest of us are gone and forgotten." Stuart Symington said George was "the greatest living American of our time;" Chapman Revercomb, a Republican, recalled "A man of impressive power and yet a kindly gentleman." John Stennis of Mississippi said, "He personified the adage, 'Simplicity is true greatness,'" and Theodore Green asserted, "Walter George is with the ages." Even Herman Talmadge said that "the nation had suffered an irreparable loss," and that "one is appalled to think what disaster probably would have befallen had it not been for the steadying influence of Walter George."[72]

Outside that body, the praise was no less. The Atlanta City Council held a minute of prayer. The *New York Times* called him "the greatest senator—Southern Style—of this century, to say the least.... Well done, George of Georgia—and farewell."[73] Editorial comments included metaphors like "a

---

[69]Ibid.

[70]"Senator George's rites...," UNC, n. d. in Sen George (NC) folder, VHPS.

[71]D. Eisenhower to Lucy Heard George, 4 August 1956, box 943, f. 347, PPF 323, Eisenhower papers.

[72]"Senators Solemnly Pay Final Tribute to George," unidentified clipping, Senator George file, VHPS; "Senate Pays Sorrowing Tribute," unidentified clipping, August 12, 1957, WFG-GSA.

[73]"Tributes to George," unidentified clipping, n. d., in Sen George (NC), VHPS.

Senator's Senator" and "one of the foremost citizens of the globe."[74]

Condolences even came from abroad. Paul Henri Spaak, the prime minister of Belgium, sent his "deepest sympathy."[75] Konrad Adenauer, the chancellor of Germany, wired Eisenhower, "I must express to you my great sorrow at the difficult loss to the American nation by the death of Senator Walter F. George.... His deep comprehension made the national union of NATO [Nordatlantikpakt] and his actions [which] made possible the solving of such difficult problems between East and West will always be remembered in Germany."[76] Georgia judge and political activist Mark Dunahoo spoke for the everyday citizen when he remembered George in his oral history for the Russell Library at the University of Georgia: "I shall never forget Senator George," he said. "I loved him dearly; I loved him until he died. He was one of the most astute men I've ever known.... No one ever questioned his integrity."[77] These types of sentiments were expressed everywhere.

George had always told his wife to keep his funeral simple and said that he wanted those who wished to honor him to give donations to the Walter F. George School of Law, his beloved alma mater. He got his wish. He was buried in a plain navy-blue suit in a solid copper casket in the Heard plot in the Vienna cemetery. Here the simplicity ended. Heard's Sunday school class had a wake all night by his coffin in the church and stood around it like an honor guard, Washington dignitaries (forty members of Congress alone) flew into Cordele airport.[78] A caravan of limousines transported them the ten miles to Vienna, where the funeral was held in the First Baptist Church. Former Massachusetts senator Henry Cabot Lodge came to represent President Eisenhower. Lyndon Johnson was there, as were senators Russell, Talmadge, Knowland, Green, Sparkman, Morse, Wiley, Byrd, Thurmond, and a number of others. Most Georgia congressmen came as well, as did Governor Marvin Griffin and Lieutenant Governor Ernest Vandiver.[79] Never had a Georgian been so honored in life or death. In a bizarre twist,

[74]"Georgia has lost one of its Greatest Men," (editorial), August 5, 1957, unidentified clipping, f. Sen. George (N.C), VHPS.

[75]P. H. Spaak to D. Eisenhower, August 5, 1957, box 943, f. 347, PPF 323, Eisenhower papers.

[76]Troute Slip to Mr. Fisher Howe, August 7, 1956, box 943, f. 327, PPF 323, Eisenhower papers

[77]Mark Dunahoo, oral history, 54, Russell Library.

[78]John Bonner interview. There was the same honor guard the next year when Miss Lucy died.

[79]*Vienna News*, August 8, 1957, 1.

newly elected Senator Herman Talmadge, whose challenge of George's reelection probably hastened his death, directed traffic outside the church.[80]

Loudspeakers were placed in the church and outside for the overflow. The church was full of flowers, including a large cross of white chrysanthemums, which were placed at the head of the coffin. The combined choirs of the Methodist and Baptist churches sang "In the Garden," a hymn chosen by Heard. His pallbearers were all prominent local citizens, including his former law partner, now federal judge, T. Hoyt Davis, and Max Conner, chairman of the county commission and a longtime friend of Heard.[81]

There was a bit of a dust-up over who would deliver the eulogy. When news of his death spread over the state, Dr. Tiny Tippet, the Georgia Baptist Sunday School Director, called the family in Vienna and more or less said that he would give the eulogy. George's pastor, D. Lee C. Cutts, the former president of Truett-McConnell College, who had grown up in Vienna and who had retired there, told him that he would be welcome to come, and he could even sit on the dais, but the eulogy was "covered," that is, by Reverend Cutts.[82] Cutts spoke from Micah 6:8: "He hath showed thee, O Man, what is good, and what doth the Lords require of thee, but to do justly and love mercy and walk humbly with thy God."[83]

After the funeral, Miss Lucy wrote to Eisenhower a thank-you note, which was a string of comma splices, but showed the gratitude that she felt for the president's attention:

> My son and I greatly appreciate your kind message of sympathy, even in the darkest hour of my life, I realize I have much to be thankful for, among them consideration and unfailing kindness to Mr. George and your appreciation of him, which you must know means more to me now than ever. May I have the courage and strength that he and his friend would expect of me and to carry on as best I can without his strong right arm.[84]

She had before George's death written Lyndon Johnson a note thanking him for flowers he had sent, but after his death, the future president wrote her one of the most profound letters she received: "I returned from

---

[80]Several citizens of Vienna told me of his action.

[81]*Vienna News*, August 8, 1956, 1; interview with Hattie Conner, wife of local politician Max Conner.

[82]John Jacob Gregory interview.

[83]John Bonner interview. He gave it as the following: "What doth the Lord require of thee? Do good and love mercy and walk with the will of God."

[84]Lucy George to D. Eisenhower, August 28, 1957, box 943, f. 347, PPF 323, Eisenhower papers.

Georgia [after the funeral] with a sense of something very real and very vital missing from my life," he told the grieving Miss Lucy. "No one has been more important in guiding my footsteps than Senator George, and my loss is deep and personal.... He will always be with me because we are bound by ties of affection and friendship. And these are some bonds too strong to be broken."[85] George's death ended a chapter in the lives of anyone who knew him well, not least in the senator-to-be-president, whose career George had so promoted.

George's estate was surprisingly small, $135,738.67, not a small sum in 1957, but puny compared to Lyndon Johnson's net worth eight years later when he ran for the presidency.[86] In 1938, the *New York Times* reported that George "is dependent upon his salary almost altogether and uses most of it in living expenses in Washington and Georgia."[87] Except for what little might have come from his farm in Vienna, there seems to have been no other income over the years. Of the $135,000 estate in 1957, his deductions were $71,140, resulting his having to pay only $137.95 in estate taxes.[88] Lucy and Heard were co-executors of his will that had been drafted on December 22, 1948. His farm was valued at $9,600, and his home in Vienna at $7,500, with his brick office building, Heard's home, and another house called "the Carter House" on Highway 41, bringing total real estate value at $39,255. There was $1,250 in stocks and bonds, $8,455 in cash in Washington and Vienna in checking accounts, $33,599.23 in eight life insurance policies, ten head of cows, $100; 6 feeder pigs, $100; and $2670 in ungathered crops (40 acres of corn, 15 acres of peanuts, 11 acres of cotton). He apparently still held the mortgage on the house on Lake Blackshear that he had sold the year before. The cost of burial was a rather pricy $4,007. 87 for that day. He left $10,000 to his granddaughter, Mary Senate. Miss Lucy received after all disbursements and expenses, an estate valued at $114,147.42.[89] George's friends used to say, probably quoting the senator himself, that "He was born poor and will die poor. But he will not die as poor as he was born."[90] These figures bear this prediction out.

Miss Lucy never returned to Washington despite receiving many invi-

---

85Lyndon Johnson to Lucy George, August 7, 1957, box 943, f. 347, PPF 323, Eisenhower papers.

86Lyndon Johnson lived well, maintained two homes, and still managed by 1964 to have amassed a net wealth of half a million dollars for every year he had been in Congress.

87"Personality...," clipping, August 18, 1938, *New York Times*, 5, RNC papers.

88T. Hoyt Davis interview. Mr. Davis allowed me access to his inheritance tax return.

89WFG Estate Tax folder, Davis & Forehand, Vienna, Georgia.

90"Old Independent," 21.

tations. Instead, she went to Florida several times in winter 1957–1958 to visit her sister and brother-in-law, who lived in Bradenton, where her visits were announced in the local paper.[91] Her feistiness and her conservatism remained with her and was feted in an anonymous poem about her:

A Democrat out in her motor
Ran over a Radical voter.
"Sakes alive," Miss Lucy cried,
"He's on the wrong side!"
"So I don't blame myself one iota!"[92]

The redoubtable lady outlived George barely a year. She had always said, "When he goes, I will go with him." She developed liver problems, hepatitis by some accounts, sclerosis of the liver by others. "There was a lot wrong with her," Frances Coley told this author; "We suspected hepatitis, but she had heart problems as well."[93] She was treated by Dr. Derrel Hazlehurst in Macon. Sclerosis of the liver was given as the official cause of death.[94] She died in the same room in their little bungalow in which the senator had died the year before. Her son conducted her service in the same Baptist church, which had honored his father the year before with an almost identical service, including the Sunday school honor guard.[95] Her will was very simple: Except for the $5,000 she left to Marcus's daughter, Mary Senate George, she left the remainder of her estate to Heard.[96]

Heard had ceased working for his father in 1955 and lived in Vienna for the rest of his life, dabbling rather unsuccessfully in real estate. He kept a garden and would always share his vegetables with his neighbors and friends. He does not seem to have been too prosperous in general, and if he needed a few dollars, he would sell a piece of property at a ridiculously small price.[97] He lived to the age of eighty-three, dying at Cohen's Retreat near

[91]"Mrs. Walter George is visitor here," *Bradenton Herald,* April 6, 1958, scrapbook, LHG-VHPS.

[92]Ibid.

[93]Frances Coley interview.

[94]US Estate Tax Return, Lucy H. George folder, Davis & Forehand, Vienna, Georgia.

[95]"George's Widow is Dead at 76," *Atlanta Journal,* October 29, 1958, clipping in LHG-VHPS.

[96]Draft of Miss Lucy's will, George, Lucy H. (will), Davis & Forehand law offices, Vienna, Georgia.

[97]Conversation with Mrs. Hattie Connor, whose husband often was involved in real estate ventures with Heard George.

Savannah. Although he received a law degree, he never really practiced. He was a captain in the Army Air Corps.[98]

Beyond the community of American historians of the twentieth century, Walter Franklin George is not well remembered outside of the state of Georgia, but within the state, monuments keep his memory alive for Georgians. Two of the first to be created were the Walter F. George Lock and Dam (formerly Ft. Gaines Lock and Dam) on the Chattahoochee River, and the lake behind it, named Walter F. George Reservoir (also called Lake George) in March 1958. A supporter described the memorial in a letter to President Eisenhower, "as a monument to the long and distinguished service of the late Senator."[99] The Georgia legislature honored him in January 1959 with a portrait still hangs in the state capitol.[100] At least one high school in the state has been named for him, and the Vienna First Baptist Church added a "George Memorial Chapel" when they remodeled in 1960. In November 1960, the US Post Office issued a commemorative stamp, and postmaster general Arthur E. Summerfield spoke at the ceremony announcing the commemoration in Vienna, where the first stamp was sold.[101] Thirteen people were presented both special bound books of the stamps, including Eisenhower, his granddaughter Mary George, nieces and nephews, and Mrs. Whiting Whittier, formerly Mrs. Marcus George.[102] Only two government servants had had stamps issued in their honor while still living: Robert Taft, Jr., and John Foster Dulles.[103] The local post office was swamped for requests for the stamp, even from abroad.[104] Summerfield continued to add to the mountain of accolades when he told the assembled crowd, "Certainly Walter F. George deserves every honor this nation can give him."[105] Congressman E. L. "Tic" Forrester of Leesburg expressed gratitude for having one more time to say, "Thank God for Senator Walter F. George."[106] Herman Talmadge praised his predecessor by noting that George could have

---

[98]Unidentified Heard George Obit, bio. Quest, RCB-5804, box 15, f. WFG-GSA.

[99]Philip S. Hughes to D. Eisenhower, March 22, 1958, box 7, f. March 28, 1958, Reports to the president, Eisenhower papers

[100]Portrait, RCB-13, box 24, f. 734, WFG-GSA.

[101]Summerfield speech, box 943, f. 347, PPF 323, Eisenhower papers.

[102]Ibid.

[103]Ibid.

[104]Conversation with Dot Morgan, who worked at the post office in Vienna at the time.

[105]"Stamp Ceremony," pamphlet in LHG-VHPS.

[106]George Landry, "Late Sen. George Lauded at Vienna," Sen. G. Misc. clippings folder, VHPS.

stayed in his law practice "and become a man of enormous wealth" but instead "he chose to serve his fellow man."[107]

Finally, in 1993, George's clapboard law office was made a museum and move to the present location on the edge of the park on the corner of Union and Fourth Streets in Vienna. The museum houses many of George's artifacts, mementoes, and what passes for his collection of papers.[108]

A giant oak had truly fallen, and to those who remained after him, his departure left an unfillable void. Alexander Pushkin, the greatest poet to use the Russian language, once stated that he would live forever in his surviving poetry. Walter Franklin George might well paraphrase this claim to his own works.

His position in his last years is best summed up in 1955 by Lyndon Johnson, who said that "in Senator George [there is] the authentic greatness that characterizes the statesmen whose names live through the ages.... And when the final chapter of these troubled times is written, the name of Walter F. George will be on every page as the man of vision...[who pointed] the way to peace and prosperity for ourselves and our posterity."[109]

When this son of a tenant farmer, who rose to become one of the most powerful men in the nation, died, there appeared an editorial that beautifully encapsulates his career: "Death has taken one of the greatest of Georgians. But his life and works will influence this nation and the world for a long time to come, and his name forever is written [prominently] in history.... He was the confidant of presidents, the friend of kings and prime ministers, and, through his unique position in the Senate, one of the most powerful figures of our time."[110] These words could not be improved upon for his epitaph.

---

[107]Ibid.

[108]At the time, I mined the George Archives housed there. The collection was in need of a curator, and the Vienna Historical Preservation Society was searching for a grant to hire a profession curator to organize the collection. As I said earlier, the notations in this book are based on the collection as I found it then. A professional archivist might well arrange the collection differently.

[109]*CR,* 84/1, 12576.

[110]"Georgia has lost one of its greatest men," editorial, August 5, 1957, unidentified clipping, WFG-VHPS.

Bibliography

1. Personal Interviews

Adams-Finn, Jane Carol
Bonner, John
Childs, Sally May
Cobb, Rena
Coley, Frances
Conner, Hattie
Crovett, Grace Slade
Davis, T. Hoyt
Drake, Judge Taylor
Dunlap, Edgar Jr.
Gregory, Justice Hardy
Gregory, John Jacob "Jake"
Hill, Hon. Ray
House, Mitchell
Johnson, Sid
McMillan, Judge Walter
McKinney, Frank
Melton, Buckner Sr.
Methvin, Gene
Newton, Elizabeth
Smathers, George
Smith, James Enlo
Stephens, Jack
Suggs, Harpe
Talmadge, Lyniece
Thompson, Tarkenton N.
Woodward, Henry

2. Oral Histories

Bennett, Wallace F. Russell Memorial Library, Athens, GA.
Bentley, James (Jimmy). Russell Memorial Library, Athens, GA.
Brooks, David William. Russell Memorial Library, Athens, GA.
Carlton, John "Jake." Russell Memorial Library, Athens, GA.
Cocke, Erle. Russell Memorial Library, Athens, GA.
Collins, Linton. Russell Memorial Library, Athens, GA.
Cox, Marvin Hill. Russell Memorial Library, Athens, GA.
Dunahoo, Robert M. Russell Memorial Library, Athens, GA.
Eastland, James O. Russell Memorial Library, Athens, GA.
Ellender, Allen. Russell Memorial Library, Athens, GA.
Grayson, Spence. Russell Memorial Library, Athens, GA.
Green, Mary Willi Russell. Russell Memorial Library, Athens, GA.
Griffin, Marvin. Russell Memorial Library, Athens, GA.
Harris, Roy Vincent. Russell Memorial Library, Athens, GA.

Hay, Isaac. Russell Memorial Library, Athens, GA.
Holt, Pat M. Chief of staff, Foreign Relations Committee, 1950–1977. Library of Congress, Manuscripts Division, Washington, DC.
Jenkins, Walter. Lyndon Baines Johnson Library, Austin, TX.
Marcy, Carl M. Chief of staff, Foreign Relations Committee, 1955–1973. Library of Congress, Manuscripts Division, Washington, DC.
Nicholas, Jesse R. Government documents clerk, 1937–1971. Library of Congress, Manuscripts Division, Washington, DC.
Peek, Scott I. Administrative assistant to Senator George Smathers, 1955–1973. Library of Congress, Manuscripts Division, Washington, DC.
Peterson, Mrs. Patience Hugh. Russell Memorial Library, Athens, GA.
Peterson, Patience. Russell Memorial Library, Athens, GA.
Peterson, Prudence R. and Fielding Dillard Russell. Russell Memorial Library, Athens, GA.
Riddick, Floyd. Senate parliamentarian, 1947–1974. Library of Congress, Manuscripts Division, Washington, DC.
Robertson, Walter. Dwight David Eisenhower Library, Abilene, KS.
Rusk, Dean. Russell Memorial Library, Athens, GA.
Russell, Russell B. Russell Memorial Library, Athens, GA.
Smathers, George. Senator, 1950–1968. Library of Congress, Manuscripts Division, Washington, DC.
St. Claire, Darrell. Assistant secretary of the Senate, 1933–1977. Library of Congress, Manuscripts Division, Washington, DC.
Stassen, Harold. Dwight David Eisenhower Library, Abilene, KS.
Troutman, Robert Jr. Russell Memorial Library, Athens, GA.
Valeo, Francis R. Secretary of the Senate, 1945–1977. Library of Congress, Manuscripts Division, Washington, DC.
Wilcox, Francis O. Chief of staff, Foreign Relations Committee, 1947–1955. Library of Congress, Manuscripts Division, Washington, DC.
———. Dwight David Eisenhower Library, Abilene, KS.

3. Archives and Private Papers

Adams-Finn, Jane Carol. Papers. Special Collections, Rare Books and Manuscripts Division, Jackson Tarver Library, Mercer University, Macon, GA.
Anderson, Katherine. Papers. Atlanta History Center, Atlanta, GA.
Bailey, Josiah. Papers. Perkins Library Special Collections, Duke University, Durham, NC.
Barker, Mary Cornelia. Papers. Manuscripts and Rare Books, Woodruff Library, Emory University, Atlanta, GA.
Besnell, Cullen Bryant. Papers. Manuscripts and Rare Books, Woodruff Library, Emory University, Atlanta, GA.
Candler, Bishop Warren Akin. Papers. Manuscripts and Rare Books, Woodruff Library, Emory University, Atlanta, GA.
Catalogue and Annual Announcements of Mercer University. Macon: Burke, 1898–1901. Jackson Tarver Library, Special Collections, Mercer University, Macon, GA.
Ciceronian Society. *Critic's Book*. Jackson Tarver Library, Special Collections, Mercer University, Macon, GA.
Ciceronian Society. *Treasurer's Book*. Jackson Tarver Library, Special Collections, Mercer University, Macon, GA.

Comptroller General (Various Records). RCB-348. Georgia State Archives, Morrow, GA.

Corcoran, Thomas G. Papers. Library of Congress, Manuscripts Division, Washington, DC.

———. Papers. Franklin Delano Roosevelt Library, Hyde Park, NY.

Cox, Eugene Papers. Georgia State Archives, Morrow, GA.

Cox, Oscar. Papers. Franklin Delano Roosevelt Library, Hyde Park, NY.

Davis, T. Hoyt. Papers. Davis and Forehand Law Firm, Vienna, GA.

Dulles, John Foster. Papers. Dwight David Eisenhower Library, Abilene, KS.

Dunlap, Edgar Sr. Scrapbook. "We're FOR George" in the possession of Edgar Dunlap Jr., Gainseville, Georgia.

Eisenhower, Dwight David. Papers. Dwight David Eisenhower Library, Abilene, KS.

Ellender, Allen. Papers. Ellender Memorial Library, Nicholls State University, Thibodaux, LA.

Foreign Office: Political Departments: General Correspondence from 1906–1966 (FO 371). America (The United States). British National Archives, London. Cited as FO-BNA.

Gardner, O. Max. Papers. Southern Historical Collection, Wilson Library, University of North Carolina, Chapel Hill, NC.

George Foreign Relations File, Vienna Historic Preservation Society, Vienna, GA. Cited as GFR-VHPS.

George, Lucy Heard. File. Vienna Historic Preservation Society, Vienna, GA. Cited as LHG-VHPS.

George, Marcus. File. Vienna Historic Preservation Society, Vienna, GA. Includes file and scrapbook.

George, Walter F. Biographical questionnaire and other documents. RCB-5804. Georgia State Archives, Morrow, GA. Cited as WFG-GSA.

———. "Christmas—Good Will Toward Men." *Mercerian* 10/3 (January 1900). Jackson Tarver Library, Special Collections, Mercer University, Macon, GA.

———. "Clean Athletics." *Mercerian* 10/4 (February 1900) Jackson Tarver Library, Special Collections, Mercer University, Macon, GA.

———. "The Dictionary of Georgia Biography," vol. 1

———. "Edwin Markham—The Man with the Hoe." *Mercerian* 10/1 (November 1899). Jackson Tarver Library, Special Collections, Mercer University, Macon, GA.

———. "The Expression of Free Thought." *Mercerian* 10/1 (November 1899). Jackson Tarver Library, Special Collections, Mercer University, Macon, GA.

———. File. Dooly County Public Library, Vienna, GA. Cited as WFG-DCPL.

———. File. Vienna Historic Preservation Society, Vienna, GA. Cited as WFG-VHPS.

———. File. Special Collections, Jackson Tarver Library, Mercer University, Macon, GA. Cited as WFG-MU.

———. Letters. Russell Memorial Library, Athens, GA. Cited as WFG-RML.

———. "On the Unveiling of Zolnay's Bust of Poe." *Mercerian* 10/1 (November 1899). Jackson Tarver Library, Special Collections, Mercer University, Macon, GA.

———. "The Oratorical Contest." *Mercerian* 10/2 (December 1899). Jackson Tarver Library, Special Collections, Mercer University, Macon, GA.

———. "Roy Fredlin to [Charles] Nadler and attachments, 23 August 1956, Walter F. George (estate founder, Davis Law Firm, Vienna, Georgia).

———. "The Story or the Essay—Which?" *Mercerian* 10/4 (February 1900). Jackson Tarver Library, Special Collections, Mercer University, Macon, GA.

Gilbert, Judge Price. Walter F. George. Papers. Davis and Forehand Law Firm, Vienna, GA.

Atlanta History Center, Atlanta, GA.
Hardwick, Thomas. Papers. Russell Memorial Library, Athens, GA.
Hartsfield, Mayor William Berry. Papers. Manuscripts and Rare Books, Woodruff Library, Emory University, Atlanta, GA.
Herty, Charles Holmes. Papers. Manuscripts and Rare Books, Woodruff Library, Emory University, Atlanta, GA.
Hicks, Mildred and Mary. Papers. Manuscripts and Rare Books, Woodruff Library, Emory University, Atlanta, GA.
House, Mitchell. Papers. Copies of the collected House papers have been deposited by the author with both the VHPS and the Rare Books and Manuscripts Division of the Tarver Library, Mercer University, Macon, GA.
Johnson Papers. Lyndon Baines Johnson Library, Austin, TX.
Kinetoscope. Volumes 2–6 (1897–1901). Macon: J. W. Burke Co., 1897–1901. Jackson Tarver Library, Special Collections, Mercer University, Macon, GA.
Lehman, Herbert H. Papers. Rare Books and Manuscripts Library, Columbia University, NY.
Martin, T. Baldwin, "Scattered Recollections." Unpublished memoir. Rare Books and Manuscripts Division of the Tarver Library, Mercer University, Macon, GA.
McGill, Ralph. Papers. Manuscripts and Rare Books, Woodruff Library, Emory University, Atlanta, GA.
Mercer Alumnus. Jackson Tarver Library, Special Collections, Mercer University, Macon, GA.
Moseley, George van Horn. Papers. Manuscripts Division, Library of Congress, Washington, DC.
Peterson, Hugh. Papers. Russell Memorial Library, Athens, GA.
Phi Delta Society. Minutes. Special Collections, Jackson Tarver Library, Mercer University, Macon, GA.
Rainey, Glenn W. Papers. Manuscripts and Rare Books, Woodruff Library, Emory University, Atlanta, GA.
Republican National Committee Papers. Dwight David Eisenhower Library, Abilene, KS. Cited as RNC papers.
Robertson, A. Willis. Papers. William and Mary University, Williamsburg, VA.
Roosevelt, Franklin Delano. Papers. Franklin Delano Roosevelt Library, Hyde Park, NY. This collection includes the presidential secretary file, cited as PSF, and the president's personal file, cited as PPF.
———. President's Alpha File (Pres. Alph. File), Roosevelt Library.
Russell, Richard B. Papers. Russell Memorial Library, Athens, GA.
———. (Winder File), Richard B. Russell Papers. Russell Memorial Library, Athens, GA.
Secretary of State Papers. Subject Files RCB-13734. Georgia State Archives, Morrow, GA.
Seydell, Mildred. Papers. Manuscripts and Rare Books, Woodruff Library, Emory University, Atlanta, GA.
Smith, Hoke. Papers. Russell Memorial Library, Athens, GA.
Ellender, Senator Allen. Special Collections. Ellender Memorial Library, Nicholls State University, Thibodaux, LA.
Stone Mountain Collection. Manuscripts and Rare Books, Woodruff Library, Emory University, Atlanta, GA.
Struby, Bert. "George Gaining the Younger Vote," March 5, 1956, unidentified clipping in a

collection given to the author by Mitchell House. Copies of the House papers have been deposited by the author with both the VHPS and the Rare Books and Manuscripts Division of the Tarver Library at Mercer University, Macon, GA.
Talmadge, Herman E. Papers. Russell Memorial Library, Athens, GA.
Truman, Harry S. Papers. Harry S Truman Library, Independence, MO.
Wallace, Henry A. Papers. Franklin Delano Roosevelt Library, Hyde Park, NY.
Wright, David McCord. Papers. Georgia Historical Society, Savannah, GA.

4. Book, Periodicals, Theses, Dissertations

"ABCs of the Bricker Amendment." *US News & World Report* 36 (January 22, 1954): 37–39.
Abels, Jules. *Out of the Jaws of Victory.* New York: Henry Holt, 1959.
Acheson, Dean. *A Citizen Looks at Congress.* New York: Harper Bros., 1957.
———. *Sketches from Life of Men I Have Known.* New York: American Heritage, 1959.
Adams. Sherman. *Firsthand Report: The Story of the Eisenhower Administration.* New York: Harper, 1961.
Allen, R. S. "Roosevelt's Defeat: The Inside Story, with editorial comment." *Nation* 145 (July 31, 1937): 123–24.
———. "The New Deal Fights for Its Life." *Nation* 145/2 (July 10, 1937): 35–36.
Alsop, Joseph, and Turner Catledge. *The 168 Days.* Garden City, NY: Doubleday, 1938.
———. *The Center: People and Power in Political Washington.* New York: Harper and Row, 1968.
Altman, O. R. "First Session of the 75th Congress." *American Political Science Review* 31/6 (December 1937): 1071–93.
———. "Second Session of the 74th Congress." *American Political Science Review* 30/6 (December 1936): 1086–107.
Ambrose, Stephen E. *Eisenhower.* 2 vols. New York: Simon & Schuster, 1983.
———. *Nixon.* New York: Simon & Schuster, 1987–1989
Amérique: Dossier Générale: Rélations Franco-Américaine [America: General File: Franco America Relations], 1952–1963. Archives du ministère des affaires étrangères [Foreign Affairs Ministry Archives], Paris, France. Cited as AMAE.
Anderson, Clinton. *Outsider in the Senate: Clinton Anderson's Memoirs.* New York: World Publishers, 1970.
Anderson, William. *Wild Man from Sugar Creek: The Political Career of Eugene Talmadge.* Baton Rouge: Louisiana State University Press, 1975.
Anderson, Terry H. *The United States, Great Britain, and the Cold War, 1944–49.* Columbia: University of Missouri Press, 1981.
"Appointments." *Time* 69 (January 14, 1957): 22.
Arnold, James R. *The First Domino: Eisenhower, the Military, and America's Intervention in Viet Nam.* New York: Morrow, 1991.
Askell, Bernard. *The FDR Memoirs.* New York: Doubleday, 1973.
"Aunt Mary's Applecart," *Time* 31/20 (May 16, 1938): 15.
"Back in the Fold." *Scholastic* 38 (February 3, 1941): 16. Harry
Baker, Bobby. *Wheeling and Dealing.* New York: Norton, 1978.
Barkley, Alben. *That Reminds Me.* Garden City: Doubleday, 1954.
"The Battle of H. R. 1776." *Scholastic* 38 (February 3, 1941): 5, 13, 16.
Baker, Leonard. *Roosevelt and Pearl Harbor.* London: Macmillan, 1970.
Bartlett, Bruce R. *Cover-up.* New Rochelle: Arlington, 1978.

Bartley, Numan V. *From Thurmond to Wallace: Political Tendencies in Georgia, 1948–1968.* Baltimore: Johns Hopkins University Press, 1970.

———. "Georgia Politics and the Disfranchisement of the Negro." *Georgia Historical Quarterly* 32 (March 1, 1948): 1–21.

———. *The Rise of Massive Resistance; Race and Politics in the South during the 1950s.* Baton Rouge: Louisiana University Press, 1969.

———, and Hugh D. Graham. *Southern Elections: County and Precinct Data, 1950–72.* Baton Rouge: Louisiana State University Press, 1978.

———. *Southern Politics and the Second Reconstruction.* Baltimore: Johns Hopkins, 1975.

Becnel, Thomas A. *Senator Allen Ellender of Louisiana.* Baton Rouge: Louisiana State University Press, 1995.

Begeman, J. "Dixiecrats Helped by the High Court: Georgia's County Unit System." *New Republic* 122 (May 1, 1950): 13–14.

Bell, Jonathan. *The Liberal State on Trial: The Cold War and American Politics in the Truman Years.* New York: Columbia University Press, 2004.

Belvin, William L. Jr. "The Georgia Gubernatorial Primary of 1946." *Georgia Historical Quarterly* 50 (March 1966): 37–53.

Bergman, Jean. "How the Supreme Court Helped the Dixiecrats." *The New Republic* 122 (May 1, 1950): 13–14.

Berman, Edgar. *Hubert: The Triumph and Tragedy of the Humphrey I Knew.* New York: Putnam, 1979.

Berman, William C. *The Politics of Civil Rights in the Truman Administration.* Columbus: Ohio State University Press, 1970.

Bernd, Joseph L. "Corruption in Georgia Primaries and Elections, 1938–1950." Master's thesis, Boston University, 1953.

———. *Grass Roots Politics in Georgia.* Atlanta: Emory University Research Committee, 1960.

———. "A Study of Primary Elections in Georgia, 1946–1954." PhD diss., Duke University, 1957.

———. "White Supremacy and the Disenfranchisement of Blacks in Georgia, 1946." *Georgia Historical Quarterly* 66 (Winter 1982): 492–513.

Beschloss, Michael R. *The Conquerors: Roosevelt, Truman, and the Destruction of Hitler's Germany, 1941–45.* New York: Simon & Schuster, 2002.

"Big Guns of Southern Revolt." *US News & World Report* 31 (November 16, 1951): 46–49.

Bloom, Sol. *The Autobiography of Sol Bloom.* New York: Putnam's Sons, 1948.

Blum, John Morton, ed. *The Price of Vision: The Diary of Henry A. Wallace, 1942–46.* Boston: Houghton Mifflin, 1973.

Bohlen, Charles E. *Witness to History, 1929–1969.* New York: Norton, 1973.

Boles, Blair. *The Armed Road to Peace: An Analysis of NATO.* New York: Foreign Policy Association, 1952.

Bolster, Paul Douglas. "Civil Rights Movements in Twentieth-Century Georgia." PhD diss., University of Georgia, 1972.

Bonner, James C. "Legislative Apportionment and the County Unit System in Georgia since 1877." *Georgia Historical Quarterly* 47/4 (1963): 351–74.

Bootle, Judge W. A. "Walter F. George Foundation Plays Key Role in the Law School's Development." *The Mercer Lawyer,* (Winter 1995): 6–8, 27.

Brauds, H. W. *Cold Warriors: Eisenhower's Generation and American Foreign Policy.* New York:

Columbia University Press, 1988.
Broadwater, Jeff. *Adlai Stevenson and American Politics.* New York: Twayne, 1994.
———. *Eisenhower and the Anti-Communist Crusade.* Chapel Hill: University of North Carolina Press, 1992.
Brownell, Herbert. *Advising Ike: The Memoirs of Attorney General Herbert Brownell.* Lawrence: University of Kansas Press, 1993.
Burns, James M. *Roosevelt: The Lion and the Fox.* New York: Harcourt, Brace, 1956.
Bryant, James C. "Walter F. George: Statesman for the World." *The Mercer Lawyer,* (Winter 1995): 2–5.
Byrnes, James F. *All in One Lifetime.* New York: Harper, 1958.
———. *Speaking Frankly.* New York: Harper, 1947.
"Can Talmadge Beat George in Georgia?" *US News & World Report* 38 (April 29, 1955): 37–39.
Cantril, Hadley, ed. *Gauging Public Opinion.* Princeton: Princeton University Press, 1944.
Carey, John, ed. *Eyewitness to History.* Cambridge: Harvard University Press, 1987.
Carlton, David L., and Peter A. Coclanis, eds. *Confronting Southern Poverty in the Great Depression: The Report on Economic Conditions of the South with Related Documents.* Boston: Bedford Books, 1996.
Caro, Robert A. *The Years of Lyndon Johnson: Master of the Senate.* New York: Knopf, 2002.
Cater, Douglas. "Foreign Policy: Default of the Democrats." *The Reporter* 12 (March 10, 1955): 21–23.
———. "Regression vs Conservatism in Georgia." *The Reporter* 13 (October 20, 1955): 13–16.
Caute, David. *The Great Fear: The Anti-Communist Purge under Truman and Eisenhower.* New York: Simon & Schuster, 1978.
"Champions of the Senate Wage Bloody War over President's Plan." *Newsweek* 10 (July 17, 1937): 8–9.
Chandler, David Leon. *The Natural Superiority of Southern Politicians: A Revisionist History.* Garden City: Doubleday, 1977.
"Changes in the Senate." *Congressional Digest* 35 (June 1956): 161.
Clapper, Raymond. "Roosevelt Tries the Primaries." *Current History* 159/2 (October 1938): 18.
———. *Watching the World.* New York: McGraw-Hill, 1944.
Cobb, James C. *Georgia Odyssey.* Athens: University of Georgia Press, 1997.
———. *The New Deal and the South.* Jackson: University of Mississippi Press, 1984.
———. "Not Gone, but Forgotten: Eugene Talmadge and the 1938 Purge Campaign." *Georgia Historical Quarterly* 59 (Summer 1975): 197–209.
Cochran, Bert. *Adlai Stevenson: Patrician among the Politicians.* New York: Funk and Wagnalls, 1969.
Cockfield, Jamie H. "The Union Sacrée." PhD diss., the University of Virginia, 1972.
Cohodas, Nadine. *Strom Thurmond and the Politics of Southern Change.* New York: Simon & Schuster, 1993.
Cole, Wayne S. *Roosevelt and the Isolationists, 1932–45.* Lincoln: University of Nebraska Press, 1983.
———. *Senator Gerald P. Nye and American Foreign Relations.* Minneapolis: University of Minnesota Press, 1962.
Coleman, Kenneth, et al. *A History of Georgia.* Athens: University of Georgia Press, 1977.

———. *A History of Georgia in Outline*. 2nd ed. Athens: University of Georgia Press, 1960.
Congressional Record. Washington: US Government Printing Office, 1922–1957. Cited as *CR*.
Connally, John with Mickey Herskowitz. *In History's Shadow: An American Odyssey*. New York: Hyperion, 1993.
Connally, Tom, as told to Alfred Steinberg. *My Name is Tom Connally*. New York: Thomas Y. Crowell, 1954.
Coode, Thomas. H. "Georgia Congressmen and the New Deal, 1933–1938." PhD diss., the University of Georgia, 1966.
Cook, James F. *Carl Vinson: Patriarch of the Armed Forces.* Macon: Mercer University Press, 2004.
———, ed. *The Governors of Georgia.* 3rd edition. Macon, GA: Mercer University Press, 2005.
Dabney, Virginius. *Liberalism in the South.* Chapel Hill: University of North Carolina Press, 1932.
Dallek, Robert. *Franklin D. Roosevelt and American Foreign Policy, 1932–1945.* New York: Oxford, 1979.
———. *Lone Star Rising: Lyndon Johnson and His Times, 1908–1960.* New York: Oxford, 1991.
Davenport, W. "States Righted." *Collier's* 89 (June 4, 1932): 11.
Davis, Kenneth. *FDR: Into the Storm, 1937–1940: A History.* New York: Random House, 1993.
———. *FDR, the New Deal Years, 1933–1927.* New York: Random House, 1986.
———. *The Politics of Honor: A Biography of Adlai E. Stevenson.* New York: Putnam, 1967.
———. *A Prophet in his Own Country: The Triumphs and Defeats of Adlai E. Stevenson.* Garden City: Doubleday, 1957.
DeWitt, William A. *The United Nations: Ten Years of Achievement.* New York: Public Affairs Committee, 1955.
Divine, Robert A. *Eisenhower and the Cold War.* New York: Oxford University Press, 1981.
Dole, Robert. *Historical Almanac of the United States Senate.* Washington: US Government Printing, 1989.
Donovan, Robert J., ed. *Confidential Secretary: Ann Whitman's Twenty Years with Eisenhower and Rockefeller.* New York: Dutton, 1988.
———. "Senator George: Ike's Favorite Democrat." *Collier's* 135/10 (May 13, 1955): 33–35.
———. *Tumultuous Years: The Presidency of Harry Truman, 1949–1953.* New York: Norton, 1982.
Douglas, Paul H. *The Fullness of Time: The Memoirs of Paul H. Douglas.* New York: Harcourt, Brace, Jovanovich, 1971.
Dowell, Spright. *A History of Mercer University.* Atlanta: Foote and Davies, 1958.
"Drama in Georgia." *Literary Digest* 121 (March 7, 1936): 9.
Drury, Allen. *Senate Journal,* New York: McGraw-Hill, 1963, 1943-45.
Dubin, Michael J. *United States Congressional Elections, 1788–1997.* Jefferson, NC: McFarland, 1998.
Duffield, E. S., ed. *The Forrestal Diaries.* New York: Viking Press, 1951.
Dulles, Allen Welsh. *The United Nations.* New York: Foreign Policy Association, 1946.
Egerton, John. *Speak Now against the Day.* New York: Alfred A. Knopf, 1995.
Eisenhower, Dwight David. *The Eisenhower Diaries.* Edited by Robert H. Ferrell. New York:

Norton, 1981.
Eisenhower, Dwight D. *Mandate for Change: 1953–56.* New York: Doubleday, 1963.
———. *Ike's Letters to a Friend, 1941–1958.* Edited by Robert Griffith. Lawrence: University Press of Kansas, 1984.
———. "The Situation in the Formosa Straits." *Vital Speeches* 21 (February 15, 1955): 1026–27.
Exhibition Commemorating the Settlement of Georgia, 1733–1948. Washington: US Government Printing Office, 1948. Exhibition held at the US Library of Congress, February 14–May 12, 1948. Library of Congress Prints and Photographs Division, Washington DC.
"Face to Face by the Blue Bermudian Sea." *Newsweek* 49 (March 25, 1957): 33–34.
Fagin, Vernon Allen. "Franklin D. Roosevelt, Liberalism in the Democratic Party, and the 1938 Congressional Elections: The Urge to Purge." PhD diss., University of California, Los Angeles, 1979.
"Famous Senator in Trouble with Voters." *US News & World Report* 40 (February 17, 1956): 32, 34.
Farley, James A. *Jim Farley's Story: The Roosevelt Years.* New York: McGraw-Hill, 1948.
Fausold, Martin L., and George T. Mazuzan, eds. *The Hoover Presidency: A Reappraisal.* Albany: State University of New York Press, 1974.
Fehrenbach, T. R. *FDR's Undeclared War, 1939–1941.* New York: McKay, 1967.
Ferrell, Robert H. *Choosing Truman: The Democratic Convention of 1944.* Columbia: University of Missouri Press, 1994.
———, and Samuel F. Bemis, eds. *American Secretaries of State and Their Diplomacy.* 18 vols. New York: Cooper Square Publishers, 1972.
———. *FDR's Quiet Confidante: The Autobiography of Frank C. Walker.* Nivot: University Press of Colorado, 1997.
Fite, Gilbert C. *Richard B. Russell, Jr., Senator from Georgia.* Chapel Hill: University of North Carolina Press, 1991.
Flanders, Ralph E. *Senator from Vermont.* Boston: Little, Brown, 1961.
———. The American Century. Cambridge: Harvard U. Press, 1986.
Fleissner, James P. "August 11, 1938: A Day in the Life of Senator Walter F. George." *The Journal of Southern Legal History,* 9/1 and 9/2 (2001): 55–101
Fleming, Thomas. *The New Dealers' War: Franklin D. Roosevelt and the War within World War II.* New York: Basic Books, 2001.
Fontenay, Charles. *Estes Kefauver: A Biography.* Knoxville: University of Tennessee Press, 1980.
"For Talk of Peace." *Newsweek* 45 (April 4, 1955): 24.
Foreman, Clark. "Georgia Kills the Poll Tax." *New Republic* 112 (February 26, 1945): 291–92.
Fossett, Roy E. "The Impact of the New Deal on Georgia Politics, 1933–1941." PhD diss., University of Florida, 1960.
Frederickson, Kari. *The Dixiecrat Revolt and the End of the Solid South.* Chapel Hill: University of North Carolina Press, 2001
Freedman, Max. "Washington in Focus: Senator George's Proposal for a Conference with Russia." *The Nation* 180 (April 2, 1955): 279–80
Fried, Albert. *FDR and His Enemies.* New York: St. Martin's, 1999.
———. *Men Against McCarthy.* New York: Columbia, 1976.

Freidel, Frank B. *FDR and the South.* Baton Rouge: Louisiana State University Press, 1965.
Gatewood, William, ""Richard B. Russell: Georgia Giant," Georgia Historic Quarterly, 76(1), 46-57.
Gabrilowitsch, Ossip. "Georgian Investigation." *Harper's Weekly* 61 (October 2, 1915): 335.
Garson, Robert. *The Democratic Party and the Politics of Sectionalism, 1941–1948.* Baton Rouge: Louisiana University Press, 1974.
Graebner, Norman. *Cold War Diplomacy: American Foreign Policy, 1945–1960.* Princeton: Van Nostrand, 1962.
———. *The New Isolationism.* New York: Ronald Press, 1956.
Gaillard, Peyre. "Georgia at Last Has a Good Governor." *American Mercury* 32 (June 1934): 241–45.
Giffith, Robert. *Politics of Fear: Joseph R. McCarthy and the Senate.* New York: Haden, 1970.
Garrettson, Charles L. III. *Hubert H. Humphrey: The Politics of Joy.* New Brunswick: Transaction Publishers, 1993.
Gay, Peter. *My German Question: Growing Up in Nazi Berlin.* New Haven: Yale University Press, 1998.
Gellman, Irwin F. *Secret Affairs: Franklin Roosevelt, Cordell Hull, and Sumner Wells.* Baltimore: Johns Hopkins University Press, 1995.
"George of Georgia." *Business Weekly* (July 7, 1956): 144.
"George of Georgia." *New Republic* 134 (May 21, 1956): 4–5.
"George of Georgia." *Newsweek* 16 (November 25, 1940): 16–17.
"George of Georgia: Ike's Friend in Need." *Newsweek* 45 (March 14, 1955).
George, W. F. *Addresses of Walter F. George in his Victorious Campaign for Reelection to the United States Senate in the Democratic Primary held September 14, 1938.* Bound typescript in the possession of the Vienna Historical Preservation Society, Vienna, GA.
———. "Democratic Tax Proposals." *Current History* 27 (August 1954): 118–19.
———. "International Law." *Vital Speeches* 11 (September 1, 1945): 687–89.
———. (Interview) "But No Neutral Zone." *Newsweek* 45 (May 30, 1955): 22.
———. "Joint Revolution on Formosa." *Vital Speeches* 21 (February 15, 1955): 1028–31.
———. "My Party and Myself." *Time* 32 (August 22, 1938): 19–20.
———. "New Methods Required to Increase Federal Income." *Vital Speeches* 10 (February 15, 1944): 273–75.
———. "Passage of Federal Aid to Education Would Not Result in Federal Bureaucratic Control of Education." *Congressional Digest* 23 (February 1944): 52–53.
———. "Russia Will Lose Power as Germany and Japan Gain." *US News & World Report* 38 (May 6, 1955): 78–81.
———. "Senator George, Finance." *US News & World Report* 34 (January 2, 1953): 34–36.
———. "Should the US Foreign Aid Program Be Curtailed?" *Congressional Digest* 35 (November 1956): 273, 275, 277, 279.
———. "Speech against Latin American Loan Bill." *Congressional Digest* 19 (December 1940): 319–20.
———. "Speech in Favor of the New Hatch Bill." *Congressional Digest* 19 (14 April 1940): 111–14.
———. "Speech on US Immigration Policy." *Congressional Digest* 35 (January 1956): 13, 15.
———. "Speech Opposing the Russell Amendment." *Congressional Digest* 19 (November 1940): 277–78.
———. "Who Needs Tax Relief Most?" *Look* 19 (December 27, 1955): 46, 48, 50.

———. "Why Taxes Must Be Cut." *US News & World Report* 27 (August 26, 1949): 32–35.

———. "Your $100,000,000,000 Tax Bill." *American Magazine* 135 (March 1943): 32–33, 104.

"Georgia Battle Smashes Talmadge." *Newsweek* 8 (September 19, 1936): 11–12.

"Georgia Loses." *Time* 67 (May 21, 1956): 22–23.

"Georgia Outcome." *Newsweek* 12/9 (August 29, 1938): 5.

"Georgia's Shame." *Independent* 83 (August 30, 1915): 280–81.

Giauque, Jeffrey Glen. *Grand Designs and Visions of Unity: The Atlantic Powers and the Reorganization of Western Europe, 1955–1963.* Chapel Hill: University of North Carolina Press, 2002.

Glad, Betty. *Charles Evans Hughes and the Illusion of Innocence.* Urbana: University of Illinois Press, 1966.

———. *Key Pittman: A Tragedy of a Senate Insider.* New York: Columbia University Press, 1986.

Goldsmith, John A. *Colleagues: Richard B. Russell and his Apprentice Lyndon B. Johnson.* Washington: Seven Locks Press, 1993.

Goodwin, Doris Kearns. *Lyndon Johnson and the American Dream.* New York: Harper and Row, 1976.

———. *No Ordinary Time: Franklin and Eleanor Roosevelt.* New York: Simon & Schuster, 1994.

Gorman, Joseph B. *Kefauver: A Political Biography.* New York: Oxford, 1971.

Graebner, Norman. *New Imperialism.* New York: Ronald Press, 1956.

Graham, Katharine. *Person History.* New York: Knopf, 1997.

Grantham, Dewey W. *The Democratic South.* Athens: University of Georgia Press, 1963.

———. *Hoke Smith and the Politics of the New South.* Baton Rouge: Louisiana University Press, 1958.

———. *The Life and Death of the Solid South.* Lexington: University of Kentucky Press, 1988.

Griffith, Winthrop. *Humphrey: A Candid Biography.* New York: Morrow, 1965.

Hagerty, James C. *The Diary of James C. Hagerty: Eisenhower in Mid-Course, 1954–55.* Edited by Robert H. Ferrell. Bloomington: Indiana University Press, 1982.

Halberstam, David. *The Fifties.* New York: Villard, 1993.

Hamby, Alonzo L. *Liberalism and Its Challengers.* 2nd ed. New York: Oxford, 1992.

Hartmann, Susan M. *Truman and the 80th Congress.* Columbia: University of Missouri Press, 1971.

Hassett, William D. *Off the Record with F. D. R., 1942–45.* New Brunswick, NJ: Rutgers University Press, 1958.

Havard, William C. *The Changing Politics in the South.* Baton Rouge: Louisiana State University Press, 1972.

Heacock, Walter J. "William B. Bankhead and the New Deal." *Journal of Southern History* 21/3 (August 1955): 347–56.

Heard, Alexander. *A Two-Party South.* Chapel Hill: University of North Carolina Press, 1952.

———, and Donald S. Strong. *Southern Primaries and Elections, 1920–1949.* Tuscaloosa: University of Alabama Press, 1950.

Heinemann, Ronald. *Harry Byrd of Virginia.* Charlottesville: University Press of Virginia, 1996.

Heinrichs, Waldo. *Threshold of War: Franklin D. Roosevelt and the American Entry into World*

War II. New York: Oxford University Press, 1988.

Henderson, Harold Paulk. *The Politics of Change in Georgia: A Political Biography of Ellis Arnall.* Athens: University of Georgia Press, 1991.

Hero, Alfred O., Jr. *The Southerner and World Affairs.* Baton Rouge: Louisiana State University Press, 1965.

"High Bid for Favor." *Newsweek* 43 (March 1, 1954): 19.

Hilderbrand, Robert C. *Dumbarton Oaks: The Origins of the United Nations and the Search for Post-War Security.* Chapel Hill: University of North Carolina Press, 1990.

Hooper, John E. "The Purge: Franklin D. Roosevelt and the 1938 Democratic Nominations." PhD diss., University of Chicago, 1966.

Hoopes, Townsend. *The Devil and John Foster Dulles.* Boston: Little, Brown, 1973.

Hoover, Calvin B. *Economic Resources and Politics of the South.* New York: Macmillan, 1951.

"How Big a Revolt against F. D. R." *Business Week* (June 19, 1937): 26–27.

"How a Democrat Guides Republican Tax Policy." *US News & World Report* 36 (March 5, 1954): 60, 62–63, 64.

Hughes, Emmett J. *The Ordeal of Power: A Political Memoir of the Eisenhower Years.* New York: Atheneum, 1963.

Hull, Cordell. *The Memoirs of Cordell Hull.* 2 vols. New York: Macmillan, 1948.

Humphrey, Hubert H. *The Education of a Public Man: My Life and Politics.* Minneapolis: University of Minnesota Press, 1991.

Huthmacher, J. Joseph. *Senator Robert F. Wagner and the Rise of Urban Liberalism.* New York: Atheneum, 1968.

I Accept the Challenge. Published by the Friends of Walter F. George, 1938.

Ickes, Harold L. *The Secret Diary of Harold L. Ickes.* 3 vols. New York: Simon & Schuster, 1953–54.

Israel, Fred L., ed. *The War Diary of Breckinridge Long.* Lincoln: University of Nebraska Press, 1966.

Jackson, Robert. *That Man: An Insider's Portrait of Franklin D. Roosevelt.* Oxford, England: Oxford University Press, 2003.

Jarman, Rufus. "Taxpayer's Senator." *Saturday Evening Post* 217 (May 19, 1945): 22–23, 39, 41–42.

Jessup, Philip C. *The Birth of Nations.* New York: Columbia University Press, 1974.

Johnson, Lyndon B. *The Vantage Point.* New York: Holt, Rinehart and Winston, 1971.

Johnson, Robert David. *Congress in the Cold War.* Cambridge: Cambridge University Press, 2006.

Johnson, Sam Houston. *My Brother Lyndon.* New York: Cowles, 1970.

Johnston, Alva. "President Tamer." *Saturday Evening Post* 210 (November 13, 1937).

Jones, Carter B. "The Georgia Plan." *American Mercury* 23 (July 1931): 311–20.

Jones, Jesse. *Fifty Billion Dollars.* New York: Macmillan, 1951.

"The Journal Salutes Georgia." *American Vocational Journal* 27 (October 1954): 4–11.

Kaufman, Burton Iva. *Trade and Aid: Eisenhower's foreign Economic Policy, 1955–1961.* Baltimore: Johns Hopkins, 1982.

Key, V. O., Jr. *Southern Politics in the State and Nation.* Knoxville: University of Tennessee Press, 1984.

Kilpatrick, Carroll, ed. *Roosevelt and Daniels: A Friendship in Politics.* Chapel Hill: University of North Carolina Press, 1952.

Kimball, Warren F. *The Most Unsordid Act: Lend-Lease, 1939–1941.* Baltimore: Johns Hopkins University Press, 1969.

Kingseed, Cole C. *Eisenhower and the Suez Crisis.* Baton Rouge: Louisiana State University Press, 1995.

Kirby, Jack T. *Darkness at the Dawning: Race and Reform in the Progressive South.* Philadelphia: Lippincott, 1972.

Kirkendall, Richard. "The Presidential Election of 1948." *The American Scene.* Edited by Robert D. Marcus and David Burner. New York: Appleton-Century-Crofts, 1971.

Kytle, C. "A Long, Dark Night for Georgia?" *Harper's* 197 (September 1948): 55–64.

Langer, William L., and S. Everett Gleason. *The Undeclared War, 1940–1941.* New York: Harper, 1953.

———. *Challenge to Isolationism, 1937–1940.* New York: Harper, 1952.

Larres, Klaus, and Kenneth Osgood. *The Cold War after Stalin's Death.* New York: Rowan and Littlefield, 2006.

Lash, Joseph P. *Roosevelt and Churchill, 1939–1941: The Partnership that Saved the West.* New York: Norton, 1976.

"Law and Lynching in Georgia." *Outlook* 112 (March 1, 1916): 484.

Lawrence, David. "Four-Power Fantasy." *Newsweek* 38 (May 6, 1955): 136.

Lawson, Steven F. *Black Ballots: Voting Rights in the South, 1944–1969.* New York: Columbia University Press, 1976.

Lee, R. Alton. *Truman and Taft-Hartley.* Lexington: University of Kentucky Press, 1966.

Leuchtenburg, William E. *Franklin Roosevelt and the New Deal.* New York: Harper and Row, 1963.

———. *The White House Looks South.* Baton Rouge: Louisiana State University Press, 2005.

Lewis, George. Massive Resistance. London: Hodder Arnold, 2006.

Lindley, E. K. "Way to Win an Election?" *Newsweek* 43 (March 1, 1954): 26.

Lisio, Donald J. *Hoover, Blacks, and Lily-Whites: A Study of Southern Strategies.* Chapel Hill: University of North Carolina Press, 1985.

Littell, Norman M. *My Roosevelt Years.* Edited by Jonathan Dembo. Seattle: University of Washington Press, 1987.

Lubell, Samuel. *The Revolt of the Moderates.* New York: Harper, 1956.

Maddox, Robert Franklin. *The Senatorial Career of Harley Martin Kilgore.* New York: Garland Publishing, 1981.

"The Majority Loses." *New Republic* 115 (July 29, 1946): 92–93.

Maney, Patrick J. *"Young Bob" La Follette: A Biography of Robert M. La Follette, Jr., 1895–1953.* Columbia: University of Missouri Press, 1978.

Manly, Chesly. *The UN Record: Ten Fateful Years for America.* Chicago: H. Regnery, 1955.

Mann, Robert. *The Walls of Jericho. Lyndon Johnson, Hubert Humphrey, Richard Russell and the Struggle for Civil Rights.* New York: Harcourt Brace, 1996.

Marcus, Robert D., and David Burner, editors. *The American Scene: Varieties of American History.* New York: Appleton-Century-Crofts, 1971.

Martin, John Bartlow. *Adlai Stevenson and the World.* New York: Doubleday, 1977.

Martin, Joseph W. *My First Fifty Years in Politics.* New York: McGraw-Hill, 1960.

Maverick, Mawry. *A Maverick American.* New York: Covici, Friede, 1937.

Mazuzan, George T. *Warren R. Austin at the UN, 1946–1953.* Kent: Kent State University Press, 1977.

———. *The Hoover Presidency.* Albany, NY: State U. of New York, 1974.

McCoy, Donald R., and Richard T. Ruetten. *Quest and Response: Minority Rights and the*

Truman Administration. Lawrence: University of Kansas Press, 1973.
McGill, Ralph. *The South and the Southerner.* Boston: Little, Brown, 1963.
McKinney, John C., and Edgar T. Thompson, eds. *The South in Continuity and Change.* Durham: Duke University Press, 1965.
McPherson, Harry. *A Political Education.* Boston: Little, Brown, 1972.
Michie, Allen A. Dixie Demagogue, New York: Vanguard Press, 1938.
Miller, Nathan. *FDR: An Intimate History.* New York: Doubleday, 1983.
Moore, John Robert. "Senator Josiah Bailey and the 'Conservative Manifesto.'" *Journal of Southern History* 31 (1965): 21–39.
———. *Senator Josiah William Bailey of North Carolina.* Durham: Duke University Press, 1968.
Moseley, Clement Charlton. "Invisible Empire: A History of the Ku Klux Klan in Twentieth Century Georgia, 1915–1965." PhD diss., University of Georgia, 1968.
McConaughy, J. L. "Patriarch." *Life* 36 (April 19, 1954): 112.
———. "The World's Most Exclusive Club." *Life* 36 (April 26, 1959): 118-120.
McGill, Ralph. *The South and the Southerner.* Boston: Little, Brown, 1963.
McKeever, Porter. *Adlai Stevenson: His Life and Legacy.* New York: Morrow, 1989.
McLaurin, Ann Mathison. "The Role of the Dixiecrats in the 1948 Election." PhD diss., University of Oklahoma, 1972.
McMillan, G. "So Goes the South." *Collier's* 137 (June 8, 1956): 42–47.
Melanson, Richard A. *Reevaluating Eisenhower: American Foreign Policy in the 1950s.* Urbana: University of Illinois Press, 1987.
Mellichamp, Josephine. *Senators from Georgia.* Huntsville: Strode Publishers, 1976.
Messer, Robert L. *The End of the Alliance: James F. Byrnes, Roosevelt, Truman and the Origins of the Cold War.* Chapel Hill: University of North Carolina Press, 1982.
Michie, Allan A., and Frank Ryhlick. *Dixie Demagogues.* New York: Vanguard, 1939.
Miller, William D. *Mr. Crump of Memphis.* Baton Rouge: Louisiana University Press, 1964.
Miller, Zell. *Great Georgians.* Franklin Springs, GA: Advocate Press, 1983.
Mitchell, Margaret. *Margaret Mitchell's Gone with the Wind Papers, 1936–1949.* Edited by Richard Harwell. New York: MacMillan Publishing Co., Inc., 1976.
Moley, Raymond. *After Seven Years.* New York: Harper, 1939.
———. "Men in Harness." *Newsweek,* 12 (August 22, 1938): 40.
———. "Perspective," *Newsweek,* 12 (July 25, 1938): 40.
Moore, John Hammond. "Jim Crow in Georgia." *South Atlantic Quarterly* 66 (Autumn 1967): 554–65.
Moore, John L. *Elections A to Z.* 2nd ed. Washington: CQ Press, 2003.
Moore, S. T. "Public Office on Easy Payments: the GOP in Georgia." *Independent* 118 (February 19, 1927): 203–206.
Morrison, Joseph L. *Governor O. Max Gardner.* Chapel Hill: University of North Carolina Press, 1971.
Morrison, Samuel Elliot. *The Oxford History of the American People* (New York: Oxford University Press, 1965).
Moseley, Clement Charlton. "Invisible Empire: A History of the Ku Klux Klan in Twentieth Century Georgia, 1915–1965." PhD diss., University of Georgia, 1968.
Moskin, J. Robert. *Mr. Truman's War: The Final Victories of World War II and the Birth of the Post-War World.* Lawrence: University Press of Kansas, 1996.
"Mr. Roosevelt's Court Plan Dies." *Newsweek* 10 (July 31, 1937): 5–6.

Mulder, Ronald A. *The Insurgent Progressives in the United States Senate and the New Deal.* New York: Garland, 1979.
Muller, Hubert. *Adlai Stevenson: A Study of Values.* New York: Harper and Row, 1967.
Murry, Gilbert. *From the League to the UN.* London: Oxford, 1948.
Nevins, Allan. *Herbert A. Lehman and His Era.* New York: Scribner's, 1963.
"New Team." *Time* 38 (August 11, 1941): 14.
"New Voice for the South in Congress." *US News & World Report* 40 (May 25, 1956): 81, 82, 84, 86.
Nixon, Richard M. *RN: The Memoirs of Richard Nixon.* New York: Grosset and Dunlop, 1978.
———. *Six Crises.* Garden City: Doubleday, 1962.
Norris, George W. *Fighting Liberal: The Autobiography of George W. Norris.* New York: Macmillan, 1945.
Oberdorfer, Don. *Senator Mansfield.* Washington: Smithsonian Books, 2003.
"Old Independent." *Time* 42 (July 19, 1943): 20–22.
"One of the Greatest." *Newsweek* 50 (August 12, 1957): 34–35.
"Outlaw State: Lynching of Leo Frank." *Outlook* 110 (August 25, 1915): 945–47.
Parmet, Herbert S. *Eisenhower and the American Crusade.* New York: Macmillan Co., 1972.
"Parting Moment." *Newsweek* 48 (July 9, 1956): 30.
Patterson, James T. *Congressional Conservatism and the New Deal: The Growth of the Conservative Coalition in Congress, 1933–1939.* Lexington: University of Kentucky Press, 1967.
———. "A Conservative Coalition Forms in Congress, 1933–1939." *Journal of American History* 52 (March 1966): 757–772.
———. *Mr. Republican: A Biography of Robert A. Taft.* Boston: Houghton Mifflin, 1972.
"People of the Week." *US News & World Report* 36 (February 12, 1954): 12; 38 (April 1, 1955): 20; 38 (May 6, 1955): 14; 39 (August 12, 1955): 12; 39 (December 23, 1955): 20; 41 (July 27, 1956): 20; 41 (November 9, 1956): 20.
Pepper, Claude. *Eyewitness to a Century.* San Diego: Harcourt, Brace, 1987.
———. "The Influence of the Deep South upon the presidential Election of 1952." *The Georgia Review* 6/2 (Summer 1952): 125–37.
Perkins, Dexter. *Charles Evens Hughes and American Democratic Statesmanship.* Boston: Little, Brown, 1956.
Perkins, Frances. *The Roosevelt I Knew.* New York: Viking, 1947.
Perret, Geoffrey. *Eisenhower.* New York: Random House, 1999.
Pleasants, Julian M. *Buncombe Bob: The Life and Times of Robert Rice Reynolds.* Chapel Hill: U. of North Carolina Press, 2009.
———. "Claude Pepper, Strom Thurmond, and the 1948 Presidential Election in Florida." *Florida Historical Quarterly* 76/4 (1998): 439–73.
Plesur, Milton. "Republican Congressional Comeback of 1938." *Review of Politics* 24 (October 1962): 525–62.
"Political Test." *Newsweek* 46 (November 21, 1955): 32–34.
Porter, David L. *The Seventy-sixth Congress and World War II, 1939–1940.* Columbia: University of Missouri Press, 1979.
Potenziani, David Daniel. "Look to the Past: Richard B. Russell and the Defense of Southern White Supremacy." PhD diss., University of Georgia, 1981.
Prudent, Caroline. *Conditional Partners: Eisenhower, the United Nations, and a Search for a Permanent Peace.* Baton Rouge: Louisiana State University Press, 1998.

Purcell, M. "George of Georgia: The Talmadge Threat." *The Nation* 181 (August 6, 1955): 105–106, 115–16.

"Purge Resumed." *Newsweek* 12 (July 1938): 3.

"The Purge Spreads: Notes on New York, Maryland, New Jersey, and Georgia." *Newsweek* 12/9 (August 29, 1938): 8–9.

Raines, Howell. *My Soul is Rested: Movement Days in the Deep South Remembered.* New York: Putnam, 1977.

Reedy, George. *Lyndon B. Johnson: A Memoir*. New York: Andrews and McMeel, 1982.

Reeves, Thomas C. *The Life and Times of Joe McCarthy.* New York: Stein and Day, 1982.

Reid, I. D. "Georgia's Negro Vote." *Nation* 163 (July 6, 1946): 12–14.

Rigdon, Louis T. *Georgia's County Unit System.* Decatur, GA: Selective Books, 1961.

Ripley, Randall. *Power in the Senate.* New York: St. Martin's, 1969.

Roberts, Chalmers. "Strong Man from the South." *Saturday Evening Post* 227 (June 25, 1955): 30–31.

Robertson, David. *Sly and Able: A Political Biography of James F. Byrnes.* New York: Norton, 1994.

Roberts, Gene, and Hank Klebanoff. *The Race Beat.* New York: Knopf, 2006.

Roosevelt, Eleanor. *This I Remember.* New York: Harper, 1949.

Roosevelt, Elliott, ed. *F. D. R.: His Personal Letters, 1928–1945.* New York: Duell, Sloan, and Pearce, 1947–50.

Roosevelt, Franklin Delano. *The Public Papers and Addresses of Franklin D. Roosevelt.* 1938 volume. New York: Macmillan, 1941.

Roosevelt, James, and Sidney Shalett. *Affectionately, F. D. R.* New York: Harcourt, Brace, 1959.

Roseman, S. I. *Working with Roosevelt.* New York: Harper, 1952.

Rostow, W. W. *Eisenhower, Kennedy, and Foreign Aid.* Austin: University of Texas Press, 1985.

———. *Europe After Stalin: Eisenhower's Three Decisions of March 11, 1953*. Austin: University of Texas Press, 1953.

Rovere, Richard H. *The Eisenhower Years.* New York: Farrar, Straus, and Cudahy, 1956.

Russell, Ina Dillard. *Roots and Ever Green: The Selected Letters of Ina Dillard Russell.* Edited by Sally Russell. Athens: University of Georgia Press, 1999.

Russell, Sally. *A Heart for Any Fate; A Biography of Richard Brevard Russell, Sr.* Macon: Mercer University Press, 2004.

Ryskind, Allan A. *Hubert: An Unauthorized Biography of the Vice President.* New Rochelle, NY: Arlington House, 1968.

Saye, Albert Berry. *A Constitutional History of Georgia, 1732–1968.* Athens: University of Georgia Press, 1970.

Schewe, Donald B., ed. *Franklin D. Roosevelt and Foreign Affairs.* 17 vols. New York: Clearwater Pub., 1983.

Schlessinger Arthur. *The Coming of the New Deal.* Boston: Houghton-Mifflin, 1960.

Scobie, Ingrid W. *Center Stage: Helen Gahagan Douglas.* New York: Oxford University Press, 1992.

Senate of the United States. 84th Congress, 2nd. Session. *Expressions of Tribute...on the Retirement of Honorable Walter F. George.* Washington: US Government Printing Office, 1956.

"Senator George." *Commonweal* 64 (July 27, 1956): 410.

"Sentimental Send-off." *Life* 41 (July 30, 1956): 95–96.
"Senator George, Who Is Saying 'No' to President on Tax Rise." *US News & World Report* 26 (April 15, 1949): 39–42.
"Senator and Senator-to-be." *Newsweek* 47 (May 21, 1956): 36–37.
"Senators Byrd and George: Leaders in the Conservative Coalition." *US News & World Report* 22 (June 6, 1947): 50–52.
Shannon, J. B. "Presidential Politics in the South: 1938, I." *The Journal of Politics* 1 (1939): 146–70.
———. "Presidential Politics in the South: 1938, II." *The Journal of Politics* 1 (1939): 278–300.
Sharrill, Roberts and Harry Ernst. *Drugstore Liberal,* New York: Grossman, 1968.
Sievers, Rodney. M. *The Last Puritan? Adlai Stevenson in American Politics.* Port Washington, NY: Associated Faculty Press, 1983.
Smith. A. Robert. *Tiger in the Senate: The Biography of Wayne Morse.* New York: Doubleday, 1962.
Smith, Gaddis. *Dean Acheson.* Volume 16 of The American Secretaries of State and Their Diplomacy. Edited by Samuel Flagg Bemis and Robert H. Ferrell. New York: Cooper Square Publishers, 1972.
Solberg, Carl. *Hubert Humphrey: A Biography.* New York: Norton, 1984.
"Southern Delegation." *Fortune* 45 (February 1952): 85–87.
"Sorry Spectacle." *New Republic* 116 (February 3, 1947): 10.
Stettinius, Edwards, Jr. *Lend-Lease: Weapon for Victory.* New York: Macmillan, 1944.
Stevens, Ruth. *Hi-Ya Neighbor: Intimate Glimpses of Franklin Delano Roosevelt at Warm Springs, Georgia 1924–45.* New York and Atlanta: Tupper and Lone, 1947.
Stevenson, Adlai E. *The Papers of Adlai E. Stevenson.* 7 vols. Boston: Little, Brown, 1972.
Stokes, Thomas. *Chip Off My Shoulder.* Princeton: Princeton University Press, 1940.
Stolberg, B. "Buzz Windrip, Governor of Georgia." *Nation* 142 (March 11, 1936): 316–18.
Stone, I. F. *The Haunted Fifties.* New York: Random House, 1963.
———. "Swastika over the Senate." *The Nation* 162 (February 9, 1946): 158–59.
Stoney, G. C. "Georgia's Rotten Boroughs." *New Republic* 103 (August 19, 1940): 248–49.
Strong, Donald S. *The 1952 Presidential Election in the South.* Tuscaloosa: Bureau of Public Administration, University of Alabama, 1956.
———, and Alexander Heard. *Southern Primaries, 1920–1949.* Freeport, NY: Books for Libraries Press, 1970.
Swint, Henry. "Northern Interests in the Shoeless Southerners." *Journal of Southern History* 41 (November 1950): 450–544.
Talmadge, Herman E. *Talmadge: A Political Legacy, A Politician's Life: A Memoir.* Atlanta: Peachtree Publishers, 1987.
Talmadge, John E. *Rebecca Latimer Felton.* Athens. University of Georgia Press, 1960.
"Talmadge's Target?" *Newsweek* 45 (April 11, 1955): 38.
Tananbaum, Duane. *The Bricker Amendment Controversy: A Test of Eisenhower's Political Leadership.* Ithaca: Cornell University Press, 1988.
This is Senator George of Georgia Campaign brochure for 1956 campaign. N. P.: Georgians for Georgia, 1956. In possession of George Museum, Vienna Historical Preservation Society, Vienna, GA.
Thomas, David Noland. "Roosevelt vs. George: The Presidential Purge Campaign of 1938." Master's thesis, University of North Carolina, 1953.

Thompson, Robert Smith. *A Time for War: Franklin Delano Roosevelt and the Path to Pearl Harbor.* New York: Prentice Hall, 1991.
Timmons, Bascom N. *Jesse H. Jones: The Man and the Statesman.* New York: Henry Holt, 1956.
Tindall, George Brown. *The Emergence of the New South: 1913–1945.* Baton Rouge: Louisiana State University Press, 1967.
Toland, John. *Infamy. Pearl Harbor and its Aftermath.* New York: Berkley Books, 1972.
Tomkins, C. David. *Senator Arthur H. Vandenberg: The Evaluation of a Modern Republican, 1884–1945.* East Lansing: Michigan State University Press, 1970.
"Treachery?" *Newsweek* 51 (April 28, 1958): 23–24.
Truman, Harry S. *Dear Bess; The Letters from Harry to Bess Truman.* Edited by Robert H. Ferrell. New York: Norton, 1983.
———. *Memoirs.* 2 vols. Garden City, NY: Doubleday, 1955–56.
———. *Off the Record; The Private Papers of Harry S.* [sic] *Truman.* Edited by Robert H. Ferrell. New York: Harper and Row, 1980.
Tucker, P. "Nine Orphan Counties." *New Republic* 117 (July 21, 1947): 22.
Tully, Grace. *F. D. R.: My Boss.* New York: Charles Scribner's Sons, 1949.
"Twelve Key Members of the New Congress." *New York Times Magazine* (January 2, 1949): 6.
The United Nations: A Handbook on the United Nations. New York: Worldmark Press, 1977.
Vandenberg, Arthur H., Jr. *The Private Papers of Senator Vandenberg.* Boston: Houghton Mifflin, 1952.
Varney, H. L. "Meet Senator Talmadge." *American Mercury* 86 (February 1958): 7–17.
Vienna Historic Preservation Society. *The Kingdom of Dooly.* Virginia Beach, VA: Donning Co., 1997.
Vienna Historic Preservation Society (VHPS) News. February 23, 2005. Vienna, GA.
"Vilifying a State." *The Nation* 101 (August 26, 1915): 251–52.
Villard, O. G. "Senators Wagner, Nye and Others." *Nation* 141 (September 4, 1935): 259.
"Voice of the 84th." *Time* 65 (April 25, 1955): 22–25.
Wade, William W., ed. *The UN Today.* New York: Wilson, 1954.
Warren, Earl. *The Memoirs of Chief Justice Earl Warren.* Garden City, NY: Doubleday, 1977.
Warren, Harris Gaylord. *Herbert Hoover and the Great Depression.* New York: Oxford, 1959.
"Washington Bulletin," *Business Week,* August 13, 1938, 7.
Webb, Clive. *Massive Resistance.* New York: Oxford, 2005.
Weiler, Lawrence D., and Anne Patricia Simons. *The United States and the United Nations: The Search for International Peace and Security.* New York: Manhattan Publishing Co., 1967.
Weintraub, Stanley. *Journey into War: December 7, 1941.* New York: Dutton, 1991.
"We'll Miss Them." *The Reporter* 15 (August 9, 1956): 4.
Western Woman's [*sic*] Club. *The History of Webster County.* Roswell, GA: Wolfe Association, 1980.
"What Senator George Said about…Red China." *Newsweek* 38 (May 6, 1955): 80.
Wheeler, Burton K. *Yankee from the West.* Garden City: Doubleday, 1962.
"When Senator George Steps Out." *US News & World Report* 40 (May 18, 1956): 46, 48.
"Where Does the New Deal Go from Here? Revolt at the Capitol." *Literary Digest* 123 (June 26, 1937): 3–4.
White. W. S. "Senator George, Monument Determined." *New York Times Magazine* (March

13, 1955): 12, 42, 44, 47.

———. *Citadel: The Story of the US Senate.* New York: Harper, 1957.

"Who's Who in the New Congress." *Business Week* (January 9, 1937), 38–40.

"Why Was Frank Lynched?" *Forum* 56 (December 1916): 677–92.

Wicker, Tom. *Shooting Star: The Brief Arc of Joe McCarthy.* New York: Harcourt, 2006.

Wilhoit, Frances M. *The Politics of Massive Resistance.* New York: Braziller, 1973.

Wilkinson, J. Harvie III. *Harry Byrd and the Changing Face of Virginia Politics, 1945–1966.* Charlottesville: University Press of Virginia, 1968.

Williams, Juan. *Eyes on the Prize: America's Civil Rights Years, 1954–1965.* New York: Viking, 1987.

Williams, T. Harry. *Huey Long.* New York: Knopf, 1969.

Williamson, Daniel C. *Separate Agendas: Churchill, Eisenhower, and Anglo-American Relations, 1953–1955.* New York: Lexington Books, 2006.

Winant, Howard. *The World Is a Ghetto.* New York: Basic Books, 2001.

Woods, Randell Bennett. *Fulbright: A Biography.* Cambridge: Cambridge University Press, 1995. R

Woodward, C. Vann. *The Strange Career of Jim Crow.* 3rd ed. London: Oxford University Press, 1966.

———. *Tom Watson, Agrarian Rebel.* Savannah: Beeline Press, 1973.

World Citizens Association. *The World at the Crossroads.* Chicago: World Citizens Association, 1946.

World Peace Foundation. *The United Nations in the Making.* Boston: The Foundation, 1945.

"Wrong Target." *Time* 72 (August 4, 1958): 17.

Wunderlin, Clarence E., Jr. *The Papers of Robert A. Taft.* 2 vols. Kent: Kent State University Press, 2001.

Yoder, Amos. *The Evolution of the United Nations System.* New York: Crane Russak, 1989.

Zeigler, Luther, Jr. "Senator Walter George's 1938 Campaign." *Georgia Historical Quarterly* 63/4 (December 1959): 333–52.

5. Newspapers

Atlanta Constitution

Atlanta Journal

Augusta Herald

Macon [Daily] Telegraph

Mercer Cluster, Tarver Library Special Collections

New York Times

Vienna [Progress] News

Savannah Morning News

Washington Post

Clippings from many other newspapers that appear in archival collections

INDEX

INDEX